Dreams are Born in
the
Heart !

Strategic Entrepreneurial Growth

Donald F. Kuratko
Ball State University

Harold P. Welsch
DePaul University

Harcourt College Publishers

Fort Worth   Philadelphia   San Diego   New York   Orlando   Austin   San Antonio
Toronto   Montreal   London   Sydney   Tokyo

Publisher	Mike Roche
Acquisitions Editor	Tracy Morse
Developmental Editor	Jana Pitts
Marketing Strategist	Beverly Dunn
Project Manager	Angela Williams Urquhart

ISBN: 0-03-031936-6
Library of Congress Catalog Card Number: 00-111719

Address for Domestic Orders
Harcourt College Publishers, 6277 Sea Harbor Drive, Orlando, FL 32887-6777
800-782-4479

Address for International Orders
International Customer Service
Harcourt College Publishers, 6277 Sea Harbor Drive, Orlando, FL 32887-6777
407-345-3800
(fax) 407-345-4060
(e-mail) hbintl@harcourtbrace.com

Address for Editorial Correspondence
Harcourt College Publishers, 301 Commerce Street, Suite 3700, Fort Worth, TX 76102

Web Site Address
http://www.harcourtcollege.com

Harcourt College Publishers will provide complimentary supplements or supplement packages to those adopters qualified under our adoption policy. Please contact your sales representative to learn how you qualify. If as an adopter or potential user you receive supplements you do not need, please return them to your sales representative or send them to: Attn: Returns Department, Troy Warehouse, 465 South Lincoln Drive, Troy, MO 63379.

Printed in the United States of America

1 2 3 4 5 6 7 8 9 0   066   9 8 7 6 5 4 3 2

Harcourt College Publishers

Entrepreneurship has evolved into one of the most popular and, arguably, one of the most important fields of study in contemporary schools of business. This academic emergence has coincided with the economic emergence of entrepreneurs throughout the past two decades. During the last ten years, the annual number of new incorporations has averaged 600,000 while most of the employment growth, innovation, and overall vitality of the U.S. economy has been sparked by the entrepreneurial sector.

This remarkable entrepreneurial growth, both economic and academic, has ignited contemporary research to examine all of the particular facets of entrepreneurship. For example, within major *Fortune* 500 corporations there has been a recognition and new respect for the entrepreneurial perspective within individuals. Thus, "corporate entrepreneurship" or "intrapreneurship" has been adopted by many firms as a strategy for innovation and growth. This strategy attempts to capitalize upon the entrepreneurial abilities of individuals *within* the corporate framework.

Additional facets of strategic entrepreneurial growth include the Internet revolution, global expansion, the franchise expansion, entrepreneurial leadership, family business, and the challenge of managing entrepreneurial growth. All of these topics provide clear examples of the particular areas of research within entrepreneurship that are emerging.

Organization

Strategic Entrepreneurial Growth is designed to be a contemporary view of several important dimensions of just what the title implies. As this field matures into major differentiated segments, the latest innovations and writings must be communicated to a growing audience of entrepreneurship students. *Strategic Entrepreneurial Growth* was developed as a graduate-level book that invites the exploration of some of these particular facets of entrepreneurship. While there are 11 selected topics of text material provided, the major focus of this book is for analysis of the comprehensive cases and readings that illustrate various strategies for entrepreneurial firms. As professors and students examine, discuss, and develop the critical issues of these cases and readings, there will emerge a greater understanding of and insight into the entrepreneurial process.

Because entrepreneurial growth is dynamic and evolving, professors are encouraged to add other topics for their students. However, it is our hope that this book provides a solid foundation for examining the emerging issues of strategic entrepreneurial growth. Through this contemporary examination, students will become more aware of today's entrepreneurial process and more prepared to accept their challenge for tomorrow's business environment.

Ancillary Materials

Instructor's Manual

Comprehensive teaching notes are included in the *Instructor's Manual* for the cases in the text as well as chapter outlines, chapter summaries, and suggestions for discussion points in the readings.

Companion Web Site

This tool, found on the publisher's Web site at **http://www.harcourtcollege.com/ management/kuratkoseg/,** contains more than 30 supplemental cases for this text. Also included is an appendix on women and minority entrepreneurs. Students will be able to access the site easily and will gain access to other topics relating to entrepreneurship. Teaching notes for these cases will be located in the Instructor's Home section.

Acknowledgments

Many individuals played an important role in helping us write, develop, and refine our text, and they deserve special recognition. Our families, from whom we took so much time, deserve our deepest love and appreciation, especially our wives, Deborah A. Kuratko and Gemma M. Welsch. We would also like to express our appreciation to the staff at Harcourt College Publishers who worked closely with us on this project, in particular: Tracy Morse, Acquisitions Editor; Jana Pitts, Developmental Editor; Beverly Dunn, Marketing Strategist; and Angela Urquhart, Project Manager.

We would like to acknowledge the authors of our comprehensive entrepreneurial cases. These professors and case researchers developed the excellent comprehensive cases that provide the focus of this text. Without their contributions, a book such as this could not be developed: Todd J. Bacon, *Eastern Michigan University*; Philip Baron, *Florida Atlantic University*; William D. Bygrave, *Babson College*; James W. Camerius, *Northern Michigan University*; James W. Clinton, *University of Northern Colorado*; Patrick J. Conway, *Iona College*; Roy A. Cook, *Fort Lewis College*; Cheryl Crofton, *Sam Houston State University*; Robert P. Crowner, *Eastern Michigan University*; Jo Ann Duffy, *Sam Houston State University*; Todd A. Finkle, *University of Akron*; Frank J. Fish, *Panasonic Communications Systems Co.*; Darin M. Floyd, *Ball State University*; David W. Frantz, *Purdue University*; Michael Jay Garrison, *Sam Houston State University*; Brian G. Gnauck, *Northern Michigan University*; J. Larry Goff, *Fort Lewis College*; Lynda L. Goulet, *University of Northern Iowa*; Peter J. Goulet, *University of Northern Iowa*; Patricia G. Greene, *University of Missouri–Kansas City*; Walter Greene, *University of Texas–Pan Am*; Philip Greenwood, *Caminar Business Strategies Group*; Donald Grunewald, *Iona College*; Keith R. Hausman, *Iowa State University*; Marilyn M. Helms, *University of Tennessee at Chattanooga*; Deborah Howard, *University of Evansville*; J. David Hunger, *Iowa State University*; Richard C. Insinga, *State University of New York at Oneonta*; Beth Jack, *University of Tennessee at Chattanooga*; Kellye Jones, *University of Texas, San Antonio*; Vladimir A. Kureshov, *Higher Business School in Krasnoyarsk, Russia*; Robert Letovsky, *Saint Michael's College*; Henry S. Maddux, *Samford University*; Hugh B. McSurely, *Eastern Michigan University*; Ed P. Moura, *University of Evansville*; Rick Mull, *Fort Lewis College*; John Mullane, *Middle Tennessee State University*; Tamara Mullarky, *Saint Michael's College*; Nathan Nebbe, *Iowa State University*; Jason O'Neil, *Ball State University*; Sam Perkins, *Babson College*; Steven A. Rallis, *Iowa State University*; Marlene M. Reed, *Samford University*; Patricia A. Roberts-Grandoff, *University of South Florida*; Rebecca Roseberry, *Sam Houston State University*; Patricia A. Ryan, *Drake University*; Robert W. Service, *Samford University*; Charles Shanabruch, *Saint Xavier University*; Jerry Sheppard, *Simon Fraser University*; Anand G. Shetty, *Iona College*; Charles B. Shrader, *Iowa State University*; Mark Sloan, *Sam Houston State University*; Thomas A. Teal, *Harvard University*; Joe G. Thomas, *Middle Tennessee State University*; Jeff Totten, *Bemidji State University*; Joan L. Twenter, *Iowa State University*; John L. Vollmer, *Indiana University–Purdue University at Fort*

Wayne; Ann Walsh, *Iowa State University*; William B. Walstad, *University of Nebraska, Lincoln*; Benjamin Weeks, *Saint Xavier University*; Thomas L. Wheelen, *University of South Florida*; Timothy E. Williams, *University of Northern Iowa*; Geraldine E. Willigan, *Harvard University*; Janet Bear Wolverton, *Oregon Institute of Technology*; John K. Wong, *Iowa State University*; Laura J. Yale, *Fort Lewis College*; and Irvin Zaenglein, *Northern Michigan University*.

We would also like to recognize the authors of the journal articles that appear at the end of each chapter. These readings, entitled, "The Entrepreneurial Library," contain research articles on topics related to the chapter material. We are grateful to the following scholars for sharing their unique contributions with us: Lloyd W. Fernald, Jr., *University of Central Florida*; George T. Solomon, *George Washington University*; Victoria Williams, *U.S. Small Business Administration*; Bruce D. Phillips, *U.S. Small Business Administration*; Donald F. Kuratko, *Ball State University*; Jeffrey S. Hornsby, *Ball State University*; Laura M. Corso, *Ball State University*; R. Duane Ireland, *University of Richmond*; Michael A. Hitt, *Arizona State University*; Norris F. Krueger, Jr., *Boise State University*; David Forlani, *University of Colorado at Denver*; John W. Mullins, *University of Denver*; William A. Sahlman, *Harvard University*; James J. Chrisman, *University of Calgary*; Jess H. Chua, *University of Calgary*; Pramodita Sharma, *Dalhousie University (Halifax)*; Shaker A. Zahra, *Georgia State University*; Daniel F. Jennings, *Texas A&M University*; Patrick J. Kaufman, *Boston University*; William B. Walstad, *University of Nebraska–Lincoln*; Marilyn L. Kourilsky, *The Kauffman Foundation*; James A. Wolff, *Wichita State University*; and Timothy L. Pett, *Wichita State University*.

Finally, we would like to express our appreciation to our colleagues at Ball State University and DePaul University. In particular, we acknowledge Ray V. Montagno, Chairman of the Management Department, Ball State University, and Neil A. Palomba, Dean of the College of Business, Ball State University, for their enthusiastic support. Also thanks to Maggie A. Ailes, executive assistant for the Midwest Entrepreneurial Education Center; the Coleman Foundation; Ilya Meiertal, Administrative Assistant, DePaul University; Kenneth Thompson, former Chairman of the Management Department, DePaul University; Gerhard Plaschka, Chairman of the Management Department, DePaul University; and Arthur Kraft, Dean of the Kellstadt Graduate School of Business, DePaul University, for their assistance and support.

Donald F. Kuratko
Ball State University

Harold P. Welsch
DePaul University

Dr. Donald F. Kuratko is the Stoops Distinguished Professor of Entrepreneurship and Founding Director of Entrepreneurship Program, College of Business, Ball State University. In addition, he is Executive Director of The Midwest Entrepreneurial Education Center. He has published eight books and more than 150 articles on aspects of entrepreneurship, new venture development, and corporate entrepreneurship. His work has been published in journals such as *Academy of Management Executive, Strategic Management Journal, Journal of Small Business Management, Journal of Business Venturing,* and *Entrepreneurship Theory & Practice.*

The academic program in entrepreneurship that Dr. Kuratko developed at Ball State University has continually earned national rankings including: Top 20 in *Business Week* and *Success* magazines; Top 10 business schools for entrepreneurship research over the last ten years (MIT study); and Top 5 in *U.S. News & World Report*'s elite ranking (including the no. 1 state university for entrepreneurship). The program has also been honored with the NFIB Entrepreneurship Excellence Award (1993), the National Model Entrepreneurship Undergraduate Program Award (1990), and the National Model Entrepreneurship Graduate Program Award (1998).

In addition to earning the Ball State University College of Business Teaching Award 14 consecutive years, Dr. Kuratko holds the distinction of being the only professor in the history of Ball State University to achieve all four of the university's major lifetime awards which include Outstanding Young Faculty (1987), Outstanding Teaching Award (1990), Outstanding Faculty Award (1996), and Outstanding Researcher Award (1999). Dr. Kuratko was also honored as the Entrepreneur of the Year for the state of Indiana (sponsored by Ernst & Young) and was inducted into the Institute of American Entrepreneurs Hall of Fame. Dr. Kuratko was named the National Outstanding Entrepreneur Educator (by the U.S. Association for Small Business and Entrepreneurship).

Dr. Harold P. Welsch holds the Coleman Foundation Endowed Chair in Entrepreneurship at DePaul University and has been active in entrepreneurship development for more than 20 years in his role as educator, consultant, researcher, entrepreneur, author, and editor. Dr. Welsch received his Ph.D. degree from Northwestern University's Kellogg Graduate School of Management.

Dr. Welsch's work has appeared in several publications, including *Entrepreneurship Theory & Practice, International Small Business Journal, Journal of Small Business Management,* and *Frontiers of Entrepreneurship Research.* His current research carries him throughout the world in his efforts to promote entrepreneurship development and education internationally.

In addition to his role as founder/director of the Entrepreneurship Program at DePaul University, Dr. Welsch has served as Chairman of the Academy of Management Entrepreneurship Division, president of the International Council for Small Business (ICSB), and president of the U.S. Association for Small Business and Entrepreneurship (USASBE). He was instrumental in establishing small business development centers in Poland and served in a pilot program in establishing an MBA program in Prague, Czechoslovakia. Dr. Welsch has received grants from the Coleman Foundation, the Booz-Allen-Hamilton Foundation, and NASA.

CONTENTS

PART TWO

Strategic Issues for
Emerging Ventures
109

Chapter 4

Chapter 5

Chapter 6

Chapter 7

Chapter 8

PART THREE

Growth Options for
Strategic Impact
343

Chapter 9

I

Understanding the Entrepreneurial Challenge

1

Entrepreneurial Leadership for the New Millennium

Key Topics

- **Strategic Leadership for Emerging Ventures**

- **The Revolutionary Impact of Entrepreneurial Firms**

- **Entrepreneurial Growth in the Economy**

- **The Age of the Gazelles**

- **Effective Strategic Leadership in the New Millennium**

Strategic Leadership for Emerging Ventures

The pace and magnitude of change in the business environment will continue to accelerate in the new millennium. The evolution and transformation of entrepreneurial firms within this pace will be critical. Building dynamic capabilities that differentiate them from their emerging competitors is the major challenge for growing firms as they evolve and transform themselves to accommodate the changing landscape. Two ways of building dynamic capabilities are internal (utilization of the creativity and knowledge from employees) and external (the search for external competencies to complement the firm's existing capabilities).[1]

Globalization, technology, and information movement are all examples of forces in this new millennium that are causing firms to reexamine their cultures, structures, and systems in terms of their flexibility and adaptability. Innovation and entrepreneurial thinking are essential elements in the strategies of growing ventures. As researcher Shaker A. Zahra points out:

> In tomorrow's entrepreneurial economy, managers and their companies are likely to face important but exciting challenges. Innovation will become even more important in tomorrow's economy than it already is today. Innovation in every part of the firm's systems, operations, culture and organization will gain greater importance. Process innovations, too, will increase in importance. Managing and fostering these innovations will continue to be a key managerial challenge.[2]

The Revolutionary Impact of Entrepreneurial Firms

Entrepreneurship is the very symbol of business tenacity and achievement. Entrepreneurs were the pioneers of today's business successes. Their sense of opportunity, their drive to innovate, and their capacity for accomplishment have become the standard by which free enterprise is now measured. Indeed, an entrepreneurial revolution has taken hold throughout the entire world. This revolution will be as powerful to the twenty-first century as the Industrial Revolution was to the twentieth century (if not more!). Entrepreneurial firms will continue to be critical contributors to economic growth through their leadership, management, innovation, research and development effectiveness, job creation, competitiveness, productivity, and formation of new industries.

Entrepreneurial Growth in the Economy

The past decade has experienced the powerful emergence of entrepreneurial activity in the United States. Many statistics can be cited to illustrate this fact. For example, during the past ten years, new business incorporations averaged 600,000 *per year*. Although many of these incorporations may have been sole proprietorships or partnerships previously, it still demonstrates venture activity, whether it was through start-ups, expan-

---

[1]Shaker A. Zahra, "The Changing Rules of Global Competitiveness in the 21st Century," *Academy of Management Executive* 13, no. 1, (1999): 36–42.

[2]Zahra, 38.

sions, or development. More specifically, 807,000 new small firms were established in 1995, an all-time record.

The net result, then, is that the United States has a very robust level of firm creation. Among the 6 million establishments with employees, approximately 600,000 to 800,000 are added each year. That number translates into an annual birth rate of 14 to 16 per 100 establishments.[3]

Small firms constitute more than 90 percent of the entire business population. Granted, this figure depends on the definition of the term "small"; however, the Internal Revenue Service (IRS) reports that 21 million businesses exist based on business tax returns. Figure 1.1 was developed by the **National Federation of Independent Business (NFIB)** to demonstrate the breakdown. Approximately 12 million businesses have owners whose principal occupations is owning and operating them. Approximately 7 million businesses (out of these 12 million) have owners who work for themselves without employing anyone else. Of the 5 million remaining firms, only 15,000 employ 500 or more people.

Keep in mind that when a business consists of a single establishment, the enterprise and establishment concepts are identical. Sometimes, however, small establishments may be owned by larger enterprises; in that case, they may not be considered small firms.

FIGURE 1.1	WHAT CONSTITUTES SMALL FIRMS IN AMERICA

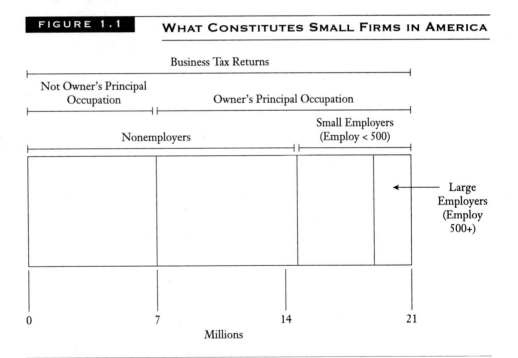

SOURCE: William J. Dennis, Jr., *A Small Business Primer* (Washington, DC: The NFIB Foundation, 1993), 3.

---

[3]Paul D. Reynolds, Michael Hay, and S. Michael Camp, *Global Entrepreneurship Monitor* (Kansas City, MO: Kauffman Center for Entrepreneurial Leadership, 1999).

Three types of establishments have been identified by the U.S. Small Business Administration:

1. "Small" establishments owned by small enterprises

2. "Apparent small" establishments owned by large enterprises

3. "Large" establishments owned by large enterprises.

Small enterprises are defined as having 100 or fewer employees; large enterprises have more than 100 employees.

Small enterprises are the most common form of enterprise-established relationships, regardless of industry, and most small businesses consist of a single establishment. More significantly, almost 90 percent of all firms employ fewer than 20 people. This employment number is important, as small entrepreneurial firms have created the most *net* new jobs in the U.S. economy. In addition, the smallest of our enterprises have created a *steady supply* of net new jobs over the business cycle from 1977 to 1990. It is important to recognize that historically, employment growth in the United States is correlated directly with new-business growth. This fact has been tracked back to 1960, demonstrating that new-business formations are critical for any net increase in U.S. employment. To further illustrate the importance of small enterprises and employment, Table 1.1 outlines the projected growth industries through the year 2005, indicating how small firms dominate these groups. Thus our employment growth and industry expansions are closely tied to new-venture development.

In summary, entrepreneurial firms make two indispensable contributions to the U.S. economy. First, they represent an integral part of the renewal process that pervades and defines market economies. Entrepreneurial firms play a crucial role by fostering the innovations that lead to technological change and productivity growth. In short, they are about change and competition because they change market structure. The U.S. economy is a dynamic organic entity always in the process of "becoming," rather than an established one that has already arrived. It is all about prospects for the future, not about the inheritance of the past.

Second, entrepreneurial firms are the essential mechanism by which millions of people enter the economic and social mainstream of American society. Small businesses enable millions of people, including women, minorities, and immigrants, to access the American Dream. The greatest source of U.S. strength has always been the American Dream of economic growth, equal opportunity, and upward mobility. In this evolutionary process, entrepreneurship plays the crucial and indispensable role of providing the "social glue" that binds together high-tech and "Main Street" activities.[4]

The Age of the Gazelles

The United States' economic future may well depend on the development of our entrepreneurial abilities. Indeed, entrepreneurial firms create the most jobs in the U.S. economy, and the vast majority of these job-creating companies are fast-growing busi-

---

[4]"The New American Revolution: The Role and Impact of Small Firms" (Washington, DC: U.S. Small Business Administration, Office of Economic Research, 1998).

TABLE 1.1	SMALL BUSINESS DOMINATION OF EXPANDING INDUSTRIES

Industries Projected to Grow Most Rapidly (1990–2005) by Dominant Firm Group

Fastest Growing in Output (percentage basis)[a]

✓Manufacturers of computer equipment—*large dominated*

✓Manufacturers of semiconductors and related devices—*large dominated*

✓Residential care—*small dominated*

✓Health services, necessary—*small dominated*

✓Manufacturers of medical instruments and supplies—*indeterminant*

✓Computer/data processing services—*small dominated*

✓Business services—*small dominated*

✓Manufacturers of miscellaneous plastic products—*small dominated*

Fastest Growing in Employment (percentage basis)[b]

✓Residential care—*small dominated*

✓Computer/data processing services—*small dominated*

✓Health services—*small dominated*

✓Offices of health practitioners—*small dominated*

✓Individual and miscellaneous social services—*small dominated*

✓Legal services—*small dominated*

✓Nursing and personal care facilities—*small dominated*

✓Elementary and secondary schools—*small dominated*

[a] Includes only industries projected to employ 200,000 or more.

[b] Includes only industries projected to employ 500,000 or more.

SOURCE: William J. Dennis, Jr., *A Small Business Primer* (Washington, DC: THE NFIB Foundation, 1993), 15.

nesses. David Birch of Cognetics, Inc., has dubbed these firms "gazelles."[5] A **gazelle,** by Birch's definition, is a business establishment with at least 20 percent sales growth, starting with a base of at least $100,000. Despite the continual downsizing in major corporations, the gazelles produced 5 million jobs and brought the net employment growth to 4.2 million jobs during the 1980s. More recently, these gazelles (currently about 358,000 firms, or 4 percent of all ongoing companies) generated practically as many jobs (10.7 million) as the entire U.S. economy (11.1 million) during the 1990s. Their extraordinary performance and contribution warrants their recognition on several fronts.[6]

---

[5]David Birch's research firm, Cognetics, Inc., traces the employment and sales records of some 9 million companies with a Dun & Bradstreet file.

[6]David Birch, Jan Gundersen, Anne Haggerty, and William Parsons, *Corporate Demographics* (Cambridge, MA: Cognetics, Inc., 1999).

TABLE 1.2	GROWTH BY GAZELLES, 1990–1994
Jobs created by gazelles	5.0 million
Jobs lost by other companies	−0.8 million
Net employment growth	**4.2 million**

Innovation

Gazelles are leaders in innovation, as shown by the following facts:

- New and smaller firms have been responsible for 55 percent of the innovations in 362 different industries and 95 percent of all radical innovations.

- Gazelles produce twice as many product innovations per employee as do larger firms.

- New and smaller firms obtain more patients per sales dollar than do larger firms.

Growth

Note how these growth data indicate the current "Age of the Gazelles":

- The past ten years have seen an average of more than 600,000 business incorporations per year, with an all-time high of 807,000 incorporations in 1995.

- Of approximately 21.5 million businesses in the United States (based on IRS tax returns), only 14,000 qualify as "large" businesses.

- The compound growth rate in the number of businesses over a 12-year span is 3.9 percent.

- Each year approximately 14 percent of firms with employees drop from the unemployment insurance rolls and approximately 16 percent new and successor firms—firms with management changes—are added. This shift represents the disappearance or reorganization of half of all listed firms every five years!

- By 2010, demographers estimate, 30 million firms will exist in the United States, up significantly from the 22.5 million firms existing in 2000.

Effective Strategic Leadership in the New Millennium

Strategic leadership is defined as a person's ability to anticipate, envision, maintain flexibility, think strategically, and work with others to initiate changes that will create a viable future for the organization.[7] If strategic leadership processes are difficult for competitors to understand and hence to imitate, the firm will create a competitive advantage.

---

[7]Michael A. Hitt, R. Duane Ireland, and Robert E. Hoskisson, *Strategic Management: Competitiveness and Globalization*, 3rd ed. (Cincinnati, OH: Southwestern Publishing, 1999).

Today's fast-paced economy has created a new competitive landscape—one marked by constant and unpredictable change. The changes are revolutionary in nature—that is, they happen swiftly and are relentless in their frequency, affecting virtually all parts of an organization simultaneously.[8] The ambiguity and discontinuity resulting from revolutionary changes challenge firms and their strategic leadership to increase the speed of the decision-making processes through which strategies are formulated and implemented.[9]

Growth-oriented firms need to adopt a new competitive mindset—one in which flexibility, speed, innovation, and strategic leadership are valued highly. With this mindset, firms can identify and competitively exploit opportunities that emerge in the new competitive landscape. These opportunities surface primarily because of the disequilibrium that is created by continuous changes (especially technological changes). More specifically, although uncertainty and disequilibrium often result in seemingly hostile and intensely rivalrous conditions, these conditions may simultaneously yield significant product-driven growth opportunities.[10] Through effective strategic leadership, growth firms can adapt their behaviors and exploit different growth opportunities.[11]

In the previous three decades, change was often treated as linear in many industries; major competitors were largely domestic firms, rather than global companies; organizations were structured in hierarchical configurations that were supported by selection and promotion practices. Today, however, conditions associated with the new competitive landscape—shorter product life cycles, ever-accelerating rates and types of change, the explosion of data and the need to convert it to usable information—prevent single individuals from having all of the insights necessary to chart a firm's direction.

Constrained by their abilities to deal with rapidly increasing amounts of data and the general complexity of the global economy, managers of growth firms are now challenged to discharge their strategic leadership responsibilities differently. Insightful leaders recognize that it is impossible for them to have all of the answers, are willing to learn along with others, and understand that the uncertainty created by the new competitive economy affects people at the top as well as those lower down in the organization.[12]

As a way of conceptualizing the importance of strategic leadership for growth companies, researchers R. Duane Ireland and Michael A. Hitt identified some of the most important steps for effective strategic leadership.[13] Table 1.3 summarizes the key components needed for effective strategic leadership.

A Growth Orientation The new, fast-paced environment demands our emphasis on growth rather than downsizing or cost containment. Acquisition, product development, innovation, decentralization, and product line extension are all possible strategies that managers of emerging firms must be ready to implement.

---

[8]Royston Greenwood and C. R. Hinings, "Understanding Radical Organizational Change: Bringing Together the Old and the New Institutionalism," *Academy of Management Review* 21 (1996): 1022–1054.

[9]Eric H. Kessler and Alok K. Chakrabarti, "Innovation Speed: A Conceptual Model of Context, Antecedents, and Outcomes," *Academy of Management Review* 21 (1996): 1143–1191.

[10]Shaker A. Zahra, "Environment, Corporate Entrepreneurship, and Financial Performance: A Taxonomic Approach." *Journal of Business Venturing* 8 (1993): 319–340.

[11]Ronald A. Heifetz and Donald L. Laurie, "The Work of Leadership," *Harvard Business Review* 7, no. 1 (1997): 124–134.

[12]Albert A. Cannella, Jr., and Martin J. Monroe, "Contrasting Perspectives on Strategic Leaders: Toward a More Realistic View of Top Managers," *Journal of Management* 23, (1997): 213–237.

[13]R. Duane Ireland and Michael A. Hitt, "Achieving and Maintaining Strategic Competitiveness in the 21st Century: The Role of Strategic Leadership," *Academy of Management Executive*, 13, no. 1 (1999): 43–57.

TABLE 1.3	COMPONENTS OF STRATEGIC LEADERSHIP

1. Determining the firm's purpose or vision
2. Exploiting and maintaining core competencies
3. Developing human capital
4. Sustaining an effective organizational culture
5. Emphasizing ethical practices
6. Establishing balanced organizational controls

SOURCE: R. Duane Ireland and Michael A. Hitt, "Achieving and Maintaining Strategic Competitiveness in the 21st Century: The Role of Strategic Leadership," *Academy of Management Executive* 13, no. 1 (1999): 43–57.

Knowledge Management The development of pathways through which knowledge may be transmitted, exploited, protected, or developed will be a continual challenge during this new millennium.

Exploring the Entrepreneurial Concepts

The following sections provide an "entrepreneurial library" that contains a journal reading on this chapter's subject and a comprehensive case study to illustrate the concept in practice. It is hoped that through the reading and discussion of the case, you will gain a greater understanding of the chapter.

THE ENTREPRENEURIAL LIBRARY

Reading for Chapter 1

ENTREPRENEURIAL LEADERSHIP: OXYMORON OR NEW PARADIGM?

Lloyd W. Fernald, Jr. University of Central Florida
George T. Solomon The George Washington University

Abstract

It appears that a new form of leadership may be evolving as a result of the rapid and fast-paced changes taking place in the business world. Flatter organizational structures, scarcer resources, changing consumer demands, the information/technology revolution, and the global competition are forcing

Requests for reprints or correspondence concerning this article should be sent to Lloyd Fernald, Department of Management, College of Business Administration, University of Central Florida, P.O. Box 161400, Orlando, FL.

changes in the way business is conducted world-wide. This study provides support for suggesting that a new leadership style is emerging in order to cope with these changes. It is a form which combines the best leadership characteristics with the characteristics most associated with successful entrepreneurs. The study reviews the literature relative to the characteristics of both entrepreneurs and leaders with the intent of revealing those characteristics common to each. It suggests that the combined characteristics provide a model for *entrepreneurial leadership*, a new form of leadership needed in business organizations of the future.

Literature Review

As the 1990s give way to the next millennium, the current social, economic, and political environment is constantly being affected by the actions of entrepreneurs and entrepreneurial ventures. The current literature in entrepreneurship devotes considerable discussion to the role entrepreneurs play within their businesses and as opinion leaders in their markets and the general economy. Often described as innovators, paradigm pioneers and visionaries, entrepreneurs are confronted with the issue of developing leadership qualities in order to grow their businesses and to transform them to a level of professionalism.

Beginning in the 1980s, there has been an increased level of entrepreneurial activity which has been spawned, not only because of the electronic age, but also by the plethora of new materials, new products, new financial networks, new joint venture possibilities and paradigmatic changes in politics, economics and societies. The fact is there is now a whole new remodeling of the ways we do business, communicate and govern. Thus, it is imperative for anyone involved in and concerned about entrepreneurial ventures, especially the entrepreneur, to fully comprehend the importance of sound leadership practices as the business grows and moves through the various organizational life cycle stages.

This article will attempt to reveal those characteristics common to both successful leaders and entrepreneurs who operate in a dynamic, changing environment, needed to propel their ventures forward to new heights and successes. Also, it will attempt to show the characteristics entrepreneurs use to cope with their need to excel and explore new vistas while ensuring that they provide the guidance and encouragement needed to their respective staffs. In essence, we will try to show that a new form of leadership is evolving, *entrepreneurial leadership*, which is needed to break from the past and move into the future.

Entrepreneurship is a relatively new, sometimes controversial, and burgeoning field of management research. *Leadership* has been studied since around 500 B.C. New to the field is the subject of *entrepreneurial leadership*. Each will be briefly discussed in turn.

Entrepreneurship

Selection of the appropriate basis for defining and understanding entrepreneurs created a challenging problem for entrepreneurial research. Over ten years ago, the field of research was described as young, i.e., in its formative stage (Paulin et al., 1982; Perryman, 1982; Peterson & Horvath, 1982; Sexton, 1982). Even now there is no generally accepted definition of an entrepreneur, and the literature is replete with criteria ranging from creativity and innovation to personal traits such as appearance and style. Models of the entrepreneur are almost as plentiful as the number of researchers studying entrepreneurs (Churchill & Lewis, 1986; Cunningham & Lischron, 1991).

Krackhardt (1995) stated that research on entrepreneurship has defined entrepreneurship in two ways, the entrepreneurial firm and entrepreneurial people. Entrepreneurial firms are small (Aldrich & Austen, 1986), fast-growing (Drucker, 1985), organic and network-based rather than mechanistic and bureaucratic (Birley, 1986). In studying work flow working leadership, a form of firm-level entrepreneurship, Sayles and Stewart (1995) defined entrepreneurship as having three components: (1) it is activity that seizes profit opportunities without regard to resources currently controlled (Stevenson & Jarillo, 1990); (2) it expands existing resources through enhanced learning, synergies, or bootstrapping (Burgelman, 1983; Leibstein, 1968; Stewart, 1989; Venkataraman, McMillan & McGrath, 1992); and (3) it promotes change and innovation leading to new combinations of resources and new ways of doing business (Burgelman, 1983; Schumpeter, 1943). Entrepreneurial people take advantage of opportunities to acquire added value. This definition sees entrepreneurship as a behavioral characteristic of employees and managers in a firm, not as a characteristic of the firm itself.

Stevenson et al. (1989) argued that entrepreneurship is an approach to management. They distinguished between "promoters," individuals whose strategic direction is driven by the perception of opportunity, and "trustees," who are driven by resources they currently control. One could argue from this that "promoters" are actually leaders while "trustees" are managers. But others have written that both management and leadership skills play important roles in determining the growth rate of a small business. The skills required include: (1) seeing and clearly communicating a clear direction for the future, (2) leading and motivating others, (3) recognizing shortcomings in the team and supplementing those skills, and (4) having the business skills from an educational and experience viewpoint (Eggers et al., 1994).

Over the years several schools of thought on entrepreneurship have been generated which combine psychological traits with management/leadership skills. With respect to entrepreneurial activities, most important to entrepreneurs are: (1) seeking opportunities, (2) needing to achieve set goals, (3) being independence-minded, (4) taking risks, and (5) innovating (Lepnurm & Bergh, 1995). McClelland (1961) believed that entrepreneurial behavior was embedded in an individual's personality, the result of one's upbringing. Stewart (1989) documented the "fire in the belly" of employees who are always "running hot" within the firm. Thus, entrepreneurial behavior appears to be internal, similar to what often is described as characteristic of leaders.

Leadership

Zaleznik (1977) has reported that managers and leaders are different. They differ in what they attend to and how they think, work and interact. Also, managers and leaders have different personalities and experience different developmental paths from childhood to adulthood. Further, managers perceive life as a steady progression of positive events, resulting in security at home and at work. Leaders are "twice born." They ". . . endure major events that lead to a sense of separateness, or perhaps estrangement, from their environments" (James, 1985). As a result, they turn inward in order to reemerge with a created rather than an inherited sense of identity. This may be a necessary condition for the ability to lead. Finally, managers appear to be narrowly engaged in maintaining their identity and self-esteem through others. Leaders have self-confidence growing out of the awareness of who they are and the visions that drive them to achieve (Zaleznik, 1990). They appear to be different from those around them for the reasons stated.

Although research shows that certain traits alone do not guarantee leadership success, there is evidence that effective leaders are different from other people in certain key aspects. Key leader characteristics are: (1) drive, which includes achievement motivation, ambition, energy, tenacity, and initiative; (2) leadership motivation; (3) honesty and integrity; (4) self-confidence; (5) cognitive ability, and (6) knowledge of the business. The key leader characteristics help the leader acquire necessary skills, formulate an organizational vision and an effective plan for pursuing it, and take the steps needed to implement the vision into reality (Kirkpatrick and Locke, 1991).

It is not necessarily the individual possessing the most formal authority who is the leader in an organization, large or small. The leader is anyone who exerts influence over others. Specific traits, characteristics, and personal attributes that will predict superior performance in any given role, team, and organization can be identified and defined.

Entrepreneurial Leadership

On the surface, one can associate entrepreneurs with leadership functions such as providing vision to the development of a new product, service, or organization. A leader has to be entrepreneurial as well. It has been written that entrepreneurial leadership deals with concepts and ideas, and these are often related to problems which are not of an organizational nature. Instead, they tend to be individual characteristics or behaviors. They include vision, problem solving, decision making, risk taking, and strategic initiatives. A short discussion of each follows:

1. *Vision*—Only in this decade has the role of vision in the strategic management process, and the possible relationship between vision and creativity, leadership, and entrepreneurship, been given much attention. A vision is formulated by explicitly identifying a domain for competitive behavior, a set of sources of competitive strength, and a profile for resource capability. A vision implies a capability construct. This capability construct is determined by many factors including the managerial vision, competence and capacity, the logistic and technological profile, as well as the financial resource access of the firm. A good vision is realistic and feasible. It provides a challenge for the whole organization and mirrors the goals of the constituents. Visions may be killed by fear of mistakes, inability to tolerate ambiguity, and lack of challenge.

2. *Problem Solving*—Task-oriented leadership gets best results with purely technical, fact-based problems. Consideration-oriented leadership copes more effectively with emotional, personal, and interpersonal problems. Effective leadership must solve, or face, problems quickly and forcefully, regardless of their nature.

3. *Decision Making*—Managers are more likely to seek assistance from subordinates in solving problems than they are when making decisions. As a general

rule, whether leaders are directive or supportive, they know they must make the decisions that commit the organization to critical actions. If a leader avoids this responsibility, he/she will be poorly judged by subordinates and the organization will suffer accordingly.

4. *Risk Taking*—Balancing risk is a necessity of leadership. One must weigh the multitudinous factors involved, while understanding that no one can predict the future with certainty. Inability to deal with uncertainty precludes an organization from achieving its goals.

5. *Strategic Initiatives*—A leader must have a vision and plan for beyond a year or two to achieve long-term success (El-Namaki, 1992).

Entrepreneurial leadership has been coined by those who realize there must be a change in leadership style in order for America's businesses, large and small, to be competitive with the rest of the world. Knowdell et al. (1994) have noted that corporations now undergo paradigm shifts rather than linear change. One such paradigm shift is from a "producer mentality" which seeks instructions to an "entrepreneurial mentality" which seeks results. This had led to structural changes in organizations and new ways of doing business. The development of the Macintosh computer perhaps is a prime example. Other similar "skunk works," or entrepreneurial projects, are increasing in number throughout corporate America.

One might question whether or not entrepreneurial leadership, however, is truly a new form of leadership, an escape from management, or both. For the past twenty years, there has been a concern that major business corporations have lost their competitiveness primarily through an emphasis on management, rather than leadership.

A survey of 90 top executives and entrepreneurs revealed that four basic competencies are common to all leaders—management of attention, meaning, trust and self-esteem (Bennis, 1988). Bennis's research indicated that potential entrepreneurs are much more likely to have had business-owning fathers or relatives and to have owned their own firm at some stage of their careers. While no differences were found between subgroups in terms of their needs for achievement or their locus of control, the likely entrepreneurs were found to have a greater need for autonomy, creative tendencies, and higher calculated risk-taking orientations than other managers. In all, factors in the family background or personal profile of managers that may attract them to entrepreneurship have some potential for detecting entrepreneurs among managers (Cromie et al. 1992).

It is argued that the organizational archetype of the future will be entrepreneurial. Its leadership, strategies, and structure will reflect entrepreneurial thinking with associated characteristics, e.g., a problem-solving and action orientation. The characteristics and behaviors that spell success in entrepreneurial firms and small businesses now are being considered as vital for success in the 1990s, even for large transnational corporations. That even large companies are interested in this phenomenon is reflected in the popularity of what has been coined as "Intrapreneurship" by Pinchot (1985). Intrapreneurship is said to exist in situations in which individuals utilize entrepreneurial thinking to initiate and implement new ideas within large corporations (Chittipeddi and Wallet, 1991).

Based on the above, and a myriad of other sources too numerous to mention here, the similarities between what we know as leaders and what we know as entrepreneurs are considerable. Regardless of the amount of study each has been given, particularly with respect to leaders, there is much we have yet to learn. The "leadership literature includes over 5,000 studies; but the confused state of the field can be attributed in large part to the sheer volume of publications, the disparity of approaches, confusing terms, many trivial studies and the preference for simplistic explanations." (Yukl, 1994) This same charge has been levied at the research involving entrepreneurship (Vesper, 1996; Sexton and Kasarda, 1992; Zimnerer and Scarborough, 1996).

Nevertheless, there is much that is known about both leaders and entrepreneurs. Both leaders and entrepreneurs have been studied relative to their traits, skills, and behavioral characteristics. Numerous studies have been conducted in an attempt to profile what is a successful leader or a successful entrepreneur (Welsh & White, 1983). There is general agreement that a leader influences others toward the attainment of a vision and goals (Zaleznik, 1990; Stoner, 1995). A successful entrepreneur likewise influences those who can help achieve a desired goal or vision, whether it be a banker or other financial lender or those who can help to manufacture or distribute a product or service. Many also agree that leaders are visionary. They know what they want and where they want to go. They have a vision of their goals (Locke & Kirkpatrick, 1995; Hajek, 1995). This is best stated in a quote from Theodore Hesburgh: "The very essence of leadership is that you have a vision. It's got to be a vision you articulate clearly and forcefully on every occasion. You can't blow an uncertain trumpet." Successful entrepreneurs also envision the need for a product or service and how to provide the needed product or service.

In summary, based on a review of the literature, both leaders and entrepreneurs are successful largely to the extent that they provide: (1) strategic leadership (vision and long-term goals); (2) problem-solving skills; (3) timely decision making; (4) a willingness to accept risks; and (5) good negotiating skills. Successful is a key adverb and a vital factor in this review. Clearly, there are many leaders and entrepreneurs who fail. Whenever possible, the authors have made an effort to include only those behavioral characteristics shared by leaders and entrepreneurs which lead to successful attainment of vision and goals.

The above is intended to provide sufficient information to support a basis for the argument that leader and entrepreneur behavioral characteristics are more similar than different. In addition, it provides a basis for viewing entrepreneurial behavior as another type of leadership. This is particularly evident in view of the fact that changes in the workplace are demanding a new form of leadership. A flatter organizational hierarchy with its shrinking management ranks and less bureaucracy, coupled with the push for greater speed, better customer responsiveness and ongoing innovation, will require such. Every employee will be required to think and act like an owner/entrepreneur (Turknett, 1995).

Methodology

Characteristics possessed by entrepreneurs and by leaders were collected from various sources, including those discussed in the review of the literature, such as journal articles, dissertations and theses, books and magazine articles. These characteristics were then compared, resulting in a list of common characteristics. Appendix A contains the most frequently cited characteristics of both entrepreneurs and leaders, as well as the sources from which the characteristics were found.

There was no scale attached to these characteristics. The existence of the characteristics and the degree to which they exist in any individual can be most reliably determined by an in-depth, structured interview by an experienced and trained psychologist. Nevertheless, the number of times each characteristic was cited in the review of literature was used to compare the characteristics of a leader and an entrepreneur.

Results

Table 1 identifies characteristics that are particular to successful entrepreneurs and leaders, and the number of times those characteristics have been cited in the literature reviewed. By comparing the characteristics of entrepreneurs and leaders, a model of these competencies can be developed that specifies the personal characteristics that lead to entrepreneurial leadership.

Characteristics that are associated with both entrepreneurs and leaders, that is, those characteristics that are common to both, are presented in Table 2.

The actions of entrepreneurs and leaders speak louder than do their characteristics. Ten leadership initiatives which represent the ten actions successful leaders take to ensure the ongoing success of their organizations are: (1) envisioning; (2) managing mindsets; (3) modeling; (4) clarifying values; (5) aligning; (6) bridging; (7) managing breakdowns; (8) coaching; (9) renewing; and (10) acknowledging accomplishments (Krisco, 1995).

TABLE 1	CHARACTERISTICS OF ENTREPRENEURS AND LEADERS
Entrepreneurial Characteristics	**Leadership Characteristics**
Ability to motivate (3)	Ability to communicate/listen (17)
Achievement motivation (19)	Ability to motivate (16)
Autonomous (9)	Ability to work with others (21)
Creative (11)	Achievement orientation (15)
Flexibility/high tolerance (7)	Charisma (13)
Passion (4)	Creative (9)
Persistence (3)	Flexibility (12)
Risk taking (25)	Honesty and integrity (12)
Vision (6)	Persistence (11)
	Risk taking (8)
	Strategic thinking (9)
	Vision (31)

TABLE 2	COMMON CHARACTERISTICS	
	Entrepreneur	Leader
Ability to motivate	3	16
Achievement orientation	19	15
Creativity	11	9
Flexibility	7	12
Persistence	3	11
Risk taking	25	8
Vision	6	31

Table 2 reveals that the most common characteristics of both an entrepreneur and a leader are risk-taking, creativity, achievement motivation, ability to motivate, vision, flexibility, and persistence.

Risk-taking is the most highly cited characteristic among entrepreneurs whereas team management, i.e., ability to work with others, is the most common characteristic among leaders. According to the statistics entrepreneurs are also able to solve problems creatively.

Conclusions

The findings of this study, the common characteristics shared by both entrepreneurs and leaders, represents an attempt to provide a base for further studies on entrepreneurial leadership. The lists shown in Table 1 describe those characteristics one might anticipate in a successful leader or entrepreneur. They may provide information important to individuals considering the entrepreneurial life or seeking other leadership positions.

Support for this study is reflected in those leadership skills reported by CEOs on the Entrepreneurial Leadership Questionnaire (Eggers and Leahy, 1995). In that particular study, the results of which are shown in Table 3 below, we have annotated the individual leadership skills which we found to be common to the Entrepreneur/Leader characteristics in this study. Only five of these characteristics are so denoted. They are listed in the order provided in Table 3 as: (1) ability to communicate; (2) ability to motivate; (3) vision; (4) creative; and (5) risk taking. Clearly, many of the other characteristics apply in individual cases whenever entrepreneurs and leaders are studied. It should be noted that, as listed in Table 2, there are seven characteristics which were shown to be common among both entrepreneurs and leaders. They are the same as the above; the other two are flexibility and persistence.

TABLE 3	LEADERSHIP SKILLS REPORTED BY CEOs ON THE ENTREPRENEURIAL LEADERSHIP QUESTIONNAIRE		
	No. of Statements		No. of Statements
* Financial mgmt.	900	* Delegating	297
** Communication	653	* Personal adaptability	290
** Motivating others	615	* Time management	299
** Vision	522	* Product and business dvlpt.	204
** Motivating self	496	* Systems development	222
* Planning/goal setting	488	* Quality control	201
* Marketing	414	** Creativity and innovation	116
* Relationship building	425	** Listening	111
* Human resources	417	* Results orientation	100
* Problem solving	395	** Risk taking	87
* Business/tech. knowledge	384	* Negotiation	98
* Sales	335	* Informing	92
* Leadership and mgmt.	334	* Oral communication	59
* Employee development	340	* Self-development	49
* Customer/vendor relation	289	* Administration	56
* Ethics/org. culture	272	* Miscellaneous	43
* Organizing	311	* Written communication	33

Clearly, much remains to be done in clarifying the role and characteristics of tomorrow's leaders. New organizational designs, new thinking patterns, and new information systems will require new leadership styles. Entrepreneurial leadership offers one answer. The question remains, however, as to whether entrepreneurial leadership will consist of the characteristics found common to both the successful entrepreneur and leader.

In addition, there are those who will argue that entrepreneurs are not necessarily "good" or successful leaders. Such doubters can find support in the literature for the iconoclastic characteristics found in many entrepreneurs which are inconsistent with "good" leadership characteristics. For doubters, the term "entrepreneurial leadership" is seen as an oxymoron, a combination of terms which is contradictory to what we have been accustomed in the past. Successful entrepreneurs, however, have provided the vision and motivational factors that have led to the birth and growth of numerous major firms in the U.S., as well as the rest of the world, and they continue to do so. Entrepreneurial thinking is being increasingly demanded in even the largest corporations.

As stated above, more research in this area is essential. For example, future studies may include surveys which contain rank order preferences of the characteristics of a leader and an entrepreneur. Such studies will permit a rank order or other statistical analyses of the characteristics of leaders and entrepreneurs, helping further to define what we believe are the characteristics needed for entrepreneurial leadership.

References

Aldrich, H. & Austen, E. R. (1986). "Even dwarfs started small: Liabilities of age and size and their strategic limitations," *Research in Organizational Behavior*, 8, 165–198.

Bennis, W. (1988). "Ten traits of dynamic leaders," *Executive Excellence*, pp. 8–9.

Birley, S. (1986). "The role of networks in the entrepreneurial process," *Journal of Business Venturing*, 1, 107–117.

Burgelman, R. A. (1983). "Corporate entrepreneurship and strategic management: Insights from a process study," *Management Science*, 29, 2, 1349–1363.

Chittipeddi, K. & Wallet, T. A. (1991). "Entrepreneurship and competitive strategy for the 1990's," *Journal of Small Business Management*, pp. 94–98.

Churchill, N. C. & Lewis, V. (1986). "Entrepreneurial research: Directions and methods." In *The Art and Science of Entrepreneurship*, pp. 333–365, D. L. Sexton & R. W. Smilor (Eds.). Cambridge: Ballinger.

Cromie, S. & O Donaghue, J. (1992). "Research note: Assessing entrepreneurial inclinations," *International Small Business Journal*, pp. 66–73.

Cromie, S., Callaghan, I., & Jansen, M. (1992). "The entrepreneurial tendencies of managers: A research note," *British Journal of Management*, pp. 1–5.

Cunningham, J. B. & Lischeron, J. (1991). "Defining entrepreneurship." *Journal of Small Business Management*, 6, 45–60.

Drucker, P. (1985). *Innovation and entrepreneurship in the American corporation*. New York: Harper & Row.

Eggers, J. H., Leahy, K. T., & Churchill, N. C. (1994). "Entrepreneurial leadership in the development of small businesses." Paper presented at the 14th Annual Entrepreneurial Research Conference, Babson College, MA.

Eggers, J. H. & Leahy, K. T. (1995). "Entrepreneurial Leadership." *Business Quarterly*, Summer 1995; p. 73.

El-Namaki, M. S. S. (1992). "Creating a corporate vision," *Long Range Planning*, pp. 25–29.

Hajek, M. (1995). *What is leadership? Leading the world in aviation/aerospace education*. Titusville, FL: Embry-Riddle Aeronautical University.

James, B. G. (1985). *Business Wargames*. Cambridge, MA: Abacus Press.

Kirkpatrick, S. A. & Locke, E. A. (1991). "Leadership: Do traits matter?" *Academy of Management Executive*, pp. 48–60.

Knowdell, R. L., Branstead, E., & Moravec, M. (1994). *From downsizing to recovery*. Palo Alto, CA: CPP Books.

Krackhardt, T. (1995). "Entrepreneurial opportunities in an entrepreneurial firm: A structural approach," *Entrepreneurship: Theory and Practice*, pp. 53–69.

Krisco, K. H. (1995). *Leadership your way.* Miles River Press, Alexandria, VA.

Leibstein, H. (1968). "Entrepreneurship and economic development." *American Economic Review*, 58, 72–83.

Lepnurm, R. & Bergh, C. (1995). "Small business: Entrepreneurship or strategy?" *The Center for Entrepreneurship Review*, p. 4.

Locke, E. A. & Kirkpatrick, S. A. (1995). "Promoting creativity in organizations." In *Creative Action in Organizations*, C. M. Ford & D. A. Gioia (Eds.). Thousand Oaks: Sage Publications.

McClelland (1961). *The Achieving Society.* Princeton, NJ: van Nostrand.

McEnroe, J. (1995). "Portrait of Outstanding Leaders." *Trustee*, Feb. pp. 6–9.

Paulin, W. L., Coffey, R. E., & Spaulding, M. E. (1982). "Entrepreneur research: Methods and directions." In *The Encyclopedia of Entrepreneurship*, pp. 352–373, C. A. Kent, D. L. Sexton, & K. H. Vesper (Eds.). Englewood Cliffs, NJ: Prentice-Hall.

Perryman, R. (1982). "Commentary on research in the field of entrepreneurship." In *The Encyclopedia of Entrepreneurship*, C. A. Kent, D. L. Sexton, & K. H. Vesper (Eds.). Englewood Cliffs, NJ: Prentice-Hall.

Peterson, R. & Horvath, D. (1982). "Commentary on research in the field of entrepreneurship." In *The Encyclopedia of Entrepreneurship*, C. A. Kent, D. L. Sexton, & K. H. Vesper (Eds.). Englewood Cliffs, NJ: Prentice-Hall.

Pinchot, G. (1985). "Intrapreneurs innovate," *Management Today*, p. 54–61.

Sayles, L. R. & Stewart, A. (1995). "Belated recognition for work flow entrepreneurs: A case of selected perception and amnesia in management thought," *Entrepreneurship: Theory and Practice*, 19, 3, 7–23.

Schumpeter, J. A. (1943). *Capitalism, socialism, and democracy.* London: George Allen & Unwin.

Sexton, D. L. (1982). "Research needs and issues in entrepreneurship." In *The Encyclopedia of Entrepreneurship*, C. A. Kent, D. L. Sexton, & K. H. Vesper (Eds.). Englewood Cliffs, NJ: Prentice-Hall.

Sexton, D. & Kasarda, J. (1992). *The State of the Art of Entrepreneurship.* Boston, MA: PWS-Kent Publishing Company.

Stevenson, H. H. & Jarillo, J. C. (1990). "A paradigm of entrepreneurship: Entrepreneurial management," *Strategic Management Journal*, 11, pp. 17–27.

Stevenson, H. H., Roberts, M. J., & Grousbeck, H. I. (1989). *New business ventures and the entrepreneur.* Homewood, IL: Richard D. Irwin.

Stewart, A. (1989). *Team entrepreneurship.* Newbury Park, CA: Sage.

Stoner, J. A. *Management*, 7th Edition (1995). Englewood Cliffs, NJ: Prentice-Hall.

Turknett, R. (1995). "New work place to require leadership qualities in all," *The Atlanta Journal/Constitution*, pp. 3–12, B3.

Venkataraman, S., McMillan, I. C., & McGrath, R. G. (1992). "Progress in research on corporate venturing." In *The State of the Art in Entrepreneurship*, D. L. Sexton & J. D. Kasarda (Eds.). Boston: PWS-Kent.

Vesper, K. (1996). *New Venture Experience.* Seattle, WA: Vector Books.

Welsh, J. A. & White, J. F. (1983). *The entrepreneur's master planning guide.* Englewood Cliffs, NJ: Prentice-Hall.

Yukl, G. (1994). *Leadership in organizations*, Third Edition. Englewood Cliffs, NJ: Prentice-Hall.

Zaleznik, A. (1977). "Managers and leaders: Are they different?" *Harvard Business Review*, pp. 5–6.

Zaleznik, A. (1990). "The leadership gap," *Academy of Management Executive*, pp. 7–22.

Zimnerer, T. & Scarborough, N. (1996). *Entrepreneurship and New Venture Formation.* Upper Saddle River, NJ: Prentice-Hall.

Appendix A: Entrepreneur and Leader Characteristics

Characteristics of an Entrepreneur

(1) Ability to Motivate

Cromie, S., Callaghan, I., & Jansen, M. (1992). "The entrepreneurial tendencies of managers: A research note," *British Journal of Management*, pp. 1–5.

Poe, R. (1991). "Take charge now: Do you have the seven traits of a franchise leader?" *Success;* June 1991; pp. 53–62.

Stevenson, H. (1995). "We create entrepreneurs," *Success*, p. 50.

(2) Achievement Motivation

Boyd, N. & Vozikis, G. (1994). "The influence of self-efficacy on the development of entrepreneurial intentions and actions," *Entrepreneurship: Theory and Practice*, p. 3.

Broberg, L. (1993). "The entrepreneurial touch: The mark of the special breed," *Providence Business News,* p. 19.

Caird, S. (1993). "What do psychological tests suggest about entrepreneurs?" *Journal of Managerial Psychology*, pp. 11–20.

Cromie, S. & O'Donaghue, J. (1992). "Research note: Assessing entrepreneurial inclinations," *International Small Business Journal*, pp. 66–73.

Gupta, S. K. (1989). "Entrepreneurship development: The Indian case," *Journal of Small Business Management*, pp. 67–69.

Gutner, T. (1994). "Junior entrepreneurs," *Forbes*, pp. 188–189.

Herron, L. (1992). "Cultivating corporate entrepreneurs," *Human Resource Planning*, p. 3.

Hornaday, J. (1982). "Research about living entrepreneurs." In *Encyclopedia of Entrepreneurship*, C. A. Kent, D. L. Sexton, K. H. Vesper, eds. Englewood Cliffs, NJ: Prentice-Hall.

Larson, A. & Starr, J. (1993). "A network model of organization formation," *Entrepreneurship: Theory and Practice*, p. 5.

Learned, K. (1992). "What happened before the organization? A model of organization formation," *Entrepreneurship: Theory and Practice*, p. 39.

Lepnurm, R. & Bergh, C. (1995). "Small business: Entrepreneurship or strategy?" *The Center for Entrepreneurship Review*, p. 4.

McEnroe, J. (1995). "Portrait of Outstanding Leaders," *Trustee*, Feb. pp. 6–9.

Olson, Philip D. (1987). "Entrepreneurship and management," *Journal of Small Business Management*, pp. 7–13.

O'Neal, M. (1993). "Just what is an entrepreneur?" *Business Week*, Special Enterprise Issue, pp. 104–112.

Poe, R. (1991). "Take charge now: Do you have the seven traits of a franchise leader?"; *Success;* June 1991, pp. 53–62.

Shaver, K. & Scott, L. (1991). "Person, process, choice: the psychology of new venture creation," *Entrepreneurship: Theory and Practice*, p. 23.

Silver, D. A. (1988). "A portrait of the entrepreneur," *Accountancy;* pp. 77–80.

Starr, J. & Fondas, N. (1992). "A model of entrepreneurial socialization and organization formation," *Entrepreneurship: Theory and Practice*, p. 67.

Warshaw, M. (1994). "The entrepreneurial mind," *Success*, pp. 48–51.

(3) Autonomous

Cromie, S., Callaghan, I., & Jansen, M. (1992). "The entrepreneurial tendencies of managers: A research note," *British Journal of Management*, pp. 1–5.

Cromie, S. & O Donaghue, J. (1992). "Research note: Assessing entrepreneurial inclinations," *International Small Business Journal*, pp. 66–73.

Goodman, J. P. (1994). "What makes an entrepreneur?" *Inc.*, p. 29.

Gupta, S. K. (1989). "Entrepreneurship development: The Indian case," *Journal of Small Business Management*, pp. 67–69.

Larson, A. & Starr, J. (1993). "A network model of organization formation," *Entrepreneurship: Theory and Practice*, p. 5.

Learned, K. (1992). "What happened before the organization? A model of organization formation," *Entrepreneurship: Theory and Practice*, p. 39.

Olson, Philip D. (1987). "Entrepreneurship and management," *Journal of Small Business Management*, pp. 7–13.

Poe, R. (1991). "Take charge now: Do you have the seven traits of a franchise leader?" *Success*, 1991, pp. 53–62.

Sexton, D. L. & Bowman, N. (1985). "The entrepreneur: A capable executive and more," *Journal of Business Venturing*, pp. 129–140.

(4) Creative/Innovative/Creative Problem Solving

Broberg, L. (1993). "The entrepreneurial touch: The mark of the special breed," *Providence Business News,* p. 19.

Caird, S. (1993). "What do psychological tests suggest about entrepreneurs?" *Journal of Managerial Psychology*, pp. 11–20.

Chittipeddi, K. & Wallet, T. A. (1991). "Entrepreneurship and competitive strategy for the 1990's," *Journal of Small Business Management*, pp. 94–98.

Cromie, S. & O Donaghue, J. (1992). "Research note: Assessing entrepreneurial inclinations," *International Small Business Journal*, pp. 66–73.

Cromie, S., Callaghan, I., & Jansen, M. (1992) "The entrepreneurial tendencies of managers: A research note," *British Journal of Management*, pp. 1–5.

Goldsmith, R. E. & Kerr, J. R. (1991). "Entrepreneurship and adaptation-innovation theory," *Technovation*, pp. 373–382.

Grigg, T. (1994). "Adopting an entrepreneurial approach in universities," *Journal of Engineering & Technology Management;* pp. 273–298.

Gutner, T. (1994). "Junior entrepreneurs," *Forbes*, pp. 188–189.

Hornaday, J. (1982). "Research about living entrepreneurs." In *Encyclopedia of Entrepreneurship*, C. A. Kent, D. L. Sexton, K. H. Vesper, eds. Englewood Cliffs, NJ: Prentice-Hall.

Learned, K. (1992). "What happened before the organization? A model of organization formation," *Entrepreneurship: Theory and Practice*, p. 39.

O'Neal, M. (1993). "Just what is an entrepreneur?" *Business Week*, Special Enterprise Issue, pp. 104–112.

(5) Flexibility/High Tolerance for Ambiguity

Boyd, N. & Vozikis, G. (1994). "The influence of self-efficacy on the development of entrepreneurial intentions and actions," *Entrepreneurship: Theory and Practice*, p. 63.

Chittipeddi, K. & Wallet, T. A. (1991). "Entrepreneurship and competitive strategy for the 1990's," *Journal of Small Business Management*, pp. 94–98.

Hornaday, J. (1982). "Research about living entrepreneurs." In *Encyclopedia of Entrepreneurship*, C. A. Kent, D. L. Sexton, K. H. Vesper, eds. Englewood Cliffs, NJ: Prentice-Hall.

Learned, K. (1992). "What happened before the organization? A model of organization formation," *Entrepreneurship: Theory and Practice*, p. 39.

Olson, Philip D. (1987). "Entrepreneurship and management," *Journal of Small Business Management*, pp. 7–13.

Sexton, D. L. & Bowman, N. (1985). "The entrepreneur: A capable executive and more," *Journal of Business Venturing,* pp. 129–140.

Shaver, K. & Scott, L. (1991). "Person, process, choice: The psychology of new venture creation," *Entrepreneurship: Theory and Practice*, p. 23.

(6) Passion

Goodman, J. P. (1994). "What makes an entrepreneur?" *Inc.*, p. 29.

Luczkiw, G. & Loucks, K. (1992). *Creativity in Business.* Toronto: Copp Clark Pitman Ltd.

Silver, D. A. (1988). "A portrait of the entrepreneur," *Accountancy*, pp. 77–80.

Warshaw, M. (1994). "The entrepreneurial mind," *Success*, pp. 48–51.

(7) Persistence

Broberg, L. (1993). "The entrepreneurial touch: The mark of the special breed," *Providence Business News,* p. 19.

Larson, A. & Starr, J. (1993). "A network model of organization formation," *Entrepreneurship: Theory and Practice*, p. 5.

Pinchot, G. (1994). "Entrepreneurial leadership," *Executive Excellence*, pp. 15–16.

(8) Risk Taking

Bordeaux, D. B. (1987). "Entrepreneurship," *Manage*, pp. 2–4.

Boyd, N. & Vozikis, G. (1994). "The influence of self-efficacy on the development of entrepreneurial intentions and actions," *Entrepreneurship: Theory and Practice*, p. 63.

Broberg, L. (1993). "The entrepreneurial touch: The mark of the special breed," *Providence Business News,* p. 19.

Caird, S. (1992). "Problems with the identification of enterprise competencies and the implications for assessment and development," *Management Education and Development,* pp. 6–17.

Caird, S. (1993). "What do psychological tests suggest about entrepreneurs?" *Journal of Managerial Psychology,* pp. 11–20.

Cromie, S., Callaghan, I., & Jansen, M. (1992) "The entrepreneurial tendencies of managers: A research note," *British Journal of Management,* pp. 1–5.

Cromie, S. & O Donaghue, J. (1992). "Research note: Assessing entrepreneurial inclinations," *International Small Business Journal,* pp. 66–73.

Ennew, C., Robbie, K., Thompson, S., & Wright, M. (1994). "Small business entrepreneurs and performance: Evidence for management buy-ins," *International Small Business Journal,* pp. 28–44.

Goldsmith, R. E. & Kerr, J. R. (1991). "Entrepreneurship and adaptation-innovation theory," *Technovation,* pp. 373–382.

Gupta, S. K. (1989). "Entrepreneurship development: The Indian case," *Journal of Small Business Management,* pp. 67–69.

Gutner, T. (1994). "Junior entrepreneurs," *Forbes,* pp. 188–189.

Hornaday, J. (1982). "Research about living entrepreneurs." In *Encyclopedia of Entrepreneurship,* C. A. Kent, D. L. Sexton, K. H. Vesper, eds. Englewood Cliffs, NJ: Prentice-Hall.

Larson, A. & Starr, J. (1993). "A network model of organization formation," *Entrepreneurship: Theory and Practice,* p. 5.

Learned, K. (1992). "What happened before the organization? A model of organization formation," *Entrepreneurship: Theory and Practice,* p. 39.

Lepnurm, R. & Bergh, C. (1995). "Small business: Entrepreneurship or strategy?" *The Center for Entrepreneurship Review,* p. 4.

Luczkiw, G. & Loucks, K. (1992). *Creativity in Business.* Toronto: Copp Clark Pitman Ltd.

Miles, M., Arnold, D., & Thompson, D. (1993). "The interrelationship between environmental hostility and entrepreneurial orientation," *Journal of Applied Business Research,* pp. 12–23.

Olson, Philip D. (1987). "Entrepreneurship and management," *Journal of Small Business Management,* pp. 7–13.

O'Neal, M. (1993). "Just what is an entrepreneur?" *Business Week,* Special Enterprise Issue, pp. 104–112.

Rubenson, G. & Gupta, A. (1992). "Replacing the founder: exploding the myth of the entrepreneur's disease," *Business Horizons,* p. 53.

Sexton, D. L. & Bowman, N. (1985). "The entrepreneur: A capable executive and more," *Journal of Business Venturing,* pp. 129–140.

Shaver, K. & Scott, L. (1991). "Person, process, choice: The psychology of new venture creation," *Entrepreneurship: Theory and Practice,* p. 23.

Silver, D. A. (1988). "A portrait of the entrepreneur," *Accountancy,* pp. 77–80.

Stevenson, H. (1995). "We create entrepreneurs," *Success,* p. 50.

Warshaw, M. (1994). "The entrepreneurial mind," *Success,* pp. 48–51.

(9) Vision

Bedi, H. (1994). "Success starts with a vision," *Asian Business,* pp. 46–47.

Broberg, L. (1993). "The entrepreneurial touch: The mark of the special breed," *Providence Business News,* p. 19.

Larson, A. & Starr, J. (1993). "A network model of organization formation," *Entrepreneurship: Theory and Practice,* p. 5.

Luczkiw, G. & Loucks, K. (1992). *Creativity in Business.* Toronto: Copp Clark Pitman Ltd.

Stevenson, H. (1995). "We create entrepreneurs," *Success,* p. 50.

Warshaw, M. (1994). "The entrepreneurial mind," *Success,* pp. 48–51.

Characteristics of a Leader

(1) Ability to Communicate

_____ . (1994). *Sales & Marketing Management,* Nov., Performance Supplement, p. 37.

Al-Shammari, M. (1992). "Organizational climate," *Leadership and Organization Development Journal*, pp. 30–32.

Grassell, M. (1990). "Supervisory leadership skills for supervisors (Part 1)," *Supervision*, pp. 3–4.

Jolson, M., Comer, L., Dubinsky, A., & Yammarino, F. (1993). "Transforming the salesforce with leadership," *Sloan Management Review*, p. 95.

Kouzes, J. & Posner, B. (1992). "Ethical leaders: An essay about being in love," *Journal of Business Ethics*, pp. 479–484.

Lee, C. (1989). "Can leadership be taught?" *Training: The Magazine of Human Resources Development*, p. 19.

Martin, W. B. (1985). "Are you a manager or a leader?" *Industry Week*, pp. 93–97.

Pollock, T. (1994). "Seven signposts to stardom," *Production*, Aug., pp. 10–11.

Rifkin, G. (1996). "Leadership: Can it be learned?" *Forbes*, p. 100.

Rodriques, C. (1993). "Developing three-dimensional leaders," *Journal of Management*, pp. 4–11.

Russell, C. A. (1989). "Openness & trust," *Executive Excellence*, p. 12.

Sarros, J. (1992). "What leaders say they do: An Australian example," *Leadership and Organization Development Journal*, pp. 21–27.

Smith, R. (1994). "Inspirational leadership: A business imperative," *Executive Speeches*, pp. 20–23.

Stanford, J., Oates, B., & Flores, D. (1995). "Women's leadership styles: A heuristic analysis," *Women in Management Review*, pp. 9–16.

Thornton, S. J. (1990). "Leadership traits that work worldwide," *Association Management*, pp. 22, 24.

Tice, L. (1994). "Limitless leadership," *Executive Excellence*, pp. 17–18.

Warn, R. S. (1994). "Characteristics of leadership," *Manage*, Second Quarter, 1986, p. 14.

(2) Ability to Motivate

Al-Shammari, M. (1992). "Organizational climate," *Leadership and Organization Development Journal*, pp. 30–32.

Buono, A. (1994). "Impact of leadership," *Personnel Psychology*, pp. 189–193.

Gardner, J. W. (1988). "The context and attributes of leadership," *New Management*, pp. 15–22.

Grassell, M. (1990). "Supervisory leadership skills for supervisors (Part 1)," *Supervision*, pp. 3–4.

Holland, D. & Williams, J. B. (1994). "Sharpening your executive competencies," *Healthcare Executive*, pp. 13–17.

Kets de Vries, M., Loper, M., & Doyle, J. (1994). "The leadership mystique: executive commentary," *Academy of Management Executive*, pp. 73–92.

Kirkpatrick, S. A. & Locke, E. A. (1991). "Leadership: Do traits matter?" *Academy of Management Executive*, pp. 48–60.

Kouzes, J. & Posner, B. (1991). "Credible leaders," *Executive Excellence*, pp. 9–10.

Lee, C. (1989). "Can leadership be taught?" *Training: The Magazine of Human Resources Development*, p. 19.

Rasberry, R. & Fletcher, L. L. (1989). "Management traits & styles: What makes a manager a leader?" *Legal Professional*, pp. 26–34.

Reinmann, B. (1995). "Leading strategic change: Innovation. Value. Growth; humility in leadership," *Conference Overview. Planning Review*, p. 6.

Rifkin, G. (1996). "Leadership; can it be learned?" *Forbes*, p. 100.

Rodriques, C. (1993). "Developing three-dimensional leaders," *Journal of Management*, pp. 4–11.

Sharma, K. (1993). "Childlike leaders," *Executive Excellence*, pp. 16–17.

Tollgerdt-Anderson, I. (1993). "Attitudes, values, and demands on leadership—A cultural comparison," *Management Education and Development*, pp. 48–57.

Vallely, I. (1993). "Leadership: Do you have the right stuff?" *Works Management*, pp. 24–27.

(3) Ability to Work with Others/Trust

_____ . (1994). *Sales & Marketing Management*, Nov., Performance Supplement, p. 37.

Al-Shammari, M. (1992). "Organizational climate," *Leadership and Organization Development Journal*, pp. 30–32.

Bennis, W. (1987). "Four competencies of great leaders," *Executive Excellence*, Dec., p. 14.

Bennis, W. (1991). "Creative leadership," *Executive Excellence*, pp. 5–6.

Capowski, G. (1994). "Anatomy of a leader: Where are the leaders of tomorrow?" *Management Review*, p. 10.

Carlson, D. & Perrewe, P. (1995). "Institutionalization of organizational ethics through transformational leadership," *Journal of Business Ethics*, pp. 829–838.

Christmas, B. (1994). "Companies need new yardsticks to evaluate modular managers," *Apparel Industry Magazine*, pp. 66–70.
Frank, M. (1993). "The essence of leadership," *Public Personnel Management*, p. 381.
Holland, D. & Williams, J. B. (1994). "Sharpening your executive competencies," *Healthcare Executive*, pp. 13–17.
Kets de Vries, M., Loper, M., & Doyle, J. (1994). "The leadership mystique: executive commentary," *Academy of Management Executive*, pp. 73–92.
Kouzes, J. & Posner, B. (1991). "Credible leaders," *Executive Excellence*, pp. 9–10.
Lee, C. (1989). "Can leadership be taught?" *Training: The Magazine of Human Resources Development*, p. 19.
Pollock, T. (1994). "Seven signposts to stardom," *Production*, Aug., pp. 10–11.
Rasberry, R. & Fletcher, L. L. (1989). "Management traits & styles: What makes a manager a leader?" *Legal Professional*, pp. 26–34.
Reinmann, B. (1995). "Leading strategic change: Innovation. Value. Growth; humility in leadership," *Conference Overview. Planning Review*, p. 6.
Russell, C. A. (1989). "Openness & trust," *Executive Excellence*, p. 12.
Smith, R. (1994). "Inspirational leadership: A business imperative," *Executive Speeches*, pp. 20–23.
Stanford, J., Oates, B. & Flores, D. (1995). "Women's leadership styles: A heuristic analysis," *Women in Management Review*, pp. 9–16.
Taylor, B. (1993). "The values of leadership," *Optimum*, p. 82.
Thornton, S. J. (1990). "Leadership traits that work worldwide," *Association Management*, pp. 22, 24.
Vallely, I. (1993). "Leadership: Do you have the right stuff?" *Works Management*, pp. 24–27.

(4) Achievement Orientation

_____ . (1990). "Leadership Qualities of Executive Chiefs," *Supervision*, Nov., pp. 19–20.
Chapman, D. (1994). "Secrets of successful people," *Management-Auckland*, pp. 68–69.
Cusiman, R. & Davis, D. (1994). "Ten top traits to consider when hiring a manager," *Telemarketing Magazine*, p. 33.
Dubinsky, A. J., Yammarino, F. J., & Jolson, M. A. (1995). "An examination of linkages between personal characteristics and dimensions of transformational leadership," *Journal of Business & Psychology*, pp. 315–335.
Holland, D. & Williams, J. B. (1994). "Sharpening your executive competencies," *Healthcare Executive*, pp. 13–17.
Kahn, W. & Kram, K. (1994). "Authority at work: internal models and their organizational consequences." *Academy of Management Review*, p. 17.
Kets de Vries, M., Loper, M., & Doyle, J. (1994). "The leadership mystique: executive commentary," *Academy of Management Executive*, pp. 73–92.
Kirkpatrick, S. A. & Locke, E. A. (1991). "Leadership: Do traits matter?" *Academy of Management Executive*, pp. 48–60.
Mani, B. (1995). "Progress on the journey to total quality management: Using the Myers-Briggs type indicator and the adjective check list in management development," *Personnel Management*, p. 365.
Martin, W. B. (1985). "Are you a manager or a leader?" *Industry Week*, pp. 93–97.
Parker, W. N. (1994). "Better leadership," *Executive Excellence*, p. 14.
Pollock, T. (1994). "Seven signposts to stardom," *Production*, Aug., pp. 10–11.
Rasberry, R. & Fletcher, L. L. (1989). "Management traits & styles: What makes a manager a leader?" *Legal Professional*, pp. 26–34.
Stanford, J., Oates, B., & Flores, D. (1995). "Women's leadership styles: A heuristic analysis," *Women in Management Review*, pp. 9–16.
Ward, J. L. & Aronoff, C. E. (1994). "Preparing successors to be leaders," *Nation's Business*, pp. 54–55.

(5) Charisma

Atwater, L. & Yammarino, F. (1993). "Personal attributes as predictors of superiors' and subordinates' perceptions of military academy leadership," *Human Relations*, p. 645.
Buono, A. (1994). "Impact of leadership," *Personnel Psychology*, pp. 189–193.

Capowski, G. (1994). "Anatomy of a leader: Where are the leaders of tomorrow?" *Management Review*, p. 10.

Carlson, D. & Perrewe, P. (1995). "Institutionalization of organizational ethics through transformational leadership," *Journal of Business Ethics*, pp. 829–838.

Dubinsky, A. J., Yammarino, F. J., & Jolson, M. A. (1995). "An examination of linkages between personal characteristics and dimensions of transformational leadership," *Journal of Business & Psychology*, pp. 315–335.

Gibbons, P. (1992). "Impacts of organizational evolution on leadership roles and behaviors," *Human Relations*, p. 1.

Kets de Vries, M., Loper, M., & Doyle, J. (1994). "The leadership mystique: executive commentary," *Academy of Management Executive*, pp. 73–92.

Kirkpatrick, S. A. & Locke, E. A. (1991). "Leadership: Do traits matter?" *Academy of Management Executive*, pp. 48–60.

Mink, O. (1992). "Creating new organizational paradigms for change," *International Journal of Quality and Reliability Management*, pp. 21–35.

Pollock, T. (1994). "Seven signposts to stardom," *Production*, Aug., pp. 10–11.

Santora, J. & Sarros, J. (1995). "Mortality and leadership succession: A case study," *Leadership and Organization Development Journal*, pp. 29–32.

Smolenyak, M. & Majumdar, A. (1992). "What is leadership?" *Journal for Quality and Participation*, pp. 28–32.

Wood, J. (1996). "The two sides of leadership," *Financial Times*, p. VIII.

(6) Creative/Creative Problem Solving

_____ . (1990). "Leadership Qualities of Executive Chiefs," *Supervision*, Nov., pp. 19–20.

_____ . (1994). *Sales & Marketing Management*, Nov., Performance Supplement, p. 37.

Bennis, W. (1988). "Ten traits of dynamic leaders," *Executive Excellence*, pp. 8–9.

Capowski, G. (1994). "Anatomy of a leader: Where are the leaders of tomorrow?" *Management Review*, p. 10.

Dubinsky, A. J., Yammarino, F. J., & Jolson, M. A. (1995). "An examination of linkages between personal characteristics and dimensions of transformational leadership," *Journal of Business & Psychology*, pp. 315–335.

El-Namaki, M. S. S. (1992). "Creating a corporate vision," *Long Range Planning*, pp. 25–29.

Kirkpatrick, S. A. & Locke, E. A. (1991). "Leadership: Do traits matter?" *Academy of Management Executive*, pp. 48–60.

Rodriques, C. (1993). "Developing three-dimensional leaders," *Journal of Management*, pp. 4–11.

Thornton, S. J. (1990). "Leadership traits that work worldwide," *Association Management*, pp. 22, 24.

(7) Flexibility/Decisiveness

_____ . (1994). *Sales & Marketing Management*, Nov., Performance Supplement, p. 37.

Bennis, W. (1988). "Ten traits of dynamic leaders," *Executive Excellence*, pp. 8–9.

Buhler, P. (1995). "Leaders vs. managers," *Supervision*, pp. 24–26.

Christmas, B. (1994). "Companies need new yardsticks to evaluate modular managers," *Apparel Industry Magazine*, pp. 66–70.

Cusiman, R. & Davis, D. (1994). "Ten top traits to consider when hiring a manager," *Telemarketing Magazine*, p. 33.

Kets de Vries, M., Loper, M., & Doyle, J. (1994). "The leadership mystique: executive commentary," *Academy of Management Executive*, pp. 73–92.

Kirkpatrick, S. A. & Locke, E. A. (1991). "Leadership: Do traits matter?" *Academy of Management Executive*, pp. 48–60.

Lonardi, E., Willower, D., & Bredeson, P. (1995). "Assessing motivational needs: The case of the school superintendent," *Journal of Educational Administration*, pp. 6–13.

Martin, W. B. (1985). "Are you a manager or a leader?" *Industry Week*, pp. 93–97.

Parker, W. N. (1994). "Better leadership," *Executive Excellence*, p. 14.

Pollock, T. (1994). "Seven signposts to stardom," *Production*, Aug., pp. 10–11.

Thornton, S. J. (1990). "Leadership traits that work worldwide," *Association Management*, pp. 22, 24.

(8) Honesty & Integrity

Buhler, P. (1995). "Leaders vs. managers," *Supervision*, pp. 24–26.

Capowski, G. (1994). "Anatomy of a leader: Where are the leaders of tomorrow?" *Management Review*, p. 10.

Carlson, D. & Perrewe, P. (1995). "Institutionalization of organizational ethics through transformational leadership," *Journal of Business Ethics*, pp. 829–838.

Grassell, M. (1990). "Supervisory leadership skills for supervisors (Part 1)," *Supervision*, pp. 3–4.

Kirkpatrick, S. A. & Locke, E. A. (1991). "Leadership: Do traits matter?" *Academy of Management Executive*, pp. 48–60.

Kouzes, J. & Posner, B. (1992). "Ethical leaders: An essay about being in love," *Journal of Business Ethics*, pp. 479–484.

Kouzes, J. & Posner, B. (1991). "Credible leaders," *Executive Excellence*, pp. 9–10.

Larkin, C. (1994). "Leadership: The challenge of the 1990's," *Executive Speeches*, pp. 56–60.

Morgan, R. (1993). "Self- and co-worker perceptions of ethics and relationships to leadership and salary," *Academy of Management Journal*, p. 200.

Taylor, B. (1993). "The values of leadership," *Optimum*, p. 82.

Ward, J. L. & Aronoff, C. E. (1994). "Preparing successors to be leaders," *Nation's Business*, pp. 54–55.

Wood, J. (1996). "The two sides of leadership," *Financial Times*, p. VIII.

(9) Persistence/Commitment

Atwater, L. & Yammarino, F. (1993). "Personal attributes as predictors of superiors' and subordinates' perceptions of military academy leadership," *Human Relations*, p. 645.

Bennis, W. (1991). "Creative leadership," *Executive Excellence*, pp. 5–6.

Buhler, P. (1995). "Leaders vs. managers," *Supervision*, pp. 24–26.

Carlson, D. & Perrewe, P. (1995). "Institutionalization of organizational ethics through transformational leadership," *Journal of Business Ethics*, pp. 829–838.

Holland, D. & Williams, J. B. (1994). "Sharpening your executive competencies," *Healthcare Executive*, pp. 13–17.

Kirkpatrick, S. A. & Locke, E. A. (1991). "Leadership: Do traits matter?" *Academy of Management Executive*, pp. 48–60.

Larkin, C. (1994). "Leadership: The challenge of the 1990's," *Executive Speeches*, pp. 56–60

Parker, W. N. (1994). "Better leadership," *Executive Excellence*, p. 14.

Pollock, T. (1994). "Seven signposts to stardom," *Production*, Aug., pp. 10–11.

Rodriques, C. (1993). "Developing three-dimensional leaders," *Journal of Management*, pp. 4–11.

Santora, J. & Sarros, J. (1995). "Mortality and leadership succession: A case study," *Leadership and Organization Development Journal*, pp. 29–32.

(10) Risk Taking

Bennis, W. (1988). "Ten traits of dynamic leaders," *Executive Excellence*, pp. 8–9.

Caird, S. (1993). "What do psychological tests suggest about entrepreneurs?" *Journal of Managerial Psychology*, pp. 11–20.

Capowski, G. (1994). "Anatomy of a leader: Where are the leaders of tomorrow?" *Management Review*, p. 10.

Dubinsky, A. J., Yammarino, F. J., & Jolson, M. A. (1995). "An examination of linkages between personal characteristics and dimensions of transformational leadership," *Journal of Business & Psychology*, pp. 315–335.

Farey, P. (1993). "Mapping the leader/manager," *Management Education and Development*, pp. 109–121.

McEnroe, J. (1995). "Portrait of outstanding leaders," *Trustee*, Feb. pp. 6–9.

Rodriques, C. (1993). "Developing three-dimensional leaders," *Journal of Management*, pp. 4–11.

Schiffman, S. (1993). "Successful salespeople know how to lead," *Supervision*, pp. 7–8.

(11) Strategic Thinking

_____ . (1990). "Leadership Qualities of Executive Chiefs," *Supervision*, Nov., pp. 19–20.

_____ . (1994). *Sales & Marketing Management*, Nov., Performance Supplement, p. 37.

Bennis, W. (1988). "Ten traits of dynamic leaders," *Executive Excellence*, pp. 8–9.

Guthrie, J., Grimm, C., & Smith, K. (1991). "Environmental change and management staffing: An empirical study," *Journal of Management*, p. 735.

Holland, D. & Williams, J. B. (1994). "Sharpening your executive competencies," *Healthcare Executive*, pp. 13–17.

Kirkpatrick, S. A. & Locke, E. A. (1991). "Leadership: Do traits matter?" *Academy of Management Executive*, pp. 48–60.

Pollock, T. (1994). "Seven signposts to stardom," *Production*, Aug., pp. 10–11.

Rosenbaum, B. (1991). "Leading today's professional," *Research-Technology Management*, pp. 30–35.

Simpson, P. & Beeby, M. (1993). "Facilitating public sector organizational culture change through the processes of transformational leadership: A study integrating strategic options development and analysis with the cultural values survey," *Management Education and Development*, pp. 316–329.

(12) Vision

Al-Shammari, M. (1992). "Organizational climate," *Leadership and Organization Development Journal*, pp. 30–32.

Bennis, W. (1991). "Creative leadership," *Executive Excellence*, pp. 5–6.

Buhler, P. (1995). "Leaders vs. managers," *Supervision*, pp. 24–26.

Capowski, G. (1994). "Anatomy of a leader: Where are the leaders of tomorrow?" *Management Review*, p. 10.

Carlson, D. & Perrewe, P. (1995). "Institutionalization of organizational ethics through transformational leadership," *Journal of Business Ethics*, pp. 829–838.

Dwyer, E. (1994). "Seven paradoxes of leadership," *Journal for Quality and Participation*, pp. 46–48.

El-Namaki, M. S. S. (1992). "Creating a corporate vision," *Long Range Planning*, pp. 25–29.

Gibbons, P. (1992). "Impacts of organizational evolution on leadership roles and behaviors," *Human Relations*, p. 1.

Gilbert, G. (1992). "Quality improvement in a federal defense organization," *Public Productivity and Management Review*, pp. 65–75.

Grant, N. (1993). "Focus on leadership and leading: So you want to be a leader?" *Public Productivity and Management Review*, pp. 195–199.

Harter, N. (1992). "Thinking about diamonds and organizational vision," *Journal for Quality and Participation*, pp. 14–16.

Kets de Vries, M., Loper, M., & Doyle, J. (1994). "The leadership mystique: executive commentary," *Academy of Management Executive*, pp. 73–92.

Klagge, J. (1995). "Unity and diversity: A two-headed opportunity for today's organizational leaders," *Leadership and Organization Development Journal*, pp. 45–47.

Kouzes, J. & Posner, B. (1992). "Ethical leaders: An essay about being in love," *Journal of Business Ethics*, pp. 479–484.

Lee, C. (1989). "Can leadership be taught?" *Training: The Magazine of Human Resources Development*, p. 19.

Montebello, A. (1994). "The learning edge: How smart managers and smart companies stay ahead," *Personnel Psychology*, pp. 420–423.

Motley, A. (1994). "Taking charge of change," *Association Management*, p. 177.

Parker, W. N. (1994). "Better leadership," *Executive Excellence*, p. 14.

Reinmann, B. (1995). "Leading strategic change: Innovation. Value. Growth; humility in leadership," *Conference Overview. Planning Review*, p. 6.

Rifkin, G. (1996). "Leadership: Can it be learned?" *Forbes*, p. 100.

Rodriques, C. (1993). "Developing three-dimensional leaders," *Journal of Management*, pp. 4–11.

Rosenbaum, B. (1991). "Leading today's professional," *Research-Technology Management*, pp. 30–35.

Sarros, J. (1992). "What leaders say they do: An Australian example," *Leadership and Organization Development Journal*, pp. 21–27.

Streib, G. (1992). "Applying strategic decision making in local government," *Public Productivity and Management Review*, pp. 341–354

Sharma, K. (1993). "Childlike leaders," *Executive Excellence*, pp. 16–17.

Taylor, B. (1993). "The values of leadership," *Optimum*, p. 82.

Tice, L. (1994). "Limitless leadership," *Executive Excellence*, pp. 17–18.

Train, J. (1995). "Look for leaders, not managers," *Financial Times*, p. II.

Vallely, I. (1993). "Leadership: Do you have the right stuff?" *Works Management*, pp. 24–27.

Ward, J. L. & Aronoff, C. E. (1994). "Preparing successors to be leaders," *Nation's Business*, pp. 54–55.

Wood, J. (1996). "The two sides of leadership," *Financial Times*, p. VIII.

About the Authors

Lloyd W. Fernald, Jr., D.B.A., is a Professor of Management at the College of Business Administration, University of Central Florida, in Orlando, Florida. He is a Past President and currently Vice President, IBC Liaison, of the International Council for Small Business (ICSB), on the Steering Committee of the International Small Business Congress, President of the Small Business Director's Association, Region IV, and Chair, Florida Small Business Development Center Certification Board. He also is a Wilford White fellow of the ICSB and recent recipient of the Galloway Professorship in Management Award. Dr. Fernald serves on the editorial boards of the *Journal of Management Systems* and *Journal of Small Business Management*. His research interests are primarily in the area of Entrepreneurship and small business, creative and innovative management and the relationship between creativity, innovation and Entrepreneurship. His articles have been published in the *Journal of Creative Behavior, Entrepreneurship: Theory and Practice, Journal of Small Business Management, Journal of Business and Entrepreneurship, Journal of Private Enterprise*, several periodicals and numerous conference proceedings.

George T. Solomon is currently Director of Special Initiatives, U.S. Small Business Administration, Office of Business Initiatives. He also is an adjunct professor of Entrepreneurship and Management at both The George Washington University School of Business and Public Management and Georgetown University's Graduate School of Nursing. Prior to his tenure at The George Washington University, he was an Assistant professor of Marketing at Bentley College, Waltham, MA. Dr. Solomon has published over 60 articles and edited a number of reference materials in both the areas of Entrepreneurship/Small Business Management and Organizational Behavior & Dynamics. He also has appeared as a featured speaker and presenter at various national and international conferences. Dr. Solomon received his Doctorate of Business Administration (DBA) from The George Washington University School of Government and Business Administration with a major in Entrepreneurship/Small Business Management and Organizational Behavior & Development. He was the first individual in the nation to receive a doctorate in Entrepreneurship/small business management from a major accredited school of business. He received his MBA from Suffolk University, Boston, MA, and his BBS from Central Connecticut State University.

COMPREHENSIVE CASE STUDY

C A S E   **SPLATTERBALL ADVENTURE GAMES, INC.**

Beth Jack and Marilyn M. Helms   The University of Tennessee at Chattanooga

Splatterball Adventure Games, Inc. conducts paintball games in the Chattanooga, Tennessee, area. The company also maintains a store located in East Ridge, Tennessee, approximately five miles outside of the Chattanooga city limits. The playing field location for the game is in Apison, Tennessee, approximately 20 miles from Chattanooga.

As of 1992, Splatterball has one principal, Mr. Doug Gray, who runs all aspects of the business including monitoring the games, conducting sales, bookkeeping, and gun repair.

What Is Paintball?

Paintball became popular nationally in the early 1980s and includes both amateur and professional players in the sport. The development of the professional player occurred in the late 1980s. Like other sports, professional status is obtained when players earn money for playing paintball. In the case of paintball, money is earned by winning tournaments. Some of these tournaments have first place prizes as high as $30,000 for a ten-member team. For a team to be designated as a professional team, three-fifths of the members must be professional players.

Paintball is played mainly in the United States. Mr. Gray estimates there are approximately 300 fields across the United States. There are some fields located around the world. It is difficult to know exactly how many fields do exist outside the United States because many are located in countries that consider the guns used in paintball illegal.

The development of the sport has also led to the development of standard governing. Although several different governing organizations do exist, the most prevalent is the International Paintball Player's Association (IPPA). This organization was set up to create tournament and field guidelines. It also monitors any pending legislation that may be harmful to the industry and attempts to bring together the participants in paintball to prevent any adverse actions.

There are several variations in the way paintball is played. These variations depend on the location of the field, the type of field, and the field operator. However, because tournaments usually follow the IPPA rules, these are the guidelines most commonly followed in field operations.

There is some standard equipment for all players. Comfortable clothing and shoes for running through the obstacles are required. Many people choose to wear camouflage although it is not necessary. All players must wear protective eye goggles whenever on the field. Also required are the guns, carbon dioxide tanks, and paintballs. All

SOURCE: This case was written and developed by Beth Jack and Marilyn M. Helms of The University of Tennessee at Chattanooga.

of the equipment, with the exception of the clothing, can be bought or rented from the field operator.

Additional equipment used by regular players includes semiautomatic guns, gun cleaners, replacement parts for guns, vests, and speedloaders. This equipment is allowed in tournament play and is used to increase the playing ability of the players. It can be ordered from vendors across the country or purchased from paintball specialty stores.

Games are usually played in densely wooded areas. This gives players obstacles to hide behind and adds to the difficulty of the game. The games can be played in backyards; however, there are usually not enough obstacles for effective play. Paintball is not played in parks unless prior approval is received from park managers. The paint used in the paintball is water-based, but it still leaves marks on trees and other obstacles until there is enough rain to wash the paint away. The paint used is environmentally safe. Also, the plastic casing around the paintball will be left behind.

The object of paintball is to capture the opponent's flag and return it to your own flag station. The flags remain at the flag stations until a member of the opposing team captures it. These flag stations are simply a small area from which a flag is hung from a tree or some type of pole placed in the clearing. The area around the flag station varies from field to field. In some cases there will be natural barrier from which a player can defend the station. In other cases it is wide and open and must be defended from its perimeter. If the person who has captured the flag is shot while carrying the flag, the flag is considered "dead." That individual must return the flag to its original station and it then must be recaptured by another team member. It cannot simply be transferred to another teammate.

There are two main differences between tournament play and casual play. In casual play the team returning the captured flag to its own station wins the game. However, in tournament play teams advance through round-robin brackets in a point system. Points are awarded for the number of opposing players shot, first flag pulled, and returning the flag to one's own flag station. There are point penalties for safety violations, foul or abusive language, and physical contact during a game. The maximum number of points awarded is 100.

Each member of the team carries a carbon dioxide-based gun that shoots the paintball. The original guns were pressed plastic with few moving parts. The carbon dioxide came in small metal tubes that were pierced when inserted into the gun and would shoot approximately 20 to 30 rounds of paintballs. The guns now used have become more complicated with more moving parts. These guns are made of metal and often more closely resemble real guns. Manufacturers have begun the introduction of new types of guns such as semiautomatics. The carbon dioxide used in the guns can be obtained in refillable tanks and can be used for an entire game.

The paintballs are about the size of a marble. They were originally made of oil-based paint enclosed in a thin plastic shell. This quickly changed because once this paint dried onto clothing, it was extremely difficult to get out. The paintballs are now water-based so the paint can easily be washed out. They come in a wide variety of colors. However, most fields avoid using red so injuries are not mistaken for paint. The manufacturing process for the paintball is constantly being improved so that a more uniform ball can be made for better accuracy.

Professional teams have developed from 15-member teams to 10- and 5-member teams. This development has occurred so that games could be played under a 45-minute time limit.

Amateur games, usually played on weekends, are not as strict about time limits and the number of members on a team. Usually the field operator will split individuals up to form two to four teams, depending on the number of people at the field. They try not to allow more than 25 players on a team, if possible. Games are usually limited to one hour, although amateur games tend to end within 30 minutes.

The typical paintball player is male. There are some females who play as amateurs and a few on professional teams. The average professional player is 22–35 years old. The average casual player is 18–30. Players come from a wide variety of backgrounds including professional managers, physicians, blue-collar workers, and students.

Tournaments are sponsored year round in the United States. A tournament circuit holds games in San Francisco, Chicago, and two in Nashville. The most prestigious tournament takes place every October in Nashville, Tennessee. This tournament, the International Masters Tournament, is the biggest of its kind with a 64-team field and a $30,000 first prize. This tournament lasts five days and includes both five-member and ten-member team competitions. This tournament usually includes at least two British teams every year. The top eight finishers of this tournament are able to get sponsorship from manufacturers of paintball equipment. This tournament is also a chance for vendors to display their new products and innovations to the players.

History of Splatterball Adventure Games, Inc.

Splatterball Adventure Games, Inc. is located in Chattanooga, Tennessee, and runs local paintball games. Also, it has a store that sells some paintball supplies and repairs guns. It is through this store that many of the games are scheduled.

The owner of Splatterball, Doug Gray, began his involvement with the sport of paintball in 1981. He was a member of a small team based out of Chattanooga. Shortly after joining, the team moved to Nashville when the field they were using was sold and was no longer available for their use. Many of the players lived in Nashville at that time, so they decided to open a field in Nashville rather than look for a new field in Chattanooga. The team in Nashville became known as the Nashville Ridgerunners. Mr. Gray is still in active member of the Nashville Ridgerunners Professional Paintball Team.

Because there was no longer a field in Chattanooga, Mr. Gray drove two hours to Nashville almost every weekend to play the sport. It was during these trips that he decided to open a field of his own in Chattanooga so he could practice closer to home.

Mr. Gray began to get his friends and acquaintances to go to Nashville with him in order to generate interest. Eventually, he was able to get enough people interested in paintball to support his field in Chattanooga.

Mr. Gray leased a parcel of land approximately 20 miles southeast of Chattanooga. According to Mr. Gray, "Since this was more of a hobby than a business, I decided to run the operation from my home." He bought some of the plastic guns to use for rentals so he could continue to bring in new players to his field.

During this time the field in Nashville became very successful at organizing paintball tournaments. Many tournaments were organized to bring in teams from the southeast region. Mr. Gray worked closely with the Nashville field in setting up his own field. His close ties enabled him to obtain many of his supplies at volume discount prices, as well as gain other advantages that would otherwise have been denied to him as an independent.

Mr. Gray's business continued to grow as paintball began to receive more attention nationally. Businesses and groups began to schedule games for their members only. As his business expanded, Mr. Gray began to carry more rental equipment and supplies for the part-time player.

Eventually the business grew so large it became difficult to manage from his home. The rental equipment took up so much room that he decided it was time to establish a center of operations. However, in order to make this feasible, Mr. Gray needed an infusion of capital for the store lease, furniture lease, and the addition of even more equipment. He figured the total cost would run approximately $7,500. It was at this time that he took in one partner and the business incorporated with each partner owning 500 shares of stock.

Unfortunately, the partnership was not successful. Both partners had differing ideas on how the income should be distributed. Mr. Gray wanted most of the money reinvested into the business for further growth. However, his partner decided he wanted his capital infusion paid back immediately. After one year the partnership was dissolved through Mr. Gray's purchase of his partner's 500 shares of stock for $11,000. The original investment was $10,000 and his partner had received approximately $1,200 in capital withdrawals when the repurchase was made.

The Situation in 1992

As of 1992, Mr. Gray is the sole stockholder of Splatterball and he has decided to reevaluate what he is trying to accomplish. What is the future of Splatterball? Where is he trying to go with the business? How does he get there?

The business itself is quickly becoming a full-time operation. The hours of operation of the store are currently 11:00 a.m. to 3:00 p.m. Monday through Friday. It is only open on weekends if no games are being played at the field. Mr. Gray would like to increase the hours of operation but currently is not in the position to do so. Mr. Gray has a full-time job as a computer programmer and he works 4:00 p.m. to 12:15 a.m. Monday through Friday. Eventually he would like to leave this position and have the business as his main source of income.

The store does bring some walk-in business, often from people who play the game on their own land. Mr. Gray offers a gun repair service on the premises. He is able to sell guns, supplies, and trade magazines at the store. Most of Splatterball's income is derived from the games. The field is available all year but games are scheduled in advance, especially during the winter months. With scheduling, the proper amount of supplies can be ordered and the appropriate number of field judges can be obtained. Splatterball only keeps 100 rental guns in stock, so if extremely large groups play, Mr. Gray has to borrow guns from another field. He has worked out an agreement with a field in Atlanta in which each field makes guns available to the other at no charge.

Splatterball has its own professional and amateur teams that play regularly at the Splatterball field and in national tournaments. These teams were started in 1990 and have no sponsorship. There is no fee to become a member as each member is responsible for all tournament entry fees and supplies. Mr. Gray relies heavily on his professional team members to give their support in running the store and in officiating games when they are not playing. Their compensation is in the form of discounts on supplies and gun repairs. New members are recruited from individuals playing the game with a group who have decided that they would like to play on a regular basis. These individuals will generally play with the team for six months before becoming a team member.

Currently, almost all of the games are scheduled on Saturday and Sunday mornings and afternoons. Groups schedule the field for an entire day. It is also possible for Mr. Gray to run the games during the week before 2:00. Splatterball continues to run walk-on games on weekends, enabling individuals to try paintball without having to find other players to make up two teams. In addition to the typical player, Mr. Gray has some school groups that regularly rent the field for an entire day.

As previously mentioned, Mr. Gray has been involved with paintball since 1981. His business background includes several years of college courses and his own trial-and-error experience when he first started Splatterball. He has taken a small-business management course at a local junior college, but feels that he learned the most about management from starting the business. When asked about his management style, Mr. Gray says, "Currently I am a doer out of necessity, but I am a delegator by nature. I am great at long-range planning and I need to be careful not to forget the small daily details that keep me in business."

The Competition

Splatterball's competition is primarily from the amusement industry and other paintball fields. Movies, music, and sport hunting are just three examples of the competition. Also, because of the great deal of physical activity involved, Mr. Gray feels he competes for the physical fitness dollar as well.

Competition between the paintball fields is actually very friendly. The closest fields to Chattanooga are in Atlanta, Knoxville, and Nashville. Each of these fields is approximately a two-hour drive from Chattanooga. Because there are no fields close by, he does not compete directly with them for local players. Instead he has worked out arrangements with many of them that enable each of them to host all of the participating regional teams in a league play. This league has ten teams from Chattanooga, Nashville, Atlanta, and Birmingham. Ten times a year, all the teams meet at different fields to play each other. This was set up to give each of the teams a chance to play different types of fields with a higher level of competition. Although a trophy is awarded to the team accumulating the most points at the end of a calendar year, the main purpose of this league is to provide a higher level of practice for the major tournaments. Most of the fields in this league are about the same size as Mr. Gray's, with the exception of the Nashville field. The Nashville field is able to handle approximately three to four times the size of the Splatterball field. Also, the Nashville field has an agreement with a local campground to use the campgrounds for major tournaments in the spring and the fall. As it is privately held, the exact earnings are unknown, but it is estimated to be around $1 million annually, including field operations, store operations, and tournaments.

In competing with the physical fitness activity, Splatterball has actually been able to work in cooperation with different programs. The game has been included as an activity in an intensive six-week fitness program in Chattanooga. This program is used to build self-confidence as well as physical fitness.

Splatterball also competes with the hobby/entertainment industry in general. Often it can be heard around the field that someone played that weekend instead of hunting or buying some personal item.

Costs

The cost of playing Splatterball depends on the experience of the player. Novice players will generally have lower costs, because they rent their equipment. Mr. Gray typically charges a $22.52 flat field fee which includes the $12 gun rental, 40 rounds of paint, and one small tank of carbon dioxide. Novice players generally shoot less than more experienced players and often do not have to purchase extra paint. The typical charge is $1.08 for one tube of paint (eight rounds).

The experienced player tends to incur much higher costs as most will purchase their own guns, which will start at about $150. Also, there is the purchase of camouflage and other extra equipment to maintain the performance of their equipment. It is not uncommon for an experienced player to shoot up to 30 tubes of paint per game. Since most play a minimum of three 45-minute games, this will add up quickly.

The players that are part of a team will often have expenses on top of those incurred by the experienced player. Many own several guns in case of gun failure. These failures are usually due to wear on parts and do not occur regularly, but if a gun fails during a tournament, then the team is short a player. Also, there is the high entrance fees for tournaments which can be as much as $200 per member.

Financial Situation

Splatterball Adventure Games, Inc. actually has a very "loose" accounting system. However, Mr. Gray has recently had an offer of free accounting services for 100 shares of stock (Mr. Gray owns 1,000 shares of the 1,500 shares; 500 shares are retained by the business.)

EXHIBIT 1	SPLATTERBALL ADVENTURE GAMES, INC. INCOME STATEMENT FOR THE QUARTER ENDING DECEMBER 31, 1991

INCOME	
Sales	7,107.00
Net Sales	7,107.00
COST OF GOODS SOLD	
Total Cost of Goods Sold	0.00
Gross Profit	7,107.00
EXPENSES	
Advertising	2,195.00
Auto Expense	15.22
Bank Service Charges	22.50
Bank Wire Transfer Fees	18.00
Casual Labor	175.00
Dues & Subscriptions	58.00
Entertainment	173.28
Entry Fees	278.00
Miscellaneous Expense	190.10
Office Expense	377.69
Paint and CO_2 Supplies	6,280.71
Postage	10.24
Rent	100.00
Field Supplies	1,204.97
Telephone	111.88

EXHIBIT 1	(CONTINUED)

Uniforms	128.56
Total Expenses	11,339.15
Net Operating Expenses	(4,232.15)
OTHER INCOME	
Interest Income	13.00
Total Other Income	13.00
OTHER EXPENSES	
Total Other Expenses	0.00
Income Before Taxes	(4,219.15)
Net Income	(4,219.15)

Splatterball Adventure Games, Inc.
Balance Sheet,
December 31, 1991

ASSETS

CURRENT ASSETS		
Cash	(1,777.58)	
Inventory	260.99	
Total Current Assets		(1,516.59)
FIXED ASSETS		
Office Equipment	189.95	
Paint Guns	8,539.10	
Field Equipment	2,592.25	
Total Fixed Assets		11,321.30
OTHER ASSETS		
Total Other Assets		0.00
Total Assets		9,804.71

LIABILITIES & EQUITY

CURRENT LIABILITIES			
Accounts Payable	1,145.00		
Notes Payable	11,363.26		
Sales Tax Payable	515.60		
Total Current Liabilities		13,023.86	
LONG-TERM LIABILITIES			
Total Long-Term Liabilities		0.00	
Total Liabilities			13,023.86
STOCKHOLDERS' EQUITY			
Common Stock		1,000.00	
Current Earnings		(4,219.15)	
Total Equity			(3,219.15)
Total Liabilities & Equity			9,804.71

Exhibit 1 shows the current financial statements for the firm. The largest debt is Mr. Gray's repayment of the $11,000 loan used to repurchase the stock from his former partner. Other expenses, such as supplies, can usually be directly matched to the sales since most supplies are received within two days of use. This helps eliminate spoilage of the supplies. The paintballs have a shelf life of several months, but they do tend to become soft. The sooner they are used, the better they perform.

Mr. Gray has also had an offer from two of the members of his team to work for 150 shares of stock each in the business. These players have helped Mr. Gray run Splatterball for two years. Neither would invest any money at this time but instead would reinvest their share of the profits plus provide free services. They would be able to assist in running the games and working in the store to increase its hours of operations. Both are experienced in gun repair and would be able to assist in this aspect of the business, as well. One is a computer programmer with a college degree in this field and the other assists in the management of his family's convenience store. The other individual is an accountant who will contribute free accounting and tax services to Splatterball. Both individuals would be able to work during the hours Mr. Gray is at his full-time job. This is currently under consideration with the attorneys in regards to fair value and distribution of future income through dividends or through salaries.

Legal Environment

The current legal environment is of great concern to Splatterball. Although every player signs a waiver form (see Exhibit 2) each time he or she plays, these waivers have not been tested through a lawsuit. Mr. Gray has had several attorneys review his form and has always received approval.

Injuries are one of the main concerns for Mr. Gray. Last year a new player was hit in the eye with a paintball and lost his vision. This player had taken his goggles off even though he had been instructed not to and had signed the waiver stating he would wear the goggles at all times. In this particular instance, Splatterball was very lucky as a spectator had just taken a picture of the injured player not wearing the required safety goggles. This picture prevented a lawsuit for negligence. However, the potential legal problems were brought to the forefront by this incident.

The entire paintball industry has worked very hard to promote safe usage practices both on and off the fields. *Paintball Sports Magazine* has published several articles regarding the usage of guns off the field. Tournaments impose penalties against teams whenever a player is found not to be wearing goggles. Off the field, barrels are required to have plugs in them so that if they accidentally are shot, the paintball breaks in the gun. Field operators also monitor how hard the guns are shooting the paintball. They chronograph the guns to ensure the guns do not shoot so hard as to injure a player who is shot. Even though the guns are carefully monitored, being hit by a paintball will hurt. If shot from a very close range it will leave a bruise and occasionally a small welt. This welt, although painful, usually disappears within 1 to 2 days with no special attention required.

Most fields, including Splatterball, and all tournaments discourage shooting other players in the head. They have simply ruled head shots do not count as "kills" or points. If a player is hit in the head, he or she may call a judge over to help him/her wipe off the paint. The judge will declare the player neutral until the paint is wiped off and then puts the player back into the game.

Whenever new players come out to the field, they are given instructions before the game begins. The field operator will walk over the field with the new player(s) to point out the boundaries and the flag stations. The field operator also points out any areas that players may want to avoid because of potential injury.

The entire industry has also worked together in regards to concerns about their equipment. There have been attempts in several states, most notably California where there are several major fields, to ban the sale of toys that closely resemble guns. This is due to the very publicized shooting of children because someone thought they had real guns. Because the newer guns do closely resemble real guns, the industry is notably concerned.

Teams, field operators, and suppliers have worked together to keep paintball games as safe as possible. Because of the nature of the sport, there are sometimes injuries, but the people involved know that when care and caution are used, most of these injuries can be avoided. These same people have also worked very hard to keep the sport legal in all states through letter-writing, campaigns, and lobbying.

The Future

Mr. Gray would eventually like to turn Splatterball into his full-time job. Currently he works evenings to supplement his income. He states, "If I could create a larger demand in the off-season, I could depend on Splatterball as my sole source of income."

Because of his expansion, the addition of shareholders to ease the financial burden is another consideration of Mr. Gray's. It would enable Splatterball to run more games, especially during the week.

There is no real marketing strategy in place for Splatterball and Mr. Gray feels it is needed. Although Mr. Gray had some informational brochures printed for distribution, the main source of new business comes from word-of-mouth advertising. Mr. Gray would like to implement a strategy that will not deplete too much of his personal financial resources yet will enable him to work full time in his hobby.

EXHIBIT 2 | **SPLATTERBALL ADVENTURE GAMES, INC. APPLICATION TO PLAY WAIVER OF LIABILITY AND ASSUMPTION OF RISK**

---

1. I, the undersigned wish to play the Splatterball Adventure game. I recognize and understand that playing the game involves running certain risks. Those risks include, but are not limited to, the risk of injury relating from the impact of the paint pellets used in the Game, injuries resulting from possible malfunction of equipment used in the Game, and injuries resulting from tripping or falling over obstacles in the Game playing field. In addition, I recognize that the exertion of playing the game could result in injury or death.

2. Despite these and other risks, and fully understanding such risks, I wish to play the Game and hereby assume the risks of playing the Game. I also hereby hold harmless Splatterball Adventure Game, Inc., hereafter called the Sponsors, and John Felts (landowner) and indemnify them against any and all claims, actions, suits, procedures, costs, expenses (including attorney's fees and expenses), damages and liabilities arising out of, connected with, or resulting from my playing

(continued)

the Game, including without limitation, those resulting from the manufacture, selection, delivery, possession, use or operation of such equipment. I hereby release the sponsors from any and all such liability, and I understand that this release shall be binding upon my estate, my heirs, my representatives and assigns. I hereby certify to the Sponsors that I am in good health and do not suffer from a heart condition or other ailment which could be exacerbated by the exertion involved in playing the Game.

3. I hereby promise to play the Game only in accordance with the rules of the Game as set forth by the Sponsors. In particular, I agree:

   a. to wear safety goggles at all times when I am on the playing field or at the target area, even after I have been marked with paint or the game is over and to keep the goggles snug by pulling the straps tight; I understand that serious eye injury, including loss of eyesight, could occur if the safety goggles are not on when marking pistols may be discharged anywhere near me. Should my safety goggles fog up or for any reason be such that I cannot see through them properly, I will ask someone near me, on the playing field or in the target area, to lead me out of the area I am into one where all marking pistols are on "SAFETY." Only then will I remove my safety goggles to clean them. I understand that any "safety goggle" is subject to fogging up or getting dirty and that if I am anywhere near a marking pistol as it discharges, and my "safety goggles" are not properly on, I may get seriously and permanently injured;

   b. to avoid any physical contact or fighting with other players;

   c. to stay within the boundaries of the playing field and not to chase or run after anyone over ledges or mountainous terrain;

   d. to keep the marking pistol I am using on "safety" (the no-shoot position) in the staging areas at all times, in the target area while not shooting and on the playing field before and after each game, to aim or point the pistol at another person ONLY during an active game and never to wave or brandish the pistol about in the staging area or the target area; and

   e. to avoid pointing or shooting at the head of any player at any time.

4. For safety reasons I agree to use only equipment and/or supplies provided to me by the Sponsors while playing the game or in the target area. Written permission of the Sponsors is necessary should I elect to use other equipment or supplies. If I have chosen not to use the goggles or marking pistol available from the Sponsors, I hereby certify that the goggles or marking pistol, which I have chosen to use, are at least as safe as the Sponsor's from claims arising out of any additional risk resulting from my use of goggles or marking pistol other than those available from the Sponsors.

5. I agree to ask the Sponsor for clarification of any rule or safety procedure, for further instruction as regards anything that I don't understand about the equipment and supplies as regards anything else that may affect the safety of playing of the Game.

6. I have read this waiver of liability and assumption of risk carefully, and understand that by signing below, I am agreeing, on behalf of myself, my estate, my

heirs, representatives and assigns not to sue the Splatterball Adventure Games, Inc. or to hold them or their insurors liable for any injury including death, resulting from my playing the Game. I intend to be fully bound by this Agreement.

By virtue of my signature, I acknowledge and agree to all terms and conditions set forth on this form.

X Signature _____

Date Signed _____

Is this your first visit to our field?   YES ( )   NO ( )

2

The Internet Revolution

Key Topics

- The Internet Explosion

- The E-Commerce Challenge

- E-Names: The Web Address

- Developing a Web Site

- Emerging E-Commerce Strategies

- Myths of the Internet

- Web Site Assistance for Small Firms

The Internet Explosion

Peter F. Drucker has stated that the "truly revolutionary impact of the Information Revolution is just beginning to be felt . . . the explosive emergence of the Internet as a major, perhaps eventually the major, worldwide distribution channel for goods, for services, and, surprisingly, for managerial and professional jobs is profoundly changing economies, markets, and industry structures; products and services and their flow; consumer segmentation, consumer values, and consumer behavior; jobs and labor markets."[1]

This statement summarizes quite succinctly the tremendous impact that the Internet is having on the global marketplace. The statistics appear to support this claim of profound change from the "Internet Explosion."

In 1999, U.S. businesses spent $85.7 billion on building up their Internet capabilities, according to International Data Corporation, Framingham, Massachusetts, up 39 percent from the amount expended a year earlier. For 2000, IDC predicts more rapid growth, with total spending nearing $120 billion.

Manufacturers and financial services companies are pushing their electronic-commerce (e-commerce) initiatives especially aggressively. Likewise, media companies, retailers, and even utilities are spending billions of dollars in hopes of mastering the Internet's promise and turning it into a revenue and profit-generating tool for themselves.

The allure of doing business on the Internet is simple. Online technology provides a low-cost, extremely efficient way to display merchandise, attract customers, and handle purchase orders. But getting all the parts of an e-commerce strategy to work smoothly can be a challenging experience. For every company that has it right, countless others are struggling to upgrade their Web sites and related infrastructure.

Internet use by small ventures is on the rise: the number of entrepreneurial businesses with access to the Internet nearly doubled over two years, increasing from 21.5 percent in 1996 to 41.2 percent in 1998. As many as 35 percent of small businesses maintain their own Web site. Research shows that smaller ventures that utilize the Web have higher annual revenues, averaging $3.79 million in 1998, compared with $2.72 million for all small ventures.[2]

Smaller ventures use the Internet for a variety of operations, including customer-based identification, advertising, consumer sales, business-to-business transactions, e-mail, and private internal networks for employees. Seventy-eight percent of small venture owners with a Web site have declared the ability to reach new and potential customers as their main reason for having one.

The E-Commerce Challenge

E-commerce—the marketing, promoting, buying, and selling of goods and services electronically, particularly via the Internet—is the new wave in transacting business. E-commerce encompasses several modes of Internet use:

- E-tailing (virtual store fronts), which involve sites for shopping and making purchases

---

[1]Peter F. Drucker, "Beyond the Information Revolution," *Atlantic Monthly* (Oct. 1999): 47–57.

[2]*E-Commerce: Small Business Ventures Online* (Washington, DC: U.S. Small Business Administration, Office of Advocacy, 1999), *www.sba.gov/advo/stats.*

- Electronic data interchange (EDI), which is business-to-business exchange of data

- E-mail and computer faxing

- Business-to-business buying and selling

- Ensuring the security of data transactions

Ultimately, e-commerce is simply the integration of business processes electronically via information and communication technologies.

According to the U.S. Small Business Administration, online retail marketing is currently experiencing about a 200 percent annual growth rate, with online traffic doubling every 100 days. Small businesses earned $3.5 billion in e-commerce sales in 1997, and projections for online sales for the beginning of the new millennium vary widely—from $25 billion to more than $300 billion—depending on the source.

Small firms encounter a number of barriers when pursuing the e-commerce route. These obstacles include initial start-up costs, difficulty attracting and keeping technologically skilled personnel to service the site and customers, maintaining security of the small business's (or its customers') data, and consumer trust. (See Table 2.1 for a list of advantages and challenges to e-commerce.) The most immediate barrier to full implementation of e-commerce is the cost. Experts estimate that a small business would need an initial investment of $10,000 to launch an e-commerce site and approximately 20 percent of the launching expense to maintain it annually. The technical barriers involve both personnel and data.[3]

E-Names: The Web Address

The first step in e-commerce is to choose an Internet brand name. However, this step isn't easy. Because customers are less likely to remember long or awkward names, short and snappy Web addresses are at a premium.

The dot-com renderings of large portions of the English vocabulary have been used up already, as have obvious techno-permutations of those words. E-toys.com, Cyber-toys.com, and NetToys.com, for example, are all taken, as is Toys.com. Network Solutions, Inc., a Herndon, Virginia, company that handles registration of domain names has assigned 5 million of the dot-com addresses to date.

Network Solutions' role began a number of years ago, when it got a $1 million contract from the National Science Foundation to dole out Internet addresses ending in .com, .net, and .org at no charge to registrants. In 1995, the company won permission from the federal government to begin charging registrants. The current cost to register a domain name: a $70 charge for the first two years, and $35 for every year after that.

Generally speaking, registering a domain name is as easy as checking with Network Solutions to see whether that name has been registered and paying a fee of $70. Domain name registrations are now undergoing the biggest makeover in the Internet's history, however, with dramatic implications for Network Solutions. The U.S. government has set up a nonprofit organization—the Internet Corporation for Assigned Names and Numbers (ICANN)—to oversee the introduction of competition into the domain name registration business. ICANN allowed five companies, includ-

---

[3]*E-Commerce: Small Business Ventures Online*, 1999.

TABLE 2.1	ADVANTAGES AND CHALLENGES OF E-COMMERCE FOR ENTREPRENEURIAL FIRMS

Advantages

- Ability of small firms to compete with other companies both locally and nationally (promotional tools)
- Creation of opportunities for more diverse people to start a business
- Convenient and easy way of doing business transactions (not restricted to certain hours of operation, virtually open 24 hours a day, seven days a week)
- An inexpensive way (compared to the cost of paper, printing, and postage prior to the Internet) for small businesses to compete with larger companies and for U.S. firms to make American products available in other countries
- Higher revenues for small businesses that utilize the Internet, averaging $3.79 million compared to $2.72 million for small business overall (IDC research)

Challenges

- Managing upgrades (anticipating business needs/application)
- Assuring security for a Web site and the back-end integration with existing company system
- Avoiding being a victim of fraudulent activities online
- Meeting the costs required to maintain the site
- Finding and retraining qualified employees

SOURCE: *E-Commerce Small Businesses Venture Online*, (Washington, DC: U.S. Small Business Administration, Office of Advocacy, July 1999).

ing America Online, Inc., and Register.Com Inc., to begin competing with Network Solutions as registrars. ICANN also gave dozens of other companies clearance to begin developing registration services.[4]

In many cases, however, the most desirable names have already been claimed. As a result, some businesses are paying anywhere from $400,000 to $1 million just to get the rights to the online names they want. (See Table 2.2 for examples of expensive domain names.)

Developing a Web Site

Designing an attractive, useful home Web page has its challenges. Some companies make their sites too flashy—in which case it can take ages to download, especially if customers aren't using high-speed modems to connect to the Internet. (Table 2.3 describes the most popular uses of Internet sites).

Increased visitor traffic—which at first glance seems highly desirable—brings its own headaches. Many first- or second-generation Web sites were patched together with

---

[4]Nick Wingfield, "The Game of the Name," *Wall Street Journal*, E-Commerce Special (Nov. 22, 1999): R14.

TABLE 2.2	FIVE OF THE MOST EXPENSIVE DOMAIN NAMES
Domain	**Price**
Bingo.com (bingo-based e-mail community)	$1.1 million
WallStreet.com (online "wagering" on stocks)	$1 million
Drugs.com (pharmaceutical and drug portal)	$823,456
University.com (a training and education "super-portal")	$530,000
Blackjack.com (online gambling)	$460,000

SOURCE: *Wall Street Journal*, E-Commerce Special, (Nov. 22, 1999).

data management systems meant to handle only light loads. Now, busy Web sites may attract 500,000 visitors per day. Customers expect detailed information on thousands or even millions of products. And pretty Web sites that don't connect flawlessly to a company's inventory system and supply chain are considered failures.[5] (See Figure 2.1.)

The do-it-yourself approach for a Web site involves a simple three-step process. First, build a Web site to display the merchandise and take orders electronically. That's not quite as easy as sending e-mail, but almost. Second, find someone to "host" your site, unless you have the programming skills and megabucks needed to buy and operate a Web server of your own. Third, advertise and promote the store.

A number of products, such as IBM's HomePage Creator, will walk a small-business owner through the process of setting up an online store—complete with product catalog and a virtual shopping cart. For an extra fee, even the smallest online

TABLE 2.3	USE OF INTERNET SITES
Company information	93%
Corporate image building	89
Product information	80
Advertising	78
Marketing	77
Customer communications	76
Recruiting	75
Customer service	72
Product sales	61
Business-to-business transactions	55
Business-to-employee communications	43

SOURCE: *Ernst & Young's 18th Annual Survey of Retail Information Technology*, 1999.

---

[5]George Anders, "Better, Faster, Prettier," *Wall Street Journal*, E-Commerce Special, (Nov. 22, 1999): R6.

THE MOST IMPORTANT FACTORS FOR CUSTOMERS TO DO BUSINESS ONLINE

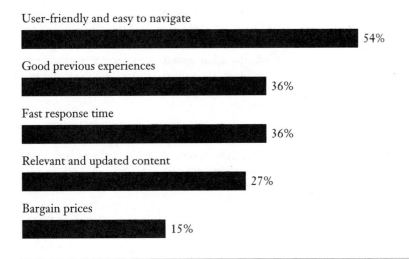

SOURCE: *Wall Street Journal*, E-Commerce Special (Nov. 22, 1999).

store can have real-time, online credit card processing. **First Data Corporation, Cardservice International, Inc.,** and other companies that specialize in authoring and billing credit-card purchases provide such services, often through a site builder.

The marketing of a site requires constant advertising and marketing. Internet shoppers can't go to a single source like the Yellow Pages to find a Web store selling what they want. Visitors enter the Net through hundreds of portals, each having its own list of sites. As an online merchant, the trick is to get your Web store listed, or cross-referenced, on as many portals as possible and to advertise the store and its products on the most popular portals. Once the site is listed, you must constantly check to ensure that it remains there.

Many companies are eager to help would-be Web entrepreneurs. **Microsoft Corporation's** Link Exchange (*www.linkexchange.com*), located in San Francisco, bills itself as a one-stop shop for the marketing needs of mom-and-pop stores online. For a yearly fee, Link Exchange's Submit It! service will register a site with as many as 400 search engines and directories. The company also provides services that let Internet stores collect customer e-mail addresses and manage online mailing lists, and that help online merchants operate "affiliate" programs, which provide referral fees to other Web sites in return for generating sales leads for them.[6]

Sticking to Your Web Site

In the world of e-commerce, "stickiness" is everything. Loyalty is fleeting when customers can click on a competing site and find a better deal. *Stickiness* refers to a host of potential value-adds, features, functions, and "gimmies"—all of which serve as

---

[6]Joelle Tessler, "Small Investment, Big Results," *Wall Street Journal*, E-Commerce Special (Nov. 22, 1999): R16.

electronic fly paper of sorts and make people want to linger at your site. The idea is that, if potential customers stay at your site long enough, they're likely to buy something eventually and then return frequently to take advantage of your offerings.

Chat is an excellent way to increase stickiness, because customers love to speak their minds and swap ideas with fellow buyers. Unfortunately, chat can also be an expensive headache for small businesses: to make chat into a robust community-building feature for your site, you must integrate a variety of software products, purchase resources to create and maintain the infrastructure, and then monitor the dialog for inappropriate activity. The last consideration is important, because inappropriate communications can taint an entire site or user community.

One way to create stickiness, without creating sticky technical situations for yourself, is to outsource the task to a company that handles chat technology and management. This option can lead to a safe, cost-effective, and efficient community experience. Unfortunately, it is expensive with setup fees ranging as high as $10,000 and ongoing fees of no less than $5,000 per month.[7]

Emerging E-Commerce Strategies

Numerous strategies are being touted to entrepreneurs who seek to enter the powerful Internet marketplace. A few of these strategies are worth summarizing.

The 3-P Growth Model, introduced by Ernst & Young (the accounting firm), defines three specific stages for a venture pursuing the e-commerce route:

- **Presence:** The ramp-up stage, where the entrepreneur builds an excitement about the specific capabilities or offerings of the venture in the marketplace.

- **Penetration:** The "hyper-growth" stage, where the entrepreneur focuses on gaining market share and establishing greater virtual integration.

- **Profitability:** The managed growth stage, where the entrepreneur focuses on expanding revenue via business-to-business transactions and increased operational efficiencies.

Another strategy aims at the so-called second generation of e-commerce. That second generation is the advancement from simply getting into e-commerce to pursuing competitive advantages through an understanding of the navigational challenges. Consultants Philip Evans and Thomas S. Wurster recommend that entrepreneurs recognize three dimensions in their pursuit of competitive advantage—reach, richness, and affiliation.[8]

Reach deals with access and connection. It means, simply, how many customers a business can connect with and how many products it can offer to those customers. Reach is the most visible difference between electronic and physical business, and it has been the primary competitive differentiator for e-business thus far.

Richness encompasses the depth and detail of information that the business can give the customer, as well as the depth and detail of information that it collects about the customer. Richness holds enormous potential for building close relationships with customers in a future dominated by e-commerce.

---

[7]Steve Bennett and Stacey Miller, "The E-Commerce Plunge," *Small Business Computing* (Feb. 2000): 48–52.

[8]Philip Evans and Thomas S. Wurster, "Getting Real About Virtual Commerce," *Harvard Business Review* (Nov.–Dec. 1999): 85–94.

Affiliation consists of the specific interests represented by the business. Until now, affiliation has not been a serious competitive factor in physical commerce because, in general, no company ever devised a way to make money by taking the consumers' side. Nevertheless, it is a natural progression for pure navigators to affiliate with customers; they aren't selling anything except, possibly, information—and therein could lie a huge competitive advantage.[9]

Myths of the Internet

Although the Internet has created a new frontier of opportunity, it has also created a world of hysteria and hype. What's real and what's fiction can be difficult to decipher in this techno-crazed economy. To better understand this new business environment, it is necessary to debunk some of the myths of the Internet.

Myth #1: Building a Web site is easy.

Reality: Details in technology can clearly shut you down. It's easy to build a bad Web site, but much more difficult to build a good one.

Myth #2: Traffic will make you rich.

Reality: There are users and customers. Driving visitors to a site is not a guarantee of viable business. Selling makes you rich. Traffic merely provides "eyeballs."

Myth #3: Smart money makes you smart.

Reality: It comes down to the entrepreneur—a bad product or service will not sell regardless of how much money is behind it.

Myth #4: Razzle-dazzle makes Web sites great.

Reality: Fancy front-end technology slows down the user experience. Ultimately, that delay will turn consumers off. What matters most is speed.

Myth #5: Brand is everything.

Reality: Just having a brand isn't enough when competitors are only a click away. People try to brand their sites but it's more important to show an image of what you are selling. Image is fine, but sales are better.

Myth #6: Wild ads make Web stars.

Reality: Everyone is trying to stand apart from the crowd. Although different and creative can be good, young dot-com companies spending enormous amounts of money to advertise during the Super Bowl can be disastrous.

Myth #7: Community, community, community.

Reality: Not everyone can build an on-line community.[10]

[9]Philip Evans and Thomas S. Wurster, *Blown to Bits: The New Economics of Information Transforms Strategy* (Boston: Harvard Business School Press, 1999).

[10]Emily Barker, Anne Marie Borrego, and Mike Hofman, "I Was Seduced by the Web Economy," *Inc.* (Feb. 2000): 48–70.

Web Site Assistance for Small Firms

A number of services are available to help small merchants get up and running quickly on the Net, as well as to host their sites. Most of these services are browser-based and require no technical knowledge. They hide the complexity of setting up an online store by providing "drag-and-drop" functions and "click-here" instructions that just about anyone can follow. They also offer lots of Web page templates and use terms that laypeople can understand—describing storage space in terms of number of pages rather than megabytes, for instance. Some of these services are profiled here.[11]

Simematic Express, offered by **Sitematic Corporation,** lets a merchant set up a simple 12-page Web site for $29.95 per month. The Sitematic Catalog allows construction of a virtual storefront selling up to 20 items for $39.95 per month. Both services require a $50 setup fee. As with many of the other services discussed here, prices for both packages rise as you add pages and catalog items.
www.sitematic.com

HomePage Creator, offered by **International Business Machines Corporation,** lets a merchant create as many as five Web pages and display up to 12 catalog items for a $25 setup fee and $24.95 per month. This service lets shoppers place orders with a credit-card number and sends those orders to an IBM server. IBM then notifies the merchant of the sale. For a $35 setup fee and $39.95 per month, IBM adds real-time credit-card authorization and processing. For 50 pages and 500 items, the service costs $200 per month with a $150 setup fee.
www.ibm.com/hpc

BigStep.Com is offering free templates, site-building tools, and hosting services. It also gives away tools to help small businesses setup and manage customer e-mail lists, as well as tools to help them track where their visitors go on their sites and what is selling well. Credit-card processing costs $14.95 per month, plus $0.15 per transaction and 2.67 percent of each sale. **Cardservice International** and **Clear Commerce Corporation** do the processing.
www.bigstep.com

Virtual Office, by **Netopia, Inc.,** includes three packages. For $19.95 per month, Netopia provides and hosts a basic 10- to 12-page Web site that essentially serves as an online brochure. For $59.95 per month, the company adds offline credit-card processing to the package—meaning that shoppers can enter their credit-card numbers for Netopia to pass along to the merchant. The company is just rolling out a $99 per month plan that includes real-time, online credit-card processing.
www.netopia.com/software/nvo

Yahoo!Store, offered by **Yahoo! Inc.,** costs $100 per month for merchants selling as many as 50 items and $300 per month for merchants that are selling as many as 1,000 items. The company automatically includes these stores in Yahoo!Shopping, its giant online shopping mall, and in its shopping search engine. The company also places links to its shopping mall in its popular online directory and search results, and recently added functions to let its retailers list their products with Yahoo's online auctions and classified services.
www.store.yahoo.com

---

[11]George Anders, "Better, Faster, Prettier," *Wall Street Journal*, E-Commerce Special (Nov. 22, 1999): R6.

ZShops, a new service from **Amazon.com, Inc.,** lets any small merchant sell on Amazon's site for $9.95 per month plus a "success fee" of 2 percent to 5 percent of each sale. Merchants may also accept credit-card payments for an additional $0.60 per transaction plus 4.75 percent of any sale.
www.amazon.com

Web Store, by **Intel Corporation's iCat Division,** costs $9.95 per month for as many as 10 items; $99.95 per month for as many as 100 items; and $249.95 per month for as many as 1,000 items.
www.icap.com

Internet Store, offered by **QSound Labs, Inc.'s Virtual Spin Division,** costs $19.95 per month for stores with as many as 25 items; $49.95 per month for as many as 100 items; and $149.95 per month for as many as 1,000 items.
www.virtualspin.com

Exploring the Entrepreneurial Concepts

The following sections provide an "entrepreneurial library" that contains a journal reading on this chapter's subject and a "comprehensive cases study" to illustrate the concept in practice. It is hoped that through the reading and discussion of the case, you will gain a greater understanding of the chapter.

THE ENTREPRENEURIAL LIBRARY

Reading for Chapter 2

E-COMMERCE: SMALL BUSINESSES VENTURE ONLINE

July 1999
The report examines the available data on small businesses' use of electronic commerce.

Written by Victoria Williams under the supervision of Bruce D. Phillips, Director of Economic Research, in the Office of Advocacy, U.S. Small Business Administration

Executive Summary

Small businesses are tapping into the Internet to conduct business and to reach new prospective consumers. This report, prepared by the Office of Advocacy at the U.S. Small Business Administration, examines the available data on small businesses' use of electronic commerce (e-commerce). For the purposes of the report, e-commerce includes: e-tailing ("virtual store fronts"), electronic data interchange, electronic mail, and computer faxing. Data sources are from different studies performed by various organizations, most of which looked at the barriers to e-commerce and the expanded use of e-commerce by businesses. Most research identified small companies as those with less than 100 employees.

The findings from various research covered in this report include:

- Over 4.5 million small employers used computer equipment in their operations in 1998.

- The percentage of small businesses with access to the Internet nearly doubled from 1996 to 1998 from 21.5 percent to 41.2 percent, respectively.

- Small businesses that utilize the Internet have higher revenues, averaging $3.79 million in 1998 compared to $2.72 million overall.

- Seventy-eight percent of small business owners declared the ability to reach new and potential customers as their primary reason for having a Web site; 35 percent of small business owners maintain a Web site.

- The most common barrier for small businesses in the adoption of e-commerce is the cost associated with it.

- Small businesses use the Internet for a variety of operations including e-mail, customer-based identification, advertising, consumer sales, business-to-business transactions, research, and internal networks for employees.

- Only 1.4 percent of Internet use among small businesses is directed toward e-commerce sales.

- Internet sales account for less than 1 percent of total retail sales in the U.S. economy.

- Over 60 percent of small businesses have inoculated themselves from Y2K (millennium bug).

- E-mail service is the number one use of e-commerce, while education is the least-used application.

- Online retail marketing is experiencing about 200 percent annual growth, and traffic online has been doubling every 100 days.

- Only 5 percent of consumers who visit the World Wide Web become customers.

- Estimates of e-commerce revenue vary widely. In 1997, it is estimated that small businesses earned $3.5 billion in e-commerce sales. Projections for the beginning of the next decade range from $25 billion to over $300 billion.

- The Internet Tax Freedom Act of 1998 has placed a three-year ban on both state and local government taxes on the Internet.

- By 2000, it is estimated that almost one-third of all business-to-business transactions will be performed via e-commerce.

This report was prepared by Victoria Williams under the general supervision of Bruce D. Phillips, director of economic research at the U.S. Small Business Administration's Office of Advocacy. Comments on this report may be directed to the Office of Economic Research at (202) 205-6530. For more information visit the Office of Advocacy's Web site at *http://www.sba.gov/ADVO/stats*.

Introduction

Small businesses are important to the U.S. economy, and they are adopting electronic commerce (e-commerce)—the marketing, promoting, buying, and selling of goods and services electronically, particularly via the Internet—as a new way of transacting business. E-commerce encompasses various modes of Internet use. E-commerce includes: e-tailing (virtual store fronts), which is a site for shopping and making purchases; electronic data interchange (EDI), which is business-to-business exchange of data; e-mail and computer faxing; business-to-business buying and selling; and ensuring the security of data and transactions (Van Ketel & Nelson, 1998). Forrester Research, Inc., an independent research firm, narrowly defines Internet commerce as the trading of goods and services in which the final order is placed over the Internet (1998).

Estimates vary, but a growing number of small businesses are tapping into the Internet to conduct business and to reach new prospective customers.

According to this study, online sales are booming, but such electronic commerce represents only a fraction of small businesses' use of the Internet. One conclusion of this report is clear: more research is needed, especially on the barriers to e-commerce use.

The data examined by this report are somewhat inconsistent. This inconsistency may have been caused by the small sample size of some studies, the time frame between which the studies were conducted and released, or because respondents were allowed more than one response in some of the studies.

This report looks at the various areas of small businesses affected by this new way of doing business, using summaries of interviews, surveys, and field studies by various research groups and organizations.

Almost all industries in the economy are beginning to use the Internet as a means of cost savings on purchasing, managing supplier relationships, streamlining logistics and inventories, planning production, and reaching new and existing customers more effectively (U.S. Department of Commerce, 1998). This medium has experienced unprecedented growth.

Information technology (IT) has made it possible for e-commerce and has enabled small, medium-sized, and home-based businesses to compete more effectively in the global market. E-commerce makes it possible for more people to start their own businesses. The number of U.S. households that have a home-based business currently exceeds 12 percent.

More than 13 million households spent an estimated $22 billion on technology in 1998. Home-based businesses represent about 18 percent of all homes with personal computers (PCs) and 22 percent of homes businesses that have made an online purchase. By 2003, home-based-business technology spending is projected to be $30 billion, and 71 percent of those businesses will be conducted online (Forrester Research, 1998). According to the National Federation of Independent Business (NFIB) Education Foundation, the number of small employers that use computer equipment in their operations exceeds 4.5 million.

Information technology has opened new avenues for businesses and individuals to get easy access to information. It has made it possible and easier for businesses and individuals to conduct transactions with the click of a mouse. As a result, e-commerce is becoming a vital tool in the economy, and small businesses are using it.

This report identifies a number of issues in the move to electronic commerce by small businesses: the cost of establishing and maintaining a Web site, the security of data collected online, potential tax liability, and the millennium bug (Y2K).

Uses of the Internet by Small Businesses

The uses of the Internet vary widely among businesses, as do the surveys on the extent of such usage. Recent surveys by Arthur Andersen's Enterprise Group and National Small Business United, ZDNet, Cahners In-Stat Group and many other organizations have evaluated the uses of the Internet by small businesses. Data inconsistencies among these studies are a result of a number of factors: the time the study was conducted and released, the sample size, and firm size of each of these studies. However, general conclusions can be drawn from the cross section of these reports, including the inevitable growth of e-commerce and the expanded use by small businesses.

Currently, 40 percent of small businesses are logged onto the Web, according to a recent report by ZDNet. The report revealed four major uses: 1) 35.4 percent use the Internet for research; 2) 19.3 percent for homepage uses; 3) 18 percent for e-mail; and 4) 13.3 percent for intranet (internal, private networks for a business's employees) purposes (Goldberg, 1998). In this survey, unlike other research examined in this report, the respondents listed a single primary use of the Internet.

Most small and medium-sized businesses, as well as large businesses, in the United States are using the Internet. Internet use by small businesses is on the rise: 47 percent of small businesses have access to the Internet, 35 percent maintain a Web site, and one in three do business transactions through it, according to a private annual small business only (Dun and Bradstreet, 1998).

According to a survey of small and medium-sized businesses conducted by Arthur Andersen's Enterprise Group and National Small Business United, e-mail and research continue to be the most popular uses of the Internet among small enterprises (1998). Half of businesses with computers reported using the Internet to send business related e-mail while 35 percent use e-mail to send personal messages. This survey found that 47 percent of small enterprises are using the Internet for research purposes, up from 32 percent in 1997. Nearly one-quarter (23 percent) of companies that use the Internet have a Web page. Among the findings, 22 percent use the Internet to sell goods and services, while 19 percent use it for purchases. Only 4 percent use it to recruit employees.

Some of the major reasons why small enterprises use a Web site according to the NSBU study include: reaching new and potential customers (78 percent); selling goods and services (65 percent); providing information more efficiently (62 percent); reaching new prospective employees (13 percent); and expanding globally (17 percent).

A study by IBM and the U.S. Chamber of Commerce (which surveyed 1,010 firms with less than 100 employees) discovered that 30 percent of small businesses surveyed use the Internet to promote their services while one-half use it to seek information about potential customers. Sixty-three percent use it to answer specific questions and 85 percent use it for e-mail purposes. They survey also revealed that one-quarter of small businesses report being conversant with "e-commerce" while some are already practicing it. Thirty-seven percent of Internet users use it to place orders while 29 percent receive orders with it; 9 percent use it to pay suppliers (Small Business and Technology, 1998). (See Table 1.)

Additionally, a study by Cahners In-Stat Group shows that about one-quarter (28 percent) of small businesses accept customers' orders via the Web (Goeler, 1998). Almost one-fifth accept or use the Web for payment information online and 36 percent use it for online catalogs, where information and pricing is provided for customers. In most of the sites, 62 percent use it to get customer feedback and technical support.

TABLE 1

Small and medium-sized uses of the Internet	%	Primary uses by ZDNet	%	IBM and the U.S. Chamber of Commerce	%
Business e-mail	51	E-mail	18	E-mail	85
Research	47	Research	35.4	Provide answers	63
Personal e-mail	35	Intranet purposes	13.3	Seek customer info.	49
Web-site	23	Homepage	19.3	Promotion/advertising	30
Online transaction	22	E-commerce	1.4	Online ordering	37
Online ordering	19	Communication	1.5	Receive orders	29
Employment	4	EDI	4.9	Pay suppliers	9
		Technical support	2		
		Education	1.3		
N = 504		**N = 50,931**		**N = 1,010**	

Note: Respondents included small and medium-sized businesses. SOURCE: Arthur Andersen's Enterprise Group and National Small Business United, Nov., 1998.

Note: Study was on businesses with less than 100 employees. SOURCE: ZDNet, Nov., 1998.

Note: Study was on businesses with less than 100 employees. SOURCE: IBM and U.S. Chamber of Commerce, June, 1998.

Business-to-Consumer and Business-to-Business E-Commerce

Source estimates differ dramatically for Internet sales for both business-to-consumer and business-to-business e-commerce. According to Roberts, analysts estimate Internet retail sales to be a minute fraction of consumer spending—between $1.3 billion and $4 billion out of $2.5 trillion that consumers spent in 1997 (1999). A study by Access Media International (AMI) estimated that small business gained $3.5 billion in e-commerce consumer sales in 1997 and projected that number to exceed $7.5 billion in 1998; this number is expected to reach $25 billion in the year 2000 (1998). See Figure 1. Business-to-consumer online shopping should rise from $2.4 billion in 1997 to $17.4 billion in 2001, according to Mehling (1998). Another report projects the growth rate of business-to-consumer Internet transactions to rise by 37 percent, from $7.17 billion in 1998 to $19.37 billion in 1999 (Zona, 1998).

The largest component of electronic commerce is business-to-business trade (Tax Features, 1998). This could be attributed to its cost saving features. Revenues of U.S. business-to-business e-commerce will grow from $17 billion in 1998 to $327 billion in the year 2002, according to Mehling (1998). Another study projects business-to-business transactions to grow by 46.5 percent, from $24.1 billion in 1998, to $51.9 billion in 1999 (Zona, 1998). Olbeter projects that by the year 2000, almost one-third of all business-to-business transactions will be performed via e-commerce (1998). . . .

Figure 2 has the various phases as building blocks toward e-commerce. . . . Brochure-ware, Pre-commerce and Simple Commerce Sites are described below according to Cahners In-Stat:

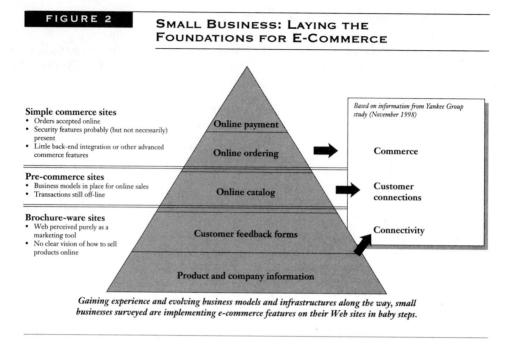

Gaining experience and evolving business models and infrastructures along the way, small businesses surveyed are implementing e-commerce features on their Web sites in baby steps.

SOURCE: Illustration adapted from Kate Von Goeler, "Internet Commerce by Degrees." © 1998, Cahners In-Stat Group. Reproduced with permission.

Brochure-ware Sites   Companies have and use their Web sites predominantly for product advertisement. Firms gather customer prospect information and improve customer service by providing forms for customer feedback and information requests. These firms have yet to install the technology that is needed to sell their goods over the Web.

Pre-commerce Sites   These firms have enough information including price to create immediate orders off their Web sites. However, they drag their feet when it comes to online point-of-sale transactions. Unlike their counterparts, they have jumped a major hurdle in implementing e-commerce and have developed a business model that allows them to make transactions and have the resources to keep their site current.

Simple Commerce Sites   These businesses accept orders over the Web, and most of the time accept payments. When compared with larger companies that have larger sites, simple commerce sites by small businesses are likely to be very primitive. They have little in security or online payment processing and virtually nothing when it comes to back-end integration. . . .

Obstacles Facing Small Businesses

While some small businesses may have been early adopters of Internet marketing, many other small businesses have been slow putting in place the tools to sell their products and services directly over the Web (Notes & News, 1998). Small businesses have been slower than big businesses to embrace e-commerce, but [are] now more interested in sales over the Web according to Mehling (1998). Although small businesses joining the Internet are on the rise, most of them face a number of obstacles to e-commerce application: costs, security concerns, technical expertise, and customer service concerns (Goeler, 1998). Cahners In-Stat released a study that showed the growth of Internet commerce by high-tech small business and the challenges that they faced (1998). In examining 47 businesses that are already using the Web to sell computer-related goods and services, they identified obstacles to implementing e-commerce, including cost, security of sites, difficulty of implementation, and customer service.

Cost is the most common and greatest impediment to expanding e-commerce. Three basic cost concerns identified by respondents were: 1) lack of funds for up-front implementation costs; 2) lack of monthly cash flows to maintain their sites; 3) the probability that there would not be a real return on their investment. Security concerns are of great concern even for this technical-savvy market segment. The major worries were customer fraud and the potential for hackers to gain access to vulnerable information. Other concerns were the security of Internet service providers and Web hosts, and the possibility that back-end integration into a company's existing system would make internal systems vulnerable to hackers. Although the businesses in the study had technical skills, they were impeded by the difficulties of implementing and integrating commerce sites. They had concerns that they would not have the available resources to maintain their sites. Finally, customer service was seen as a challenge for e-commerce. Numerous small businesses rely on knowing customers and their needs intimately and have created their business processes and quality control methods around personal communications. The majority of businesses that participated in the survey were concerned that the loss of customer contact would decrease the quality of service. Others felt that selling on the Web without providing enhanced services would make customers more resistant to their price at the point of sale.

The businesses in the Cahners In-Stat study were high-tech, computer-oriented companies, with in-house technical skills. Yet they were still hindered by the complexity of installing commerce sites. Logically, less technology-savvy firms would have greater concerns about e-commerce and online sales (Goeler, 1998).

In a recent survey of 500 small business owners and managers, E-valuations research found that most respondents believe selling on the Web will be important to their future. One-half indicated that the cost of building and maintaining a site is the biggest barrier to selling online. Other barriers were: lack of technical expertise (45 percent); the amount of site security needed (39 percent); and the cost of building a transactions-based site (36 percent) (Mehling, 1998).

The minimum initial investment in an e-commerce site is about $10,000, according to Erica Rugullies, an e-commerce analyst at research firm Giga Information Group. Small businesses should expect to spend 20 percent of the launch cost for annual maintenance and support (Mehling, 1998). Another barrier affecting the growth of e-commerce among small businesses, according to a study by Pricewaterhouse Coopers, is the lack of qualified workers (1998). Two-thirds of top technology executives cited this as a barrier to achieving their revenue goals over the next 12 months. According to the same study, 76 percent of small high-tech businesses see worker qualifications as a possible pitfall, versus 56 percent of large companies.

Factors Affecting E-Commerce

A study by Visa indicates that gender and age have a great impact on how small business owners utilize technology, whether they have computers, fax machines or use the Internet (1998). The report is based on a survey of 350 small business owners. Other factors, according to the report, that can play a role in the usage of technology are the age of the business and its industry. Visa developed four classifications for technology views among owners: 1) express lane, 2) slower traffic—stay right, 3) proceed with caution, and 4) no access.

The "express lane" represents about 34 percent of business owners who are eager, adaptive to new technologies, and younger. They typically are 30 to 49 years old and male, managing larger organizations in the business and financial services industries and generating more than $250,000 in annual revenues. Their counterparts are female business owners, who are classified as the "slower traffic—stay right" and represent 26 percent of owners and are age 40 to 49 years old. Often they are owners of smaller companies, with annual revenues less than $250,000, and engage in the hospitality, travel, construction, and nonprofit sectors. They are aware of the value of technology, but are satisfied with the level of high-tech tools they are using. "Proceed with caution" category is a socially diverse group that is a littler older (ages 50 to 59), and represents about 21 percent of this survey. Their companies typically have been in existence for fewer than five years, and they are in the insurance or transportation industries. This group viewed technology as an essential element of being competitive but felt overwhelmed by it. Older owners (aged 50 and over) with mature businesses (more than 15 years) dominated the "no access" class and represented 19 percent of owners. They are often engaged in retail trade generating annual revenues of less than $250,000, and viewed technology as adding little or no value to their business.

Strengths and Challenges

The accelerated growth that is being experienced by the Internet is attributable primarily to its strength as a medium of communication, education, entertainment, and, more recently, a tool for e-commerce (U.S. Department of Commerce 1998).

Fraudulent Misuse   As the Internet grows, so does fraudulent behavior. The risk that is involved with the use of e-commerce includes the security of proprietary information of the business online and its customers. The Internet has become an efficient medium and haven for white-collar crimes. Fraudulent operators find the Internet attractive because they can instantly communicate with millions of potential victims via professionally looking Web sites—appearing to offer legitimate information or products, online newsletters, or e-mail at relatively lower cost then traditional means of communication and doing business transactions (Hillman, 1999). According to the Securities Exchange Commission, the public submitted about 10 to 15 complaints daily about online fraud in 1996 via the e-mail system. This increased to about 120 complaints daily through September 1998. The number soared to 200 to 300 daily and stayed in this range in early 1999 (Hillman, 1999). As fraud grows exponentially, fraudulent behavior can be a disincentive for both consumers and businesses to embrace e-commerce.

Some of the advantages and challenges highlighted in various studies include:

Advantages

1. Ability of small firms to compete with other companies both locally and nationally (promotional tool);

2. Creates the possibility and opportunity for more diverse people to start a business;

3. Convenient and easy way of doing business transactions (not restricted to certain hours of operation, virtually open 24 hours a day, seven days a week);

4. An inexpensive way (compared to the cost of paper, printing and postage prior to the Internet) for small business to compete with larger companies and for U.S. firms to make American products available in other countries; and

5. Small businesses that utilize the Internet have higher revenues, averaging $3.79 million compared to $2.72 million overall (IDC research).

Challenges

1. Managing upgrades (anticipating business needs/application);

2. Assuring security for a Web site and the back-in integration with existing company system;

3. Avoiding being a victim of fraudulent activities online;

4. Costs required to maintain the site;

5. Finding qualified consultants;

6. Finding and retraining qualified employees;

7. No market for old computers; and

8. The Y2K issue. . . .

Digital Cash and the Future

Analysts predict that the number of devices used to access the Web will increase significantly, and spending on such devices would increase from $78.1 million in 1997 to $515 million in 2002 (Hu, 1998). With the number of devices increasing, more entrepreneurs will gain access to the Internet at a lower cost. . . . Securing a viable digital cash system is a key element of online security.

In studies by Cahners In-Stat, ZDNet, Giga Information Group, and E-valuations, respondents mentioned security concerns as one major hindrance to e-commerce progress. One would assume that if a more secure way of doing business on the Internet is developed, businesses and consumers will not feel so vulnerable about personal information. This concern could be alleviated if electronic money or digital cash is put into place. According to Matonis (1995), a private digital cash system would consist of ten key elements:

Security Transaction protocol must ensure that high-level security is maintained through sophisticated encoding techniques (i.e., an individual should be able to pass digital cash to another without either of them, or others, being able to alter or reproduce the electronic token).

Anonymity   Anonymity assures the privacy of a transaction on various levels. Beyond encryption, this optional feature to prevent tracing the exchange of digital cash promises to be one of the major points of competition between providers (both individuals should have the option to remain completely anonymous with regard to the payment).

Portability   Security and usage of digital cash [are] not dependent on any physical location. The money can be transferred through computer networks and off the computer network into other storage devices. Both individuals and businesses should be able to walk away with their digital cash and transport it for use within alternative delivery systems, including non-computer network channels. Importantly, digital wealth should not be restricted to a unique, proprietary computer network.

Two-way   Digital money can be transferred to other users. It is essential that peer-to-peer payments are possible without either party required to attain registered merchant status with today's card-based systems.

Off-line capability   The protocol between the two exchanging parties is executed off-line, meaning that neither is required to be host-connected in order to process, and unrestricted availability must exist. Each individual can pass value freely to another at any time without requiring third party authentication.

Divisibility   A digital cash token amount can be subdivided into smaller units of cash. The money must be fungible, so exchanges can be made. An individual should be able to visit a provider or exchange house and request digital cash breakdowns in the smallest possible units.

Infinite duration   Digital cash should have no expiration date. It continues to maintain value until lost or destroyed provided that the issuer has not debased the unit to nothing or gone out of business. Individuals should be able to store a token in a safe place for a number of years and then retrieve it for use.

Wide acceptability   Digital cash is well known and acceptable in a large commercial zone. This feature implies trust in the issuer. The individual should be able to use the preferred unit in more than just a restricted local setting.

User-friendly   Digital cash should be simple to use for spending and receiving. Simplicity in use will result in massive acceptance and increased trust in the system. The protocol machinations should be transparent to the immediate user.

Unit-of-value freedom   Digital cash should be denominated in market-determined, non-government monetary units. An individual should be able to issue non-political digital cash denominated in a defined unit, which competes with governmental-unit digital cash.

Conclusion

E-commerce has created an evolutionary change in catalog retailing and improved business methods of communication and information. These quality and productivity increases are what drive the U.S. economy forward. Consumers are on the Internet because of the price and choice that is available to them there. The use of e-commerce expands the small business's and consumer's venues for exchanging information, goods, and services. While barriers, such as security, Y2K bug, and costs, are associated with the Internet use in e-commerce, solutions such as digital cash likely will expand the market.

It is important to understand how e-commerce affects small businesses and how they are utilizing it, because small businesses generate most net new jobs in the U.S. More research is needed in this area to fully understand the experiences of small businesses with e-commerce and to find solutions for the future of e-commerce for the small business community and its customers.

The number of small businesses that use computer equipment in their operations will increase significantly in the near future. Based on the studies available, the Internet is a fast and easy medium of communication among businesses and customers. With Internet retail sales below 1 percent of total retail sales, more companies are likely to experience e-commerce in the future. Businesses that use the Internet to buy, sell, distribute and maintain products and services can realize significant cost savings and attract more customers to their business, thereby potentially increasing sales. However, e-commerce will not replace the traditional way of shopping and doing business; rather it will provide another option to the merchant and consumer.

Although the Internet Tax Freedom Act of 1998 may encourage new entrepreneurs and more buyers online by temporarily banning sales and use taxes, it also tends to discriminate against those who do business the traditional way. As e-commerce continues to grow so does the fraction of sales that escapes sales and use taxes, at least temporarily.

The business-to-consumer trend is slow when compared to business-to-business e-commerce. Until more cost-effective and secure mechanisms are in place, growth in consumer online sales could stall. Demographics have also played a role in the way that e-commerce has been implemented, particularly in the retail sector. The newest generation of consumers likely will embrace e-commerce. If e-commerce blossoms as predicted by analysts within the next five years, digital cash may become more prevalent.

The Office of Advocacy anticipates the development of e-commerce in the small business community. Through research and policy development, Advocacy will pursue a successful, secure virtual market square.

Bibliography

Publications, Journals, Magazines, Articles, etc.

Access Media International: Press, "U.S. Small Businesses Spent Record $138 Billion on Information Technology and Telecommunications Products and Services in 1997" (February 9, 1998).

Arthur Andersen and National Small Business United, "Survey of Small and Medium-sized Businesses," p. 19–20 (November 1998).

Dennis, William J. Jr., "Small Businesses and the Y2K Problem: Part 11" NFIB Education Foundation (December 28, 1998).

Hamel, Gary and Sampler, Jeff, "The E-Corporation," *Fortune Magazine* (December 7, 1998), p. 92. Quebecor Printing Corp., Clarksville, Tenn.

Hillman, Richard J., "The Internet Poses Challenges to Regulators and Investors" Securities Fraud (1998).

Olbeter, Erik R., "The Strategic Economic Importance of the Internet," *Economic Strategic Institute* (November 1998), Washington, D.C.

Schmitt, Eric, Mines, Christopher, and Rhinelander, Tom (December 1998), "People and Technology Strategies," *Forrester:* Forrester Research Inc., Cambridge, Mass. Vol. 5 No. 8, p. 2–7.

Simons, John, "States Chafe as Web Shoppers Ignore Sales Taxes" *The Wall Street Journal* (January 26, 1999) p. B1.

Tax Features, "Mismatch Between Old Tax and New E-commerce has Governments Scrambling," (November 1998) Vol. 42, No. 10, p. 4, 8.

U.S. Department of Commerce, "The Emerging Digital Economy" Washington, D.C. (1998).

Zona Research, "Challenges in the Electronic Economy"—Part 11 (November 23, 1998).

Available on the World Wide Web

Angal, David S., "Rogue Valley Y2K Task Force" (December 6, 1998). *http://www.rv-y2k.org/introy2k.htm*

CNNFn, "Tax Banned from Web" (October 15, 1998). *http://cnnfn.com/*

Dun & Bradstreet 17 Annual D&B Small Business Study (February 19, 1998). *http://www.dnb.com/newsview/0217news4.htm*

Forrester Research, "Growth Spiral in Online Retail Sales Will Generate $108 Billion in Revenues by 2003" (November 19, 1998). *http://www.forrester.com*

Goldberg, Aaron, "What Small Businesses Are Doing on the Web" (November 10, 1998). *http://www.ZdNet.com/icom/ebusiness/1998/11/small.webbies/index.html*

Hu, Jim, "E-commerce to Hit $400 Billion by 2002" (August 18, 1998). *http://www.abcnews.com/*

IBM, U.S. Chamber of Commerce, "Small Business and Technology" (June 1, 1998). *http://www.uschamber.com/news/sb980601a.htm*

International Data Corporation, "Small Business Embraces the Internet" (1998). *http://www.idc.com/F/HNR/071398.htm*

Matonis, Jon W., "Digital Cash and Monetary Freedom" (August 7, 1995). *http://info.isoc.org/HMP/PAPER/136/abst.html*

Mehling, Herman, "Small Businesses Are Eager to Sell Wares on the Web" (December 21, 1998), p. 87b. *http://www.crn.com/sections/news/7*

Pricewaterhouse Coopers, "Economic Outlook Appears Bright for Technology Businesses, Especially Smaller Ones" (November 3, 1998). *http://www.pwcglobal.com/extweb/ncsurvres.nsf/*

Robert, Victoria, "Economic Outlook: Information Technology Sector to Lead U.S. Economy's Continuing Growth in 1999" (January 27, 1999), No. 17. *http://www.newsstand.k-link.com/*

Visa, "Signs of the Times: How Small Business Owners View Technology" (1998). *http://www.visa.com/cgi-bin/vee/fb/smbiz/survey/signs/main.html?2+0*

Von Goeler, Kate, "Internet Commerce by Degrees: Small Business Early Adopters" (November 8, 1998). *http://www.instat.com*

Van Kete, Mark and Nelson, Tim D., "E-commerce" (May 18, 1998). *http://www.whatis.com/*

Yankee Group, "Yankee Group Finds Small and Business Market Missing the Internet Commerce Opportunity: Market Unsatisfied with Current Internet Solution Provider Offerings" (November 17, 1998). *http://www.yankeegroup.com/*

Zimbler, Eileen, "U.S. Small Businesses Spent Record $138 Billion on Innovation: Technology and Telecommunication Products and Services" (February 1998). *http://www.ami-usa.com/press2.html*

C A S E   FASTEN YOUR SEAT BELTS: TURBULENCE AHEAD FOR TRAVEL AGENCIES

Consider the following challenges. Your business is positioned in the middle of the supply chain and your major suppliers are trying to drive you out of business by continually assuming your value-added functions and cutting the amounts they pay you for providing these services. Your competitors, both large and small, are merging, acquiring others, or being acquired at an increasing rate. Your customers are experimenting with electronic venues that could significantly reduce your revenues. Welcome to the turbulent, competitive environment faced by travel agencies every business day. The competitive landscape is not only extremely fragmented and cutthroat, but as Scott Barry, an industry analyst, has noted, "Wall Street has historically viewed [the travel services industry] as one with low barriers to entry, not particularly technologically sophisticated, and (with) deteriorating returns."[1]

The Way It Was

The basics of the travel agency business have not changed much since 1841. That date marks the time when the first organized tour package was created, marketed, and conducted by Thomas Cook. This first tour served a group of 570 travelers who attended a temperance rally in Leicester, England. The package sold for a shilling (12 pence) and included train transportation, a picnic lunch, and a brass band for entertainment. At the time, Thomas Cook was a minister, but his first package trip was so successful that he went into the business of providing tour packages on a full-time basis.

It was not long before the idea of having someone else do the work of making travel plans found its way to the United States and took on a new role and form. In 1888, Ward G. Foster, a gift shop owner in St. Augustine, Florida, opened the first travel agency. He may have never planned to be a travel agent, but his love of geography, detailed knowledge of train schedules, and the locations of good quality hotels made his shop a natural stopping place for people seeking help with their travel plans. He soon became so famous that the name for this well-known agency, Ask Mr. Foster Travel, came from his customers who would tell others if they had any questions about travel to "Ask Mr. Foster."

Travel Agents in the Twentieth Century

Traditionally, the channel of distribution for tourism services involved a supplier (e.g., airline, hotel, or tour wholesaler) and a travel agent. The travel agent filled many important functions as a channel member. Agents were a vast sales force for suppliers, having local knowledge of and access to consumers. The travel agent was viewed by buyers as an expert in travel planning and the best source of travel information. Agents provided suppliers with a matchmaking service, placing supplier brochures into the hands of those consumers most likely to purchase. The agents facilitated the tourism service transaction by accepting payment and maintaining the client interface for the transfer of reservation confirmations, tickets, and other pertinent information.

From these small beginnings, travel agents have grown to be an important intermediary, fulfilling a significant role as service providers in the travel services industry. As intermediaries in the distribution channel for tourism services, travel agents stand between suppliers such as airlines, hotels, and car rental companies and consumers. In fulfilling their intermediary role, they can simplify the routine booking reservations processes for consumers and increase the marketing efforts of suppliers who are attempting to reach a broad cross section of consumers who are often dispersed over wide geographic areas. They furnish a wide range of services to customers from providing information and making reservations to ticketing and preparing itineraries. These services are secured from a host of suppliers including airlines, car rental companies, hotels, cruise lines, and tour operators and then sold to retail customers. While travelers have always been able to purchase these services directly from the service suppliers, many, especially business travelers, rely on the value-added services provided by intermediaries such as travel agencies to facilitate these transactions.

During the 1990s, the importance of travel agencies to tourism service providers has continued to grow. Key statistics, as shown in Table 1, reflect the continued importance of this industry grouping. Yet the apparent upward trend in the total number of travel agencies that had been exhibited in the past stopped in 1997 and is now in question. This can be attributed to new and improved forms of technology allowing travelers to access service providers directly and growing commission cuts which are squeezing already thin profit margins.

Prior to February, 1995, travel agents could earn 10 percent on all domestic ticket sales and 15 percent on international ticket sales with a potential of additional overrides which are extra commissions paid by airlines to travel agencies who meet sales

TABLE 1[2]   **TRAVEL AGENCIES**

Year	Sales (billions)	Number of Agencies	Number of Agencies Generating $1 Million or More	Number of Agencies Generating $5 Million or More
1987	$64.2	29,584	9,171	2,663
1989	79.4	30,373	8,201	2,734
1991	85.9	32,066	9,620	3,527
1993	93.5	32,446	9,409	4,218
1995	101.11	33,593	10,078	4,703
1997	126.0	33,500	6,502	5,618

targets. Then in February, 1995, the commission structure on airline ticket sales was radically altered. Delta Airlines was the first airline to cap commissions on domestic fares of $500.00 and up to no more than $50.00 per round-trip ticket, but soon all major airlines followed. In 1997, United Airlines led the second major assault on travel agency commissions by retaining the caps and reducing commissions from 10 to 8 percent for U.S. and Canadian travel agencies on domestic and international bookings. They were soon followed by all major carriers except TWA which opted to retain 10 percent commissions for international bookings.

The number of agencies dipped for the first time in 1997 and a downward trend is predicted for the future. The number of large agencies and especially mega agencies such as American Express Travel Services, Rosenbluth International, Uniglobe, Maritz Travel, Professional Travel, and Morris Travel continue to grow in importance and capture additional market share. These and other agencies that compose the top 50 largest travel agencies generate almost 30 percent of all agency sales. Small agencies, or what are known as "Mom and Pop Shops" in the industry, generate sales of less than $1 million a year and are predicted to continue to decline in numbers. In addition to classifying travel agencies based on revenues, they can also be classified by their primary service focus such as leisure, business, or cruise only.

Although the risks are high, many individuals are still attracted to the opportunity of opening a travel agency. The process is fairly easy and inexpensive. Total start-up costs can range from $15,000 to $60,000 depending on whether the decision is made to go it alone or to select the franchise route, which would add another $8,000 to $33,000 to initial costs.

In addition to paying the typical rent, utilities, labor, furniture, fixtures, and equipment expenses that face any retail operator, travel agencies must also seek and obtain accreditation from the Airlines Reporting Corporation (ARC). To receive ARC accreditation, an agency must be open for business, accessible to the public, clearly identified as a travel agency, and actively selling airline tickets. In addition, an agency must also meet minimum financial requirements, including a bond or irrevocable letter of credit for $20,000 and an adequate cash reserve to pay expenses during the first year of operation. ARC accreditation provides clearinghouse operations for commission payments from all domestic and most international airlines as well as universal ticket stock to travel agencies so they can produce tickets for all member airlines.

An Industry in Transition

No matter what their size or marketing focus, travel agents almost never take title to the services they are selling. Instead, their task is to expedite the flow of information, payment, and delivery of services from tourism service suppliers to the final consumer efficiently.[3] Tourism service suppliers have traditionally relied on a combination of internal sales forces and the assistance of travel agencies to reach potential customers. Nowhere in the industry has this been more noticeable than with the airlines. Until 1995, travel agencies booked 85 percent of all domestic airline reservations. However, since that date, this number has fallen into the 80 percent range.[4] Yet, as can be seen in Table 2, many travel-related arrangements still involve travel agents. But, with the rise of Internet connections, many transactions are beginning to bypass travel agents.

Most travel agencies work with a wide array of suppliers. However, larger agencies often focus their marketing efforts on selected preferred suppliers in each industry segment to improve service delivery through conversion privileges and to improve profitability through override commissions. For example, conversion privileges, often referred to as "waivers and favors" in the industry, allow travel agents to enhance customer service to airline passengers by converting full-fare, economy-priced airline reservations to a discounted price when all discounted seats are sold out. Override commissions are additional commissions paid to travel agencies as a bonus for increased productivity. Overrides can enhance profitability when targeted sales volumes and/or market share shifts are achieved. By achieving targeted levels of sales or shifts in market share, travel agencies gain the privilege to upgrade or confirm preferential schedules and/or services for their own preferred high-volume customers.

Tourism service suppliers still rely on intermediaries such as travel agencies and tour wholesalers and operators to help sell and market their services, but they are also becoming tenacious competitors as they strive to minimize controllable expenses. This competitiveness is being exacerbated by consolidation within the industry, rapid proliferation of technology which is providing easy consumer access to suppliers, and cost-cutting measures which are continually being implemented by suppliers.

In the face of real or perceived threats to continued profitability, travel agencies have taken several steps from searching for economies of scale and scope to embracing new technologies and implementing service fees. In addition, the merger and acquisition activity in this industry segment has continued to increase.

Is Bigger Better?

Size does make a difference when it comes to profitability. While 76 percent of all travel agencies made a profit in 1997, more than 90 percent of the agencies with sales of $5 million or more were profitable, while only 62 percent of those with less than $1 million were profitable.[5]

As agency owners and managers search for profitability through economies of scale and scope, many are seeking affiliations through franchises and memberships in consortiums. By 1997, "54 percent of all agency locations were affiliated with a leisure-oriented consortium or marketing group such as GEM, Travelsavers, or Giants. Ten years earlier, in 1987, only 36 percent of agency locations had such affiliations. . . ."[6] The large dollar volume of transactions generated through these contractual combinations allow these affiliations to increase profitability by obtaining preferred vendor status and access to override commissions while, at the same time, lowering costs on everything from advertising expenses to supplies and materials.

TABLE 2	TRAVEL TRANSACTIONS COMPLETED BY TRAVEL AGENCIES

- 95 percent of all cruise reservations
- 85 percent of all international airline reservations
- 80 percent of all domestic airline reservations
- 50 percent of all car rental reservations
- 25 percent of all domestic hotel reservations

Size can make a difference if travel agencies generate enough revenue to achieve preferred vendor status. The dollar volume increases gained through preferred vendor status [are] becoming more and more important as agencies search for new ways to serve customers who have new choices for acquiring travel services. Preferred vendor status allows agencies to offer lower rates for hotels and cruise lines as well as availability at locations and on dates that are not available to the general public. The sales or market share targets that must be achieved to gain preferred vendor status are pushing many smaller travel agencies to seek some type of affiliation to remain profitable and provide expected levels of service.

Initial public offerings of companies such as Galileo International, Navigant International, Preview Travel, and Travel Services International during 1997 and early 1998 point to yet another change that is occurring in the industry. Travel service companies which were once subsidiaries of other companies or operated as privately held companies are joining the ranks of publicly traded companies.

Travel Services International (TSI) provides an excellent example of an emerging trend in travel services. TSI, which went public in 1997, pursued an acquisition strategy that has become increasingly common in the industry. This strategy, referred to as a roll-up, is a situation where a company "rolls up" or combines several synergistic companies such as corporate, leisure, and cruise agencies under one management umbrella to gain economies of scale and enhance shareholder value. By bringing several agencies together, back office accounting and other administrative functions can be combined. In addition, cross marketing of services can enhance potential revenues. After going public, TSI bought several smaller competitors in different sectors of travel services, such as cruise-only agencies, and quickly became the market leader.

Coping with New Technology

Rapid developments in technology are already occurring in the travel industry with many companies beginning to promote and sell their products and services over the Internet. Travelers can access tourism service suppliers through the Internet, and travel agencies are learning that they can continue to fill their traditional intermediary role by facilitating this new group of information and service seekers. As travelers become more comfortable booking reservations through the Web, it has been projected that travel agents could facilitate this process through their own Web sites. However, "[t]oday, on-line travel represents barely 1 percent of travel agency sales in the U.S., but the leaders in the on-line travel space—Preview Travel, Expedia.com, and Travelocity—are poised to be among the top 50 largest U.S. travel agencies, or agency equivalents, in 1998."[7] From an almost indiscernible $300 million in sales during 1996, the dollar volume of travel spending on the Internet is projected to explode to $8.9 billion by 2002.[8] Other Internet services, such as Priceline.com, are proving to be popular with travelers shopping for bargain fares and airlines wanting to hold anonymous sales of excess inventory.

Purchasing airline tickets has been the primary focus of Internet use by travelers. This has not gone unnoticed by travel intermediaries that control the movement of airline ticket sales through sophisticated computer reservations systems such as Sabre and Galileo. These reservation systems link the airlines to travel agents. "AMR, parent of American Airlines and 80-percent owner of Sabre, the leading travel-reservations system used by agents around the country, is betting on a Web strategy that would move its biggest customers safely into cyberspace via a service called Travelocity.[9]

Other services such as Microsoft's Expedia are also being enhanced to gain market share by creating a direct link between suppliers and the final consumer.

According to Travel Industry Association research, 50 million adults in the United States were using an online service on the Internet in 1997 for information and/or reservations services. Of the online transactions they completed, 84 percent were for airline tickets. Frequent business travelers in particular have been drawn to this information source as they search and make travel plans. It is expected that this trend will continue to grow for the general population and frequent travelers in particular.[10] According to the results of a 1998 survey as shown in Table 3, the majority (65.8 percent) of Internet users were between the ages of 21 and 45, married with no children, college educated, and earned $30,000 or more per year.[11]

Corporations can now make all their travel arrangements through the power of personal computers readily available at employee's fingertips. Technological advances are also allowing companies to monitor and enforce travel policies as well as creating productivity improvements by automating the travel function. Corporate travelers can book their own itineraries to meet their personal needs while complying with restrictions on advance reservations, class of accommodations, and rental cars. These technological advances are threatening to greatly lessen the need for travel agents by

TABLE 3[12]	AGE OF INTERNET USERS		
Age	**Frequency**	**Percent**	**Cumulative Percent**
5–10	1	.0	.0
11–15	49	1.0	1.0
16–20	251	5.0	6.0
21–25	627	12.5	18.5
26–30	808	16.1	34.6
31–35	684	13.6	48.2
36–40	571	11.4	59.6
41–45	612	12.2	71.7
46–50	496	9.9	81.6
51–55	393	7.8	89.4
56–60	215	4.3	93.7
61–65	103	2.1	95.8
66–70	79	1.6	97.4
71–75	33	.7	98.0
76–80	11	.2	98.2
Over 81	6	.2	98.3
Not Say	83	1.7	100.0
Total	**5,022**	**100.0**	

allowing companies to access tourism services directly as well as monitor travel patterns and enforce cost-saving travel policies.

Searching for Profitability

Travel agencies, like most members of the tourism industry, are faced with peaks and valleys in demand, resulting in significant cash flow fluctuations due to the seasonality of their business. The travel industry is extremely seasonal and, as is true in most service industries, profit margins for travel agencies have traditionally been low. In recent years, the before tax net profit margin has hovered between 2 and 3 percent before dipping noticeably in 1998. As can be seen in the common-sized data presented in Tables 4 and 5, the industry can be characterized by a low level of fixed investments and a high level of operating expenses. The most significant operating expenses for travel agencies are salaries and benefits, rent, and computer reservations system expenses.

In the face of tightening profit margins, travel agencies have employed several tactics from seeking affiliations through franchises and memberships in consortiums to instituting service fees to improve profitability. In response to commission caps and cuts by airlines, one tactic that has been adopted by a wide range of agencies has been to add service fees to customer transactions. By early August 1998, about two-thirds of all agencies were charging service fees. The remaining one-third cited competitive pressures, fee processing difficulties, and employee resistance as reasons they were not charging service fees.[13]

Caution should be exercised when analyzing sales revenues for travel agencies. Total sales will appear to be very large, highlighting the dollar volume of transactions processed by a travel services company; however, the more important financial target in this industry grouping is not gross sales revenues but net sales revenues. Net sales revenues reflect actual receipts from standard commissions, mark-ups, volume bonuses, override commissions, and service fees. For example, a travel agency may produce an airline ticket valued at $400 (sales), but only receives $32 (net sales revenue) in a standard commission for that transaction.

Eroding profit margins may be traced to commission caps that were first instituted by all major airlines during 1995. When overrides are included, commissions on domestic airline tickets averaged around 9 percent which compares to precap averages of 11 percent. Domestic commissions have been capped at $25 on one-way tickets and $50 on round-trip tickets. Prior to the caps, agencies could earn a base rate commission of 10 percent on all sales.

Looking into the Future

Tourism activities have demonstrated a general upward trend in numbers of participants and revenues over the past 50 years. As one leading tourism scholar noted, "While other industries show declines, tourism slows down and may go flat, but it seldom falls into recession."[14] However, there is nothing like a little uncertainty about the future to create concern and a good debate. A hotly debated area in the tourism industry is the future role of the travel agent and agencies. Travel agents have historically played an important role in tourism distribution channels, performing valuable intermediary service by bringing together tourism service suppliers and the traveling public. Will the

TABLE 4*	COMPARATIVE COMMON-SIZED BALANCE SHEET DATA†				
Year Ended	**3/31/94**	**3/31/95**	**3/31/96**	**3/31/97**	**3/31/98**
ASSETS					
Cash & Equiv.	26.6%	26.3%	30.0%	29.7%	28.0%
Trade Receiv.	27.1	27.6	24.0	23.9	25.6
Inventory	1.7	1.1	0.4	0.4	0.3
All Other Current	4.2	4.0	3.8	4.5	3.3
Total Current	59.6	59.0	58.3	58.5	57.3
Fixed Assets	20.4	19.5	19.0	19.0	19.6
Intangibles	7.9	7.1	8.7	8.3	9.7
All Other nonCur.	12.1	14.4	13.9	14.2	13.4
Total	100.0%	100.0%	100.0%	100.0%	100.0%
LIABILITIES					
Notes Payable ST	10.3%	10.8%	9.3%	8.9%	10.4%
Cur.Mat.—L/T/D	3.1	5.0	2.7	2.9	3.9
Trade Payables	14.5	14.4	15.0	15.3	16.7
Income Tax Pay.	1.4	0.5	0.5	0.4	0.2
All Other Current	17.9	20.4	21.0	19.6	21.7
Total Current	47.3	51.1	48.6	47.0	52.9
Long-term Debt	12.0	10.9	10.4	10.7	12.9
Deferred Taxes	0.2	0.3	0.2	0.3	0.3
All Other nonCur.	4.1	2.6	5.1	4.0	4.5
Net Worth	36.4	35.1	35.7	38.0	29.5
Total Liabilities & Net Worth	100.0%	100.0%	100.0%	100.0%	100.0%

*The conversion of financial statement absolute dollar amounts to percentages enables the users of the statements to perform a number of comparisons. This process is frequently called common-size analysis because all the years are reduced to a "common size" in that all the amounts are expressed in percentages of some common number and always add up to 100 percent.
†Although technically totals on common-sized statements must equal 100 percent, rounding adjustments may result in slight internal variations. The percentages presented in these exhibits are as reported in Robert Morris Associates.[15]

role of the travel agent remain the same in a world that appears to be turning in ever-increasing numbers to new information sources such as the Internet?

The technology provided through the Internet has the power to make travel planning more exciting. Computer users will become more informed consumers as they

	TABLE 5	COMPARATIVE COMMON-SIZED INCOME STATEMENT DATA*			
Year Ended	**3/31/94**	**3/31/95**	**3/31/96**	**3/31/97**	**3/31/98**
Net Sales	100.0%	100.0%	100.0%	100.0%	100.0%
Op. Exp.	96.7	96.7	97.3	97.6	97.8
Op. Profit	3.3	3.3	2.7	2.4	2.2
All Other Exp.	0.7	0.2	(0.1)	(0.1)	0.4
Profit Bef. Tax	2.6%	3.0%	2.7%	2.4%	1.8%

*Although technically totals on common-sized statements must equal 100 percent, rounding adjustments may result in slight internal variations. The percentages presented in these exhibits are as reported in Robert Morris Associates.[16]

explore travel and other leisure-time options ranging from transportation and accommodations to attractions and entertainment. As networking capabilities continue to increase in availability and speed, computer terminals, serving as electronic smart agents that utilize sophisticated software and networks, will develop that can meet travelers' specific needs. Booking a preferred flight time, reserving accommodations that meet specific criteria such as price range, level of service, or driving distance from the airport, and reserving tickets for the evening play are all future possibilities. For other people, the personal service and professional expertise provided by a travel agent will continue to be the travel department store of choice.

Some experts say that the role of the travel agent will become unimportant in a world where everyone has access to travel-related information and reservation sources through personal computers. Other experts say that the role of the travel agent will become more important and specialized as people have access to more data and less time to sort through this sea of information. Some people may use the information and reservation capacities provided through the Internet to book simple travel arrangements such as traveling from point A to point B. However, as travel needs become more complex and the management of business travel expenses become more important, the services of travel professionals may prove to be invaluable. Rapid technological changes and the need to possess detailed knowledge may force more and more travel agents to focus on one particular part of the industry such as cruises or business travel.

In the face of these real or perceived threats to continued profitability, travel agencies behave taken several steps from searching for economies of scale and scope to embracing new technologies and implementing service fees. Now, as we enter the 21st century, will the role of the travel agent remain the same in a world that appears to be turning in ever-increasing numbers to new information sources such as the Internet? You be the judge in this debate.

End Notes

[1]Whitney, Daisy. "Travel Expenses Trimmed," *The Denver Post*, December 5, 1998, p. C8.

[2]"1998 Travel Agency Survey," *Travel Weekly Focus*, vol. 57 (68), August 27, section 2.

[3]Cook, Roy A., Laura J. Yale, and Joseph J. Marqua. (1999). *Tourism: The Business of Travel.* Upper Saddle River, NJ: Prentice Hall.

[4]McGee, William J. "Reshaping the Relationship," Air Transport World, 34 (12), December 1997, pp. 57–59.

[5]"1998 Travel Agency Survey," *Travel Weekly Focus*, 57 (68), August 27, 1998, Section 2.

[6]"Agency Affiliations," *Travel Weekly*, 57 (68), August 27, 1998, p. 88.

[7]"Pioneers of the 21st Century," *Travel Weekly*, 56 (45), June 8, 1998, p. F4.

[8]"Clipboard," *Travel Weekly*, June 22, 1998, p. 73.

[9]"The Travel Agents' Dilemma," *Fortune*, 137 (9), May 11, 1998, pp. 163–164.

[10]www.tia.org Travel Industry Association of America.

[11]www.cc.gatech.edu/gvu/user_surveys/survey-1998-10/graphs/graphs.html.

[12]www.cc.gatech.edu/gvu/user_surveys/survey-1998-10/graphs/graphs/html.

[13]"Clipboard," *Travel Weekly*, August 10, 1998, p. 53.

[14]RMA Annual Statement Studies 1999, Philadelphia: Robert Morris Associates.

[15]Waters, Somerset R. "The U.S. Travel Industry: Where We're Going," *The Cornell Hotel Restaurant Administration Quarterly*, February 1990, pp. 26–33.

[16]RMA Annual Statement Studies.

3

Managing Entrepreneurial Growth

Key Topics

- **Understanding the Entrepreneurial Organization**

- **The Entrepreneurial Manager**

- **Building the Adaptive Firm**

- **Transition from an Entrepreneurial Style to a Managerial Approach**

- **Balancing Entrepreneurial and Managerial Style**

- **Managing Paradox and Contradiction**

- **Growth and Decision Making**

Understanding the Entrepreneurial Organization

Managing entrepreneurial growth may be the most critical tactic for the future success of business enterprises. After initiation of a new venture, the entrepreneur needs to develop an understanding of management change. This task represents a great challenge, because it often encompasses the art of balancing mobile and dynamic factors.[1] Thus achieving the survival and growth of a new venture requires that the entrepreneur possess both strategic and tactical skills and abilities. Which specific skills and abilities are needed depend in part on the venture's current development.

It has been noted that entrepreneurs (1) perceive an opportunity, (2) pursue this opportunity, and (3) believe that success of the venture is possible.[2] This belief that the idea is unique, that the product is strong, or that the entrepreneur possesses special knowledge or skill must be instilled into the organization itself as it grows.

The Entrepreneurial Manager

It is important for the venture's manager to maintain an open, entrepreneurial frame of mind to avoid the danger of evolving into a bureaucrat who stifles innovation. In some cases, success will affect an entrepreneur's willingness to change and innovate. This situation is particularly apt to arise if the enterprise develops an aura of complacency with which the entrepreneur is comfortable. In fact, some entrepreneurs create a bureaucratic environment in which orders are issued only from the top down and change initiated at the lower levels is not tolerated.[3] As a result, no one in the venture is willing or encouraged to become innovative or entrepreneurial because the owner-founder stifles such activity.

One recent study found that the attitude of the entrepreneur directly affects the firm's growth orientation as measured by profitability goals, product/market goals, human resource goals, and flexibility goals.[4] If the entrepreneur hopes to maintain the creative climate that initially helped launch the venture, he or she must take specific steps or measures to ensure its continuation.

Building the Adaptive Firm

As was mentioned in Chapter 1, building dynamic capabilities that are differentiated from those of emerging competitors is the major challenge for growing firms that seek to adapt to this changing landscape. One critical method of building dynamic capabilities is internal—utilization of the creativity and knowledge from employees.[5]

---

[1]Jeanie Daniel Duck, "Managing Change: The Art of Balancing," *Harvard Business Review* (Nov.–Dec. 1993): 109–118.

[2]Howard H. Stevenson and Jose Carlos Jarillo-Mossi, "Preserving Entrepreneurship as Companies Grow," *Journal of Business Strategy* (Summer 1986): 10.

[3]Ibid., 11.

[4]Vesa Routamaa and Jukka Vesalainen, "Types of Entrepreneurs and Strategic Level Goal Setting," *International Small Business Journal* (Spring 1987): 19–29; Lanny Herron and Richard B. Robinson, Jr., "A Structural Model of the Effects of Entrepreneurial Characteristics on Venture Performance," *Journal of Business Venturing* (May 1993): 281–294.

[5]Morten T. Hansen, Nitin Nohria, and Thomas Tierney, "What's Your Strategy for Managing Knowledge?" *Harvard Business Review*, 77, no. 2 (1999): 106–116.

Consequently, innovation and entrepreneurial thinking are essential elements in the strategies of growing ventures.[6]

Entrepreneurs must establish a business that remains flexible beyond the start-up period. An **adaptive firm** increases opportunity for its employees, initiates change, and instills the desire to be innovative in employees. The remainder of this section discusses ways to build adaptive firms. These guidelines are not set in stone, but they do enhance a venture's chance of remaining adaptive and innovative through and beyond the growth state.[7]

Increase the Perception of Opportunity

This goal can be accomplished through careful job design. In particular, objectives for which employees will be responsible should be well defined. Keeping each level of the hierarchy informed of its role in producing the final product or service is often known as "staying close to the customer."[8] Another way to increase the perception of opportunity is through a careful coordination and integration of functional areas, which allows subordinates in different functional areas to work together as a cohesive unit.

Institutionalize Change as the Venture's Goal

This effort entails making a preference for innovation and change rather than preservation of the status quo. If opportunity is to be perceived, the environment of the enterprise must not only encourage it, but also establish it as a goal. Within this context, a desire for opportunity can exist if resources are made available and departmental barriers are reduced.

Instill the Desire to Be Innovative

Personnel's desire to pursue opportunity must be carefully nurtured. Words alone will not create this innovative climate; specific steps should be taken. The following components are key features in this effort:

A Reward System   Explicit forms of recognition should be given to individuals who attempt to capitalize on innovative opportunities. For example, bonuses, awards, salary advances, and promotions should be tied directly to employees' innovative attempts.

An Environment That Allows for Failure   Fear of failure can be minimized if employees recognize that often many attempts are needed before success is achieved. This statement does not imply that failure is sought or desired. However, learning from failure, as opposed to expecting punishment for it, is promoted. When this type of environment exists, people become willing to accept the challenge of change and innovation.

---

[6]Shaker A. Zahra, "The Changing Rules of Global Competitiveness in the 21st Century," *Academy of Management Executive* 13, no. 1 (1999): 36–42.

[7]Stevenson and Jarillo-Mossi, "Preserving Entrepreneurship," 13–16.

[8]Thomas J. Peters and Robert H. Waterman, Jr., *In Search of Excellence* (New York: Harper & Row, 1982).

Flexible Operations   Flexibility makes change possible and has a positive effect. If a venture remains too rigidly tied to plans or strategies, it will not be responsive to new technologies, customer changes, or environmental shifts. Innovation will not take place because it does not "fit in."

Transition from an Entrepreneurial Style to a Managerial Approach

A venture's transitional stages are complemented (or in some cases retarded) by the entrepreneur's ability to make a transition in style. A key transition occurs during a venture's growth stage, when the entrepreneur shifts to a managerial style. This move is not an easy one to make. As Hofer and Charan have noted, "Among the different transitions that are possible, probably the most difficult to achieve and also perhaps the most important for organizational development is that of moving from a one-person, entrepreneurially managed firm to one run by a functionally organized, professional management team."[9]

A number of problems can arise in making this transition, especially if the enterprise is characterized by factors such as (1) a highly centralized decision-making system, (2) an overdependence on one or two key individuals, (3) an inadequate repertoire of managerial skills and training, and (4) a paternalistic atmosphere.[10] These characteristics, while often effective in the start-up and survival phases of a new venture, pose a threat to the development of the firm during its growth stage. Quite often they inhibit the venture's evolution by detracting from the entrepreneur's ability to successfully manage the growth stage.

Balancing Entrepreneurial and Managerial Styles

Two important points must be remembered about managing the growth stage. First, the entrepreneur of an adaptive firm needs to retain certain entrepreneurial characteristics so as to encourage innovation and creativity in his or her personnel while personally making a transition toward a more managerial style.[11] This critical entrepreneur/manager balance is extremely difficult to achieve. As Stevenson and Gumpert have noted, "Everybody wants to be innovative, flexible, and creative. But for every Apple, Domino's, and Lotus, there are thousands of new restaurants, clothing stores, and consulting firms that presumably have tried to be innovative, to grow, and to show other characteristics that are entrepreneurial in the dynamic sense, but have failed."[12]

Remaining entrepreneurial in nature while adopting certain administrative traits is critical to successful growth of a venture.[13] Table 3.1 provides a framework for comparing the characteristics and pressures relating to five major factors: strategic

---

[9]Charles W. Hofer and Ram Charan, "The Transition to Professional Management: Mission Impossible?" *American Journal of Small Business* (Summer 1984): 3.

[10]Ibid., 4.

[11]John B. Miner, "Entrepreneurs, High Growth Entrepreneurs, and Managers: Contrasting and Overlapping Motivational Patterns," *Journal of Business Venturing* (July 1990): 221–234.

[12]Howard J. Stevenson and David E. Gumpert, "The Heart of Entrepreneurship," *Harvard Business Review* (March–April 1985): 85.

[13]Arnold C. Cooper, "Challenges in Predicting New Firm Performance," *Journal of Business Venturing* (May 1993): 241–254.

orientation, commitment to seize opportunities, commitment of resources, control of resources, and management structure. Each of these five areas is critical to the balance needed to manage entrepreneurially. At the two ends of the continuum (**entrepreneurial** focus versus **administrative** focus) are specific points of view. Stevenson and Gumpert have characterized these points in question format.[14]

The administrative point of view:

- What sources do I control?
- What structure determines our organization's relationship to its market?
- How can I minimize the impact of others on my ability to perform?
- What opportunity is appropriate?

The entrepreneurial point of view:

- Where is the opportunity?
- How do I capitalize on it?
- What resources do I need?
- How do I gain control over them?
- What structure is best?

The logic behind these questions can be presented in a number of different ways. For example, the commitment of resources in the entrepreneurial frame of mind responds to changing environmental needs, whereas the managerial point of view is focused on the reduction of risk. In controlling these resources, entrepreneurs will avoid ownership because of the risk of obsolescence and the need for greater flexibility, whereas managers will view the factors of efficiency and stability as being accomplished through ownership. In terms of structure, the entrepreneurial emphasis is on a need for flexibility and independence, whereas the administrative focus is on ensuring integration with a complexity of tasks, a desire for order, and controlled reward systems.

These examples of differences in focus help establish the important issues involved at both ends of the managerial spectrum. Both points of view—entrepreneurial and administrative—have important considerations that need to be balanced if effective growth is to occur.

Managing Paradox and Contradiction

When a venture experiences surges in growth, a number of structural factors begin to present challenges. These factors, such as cultural elements, personnel staffing and development, and appraisal and rewards systems, are a source of constant struggle, with the firm vacillating between a rigid, bureaucratic design and a flexible, organic design. Table 3.2 depicts the conflicting designs for each element.

---

[14]Ibid., 86–87.

TABLE 3.1	ENTREPRENEURIAL CULTURE VERSUS ADMINISTRATIVE CULTURE

	Entrepreneurial Focus	
	Characteristics	**Pressures**
Strategic Orientation	Driven by perception of opportunity	Diminishing opportunities Rapidly changing technology, consumer economics, social values, and political rules
Commitment to Seize Opportunities	Revolutionary, with short duration	Action orientation Narrow decision windows Acceptance of reasonable risks Few decision constituencies
Commitment of Resources	Many stages, with minimal exposure at each stage	Lack of predictable resource needs Lack of control over the environment Social demands for appropriate use of resources Foreign competition Demands for more efficient use
Control of Resources	Episodic use or rent of required resources	Increased resource specialization Long resource life compared with need Risk of obsolescence Risk inherent in the identified opportunity Inflexibility of permanent commitment to resources
Management Structure	Flat, with multiple informal networks	Coordinates of key noncontrolled resources Challenge to hierarchy Employees' desire for independence

Research has shown that new-venture managers experiencing growth—particularly those in emerging industries—need to adopt flexible, organic structures.[15] Rigid bureaucratic structures are best suited for mature, stable companies. Thus the new venture's cultural elements need to emphasize a flexible design of autonomy, risk taking, and entrepreneurship. This type of culture represents a renewal of the entrepreneur's original force that created the venture. Even if the entrepreneur makes a

---

[15]Jeffrey G. Covin and Dennis P. Slevin, "New Venture Strategic Posture, Structure, and Performance: An Industry Life Cycle Analysis," *Journal of Business Venturing* (March 1990): 123–133.

TABLE 3.1	(CONTINUED)	

	Administrative Focus	
	Characteristics	**Pressures**
	Driven by controlled resources	Social contracts Performance measurement criteria Planning systems and cycles
	Evolutionary, with long duration	Acknowledgment of multiple constituencies Negotiation about strategic course Risk reduction Coordination with existing resource base
	A single stage, with complete commitment out of decision	Need to reduce risk Incentive compensation Turnover in managers Capital budgeting systems Formal planning systems
	Ownership or employment of required resources	Power, status, and financial rewards Coordination of activity Efficiency measures Inertia and cost of change Industry structures
	Hierarchy	Need for clearly defined authority and responsibility Organizational culture Reward systems Management theory

SOURCE: Reprinted by permission of the *Harvard Business Review*. An exhibit from "The Heart of Entrepreneurship" by Howard H. Stevenson and David E. Gumpert, March–April 1985, p. 89. Copyright © 1985 by the President of Fellows of Harvard College; all rights reserved.

transition toward a more administrative style (as mentioned earlier), the spirit of innovation and entrepreneurship must continue to permeate the organization.[16]

In designing a flexible structure that can support high growth, a number of contradictory forces are at work. Consider the following structures.

---

[16]Ikujiro Nonaka and Tervo Yamanovchi, "Managing Innovation as a Self-Renewing Process," *Journal of Business Venturing* (Sept. 1989): 229–315.

Bureaucratization versus Decentralization Increased hiring stimulates bureaucracy; firms formalize procedures as staffing doubles and triples. Employee participation and autonomy decline and internal labor markets develop. Tied to growth, however, is an increased diversity in product offering that favors less formalized decision-making processes, greater decentralization, and the recognition that the firm's existing human resources lack the necessary skills to manage the broadening portfolio.

Environment versus Strategy High levels of environmental turbulence and competitive conditions favor company cultures that support risk taking, autonomy, and employee participation in decision making. Firms confront competitors, however, through strategies whose implementation depends on the design of formal systems that inhibit risk taking and autonomy.

Strategic Emphasis on Quality versus Cost versus Innovation Rapidly growing firms strive to simultaneously control costs, enhance product quality, and improve product offerings. Minimizing costs and undercutting competitors' product prices, however, are best achieved by traditional hierarchical systems of decision making and evaluations strategies. Yet, these systems conflict with the kinds of autonomous processes most likely to encourage the pursuit of product quality and innovation.[17]

TABLE 3.2	CONFLICTING DESIGNS OF STRUCTURAL FACTORS

Flexible Design	Bureaucratic Design
Cultural Elements	
Autonomous	Formalized
Risk taking	Risk averse
Entrepreneurial	Bureaucratic
Staffing and Development	
Technical skills	Administrative skills
Specialists	Generalists
External hiring	Internal hiring
Appraisal and Reward	
Participative	Formalized
Subjective	Objective
Equity based	Incentive based

SOURCE: Charles J. Fombrun and Stefan Wally, "Structuring Small Firms for Rapid Growth," *Journal of Business Venturing* (March 1989): 109.

---

[17]Charles J. Fombrun and Stefan Wally, "Structuring Small Firms for Rapid Growth," *Journal of Business Venturing* (March 1989): 107–122. See also Patricia P. McDougall, Richard B. Robinson, Jr., and Angelo S. DeNisi, "Modeling New Venture Performance: An Analysis of New Venture Strategy, Industry Structure, and Venture Origin," *Journal of Business Venturing* (July 1992): 267–290.

These factors emphasize the importance of managing paradox and contradiction. Growth involves meeting the multiple challenges of controlling costs while simultaneously enhancing quality and creating new products to maintain competitive parity, and centralizing operations to retain control while simultaneously decentralizing systems to encourage the contributions of autonomous, self-managed professionals to the embryonic corporate culture. Rapidly growing firms must attempt to strike a balance between these challenges when designing their managerial systems.

Growth and Decision Making

The **decision-making process** is a critical issue in the growth stage of emerging ventures.[18] The focus and style of decision making in this phase differ from the focus and style observed in earlier or later stages that a venture goes through, as illustrated in Table 3.3. Also, as depicted in Table 3.3, the organizational characteristics of successful early-stage firms and successful mature firms are quite different, as are the problems each type of organization encounters. Early-stage firms are often unable to define tasks regarding technology or market development that are characterized by high levels of uncertainty. As a result, they typically show little structure in terms of job specialization, rules, or formality. The owner is, in many instances, the sole decision maker, with communication being informal and face-to-face. The owner-founder usually integrates people, functions, and tasks by direct contact.

In contrast, mature firms that have several hundred employees can no longer manage in such a fashion. They require formality, structure, and specialization to effectively and efficiently control and direct the organization.

The transition from early-stage decision making to later-stage decision making must be effected during the growth stage, and the timing of this shift is critical. Premature introduction of structure and formalities may dampen the venture's creative, entrepreneurial climate. If formality and structure are adopted too late, however, management may lose control of the organization as its size increases, leading to major dislocations of the firm and even failure.[19]

Consequently, entrepreneurs need to recognize the important transition of decision-making style during the growth stage and learn to authorize others to make necessary decisions to address the multiple challenges of rapid growth. Some suggestions for handling decision making during growth follow.

One method concentrates on the use of external resources through **networking**.[20] In this system, entrepreneurs make use of resources that are external to their venture; that is, they establish personal relationships that may be used for professional assistance. The idea is to gain a competitive advantage by extending decision making and resource availability beyond the assets that are under the direct control of the venture. For example, a firm might promise a royalty on future sales so as to obtain a license to

[18]Robin Siegel, Eric Siegel, and Ian C. MacMillan, "Characteristics Distinguishing High Growth Ventures," *Journal of Business Venturing* (March 1993): 169–180.

[19]Thomas N. Gilmore and Robert K. Kanzanjian, "Clarifying Decision Making in High Growth Ventures: The Use of Responsibility Charting," *Journal of Business Venturing* (Jan. 1989): 69–83.

[20]J. Carlos Jarillo, "Entrepreneurship and Growth: The Strategic Use of External Resources," *Journal of Business Venturing* (March 1989): 133–147. See also Dean Tjosvold and David Weicker, "Cooperative and Competitive Networking by Entrepreneurs: A Critical Incident Study," *Journal of Small Business Management* (Jan. 1993): 11–21.

TABLE 3.3	DECISION-MAKING CHARACTERISTICS AND STAGE OF GROWTH		
	Early Stage(s)	**Growth Stage**	**Later Stage(s)**
Primary Focus	Product business	Volume production	Cost control
	Definition	Market share	Profitability
	Acquisition of resources	Viability	Future growth opportunity
	Development of market position		
Decision-Making Characteristics	Informal	Transitional	Formal
	Centralized		Decentralized
	Nonspecialized		Specialized
	Short time horizon		Long and short time horizon

SOURCE: Thomas N. Gilmore and Robert K. Kazanjian, "Clarifying Decision Making in High Growth Ventures: The Use of Responsibility Charting," *Journal of Business Venturing* (Jan. 1989): 71.

use a well-known name to market a product that could not otherwise achieve recognition. The firm is obviously taking advantage of a series of resources, which in this case includes all the resources needed to create a national brand that it does not own. **External resources** are those assets, physical or otherwise, that the firm uses in its pursuit of growth and over which the firm has no direct ownership.[21] Another example is the use of outside consulting assistance to help with administrative or operating problems. Strategic planning, security financing, marketing, and day-to-day operational assistance are all areas in which emerging firms may seek outside assistance.[22]

Another method suggested to entrepreneurs for handling decisions during growth is called **responsibility charting**.[23] This process assumes that decision making involves multiple roles that work together in various ways at different points over time. Its three major components are combined to form a matrix in which a respondent assigns a type of participation to each of the roles (at the top of the matrix) for a specific decision (on the left of the matrix). Responses are then analyzed either in a group setting with all participants present or by a facilitator alone when group size makes data processing unwieldy. Table 3.3 lists the steps used in responsibility charting.

In reporting the value of this process, Gilmore and Kanzanjian state:

> Responsibility charting enables better discussions of power and authority because it allows a rich range of potential solutions, rather than the win–lose dynamics that result from discussing these issues in terms of boxes and lines of a new structure.

[21]Ibid., 135.

[22]James J. Chrisman and John Leslie, "Strategic, Administrative, and Operating Problems: The Impact of Outsiders on Small Firm Performance," *Entrepreneurship Theory and Practice* (Spring 1989): 37–48.

[23]Gilmore and Kanzanjian, "Clarifying Decision Making in High Growth Ventures," 69–83.

In growth-stage ventures, team building often fails because of the influx of new executives. If responsibility charting is used to clarify major decisions, the results can orient new executives who step into key roles. Unlike a job description that only communicates one's duties, the chart shows how each manager's role interacts with the many other critical processes.[24]

Whether by using networking or responsibility charting, entrepreneurs need to develop methods to handle the increasing complexities of decision making in the growth stage.

Exploring the Entrepreneurial Concepts

The following sections provide an "entrepreneurial library" that contains a journal reading on this chapter's subject and a comprehensive case study to illustrate the concept in practice. It is hoped that through the reading and discussion of the case, you will gain a greater understanding of the chapter.

THE ENTREPRENEURIAL LIBRARY

Reading for Chapter 3

BUILDING AN ADAPTIVE FIRM

Donald F. Kuratko, D.B.A.
Jeffrey S. Hornsby, Ph.D.
Laura M. Corso, M.A.

This article is reprinted from the Small Business Forum, the Journal of the Association of Small Business Development Centers, which is published by the University of Wisconsin–Extension Small Business Development Center. For information about subscriptions, reprints or submissions, please write to us at 432 North Lake Street, Room 425, Madison, WI 53706, or call us at 608/263-7843.

Author of several best-selling entrepreneurship textbooks, Dr. Kuratko is the Stoops Distinguished Professor of Business, at Ball State University. Dr. Hornsby is an associate professor and coordinator of the Human Resource Management Program in the management department at Ball State University. Dr. Corso is an associate professor of merchandising in the College of Applied Science at Ball State University.

Let's start with something we all know is true: In order to successfully grow, a business needs to be "adaptive"—which means that it is flexible enough to manage change.

Adaptive firms don't crumble when the marketplace takes a new turn, or when technology suddenly revolutionizes the way we work, or when customers want to form new relationships.

We've all seen flexible firms change with the times—and inflexible firms become obsolete. What is at the heart of the difference between these two types of firms? Solid leadership? Appropriate technology? A solid financial foundation? Luck? What explains why some firms can manage change, and others become victims of it?

---

[24]Ibid., 81.

S O C I A L   A N D   E C O N O M I C   I S S U E S

In Focus

This article advocates role reversal. Our authors argue that the common situation—in which entrepreneurs are innovators and employees are managers—limits growth. When, instead, the entrepreneur becomes managerial and employees become entrepreneurial, the business can grow.

—Catherine Stover, Senior Editor

We believe the answer lies in the ability of the founding entrepreneur and the employees to exchange roles. It is our observation that adaptive firms have entrepreneurs who have become more managerial, while the employees have become more entrepreneurial.

Ideally, the entrepreneur transfers the spirit of innovation and creativity to the employees (to encourage them to become "entrepreneurial"). At the same time, the entrepreneur's energy shifts from the creative process to the managerial process. Instead of developing a new product or process, the entrepreneur works on increasing efficiency, lowering costs, and training employees. As a result, the firm has the best of both worlds: an entrepreneur who can manage, and employees who can create.

Frequently, these roles are reversed. In fact, we have seen many businesses where the entrepreneur is the sole creator and the employees are managers. However, these businesses often reach a point where they stop growing—because they are limited to the innovations that are generated by a single person.

It's not easy for entrepreneurs to transfer their spirit of innovation and creativity to employees. Nor is it easy for employees to feel comfortable in a risk-taking environment. Yet, we believe that when this does happen, firms become much more flexible, more adaptive, more able to grow and evolve.

In this article, we outline the steps in the process that support this reversal of roles.

THE ENTREPRENEUR BECOMES MORE MANAGERIAL, WHILE EMPLOYEES BECOME MORE ENTREPRENEURIAL

Entrepreneur $\longrightarrow$ Managerial

Entrepreneurial $\longleftarrow$ Managers/Employees

Flexibility and Independence vs. Order and Systems
Innovation and Creativity vs. Control and Planning

Step One: The Entrepreneur Decides to Change

We all know that the entrepreneur's management style must change as the firm evolves. The focus of the founder must shift from creation to exploitation (Willard, Krueger and Fesser, 1992). But shifting from the creative process to the managerial process is not easy—nor is shifting from "passionate commitment" to "dispassionate objectivity."

Why is it so hard? There are at least two strong reasons. First, the chaotic pace of the day-to-day routine leaves no time for thoughtful contemplation. Second, when things appear to be going well, there is little incentive to change (Hanks and McCarrey, 1993).

Sometimes change does not occur until the business hits a "growth wall." A growth wall is a barrier that seems too big to surmount. Researchers have identified some of the common challenges that come at this stage:

- Instant size,

- A sense of infallibility,

- Internal turmoil, and

- Extraordinary resource needs (Kuratko and Hodgetts, 1995).

Clearly, this is a time when the entrepreneur needs to become more managerial. The first step in the process is to decide to change.

When the entrepreneur decides to become more managerial, what exactly does this entail? According to Stevenson and Gumpert (1985):

Entrepreneurs ask . . .

- Where is the opportunity?

- How do I capitalize on it?

- What resources do I use?

- How do I gain control over them?

Managers ask . . .

- What sources do I control?

- What structure determines our organization's relationship to its market?

- How can I minimize the impact of others on my ability to perform?

- What opportunity is appropriate?

Without relying too much on stereotypes, it's probably safe for us to assume that most readers know what we mean when we say that entrepreneurs value creativity, managers value control and planning. While entrepreneurs need flexibility and independence, managers need order and systems. One approach is not "better" or "worse" than the other—they are just two different points of view.

After the entrepreneurs reach the point where they recognize that their role must change, the next step is possible.

Step Two: Decide to Empower Employees

At its most fundamental level, this means that the entrepreneur stops being the company's sole source of new ideas, and starts encouraging creativity in the employees.

Too often, founders fall into the trap of inadvertently destroying other people's ideas. By using certain negative phrases for reasons of efficiency or impatience, they may unintentionally stop their staff's creative process. Table 1 lists 15 of the most commonly used "idea stoppers." These phrases are symptoms of a low tolerance for new thinking from other people.

Everyone in the organization must have the perception that idea development is possible and will be rewarded. The perception is linked directly to the founder's attitude and the prevailing corporate culture. If the founder does not work to project a clearly defined culture, one will emerge anyway—but it may inhibit, rather than facilitate, change (Peak, 1993). In other words, a corporate culture will emerge, by design or default. The choice to design an adaptive culture or default to an inhibiting culture remains with the firm's founder.

Empowerment, a buzzword of the 1990s, has caught on in many organizations because it is so fundamental to managing change. How do you get people to improve constantly? Let them "own" their jobs. You can't talk them into it; you can't "control" them into it. In the long run, empowerment gives employees the motivation to improve. Empowerment is not a program; it is a culture change. Empowerment is a value for the organization. Kizilos (1990) warned that "powerlessness" is the root cause of many of the problems that management is concerned with in the workplace today.

TABLE 1	THE MOST COMMON IDEA STOPPERS

- "Naah."
- "Can't" (said with a shake of the head and an air of finality).
- "That's the dumbest thing I've ever heard."
- "Yeah, but if you did that . . ." (poses an extreme or unlikely disaster case).
- "We already tried that—years ago."
- "We've done all right so far; why do we need that?"
- "I don't see anything wrong with the way we're doing it now."
- "That doesn't sound too practical."
- "We've never done anything like that before."
- "Let's get back to reality."
- "We've got deadlines to meet—we don't have time to consider that."
- "It's not in the budget."
- "Are you kidding?"
- "Let's not go off on a tangent."
- "Where do you get these weird ideas?"

SOURCE: Adapted from *The Creative Process*, edited by Angela M. Biondi, The Creative Education Foundation, 1986.

Step Three: Decide to Focus on Big Issues

The third step in the process of becoming more managerial is for the entrepreneur to focus on the big issues instead of the day-to-day running of the business.

What are the big issues? For an adaptive firm, they are:

A Reward System   Explicit forms of recognition should be given to individuals who attempt innovative opportunities. For example, bonuses, awards, salary advances, and promotions should be tied directly to the innovative attempts of your staff.

An Environment That Allows for Failure   This may sound like a strange priority, but in fact the fear of failure must be minimized through the general recognition that often many attempts are needed before a success is achieved. This does not imply that failure is sought or desired. However, learning from failure, as opposed to expecting punishment for it, is promoted. When this type of environment exists, people become willing to accept the challenge of change and innovation.

Flexible Operations   Flexibility creates the possibility of change taking place and having a positive effect. If a venture remains too rigidly tied to plans or strategies, it will not be responsive to new technologies, customer changes, or environmental shifts. Innovation will not take place because it will not "fit in."

The Development of Venture Teams' Performance   In order for the environment to foster innovation, venture teams need to be developed and team performance needs to be established. These must not be just work groups but visionary, committed teams that have the authority to create new direction, set new standards, and challenge the status quo (Kuratko and Hodgetts, 1995).

These central issues are also the hallmarks of an adaptive firm.

How can you tell when you are working on the right things? Researchers tell us that growth-oriented firms have exhibited a few consistent themes:

- The entrepreneur is able to envision and anticipate the firm as a larger entity.

- The team needed for tomorrow is hired and developed today.

- The original core vision of the firm is constantly and zealously reinforced.

- New "big company" processes are introduced gradually as supplements to, rather than replacements for, existing approaches.

- Hierarchy is minimized.

- Employees hold a financial stake in the firm (Kuratko and Hodgetts, 1995).

These actions will also help firms manage growth.

Step Four: Create a New Reward and Incentive Program

One method of fostering an environment of employee ownership of new ideas is through reward and incentive programs. Traditional basic benefit packages have not been motivators for employee innovation. However, those benefits which go beyond

SOCIAL AND ECONOMIC ISSUES

How One Entrepreneur Let Go

Patrick Leamy, president and chief executive officer of EconoPrint, developed a dynamic management model where decisions are made by employees and true power of the company is shared. All 85 employees in his eight Madison, Wisconsin, stores are problem-solvers who are committed to providing excellent customer service. His unique model has received national attention in his industry. His management style, gross sales, and sales per employee were all cited when EconoPrint was rated the No. 1 quick printer in the north and northeast portions of the United States by *Graphic Arts Monthly*. Out of 35,000 quick printers nationally, *Quick Print Magazine* rated EconoPrint No. 13.

The purpose of his employee involvement program, Leamy says, is to bring employees into the decision-making process. "They know their own jobs better than anyone else does. And they have a lot of ideas to contribute. When we started this program in 1989, it really turned the company around. Our sales increased and so did our morale."

At the center of the EconoPrint's employee involvement program is a steering committee, which consists of seven employees who have been elected by their peers to represent all job classifications. The committee is assisted by an outside facilitator. Pat Leamy is present at the meetings, and serves as a resource, but is not an active participant. The members of the steering committee also help lead special subcommittees, which are formed to address specific problems.

For example, one subcommittee was asked to design, develop and implement an account management program, which would help the employees to learn more about how they could help their customers. The committee developed a plan, which specified how each employee would take care of a certain number of accounts. For example, under this plan, every press person calls one customer per day to say, "I operated the press on the printing job we ran for you two days ago, I'm calling to see how we did." The plan is designed to help all employees learn more about their customers. Leamy says, "It's critical to know—not to just assume you know—what your customers want. It takes extra work and an organized effort. If it were easy to do, every business would be successful."

Every EconoPrint employee undergoes an orientation program that consists of 13 two-to-six-hour sessions, all of which are taught by staff members. The members of the steering committee receive additional training. "They go to the same two-day seminar on problem solving that the management here goes to. This way, we all use the same problem-solving process, and we all use the same terminology." Leamy believes that the program has

the "basics" and address other important employee needs, such as child care and elder care assistance, company-sponsored tax deferred savings plans, or perhaps a cafeteria of flexible benefits, are perceived as more motivating (Harper, Densmore and Motwani, 1993). According to Hornsby, Kuratko and Naffziger (1993) employee benefits can be used to attract employees, increase morale, reduce turnover, increase job satisfaction, motivate employees, enhance the firm's image and remain cost-effective.

One recent study found the more the workers used work-family benefits, the more they reported helping out co-workers and their supervisors, volunteering for work and showing initiative. According to Mason (1992), workers were more likely to support changes, participate in team problem solving, and suggest twice as many product and process improvements.

Well-designed compensation plans include incentives and rewards for employee effort and innovative performance. The total package should serve as a tool in building relationships with employees. An important part of a strategic growth plan is a benefits/rewards/incentive program which mirrors the firm's mission and culture.

had a positive impact on his company in five different ways:

- It has given the employees a greater sense of accomplishment, dignity, belonging, and job satisfaction.

- It has given managers better information, a greater sense of job satisfaction, and improvements in productivity and quality.

- It has created a better work environment.

- It has improved labor relations.

- It has improved shop problem solving.

"If I had to summarize it in one word," Leamy said, "it would be *communication*. People are talking to each other now. We used to have many separate units, and now we are all working together to solve problems."

To those employers who may consider developing their own employee involvement system, Leamy has these words of advice:

Start by Selecting Employees Wisely   Leamy is the only quick-printer in the United States to employ a full-time human resources director. "Nationally, our industry has a 53 percent turnover rate. In one year, our human resources director decreased our turnover from 48 percent to 24 percent."

Don't Expect Universal Enthusiasm   When Leamy introduced his employee involvement program, about 30 percent of his staff embraced the idea. "But that is 30 percent more than we had before," he says.

Provide Training   It's not enough to give your people a voice, Leamy says. You also have to make sure they know how to proceed. Steering committees ought to have an experienced facilitator and training in problem-solving.

Be an Educated Leader   Before starting his program, Leamy was able to draw upon years of exposure to new ideas and educational resources. He has had an advisory board since 1982, he has been involved with his national association, he belongs to a local group that hosts monthly speakers, he has a group of seven peers who exchange advice, and he has read current management books. He is able to draw upon numerous sources for his ideas.

SOURCE: Catherine Stover, "EconoPrint's boss listens to input of his employees" *The Capital Times*, March 3, 1992.

Viewed as a management tool, this program can serve several purposes. It should communicate and reinforce company values as well as motivate the firm's employees. Morris, Lewis and Sexton (1994) suggest that the culture and reward system of the enterprise must be one that encourages innovative thinking, fosters proactive behaviors and most important, tolerates failure when appropriate.

In addition to benefits, both programs which reward employee efforts and incentives to motivate innovative performance are gaining in popularity as important managerial tools for adaptive firms. The entrepreneurial firm must look beyond the individual employee when designing a compensation package and must look at the employee's total environmental needs which include the extended family, his/her mental and physical health, and sense of value to the firm (Motwani, Harper, Subramanian, and Douglas, 1993).

The initial challenge is to determine what kind of program will meet the unique needs of an organization, and then develop a program based on those findings. An innovative incentive program is vital for today's business environment. Table 2 provides some recommendations for developing a rewards/incentives program.

TABLE 2	STARTING YOUR OWN REWARDS AND INCENTIVES PROGRAM

- Plan the program carefully before it is in place.
- Focus on company, employee and customer needs. (Don't reward one at the expense of the other).
- Reward good performance as quickly as possible.
- Keep the incentives accessible to as many employees as possible.
- Keep the program simple.
- Let the employees reward each other.
- Establish the right "fit" within the firm's culture.
- Run the program for a short period, and change the rewards frequently.
- Be sure that the rewards/incentives are perceived by the employees to be of value.
- Make sure that both full-time and part-time employees have an equal opportunity (if not, develop two parallel programs).
- Don't reward employees with something that they can get on their own (through their employee discount).
- Don't be afraid to have fun.
- Vary the criteria for various rewards so that *everyone* is rewarded sometime during the year.
- Remember that the incentives and rewards do not have to be costly or even financial in nature.
- Be creative.

Step Five: Have Courage to Believe in Change

Change requires courage. The founder and the employees alike must recognize that the changes in roles described so far require commitment, vision, and courage.

A tolerance for experimentation will create an atmosphere of inquiry and critical thinking, which, in turn, will lead to ideas for improving the systems or products.

But opportunities for the company will not be pursued unless the individuals within the organization believe that it is a personal opportunity for themselves. Therefore, ". . . management should ensure that the consequence of pursuing a new idea will be that a person is given a sense of satisfaction just for being *one who tried*" (Stevenson & Jarillo-Mossi, 1986).

A low tolerance for failure is sure to kill any incentive to be creative.

What should the founder do to create a company that has the courage to believe in change? Here is a brief list:

- Open channels of communication.
- Create visionaries and change agents.
- Develop a learning environment.
- Provide training.

- Stop the rumor mill.

- Begin a strong, targeted communication campaign.

- Make top management's commitment to growth clear.

- Achieve buy-in at all levels.

- Break down the barriers between employees.

- Ensure that anticipatory capability is built into the culture.

- Design rewards for the pursuit of opportunity.

- Reduce the risk of failure.

- Make people believe they can succeed.

- Make sure that one idea cannot be killed by just one negative opinion. (Goldberg, 1992; Stevenson & Jarrillo-Mossi, 1986).

SOCIAL AND ECONOMIC ISSUES

How the Incentive Program at Liebhardt Mills Increased Productivity

"Give them the target and the tools and your employees will surprise you." These are the words of William Walker, vice president of operations for Liebhardt Mills, Inc. (LMI), a leading pillow and bed products manufacturer with five plants and approximately 300 employees. After several years using a piece-rate incentive system for pillow manufacturing, corporate executives set a new course with a workteam concept. Instead of receiving pay per unit produced, the new incentive program placed greater emphasis on quality, shipment cycle time, safety, cost per unit and inventory turns ration.

Specific elements of the incentive program include:

- Base pay of $7.50 per hour.
- Annual reviews for potential base increases determined by company profitability and market equity.
- Establishment of self-directed workteams who were cross-trained in all aspects of pillow manufacturing.
- Incentive standards based on group productivity and quality where group members could earn up to 25 percent of their base pay.
- Quarterly safety, shipment cycle time, cost per unit and inventory turns ratio bonuses for

work teams. Group members could earn up to 5 percent of their base pay.

Liebhardt Mills, Inc., embarked on this ambitious organizational change effort in their largest plant in Middletown, Indiana. During the fall of 1993 and winter of 1994 workteams were formed and cross-trained, the pillow production process was totally redesigned, and the plant managerial structure was reorganized. By the end of 1994, the investment started to pay off. Workteam members were accepting their new responsibilities and productivity and quality increased dramatically. By the spring of 1995, productivity per team had risen from 2200 pillows per shift to 3200 pillows per shift, representing nearly a 46 percent improvement.

According to Bill Walker, the teams have yet to reach their full potential. He does caution that productivity and quality improvements do not occur overnight. At the start of the new workteam incentive program, productivity remained stagnant and sometimes slipped below rates established before the new program was introduced. Other adjustments cited included increased expenditures for training and some initial turnover of employees unable to fit into the work team concept.

SOURCE: Personal interview: William Walker, Vice President-Operations, Liebhardt Mills, Inc., Daleville, Indiana, April 1995.

Conclusion

In summary, the managing entrepreneur must make a decision to allow the firm to grow and then prepare himself/herself and the organization for growth. By building the adaptive firm, the entrepreneur will ensure the business will remain flexible beyond its start-up. Within the adaptive firm, benefits, rewards, and incentives are powerful tools which can be effectively used to help employees take ownership of their jobs and share in the firm's mission of growth. Creating tomorrow's vision can be accomplished only through the careful management of today's growth.

References

Goldberg, B., Manage change—not the chaos caused by change, *Management Review*, 81, 1992, pp. 39–45.

Hanks, S. H. and McCarrey, L. R., Beyond survival: reshaping entrepreneurial vision in successful growing ventures, *Journal of Small Business Strategy*, Vol. 4, 1993, pp. 1–11.

Harper, E., Densmore, M., and Motwani, J., New realities in the corporate workplace: Child care in the nineties, *Sam Advanced Management Journal*, Vol. 58, 1993, pp. 4–8.

Hornsby, J. S., Kuratko, D. F. and Naffziger, D. W., Flexible employee benefit plans for small business, *Small Business Forum*, 11, 1993, pp. 35–43.

Kizilos, P., Crazy about empowerment? *Training*, 27, 1990, pp. 47–56.

Kuratko, D. F., and Hodgetts, R. M., *Entrepreneurship: A Contemporary Approach*, Ft. Worth: Dryden Press, 1995.

Mason, J. C., Flexing more than muscle: employees want time on their side, *Management Review*, 82, 1992, pp. 25–28.

Mason, J. C., Working in the family way, *Management Review*, 82, 1993, pp. 25–28.

Morris, M. H., Lewis, P. S. and Sexton, D. L., Reconceptualizing entrepreneurship: An input–output perspective, *Sam Advanced Management Journal*, 59, 1994, pp. 21–31.

Motwani, J., Harper, E., Subramanian, R. and Douglas, C., Managing the diversified workforce: Current efforts and future directions, *Sam Advanced Management Journal*, 58, 1993, pp. 16–21.

Peak, M., Corporations prepare for change, *Management Review*, 82, 1993, pp. 42–47.

Stevenson, H. H. and Gumpert, D. E., The Heart of Entrepreneurship, *Harvard Business Review*, March–April 1985, pp. 85–94.

Stevenson, H. H. and Jarrillo-Mossi, J. C., Preserving entrepreneurship as companies grow, *The Journal of Business Strategy*, 7, 1986, pp. 10–23.

Willard, G. E., Krueger, D. A., and Fesser, H. R., In order to grow, must the founder go: A comparison of performance between founder and non-founder managed high-growth manufacturing firms, *Journal of Business Venturing*, 7, 1992, pp. 181–194.

COMPREHENSIVE CASE STUDY

C A S E **Wal-Mart Stores, Inc.: Strategies for Continued Market Dominance**

James W. Camerius

This case was prepared by James W. Camerius of Northern Michigan University and is intended to be used as a basis for class discussion rather than to illustrate either effective or ineffective handling of an administrative situation. All rights reserved to the author. Copyright © 1998 by James W. Camerius.

David Glass assumed the role of President and Chief Executive Officer at Wal-Mart, the position previously held by Sam Walton. Known for his hard-driving managerial style, Glass gained his experience in retailing at a small supermarket chain in Springfield, Missouri. He joined Wal-Mart as executive vice president for finance in 1976. He was named president and chief operating officer in 1984. In 1998, as he reflected on growth strategies of the firm, he suggested: "Seldom can you count on everything coming together as well as it did this year. We believe we could always do better, but we improved more this year than I can ever remember in the past. If Wal-Mart had been content to be just an Arkansas retailer in the early days, we probably would not be where we are today."

A Maturing Organization

In 1998, Wal-Mart Stores, Inc., Bentonville, Arkansas, operated mass-merchandising retail stores under a variety of names and retail formats including: Wal-Mart discount department stores; Sam's Wholesale Clubs, wholesale/retail membership warehouses; and Wal-Mart Supercenters, large combination grocery and general merchandise stores in all 50 states. In the International Division, it operated in Canada, Mexico, Argentina, Brazil, Germany, and Puerto Rico, and through joint ventures in China. It was not only the nation's largest discount department store chain, but had surpassed the retail division of Sears, Roebuck, & Co. in sales volume as the largest retail firm in the United States. The McLane Company, a support division with over 36,000 customers, was the nation's largest distributor of food and merchandise to convenience stores and served selected Wal-Marts, Sam's Clubs and Supercenters. Wal-Mart also continued to operate a small number of discount department stores called Bud's Discount City. A financial summary of Wal-Mart Stores, Inc., for the fiscal years ended January 31, 1997 and 1998, is shown in Appendix A.

The Sam Walton Spirit

Much of the success of Wal-Mart was attributed to the entrepreneurial spirit of its founder and Chairman of the Board, Samuel Moore Walton (1918–1992). Many considered him one of the most influential retailers of the century.

Sam Walton or "Mr. Sam" as some referred to him, traced his down-to-earth, old-fashioned, home-spun, evangelical ways to growing up in rural Oklahoma, Missouri, and Arkansas. Although he was remarkably blasé about his roots, some suggested that it was the simple belief in hard work and ambition that had "unlocked countless doors and showered upon him, his customers, and his employees . . . , the fruits of . . . years of labor in building [this] highly successful company."

"Our goal has always been in our business to be the very best," Sam Walton said in an interview, "and, along with that, we believe that in order to do that, you've got to make a good situation and put the interests of your associates first. If we really do that consistently, they in turn will cause . . . our business to be successful, which is what we've talked about and espoused and practiced." "The reason for our success," he said, "is our people and the way that they're treated and the way they feel about their company." Many have suggested it is this "people first" philosophy which guided the company through the challenges and setbacks of its early years, and allowed the company to maintain its consistent record of growth and expansion in later years.

There was little about Sam Walton's background that reflected his amazing success. He was born in Kingfisher, Oklahoma, on March 29, 1918, to Thomas and Nancy Walton. Thomas Walton was a banker at the time and later entered the farm mortgage business and moved to Missouri. Sam Walton, growing up in rural Missouri in the depths of the Great Depression, discovered early that he "had a fair amount of ambition and enjoyed working," he once noted. He completed high school at Columbia, Missouri, and received a Bachelor of Arts Degree in Economics from the University of Missouri in 1940. "I really had no idea what I would be," he said, adding as an afterthought, "at one point in time, I thought I wanted to become president of the United States."

A unique, enthusiastic, and positive individual, Sam Walton was "just your basic home-spun billionaire," a columnist once suggested. ". . . Mr. Sam is a life-long small-town resident who didn't change much as he got richer than his neighbors," he noted. Walton had tremendous energy, enjoyed bird hunting with his dogs and flew a corporate plane. When the company was much smaller he could boast that he personally visited every Wal-Mart store at least once a year. A store visit usually included Walton leading Wal-Mart cheers that began, "Give me a W, give me an A . . ." To many employees he had the air of a fiery Baptist preacher. Paul R. Carter, a Wal-Mart executive vice president, was quoted as saying, "Mr. Walton has a calling." He became the richest man in America, and by 1991 had created a personal fortune for his family in excess of $21 billion.

Sam Walton's success was widely chronicled. He was selected by the investment publication *Financial World* in 1989 as the "CEO of the Decade." He had honorary degrees from the University of the Ozarks, the University of Arkansas, and the University of Missouri. He also received many of the most distinguished professional awards of the industry like "Man of the Year," "Discounter of the Year," "Chief Executive Officer of the Year," and was the second retailer to be inducted into the Discounting Hall of Fame. He was recipient of the Horatio Alger Award in 1984 and acknowledged by *Discount Stores News* as "Retailer of the Decade" in December of 1989. "Walton does a remarkable job of instilling near-religious fervor in his people," said analyst Robert Buchanan of A. G. Edwards. "I think that speaks to the heart of his success." In late 1989 Sam Walton was diagnosed to have multiple myeloma, or cancer of the bone marrow. He planned to remain active in the firm as Chairman of the Board of Directors.

The Market Concept

Genesis of an Idea

Sam Walton started his retail career in 1940 as a management trainee with the J. C. Penney Co. in Des Moines, Iowa. He was impressed with the Penney method of doing business and later modeled the Wal-Mart chain on "The Penney Idea" as reviewed in Exhibit 1. The Penney Company found strength in calling employees "associates" rather than clerks. Penney's, founded in Kemerer, Wyoming, in 1902, located stores on the main streets of small towns and cities throughout the United States.

Following service in the U.S. Army during World War II, Sam Walton acquired a Ben Franklin variety store franchise in Newport, Arkansas. He operated this store successfully with his brother, James L. "Bud" Walton (1921–1995), until losing the lease in 1950. When Wal-Mart was incorporated in 1962, the firm was operating a chain of

EXHIBIT 1	THE PENNEY IDEA, 1913

1. To serve the public, as nearly as we can, to its complete satisfaction.

2. To expect for the service we render a fair remuneration and not all the profit the traffic will bear.

3. To do all in our power to pack the customer's dollar full of value, quality, and satisfaction.

4. To continue to train ourselves and our associates so that the service we give will be more and more intelligently performed.

5. To improve constantly the human factor in our business.

6. To reward men and women in our organization through participation in what the business produces.

7. To test our every policy, method, and act in this wise: "Does it square with what is right and just?"

SOURCE: Trimble, Vance H., *Sam Walton: The Inside Story of America's Richest Man* (New York: Dutton), 1990.

15 stores. Bud Walton became a senior vice president of the firm and concentrated on finding suitable store locations, acquiring real estate, and directing store construction.

The early retail stores owned by Sam Walton in Newport and Bentonville, Arkansas, and later in other small towns in adjoining southern states, were variety store operations. They were relatively small operations of 6,000 square feet, were located on "Main Street," and displayed merchandise on plain wooden tables and counters. Operated under the Ben Franklin name and supplied by Butler Brothers of Chicago and St. Louis, they were characterized by a limited price line, low gross margins, high merchandise turnover and concentration on return on investment. The firm, operating under the Walton 5 & 10 name, was the largest Ben Franklin franchisee in the country in 1962. The variety stores were phased out by 1976 to allow the company to concentrate on the growth of Wal-Mart discount department stores.

Foundations of Growth

The original Wal-Mart discount concept was not a unique idea. Sam Walton became convinced in the late 1950s that discounting would transform retailing. He traveled extensively in New England, the cradle of "off-pricing." After he had visited just about every discounter in the United States, he tried to interest Butler Brothers executives in Chicago in the discount store concept. The first Kmart, as a "conveniently located one-stop shopping unit where customers could buy a wide variety of quality merchandise at discount prices" had just opened in Garden City, Michigan. Walton's theory was to operate a similar discount store in a small community and in that setting, he would offer name brand merchandise at low prices and would add friendly service. Butler Brothers executives rejected the idea. The first "Wal-Mart Discount City" opened in late 1962 in Rogers, Arkansas.

Wal-Mart stores would sell nationally advertised, well-known brand merchandise at low prices in austere surroundings. As corporate policy, they would cheerfully give refunds, credits, and rain checks. Management conceived the firm as a "discount department store chain offering a wide variety of general merchandise to the customer." Early emphasis was placed upon opportunistic purchases of merchandise from whatever sources were available. Heavy emphasis was placed upon health and beauty aids (H&BA) in the product line and "stacking it high" in a manner of merchandise presentation. By the end of 1979, there were 276 Wal-Mart stores located in eleven states.

The firm developed an aggressive expansion strategy. New stores were located primarily in towns of 5,000 to 25,000 population. The stores' sizes ranged from 30,000 to 60,000 square feet with 45,000 being the average. The firm also expanded by locating stores in contiguous areas, town by town, state by state. When its discount operations came to dominate a market area, it moved to an adjoining area. While other retailers built warehouses to serve existing outlets, Wal-Mart built the distribution center first and then spotted stores all around it, pooling advertising and distribution overhead. Most stores were less than a six-hour drive from one of the company's warehouses. The first major distribution center, a 390,000 square foot facility opened in Searcy, Arkansas, outside Bentonville in 1978.

National Perspective

At the beginning of 1991, the firm had 1,573 Wal-Mart stores in thirty five states with expansion planned for adjacent states. Wal-Mart became the largest retailer and the largest discount department store in the United States.

As a national discount department store chain, Wal-Mart Stores, Inc., offered a wide variety of general merchandise to the customer. The stores were designed to offer one-stop shopping in 36 departments which included family apparel, health and beauty aids, household needs, electronics, toys, fabric and crafts, automotive supplies, lawn and patio, jewelry, and shoes. In addition, at certain store locations, a pharmacy, automotive supply and service center, garden center, or snack bar were also operated. The firm operated its stores with an "everyday low price" as opposed to putting heavy emphasis on special promotions, which called for multiple newspaper advertising circulars. Stores were expected to "provide the customer with a clean, pleasant, and friendly shopping experience."

Although Wal-Mart carried much the same merchandise, offered similar prices and operated stores that looked much like the competition, there were many differences. In the typical Wal-Mart store, employees wore blue vests to identify themselves, aisles were wide, apparel departments were carpeted in warm colors, a store employee followed customers to their cars to pick up their shopping carts, and the customer was welcomed at the door by a "people greeter" who gave directions and struck up conversations. In some cases, merchandise was bagged in brown paper sacks rather plastic bags because customers seemed to prefer them. A simple Wal-Mart logo in white letters on a brown background on the front of the store served to identify the firm. In consumer studies it was determined that the chain was particularly adept at striking the delicate balance needed to convince customers its prices were low without making people feel that its stores were too cheap. In many ways, competitors like Kmart sought to emulate Wal-Mart by introducing people greeters, by upgrading interiors, by developing new logos and signage, and by introducing new inventory response systems.

A "Satisfaction Guaranteed" refund and exchange policy was introduced to allow customers to be confident of Wal-Mart's merchandise and quality. Technological advancements like scanner cash registers, hand held computers for ordering of merchandise and computer linkages of stores with the general office and distribution centers improved communications and merchandise replenishment. Each store was encouraged to initiate programs that would make it an integral part of the community in which it operated. Associates were encouraged to "maintain the highest standards of honesty, morality, and business ethics in dealing with the public."

The External Environment

Industry analysts labeled the 1980s and early 1990s as eras of economic uncertainty for retailers. Many retailers were negatively affected by increased competitive pressures, sluggish consumer spending, slower-than-anticipated economic growth in North America, and recessions abroad. In 1995, Wal-Mart management felt the high consumer debt level caused many shoppers to reduce or defer spending on anything other than essentials. Management also felt that the lack of exciting new products or apparel trends reduced discretionary spending. Fierce competition resulted in lower margins and the lack of inflation stalled productivity increases. By 1998 the country had returned to prosperity. Unemployment was low, total income was relatively high, and interest rates were stable. Combined with a low inflation rate, buying power was perceived to be high and consumers were generally willing to buy.

Many retail enterprises confronted heavy competitive pressure by restructuring. Sears, Roebuck & Company, based in Chicago, became a more focused retailer by divesting itself of Allstate Insurance Company and its real estate subsidiaries. In 1993, the company announced it would close 118 unprofitable stores and discontinue the unprofitable Sears general merchandise catalog. It eliminated 50,000 jobs and began a $4 billion, five-year remodeling plan for its remaining multi-line department stores. After unsuccessfully experimenting with an "everyday low-price" strategy, management chose to realign its merchandise strategy to meet the needs of middle market customers, who were primarily women, by focusing on product lines in apparel, home, and automotive. The new focus on apparel was supported with the advertising campaign, "The Softer Side of Sears." A later company wide campaign broadened the appeal: "The many sides of Sears fit the many sides of your life." Sears completed its return to its retailing roots by selling off its ownership in Dean Witter Financial Services, Discovery Card, Coldwell Banker Real Estate, and Sears mortgage banking operations.

The discount department store industry by the early-1990's had changed in a number of ways and was thought to have reached maturity by many analysts. Several formerly successful firms like E. J. Korvette, W. T. Grant, Atlantic Mills, Arlans, Federals, Zayre, Heck's, and Ames had declared bankruptcy and as a result either liquidated or reorganized. Regional firms like Target Stores and Shopko Stores began carrying more fashionable merchandise in more attractive facilities and shifted their emphasis to more national markets. Specialty retailers such as Toys "R" Us, Pier 1 Imports and Oshmans were making big inroads in toys, home furnishing and sporting goods. The "superstores" of drug and food chains were rapidly discounting increasing amounts of general merchandise. Some firms like May Department Stores Company with Caldor and Venture and Woolworth Corporation with Woolco had withdrawn from the field by either selling their discount divisions or closing them down entirely. The firm's [Woolworth's] remaining 122 Woolco stores in Canada were sold to Wal-Mart in 1994. All remaining Woolworth variety stores in the United States were closed in 1997.

Several new retail formats had emerged in the marketplace to challenge the traditional discount department store format. The superstore, 100,000–300,000 square foot operation, combined a large supermarket with a discount general-merchandise store. Originally a European retailing concept, these outlets were know as "malls without walls." Kmart's Super Kmart Centers, American Fare and Wal-Mart's Supercenter Store were examples of this trend toward large operations. Warehouse retailing, which involved some combination of warehouse and showroom facilities, used warehouse principles to reduce operating expenses and thereby offer discount prices as a primary customer appeal. Home Depot combined the traditional hardware store and lumber yard with a self-service home improvement center to become the largest home center operator in the nation.

Some retailers responded to changes in the marketplace by selling goods at price levels (20 to 60 percent) below regular retail prices. These off-price operations appeared as two general types: (1) factory outlet stores like Burlington Coat Factory Warehouse, Bass Shoes, and Manhattan's Brand Name Fashion Outlet, and (2) independents like Loehmann's, T. J. Maxx, Marshall's and Clothestime which bought seconds, overages, closeouts or leftover goods from manufacturers and other retailers. Other retailers chose to dominate a product classification. Some super specialists like Sock Appeal, Little Piggie, Ltd., and Sock Market, offered a single narrowly defined classification of merchandise with an extensive assortment of brands, colors and sizes. Others, as niche specialists, like Kids Mart, a division of Woolworth Corporation, and McKids, a division of Sears, targeted an identified market with carefully selected merchandise and appropriately designed stores. Some retailers like Silk Greenhouse (silk plants and flowers), Office Club (office supplies and equipment), and Toys "R" Us (toys) were called "category killers" because they had achieved merchandise dominance in their respective product categories. Stores like The Limited, Limited Express, Victoria's Secret, and The Banana Republic became mini-department specialists by showcasing new lines and accessories alongside traditional merchandise lines.

Kmart Corporation, headquartered in Troy, Michigan, became the industry's third largest retailer after Sears, Roebuck & Co. and second largest discount department store chain in the United States in the 1990s. Kmart had 2,136 stores and $32,183 million in sales at the beginning of 1998. The firm was perceived by many industry analysts and consumers in several independent studies as a laggard. It had been the industry sales leader for a number of years and had recently announced a turn-around in profitability. In the same studies, Wal-Mart was perceived as the industry leader even though according to the *Wall Street Journal:* "they carry much the same merchandise, offer prices that are pennies apart and operate stores that look almost exactly alike." "Even their names are similar," noted the newspaper. The original Kmart concept of a "conveniently located, one-stop shopping unit where customers could buy a wide variety of quality merchandise at discount prices" had lost its competitive edge in a changing market. As one analyst noted in an industry newsletter: "They had done so well for the past 20 years without paying attention to market changes, now they have to." Kmart acquired a new Chairman, President and Chief Executive Officer in 1995. Wal-Mart and Kmart sales growth over the period 1987–1997 is reviewed in Exhibit 2. A competitive analysis is shown of four major retail firms in Exhibit 3.

Some retailers like Kmart had initially focused on appealing to professional, middle class consumers who lived in suburban areas and who were likely to be price sensitive. Other firms like Target (Dayton Hudson), which had adopted the discount concept early, attempted to go generally after an upscale consumer which had an annual household income of $25,000 to $44,000. Some firms such as Fleet Farm and Menard's served the rural consumer, while firms like Chicago's Goldblatt's Depart-

EXHIBIT 2	COMPETITIVE SALES AND STORE COMPARISON, 1987–1997			
	Kmart		Wal-Mart	
Year	Sales (000)	Stores[1]	Sales (000)	Stores[1]
1997	$32,183,000	2,136	117,958,000	3,406
1996	31,437,000	2,261	104,859,000	3,054
1995	34,389,000	2,161	93,627,000	2,943
1994	34,025,000	2,481	82,494,000	2,684
1993	34,156,000	2,486	67,344,000	2,400
1992	37,724,000	2,435	55,484,000	2,136
1991	34,580,000	2,391	43,886,900	1,928
1990	32,070,000	2,350	32,601,594	1,721
1989	29,533,000	2,361	25,810,656	1,525
1988	27,301,000	2,307	20,649,001	1,364
1987	25,627,000	2,273	15,959,255	1,198

[1]Number of general merchandise stores.

ment Stores and Ames Discount Department Stores chose to serve blacks and Hispanics in the inner city.

In rural communities Wal-Mart's success often came at the expense of established local merchants and units of regional discount store chains. Hardware stores, family department stores, building supply outlets, and store featuring fabrics, sporting goods and shoes were among the first to either close or relocate elsewhere. Regional discount retailers in the Sunbelt states like Roses, Howard's, T.G.&Y. and Duckwall-ALCO, who once enjoyed solid sales and earnings, were forced to reposition themselves by renovating stores, opening bigger and more modern units, remerchandising assortments and offering lower prices. In many cases, stores like Coast-to-Coast, Pamida, and Ben Franklin closed upon a Wal-Mart announcement that it was planning to build in a specific community. "Just the word that Wal-Mart was coming made some stores close up," indicated a local newspaper editor.

Corporate Strategies

The corporate and marketing strategies that emerged at Wal-Mart were based upon a set of two main objectives that had guided the firm through its growth years. In the first objective the customer was featured; "customers would be provided what they want, when they want it, all at a value." In the second objective the team spirit was emphasized, "treating each other as we would hope to be treated, acknowledging our total dependency on our Associate-partners to sustain our success." The approach included: aggressive plans for new store openings; expansion to additional states; upgrading, relocation, refurbishing and remodeling of existing stores; and opening new distribution centers. The plan was to not have a single operating unit that had not been updated in

EXHIBIT 3	AN INDUSTRY COMPARATIVE ANALYSIS, 1997			
	Wal-Mart	**Sears**	**Kmart**	**Target**
Sales (Millions)	$117,958	$36,37	$32,183	$20,368
Net Income (Thousands)	$ 3,526	$1,188	$ 249	$ 1,287
Net Income per Share	$ 1.56	$ 3.03	$ .51	n/a
Dividends per Share	$ .27	$ n/a	$ n/a	n/a
% Sales Change	12.0%	8.0%	2.4%	14%

Number of Stores:

Wal-Mart & Subsidiaries
    Wal-Mart Stores—2,421
    Sam's Clubs—483
    Supercenters—502

Sears Roebuck & Company (all divisions)
  Sears Merchandise Group
    Department Stores—833
    Hardware Stores—255
    Furniture Stores—129
    Sears Dealer Stores—576
    Auto/Tire Stores—780
    Auto Parts Stores
      Western Auto—39
      Parts America—576
      Western Auto Dealer Stores—800

Kmart Corporation
    General Merchandise—2,136

Dayton Hudson Corporation
    Target—796
    Mervyn's—269
    Department Stores—65

SOURCE: Corporate Annual Reports.

the past seven years. For Wal-Mart management, the 1990's were considered: "A new era for Wal-Mart; an era in which we plan to grow to a truly nationwide retailer, and should we continue to perform, our sales and earnings will also grow beyond where most could have envisioned at the dawn of the 80's."

In the decade of the 1980's, Wal-Mart developed a number of new retail formats. The first Sam's Club opened in Oklahoma City, Oklahoma, in 1983. The wholesale club was an idea which had been developed by other firms earlier but which found its greatest success and growth in acceptability at Wal-Mart. Sam's Clubs featured a vast array of product categories with limited selection of brand and model, cash-and-carry business with limited hours, large (100,000 square foot), bare-bone facilities, rock bottom wholesale prices and minimal promotion. The limited membership plan permitted wholesale members who bought membership and others who usually paid a percentage above the ticket price of the merchandise. At the beginning of 1998, there were 483 Sam's Clubs in operation. A revision in merchandising strategy resulted in fewer items in the inventory mix with more emphasis on lower prices.

Wal-Mart Supercenters were large combination stores. They were first opened in 1988 as Hypermarket*USA, a 222,000 square foot superstore which combined a discount store with a large grocery store, a food court of restaurants and other service businesses such as banks or video tape rental stores. A scaled down version of Hypermarket*USA was called the Wal-Mart SuperCenter, similar in merchandise offerings, but with about half the square footage of hypermarts. These expanded store concepts also included convenience stores, and gasoline distribution outlets to "enhance shopping convenience." The company proceeded slowly with these plans and later suspended its plans for building any more hypermarkets in favor of the smaller Supercenter. In 1998, Wal-Mart operated 502 Supercenters. It also announced plans to build several full-fledged supermarkets called "Wal-Mart Food and Drug Express" with a drive-through option as "laboratories" to test how the concept would work and what changes would need to be made before a decision [was] made to proceed with additional units. The McLane Company, Inc., a provider of retail and grocery distribution services for retail stores, was acquired in 1991. It was not considered a major segment of the total Wal-Mart operation.

On the international level, Wal-Mart management had a goal to be the dominant retailer in each country it entered. With the acquisition of 122 former Woolco stores in Canada, the company exceeded expectations in sales growth, market share, and profitability. With a tender offer for shares and mergers of joint ventures in Mexico, the company had a controlling interest in Cifra, Mexico's largest retailer. Cifra operated stores with a variety of concepts in every region of Mexico, ranging from the nation's largest chain of sit-down restaurants to a softline department store. Plans were also proceeding with start-up operations in Argentina and Brazil as well as China. The acquisition of 21 "hypermarkets" in Germany at the end of 1997 marked the company's first entry into Europe, which management considered "one of the best consumer markets in the world." These large stores offered one-stop shopping facilities similar to Wal-Mart Supercenters. The international expansion accelerated management's plans for the development of Wal-Mart as a global brand along the lines of Coca-Cola, Disney and McDonald's. "We are a global brand name," said Bobby Martin, President of the International Division of Wal-Mart. "To customers everywhere it means low cost, best value, greatest selection of quality merchandise and highest standards of customer service." Some changes were mandated in Wal-Mart's international operations to meet local tastes and intense competitive conditions. "We're building companies out there," said Martin. "That's like starting Wal-Mart all over again in South America or Indonesia or China." Although stores in different international markets would coordinate purchasing to gain leverage with suppliers, developing new technology and planning overall strategy would be done from Wal-Mart headquarters in Bentonville, Arkansas. At the beginning of 1998, the International Division of Wal-Mart operated 500 discount stores, 61 Supercenters and 40 Sam's Clubs.

Several programs were launched to "highlight" popular social causes. The "Buy American" program was a Wal-Mart retail program initiated in 1985. The theme was "Bring It Home To The USA" and its purpose was to communicate Wal-Mart's support for American manufacturing. In the program, the firm directed substantial influence to encourage manufacturers to produce goods in the United States rather than import them from other countries. Vendors were attracted into the program by encouraging manufacturers to initiate the process by contacting the company directly with proposals to sell goods that were made in the United States. Buyers also targeted specific import items in their assortments on a state-by-state basis to encourage domestic manufacturing. According to Haim Dabah, president of Gitano Group, Inc., a maker of fashion discount clothing which imported 95% of its clothing and now makes about 20% of its products here: "Wal-Mart let it be known loud and clear that if you're going to grow with them, you sure better have some products made in the U.S.A." Farris Fashion, Inc. (flannel shirts); Roadmaster Corporation (exercise bicycles); Flanders Industries, Inc. (lawn chairs); and Magic Chef (microwave ovens) were examples of vendors that chose to participate in the program.

From the Wal-Mart standpoint the "Buy American" program centered around value—producing and selling quality merchandise at a competitive price. The promotion included television advertisements featuring factory workers, a soaring American eagle, and the slogan: "We buy American whenever we can, so you can too." Prominent in-store signage, and store circulars were also included. One store poster read: "Success Stories—These items, formerly imported, are now being purchased by Wal-Mart in the U.S.A."

Wal-Mart was one of the first retailers to embrace the concept of "green" marketing. The program offered shoppers the option of purchasing products that were better for the environment in three respects: manufacturing, use, and disposal. It was introduced through full-page advertisements in the *Wall Street Journal* and *USA Today*. In store signage identified those products which were environmentally safe. As Wal-Mart executives saw it, "Customers are concerned about the quality of land, air, and water, and would like the opportunity to do something positive." To initiate the program, 7,000 vendors were notified that Wal-Mart had a corporate concern for the environment and to ask for their support in a variety of ways. Wal-Mart television advertising showed children on swings, fields of grain blowing in the wind, and roses. Green and white store signs, printed on recycled paper, marked products or packaging that had been developed or redesigned to be more environmentally sound.

Wal-Mart had become the channel commander in the distribution of many brand name items. As the nation's largest retailer and in many geographic areas the dominant distributor, it exerted considerable influence in negotiation for the best price, delivery terms, promotion allowances, and continuity of supply. Many of these benefits could be passed on to consumers in the form of quality name brand items available at lower than competitive prices. As a matter of corporate policy, management often insisted on doing business only with producer's top sales executives rather than going through a manufacturer's representative. Wal-Mart had been accused of threatening to buy from other producers if firms refused to sell directly to it. In the ensuing power struggle, Wal-Mart executives refused to talk about the controversial policy or admit that it existed. As a representative of an industry association representing a group of sales agencies' representatives suggested, "In the Southwest, Wal-Mart's the only show in town." An industry analyst added, "They're extremely aggressive. Their approach has always been to give the customer the benefit of a corporate saving. That builds up customer loyalty and market share."

Another key factor in the mix was an inventory control system that was recognized as the most sophisticated in retailing. A high-speed computer system linked virtually all the stores to headquarters and the company's distributions centers. It electronically logged every item sold at the checkout counter, automatically kept the warehouses informed of merchandise to be ordered and directed the flow of goods to the stores and even to the proper shelves. Most important for management, it helped detect sales trends quickly and speeded up market reaction time substantially. According to Bob Connolly, Executive Vice President of Merchandising, "Wal-Mart has used the data gathered by technology to make more inventory available in the key items that customers want most, while reducing inventories overall."

Decision Making in a Market-Oriented Firm

One principle that distinguished Wal-Mart was the unusual depth of employee involvement in company affairs. Corporate strategies put emphasis on human resource management. Employees of Wal-Mart became "associates," a name borrowed from Sam Walton's early association with the J. C. Penney Co. Input was encouraged at meetings at the store and corporate level. The firm hired employees locally, provided training programs, and through a "Letter to the President" program, management encouraged employees to ask questions, and made words like "we," "us," and "our" a part of the corporate language. A number of special award programs recognized individual, department, and division achievement. Stock ownership and profit-sharing programs were introduced as part of a "partnership concept."

The corporate culture was recognized by the editors of the trade publication, *Mass Market Retailers*, when it recognized all 275,000 associates collectively as the "Mass Market Retailers of the Year." "The Wal-Mart associate," the editors noted, "in this decade that term has come to symbolize all that is right with the American worker, particularly in the retailing environment and most particularly at Wal-Mart." The "store within a store" concept, as a Wal-Mart corporate policy, trained individuals to be merchants by being responsible for the performance of their own departments as if they were running their own businesses. Seminars and training programs afforded them opportunities to grow within the company. "People development, not just a good program for any growing company but a must to secure our future," is how Suzanne Allford, Vice President of the Wal-Mart People Division, explained the firm's decentralized approach to retail management development.

"The Wal-Mart Way" was a phase that was used by management to summarize the firm's unconventional approach to business and the development of the corporate culture. As noted in a report referring to a recent development program: "We stepped outside our retailing world to examine the best managed companies in the United States in an effort to determine the fundamentals of their success and to 'benchmark' our own performances." The name "Total Quality Management (TQM) was used to identify this vehicle for proliferating the very best things we do while incorporating the new ideas our people have that will assure our future."

The Growth Challenge

And what of Wal-Mart without Mr. Sam? "There's no transition to make," said Glass, "because the principles and the basic values he used in founding this company were so sound and so universally accepted." "As for the future," he suggested, "there's more opportunity ahead of us than behind us. We're good students of retailing and we've studied the mistakes that others have made. We'll make our own mistakes, but we won't repeat theirs. The only thing constant at Wal-Mart is change. We'll be fine as long as we never lose our responsiveness to the customer." Management identified four key legacies of Sam Walton to guide the company's "quest for value" in the future: (1) Everyday Low Prices, (2) Customer Service, (3) Leadership, and (4) Change.

Wal-Mart Stores, Inc., had for over twenty-five years experienced tremendous growth and as one analyst suggested, "been consistently on the cutting edge of low-markup mass merchandising." Much of the forward momentum had come from the entrepreneurial spirit of Samuel Moore Walton. The company announced on Monday, April 6, 1992, following Walton's death, that his son, S. Robson Walton, Vice Chairman of Wal-Mart, would succeed his father as Chairman of the Board. David Glass would remain President and CEO. The Wal-Mart Board of Directors and Executive Officers in 1998 are listed in Appendix B.

A new management team was in place. Management felt it had positioned the firm as an industry leader. A number of new challenges, however, had to be met. It had predicted as early as 1993 that Wal-Mart's same-store growth would likely slip into the 7% to 8% range in the near future. Analysts were also concerned about the increased competition in the warehouse club business and the company's move from its roots in Southern and Midwestern small towns to the more competitive and costly markets of the Northeast. Wal-Mart "supercenters" faced more resilient rivals in the grocery field. Unions representing supermarket workers delayed and in some cases killed expansion opportunities. Some analysts said: "the company is simply suffering from the high expectations its stellar performance over the years has created." In early 1996, management acknowledged that 1995 had not been a "Wal-Mart year." After 99 consecutive quarters of earnings growth, Wal-Mart management said profit for the fiscal fourth quarter, ending January 31, would decline as much as 11% from the year before. Much of the company sales growth in 1996 and 1997 was attributed to the opening of new stores in an expansion program. Same store sales growth in 1996 and 1997 was 5% and 6%, respectively, when compared with the previous year's sales performance.

References

"A Supercenter Comes to Town," *Chain Store Age Executive*, (December 1989), pp. 23–30+.

Barrier, Michael, "Walton's Mountain," *Nation's Business*, (April 1988), pp. 18–20+.

Bergman, Joan, "Saga of Sam Walton," *Stores*, (January 1988), pp. 129–130+.

Blumenthal, Karen, "Marketing with Emotion: Wal-Mart Shows the Way," *Wall Street Journal*, (November 20, 1989), p. B3.

Bragg, Arthur, "Wal-Mart's War on Reps," *Sales & Marketing Management*, (March 1987), pp. 41–43.

Brauer, Molly, "Sam's: Setting a Fast Pace," *Chain Store Age Executive*, (August 1983), pp. 20–21.

Corwin, Pat, Jay L. Johnson and Renee M. Rouland, "Made in U.S.A.," *Discount Merchandiser*, (November 1989), pp. 48–52.

"David Glass's Biggest Job Is Filling Sam's Shoes," *Business Month*, (December 1988), p. 42.

Fisher, Christy and Patricia Strnad, "Wal-Mart Pulls Back on Hypermart Plans," *Advertising Age*, (February 19, 1990), p. 49.

Fisher, Christy and Judith Graham, "Wal-Mart Throws 'Green' Gauntlet," *Advertising Age*, (August 21, 1989), pp. 1+.

Friedland, Johnathan and Louise Lee, "The Wal-Mart Way Sometimes Gets Lost in Translation Overseas," *The Wall Street Journal*, (October 8, 1997), pp. A1, A12.

"Glass Is CEO at Wal-Mart," *Discount Merchandiser*, (March 1988), pp. 6+.

Helliker, Kevin, "Wal-Mart's Store of the Future Blends Discount Prices, Department-Store Feel," *The Wall Street Journal*, (May 17, 1991), p. B1, B8.

Helliker, Kevin, and Ortega, Bob, "Falling Profit Marks End of Era at Wal-Mart," *The Wall Street Journal*, (January 18, 1996), p. B1.

Huey, John, "America's Most Successful Merchant," *Fortune*, (September 23, 1991) pp. 46–48+.

Johnson, Jay L., "Are We Ready for Big Changes?," *Discount Merchandiser*, (August 1989), pp. 48, 53–54.

Johnson, Jay L., "Hypermarts and Supercenters—Where Are They Heading?," *Discount Merchandiser*, (November 1989), pp. 60+.

Johnson, Jay L., "Internal Communication: A Key to Wal-Mart's Success," *Discount Merchandiser*, (November 1989), pp. 68+.

Johnson, Jay L., "The Supercenter Challenge," *Discount Merchandiser*, (August 1989), pp. 70+.

Kelly, Kevin, "Sam Walton Chooses a Chip Off the Old CEO," *Business Week*, (February 15, 1988), p. 29.

Kerr, Dick, "Wal-Mart Steps Up 'Buy American'," *Housewares*, (March 7–13, 1986), pp. 1+.

Lee, Louise, "Discounter Wal-Mart Is Catering to Affluent to Maintain Growth," *The Wall Street Journal*, (February 7, 1996), pp. A1.

Lee, Louise, and Joel Millman, "Wal-Mart to Buy Majority Stake in Cifra," *The Wall Street Journal*, (June 4, 1997), pp. A3+.

"Management Style: Sam Moore Walton," *Business Month*, (May 1989), p. 38.

Marsch, Barbara, "The Challenge: Merchants Mobilize to Battle Wal-Mart in a Small Community," *The Wall Street Journal*, (June 5, 1991), p. A1, A4.

Mason, Todd, "Sam Walton of Wal-Mart: Just Your Basic Homespun Billionaire," *Business Week*, (October 14, 1985), pp. 142–143+.

Nelson, Emily, "Wal-Mart to Build a Test Supermarket in Bid to Boost Grocery-Industry Share," *The Wall Street Journal*, (June 19, 1998), p. A4.

"Our People Make the Difference: The History of Wal-Mart," Video Cassette, (Bentonville, Arkansas: Wal-Mart Video Productions, 1991).

Peters, Tom J., and Nancy Austin, *A Passion for Excellence*, (New York: Random House), pp. 266–267.

Rawn, Cynthia Dunn, "Wal-Mart vs. Main Street," *American Demographics*, (June 1990), pp. 58–59.

Reier, Sharon, "CEO of the Decade: Sam M. Walton," *Financial World*, (April 4, 1989), pp. 56–57+.

"Retailer Completes Purchase of Wertkauf of Germany," *The Wall Street Journal*, (December 31, 1997), p. B3.

Rudnitsky, Howard, "How Sam Walton Does It," *Forbes*, (August 16, 1982), pp. 42–44.

Rudnitsky, Howard, "Play It Again, Sam," *Forbes*, (August 10, 1987), p. 48.

"Sam Moore Walton," *Business Month*, (May 1989), p. 38.

Schwadel, Francine, "Little Touches Spur Wal-Mart's Rise," *The Wall Street Journal*, (September 22, 1989), p. B1.

Sheets, Kenneth R., "How Wal-Mart Hits Main St.," *U.S. News & World Report*, (March 13, 1989), pp. 53–55.

Smith, Sarah, "America's Most Admired Corporations," *Fortune*, (January 29, 1990), pp. 56+.

Sprout, Alison L., "America's Most Admired Corporations," *Fortune*, (February 11, 1991), pp. 52+.

"The Early Days: Walton Kept Adding 'a Few More' Stores," *Discount Store News*, (December 9, 1985), p. 61.

Thurmond, Shannon, "Sam Speaks Volumes About New Formats," *Advertising Age*, (May 9, 1988), p. S–26.

Trimble, Vance H., *Sam Walton: The Inside Story of America's Richest Man*, (New York: Dutton), 1990.

"Wal-Mart Spoken Here," *Business Week*, (June 23, 1997), pp. 138+.

Wal-Mart Stores, Inc., *Annual Report*, Bentonville, Arkansas, 1996.

Wal-Mart Stores, Inc., *Annual Report*, Bentonville, Arkansas, 1997.

Wal-Mart Stores, Inc., *Annual Report*, Bentonville, Arkansas, 1998.

"Wal-Mart's 'Green' Campaign to Emphasize Recycling Next," *Adweek's Marketing Week*, (February 12, 1990), pp. 60–61.

"Wal-Mart Rolls Out Its Supercenters," *Chain Store Age Executive*, (December 1988), pp. 18–19.

"Wal-Mart: The Model Discounter," *Dun's Business Month*, (December 1982), pp. 60–61.

"Wal-Mart to Acquire McLane, Distributor to Retail Industry," *The Wall Street Journal*, (October 2, 1990), p. A8.

"Wholesale Clubs," *Discount Merchandiser*, (November 1987), pp. 26+.

"Work, Ambition—Sam Walton," Press Release, Corporate and Public Affairs, Wal-Mart Stores, Inc.

Zweig, Jason, "Expand It Again, Sam," *Forbes*, (July 9, 1990), p. 106.

| APPENDIX A | WAL-MART STORES, INC. FINANCIAL SUMMARY |

Consolidated Statements of Income

(Amounts in millions except per share data)

Fiscal years ended January 31,	1998	1997	1996
Revenues:			
Net sales	$117,958	$104,859	$93,627
Other income-net	1,341	1,319	1,146
	119,299	106,178	94,773
Costs and Expenses:			
Cost of sales	93,438	83,510	74,505
Operating, selling and general and administrative expenses	19,358	16,946	15,021
Interest Costs:			
Debt	555	629	692
Capital leases	229	216	196
	113,580	101,301	90,414
Income Before Income Taxes, Minority Interest and Equity in Unconsolidated Subsidiaries	5,719	4,877	4,359
Provision for Income Taxes			
Current	2,095	1,974	1,530
Deferred	20	(180)	76
	2,115	1,794	1,606
Income Before Minority Interest and Equity in Unconsolidated Subsidiaries	3,604	3,083	2,753
Minority Interest and Equity in Unconsolidated Subsidiaries	(78)	(27)	(13)
Net Income	$3,526	$3,056	$2,740
Net Income Per Share—Basic and Dilutive	$1.56	$1.33	$1.19

Consolidated Balance Sheets

(Amounts in millions)

January 31,	1998	1997
Assets		
Current Assets:		
Cash and cash equivalents	$1,447	$883
Receivables	976	845
Inventories		
At replacement cost	16,845	16,193
Less LIFO reserve	348	296
Inventories at LIFO cost	16,497	15,897
Prepaid expenses and other	432	368
Total Current Assets	19,352	17,993
Property, Plant and Equipment, at Cost:		
Land	4,691	3,689
Building and improvements	14,646	12,724

APPENDIX A	WAL-MART STORES, INC. FINANCIAL SUMMARY

Consolidated Balance Sheets (continued)

Fixtures and equipment	7,636	6,390
Transportation Equipment	403	379
	27,376	23,182
Less accumulated depreciation	5,907	4,849
Net property, plant and equipment	21,469	18,333
Property Under Capital Lease:		
Property under capital lease	3,040	2,782
Less accumulated amortization	903	791
Net property under capital leases	2,137	1,991
Other Assets and Deferred Charges	2,426	1,287
Total Assets	$45,384	$39,604
Liabilities and Shareholders' Equity		
Current Liabilities:		
Accounts payable	$9,126	$7,628
Accrued liabilities	3,628	2,413
Accrued income taxes	565	298
Long-term debt due within one year	1,038	523
Obligations under capital leases due within one year	102	95
Total Current Liabilities	14,460	10,957
Long-Term Debt	7,191	7,709
Long-Term Obligations Under Capital Leases	2,483	2,307
Deferred Income Taxes and Other	809	463
Minority Interest	1,938	1,025
Shareholders' Equity		
Preferred stock ($.10 par value; 100 shares authorized, none issued)		
Common stock ($.10 par value; 5,500 shares authorized, 2,241 and 2,285 issued and outstanding in 1998 and 1997, respectively)	224	228
Capital in excess of par value	585	547
Retained earnings	18,167	16,768
Foreign currency translation adjustment	(473)	(400)
Total Shareholders' Equity	18,503	17,143
Total Liabilities and Shareholders' Equity	$45,384	$39,604

APPENDIX B

WAL-MART STORES, INC.
BOARD OF DIRECTORS AND CORPORATE OFFICES, 1998

Directors

Jeronimo Arango
Paul R. Carter
John A. Cooper, Jr.
Stephen Friedman
Stanley C. Gault
David D. Glass
Frederick S. Humphries
E. Stanley Kroenke
Elizabeth A. Sanders
Jack C. Shewmaker
Donald G. Soderquist
Dr. Paula Stern
John T. Walton
S. Robson Walton

Chairman of the Board	S. Robson Walton
CEO, President	David D. Glass
Vice Chairman, COO	Donald G. Soderquist
Executive VP, President–Wal-Mart Realty	Paul R. Carter
Executive VP–Merchandising	Bob Connolly
Executive VP, COO–Operations Wal-Mart Stores Division	Thomas M. Coughlin
Executive VP–Specialty Division	David Dible
Executive VP, President–Sam's Club Division	Mark Hansen
Executive VP, President–International Division	Bob L. Martin
Executive VP, CFO	John B. Menzer
Executive VP, President–Wal-Mart Stores Division	H. Lee Scott
Executive VP–Supercenter	Nick White
Senior VP, Secretary–General Counsel	Robert K. Rhoads
Senior VP, Finance–Treasurer	J. J. Fitzsimmons

II

Strategic Issues for Emerging Ventures

4

Understanding the Strategic Process

Key Topics

- **The Nature of Planning in Emerging Firms**

- **Strategic Planning**

- **Key Dimensions Influencing
  Strategic Planning Activities**

- **The Lack of Strategic Planning**

- **The Value of Strategic Planning**

- **Fatal Visions in Strategic Planning**

- **Strategic Positioning:
  The Entrepreneurial Edge**

The Nature of Planning in Emerging Firms

Although most entrepreneurs do some form of planning for their ventures, it often tends to be informal and unsystematic.[1] The actual need for systematic planning will vary with the nature, size, and structure of the business. In other words, a two-person operation may successfully use informal planning because little complexity is involved. In contrast, an emerging venture that is rapidly expanding with constantly increasing staff size and market operations will need to formalize its planning because a great deal of complexity exists.

An entrepreneur's planning may need to shift from an informal to a formal systematic style for other reasons as well. First, the degree of uncertainty that the venture faces in attempting to become established and to grow will affect the planning process. With greater levels of uncertainty, entrepreneurs have a more pressing need to deal with the challenges facing their ventures, and a more formal planning effort can help them to achieve this goal. Second, the strength of the competition (in terms of both numbers and quality of competitors) will make more systematic planning more important for a new venture as it seeks to monitor its operations and objectives more closely.[2] Finally, the amount and type of experience the entrepreneur has may be a factor in deciding the extent of formal planning. A lack of adequate experience—either technological or business—may constrain the entrepreneur's understanding and thus necessitate formal planning to help determine future paths for the organization.

Strategic Planning

Strategic planning is the formulation of long-range plans for the effective management of environmental opportunities and threats in light of a venture's strengths and weaknesses. It includes defining the venture's mission, specifying achievable objectives, developing strategies, and setting policy guidelines.[3] Thus strategic planning is the primary step in determining the future direction of a business. The "best" strategic plan will be influenced by many factors, including the abilities of the entrepreneur, the complexity of the venture, and the nature of the industry. Yet, whatever the specific situation, five steps must be followed in strategic planning:

1. Examine the internal and external environments of the venture (strengths, weaknesses, opportunities, threats).

2. Formulate the venture's long-range and short-range strategies (mission, objectives, strategies, policies).

3. Implement the strategic plan (programs, budgets, procedures).

---

[1]Douglas W. Naffziger and Donald F. Kuratko, "An Investigation into the Prevalence of Planning in Small Business," *Journal of Business and Entrepreneurship* (Oct. 1991). See also Amar Bhide, "How Entrepreneurs Craft Strategies That Work," *Harvard Business Review* (March/April 1994): 150–161.

[2]Radha Chaganti, Rajeswararao Chaganti, and Vijay Mahajan, "Profitable Small Business Strategies Under Different Types of Competition," *Entrepreneurship Theory and Practice* (Spring 1989): 21–36.

[3]Thomas L. Wheelen and J. David Hunger, *Strategic Management and Business Policy*, 7th ed. (Upper Saddle River, NJ: 2000). See also Michael A. Hitt, R. Duane Ireland, and Robert E. Hoskisson, *Strategic Management: Competitiveness and Globalization*, 3rd ed. (Cincinnati, OH: South-Western Publishing, 1999).

4. Evaluate the performance of the strategy.

5. Take follow-up action through continuous feedback.

Figure 4.1 illustrates these basic steps in a flow diagram.

The first step—examining the environment—can be one of the most critical for an emerging venture. A clear review of a venture's internal and external factors (including those external factors most likely to affect the implementation of present and future strategic decisions) is needed, and both sets of factors must be considered when performing an environmental analysis. This analysis is often called a **SWOT analysis;** *SWOT* is an acronym for a venture's internal *s*trengths and *w*eaknesses and its external *o*pportunities and *t*hreats. By carrying out such an analysis, an emerging venture will be prepared to proceed through the other steps of strategic planning—namely, formulation, implementation, evaluation, and feedback.

The greatest value of the strategic planning process is the "strategic thinking" that it promotes among business owners. Although not always articulated formally, strategic thinking synthesizes the intuition and creativity of an entrepreneur into a vision for the future.[4]

We now examine the different aspects of strategic planning for emerging ventures.

Key Dimensions Influencing Strategic Planning Activities

Five factors shape the strategic management activities of growing companies: (1) demands on strategic managers' time, (2) decision-making speed, (3) problems of internal politics, (4) environmental uncertainty, and (5) the entrepreneur's vision.

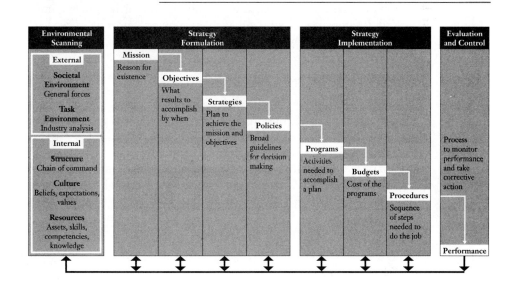

FIGURE 4.1   STRATEGIC PLANNING MODEL

---

[4]Henry Mintzberg, "The Fall and Rise of Strategic Planning," *Harvard Business Review* (Jan./Feb. 1994): 107–114.

Demands on Strategic Managers' Time

The increasing demands on key owner-managers' time that accompany the complexity brought on by growth of the entrepreneurial firm bring about a need for more rigorous strategic management practices. This logically appealing proposition has been offered in the past by many researchers. From their perspective, increased strategic planning activity provides the means to accommodate the owner-manager's need to maintain control and direction of the enterprise, even as the entrepreneur relinquishes some activities in recognition of his or her increased time pressures.

Decision-Making Speed

As the firm expands, the decisions to be made can be expected to increase both in number and frequency. These pressures are referred to as "delegation demands" on the growing firm's management. More systematic strategic planning practices are needed to enable entrepreneurs to guide and control the increasing decision making within the firm.

Problems of Internal Politics

Strategic planning practices are seen as one way to alleviate the difficulties associated with the dysfunctional effects of internal politics on organizational decision making. By providing a formal process by which to channel partisan organizational priorities, strategic planning helps to control the politics that inevitably emerge as an entrepreneurial firm grows and develops organizational power seekers.

Environmental Uncertainty

Research has suggested that the need for strategic planning is greater in the presence of increased environmental uncertainty. Thus environmental uncertainty is a key factor influencing the strategic management activities of entrepreneurial firms with an increasingly life-cycle-diverse product and market base.[5]

The Entrepreneur's Vision

To a large degree, venture planning is an extension of the entrepreneurial ego. Planning is the process of transforming entrepreneurial vision and ideas into action. This process involves basic steps.

Step 1: Commitment to an Open Planning Process   Many entrepreneurs are suspicious of planning, because they fear the loss of control and of flexibility. Quite often this fear represents the chief obstacle to future success, as it can blind the entrepreneur to the ideas of other knowledgeable people. This narrow-mindedness, in turn, closes the door on new ideas and greatly limits the benefits associated with an open planning process.

---

[5]Richard B. Robinson Jr. and John A. Pearce II, "Product Life-Cycle Considerations and the Nature of Strategic Activities in Entrepreneurial Firms," *Journal of Business Venturing* (Spring 1986): 207–224. See also Charles H. Matthews and Susan G. Scott, "Uncertainty and Planning in Small Entrepreneurial Firms: An Empirical Assessment," *Journal of Small Business Management* (Oct. 1995): 34–52.

Step 2: Accountability to a Corporate Conscience   The implementation of such accountability often takes the form of an advisory board, which is a highly effective form of corporate conscience. The advisory board can substantially enhance the functioning of entrepreneurial ego. This committee differs from a board of directors by its lack of legal standing and its primary objectives, which are to increase the owner's sensitivity to larger issues of direction and to make the owner accountable, albeit on a voluntary basis.

Step 3: Establishment of a Pattern of Subordinate Participation in Strategic Planning   The planning process can create organizational energy, especially if key members of the organization are instrumental in creating the strategic plan. Interviews with key subordinates have revealed that an absence of the organizational and personal guideposts needed to chart and monitor a successful course of executive action tend to result in little support for the plan.[6]

These three steps may seem obvious to any entrepreneur attempting to translate his or her vision into a planning process. The fact remains, however, that such planning is too often lacking in new small ventures.

The Lack of Strategic Planning

The importance of new ventures to the economy is substantial in terms of innovation, employment, and sales, and effective planning can help these new firms survive and grow. Unfortunately, research has shown a distinct lack of planning on the part of many new ventures. Five reasons for the lack of strategic planning have been identified:

- **Time scarcity.** Managers report that their time is scarce and difficult to allocate to planning in the face of day-to-day operating problems.

- **Lack of knowledge.** Small-firm owners/managers have minimal exposure to, and knowledge of, the planning process. They are uncertain of the components of the process and the sequence in which those components should be addressed. Many entrepreneurs are also unfamiliar with planning information sources and their relevance to the planning process.

- **Lack of expertise/skills.** Small-business managers typically are generalists, and they often lack the specialized expertise necessary for the planning process.

- **Lack of trust and openness.** Small-firm owners/managers are often highly sensitive and guarded about their businesses and the decisions that affect them. Consequently, they may hesitate to formulate a strategic plan that requires participation by employees or outside consultants.

- **Perception of high cost.** Small-business owners perceive the cost associated with planning to be very high. Their fear of expensive planning causes many business owners to avoid or ignore planning as a viable process.[7]

---

[6]Richard L. Osborne, "Planning: The Entrepreneurial Ego at Work," *Business Horizons* (Jan./Feb. 1987): 20–24.

[7]Richard B. Robinson, Jr., and John A. Pearce II, "Research Thrusts in Small Firm Strategic Planning," *Academy of Management Review* (Jan. 1984): 129; and Charles B. Shrader, Charles L. Mumford, and Virginia L. Blackburn, "Strategic and Operational Planning, Uncertainty, and Performance in Small Firms," *Journal of Small Business Management* (Oct. 1989): 52.

Other factors have also been reported as difficulties of the planning process. For example, both high-performing and low-performing small ventures often struggle with long-range planning. Both the time and the expense involved are perceived as major obstacles. Additionally, low-performing firms report that a poor planning climate, inexperienced managers, and unfavorable economic conditions are common problems. Quite obviously, strategic planning is no easy chore for new ventures. On the other hand, many benefits can be gained from such planning.

The Value of Strategic Planning

Does strategic planning pay off? Research shows that it does.

A number of studies have examined the effects of planning on small firms.[8] These studies support the contention that strategic planning is of value to a venture. Most of their results imply, if they do not directly state, that planning influences a venture's survival. In Robinson and Pearce's study, for example, planning was found to be an important criterion for differentiating successful from unsuccessful firms.[9] In another study of 70,000 failed firms, lack of planning was identified as a major cause of failure.[10] Yet another investigation demonstrated that firms engaged in strategic planning outperformed those that did not undertake such planning.[11]

In a study of 220 small firms, Ibrahim established the importance of selecting an appropriate strategy (niche strategy) for a venture to build distinctive competence and a sustainable competitive advantage.[12] Another researcher, Mosakowski, examined the dynamic effects of strategies on company performance in the software industry. Her findings showed that when focus or differentiation strategies were established, performance by those firms was enhanced.[13]

More recently, Rue and Ibrahim examined 253 smaller firms to determine the relationship between performance and planning sophistication. They classified companies into these categories:

Category I—no written plan (101 firms, or 39.9 percent)

Category II—moderately sophisticated planning, including a written plan and/or some quantified objectives, some specific plans and budgets, identification of some factors in the external environment, and procedures for anticipating or detecting differences between the plan and actual performance (89 firms, or 35.2 percent)

Category III—sophisticated planning, including a written plan with all of the following: some quantified objectives, some specific plans and budgets, identification of

[8]Robinson and Pearce, "Research Thrusts," 132–133.

[9]Ibid.

[10]"The Business Failure Record," *Dun & Bradstreet*, 1995.

[11]Richard B. Robinson, "The Importance of Outsiders in Small Firm Strategic Planning," *Academy of Management Journal* (March 1982): 80–93.

[12]A. Bakr Ibrahim, "Strategy Types and Small Firm's Performance: An Empirical Investigation," *Journal of Small Business Strategy* (Spring 1993): 13–22.

[13]Elaine Mosakowski, "A Resource-Based Perspective on the Dynamic Strategy—Performance Relationship: An Empirical Examination of the Focus and Differentiation Strategies in Entrepreneurial Firms," *Journal of Management* 19, no. 4 (1993): 813–839.

some factors in the external environment, and procedures for anticipating or detecting differences between the plan and actual performance (63 firms, or 24.9 percent)

Their results indicated that more than 88 percent of firms with Category II or Category III planning performed at or above the industry average, compared with only 40 percent of those firms with Category I planning.[14]

In summary, all of the research to date indicates that firms that engage in strategic planning are more effective than those that do not. Most importantly, the studies emphasize the significance of the planning process—rather than merely the plans—as a key to successful performance.[15]

Fatal Visions in Strategic Planning

The actual execution of a strategy is almost as important as the strategy itself. Many entrepreneurs make unintentional errors while applying a specific strategy to their particular venture. Competitive situations differ, and the particular application of known strategies must be tailored to those unique situations.

Researcher Michael E. Porter has noted five fatal mistakes to which entrepreneurs continually fall prey in their attempt to implement a strategy:[16]

Flaw 1: Misunderstanding industry attractiveness. Too many entrepreneurs associate attractive industries with those that are growing the most rapidly, appear to be glamorous, or use the fanciest technology. This assumption is wrong, because attractive industries have high barriers to entry and the fewest substitutes. The more high-tech or high-glamour a business is, the more likely that many new competitors will enter it and make it unprofitable.

Flaw 2: No real competitive advantage. Some entrepreneurs merely copy or imitate the strategy of their competitors. That may be an easy tactic, and it is certainly less risky, but it means that an entrepreneur has no competitive advantage. To succeed, new ventures must develop unique ways to compete.

Flaw 3: Pursuing an unattainable competitive position. Many aggressive entrepreneurs pursue a position of dominance in a fast-growing industry. However, they are so busy getting off the ground and finding people to buy their products that they forget what will happen if the venture succeeds. For example, a successful software program will be imitated quickly. As a consequence, the advantage it alone gives cannot be sustained. Real competitive advantage in software comes from servicing and supporting buyers, providing regular upgrades, and getting a company online with customers so their computer departments depend on the organization. Those activities create barriers to entry. Sometimes, small companies simply cannot sustain their initial advantage.

[14]Leslie W. Rue and Nabil A. Ibrahim, "The Relationship Between Planning Sophistication and Performance in Small Business," *Journal of Small Business Management* (Oct. 1998): 24–32.

[15]Charles R. Schwenk and Charles B. Shrader, "Effects of Formal Strategic Planning on Financial Performance in Small Firms: "A Meta Analysis," *Entrepreneurship Theory and Practice* (Spring 1993): 53–64. See also Philip D. Olson and Douglas W. Boker, "Strategy Process—Content Interaction: Effects on Growth Performance in Small, Startup Firms," *Journal of Small Business Management* (Jan. 1995): 34–44.

[16]Michael E. Porter, "Knowing Your Place—How to Assess the Attractiveness of Your Industry and Your Company's Position in It." *Inc.* (Sept. 1991): 90–94.

Flaw 4: Compromising strategy for growth. A careful balance must exist between growth and the competitive strategy that makes a new venture successful. If an entrepreneur sacrifices his or her venture's unique strategy to realize fast growth, then the venture may grow out of business. Although fast growth can be tempting in certain industries, it is imperative that entrepreneurs maintain and grow their strategic advantage as well.

Flaw 5: Failure to explicitly communicate the venture's strategy to employees. It is essential for every entrepreneur to clearly communicate the company's strategy to every employee. Never assume employees already know the strategy. Always be explicit.

"One of the fundamental benefits of developing a strategy is that it creates unity, or consistency of action, throughout a company. Every department in the organization works toward the same objectives. But if people do not know what the objectives are, how can they work toward them? If they do not have a clear sense that low cost, say, is your ultimate aim, then all their day-to-day actions are not going to be reinforcing that goal. In any company, employees are making critical choices every minute. An explicit strategy will help them make the right ones," Porter says.[17]

Strategic Positioning: The Entrepreneurial Edge

Strategic competition can be envisioned as the process of perceiving new positions that attract customers from established positions or draw new customers into the market. In principle, incumbents and entrepreneurs face the same challenges in finding new strategic positions. In practice, entrepreneurs often have the edge.

Strategic positionings are often not obvious, and finding them requires creativity and insight. Entrepreneurs often discover unique positions that have been available but simply overlooked by established competitors. In addition, entrepreneurial ventures may prosper by occupying a position that a competitor once held but has ceded through years of imitation and straddling. (See Table 4.1 for alternative views of strategy.)

Most commonly, new positions open up because of change. New customer groups or purchase occasion arise; new needs emerge as societies evolve; new distribution channels appear; new technologies are developed; new machinery or information systems become available. When such changes happen, entrepreneurial ventures unencumbered by a long history in the industry can often more easily perceive the potential for a new way of competing. Unlike incumbents, these organizations can be more flexible because they face no trade-offs with their existing activities.[18]

Exploring the Entrepreneurial Concepts

The following sections provide an "entrepreneurial library" that contains a journal reading on this chapter's subject and a comprehensive case study to illustrate the concept in practice. It is hoped that through the reading and discussion of the case, you will gain a greater understanding of the chapter.

---

[17]Ibid., 93.

[18]Michael E. Porter, "What Is Strategy?" *Harvard Business Review* (Nov.–Dec. 1996): 61–78.

TABLE 4.1	ALTERNATIVE VIEW OF STRATEGY	

The Implicit Strategy Model of the Past Decade	Sustainable Competitive Advantage
• One ideal competitive position in the industry • Benchmarking of all activities and achieving best practice • Aggressive outsourcing and partnering to gain efficiencies • Advantages rest on a few key success factors, critical resources, and core competencies • Flexibility and rapid responses to all competitive and market changes	• Unique competitive position for the company • Activities tailored to strategy • Clear trade-offs and choices vis-à-vis competitors • Competitive advantage arises from fit across activities • Sustainability comes from the activity system, not the parts • Operational effectiveness is a given

SOURCE: Michael E. Porter, "What Is Strategy?" *Harvard Business Review* (Nov.–Dec. 1996): 74.

THE ENTREPRENEURIAL LIBRARY

Reading for Chapter 4

ACHIEVING AND MAINTAINING STRATEGIC COMPETITIVENESS IN THE 21ST CENTURY: THE ROLE OF STRATEGIC LEADERSHIP

R. Duane Ireland University of Richmond
Michael A. Hitt Arizona State University

Executive Overview

Competition in the 21st century's global economy will be complex, challenging, and filled with competitive opportunities and threats. Effective strategic leadership practices can help firms enhance performance while competing in turbulent and unpredictable environments. The purpose of this paper is to describe six components of effective strategic leadership. When the activities called for by these components are completed successfully, the firm's strategic leadership practices can become a source of competitive advantage. In turn, use of this advantage can contribute significantly to achieving strategic competitiveness and earning above-average returns in the next century.

> It is possible—and fruitful—to identify major events that have already happened, irrevocably, and that will have predictable effects in the next decade or two. It is possible, in other words, to identify and prepare for the future that has already happened.
>
> Peter Drucker, 1997.

SOURCE: R. Duane Ireland, University of Richmond, and Michael A. Hitt, Arizona State University. Reprinted with permission.

Grounded in the insights and understanding that experience provides, conventional wisdom holds that it is very difficult to predict the future with high degrees of accuracy. In fact, Peter Drucker goes so far as to suggest that "In human affairs—political, social, economic, or business—it is pointless to try to predict the future, let alone attempt to look ahead 75 years."[1] Notwithstanding this difficulty, the capability implied by Drucker's comment above is encouraging. It is both possible and productive for firms to identify and prepare for a future that has already happened. Thus, although it is difficult for organizations to predict their future accurately, examining events that have already taken place allows them to know how to prepare for a future whose state has been influenced.

Based on this approach, we present a description of the strategic leadership practices that will contribute to corporate success during the 21st century. More precisely, our position is that the global economy is a major irrevocable event whose existence has already had a major influence on today's strategic leadership practices and offers insights about practices that should be used in the future. By examining appropriate and often innovative strategic leadership practices currently being used successfully by visionary organizations, it is possible to identify and understand practices that will be effective in the next century. This analysis is important, because strategic leadership may prove to be one of the most critical issues facing organizations. Without effective strategic leadership, the probability that a firm can achieve superior or even satisfactory performance when confronting the challenges of the global economy will be greatly reduced.[2]

Strategic leadership is defined as a person's ability to anticipate, envision, maintain flexibility, think strategically, and work with others to initiate changes that will create a viable future for the organization.[3] When strategic leadership processes are difficult for competitors to understand and, hence, to imitate, the firm has created a competitive advantage.[4] Because the creation of sustainable competitive advantage is the universal objective of all companies,[5] being able to exercise strategic leadership in a competitively superior manner facilitates the firm's efforts to earn superior returns on its investments.

The Global Economy

There is virtually uniform agreement that the complexity, turbulence, and extraordinary changes during the 1980s and 1990s are contributing to the rapid development of an ultracompetitive global economy. Joseph Gorman, TRW's CEO, suggests that a transformational change is occurring, from regional economies and industries to global ones.[6] A key reality of our time, the commercial interactions that are taking place in the global economy are becoming the dominant force shaping relationships among nations. The fact that ". . . the proportion of trade among nations as a share of global income has increased from 7 percent to 21 percent since the end of World War II demonstrates why the globalization of commercial markets has an important effect on individual countries"[7] Thus, in the global economy, products are shipped anywhere in the world in a matter of days; communications are instant; and new product introductions and their life cycles have never been shorter, with six months the norm in some high-tech industries.[8]

The incredible breadth and depth of the global economy's effects are shown by the suggestion that in the 21st century, nation-states will lose their sovereignty, technology may replace labor, and corporations may come to resemble amoebas—collections of workers that are subdivided into dynamic, ever-changing teams to competitively exploit the firm's unique resources, capabilities, and core competencies. Thus, some analysts argue with conviction that the large number of structural changes occurring simultaneously in the international system are resulting in economies and communication systems that are more integrated. For example, it has been predicted that by 2150, all or most of the global economy will be part of a "... single market, perhaps complete with a single currency and monetary authority."[9] However, others believe that the political structures supporting various economies and their communication systems will remain somewhat fragmented and may even be reduced to ethnic units during the 21st century.[10] Changes such as these may culminate in corporations that would be unrecognizable to many employees and world citizens today.[11] The global economy may create a need for individual citizens to maintain separate loyalties—one to their own unique traditions and institutions, the other to the characteristics of a rapidly evolving international culture.

The New Competitive Landscape

The global economy has created a new competitive landscape—one in which events change constantly and unpredictably.[12] For the most part, these changes are revolutionary, not evolutionary in nature. Revolutionary changes happen swiftly, are constant, even relentless in their frequency, and affect virtually all parts of an organization simultaneously.[13] The uncertainty, ambiguity, and discontinuity resulting from revolutionary changes challenge firms and their strategic leadership to increase the speed of the decision-making processes through which strategies are formulated and implemented.[14] In the global economy, knowledge work and knowledge workers are the primary sources of economic growth—for individual firms and for nations. Thus, in the 21st century, the ability to build, share and leverage knowledge will replace the ownership and/or control of assets as a primary source of competitive advantage.[15]

However, certain conditions of the new competitive landscape, including the expectation that the world's economy will grow substantially during the first 20 years of the next century, also create opportunities for companies to improve their financial performance.[16] Organizations in which strategic leaders adopt a new competitive mindset—one in which mental agility, firm flexibility, speed, innovation, and globalized strategic thinking are valued highly—will be able to identify and competitively exploit opportunities that emerge in the new competitive landscape. These opportunities surface primarily because of the disequilibrium that is created by continuous changes (especially technological changes) in the states of knowledge that are a part of a competitive environment. More specifically, although uncertainty and disequilibrium often result in seemingly hostile and intensely rivalrous conditions, these conditions may simultaneously yield significant product-driven growth opportunities.[17] Through effective strategic leadership, an organization can be mobilized so that it can adapt its behaviors and exploit different growth opportunities.[18]

Strategic Leadership

In the 1960s and early 1970s, situations facing the firm were thought to be the primary determinant of managerial behaviors and organizational outcomes. Compared with the influence of conditions in the firm's external environment, managers were believed to have little ability to make decisions that would affect the firm's performance.

The Great Leader View of Strategic Leadership

In 1972, John Child, a prominent organization theorist, argued persuasively that an organization's top-level managers had the discretion or latitude to make choices that would, indeed, affect their firm's outcomes.[19] In particular, because top managers have the responsibility for the overall performance of their firms, these individuals have the strongest effect on the firm's strategic management process. In Child's view, strategic leaders, armed with substantial decision-making responsibilities, had the ability to influence significantly the direction of the firm and how it was to be managed in that pursuit. Strategic leadership theory holds that companies are reflections of their top managers, and, in particular, of the chief executive officers, and that ". . . the specific knowledge, experience, values, and preferences of top managers are reflected not only in their decisions, but in their assessments of decision situations."[20]

Substantial numbers of CEOs have adopted the notion that strategic leadership responsibilities are theirs alone. One of their primary tasks is to choose a vision for the firm and create the conditions to achieve that vision. Thus, as a result of the significant choice options available to the CEO as the firm's key strategic leader, this individual often worked as a Lone Ranger when shaping the firm. Isolated from those being led, the firm's key strategic leader commanded his/her organization primarily through use of top-down directives.[21] Particularly when these choices resulted in financial success for the company, the key strategic leader was recognized widely as the "corporate Hercules."[22]

Appropriate for its time, the theory of strategic leadership contributed to organizational success. But the environmental conditions in which this theory was used have changed dramatically because of the global economy. In the past few decades, environmental conditions were relatively stable and predictable compared with the current and predicted states of these conditions in the 21st century.

The relative stability and predictability of the past few decades resulted in manageable amounts of uncertainty and ambiguity. Change was often treated as linear in many industries; major competitors were largely domestic, not global companies; organizations were structured in hierarchical configurations that were supported by selection and promotion practices. However, conditions associated with the global economy's new competitive landscape—shorter product life cycles, ever-accelerating rates and types of change, the explosion of data and the need to convert it to useable information—prevent single individuals from having all of the insights necessary to chart a firm's direction. Moreover, some believe that having strategic leadership centered on a single person or a few people at the top of a hierarchical pyramid is increasingly counterproductive.[23] Constrained by their abilities to deal with rapidly increasing amounts of data and the general complexity of the global economy, top managers are now challenged to discharge their strategic leadership responsibilities differently.[24] Insightful top managers recognize that it is impossible for them to have all of the answers, are willing to learn along with others, and understand that the uncertainty created by the global economy affects people at the top as well as those lower down in the organization.[25]

The Great Groups View of Strategic Leadership

In the 21st century, the nature of the organization in which effective strategic leadership practices occur will be different. In the view of noted business thinker Charles Handy, a public corporation should and will be regarded not as a piece of property owned by the current holders of its shares, but as a community. More properly thought of as citizens than as employees, people involved with an organizational community remain together to pursue a common purpose. A community is something to which a person belongs and that belongs to no one individual. The community's citizens have both responsibilities to pursue the common good and rights to receive benefits earned through its attainment.

In an organizational community, strategic leadership is distributed among diverse individuals who share the responsibility to create a viable future for their firm. Handy argues that many citizens will need to serve their communities as leaders and will need to be dispersed throughout the firm.[26] When allowed to flourish as involved leaders, people spark greatness in each other. As Italian author Luciano De Crescenzo noted, "We are all angels with only one wing, we can only fly while embracing each other."[27]

Combinations or collaborations of organizational citizens functioning successfully have been labeled great groups. These collaborations usually feature managers with significant profit and loss responsibilities, internal networkers "who move about the organization spreading and fostering commitment to new ideas and practices," and community citizens with intellectual capital that stimulates the development and/or leveraging of knowledge.[28] Members of great groups rely on one another to create an environment in which innovations occur regularly and knowledge is generated and dispersed constantly. Consistent leadership between and among all of the firm's great groups results in innovative strategic thinking and rapid acceptance of organizational changes that, even when difficult, are required to enhance firm performance. Top managers who facilitate the development of great groups—groups in which strategic leadership takes place among a range of people with different talents—have shifted the locus of responsibility to form adaptive solutions to issues from themselves to the organization's full citizenry.[29]

As knowledge sharing and developing entities, great groups have several characteristics.[30] First, members of great groups have accepted their responsibility for firm outcomes. Involved and committed, these people understand the significance of their work and their responsibility to each other.[31] Second, great groups seek to learn from multiple parties, including contractors, suppliers, partners, and customers. Group members are committed to the position that "No matter where knowledge comes from, the key to reaping a big return is (for the group) to leverage that knowledge by replicating it throughout the company so that each unit is not learning in isolation and reinventing the wheel again and again."[32]

The third great group characteristic concerns information and knowledge. Increasingly, the information great groups gather to form knowledge and to understand how to use knowledge already possessed must come from events and conditions outside the organization. In Peter Drucker's view, it is primarily information from outside that allows a business to decide ". . . how to allocate its knowledge resources in order to produce the highest yield. Only with such information can a business also prepare for new changes and challenges arising from sudden shifts in the world economy and in the nature and content of knowledge. The development of rigorous methods for gathering and analyzing outside information will increasingly become a major challenge for businesses and for information experts."[33] Great groups respond positively to Drucker's challenge and are learning how to interpret external information in competitively relevant terms. In the 21st century, it will be increasingly vital for the firm's strategic leadership processes to adopt this perspective regarding the acquisition and use of information flows.

Another characteristic of great groups is their maintenance of records of individuals' knowledge stocks. With these records, people can quickly find others who possess the knowledge required to solve problems as they arise. Maintaining and using these records demonstrates these groups' ability to work smarter through their collective insights and the skills resulting from them.[34] Finally, great groups understand that the firm's method of strategic leadership results in a constantly changing configuration of responsibilities. Across tasks, every member of a great group serves, at different times, as a leader, peer, or subordinate. The operationalization of this understanding results in mutual influence relationships among the firm's top managers and all organizational citizens, including those with formal managerial responsibilities.[35]

Perhaps the most important "great group" in an organization is the top management team (TMT) formed by the CEO. The top management team is a relatively small group of executives, usually between three and ten people. These individuals are at the apex of the organization and provide strategic leadership.[36]

Because of the complexity of the new competitive landscape, both in its structure and dynamism, the collective intellect generated by a top management team is necessary for effective strategic leadership to occur in the firm. A philosopher's view demonstrates this point: "None of us is as smart as all of us."[37] The large number of organizational stakeholders alone makes it necessary to depend on a team of top executives for strategic leadership. The global economy, more than any other factor, has created the need for the top management team to effectively exercise strategic leadership in organizations. The knowledge needed to understand and operate in many global markets is substantial, thereby requiring a team effort. In fact, global firms such as Asea Brown Boveri (ABB) believe that it is necessary to have a culturally diverse TMT to successfully operate in such markets. This is particularly important because of the emphasis on gaining the external knowledge necessary to develop a collective vision for the organization and to gain the multiple constituencies' commitment to pursuit of the vision.

Because of the multiple stakeholders with competing interests, there is need for a heterogeneous TMT, one with members having different knowledge sets and skills.[38] The CEO remains the top leader, but must use these different knowledge sets and skills to successfully manage the organization. Viewing the other members of the TMT as partners allows the CEO to do this effectively. Beyond this, top managers should treat all employees as partners, especially in flatter, matrix-type organizations—an organizational form that will be used increasingly in 21st century firms. In such organizations, top managers manage across traditional boundaries (e.g., functions), building the horizontal organization in the process.[39]

Even though the operational details of effective strategic leadership are continuing to change as the global economy evolves, the CEO remains accountable for the entire firm's performance. The board of directors will hold the CEO accountable for guiding the firm in ways that best serve the interests of owners (e.g., shareholders) and other stakeholders. Tomorrow's organizations will still require a great leader to be successful. Great leaders are able to share responsibility for leading and managing business units, sharing information and ideas widely with others and seeking mutual influence among all who have accepted the responsibility to contribute to the formation and achievement of the firm's direction.

Six Components of Strategic Leadership

What will be different in 21st century companies is how top managers discharge their strategic leadership responsibilities. They will no longer view their leadership position as one with rank and title, but rather as a position of significant responsibility to a range of stakeholders. Instead of seeking to provide all the right answers, they will strive to ask the right questions of community citizens they have empowered to work as partners with them. They can choose to form a community of colleagues rather than a company of employees constrained by traditional hierarchical configurations.

The top managers must affect the behaviors of many stakeholders, especially those of organizational citizens, working often as a coach. The organizational community is one in which citizens' creative energy is released, and their self-confidence enhanced, when they are inspired to assume responsibility for leading themselves through the work of great groups.[40] Sharing among inspired and committed citizens facilitates the emergence of the collective magic that creates intellectual capital and knowledge. An effective strategic leader "finds glory in the whole team reaching the summit together."[41]

John Browne, CEO of British Petroleum Company, believes that the top manager must stimulate the organization rather than control it. The top manager provides strategic directives, encourages learning that results in the formation of intellectual capital, and verifies that mechanisms exist to transfer intellectual capital across all of the firm's parts. Browne believes that "the role of leaders at all levels is to demonstrate to people that they are capable of achieving more than they think they can achieve and that they should never be satisfied with where they are now."[42] Heinrch von Pierer, president and CEO of Siemens AG, says that "As we move into what will be a century of unprecedented challenges, successful leaders will rely even more intensely on strengths that have become crucial in recent years—speed of decisions, flexibility, capable delegation, teamwork, the ability to build for the long term while meeting short-term needs—and vision. Increasingly, networked and globalized thinking will be essential for coping with the accelerating pace of change."[43]

Based on the evidence discussed above, we believe that 21st century strategic leadership should be executed through interactions that are based on a sharing of insights, knowledge, and responsibilities for achieved outcomes. These interactions should occur between the firm's great leaders—the top managers—and its citizens. These interactions take place as the firm satisfies the requirements associated with six key effective strategic leadership practices. Although considered individually, it is through the configuration of all six activities that strategic leadership can be effective in the 21st century organization.

Determining the Firm's Purpose or Vision

The task of determining the direction of the firm rests squarely on the CEO's shoulders. Joe Gorman, TRW's CEO, believes that the top manager, often working in concert with the TMT, must provide general guidelines as to where the firm intends to go and the key steps to be taken to reach that end.[44] J. Tracy O'Rourke, CEO of Varian Associates, Inc., endorses Gorman's view: "Clearly, if you're going to do well over time, you have to have some ability—yourself or in combination with others—to come up with a vision . . . and then follow it up with believable and implementable action plans. In most corporate structures, the only person who can do that is the CEO."[45] A recent survey of 1,450 executives from 12 global corporations found that the ability to "articulate a tangible vision, values, and strategy" for their firm was the most important of 21 competencies considered to be crucial skills for global leaders to possess in the future.[46]

Various definitions of purpose or vision have been offered. However, the one advanced recently by John Browne, British Petroleum's CEO, captures the attributes of an effective organizational purpose for 21st century firms. Browne argues that as a description of who the firm is and what makes it distinctive, purpose indicates what a company exists to achieve and what it is willing and not willing to do to achieve it. Browne also believes that a clear purpose ". . . allows a company to focus its learning efforts in order to increase its competitive advantages."[47] Visions that facilitate development of this type of focus make sense to all organizational citizens, stretch citizens' imaginations but are still within the bounds of possibility, are understood easily, and create a cultural glue that allows units to share knowledge sets.[48]

Once the CEO and the TMT have set the general organizational purpose, all other citizens, including the TMT, will be empowered to design and execute strategies and courses of action to accomplish that end.[49] Empowered organizational citizens working individually or as members of great groups in pursuit of the firm's purpose will be able to provide valuable feedback to the CEO and the TMT. This feedback will help the top executives develop the type of insights required to revisit the purpose regularly to verify its authenticity.

Rockwell International's new vision is for the company to become "the world's best diversified high-technology company." The CEO and TMT believe that the actions necessary for this vision to be reached are the aggressive pursuit of global growth, the execution of leading-edge business practices, and the manufacture and distribution of products that will allow the firm's customers to be the most successful in the world in their business operations.

Critical efforts to achieve the firm's vision is the active involvement of Rockwell employees (organizational citizens). At locations throughout the world, employees are to be challenged to take determined actions that will help the firm achieve its purpose. To select appropriate actions, employees/citizens are formed into 23 implementation teams (or great groups) that are asked to identify strengths and weaknesses. Each unit is to develop recommendations that when accomplished will allow it to become the best in the world at completing a particular task or set of activities.[50] This pattern—wherein organizational citizens work as members of a community that is seeking to serve the common good—will be linked with effective strategic leadership practices in the 21st century.

The blurring of industry boundaries stimulates the emergence of new and sometimes aggressive competitors with significant resource bases and creates interesting challenges for firms' strategic leadership processes.

The announced entrance in early 1998 of the Korean giant, Samsung Group, into the world's automobile manufacturing industry demonstrates this challenge. Although as of mid-1997 Samsung had never built and delivered to a customer a passenger car, it was in the midst of a $13 billion investment to manufacture 1.5 million cars annually. The vision driving these commitments and actions was for Samsung to rank among the world's top ten automakers by 2010. A demonstration of this vision is the billboard outside Samsung's new automobile manufacturing facility in Pusan: "Our dream and Korea's future."

Samsung Group's ambitious auto manufacturing goal surprised at least some industry analysts who noted that the global auto industry was awash in excess production capacity—a problem not expected to abate in the foreseeable future. One noted industry observer said "the world is not waiting breathlessly for a Samsung car . . . There's no logical opening in the marketplace where Samsung can step in and fill a vacuum. Its sales will have to come out of someone else's hide."[51] Evidence was also emerging in mid-1997 that at least some of South Korea's conglomerates were encountering difficult performance challenges because of too much diversification at too rapid a pace. Although Samsung's future competitive intentions could be affected by these general problems,[52] some believe it would be a serious mistake to underestimate Samsung's ability to make its vision a reality. In the words of Richard Pyo of Credit Suisse First Boston in Seoul, "Many people say that Samsung's plans are crazy and too risky, but the Korean economy has developed on gambles.[53]

As this example suggests, every automobile manufacturing company's strategic leadership is challenged to analyze carefully Samsung Group's ability to achieve its vision in the world's auto marketplace. To respond successfully to this challenge, both the top managers (strategic leaders) and organizational citizens (through their work in great groups) in companies competing against Samsung Group's auto unit should use significant amounts of external information to select appropriate competitive responses.

Exploiting and Maintaining Core Competencies

Core competencies are the resources and capabilities that give a firm a competitive advantage over its rivals. The relatively unstable market conditions resulting from innovations, diversity of competitors, and the array of revolutionary technological changes occurring in the new competitive landscape have caused core competencies rather than served markets to become ". . . the basis upon which firms establish their long-term strategies."[54] In the 21st century, an ability to develop and exploit core competencies will be linked even more positively and significantly with the firm's success.

Only the combinations of a firm's resources and capabilities that are valuable, rare, costly to imitate, and for which there are no equivalent strategic substitutes can be rightly identified as core competencies.[55] Only when uniform agreement exists within the organizational community about which resources and capabilities are indeed core competencies can appropriate actions be designed to exploit them in the marketplace.[56] The large retailer Nordstrom Inc., for example, is thought to have core competencies in its customer service and ability to package merchandise in ways that provide unique value to customers. Dell Computer Corporation's distribution system is a key competitive advantage. Competencies in the general area of marketing and specific applications of special skills in advertising campaigns and its global brand name are recognized as core competencies for Philip Morris. In each of these cases, following agreement about their identification as core competencies, strategic leaders work tirelessly to apply the competencies in ways that will improve company performance.

The sharing of knowledge or intellectual capital that is unique to a particular organization will influence significantly the choices strategic leaders make when seeking to use core competencies in novel, yet competitive ways. Through the reciprocal sharing of knowledge and the learning that results from it are a firm's core competencies nurtured effectively.

Knowledge is shared and learning occurs through superior execution of the human tasks of sensing, judging, creating, and building relationships.[57] The importance of knowledge for firms seeking competitive advantage in the global economy is shown by the following comment about Owens Corning's positive financial performance. "In the past year a series of moves in sales and marketing, information systems, and manufacturing and distribution have come together in a coherent strategy that is transforming this Midwestern maker of humdrum materials into a global competitor whose real business is knowledge."[58] Indeed, with rare exceptions, in the 21st century, a firm's productivity will lie more in its collective intellect—that is, in its collective capacity to gain and use knowledge—rather than in its hard assets such as land, plant, and equipment.[59]

The competitive value of core competencies increases through their use and continuing development.[60] A firm's privately held knowledge is the foundation of its competitively valuable core competencies and is increasing in importance as a driver of strategic decisions and actions. The most effective strategic leadership practices in the 21st century will be ones through which strategic leaders find ways for knowledge to breed still more knowledge. While physical assets such as land, machinery, and capital may be relatively scarce on a global basis, ideas and knowledge "are abundant, they build on each other, and they can be reproduced cheaply or at no cost at all. In other words, ideas don't obey the law of diminishing returns, where adding more labor, machinery or money eventually delivers less and less additional output.[61]

Johnson & Johnson's CEO is a strategic leader who believes in developing and nurturing his firm's knowledge base. Asked to describe factors that account for his company's success, he suggested that his company is "not in the product business. (It) is in the knowledge business."[62] However, knowledge cannot breed knowledge and core competencies cannot be emphasized and exploited effectively in the global marketplace without appropriate human capital.

Developing Human Capital

Human capital is the knowledge and skills of a firm's entire workforce or citizenry. Strategic leaders are those who view organizational citizens as a critical resource on which many core competencies are built and through which competitive advantages are exploited successfully. In the global economy, significant investments will be required for the firm to derive full competitive benefit from its human capital. Some economists argue that these investments are "essential to robust long-term growth in modern economies that depend on knowledge, skills, and information.[63] Continual, systematic work on the productivity of knowledge and knowledge workers enhances the firm's ability to perform successfully. Citizens appreciate the opportunity to learn continuously and feel greater involvement with their community when encouraged to expand their knowledge base. Ongoing investments in organizational citizens result in a creative, well-educated workforce—the type of workforce capable of forming highly effective great groups.

The importance of educational investments in citizens is being supported in a growing number of corporations. Andersen Consulting, for example, allocates six percent of its annual revenue to education and requires each professional employee to complete a minimum of 130 hours of training annually. Intel Corp. spends $3,500 per year per person on education. General Motors Corp. and General Electric have appointed chief knowledge officers. Warren Bennis suggests that "this institutionalization of education is not some fringe, feel-good benefit. It is tangible recognition that education gives the biggest bang for the corporate buck." A recent study showed that companies that invest 10 percent [or] more in education receive an 8.5 percent increase in productivity. In contrast, companies boosted their productivity by only three percent as a result of a 10 percent increase in capital expenditures.[64]

The global economy allows firms to earn a financial premium by using competitively superior practices in the location, selection, and subsequent development of human capital. One key reason is that skilled labor is expected to be in short supply during the first part of the 21st century. For example, a million new jobs in high technology will be created over the next decade with almost no increase in the supply of human resources to fill these jobs.[65]

A survey of human resource managers conducted by the American Management Association revealed that 47 percent of the respondents worked in firms that faced skilled labor shortages. Interestingly, 54.7 percent of the same group of respondents also believe that the shortages in skilled personnel will be worse in 2000 and beyond. As of mid-1997, at least 190,000 information technology jobs were vacant in U.S. companies. A 43 percent decline in the number of college graduates earning undergraduate degrees in computer science between 1988 and 1997 suggests more serious labor shortages ahead.[66]

Skilled labor shortages have unintended negative consequences. Talented, dedicated, and motivated employees often become frustrated and dissatisfied when asked to work continuously with those without equivalent skills and commitments. As a successful financial analyst explained: "I could not fathom, let alone accept, the extreme variations in work ethic, attention to detail, and commitment to job and company. All my prior work and school experience had been with creative, energized, self-starters. It took me months, if not years, the value the diverse work styles and varying motivators of the work force I encountered."[67] Thus, a challenge for tomorrow's strategic leaders is to find ways to encourage each employee to fulfill her or his potential. Especially when faced with labor shortages, the organizational community's common good can be reached only when each member of the great group is committed to full participation.

Greater workforce diversity is another issue that will confront 21st century strategic leaders. Organizational communities will comprise individuals from multiple countries and cultures that may have unique and idiosyncratic value structures. CEOs and TMTs should learn to appreciate the beliefs, values, behaviors, and business practices of companies competing in a variety of regions and cultures. Organizational citizens can then better understand the realities and preferences that are a part of the region and culture in which they are working.

Peter Brabeck-Letmathe, CEO of Nestle SA, believes that it is increasingly important for top managers to speak at least two to three languages.[68] Cross-border and culture transfers among organizational citizens will be used prominently in the 21st century, as will experts who help people understand the nuances of other cultures. As at ABB today, many firms' TMTs will be culturally diverse. Success will depend on the ability of a firm's top managers to form a community of citizens rather than a band of employees working for a firm.

Sustaining an Effective Organizational Culture

Organizational culture refers to the complex set of ideologies, symbols, and core values shared throughout the firm. Several business writers believe that the challenges to firms in the 21st century will be not so much technical or rational as cultural—"how to lead the organizations that create and nurture knowledge; how to know when to set our machines aside and rely on instinct and judgment; how to live in a world in which companies have ever increasing visibility; and how to maintain, as individuals and organizations, our ability to learn."[69]

Culture provides the context within which strategies are formulated and implemented. Organizational culture is concerned with decisions, actions, communication patterns, and communication networks. Formed over the life of a company, culture reflects what the firm has learned across time through its responses to the continuous challenges of survival and growth. Culture is rooted in history, held collectively, and is of sufficient complexity to resist many attempts at direct manipulation. Because it influences how the firm conducts its business, as well as the methods used to regulate and control the behavior of organizational citizens, culture can be a competitive advantage.

In the global economy, strategic leaders capable of learning how to shape a firm's culture in competitively relevant ways will become a valued source of competitive advantage. Chrysler's CEO Robert Eaton and President Robert Lutz are strategic leaders thought to be sources of competitive advantage for their firm. The secret to his company's recognition as "Detroit's profitability champion," Eaton suggested, is the "Chrysler difference; a corporate culture that rejects Motown's hidebound bureaucratic traditions." Some analysts support this suggestion, noting that "no group of managers has stirred up Detroit more than Ford's fabled Whiz Kids of the 1950s." In one writer's view, the firm's tone "is set by Eaton, whose low-key demeanor belies a fierce competitive streak, and Lutz, the swashbuckling ex-Marine with a flair for product creation. But behind Eaton and Lutz, Chrysler boasts a little-known cast of managers who've become the envy of the industry."[70] Integrating this culture with Daimler-Benz's may prove to be challenging. On the other hand, a successful integration of these cultures could result in a competitive advantage for the new firm.

The social energy that drives Southwest Airlines is largely a product of CEO Herb Kelleher and the managers who surround him. The firm's culture is responsible for the company's steady growth, above-average profitability, and the avoidance of employee layoffs for more than 25 years. Actions that exemplify Southwest's culture include: "Pilots hold barbecues to thank mechanics; flight attendants sing safety instructions on board; agents hang mirrors on their computers to make sure they're smiling when taking reservations; Kelleher is generous with hugs and kisses." Employees are committed to treating coworkers and customers with respect and dignity, having fun, and working hard. An indication of the culture's desirability is that 137,000 people applied in 1996 for only 5,000 Southwest Airlines' job openings.[71]

Effective cultures are ones in which organizational citizens understand that competitive advantages do not last forever and that the firm must move forward continuously. When citizens are comfortable with the reality of constant change and the need for a never-ending stream of innovations, patterns and practices are in place that can enhance global competitiveness.

Emphasizing Ethical Practices

Ethical practices serve as a moral filter through which potential courses of action are evaluated.[72] The influence of top managers on the firm's ethical practices and outcomes is accepted by business practitioners, academics, and society. In the 21st century, effective strategic leaders will use honesty, trust, and integrity as the foundations for their decisions. Strategic leaders displaying these qualities are capable of inspiring their employees and developing an organizational culture in which ethical practices are the behavioral norm. Acer CEO Stan Shih notes that for his employees there is simply no alternative to dealing honestly with all of the firm's stakeholders. Shih's belief that human nature is basically positive and good could be the force driving his forthright and ethical business practices.[73]

The challenge for strategic leaders is how to instill normative values that guide corporate action and individuals' behaviors.[74] In the final analysis, ethical decision-making processes result in the use of organizational resources to obtain benefits desired by legitimate stakeholders. A strategic leader's commitment to pursuits in which legal, ethical, and social concerns have been taken into account is thought to be both morally right and economically efficient.

Establishing ethical practices will be difficult for strategic leaders in the 21st century's global economy because of the significant diversity of the cultures and economic structures within which firms will compete. An understanding of the interests of all legitimate stakeholders will come only through analysis of and sensitivity to cultural diversity. A strategic leader's commitment to serve stakeholders' legitimate claims will contribute to the establishment and continuation of an ethical organizational culture. Employee practices that take place in such a culture become the set of accepted and expected commitments, decisions, and actions that should be taken when dealing with the firm's stakeholders.

Establishing Balanced Organizational Controls

Organizational controls are the formal, information-based procedures that strategic leaders and managers use to frame, maintain, and alter patterns of organizational activities.[75] The new competitive landscape makes it difficult to establish such controls, which, by their nature, limit employees' behaviors. Controls influence and guide work in ways necessary to achieve performance objectives. The new competitive landscape is replete with opportunities that are addressed most effectively through innovation and creativity. Strategic leaders able to establish controls that facilitate flexible, innovative employee behaviors will earn a competitive premium for their firm.

Top managers are responsible for the development and effective use of two types of internal controls—strategic controls and financial controls.[76] Strategic controls require information-based exchanges among the CEO, top management team members, and organizational citizens. To exercise effective strategic control, top managers must acquire deep understandings of the competitive conditions and dynamics of each of the units or divisions for which they are responsible. Exchanges of information occur through both informal, unplanned meetings and interactions scheduled on a routine, formal basis. The effectiveness of strategic controls is increased substantially when strategic leaders are able to integrate disparate sets of information to yield competitively relevant insights. Because their emphasis is on actions rather than outcomes, strategic controls encourage lower-level managers to make decisions that incorporate moderate and acceptable levels of risk. Moreover, a focus on the content of strategic actions provides the flexibility managers and other great group members require to take advantage of competitive opportunities that develop rapidly in the new competitive landscape.

Financial controls entail objective criteria (e.g., various accounting-based measures) that strategic leaders use to evaluate returns earned by company units and those responsible for their performance. By focusing on performance-induced outcomes, financial controls encourage the accomplishment of short-term performance goals. An emphasis on financial rather than strategic controls makes managerial rewards contingent on achievement of financial outcomes. Therefore, an emphasis on short-term financial performance goals encourages risk-adverse managerial decisions and behaviors.

Effective top managers seek to develop and use a balanced set of strategic and financial controls. Typically, this outcome is achieved by using strategic controls to focus on positive long-term results while pursuing simultaneously the requirement to execute corporate actions in a financially prudent and appropriate manner. In this fashion, strategic leaders are able to use strategic controls to increase the probability that their firm will gain the benefits of carefully formulated strategies, but not at the expense of the type of financial performance that is critical to successful strategy implementation processes and to the firm's ability to satisfy selected stakeholders. Nonetheless, the diversity of the global economy, coupled with the dynamic challenges embedded within the new competitive landscape, highlight the increasing importance of strategic controls. Providing the leadership required for the firm to compete successfully in multiple countries and cultures demands strategic leadership practices that are oriented largely to the integration of disparate competitive information and the use of broad-based strategic controls.

Recommendations for Effective Strategic Leadership Practices

Competition in the 21st century's global economy will occur in postindustrial societies that differ dramatically from the industrial societies they are replacing.

Industrial societies and the commercial enterprises operating within them have been focused primarily on activities intended to create wealth. Technological and scientific advances were the principal means through which wealth was created in such sectors as medicine, agriculture, communications, energy, transportation, and electronics. In the postindustrial era, information-based technology and internationalization are the primary wealth-creation activities. In this era, "(1) much of the economic production occurs in service and high-technology sectors, (2) there is increasing globalization of finance, production, labor, and product markets, (3) economic growth is confronted with ecological limits, and (4) there is a movement toward democratization of markets and politics" in many of the world's countries.[77]

The attributes of the postindustrial era create more risk for firms that attempt to create wealth by competing in multiple marketplaces. Strategic leaders face challenges that may become pervasive as more market democratization processes occur throughout the world. These leaders are offered the following recommendations.

A Growth Orientation

The realities of competition in the global economy demand a corporate focus on growth rather than on downsizing and cost reductions. A variety of strategic approaches can be used in the pursuit of growth, including acquisition, innovation and product development, extreme decentralization, and concentration on product line extensions to provide customers with additional value. The means are less critical than the desired outcome. The most effective strategic leaders will be capable of working with all organizational citizens to find ways to match the firm's resources, capabilities, and core competencies with relevant growth-oriented opportunities.

Knowledge Management

Strategic leaders must enable their organizations to develop, exploit, and protect the intellectual capital contained in their citizens' knowledge bases. They are challenged to develop pathways through which knowledge can be transferred to people and units where it can be further developed and used to pursue strategic competitiveness. Managing knowledge in this manner challenges conventional thinking and increases the likelihood that the firm will be able to create new competitive space in its markets. In the words of Warren Bennis, "the key to competitive advantage in the 1990s and beyond will be the capacity of leadership to create the social architecture that generates intellectual capital. Success will belong to those who unfetter greatness within their organizations and find ways to keep it there."[78]

Through voluntary arrangements such as strategic alliances, joint ventures, technology exchanges, and licensing agreements, firms pool their resources to create goods and services with economic value. They create knowledge that, in turn, facilitates the development of competitively valuable goods or services.[79] Strategic leaders who learn how to manage such collaborations will become a source of competitive advantage for their organizations. The most effective strategic leaders will develop the skills required to engage simultaneously in competitive and cooperative behaviors.[80] Companies that both effectively cooperate and compete with other enterprises will earn above-average financial returns. The creativity of great groups will be instrumental in isolating cooperative projects from those for which competitive behaviors are more appropriate.

Mobilization of Human Capital

Implied throughout is the need for companies to adapt to the significant changes in the global economy. To cope with changes in the world's societies, technologies, and markets, 21st century strategic leaders will be challenged to mobilize citizens in ways that increase their adaptive abilities. Leaders should refrain from providing answers; instead, their focus should be on asking challenging questions. They should request that citizens working as members of great groups consider relevant information to determine how the firm can use its knowledge base to achieve strategic competitiveness. Asking citizens to accept their roles as leaders and colleagues while working in great groups can be expected to mobilize their efforts around key strategic issues. Facilitating citizens' efforts to challenge the historical conduct of business in the firm also can galvanize them as they seek to accomplish relevant goals. The development and mobilization of human capital is vital if the firm is to achieve flexibility that is linked with success in the new competitive landscape.[81]

Developing an Effective Organizational Culture

As the social energy that drives the firm, culture exerts a vital influence on performance. To facilitate the development of values oriented to growth and success, 21st century strategic leaders should commit to being open, honest, and forthright in their interactions with all stakeholders, including organizational citizens.

Such a commitment supported James Bonini's work as the manager of Chrysler Corp.'s big-van plant in Windsor, Ontario. At the young age of 33 and with limited manufacturing experience, Bonini needed the support of the plant's 84 managers, 1,800 workers, and officials of the local Canadian autoworkers' union. In a display of candor and honesty, Bonini acknowledged his youth and inexperience to those he was to lead and solicited help from everyone involved with the plant. He scheduled town hall meetings to hear workers' ideas and complaints, met with union officials, and made certain that each employee knew him. He made frequent visits to the plant floor to verify that work was proceeding as intended and to request workers' insights regarding improvements. Employees responded positively to Bonini's candor, honesty, and integrity.[82]

Remaining Focused on the Future

The significant differences between effective strategic leadership practices in the 20th and the 21st centuries are presented in Table 1. CEOs who apply practices associated with 21st century strategic leadership can create sources of competitive advantage for their organizations. The competitive advantages resulting from the work of CEOs as chief leaders and the contributions of great groups as members of organizational communities will allow firms to improve their global competitiveness.

Strategic leaders must use some of their time and energies to predict future competitive conditions and challenges. Companies in the United States, Europe, and Japan have intensified their competitive actions in the world's emerging markets. This emphasis is understandable, given that emerging markets constitute a new and important competitive frontier. However, high levels of risk are associated with these significant opportunities. Major reversals in the trend toward democratization of countries' markets and their accompanying political structures could have significant implications for strategic leaders and their firms.[83] Effective strategies leaders should seek information that will allow them to predict accurately changes in various global markets. Strategic collaborations, with host governments and other companies, are a valuable means of dealing with changing conditions in emerging economic structures. By aligning their strategies with an emerging country's best interests, firms increase their chance of competitive success in volatile situations. Failure to develop these understandings will inhibit strategic leaders' efforts to lead their firms effectively in the 21st century.

TABLE 1	STRATEGIC LEADERSHIP PRACTICES
20th Century Practices	**21st Century Practices**
Outcome focused	Outcome and process focused
Stoic and confident	Confident, but without hubris
Sought to acquire knowledge	Seeks to acquire and leverage knowledge
Guided people's creativity	Seeks to release and nurture people's creativity
Work flows determined by hierarchy	Work flows influenced by relationships
Articulated the importance of integrity	Demonstrates the importance of integrity by actions
Demanded respect	Willing to earn respect
Tolerated diversity	Seeks diversity
Reacted to environmental change	Acts to anticipate environmental change
Served as the great leader	Serves as the leader and as a great group member
Views employees as a resource	Views organizational citizens as a critical resource
Operated primarily through a domestic mindset	Operates primarily through a global mindset
Invested in employees' development	Invests significantly in citizens' continuous development

End Notes

[1] Five business thinkers, Peter F. Drucker, Esther Dyson, Charles Handy, Paul Saffo, and Peter M. Senge, were asked recently by *Harvard Business Review* to describe the challenges they see already taking shape for executives as they move into the next century. See P. F. Drucker, E. Dyson, C. Handy, P. Saffo and P. M. Senge, Looking Ahead: Implications of the Present, *Harvard Business Review*, 75(5), 1997, 18–32.

[2] The importance of strategic leadership for 21st century firms is described in: M. Davids, Where Style Meets Substance, *Journal of Business Strategy*, 16(1), 1995, 48–60; R. P. White, P. Hodgson, and S. Crainer. *The Future of Leadership* (London: Pitman Publishing, 1997).

[3] Additional definitional information about strategic leadership can be found in: C. M. Christensen, Making Strategy: Learning by Doing, *Harvard Business Review*, 75(6), 1997, 141–156; M. A. Hitt, R. D. Ireland, and R. E. Hoskisson, *Strategic Management: Competitiveness and Globalization*, Third Edition (Cincinnati: South-Western College Publishing Company, 1999).

[4] John Browne, CEO of British Petroleum, describes a wide range of competitive approaches being used at BP. See S. E. Prokesch, Unleashing the Power of Learning: An Interview with British Petroleum's John Browne, *Harvard Business Review*, 75(5), 1997, 147–168.

[5] The universal need for each firm to develop a competitive advantage serves as a foundation for two authors' analysis of how strategic management can be improved. For additional information on this subject, see: A. Campbell and M. Alexander, What's Wrong with Strategy? *Harvard Business Review*, 75(6), 1997, 42–51.

[6] Mr. Gorman's viewpoint is included in an article in which potential reasons for the recent success of U.S. firms in the global economy are examined. For further information see: G. P. Zachary, Behind Stocks' Surge Is an Economy in Which Big U.S. Firms Thrive, *Wall Street Journal*, November 22, 1995, A1,A3.

[7] Based on an argument that globalization is a reality of our time, one business writer offers intriguing perspectives regarding the level and degree of economic interdependence of the world's nations. To explore his views further, see: R. Ruggiero, The High Stakes of World Trade, *Wall Street Journal*, April 28, 1997, A18.

[8] In light of the global economy, an interesting set of predictions about the nature of business firms and their leaders in the 21st century can be found in: S. Makridakis, Management in the 21st Century, *Long Range Planning*, 22, April, 1989, 37–53.

[9] The director of the Institute for International Economics offers his optimistic perspective about the characteristics of a global economy in: C. F. Bergsten, The Rationale for a Rosy View, *The Economist*, September 11, 1993, 57–58.

[10] Peter Drucker made these observations in an address to the Knowledge Advantage Conference sponsored by the Ernst & Young Center for Business Innovation. See Peter Drucker on The Next 20 Years, *Executive Upside*, March, 1997, 3.

[11] To better understand the possible nature of the global marketplace in the future, a senior writer reviewed several books. His reviews can be found in: F. R. Bleakley, The Future of the Global Marketplace, *Wall Street Journal*, March 15, 1996, A13.

[12] Unpredictable events affect firms of all sizes. An analysis of the effects of the new competitive landscape on high-growth entrepreneurial firms is presented in: R. D. Ireland and M. A. Hitt, Performance Strategies for High-Growth Entrepreneurial Firms, *Frontiers of Entrepreneurship Research*, 1997, 90–104.

[13] In a recent article, two prominent researchers argue convincingly that "the complexity of political, regulatory, and technological changes confronting most organizations has made radical organizational change and adaptation a central research issue." To further explore this central issue see: R. Greenwood and C. R. Hinings, Understanding Radical Organizational Change: Bringing Together the Old and the New Institutionalism, *Academy of Management Review*, 21, 1996, 1022–1054.

[14] Rapidly changing business conditions result in a premium being placed on the firm's ability to speed up its operations. Recent research suggests that this ability is especially important to develop a competitive advantage in firms in industries with shortened product life cycles. Arguments supporting this position are presented in: E. H. Kessler and A. K. Chakrabarti, Innovation Speed: A Conceptual Model of Context, Antecedents, and Outcomes, *Academy of Management Review*, 21, 1996, 1143–1191.

[15] Both Drucker and Senge emphasize this point in their descriptions of events that have already happened that are shaping the future for 21st century firms. For more information,

see: Drucker, Dyson, Handy, Saffo, and Senge, "Looking Ahead: Implications of the Present," 18–32.

[16]This positive projection of growth for at least the beginning part of the 21st century is presented in: *Dallas Morning News*, Futurists See Bright 21st Century, June 11, 1997, D2.

[17]An insightful treatment of the link between corporate entrepreneurship and the pursuit of organizational growth in firms facing challenging competitive environments is presented in: S. A. Zahra, Environment, Corporate Entrepreneurship, and Financial Performance: A Taxonomic Approach, *Journal of Business Venturing*, 8, 1993, 319–340.

[18]For additional information about how firms can mobilize to adapt their behaviors for competitive reasons, see: R. A. Heifetz and D. L. Laurie, The Work of Leadership, *Harvard Business Review*, 75(1), 1997, 124–134.

[19]Further arguments regarding the choices firms can make through the work of their strategic leaders and other key decision makers can be found in the following classic: J. Child, Organizational Structure, Environment, and Performance: The Role of Strategic Choice, *Sociology* 6, 1972, 1–22.

[20]In a recent article, two researchers present a detailed analysis of different perspectives of strategic leadership that appear in the academic literature. This work is intended to present what the authors consider to be a "more realistic view of top managers' work." To examine the researchers' perspectives, see: A. A. Cannella, Jr., and M. J. Monroe, Contrasting Perspectives on Strategic Leaders: Toward a More Realistic View of Top Managers, *Journal of Management*, 23, 1997, 213–237 (the quote in our article appears on page 213 of the Cannella and Monroe publication).

[21]The historical isolation between strategic leaders and those they led is described in: P. M. Senge, Communities of Leaders and Learners, *Harvard Business Review*, 75(5), 1997, 30–32.

[22]W. Bennis, Cultivating Creative Genius, *Industry Week*, August 18, 1997, 84–88.

[23]This point is described in greater detail in Bennis, Cultivating Creative Genius.

[24]Some believe that understanding how to gather and interpret data is the organizational challenge of the next century. To evaluate this possibility, see: J. Teresko, Too Much Data, Too Little Information, *Industry Week*, August 19, 1996, 66–70.

[25]For a discussion of how uncertainty affects people at both upper and lower organizational levels, see: R. P. White, Seekers and Scalers: The Future Leaders, *Training & Development*, January, 1997, 21–24.

[26]Known widely as a preeminent business thinker, Charles Handy explains his thoughts about organizational communities in: C. Handy, *The Age of Unreason* (Boston: Harvard Business School Press, 1989).

[27]This quotation appears in: Bennis, Cultivating Creative Genius, 88.

[28]To explore the concept of great groups further, see W. Bennis, *Organizing Genius: The Secrets of Creative Collaboration* (Reading, MA: Addison-Wesley Publishing Company, 1997).

[29]To learn how effective leaders allow all organizational employees to play an active role in helping firms become adaptive, see: Heifetz and Laurie, The Work of Leadership.

[30]To learn the views of British Petroleum's CEO about the value and nature of teams (or great groups) in the global economy, see: Prokesch, Unleashing the Power of Learning: An Interview with British Petroleum's John Browne.

[31]The importance of group members accepting the responsibility to support one another in their work is discussed in another one of Charles Handy's books: C. Handy, *The Age of Paradox* (Boston: Harvard Business School Press, 1994).

[32]Among many points discussed by John Browne, the importance of learning how to leverage knowledge is given the most attention. See Prokesch, op. cit.

[33]The criticality of external information for firms seeking high performance in the global economy is described in: P. F. Drucker, The Future That Has Already Happened, *Harvard Business Review*, 75(5), 1997, 20–24.

[34]The importance of collective work, and how such work can be stimulated, is discussed in: P. B. Vaill, *Managing as a Performing Art: New Ideas for a World of Chaotic Change* (San Francisco: Jossey-Bass, 1989).

[35]The inclusive roles of organizational leaders is noted in: G. Dutton, Leadership in a Post-Heroic Age, *Management Review*, October 1996, 7.

[36]An excellent, comprehensive analysis of strategic leadership and the role of the top management team as part of strategic leadership, appears in: S. Finkelstein and D. C. Hambrick, *Strategic Leadership: Top Executives and Their Effects on Organizations* (St. Paul: West Publishing, 1996).

[37]This quote is taken from: Bennis, Cultivating Creative Organizations.

[38]Research results regarding the value of heterogeneous top management teams are explored carefully and in a detailed manner in: Finkelstein and Hambrick, *Strategic Leadership*.

[39]D. F. Abell, Mastering Management—Part 16, *Financial Times*, February 23, 1996, 13.

[40]The important link between self-confidence and the successful completion of significant types of organizational work is discussed in: R. D. Ireland, M. A. Hitt, and J. C. Williams, Self-confidence and Decisiveness: Prerequisites for Effective Management in the 1990s, *Business Horizons*, 35(1), 1992, 36–43.

[41]B. A. Nagle, Wanted: A Leader for the 21st Century, *Industry Week*, November 20, 1995, 29.

[42]This quote, and the importance of letting organizational citizens know that their strategic leaders want them to try different methods to satisfy the demands of new challenges, appears on page 158 of Prokesch, op. cit.

[43]Viewpoints of other leaders, in addition to von Pierer, can be found in: W. H. Miller, Leadership at a Crossroads, *Industry Week*, August 19, 1996, 43–57.

[44]Other aspects of Mr. Gorman's perspectives about the value of a corporate purpose are included in: Miller, Leadership at a Crossroads.

[45]Mr. O'Rourke offered this viewpoint as part of his description of what a leader must do to lead effectively. His perspectives can be studied fully by reading: W. H. Miller, Leadership's Common Denominator, *Industry Week*, August 19, 1997, 97–100.

[46]A full list of 21 competencies identified by the survey's 1,450 participants can be viewed by reading: Davids, Where Style Meets Substance.

[47]This view is explained more fully in Prokesch, op. cit.

[48]Charles Handy considers these points in two books: *The Age of Paradox* and *The Age of Unreason*.

[49]This point is articulated in: *The Economist*, The Changing Nature of Leadership, June 10, 1995, 57.

[50]Full details regarding actions framed by Rockwell's strategic leaders to achieve the firm's vision can be found in: It's Time to Change Your Perception of Rockwell, Rockwell International Corporation Annual Report, 1995.

[51]An intriguing analysis of decisions made by Samsung Group's strategic leaders regarding the firm's entry into the world's automobile manufacturing industry is featured in: L. Kraar, Behind Samsung's High-Stakes Push into Cars, *Fortune*, May 12, 1997, 119–120.

[52]Large conglomerates, called chaebols, have played important roles in the growth of South Korea's economy. However, some evidence suggests that these huge firms may encounter additional competitive challenges in the future. Details of these challenges, and some of the chaebols' responses to them, are presented in: M. Schuman and N. Cho, Troubles of Korean Conglomerates Intensify, Signaling End of an Era, *Wall Street Journal*, April 25, 1997, A11.

[53]Kraar, Behind Samsung's High-Stakes Push into Cars, 119.

[54]Some research proposes that knowledge is the most strategically significant source of core competence and thus of competitive advantage for firms competing in the complex global economy. In a recent publication, this issue is explored through the development of a knowledge-based theory of organizational capability. To examine this theory see: R. M. Grant, Prospering in Dynamically-Competitive Environments: Organizational Capability as Knowledge Integration, *Organization Science*, 7, 1996, 375–387.

[55]Jay Barney's work informs our understanding of the criteria of sustainability. Two publications in which Barney's arguments are detailed are: J. B. Barney, Looking Inside for Competitive Advantage, *Academy of Management Executive*. IX(4), 1995, 49–61; J. B. Barney, Firm Resources and Sustained Competitive Advantage, *Journal of Management*, 17, 1991, 99–120.

[56]The value of understanding the nature of a firm's core competencies is accepted widely. However, one researcher suggests that little guidance is available to help strategic leaders and their co-workers to define carefully their firm's capabilities and core competencies. The experiences of three top-level mangement teams are described in: K. E. Marino, Developing Consensus on Firm Competencies and Capabilities, *Academy of Mangement Executive*, X(3), 1996, 40–51.

[57]T. A. Stewart, *Intellectual Capital* (New York: Doubleday/Currency, 1997).

[58]T. A. Stewart, Owens Back from the Dead, *Fortune*, May 26, 1997, 118–126.

[59]Three researchers have identified actions effective strategic leaders and their firms take to maximize the value of this critical organizational resource. These guidelines are offered in: J. B. Quinn, P. Anderson, and S. Finkelstein, Leveraging Intellect, *Academy of Management Executive*, X(3), 1996, 7–27.

[60]Based on organizational meta-learning processes, firms are able to continue gaining competitive advantages by exploiting dynamic core competencies. How this is accomplished is

described in: D. Lei, M. A. Hitt, and R. Bettis, Dynamic Core Competences Through Meta-Learning and Strategic Context, *Journal of Management*, 22, 1996, 549–569.

[61]Economist Paul M. Romer's work is thought by some to be controversial. Romer's analyses suggest that ideas and technological discovery are the main drivers of a nation's economic growth. An introduction of these arguments is offered in: B. Wysocki, Jr., For This Economist, Long-Term Prosperity Hangs on Good Ideas, *Wall Street Journal*, January 21, 1997, A1, A8.

[62]H. Rudnitsky, One Hundred Sixty Companies for the Price of One, *Forbes*, February 26, 1996, 56–62.

[63]The potential value of additional national expenditures being allocated to education and training initiative is explored by a prominent economist in: G. S. Becker, Why the Dole Plan Will Work, *Business Week*, August 26, 1996, 16.

[64]These points are discussed in Bennis, Cultivating Organizational Genius.

[65]J. Katkin, Close the Talent Gap, *Houston Chronicle*, November 9, 1997, C1, C5.

[66]These statistics are drawn from the following two sources: S. Baker, A. Barrett, and L. Himelstein, Calling All Nerds, *Business Week*, March 10, 1997, 36–37; D. Kunke, In Search of Expertise, *Dallas Morning News*. April 16, 1997, D1, D10.

[67]A business practitioner who participated in a debate expressed this view. The focus of the debate was the extent to which the traditional model of the MBA degree is outdated. The full text of this debate appears in: MBA: Is the Traditional Model Doomed? *Harvard Business Review*, 70(6), 1992, 128–140.

[68]For more information about Mr. Brabeck-Letmathe's views, see: Miller, Leadership's Common Denominator.

[69]These questions appear at the beginning of the interviews with Drucker, et al., op. cit.

[70]B. Vlasic, Can Chrysler Keep It Up? *Business Week*, November 25, 1996, 108–120.

[71]Southwest Airlines' culture has been cited frequently as a competitive advantage for the firm. Interestingly, everyone (except consultants and U.S. competitors) is welcome to attend the sessions in which the company's culture is discussed. Additional details about the firm's culture sessions are offered in: W. Zellner, Southwest's Love Fest at Love Field, *Business Week*, April 28, 1997, 124.

[72]To explore in greater detail how ethical practices can be used as decision filters, see: J. M. Lozano, Ethics and Management: A Controversial Issue, *Journal of Business Ethics*, 15, 1996, 227–236; J. Milton-Smith, Ethics as Excellence: A Strategic Management Perspective, *Journal of Business Ethics*, 14, 1995, 683–693.

[73]L. Kraar, Acer's Edge: PCs to Go, *Fortune*, October 30, 1995, 187–204.

[74]The developing relationship between corporate social responsibility and society's expectations of corporations was considered through a special issue of *Academy of Management Review*. To examine the special issue's topics, consult the introductory comments included in: S. P. Sethi, Introduction to *AMR*'s Special Topic Forum on Shifting Paradigms: Societal Expectations and Corporate Performance, *Academy of Management Review*, 20, 1995, 18–21.

[75]R. Simons, How New Top Managers Use Control Systems as Levers of Strategic Renewal, *Strategic Management Journal*, 15, 1994, 169–189.

[76]Extensive considerations of the differences between strategic controls and financial controls are presented in several publications including: M. A. Hitt, R. E. Hoskisson, R. A. Johnson, and D. D. Moesel, The Market for Corporate Control and Firm Innovation, *Academy of Management Journal*, 39, 1996, 1084–1119; M. A. Hitt, R. E. Hoskisson, and R. D. Ireland, Mergers and Acquisitions and Managerial Commitment to Innovations in M-form Firms, *Strategic Management Journal*, 11 (Special Issue), 1990, 29–47.

[77]P. Shrivastava, Ecocentric Management for a Risk Society, *Academy of Management Review*, 20, 1995, 119.

[78]Bennis, Cultivating Creative Genius, 87.

[79]Three researchers explain theoretically the value firms can derive through implementation of cooperative strategies formed through interfirm collaborations: A. A. Lado, N. G. Boyd, and S. C. Hanlon, Competition, Cooperation, and the Search for Economic Rents: A Syncretic Model, *Academy of Management Review*, 22, 1997, 110–141. See also K. M. Eisenhardt and C. B. Schoonhoven, Resource-based View of Strategic Alliance Formation: Strategic and Social Effects in Entrepreneurial Firms, *Organization Science*, 7, 1996, 136–150.

[80]Lado, Boyd, and Hanlon argue that "Success in today's business world often requires that firms pursue both competitive and cooperative strategies simultaneously." They define syncretic rent-seeking behavior as actions firms can take to earn economic rents while engaging jointly in competitive and cooperative behaviors.

[81]This point is discussed in some detail in: M. A. Hitt, B. W. Keats and S. DeMarie, Navigating in the New Competitive Landscape: Building Strategic Flexibility and Competitive Advantage in the 21st Century. *Academy of Management Executive*, 12(4), 22–42.

[82]A comprehensive description of James Bonini's experiences as a young, inexperienced manager at a Chrysler Corp. plant is offered in: G. Stern, How a Young Manager Shook Up the Culture at Old Chrysler Plant, *Wall Street Journal*, April 21, 1997, A1, A6.

[83]These possibilities, and their accompanying competitive implications for firms committed to achieving success in the global marketplace are examined in: J. E. Garten, Troubles Ahead in Emerging Markets, *Harvard Business Review*, 1997, 75(3), 38–49.

About the Authors

R. Duane Ireland holds the W. David Robbins Chair in Business Policy at the University of Richmond. Previously, he was the Curtis Hankamer Chair in Entrepreneurship at Baylor University and is the director of the Entrepreneurship Studies Program at Baylor's Hankamer School of Business. He received his PhD from Texas Tech University. He has been an associate editor of the *Academy of Management Executive* and a consulting editor for *Entrepreneurship: Theory and Practice*. He is now serving as a member of the editorial review boards for *Academy of Management Review* and *Journal of Management*. His research examines questions related to corporate-level strategy, innovation, and core competencies. Currently, he is studying issues related to the intersection between the entrepreneurship and strategic management literatures and factors that differentiate success from failure in mergers and acquisitions. He is the coauthor of *Strategic Management: Competitiveness and Globalization* and is working on three books. He has been selected as Baylor University's outstanding researcher (1988) and as the distinguished professor in the Hankamer School of Business (1986).

Michael A. Hitt holds the Paul M. and Rosalie Robertson Chair in Business Administration at Texas A&M University. He received his PhD from the University of Colorado and has been selected to receive an honorary doctorate from the Universidad Carlos III de Madrid for his contributions to the field. He is a former editor of the *Academy of Management Journal* and a past president of the Academy of Management. A frequent contributor to the literature, he focuses on international strategy, corporate governance, innovation, importance of intangible resources and the new competitive landscape. He is the coauthor or coeditor of several recent books, including *Downscoping: How to Tame the Diversified Firm; Strategic Management: Competitiveness and Globalization; Managing Strategically in an Interconnected World;* and *New Managerial Mindsets.* He is a fellow of the Academy of Management and received the 1996 Award for Outstanding Academic Contributions to Competitiveness from the American Society for Competitiveness.

C A S E AMERICAN FAMILY HOUSING, INC.

Rebecca Roseberry
Michael Jay Garrison
Jo Ann Duffy
Department of Management and Marketing
College of Business Administration
Sam Houston State University
Huntsville, Tx 77341
tele. 409 294 1518
fax 409 294 3957
e-mail mgt_jxd@shsu.edu

"Did you hear that by the year 2000 forty percent of all homes owned will be mobile?" said Russell Dawson in 1992 prior to opening their first dealership. "That's great. But how can we take advantage of this opportunity?" queried Stephen Dawson. Looking out over the 400 units sitting on the Cleveland lot, Russell said, "If we figure it out, someday we're gonna be the Wal-Mart of this industry." "Well, we definitely have some important decisions to make," replied Stephen. "You're right. I wonder what Dad would do?" said Russell. Stephen replied, "I don't know. Maybe we should ask him. After all, he is the one who's been in this business for almost twenty years."

As young children, Russell and Stephen became acquainted with the mobile home business. Their parents, Mr. and Mrs. Stephen Dawson, started their first dealership in Huntsville, Texas, in 1967, so Russell and Stephen were exposed to every phase of the business. Russell became interested in the sales aspect while Stephen became interested in the moving and service area. By the time Stephen was 14 years old, he was driving the unwieldy trucks pulling mobile homes down hilly, winding country roads. Together they had over twenty-two years experience in the mobile home industry when they decided to start their own mobile home business which they named American Family Housing, Inc. They opened their first dealership in Cleveland, Texas, which served as the home office. Their father loaned Russell and Stephen the money they needed to start. Since the startup in 1992, the two brothers have opened another facility twenty-eight miles from Cleveland and plan to open at least one more facility. By the end of 1994 Russell and Stephen had repaid the loan to their dad in full.

Industry Background[1]

Mobile homes have come a long way from the familiar rickety boxes that were once rolled off factory assembly lines and perched on cinder blocks. Today these homes are redesigned to look more like the traditional single unit home. They can be set on a foundation making it more difficult to tell the difference between a manufactured house and a constructed house.

From a sociocultural standpoint, major changes are occurring with the mobile home market. The demographics of the mobile home market have broadened to include not only the lower and middle class but also professionals. There are now mobile homes in the $70,000 to $120,000 range with as much as 7000 square feet of living area. These houses appeal to professionals who see mobile homes as a way to get more value for their housing dollar than they would for a traditional on-site built home. The greatest demand, however, continues to be from lower and middle class families who choose mobile homes because they are an affordable way to own a home. The lower cost of the manufactured home means that some buyers can afford to buy more land than they could have if they had purchased a constructed home. Mobile home buyers are price sensitive. Most purchase mobile homes based on their income: quality is of secondary importance. The alternatives to buying a mobile home include: buying an on-site constructed house or renting an apartment or house.

The continuing increase in new on-site home construction costs has excluded some middle income families from the American dream of home ownership. The shortage of affordable homes in the U.S. has directed middle income families' attention to the mobile home industry. The lower price, changes in construction, quality, and appearance have caused these households to take a new look at mobile homes. The average price of a constructed home in 1994 was $126,500 while the average cost of a mobile home was about $30,000. Modern mobile homes are attractive in appearance and come in various floorplans and square footage. Moreover, they offer many luxury amenities in the bathrooms and kitchens.

Sales in the industry increased 23% to 26% during the last few years and industry analysts estimate an average annual growth rate of 10% through the year 2000. One of every sixteen U.S. homeowners lives in a mobile home. Major new international markets have opened up; these include Mexico, Russia, South Africa, and Poland. Because of the shortage of available housing in these countries, space limitations, price limitations, and the low wage rates, mobile homes are appealing.

At one time a mobile home loan was not considered by financial institutions as a home loan but rather a consumer loan. This meant much higher interest rates and short term loans of 3–5 years. Now mobile homes have been redefined as "manufactured housing" and qualify for home loans. They can be financed for up to 30 years at the going rate of other similarly priced homes. The new lower financing rates and terms have contributed to the dramatic increase in mobile home sales. However, the fact that most mobile homes are financed makes the industry susceptible to fluctuations in interest rates.

Financing can also be done "in-house." During the 1980's some lenders required mobile home dealers to guarantee loans. If the homeowner defaulted on the loan the dealer had to agree to take the home back. Some mobile home dealers spent millions of dollars to repay the defaulted loans. Today some of the larger dealerships offer in-house financing as not only a convenience to their customers but also as a profit center.

[1]Four sources provided information about the mobile home industry.

1. Babej, Marc E. "Lesson Learned." *Forbes* May 23, 1994: 85–86.
2. Giltenan, Edward. "Standing Out." *Forbes* Dec. 23, 1991: 132–33.
3. O'Hare, William and Barbara Clark O'Hare. *American Demographics* Jan. 1993: 26–34.
4. Fefer, Mark D. "More New Homes Hit the Road." *Fortune* Feb. 7, 1994: 16.

New building codes and national safety regulations established by the Department of Housing and Urban Development (HUD), the government agency that regulates the mobile home industry, has made financing and insuring mobile homes easier. More insurance companies are willing to provide coverage at a lower rate than the traditional rates that were about 10–15% higher than on-site homes.

While the image is changing, there are still many hurdles to overcome. Zoning laws in some states prohibit mobile homes in middle class neighborhoods while some zoning laws prohibit installing a manufactured home in any area where there are existing "site-built" homes. Other areas have adopted broad ordinances aimed at banning single-wide trailers. Mobile home manufacturers continue to lobby state and local governments in an effort to get these laws changed.

Two types of Mobile Home dealerships characterize the industry: (1) manufacturer-owner retail dealerships and (2) independent dealerships. Most manufacturers regulate the dealerships; they allow no more than one dealership within a geographic radius to sell their homes; otherwise, they would be competing against themselves. There are no economies of scale with respect to independent mobile home dealers. Most of the customers are "walk-ins"; price and quality are usually the primary differentiating factors, rather than brand identification. Capital requirements are fairly significant, usually averaging around $1.5 million for start-up costs that include land, building, equipment, and floorplanning. Technological factors are not a significant concern to dealers although they are a major concern to the manufacturer. Mobile homes are shipped from the factory with new technological changes already built-in. While some manufacturers construct, sell, and finance their own products, most manufacturers use authorized retail dealerships.

The mobile home industry exists in a complex legal environment. HUD regulates manufactured housing safety and building codes such as insulation guidelines, wind resistance, and ventilation. Zoning laws at both state and local levels, hauling laws, and certain state and local restrictions may apply.

The economy significantly affects the industry since affordability is the primary criteria of mobile home buyers. An economic slump has a mixed effect on mobile home sales. Poor economic conditions result in a decrease in the demand for mobile home by lower income families. However, middle income family demand for mobile homes may actually increase as the price of on-site housing becomes unaffordable.

A relatively new development in the mobile home industry is the land-lease community. In this type of planned community, the dealer owns the property and either sells [homes] or offers long-term leases to the mobile home owners. The leases can be for new or repossessed mobile homes. Upkeep of the property is covered by maintenance fees assessed to the mobile home resident. An example of a planned community is in Pinehurst, N.C., where the mobile homes are located on a golf course and sell for $75,000–$85,000.

Competitors

The Cleveland area has been growing in population for several years and is projected to continue growing. Cleveland is the gateway to the East Texas area which—along with the Austin area—shows the strongest growth in Texas. Cleveland is in the corridor connecting Houston and Dallas. Its proximity to Houston is the main reason for the population growth experienced in Cleveland and the surrounding area.

At the time Russell and Stephen opened their facility in Cleveland, there were no other "new" mobile home dealers in the immediate Cleveland area. There was another mobile home dealer located in the city, but it sold only "used" homes and repossessed mobile homes on consignment. Since opening in 1992, Russell and Stephen have seen their competition increase to ten competitors; all located within an eight mile radius of their home office. The closest and largest firms are Nationwide Mobile Homes and Advanced Housing. The competition uses low prices to gain competitive advantage. Unlike American Family, they do not keep large inventories on hand. The competitors are manufacturer-owner retail dealerships, an arrangement which limits them to the products sold by a specific manufacturer. American Family, however, is an independent dealer, able to order models from more than one manufacturer.

The Company

American Family Housing, Inc., operates an independent dealership. The company has a Sales Department, Service Department, Set-up (Trucking) Department, Parts Department, and a Finance and Insurance Department. The organizational structure and distribution of the 40 employees are shown in Figure 1.

Currently, American Family offers four major selections of mobile homes: The Schult, which is considered the Rolls Royce of mobile homes, The Fleetwood, The Patriot, and The Masterpiece. The company carries a large inventory of mobile homes, which means that a customer can come in today, pick out a home and have it delivered in 3–4 days, depending on loan processing. This is unique because most of their local competitors stock only models and, while the customer can pick the model they like, and customize it with their preferences, there is a wait of 2–4 weeks depending on the manufacturer. This option is also available through American Family as shown in the workflow diagram (Figure 2). Recently, the company added RV sales

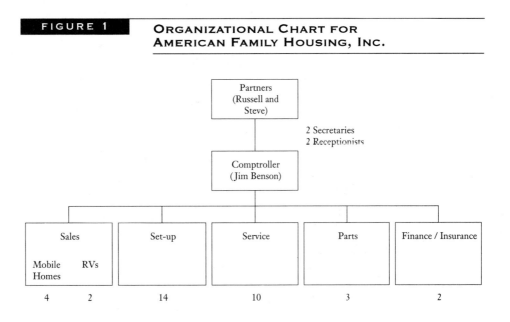

FIGURE 1   ORGANIZATIONAL CHART FOR AMERICAN FAMILY HOUSING, INC.

FIGURE 2	FLOW CHART FOR AMERICAN FAMILY HOUSING, INC., OPERATIONS

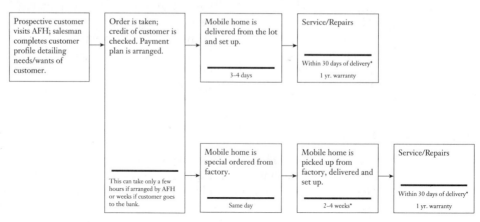

*Potential bottlenecks

and service at the Cleveland site. Although it is too early to evaluate the financial success of this new addition the two brothers feel that RV sales are a natural complement to mobile home sales.

In order to have an extensive inventory of homes, American Family uses what is referred to in the industry as floorplanning. The manufacturer ships and invoices American Family for the mobile home. Simultaneously, the manufacturer sends the title to a lender, who owns the home until it is sold. American Family owes the lender interest for each day the home remains unsold. This process allows American Family to have several of the same model mobile home available on the lot at one time for the convenience of the customer. This allows the consumer to choose the model mobile home they like instantly instead of having to order it from the manufacturer and wait for several weeks before receiving their home. The disadvantage of floorplanning to the company is the high carrying costs. Currently, American Family floorplans approximately $\frac{2}{3}$ of their homes at an interest rate of prime plus two percent; their goal is to floorplan no more than $\frac{1}{3}$ of their inventory. This will eventually occur as units are sold and not replaced on the lot. When this goal is achieved, American Family would be able to enjoy higher profit margins because there would be lower carrying costs. The proportion that is not floorplanned represents models of mobile homes. This is the alternative to floorplanning. Buyers use these models to decide what to special order directly from the manufacturers; this type of purchase involves no carrying costs to the dealer.

American Family Housing, Inc.'s mission is to provide quality standard housing in Mobile Homes that is acceptable to its customers and that will provide a long-term benefit to those customers. In support of this, the company is committed to being recognized by customers as responsive to their service needs and as a technically superior and innovative supplier of high quality housing. They aspire to be recognized by employees, as well as the business community, for excellence and integrity in managing the company's business. The company is also committed to providing programs and services in the most cost-effective manner and in maintaining a visible reputation for consistently achieving internal planning results.

EXHIBIT 1	**BALANCE SHEET**				

	12/31/93 %	12/31/94 %	25% of yr. Annualized 03/31/95 %	RMA SIC # 52712 %	VAR %
Cash and Equiv	−7.54	−4.94	−0.49	12.2	−104.0
Accts Rcvbl	0.00	0.00	0.00	7.6	−100.0
Inventory	82.22	64.12	65.89	57.7	14.2
All other Current	0.00	0.00	0.00	2.5	−100.0
TOTAL CURR ASSESTS	74.68	59.18	65.40	80.00	−18.3
Fxd Assts—Net	11.58	14.41	11.06	12.7	−12.9
Jt Vent & Invst	0.00	0.00	0.00	0.0	inf
Intangibl—Net	0.00	0.00	0.00	0.3	−100.0
Oth N-Current	13.74	26.41	23.54	6.90	241.2
TOTAL ASSETS	100.0	100.0	100.0	100.0	241.2
Nts Pay—shtrm	0.00	0.00	0.00	43.4	−100.0
Cur Matur LTD	0.00	0.34	1.67	1.8	−7.2
Accts Payable	0.00	0.00	0.00	4.5	−100.0
Inc Tax Paybl	0.00	0.00	0.00	0.5	−100.0
All oth Curr	3.03	2.67	2.37	8.2	−71.1
TOTAL CURR LIAB	3.03	3.00	4.04	58.4	−93.1
Long Term Debt	73.69	64.77	66.62	8.7	665.7
Deferred Taxes	0.00	0.99	0.18	0.4	−55.4
All oth N-Cur	0.00	0.00	0.17	3.3	−94.7
Net Worth	23.28	31.23	28.99	29.3	−1.0
TOTAL LIAB & NW	100.00	100.00	100.0	100.0	

	Income Statement				
Net Sales	100.0	100.0	100.0	100.0	
Gross Profit	15.07	13.84	19.94	21.9	−9.0
Opertng Costs	8.19	7.32	7.53	19.4	−16.2
Opertng Prof	6.88	6.52	12.40	2.5	396.0
All oth Exp	1.27	1.44	2.06	−0.3	−788.1
Prft Bef Tax	5.61	5.08	10.34	2.8	269.2

| EXHIBIT 2 | INCOME STATEMENT | | | | | |

	12/31/93	%	12/31/94 $000	%	25% of Yr Annualized 03/31/95 $000	%
GROSS SALES	6,432.2	100.0	10,896.5	100.0	10,333.0	100.0
Less: dis/Ret	—	—	—	—	—	—
NET SALES	6,432.2	100.0	10,896.5	100.0	10,333.0	100.0
Less: COGS	5,463.0	84.9	9,388.6	86.2	8,273.0	80.1
GROSS PROFIT	969.2	15.1	1,507.9	13.8	2,059.9	19.9
OPERATING EXPENSES						
Adver & Promo	41.2	0.6	60.2	0.6	77.3	0.7
Bad Debts	—	—	—	—	—	—
Bank Svc Chrg	—	—	—	—	—	—
Auto	6.2	0.1	—	—	—	—
Fuel	29.3	0.5	—	—	—	—
Undistrib.	—	—	33.5	0.3	8.2	0.1
Total	35.5	0.6	33.5	0.3	8.2	0.1
Comissions	—	—	—	—	—	—
Amort Intang	—	—	—	—	—	—
Deprec/Depltn	53.2	0.8	0.0	0.0	—	—
Dues & Pubs	0.7	0.0	3.7	0.0	2.4	0.0
Emply Ben Prg	—	—	—	—	—	—
Freight	3.3	0.1	6.1	0.1	7.2	0.1
Insurance						
Veh	0.0	0.0				
Group	0.5	0.0				
Lot	14.9	0.2				
Other	1.2	0.0				
Undistrib.	—	—	48.4	0.4	74.7	0.7
Total	16.6	0.3	48.4	0.4	74.7	0.7
Laundry & Clg	4.3	0.1	9.8	0.1	16.8	0.2
Leased Equip	—	—	—	—	—	—
Legal/Profess	3.2	0.0	10.0	0.1	10.5	0.1
Office Expense	21.9	0.3	26.3	0.2	24.9	0.2
Outside Labor	—	—	—	—	—	—
Pens P/R Tax	19.0	0.3	54.7	0.5	82.6	0.8
Rent	35.3	0.5	58.1	0.5	70.5	0.7
Rprs & Maint	40.2	0.6	73.2	0.7	80.3	0.8
Operating Sup	7.1	0.1	20.7	0.2	—	—
Taxes & Licen						
Oth	5.3	0.1				
Pers	7.0	0.1				
Real	3.7	0.1				
Undistr	—	—	52.3	0.5	69.0	0.7
Total	16.0	0.2	52.3	0.5	69.0	0.7
Travel & Ent	11.2	0.2	46.5	0.4	47.8	0.5
Util & Tele						
Tele	26.9	0.4	—	—	—	—
Util	16.2	0.3	—	—	—	—

| EXHIBIT 2 | INCOME STATEMENT (CONTINUED) | | | | | |

	12/31/93	%	12/31/94 $000	%	25% of Yr Annualized 03/31/95 $000	%
Undistrib.	—	—	65.2	0.6	79.4	0.8
Total	43.1	0.7	65.2	0.6	79.4	0.8
WAGES Salary—Offcrs						
Bon	103.3	1.6	—	—	—	—
Sal	39.0	0.6	—	—	—	—
Undistrib	—	—	131.3	1.2	24.0	0.2
Total	142.0	2.2	131.3	1.2	24.0	0.2
Payroll						
Sal	31.5	0.5	—	—	—	—
Bon	1.3	0.0	—	—	—	—
Undistrib.	—	—	97.3	0.9	103.1	1.0
Total	32.8	0.5	97.3	0.9	103.1	1.0
Fixed 1	—	—	—	—	—	—
Fixed 2	—	—	—	—	—	—
VAR 1	—	—	—	—	—	—
VAR 2	—	—	—	—	—	—
TTL OPER EXP	526.6	8.2	797.3	7.3	778.6	7.5
OPERTNG PROF	442.6	6.9	710.7	6.5	1,218.4	12.4
Interest						
Floor	67.8	1.1	—	—	—	—
Oth	3.1	0.0	—	—	—	—
Undistrib.	—	—	138.3	1.3	195.9	1.9
Total	70.9	1.1	138.3	1.3	195.9	1.9
Misc Expenses						
Con	0.1	0.0	—	—	—	—
Cred	5.0	0.1	—	—	—	—
Cust	3.2	0.0	—	—	—	—
Ext	0.1	0.0	—	—	—	—
Lawn	0.7	0.0	—	—	—	—
Train	0.3	0.0	—	—	—	—
Uni	1.2	0.0	—	—	—	—
Undistrib.	0.0	0.2	18.3	0.2	17.3	0.2
Total						
Oth Exp (Inc) TOTAL OTH EXP	81.5	1.3	156.6	1.4	213.3	2.1
PROF BEF TAX	361.1	5.6	554.1	5.1	1,068.1	10.3
Inc Tax	—	—	—	—	—	—
PROF AFT TAX	361.1	5.6	554.1	5.1	1,068.1	10.3
Div/Distribtn	—	—	—	—	—	—
Ret Earnings	361.1	5.6	554.1	5.1	1,068.1	10.3

Financial Data

American Family completed their second full year of operation in December, 1994. The company's financial reports are presented in Exhibits 1 and 2 along with Robert Morris Associates (RMA) industry data for Standard Industrial Code (SIC) #52712.

Comparisons between American Family and the industry are possible but complex because:

- The mobile home industry, as a whole, encompasses both independent dealers and manufacturer-dealers. The two very different types of dealers are not tracked separately by the industry so it is not possible to compare an independent dealer, such as American Family, with only independent dealers.

- Industry tracks public-owned companies/manufacturers like Schult, Fleetwood, Clayton, and Oakwood. These companies manufacture and maintain their own retail sales facilities. Using industry ratios when comparing small independent dealerships like American Family can provide a distorted view of the operations, if these exceptions are not considered.

American Family maintains inventory on the lot for customer convenience—this is unique to the industry. Most dealerships stock only models which customers use to choose decor and options. Then the order is placed with the manufacturer. This means that most dealers have no inventory. The fact that American Family does have a high inventory results in some unfavorable ratio variances in the liquidity ratios when American Family is compared to other dealerships in the industry.

Company Operations

American Family's sales can be broken down into two parts. First, and most important, are the sales from mobile homes. At least 90% of the revenues generated come from the sales of its mobile homes. In Russell's words: "We are in the business to sell, sell, sell." Parts sales are the second type of sales generated by the company. They have a fairly large store which contains many smaller parts used to repair mobile homes and RVs. They also have a program in place which allows customers to order larger parts, such as dishwashers, bathtubs, refrigerators, etc., that are not stocked in the store due to their size. The convenience provided by this type of sales facility is appreciated by customers and helps to generate additional revenues.

Service is an important aspect of the company's operations, primarily because they are under contract to service their sales for one full year after the purchase date. This service is considered warranty work, but it must be done in a timely manner in order to keep a good relationship with customers. However, customer surveys mailed to all buyers indicate that services after-the-sale are not being provided in a timely manner. Other types of services offered to their customers include installation of decking or skirting. These services are offered to provide the customer with the needed assistance to make their mobile home "look" complete. These types of services are only provided to the customers who buy a mobile home from the company.

The service department has shown a consistent loss. Part of the problem is the requirement to provide the warranty work. The work is performed and then invoiced to the manufacturer for a refund. The manufacturer is sometimes slow in reimbursing the company and may make deductions from the invoice resulting in a loss on the warranty work. The service department has also been slow to invoice customers for billable services. During the first 3–4 months of 1995 no services were billed and the service department showed a substantial loss. The goal for the service department is to operate at break-even or no more than $3,000 loss. Employee turnover and lack of experience and supervision in determining what is billable and what is warranty work to the customer [have] contributed to losses incurred by the service department.

The service department is also responsible for refurbishing trade-ins and repossessions. The mobile home is moved into the shop and is worked on when employees aren't busy doing something else. No records or logs are kept of time and materials used in refurbishing the mobile homes. The service manger is responsible for estimating what needs to be done, how long it should take, and what parts are needed. The company needs to reach 60% utilization of its service capacity to cover costs since currently service employees are guaranteed pay for an eight hour workday.

Marketing

Newspapers are the company's most costly advertising medium. They spend approximately $6,000 per month on newspaper ads. However, the company has not been pleased by the customer response to these ads. The company feels that word of mouth and by-sight marketing are their most effective marketing practices. Customer surveys indicate that many people visit their dealership due to word of mouth from former customers. While word of mouth has proven to be one of the most beneficial types of promotion, by-sight marketing has also proven to be effective. By-sight marketing involves the selection of high trafficked locations with easy access for potential customers. Because of their high visibility locations off freeways, American Family has seen customer traffic remain steady over the past two years.

Management

American Family is a partnership. Management consists of two equal owners and a controller. The owners have two different management styles; Russell wants to be the Wal-Mart of the mobile home industry while Stephen wants to be a hands on person in all aspects of the operations. The controller of the operation, Jim Benson, is relied on very heavily for his skills and expertise. He handles many complex aspects of the daily business operations. His main duties consist of general accounting, writing all software programs, hiring and training all personnel, including department managers, tracking all internal information. He is also the liaison between the staff and Russell and Stephen. There are plans to hire a full-time accountant in the near future to handle the accounting work in-house. This would take a great deal of responsibility off Jim's hands. Jim has written many unique programs that will enable him to track all procedures and activities within the organization. This tracking system has decreased the time required to monitor these activities.

The number of employees has increased from the original seven to over forty. Employees are selected using a national recruiting firm which does the initial background checks, drug testing, and qualifying of potential employees. The potential employee is then interviewed by an American Family division manager. If the division manager decides the applicant is qualified, Jim meets with the potential employee. If the employee is hired, he or she works on probation for 30 to 60 days to see if they can "cut the mustard." If not, they are let go and the process starts over again. Over the last two years the company has turned over its entire staff at least once. Since employees have less than two years experience at American Family, continuity and coordination of services suffer. The high turnover also increases the training needs.

For the most part, training is done by the manager of each division. After successfully completing the probation period, employees are given a raise and sent out on their own. If a new manager needs to be trained, Jim is responsible for that training. The training of a manager usually takes much longer, because of the number of duties placed on their shoulders. Managers must be capable of performing all aspects of the jobs in their department.

The managers from each division meet every Wednesday morning to discuss any suggestions, problems, and conflicts they might have. These meetings are also designed to keep the division managers and upper management aware of all current situations that are happening throughout the company. The meetings are used to coordinate time schedules between delivery, setup, and servicing since these departments share the same personnel. A great deal of time is spent struggling with the effects of high turnover and the bottlenecks in the system (shown in the work flow chart, Figure 2). The company also has yearly meetings to discuss what has taken place over the past year and to determine if their goals and objectives were met and to suggest ways to make changes. They also meet near the end of the year to discuss and plan goals and objectives for the coming year.

At the end of year meeting in 1995, Russell, Steve and Jim met to review the company's long term objectives to be achieved by the year 2000:

1. At least an 18% gross profit from sales;

2. A management by objective process involving all departments in the organization;

3. 3 satellite operations; and

4. The position of industry leader in terms of sales and service.

"Well," said Russell, "Dad will be proud of us! I think we're well on our way to meeting the objectives he helped us set back in 1992. Remember, we asked him then what he would do with the business and he helped us determine those four objectives to work on? We've certainly met the first one!" "Yes," agreed Jim, "but what about the other objectives? To be the industry leader we're going to have to improve our service. We've been receiving a number of complaints about how long it takes to get the service . . . and our turnover rate really worries me." "You're both right," observed Steve, "now, let's decide what we need to do to stay ahead of the competition. Remember, we said we want to be the Wal-Mart of the mobile home business.

Opportunity Recogn...
Developing Distinctive Competencies

Key Topics

- **Sources of Business Ideas**

- **The Role of Creativity**

- **The Nature of the Creative Process**

- **Product/Market Matrix**

- **New Product Development Process**

Business Ideas

The origin of an entrepreneurial business starts with a creative idea. Where do creative ideas come from? How are they generated, nurtured, and moved along in the process of developing them into the full splendor of a business opportunity? Can a person develop a series or a plethora of good ideas that can be turned into entrepreneurial endeavors?

Sources of good ideas are all around us. Likely places to find them include jobs, hobbies, friends, newspapers, television, the Internet, advertisements, social gatherings, special interests, and family life. Other ideas may come from unlikely sources, such as a vacation, the process of confronting a particular problem, stress, historical events, and technological and environmental changes. Still other ideas come from individuals themselves, through brainstorming, free association, matching (or opposite) strategies, library visits, bookstores, or magazine racks. The National Federation of Independent Business has found, however, that most business ideas come from work or hobbies (Figure 5.1).

The Role of Creativity

It is important to recognize the role of creativity in the innovative process because creativity—that is, the generation of ideas—results in the improved efficiency and effectiveness of a system.[1] Although the origin of an idea is important, creative thinking

FIGURE 5.1   **SOURCES OF NEW BUSINESS IDEAS AMONG MEN AND WOMEN**

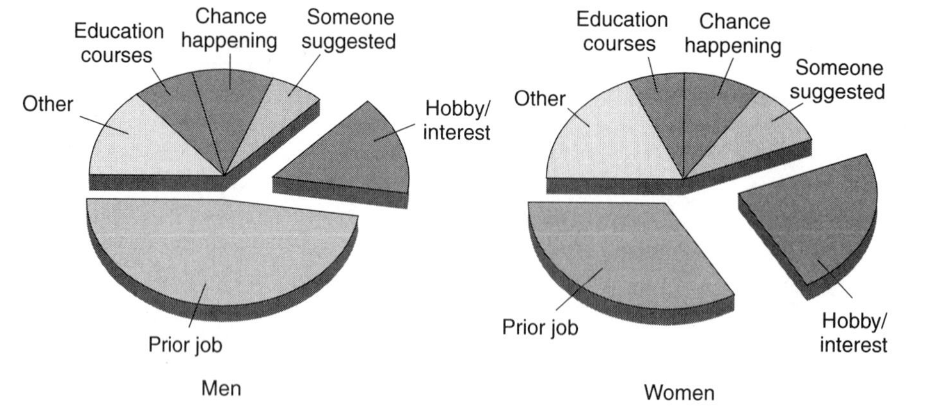

SOURCE: William J. Dennis, *A Small Business Primer* (Washington, DC: National Federation of Independent Business, 1993), 27. Reprinted with permission.

---

[1]Lloyd W. Fernald, Jr., "The Underlying Relationship between Creativity, Innovation, and Entrepreneurship," *Journal of Creative Behavior* 22, no. 3 (1988): 196–202.

plays a critical role in its development.[2] In other words, there is a major difference between speculating about an idea and initiating one that is the product of extended thinking, research, experience, and work. More importantly, a prospective entrepreneur must have the desire to take a good idea through the various development stages. Thus innovation represents a marriage of the vision to create a good idea and the perseverance and dedication to stick with the concept through its implementation.

Successful entrepreneurs are able to blend imaginative, creative thinking with systematic, logical processing abilities; this combination is the key to their success. In addition, potential entrepreneurs should always look for unique opportunities to fill unmet needs and wants. If they can sense economic potential in business problems by continually asking "What if . . . ?" or "Why not . . . ?", they will develop an ability to see, recognize, and develop opportunities where others find only problems.

The Nature of the Creative Process

Thinking creatively is a process that can be developed and improved.[3] Everyone is creative to some degree; as is the case with many abilities and talents (for example, athletic, artistic), however, some individuals have greater aptitudes for creativity than do others. Also, some people have been raised and educated in environments that encourage them to think and act creatively. For others, the process is more difficult because their creativity has not been positively reinforced. If those individuals are to become creative, they must learn how to implement the creative process.

Creativity is not some mysterious and rare talent reserved for a selected few. It is a distinct, sometimes illogical, way of looking at the world. The creative process depends on seeing relationships between things that others cannot see (for example, modems—that is, using telephones to transfer data between computers).[4]

The creative process involves four phases or steps. Most experts agree on the general nature and relationship between these phases, although they refer to them by a variety of names.[5] Experts also agree that these phases do not always occur in the same order for every creative activity. For creativity to occur, chaos must exist, but it should be a chaos that can be structured and focused. We will examine this four-step process using the most typical structural development.

Phase 1: Background or Knowledge Accumulation

Successful creations are generally preceded by investigation and information gathering. This research usually involves extensive reading, conversations with others working in the field, attendance at professional meetings and workshops, and a general absorption of information relative to the problem or issue under study. Additional investigation in

[2]Timolthy A. Matherly and Ronald E. Goldsmith, "The Two Faces of Creativity," *Business Horizons* (Sept.–Oct. 1985): 8. See also Bruce G. Whiting, "Creativity and Entrepreneurship: How Do They Relate?" *Journal of Creative Behavior* 22, no. 3 (1988): 178–183.

[3]See Edward deBono, *Serious Creativity: Using the Power of Creativity to Create New Ideas* (New York: Harper Business, 1992).

[4]See Dale Dauten, *Taking Chances: Lessons in Putting Passion and Creativity in Your Work Life* (New York: New Market Press, 1986).

[5]Edward deBono, *Six Thinking Hats* (Boston: Little Brown, 1985); and Edward deBono, "Serious Creativity," *The Journal of Quality and Participation* 18, no. 5 (1995): 12.

both related and unrelated fields is sometimes involved. This exploration gives the individual a variety of perspectives on the problem, and it is particularly important to the entrepreneur, who needs a basic understanding of all aspects of the development of the new product, service, or business venture.

Some of the more useful ways to practice the creative search for background knowledge include the following:

- Read informational material from a variety of fields.
- Join professional groups and associations.
- Attend professional meetings and seminars.
- Travel to new places.
- Talk to anyone and everyone about your subject.
- Scan magazines, newspapers, and journals for articles related to your subject.
- Develop a subject library for future reference.
- Carry a small notebook and record useful information.
- Devote time to pursuing your natural curiosities.[6]

Phase 2: The Incubation Process

Creative individuals allow their subconscious thoughts to mull over the tremendous amounts of information they gather during the preparation phase. This incubation process often occurs while they are engaged in activities totally unrelated to the subject or problem. It happens even when they are sleeping, which accounts for the advice frequently given to a person who is frustrated by what appears to be an unsolvable problem: "Why don't you sleep on it?"[7] Getting away from a problem and letting the subconscious mind work on it often allows creativity to spring forth. Some of the most helpful steps to induce incubation include the following:

- Engaging in routine, mindless activities (cutting the grass, painting the house).
- Exercising regularly.
- Playing (sports, board games, puzzles).
- Thinking about the project or problem before falling asleep.
- Meditating and/or practicing self-hypnosis.
- Sitting back and relaxing on a regular basis.[8]

---

[6]For a discussion on the development of creativity, see Eugene Raudsepp, *How Creative Are You?* (New York: Perigee Books, 1981); and Arthur B. Van Gundy, *108 Ways to Get a Bright Idea and Increase Your Creative Potential* (Englewood Cliffs, NJ: Prentice-Hall, 1983).

[7]T. A. Nosanchuk, J. A. Ogrodnik, and Tom Henigan, "A Preliminary Investigation of Incubation in Short Story Writing," *Journal of Creative Behavior* 22, no. 4 (1988): 279–280. This study reported that an eight-day incubation period was associated with significantly elevated story writing creativity.

[8]W. W. Harman and H. Rheingold, *Higher Creativity: Liberating the Unconscious for Breakthrough Insights* (Los Angeles: Tarcher, 1984); and Daniel Goleman, Paul Kaufman, and Michael Ray, *The Creative Spirit* (New York: Penguin Books, 1993).

Phase 3: The Idea Experience

The third phase of the creative process is often the most exciting because it is at this time that the individual discovers the idea or solution that he or she is seeking. The average person often—and incorrectly—perceives this phase to be the only component of creativity.

As with the incubation process, new and innovative ideas often emerge while the person is doing something unrelated to the enterprise, venture, or investigation (for example, taking a shower, driving on an interstate highway, leafing through a newspaper). Sometimes the idea appears as a bolt out of the blue, but usually the answer comes to the individual incrementally—slowly but surely the person begins to formulate the solution. Because it is often difficult to determine when the incubation process ends and the idea experience phase begins, many people are unaware of when they move from Phase 2 to Phase 3.

In any event, there are several ways to speed up the idea experience:

- Daydream and fantasize about your project.

- Practice your hobbies.

- Work in a leisurely environment (for example, at home instead of the office).

- Put the problem on the back burner.

- Keep a notebook at bedside to record late-night or early-morning ideas.

- Take breaks while working.[9]

Phase 4: Evaluation and Implementation

The fourth phase is the most difficult step of a creative endeavor and requires a great deal of courage, self-discipline, and perseverance. Successful entrepreneurs are able to identify those ideas that are workable and that they have skills to implement. More importantly, they do not give up when they encounter temporary obstacles.[10] Often they will fail several times before they successfully develop their best ideas, and in some cases they may take the idea in an entirely different direction or discover a new and more workable ideal while struggling to implement the original idea. Another important part of this phase is to rework ideas to get them into final form. Because an idea frequently emerges from Phase 3 in rough form, it needs to be modified or tested to determine its final shape.

Some of the most useful suggestions for carrying out this phase follow:

- Increase your energy level with proper exercise, diet, and rest.

- Educate yourself about the business planning process and all facets of business.

- Test your ideas with knowledgeable people.

---

[9]For more on idea development, see A. F. Osborn, *Applied Imagination*, 3rd ed. (New York: Scribners, 1963); William J. Gordon, *Synetics* (New York: Harper & Row, 1961); and Ted Pollock, "A Personal File of Stimulating Ideas, Little Known Facts and Daily Problem Solvers," *Supervision* 4 (April 1995): 24.

[10]Martin F. Rosenman, "Serendipity and Scientific Discovery," *Journal of Creative Behavior* 22, no. 2 (1988): 132–138.

- Take notice of your intuitive hunches and feelings.

- Educate yourself about the selling process.

- Learn about organizational policies and practices.

- Seek advice from others.

- View the problems that you encounter while implementing your ideas as challenges.[11]

Acceptance of New Ideas

Behavioral scientists have long studied the reactions of consumers to new ideas. Their research has shown that common attributes of successful ideas include the following:

- The idea should have a relative advantage over existing products or services. For example, the innovation might allow a person to perform a task more efficiently.

- The innovation must be compatible with existing attitudes and beliefs. It should not require a dramatic change in the buyer's behavior.

- It should not be so complex that the buyer has a difficult time understanding how it should be used.

- The results or benefits of the innovation must be easily communicable to potential users.

- It is helpful if the innovation is divisible, meaning that users can try the innovation without incurring a large risk. The distribution of samples or the acceptance of trial users, for examples, would allow potential buyers to use the innovation without risking a purchase.

- The innovation must be readily available for purchase once the buyer decides to make a purchase.

- The buyer must believe that the innovation satisfies one of his or her needs by giving some immediate benefit.[12]

Product/Market Matrix

Opportunities may be recognized and exploited in a variety of ways. New markets may open up that are receptive to both new and old products or services. Life cycles of declining products or services may be rejuvenated by improvements, updating, repackaging, or renovating. New products or services are often welcome in both old and new markets. In many cases, a new channel of distribution such as the Internet and e-commerce represents an innovative idea that contributes to the new idea's success.

---

[11]For more on implementation, see John M. Keil, *The Creative Mystique: How to Manage It, Nurture It, and Make It Pay* (New York: Wiley, 1985). See also James F. Brandowski, *Corporate Imagination Plus: Five Steps to Translating Innovative Strategies into Action* (New York: The Free Press, 1990).

[12]Everett M. Rogers and Floyd Shoemaker, *Communication of Innovations* (New York: The Free Press, 1971), 50–51.

TABLE 5.1	PRODUCT/MARKET MATRIX	
	Markets	
Products or Services	**Existing**	**New**
Existing	Increased demand and penetration	Market diversification and geographic expansion
New	Product or service modification and diversification	Pure invention of new product or service for a new market

Table 5.1 depicts the product/market matrix. Ideally, entrepreneurs would prefer to operate in the lower-right quadrant, in which they are providing a new product or service to a new market. Given the rapid pace of change in our society, new opportunities will most certainly arise in both dimensions of the model.

Recognizing such opportunities is one of the key elements that defines entrepreneurship and makes it unique.[13] In fact, one researcher believes that understanding the opportunity identification process represents the primary intellectual issue for scholars developing a theory of entrepreneurship that makes it theoretically distinct from other disciplines.[14] Entrepreneurial innovations create and destroy entire industries; in comparison, efficient markets appropriate incremental innovations. Joseph Schumpeter has identified several entrepreneurial innovations:

- The introduction of a new product of service.

- The introduction of a distinctive improvement in the level of quality for a product of service.

- The introduction of a new method of production or distribution.

- The opening of a new market.

- The capture or creation of a new source of supply.

- New forms of organization within an industry.[15]

Every plant is a weed and every mineral is just a rock in nature until an entrepreneur comes along and endows them with a new capacity to create wealth. According to Peter Drucker, innovation is the specific instrument of entrepreneurship and entrepreneurs are expected to learn to practice systematic innovation.

Successful entrepreneurs, whatever their individual motivation—be it money, power, curiosity, or the desire for fame and recognition—try to create

[13]Alexander Ardichvili, Richard Cardozo, and Sourav Ray, "A Theory of Entrepreneurial Opportunity Identification and Development," *Marketing-Entrepreneurship Interface Conference*, August 3–5, 2000, Chicago.

[14]Connie Marie Gaglio, "Opportunity Identification: Review, Critique and Suggested Research Directions." In Jerome Katz (ed.), *Advances in Entrepreneurship, Firm Emergence and Growth*, vol. 3 (Greenwich: JAI Press, 3, 1997).

[15]Joseph Schumpeter, *The Theory of Economic Development* (Cambridge, MA: Harvard University Press, 1934.)

value and to make a contribution. Still, successful entrepreneurs aim high. They are not content simply to improve on what already exists, or to modify it. They try to create new and different satisfactions, to convert a "material" into a "resource," or to combine existing resources in a new and more productive configuration.[16]

Innovative opportunities arise from seven sources:

- Unexpected events.

- Incongruity between the actual and the possible.

- Innovation based on a process need.

- Changes in industry or market structure.

- Demographic changes.

- Changes in perception mood and meaning.

- New knowledge created by research.

Unexpected Events

Unexpected events or unpremeditated discovery implies that the entrepreneur experienced an external sudden revelation that led to a good idea. "It is precisely because the unexpected jolts us out of our preconceived notions, our assumptions, our certainties, that it is such a fertile source of innovation."[17] The unexpected event often happens without much clue as to why. Penicillin and nylon resulted from unexpected accidents. In the latter case, an assistant left a burner turned on over the weekend and on Monday morning the chemist in charge at DuPont found that the contents of the kettle had congealed into fibers.

If such serendipitous events occur, entrepreneurs should be ready to exploit them by asking what effects it would have if the events were fully exploited. In which directions could they lead? Is the event a convertible opportunity? How might one go about implementing the change in a series of deliberate steps?

Accidental discovery is based on the premise that entrepreneurs do not search for opportunities but recognize the value of new information when it falls into their laps. In a review of the literature on this topic, several authors[18] documented Kirzner,[19] who distinguished between discovery and successful search by noting that the former involves a surprise that accompanies the realization that one had overlooked something readily available. In fact, firms founded on accidental discovery venture ideas, which were not subjected to formal screening, reached the break-even point more rapidly than those whose ideas resulted from a formal search.[20] In researching styles

---

[16]Peter Drucker, *Innovation and Entrepreneurship*, (New York: Harper and Row, 1985), 35.

[17]Peter Drucker, p. 50.

[18]Ardichvili, Cardozo, and Ray.

[19]I. Kirzner "The Primacy of Entrepreneurial Discovery." In A. Seldon (ed.), *The Prime Mover of Progress* (London: The Institute of Economic Affairs, 1980) 5–30.

[20]R. Teach, R. Schwarz, and F. Tarpley, *"The Recognition and Exploitation of Opportunity in the Software Industry: A Study of Surviving Firms."* In R. H. Brockhaus, et al (eds.), *Frontiers of Entrepreneurship Research* (Wellesley, MA: Babson College, 1989) 383–397.

of opportunity recognition, the experts found that only about one-half of the software firm presidents studied favored systematic approaches to searching for opportunities. In an earlier study, most entrepreneurs were found to recognize rather than actively seek out opportunities for their firms.[21]

Incongruity between the Actual and the Possible

Another source of innovation is the incongruity between normative positions and reality—that is, between what is and what everyone assumes the situation to be or would like it to be. Entrepreneurs who are able to spot these trends can focus their new enterprise on a new product or new service by exploiting the incongruity or gap. These innovators can silently creep into the industry before existing businesses or suppliers wake up to the fact that they have new and dangerous competition.

Peter Drucker cites examples of incongruity such as the integrated steel process versus the mini-steel mills, health care expenditures of 1 percent of GNP in 1929 versus 11 to 13 percent today, the hardware clerk who was willing to listen to customers' frustrations, and the pharmaceutical company salesman who reacted to the concerns of eye surgeons.

Incongruities can also exist between where we are and where we would like to be. Burch lists several "frustrating" situations that are less than ideal:

- When work ends, people are tired.
- Traffic frustrations are encountered on the way home from work.
- Feet are hot and tired.
- Clothes are rumpled, seem to cling, and are uncomfortable.
- A wife or husband is tired and grouchy.
- People experience postwork blahs.
- The grocery store seems crowded and slow.
- Parents must shout at children to get them in for their baths.
- People who have dogs must walk and curb them.
- Perhaps the dog is female and in heat, and every stray mutt within a mile is making passes.
- Predinner cocktails are needed to unwind.
- The TV news is depressing.
- The lawn needs mowing; the garden needs weeding; the roses have to be clipped; and so on.
- The kids are grouchy and hungry.

---

[21]R. H. Koller, "On the Source of Entrepreneurial Ideas." In *Frontiers of Entrepreneurship Research* (Wellesley, MA: Babson College, 1988).

- Dinner preparations are slow, noisy, and smelly.
- Telephone solicitors are irritating.[22]

Each of these situations identifies a state where we would rather not be—incongruous with our ideal—thus setting up opportunities to resolve the disparity. Ingenious entrepreneurs can devise inventive or innovative solutions to reach the desired/normative state.

Innovation Based on a Process Need

A process need existing within a functioning operation can also lead to innovations. It often supplies the missing link of a task to be done, perhaps it perfects a process that already exists, replaces a link that is weak, or redesigns an existing old process around newly available knowledge.

In 1885, printed material of all kinds was growing at an exponential rate, but typesetting had gone unchanged since Gutenberg, who had developed his printing press 400 years earlier. Printing was slow and labor-intensive work, requiring high skill and long years of apprenticeship. Ottmar Mergenthaler designed a keyboard that made possible the mechanical selection and assembly of letters, adjusting them in line, with a mechanism that returned each letter to its proper receptacle for future use. His innovation was based on an incongruity, as there were already high-speed presses and paper washing made on high-speed paper machines.

Changes in Industry or Market Structure

Industry and market structures appear so stable that many people are likely to view them as a foreordained part of the order of nature and certain to endure forever. Consider United Airlines, the world's largest air carrier, which was scheduled to merge with a competitor and thereby to control a significant part of the airline industry. Suddenly the company's pilots initiated a work slowdown, fuel prices rose, schedules were disrupted, flights were canceled, and United was unable to stop the hemorrhaging of customer losses who voted with their feet and dollars and flew with more reliable competitors. The firm's strong reputation became weak and its stock price dropped 33 percent in eight months. The airline's employee stock ownership plan, which was originally created to help avoid acrimonious labor situations, may have been doomed from the start.

As demonstrated by this case, market and industry structures are actually quite brittle, with small disruptions sometimes leading to a rapid disintegration. To continue to do business as before is an invitation to disaster and might well condemn a company to extinction. Such a major change in market or industry structure is also a major opportunity for innovation, as it offers exceptional opportunities that are highly visible and quite predictable to outsiders. Perceptive entrepreneurs who think innovatively can become a major factor in the industry with relatively little risk. Four highly visible indicators point toward impending change in industry structure:

---

[22]John G. Burch, *Entrepreneurship* (New York: John Wiley & Sons, 1986), 55.

- Rapid growth of an industry, with the industry growing significantly faster than the economy or population. No one is inclined to tamper with existing practices that are perceived to be highly successful, yet they are becoming obsolete.

- Ways in which traditional leaders define and segment the market that no longer reflect reality. Reports and figures still represent the traditional, historical view of the market, however.

- Convergence of technologies that were previously seen as distinctly separate (for example, telephone technology and computer technology).

- An industry in which the manner of doing business is changing rapidly. Such an industry is ripe for basic structural change. The shift of American physicians from private practice to HMOs was brought about by the advent of an innovative service company that could design the group's office, offer advice on equipment, and either train or manage the group practice.

Large dominant producers and suppliers tend to become complacent and arrogant after having remained successful and unchallenged for many years. They tend to review the newcomer as insignificant or amateurish. But when a newcomer carves out its own share of the market, the traditional firms often find it difficult to mobilize themselves for counteraction. Their tendency to neglect the fastest-growing market segments and cling to dysfunctional and obsolete practices allows the innovator a good chance to capture a share of the market.

Perceptive entrepreneurs can take advantage of the turbulence resulting from the changes in the market and industry. "In a free enterprise system, *opportunities* are spawned when there are changing circumstances, chaos, confusion, inconsistencies, lags or leads, knowledge and information gaps, and a variety of other vacuums in an industry or market. Changes in the business environment and, therefore, anticipation of these changes, are so critical in entrepreneurship that constant vigilance for changes is a valuable habit. It is thus that an entrepreneur with credibility, creativity, and decisiveness can seize an opportunity while others study it."[23]

Demographic Changes

Demographic changes are often easy to spot or predict because they are clear and unambiguous. Changes in population size, age structure, composition, employment age structure, educational status, and income have known lead times and predictable consequences. Demographics provoke the next series of questions in the entrepreneurial development process:

What's the fastest-growing segment of the population?

What's their labor force participation?

What's their level of education?

Into which socioeconomic class do they fall?

---

[23]Jeffry Timmons, *New Venture Creation: Entrepreneurship for the 21st Century*, 5th ed. (Boston: Irwin McGraw Hill, 1999), 81.

What's their level of mobility?

What's their income distribution? Disposable income? Discretionary income?

What's the propensity to spend in a two-income family?

What's their occupational segmentation?

What opportunities do these developments offer?

What are the various values, aspiration levels, and needs and wants of these various groups?

Finding answers to these questions allows entrepreneurs to market automobiles, clothing, housing, education, and grooming and leisure services, among others, to their customers. Peter Drucker has cited a fine-tuned example of how to market to a specific demographic group:

> The success of Club Mediterranee in the travel and resort business is squarely the result of exploiting demographic changes: the emergence of large numbers of young adults in Europe and the United States who are affluent and educated but only one generation away from working-class origins. Still quite unsure of themselves, still not self-confident as tourists, they are eager to have somebody with the know-how to organize their vacations, their travel, their fun—and yet they are not really comfortable either with their working-class parents or with older, middle-class people. Thus, they are ready-made customers for a new and "exotic" version of the old teenage hangout.[24]

Demographics can also be analyzed to determine which groups are early or late consumer adopters of innovations. Hills[25] has summarized the characteristics of these two groups (Table 5.2).

Changes in Perception and Meaning

Changes in perception often create opportunities. The unprecedented advance in the improvement of health care for Americans, for example, has led to a decrease in mortality rates for infants and increase in the lifespan of the elderly. Yet the nation remains gripped by a collective hypochondria, with much concern and fear of illness and dying despite the fact that all indicators of physical health and functioning have been moving upward.

Whatever the reasons for these misperceptions, they have created substantial innovative opportunities, including opportunities for diet and health-related magazines. *American Health*, for instance, reached a circulation of 1 million within two years. The change in perception has created the opportunity for a substantial number of new and innovative businesses to exploit the public's fears about traditional foods' ability to cause irreparable damage. Gourmet cookbooks have become best-sellers,

---

[24]Peter Drucker, *Innovation and Entrepreneurship*, (New York: Harper and Row, 1985), 95.

[25]Gerald Hills, "Market Opportunities and Marketing." In W. Bygrave (ed.), *The Portable MBA in Entrepreneurship*, 2nd ed. (New York: John Wiley & Sons, 1997).

TABLE 5.2	COMPARATIVE PROFILES OF THE CONSUMER INNOVATOR AND THE LATER ADOPTER	

Characteristic	Innovator	Noninnovator (or Later Adopter)
Product interest	More	Less
Opinion leadership	More	Less
Personality		
Dogmatism	Open-minded	Closed-minded
Social character	Inner-directed	Other-directed
Category width	Broad categorizer	Narrow categorizer
Venturesome	More	Less
Perceived risk	Less	More
Purchase and consumption traits		
Brand loyalty	Less	More
Deal proneness	More	Less
Usage	More	Less
Media habits		
Total magazine exposure	More	Less
Special-interest magazines	More	Less
Television	Less	More
Social characteristics		
Social integration	More	Less
Social striving (e.g., social, physical, and occupational mobility)	More	Less
Group memberships	More	Less
Demographic characteristics		
Age	Younger	Older
Income	More	Less
Education	More	Less
Occupational status	More	Less

SOURCE: Gerald Hills, "Market Opportunities and Marketing." In W. Bygrave (ed.), *The Portable MBA in Entrepreneurship*, 2nd ed. (New York: John Wiley & Sons, 1997).

for example, and traditional supermarkets have opened gourmet boutiques with a higher rate of return per square foot than is offered by traditional food sections.

New Knowledge Created by Research

New knowledge innovations are currently the most important opportunities, especially in high technology. Edward Roberts has documented the movement of scientific talent from Massachusetts Institute of Technology's many laboratories to literally hundreds of start-up technology-based firms, with Digital Equipment being the most prominent.[26]

The diffusion of knowledge has traveled in the minds of nascent entrepreneurs since the beginning of the Industrial Revolution, and their movements are difficult to

---

[26]Edward Roberts, *Entrepreneurs in High Technology* (New York: Oxford University Press, 1991).

control. British laws were once passed to impede the emigration of knowledge workers to foreign rivals but proved largely unsuccessful, as trained workers disguised themselves or stowed away in barrels to reach promising opportunities in America.

Knowledge information is now regarded as a form of intellectual capital. As the brainpower of an enterprise, it can be codified and put into an explicit, transferable form such as a software package or document. The competitive advantage of such an enterprise is therefore a function of what it knows, how it uses what it knows, and how fast it can know something new. Currently, intellectual capital is undergoing a change from craft production, where skilled individuals are the primary source of value, to mass production, where skills are embedded in tooling (similar to the dies, molds, and jigs that once transferred knowledge from the craftsman).[27] Today, companies such as Teltec, SAP, and Oracle embed their intellectual capital in their commercial products.

New Product Development Process

Creating a new product or service has been on the business agenda for a long time. The message to entrepreneurs is "innovate or die." Historical studies continue to pile up identifying firms that simply disappeared because they failed to keep current and competitive and were surpassed by more innovative competitors.

This constant pressure emphasizing innovation is being driven by four factors:

Technology Advances   Technical knowledge and information are increasing at an exponential rate, making possible innovative products that were once not even dreamed about, such as hand-held computers and noninvasive surgery. Annual research and development expenditures are reported to be $166 billion, with spending especially generous in certain industries noted by their growth and profitability. The software industry spends 20 percent of its sales on research and development, for example, whereas computer communication equipment averages 12.5 percent (Table 5.3).

Changing Consumer Needs   Expectations among customers are rising and have come to include the introduction of new product with significant improvements. Witness the following statement from the Cluetrain's manifesto: "We want you (the firm) to take 50 million of us as seriously as you take one reporter from the *Wall Street Journal*."[28] Now the Web is enabling the market to converse even more rapidly, as people tell one another about new products and companies and their own desires—learning faster than business. Marketplaces are in turmoil and customer preferences changing regularly.

Shortening Product Life Cycles   The world is speeding up and moving faster as improved communication and efficiencies cut the product life cycle. One study reported that product life cycles have been trimmed by a factor of 4 over the past 50 years (Figure 5.2).[29] New products no longer have life cycles of 5 to 10 years. Instead, within

---

[27]Stan Davis and Christopher Meyer, *Blur: The Speed of Change in the Connected Economy* (Reading, MA: Addison-Wesley, 1998).

[28]Rick Levine, Christopher Locke, Doc Seals, and David Weinberger, *The Cluetrain Manifesto* (New York: Perseus, 2000), viii.

[29]C. F. von Braun, *The Innovation War* (Upper Saddle River, NJ: Prentice Hall, 1997).

TABLE 5.3	TWENTY LARGEST R&D SPENDING INDUSTRIES IN THE UNITED STATES, 1997

Industry	R&D Spending, 1997 (millions $)	R&D Spending as a Percent of Sales (%)	R&D Spending as a Percent of Margin (%)	Annual R&D Percent Growth (1997 vs. 1996)
Aircraft	2,183	4.2	24.4	–4.6
Chemicals and allied products	6,593	5.9	14.7	8.2
Computer and office equipment	20,938	6.1	15.8	4.5
Computer communication equipment	3,449	12.5	21.5	20.0
Computer peripheral equipment	2,240	6.3	14.9	11.7
Electronic equipment	11,212	4.8	16.6	4.2
Electronic computers	3,449	4.6	18.2	8.7
Food and kindred products	3,595	1.4	4.3	5.8
Household audio and video equipment	7,657	6.2	23.4	8.9
Motor vehicle parts, accessories	1,928	3.2	15.7	5.9
Motor vehicles and car bodies	28,316	4.7	26.3	8.7
Petroleum refining	5,254	0.5	2.2	4.8
Pharmaceuticals	25,562	11.5	16.3	11.6
Phone communication, radio–telephone	24,504	4.8	10.6	2.0
Photographic equipment and supplies	3,569	6.5	11.2	3.6
Prepackaged software	11,506	19.9	26.8	17.9
Radio, TV, broadcast, communication equipment	5,344	9.1	28.7	15.3
Semiconductor, related devices	9,897	8.2	17.7	13.1
Special industry machinery	2,102	10.3	22.6	21.0
Telephone equipment	9,207	9.8	29.3	13.7

SOURCE: *R&D Ratios & Budgets* (Lincolnshire, IL: Schonfield & Associates, June 1997).

a few years or sometimes months, they may be superseded by a competitive entry, rendering earlier products obsolete and necessitating a new product. Speed has become the new competitive weapon, with successful entrepreneurs being able to respond to customer needs and changing markets faster than the competition can. Beating the competitors to market, or being first to set the standard, is often the key to success. Also, given the time value of money, the revenue from the sale of the product is realized earlier, as the narrower time frame reduces the odds that market conditions will dramatically change as development proceeds.

| FIGURE 5.2 | DECREASING PRODUCT LIFE CYCLES |

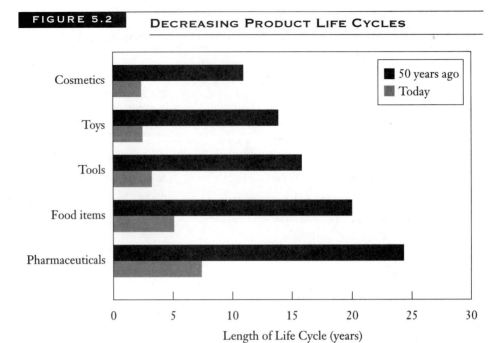

Increased World Competition   Today there is only one market—the global one. The globalization of markets has created significant opportunities for forward-thinking entrepreneurs. The standard is have a world product for a world market. Of course, the domestic market has also become someone else's international market, thus intensifying competition and speeding up the pace of product innovation.

Researcher Gerald Hills[30] points out that all products eventually die. Likewise, without product/service improvements and new products, the firm will eventually die. But product innovations are fraught with danger and pitfalls, and launching a steady stream of successful new products is no small feat.

The success rate of a new product is sometimes disappointing. For every 7 product ideas, about 4 enter development, 1.5 are launched, and only 1 succeeds (Figure 5.3).[31]

A recent Product Development and Management Association (PDMA) study revealed that new products have had a success rate of only 59 percent at launch over the past five years.[32] Cooper summarized additional statistics to arrive at a median success rate of 66 percent for consumer products and 64 percent for industrial goods.[33] Booz-Allen & Hamilton cite a 65 percent success rate for new product launches. In terms of dollar investments, an estimated 46 percent of all resources allocated to product development and commercialization is spent on projects that are canceled or fail to yield an adequate financial return.

[30]Gerald Hills, 1997.

[31]Booz-Allen & Hamilton, *New Product Management for the 1980s* (New York: Booz-Allen & Hamilton, Inc., 1982).

[32]PDMA Best Practices Study. See also Abbie Griffin, *Drivers of NPD Success: The 1997 PDMA Report* (Chicago: Product Development & Management Association, 1997).

[33]Robert Cooper, *Product Leadership* (Cambridge, MA: Perseus, 2000), 20.

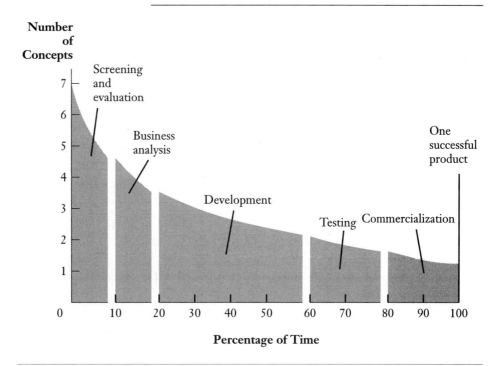

FIGURE 5.3 THE ATTRITION RATE OF NEW PRODUCT PROJECTS

Nevertheless, some firms are able to outperform the average, achieving an 80 percent success rate. Thus it is possible to identify new opportunities by engaging in a thorough planning process, such as the Booz-Allen & Hamilton model (Figure 5.4). While many entrepreneurs use a formal new product planning model, others do not follow a process that is so logical and sequential.

Conclusion

Entrepreneurs go about establishing their businesses in a variety of ways (Figure 5.5). Some engage in formal planning based on a product that was found through deliberate search. Others stumble on an idea through chance, good fortune, or unpredictable luck, such as by plunging into a particular calamity that must be worked out and realizing that the solution will prove valuable in the marketplace. Another method of establishing a business is by making a career choice where an entrepreneur knows he or she would like to be self-employed, yet has no idea, product, or service to offer yet. In the last case, the opportunity and choice of industry come later after the would-be business owner receives some training in entrepreneurship.

In all cases, the entrepreneur has a vision but that vision is unique and comes at a different time. All three types of entrepreneurs may wind up successful, but each undergoes the transformation in a different sequence. The process of opportunity recognition may come earlier for the deliberate-search entrepreneur than for the career-choice entrepreneur, whereas a career-decision entrepreneur may realize success later than the spontaneous/serendipity entrepreneur. There is no one correct path, but rather many paths that can lead to entrepreneurial success.

| FIGURE 5.4 | NEW PRODUCT DEVELOPMENT PROCESS |

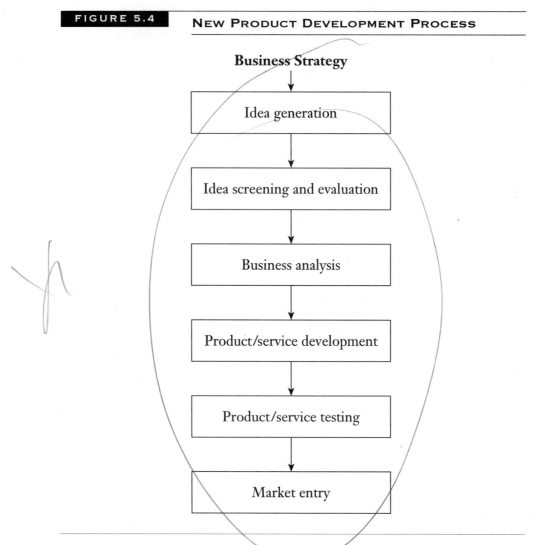

SOURCE: Adapted from Booz-Allen & Hamilton, *New Product Mangaement for the 1980s* (New York: Booz-Allen & Hamilton, 1982), 11.

Exploring the Entrepreneurial Concepts

The following sections provide an "entrepreneurial library" that contains a journal reading on this chapter's subject and a comprehensive cases study to illustrate the concept in practice. It is hoped that through the reading and discussion of the case, you will gain a greater understanding of the chapter.

TABLE 5.5	THREE PATHS TO ENTREPRENEURSHIP			
Phase	I	II	III	IV
1. Deliberate search	Product-based	Product development	Market testing	Formal business plan
2. Spontaneous/ serendipity	Problem-based	Search for product/service	Decides on entrepreneurial career	Business plan in head
3. Career choice	Occupation-based	Search for training	Search for opportunity	Evolving temporary business plan

THE ENTREPRENEURIAL LIBRARY

Reading for Chapter 5

THE COGNITIVE INFRASTRUCTURE OF OPPORTUNITY EMERGENCE

Norris F. Krueger, Jr.

Before we can act on opportunities we must first identify those opportunities. Understanding what promotes or inhibits entrepreneurial activity thus requires understanding how we construct perceived opportunities. Seeing a prospective course of action as a credible opportunity reflects an intentions-driven process driven by known critical antecedents. Based on well-developed theory and robust empirical evidence, we propose an intentions-based model of the cognitive infrastructure that supports or inhibits how we perceive opportunities. We discuss how this model both integrates past findings and guides future research. We also show the practical diagnostic power this model offers to managers.

Some organizations find their pursuit of new opportunities a difficult challenge, yet other similar organizations seem to have little difficulty. Based on well developed theory and robust empirical evidence, we propose that perceptions of organization members, channeled through intentions, can inhibit or enhance the identification and pursuit of new opportunities. This analysis proposes an intentions-based model of how opportunities emerge. Also offered are suggestions on how to develop an opportunity-friendly cognitive infrastructure.

Norris Krueger is Assistant Professor of Management at Boise State University.

The author would like to thank all those who have commented on prior versions of this research and supported this line of inquiry: Gayle Baugh, Deborah Brazeal, Alan Carsrud, Per Davidsson, William Guth, Dean Shepherd, Mike Reilly, Bjornar Reitan, and again to the late Al Shapero. The author further thanks the editors and the anonymous reviewers. Their ideas improved this manuscript dramatically. Any remaining errors of fact or judgment are solely mine.

Consider downsizing: It often arises because firms cannot identify profitable growth opportunities, even in firms that appear to have ample human resources to seek opportunities (Gertz & Baptista, 1996; Krueger & Gertz, 1996). Why is it that these firms cannot find new opportunities, but instead their thinking is dominated by threats? Consider firms that are frustrated by an inability to innovate despite having the requisite resources. Could it be that organization members do not perceive a focus on innovation as an opportunity? In both cases, we know the right questions to ask to understand why firm members do not perceive an opportunity.

An inadequate level of entrepreneurial activity may reflect an inadequate supply of opportunities perceived by organization members, not enough "entrepreneurial" thinking. If we want to understand how corporate ventures emerge, we need to understand how opportunities emerge. Organizations do not innovate; individuals within those organizations innovate. As Shapero argued, we can increase an organization's entrepreneurial potential by increasing the quality and quantity of potential entrepreneurs within that organization. In turn, we do that by increasing the quality and quantity of opportunities perceived by organization members (Shapero, 1982, 1985; Krueger & Brazeal, 1994). Any theory of venturing might wish to consider the process by which individuals identify credible opportunities and the important role of perceptions in that process.

One thing we know about innovative activity is that the adoption of an innovation entails some sort of supporting infrastructure, both tangible and intangible. We focus here on the intangible infrastructure. Individuals need to perceive a prospective new course of action as a credible opportunity, which requires the opportunity to not just be viable, but be perceived as viable.

Thinking "Entrepreneurially": The Need for Cognition-Based Models

The centrality of perceptions in opportunity identification argues for taking a cognitive approach for insights into the nature of innovative activity and how to nurture it. In particular, social psychology offers the construct of intentions as a consistently useful device to integrate past findings from a theory-driven, empirically robust vantage (Ajzen, 1987; Tubbs & Ekeberg, 1991). From a research perspective, intentions models have proven consistently robust both in explanatory power and in predictive validity (Ajzen, 1987; Tubbs & Ekeberg, 1991). From a managerial perspective, the conceptual framework offers a parsimonious mechanism for diagnosing barriers to entrepreneurial activity.

Entrepreneurship research sorely needs a framework solidly grounded in well-established theory (MacMillan & Katz, 1992; Jelinek & Litterer, 1994). Intentions-based models provide us a comprehensive theory-driven conceptual framework. This allows us to explain why (and how) phenomena such as champions operate. We need models that reflect how individuals actually make decisions and take action; these models include scripts and schemata (Lord & Maher, 1990). Intentions models do exactly that.

We can construct a tangible infrastructure to support the pursuit and implementation of existing opportunities. However, what about future opportunities? We do not find opportunities; we construct them. Opportunities are thus very much in the eye of the beholder. This tells us that perceptions and other cognitive phenomena are critical. So again we ask, what enhances the perception of viable, credible opportunities? (Another way of looking at this might be: What inhibits the perception of opportunities? Or even, what increases the perception of threats?)

What sort of infrastructure enables a greater orientation toward seeing opportunities and acting on them? The "heart of entrepreneurship" is an orientation toward seeing (and acting on) opportunities regardless of existing resources (Stevenson & Jarillo, 1990). In a rapidly changing world organizations need to continually identify new opportunities beyond existing competencies (Hamel & Prahalad, 1989, 1994; Mintzberg, 1994) if they are to survive. This argues that organizations must adopt what Hamel and Prahalad call a "strategic intent" (1989) or what Covin and Slevin describe as an "entrepreneurial orientation" (1991; Lumpkin & Dess, 1996). In short, organizations need to focus strategically on the identification of viable new opportunities.

This note will propose that organizations that successfully identify new opportunities have an intangible infrastructure—a cognitive infrastructure—that supports its members in perceiving opportunities (and acting on them). Fortunately, we already have a strong knowledge base regarding how we learn to perceive opportunities, knowledge that we can use to explain how organizations can build an opportunity-friendly cognitive infrastructure.

What Do We Know about Opportunity Perceptions?

First of all, we cannot lose sight of the reality that organizations do not see opportunities, individuals do. In Krueger and Brazeal's words, entrepreneurial potential requires potential entrepreneurs (1994). In other words, an organization with a strong orientation toward seeing opportunities must support individual organization members who have that orientation toward opportunities.

Second, we have a natural tendency to simplify the world around us by categorizing situations. Here, we tend to categorize strategic issues into opportunities and threats, something that is an ongoing, continuous process (Dutton, 1993). More important, we understand what drives this categorization process. Jackson and Dutton (1988) showed that perceptions of opportunity depend closely on perceptions that a situation is positive and that it is controllable. Perceptions of threat depend on perceptions that the situation is negative and uncontrollable.

Third, opportunity perceptions reflect an intentional process. Mental models of what we intend reflect why we intend an action. Dutton and Jackson's antecedents of opportunity perceptions are largely isomorphic with the known antecedents of intentions. In short, intentions are driven by perceptions of feasibility (e.g., controllability) and by perceptions of desirability (e.g., positiveness). Martin Fishbein and Icek Ajzen have developed a theoretically sound, empirically robust framework for understanding intentions that appears applicable to most planned behaviors, whether the action is narrowly or broadly defined or whether it is proximal or distal.

A wide variety of disciplines have independently found this same near-isomorphism (see Ajzen, 1987), suggesting that this framework is at the heart of human decision making. The intentions literature teaches us that information is important, but the impact of that information is even more important.

Fourth, we have some understanding of the mental models that entrepreneurs share, the scripts and schema that differentiate entrepreneurs (Bird, 1988; Mitchell & Chesteen, 1995). It seems probable that we have cognitive access to both an "opportunity" schema and a "threat" schema. Which schema is activated first (or activated more strongly) depends on critical cues from the environment. We know that humans process negative situations differently from positive situations: We differ in how we value information; we may we even use different parts of our brain. Yet, one individual facing the same cues may see a threat while another sees an opportunity.

Fifth, a review of the literatures on entrepreneurship finds strong arguments for intentionality (Bird, 1988; Katz & Gartner, 1988). Existing applications of intentions models or self-efficacy show consistent support (Krueger & Brazeal, 1994). For example, Shapero's model of the "entrepreneurial event" (1982) is homologous to the Ajzen-Fishbein framework (Krueger, 1993; Krueger, Reilly, & Carsrud, in press). He argued that the decision to undertake entrepreneurial activity required a pre-existing belief that the activity both desirable and feasible, coupled with some personal propensity to act on opportunities and some sort of precipitating factor.

Sixth, at the heart of these scripts and schemas are critical perceptions that map elegantly onto the common framework of intentionality. For example, we know that perceptions of competence strongly influence our perceptions of whether a situation is controllable. Perception of self-efficacy is a substantial antecedent of perceived opportunity (Krueger & Dickson, 1994). If we see ourselves as competent we are more likely to see a course of action as feasible, thus we are more likely to see an opportunity.

The critical task for this research note is to go into a bit more detail about the intentional nature of how opportunities emerge in an organization. The perceptual basis of opportunity emergence argues that we carefully consider this intangible infrastructure—this cognitive infrastructure that facilities (or inhibits) the perception of opportunities by organization members and thus the organization's ability to identify viable, credible future opportunities. Only then can we propose mechanisms for building a supportive cognitive infrastructure.

First, however, let us address why this is important, not just to researchers but to managers.

Strategic Intent, or Why Managers Should Care about Intentionality

Hamel and Prahalad (1989, 1994) argue that organizations need to exhibit some degree of "strategic intent" toward new opportunities. Identifying their core competencies will permit an organization to formulate a coherent strategic intent to explore and guide future strategic action. We also know that building new competencies to address new opportunities is a critical antecedent to capturing rents from innovation (McGrath, Tsai, Venkataraman, & MacMillan, 1996).

However, what influences an organization's readiness for the change required to pursue new opportunities? What is necessary for an organization to learn how to identify new opportunities? Senge focuses on what he labels simply "mental models": Managers' and employees' internalized cognitive schemata that guide much of their daily activity. We all need multiple schemata to adapt to a changing world. In turn, this requires that we learn multiple mental models and that we learn how to learn new schemata (Senge, 1992).

Intentions are at the heart of all this. Intentionality is deeply ingrained in how we process information into action. Any planned behavior is intentional by definition, thus strategic behaviors are inherently intentional. As such, it becomes useful to understand that intentions depend on a handful of critical antecedents. Personal and situational influences affect intent only by affecting these critical antecedents. For example, role models can help promote entrepreneurial activity, but only if they influence perceptions of desirability or, more likely, perceptions of feasibility.

Consider the notion of "entrepreneurial orientation" (Covin & Stevin, 1991). An entrepreneurial orientation seems useful in supporting strategic intent. We have an increasing understanding of what comprises the dimensions of entrepreneurial orientation (Lumpkin & Dess, 1996), but we know relatively little about its antecedents. Again, for an organization to be more entrepreneurial first requires that its members see more opportunities. Before acting on opportunities they must first see the opportunities. Seeing more possible opportunities increases the chances of finding appropriate ones to pursue. Thus, it is vital to understand how we perceive opportunities. This will help us understand how we can support (or avoid inhibiting) the perception of opportunities. It will help us to diagnose why attempts to innovate fall short. If organization members do not perceive a proposed innovation as an opportunity (or worse, see it as a threat), we can ask intelligent questions to understand why a particular innovation was not perceived as an opportunity.

In sum, models of intentions appear useful and potentially enlightening in diagnosis: how to understand and how to increase an organization's potential for entrepreneurial activity. Let us examine the nature of intentions and their antecedents more closely. To successfully apply this model requires a better understanding of the key conceptual and empirical issues.

The Nature of Intentions

Absent intention, action is unlikely. Intentions represent the belief that I will perform a certain behavior, the belief I will act. Logically, intent thus precedes action. In other words, innovation usually entails taking significant planned (intentional) action. Action requires effort; if we are to try, we must first intend to try. We all have mental models of what we intend to do (and, by extension, what we do not intend). At a deeper level, these mental models reflect why we intend a given action. If we can better understand why, we can better understand what.

The theoretical underpinnings for intentions models are nicely reviewed in Ajzen (1987). Ajzen argues persuasively that intentions-based models capture how individuals actually think. Even routine behaviors are anchored by intentions; the intentionality is simply more deeply placed. The process depicted in Figure 1 shows how the intentions framework serves as a conduit to channel our interpretations of events into action. This implies that intentions are constructed, even where they appear to arise spontaneously.

The latest version of the framework, Ajzen's "theory of planned behavior" posits that intentions toward a given target behavior depend on certain fundamental underlying attitudes. These specific attitudes reflect decision makers' attributions about a potential course of action. Decision makers should perceive the course of action as (a) within their competence and control (thus feasible), (b) personally desirable, and (c) consonant with social norms.

Barriers to any of the critical antecedents will represent a substantive inhibition to an organization's intent to seek and act on opportunities. If we inhibit the intent, we inhibit the action.

Critical Attitudes

The theory of planned behavior argues that perceptions of desirability and feasibility explain (and predict) intentions significantly. Intentions are driven by perceptions that outcomes from the behavior are personally desirable and that they are socially desirable.

Figure 1 shows that intentions toward innovation are best predicted by three critical perceptions: that the innovative activity (e.g., a new venture) is (a) perceived as personally desirable, (b) perceived as supported by social norms, and (c) perceived as feasible.

Exogenous Factors

How do intentions models handle other variables, those that are exogenous to the attitude–intention–behavior process? Exogenous factors such as individual differences and purely situational influences operate indirectly on intentions (and thus behavior) by changing these antecedents, not by directly affecting intentions. That is, a change in objective circumstances would thus change intentions if and only if the change altered a decision maker's attitudes. Path analyses using meta-analysis clearly support the causal linkage from attitudes to intentions to behavior (Kim & Hunter, 1993).

Precipitating Factors

Research also suggests that certain exogenous variables can serve to facilitate or "precipitate" the realization of intentions into behavior (Shapero, 1982; Krueger & Brazeal, 1994; Stopford & Baden-Fuller, 1994).

The Robustness of Intentions Models

Empirically, meta-analyses demonstrate clearly that this framework is remarkably robust with very large effect sizes. While designed to predict specific, proximal behaviors, this

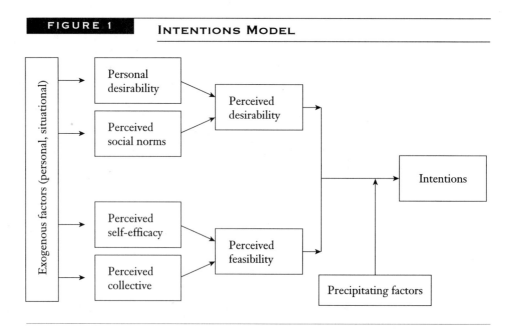

FIGURE 1 **INTENTIONS MODEL**

SOURCE: Shapero, 1982: Krueger, 1993; Krueger & Brazeal, 1994.

class of models appears to apply equally well to behaviors that are distal or less specific (e.g., Kim & Hunter, 1993). Again, this permits us to apply this model to relatively broad (innovation in general) or to relatively narrow phenomena (a specific innovation).

Kim and Hunter (1993) found that personal desirability and social norms explained 76% of the variance in intentions, while intentions explained 67% of the variance in behavior (after adjusting for statistical artifacts). Ajzen (1991) found that adding a measure of perceived feasibility explains an additional 10% of variance in intentions. Such findings compare rather favorably with the 10% of variance typically explained by traits or other dispositional measures (Ajzen, 1987).

More important, the model held in virtually every study, even where researchers took considerable liberties with model specification or measurement. That is, path analysis confirms that the correlation between attitudes and behavior is fully explained by the attitude–intention and intention–behavior links (Kim & Hunter, 1993). Moreover, formal intentions models have already been applied successfully to entrepreneurial behavior (e.g., Davidsson, 1991; Krueger & Brazeal, 1994; Reitan, 1997).

Applying the intentions framework to work motivation proved enlightening (Tubbs & Ekeberg, 1993), thus so should research applying intentions to the processes of corporate venturing. For example, if an organization's members had the requisite skills to launch a new venture that it would deem desirable, but failed to do so, the model would diagnose a potential shortfall in perceived feasibility.

Known Antecedents of Intentions

Perceived Desirability: Personal Attitude

In the Ajzen–Fishbein framework, personal attitude depends on perceptions of the consequences of outcomes from performing the target behavior: their likelihood as well as magnitude, negative consequences as well as positive, and especially intrinsic rewards as well as extrinsic (in short, an expectancy framework). However, the model also argues that these perceptions are learned. Thus, organizations influence those perceptions, often indirectly and often unintentionally.

For example, a successful innovation might lead to a promotion from R&D into management; this need not be perceived as positive (e.g., it might entail a transfer to another location). To increase attitude, increase expectancies by raising perceptions of positive outcomes (or their likelihood) or lowering perceptions of negative events (or their likelihood). Exposure to multiple perspectives (e.g., multiple mentors) and diverse life experiences (development experiences) will help individuals to recognize a broader range of desirable options.

Perceived Desirability: Social Norms

Social norms represent perhaps the most interesting component of the Ajzen–Fishbein framework. This measure is a function of perceived normative beliefs of significant others (e.g., family, friends, co-workers) weighted by the individual's motive to comply with each normative belief. Social norms often reflect the influence of organizational culture. That is, the impact of climate and culture on intent operates by its impact on perceptions of desirability (and perhaps feasibility as well). For example, work group relationships do influence individual innovation (Scott & Bruce, 1994).

Measuring social norms requires identifying the appropriate reference groups. A potential corporate entrepreneur's reference group may not be family and friends, but rather the top management and their colleagues (including those who have already started a venture).

Perceptions of Feasibility: Self-Efficacy

Albert Bandura and associates have developed and elaborated a social-cognitive model of human agency (e.g., Bandura, 1986, 1995). This model argues that taking action requires consideration of not just outcome expectancies (i.e., desirability) but also perceived self-efficacy (i.e., feasibility). This becomes particularly critical with significant strategic change (e.g., a new venture).

Bandura defines self-efficacy as an individual's perceived ability to execute some target behavior. Thus, it reflects the perception of a personal capability to do a particular job or set of tasks. Measuring perceived efficacy is relatively straightforward; one can use simple self-report measures (Bandura, 1986; Eden, 1992).

Self-efficacy perceptions play a powerful role in managerial and employee behavior. For instance, gender and ethnicity differences in work interest and performance can often be traced to differences in self-efficacy. This illustrates the vital role of self-efficacy in the empowerment of organization members. Increases in self-efficacy lead to increased initiative and persistence and thus subsequent performance; low self-efficacy reduces effort and thus performance (Eden, 1992).

Increasing self-efficacy requires more than just teaching competencies; students and trainees must fully internalize the competencies by experiencing mastery of the skills in question. Also, psychological and emotional support from management and peers reinforces perceptions of increased self-efficacy. A common mechanism is to provide credible models of key behaviors through effective mentors and champions.

Even better are developmental experiences that provide opportunities to experience mastery at those competencies (McCall, 1992; Senge, 1992). Exposure to diverse life and work experiences broadens individuals' range of what they perceive as feasible. These offer opportunities for behavioral modeling where organization members can experience mastery. This behavioral modeling can work either vicariously using credible experts or directly by affording members the hands-on experience in "safe" settings (Bandura, 1986; Weick, 1979). Providing opportunities for diverse mastery experiences is an even better way to increase individuals' evoked set of feasible alternatives.

Perceptions of Feasibility: Collective Efficacy

However, perceptions of personal competence need not translate into perceptions of organizational competence. If fellow organization members are needed to support an intended behavior, perceptions of collective efficacy are likely to be important (Bandura, 1986, 1995). This point is crucial: organization members may be perfectly capable of finding and promoting new opportunities and their self-efficacy beliefs may be high. Yet, perceptions that collective efficacy is low can inhibit opportunity seeking. Empowering organization members to be more entrepreneurial thus rests on beliefs about both personal and collective efficacy, just as perceived desirability has personal and social components. Organizations can employ the same behavioral modeling discussed above to enhance perceptions of collective efficacy.

Exogenous Factors

Research often examines variables other than attitudes and intentions, but intentions models posit that these exogenous variables operate indirectly on intentions (and thus behavior). As the model suggests, most exogenous factors influence intentions (and behavior) through influencing one or more critical attitudes. The various literatures on innovation management and entrepreneurship offer numerous examples of exogenous factors logically related to innovative or entrepreneurial activity, though often with disappointing results. If effects are actually indirect, then applying this framework may strengthen the findings. For example, the presence of role models may increase entrepreneurial behavior only if the role models actually change a key attitude such as self-efficacy (Krueger & Brazeal, 1994).

Precipitating Factors

As Figure 1 suggests, exogenous factors may also influence the intention–behavior relationship by precipitating, or facilitating the realization of intentions (Shapero, 1982; Ajzen, 1987; Stopford-Fuller & Baden, 1994). One such factor may be perceptions of resource availability (Triandis, 1967). Another might be a personal propensity to act on opportunities (Shapero, 1982).

Tangible barriers may serve to prevent an intention from coming to fruition, but the subtleness of cognitive barriers can present even greater obstacles. While Shapero notes that purely subjective conditions can precipitate action, such as facing a fortieth birthday, it appears that the typical precipitating event reflects some sort of displacement, a disruption of one's inertia such as getting fired or being offered a big contract. Yet, how we react to displacement depends on our perceptions of the impact of that event; Shapero argues that our reaction also depends on the believable options that we perceive.

External conditions may lie beyond what an organization can influence, but organizations can provide explicit, credible cues that the new circumstances represent an opportunity. Precipitating factors are not well understood, so research in this area is very likely to shed some new light.

Let us now turn the discussion in a more practical direction. Not everyone accepts the role of subjective elements (e.g., Weick, 1979), but if we accept the notion of intentions and their antecedents, how might an organization promote an appropriate cognitive infrastructure?

Building a Supportive Cognitive Infrastructure

Shapero (1982, 1985) argues that for an organization to maintain a reasonable supply of opportunity-seeking individuals requires that organizations provide a congenial environment, from the perspective of the prospective opportunity-seekers. Opportunity-seekers may enact an organizational environment that is personally favorable, but doing so requires a learning-supportive cognitive infrastructure. How do we help organization members perceive more things as desirable and feasible?

Consider the useful metaphor of the antenna. We are much more likely to notice (and take seriously) signals from directions in which we are already looking. Intentions contribute to how an organization's antennae are "tuned." We are less likely to notice opportunities from directions that do not appear desirable and feasible.

On the other hand, entrepreneurial activity (especially activity that is disruptive of existing products and markets) will generally lack legitimacy with the rest of the organization (Dougherty, 1994). We thus need to set explicit, credible organizational policies that increase both the perceived feasibility and the perceived desirability of entrepreneurial activity.

However, an objectively supportive infrastructure is not enough; organization members must perceive it as supportive. Brazeal finds that supportive reward systems and supportive top management need not be seen as such (1993). No matter how supportive an organization may be objectively (e.g., in terms of reward systems), the perceived supportiveness appears crucial. Entrepreneurial organizations appear to provide exactly this kind of supportive cognitive infrastructure (Brazeal, 1993; Krueger & Brazeal, 1994).

Returning to the "antenna" metaphor, organization members are obviously more likely to respond to highly credible cues. Increasing the credibility of cues may require that the signals be perceived as coming from more credible sources such as top management, a visible champion, or a trusted mentor.

The cognitive infrastructure should enhance perceptions in organization members that opportunity-seeking is personally and socially desirable and that members are personally and collectively competent to pursue new opportunities. Such a cognitive infrastructure would provide the empowerment needed to promote opportunity-seeking.

Increasing Feasibility Perceptions

To promote feasibility perceptions, we need to increase perceptions of personal ("*I* can do this") and collective ("*We* can do this") efficacy. Perceived feasibility entails perceptions that resources are available and obstacles are surmountable (including the obstacle of having tried and failed). Fortunately, promoting perceived efficacy is relatively straightforward and reasonably well understood; we already know how to do this (Eden, 1992). Organizations need to be vigilant in providing the necessary explicit cues and explicit support.

As already noted, providing mastery experiences that increase perceptions of personal (and collective) efficacy are invaluable. For example, providing experiences that demonstrate mastery in even a limited domain can increase efficacy perceptions if the individuals perceive their master as generalizable ("If I can launch a minor new product, I can launch a major new product!") This, of course, requires that organizations provide salient, credible cues that the skills are transferable to newer, larger domains by providing multiple low-risk mastery experiences (see Weick's (1979) notion of "small wins.").

Finally, it is just as important to dispel spurious beliefs of infeasibility. One useful mechanism is benchmarking, which can offer concrete evidence that, yes, this opportunity is feasible.

Increasing Desirability Perceptions

However, desirability perceptions may require more complicated interventions. Increasing perceived desirability requires that individuals perceive mostly positive outcomes for their innovative activity, including intrinsic rewards such as a supportive culture. For example, objectively supportive reward systems need not be perceived as such by the person rewarded. Innovation is often its own reward. Extrinsic rewards can interfere with intrinsic motivation. Some innovators even enjoy being "illegitimate" (Dougherty, 1994).

Also, the most skillfully designed formal reward system may be overridden by informal punishments. We would recommend examining the entire set of rewards (and punishments), both intrinsic and extrinsic, formal and informal. It may also prove more useful to counter spurious beliefs about an innovation's downside. Most important, reward systems must be viewed from the perspective of potential innovators, not those far removed from the trenches. For example, what about the informal rewards from other innovators for developing a cutting-edge technology, even if it's not marketable?

Shapero (1985) proposed that organizations seeking to innovate should provide what he called a "nutrient-rich" environment for potential innovators. This "seedbed" would provide "nutrients" such as credible information, credible role models, and emotional/psychological support as well as more tangible resouces. McGrath (1995) points out that organizations need to support its members in learning from adversity. Organizations should provide opportunities to attempt innovative things at relatively low risk (i.e., trying and failing is not career-threatening).

Potential Mechanisms

The literature offers some interesting prescriptions that we might consider: providing clear signals from top management, encouraging the role of teams, encouraging the role of mentors and champions (including multiple mentors), and providing explicit developmental experiences.

Explicit Cues

One of the most common recommendations one finds is that top management give clear, unambiguous signals of support for key elements of innovative activity (Guth & Ginsberg, 1990). For instance, senior management should visibly encourage the risk taking associated with the pursuit of new opportunities with clear cues that setbacks can be learning experiences (Shapero, 1985). Many are familiar with the legendary Jack Welch who describes his role as a cheerleader and facilitator. Welch clearly seems bent on promoting the perceived desirability of seeking new opportunities and promoting perceptions of feasibility, removing cognitive as well as more tangible barriers.

Strategic Controls

Yes, even bureaucratic mechanisms can help. Organizations' control mechanisms exert considerable influence over the intensity of R&D spending: long-term strategic controls help much better than short-term financial controls. Long-term controls can reward opportunity seeking while short-term controls inadvertently cause short-term setbacks (Hoskisson, Hitt, & Hill, 1993).

Consider the Enter-Prize Program at Ohio Bell (Kanter & Richardson, 1991) which allows fledgling intrapreneurs to test the waters. This program encourages employees to develop "newstreams" of new products or services that will compete for funding by top management. If the "newstream" proves successful, its developers participate in the profits, sending the clear message that Ohio Bell values both innovation and innovators and that innovation is both feasible and desirable. The strategic controls reward success at opportunity-seeking, but do not punish those whose attempt was unsuccessful.

Information Flows

Similarly, information systems can play a surprising role. If information supportive of innovative activity is relatively unavailable, but data about its downside is easily accessible, innovation may not occur. While this is true of both informal and formal flows of information, making innovation-supportive information readily available through formal channels sends a signal of its true importance to the organization about its mission. For example, how easily can one find external information about markets and competitors? Brazeal (1993) argues for making such a knowledge bank readily available to employees.

Benchmarking and Best Practices

This model tells us why benchmarking and best practices can be so useful. Increasing the visibility of what is truly feasible is central to benchmarking, but it also increases the credibility of what is feasible: "If a competent competitor can do this, so can we." The credible example of a competitor's success may also increase the desirability of the new opportunity. For example, the success of a competitor may spur the perceived need to innovate.

Teams

Teams represent an especially useful means for promoting perceptions of feasibility and desirability. Objectively, teams provide tangible resources for innovation. Teams also provide the multiple perspectives and schemata offered by different team members, thus teams, not "lone wolves," are the best internal source of feasible ideas. Teams also provide a cognitive and emotional buffer from the rest of the organization. The social reinforcement of one's team can promote perceptions of collective efficacy and supportive social norms without the perception of negative reinforcements by the bureaucracy. Encouragement and support from team members can also promote perceptions of personal desirability and of personal efficacy.

Most important, a well-constructed team is best suited to help innovators actually implement an idea. A supportive team does not ask "*Can* we do this?" Rather, it asks "*How* do we do this?" The diversity of perspectives in a good team helps defuse the potential negative ramifications—and raises perceptions of feasibility—that might arise from the innovation.

Changing Structure

In the extreme, organizations have chosen to physically separate innovative groups from the rest of the organization (e.g., the "skunkworks" concept). Such separation has symbolic implications for reducing barriers to opportunity-seeking. For example, the separation can reduce rivalry for resources. This also serves as a de facto flattening of the organization, improving speed of decision making.

Mentors and Champions

Mentoring is often promoted as vital for management development in general and for innovation development in particular. One specific variation on the mentoring process is the concept of "champions" or "change masters" (Kanter & Richardson, 1991; Day, 1994; Shane, 1994). The existence of a "champion," someone who will fight for a new venture; sends a clear signal that the organization at least tolerates entrepreneurial activity. That signal alone should increase perceptions of supportive social norms. However, mentors and roles affect entrepreneurial intentions only insofar as they first affect key attitude such as self-efficacy. We should expect that a skillful champion would contribute to stronger perceptions among organization members of an innovation's desirability and feasibility.

Multiple Mentors

Let us propose a notion founded in the practices of academe, that of multiple mentors.[1] Multiple mentors can provide multiple perspectives and multiple schemata that should broaden proteges' perceptions of desirability and feasibility. Multiple influences (particularly those that enhance self-efficacy) are also associated with entrepreneurship (Krueger & Brazeal, 1994). The multiple mentors should include one or more successful innovator. As in academe, multiple mentors are likely to transcend functional boundaries and even organizational boundaries. Successful innovators typically engage in considerable boundary-spanning themselves, proactively seeking such multiple influences (Shapero, 1985). An organization may wish to tangibly and visibly encourage successful innovators to mentor others.

For example, recent evidence suggests that successful innovators can be committed to both their profession and their organization. "Serving two masters" is actually associated with high performance, contrary to many organizations' norms (Baugh & Roberts, 1994), perhaps by multiple mentors providing multiple behavioral models (Bandura, 1995).

Developmental Experiences

Any organization can profit by providing its members with a diverse range of developmental experiences (McCall, 1992). Here, experiences can provide explicit cues that the organization supports innovation and members can internalize those into appropriate attitudes, thus intentions. The more that we expose organizational members to innovation and the more they understand its nature, the more likely they are to see innovation as feasible and desirable. McCall notes that for managers, there is no substitute for having "bottom-line" responsibilities in charge of a new or turnaround venture.

Moreover, promoting the ability of organization members to identify a broader range of alternatives as desirable and feasible yields an increased ability to learn new mental models. This ability to learn offers value beyond any particular innovation in question, helping organization members perceive the ability to learn and implement new competencies (Senge, 1992). Organizations should consider such development as an integral part of their strategy (McCall, 1992) and thus provide the right kind of cognitive infrastructure.

Implications

The robust empirical track record of intentions models and their firm theoretical grounding both argue that we do have a sound grasp of the critical antecedents of opportunity

---

[1] Thanks to Gayle Baugh for this useful insight.

perception. We also know how to overcome inhibitions to opportunity perception by influencing these critical antecedents. The perception-driven nature of intentions implies that a healthy cognitive infrastructure will change as circumstances (and our perceptions) change. Thus, there are no specific universal prescriptions. Instead we must continually maintain a healthy cognitive infrastructure by keeping a close eye on the perceptions of organization members. An organization that wishes to innovate must accept that it needs to empower its members to help them see a broader range of new opportunities. Meanwhile, it should minimize activities that inhibit opportunity-seeking.

Exploring questions such as these should prove both interesting and useful.

Integrating Past Research

One useful exercise might be to test these propositions by examining past research efforts that explored the dimensions of successful (and unsuccessful) innovation. For instance, the work of Eisenhardt and Schoonhoven (1990) illustrates the importance of initial decisions, a fundamental characteristic of intentional behavior. We might examine the specific activities of leaders such as Welch to assess their impact on perceptions of desirability and feasibility. We can see how initial strategies and intentions depend upon perceptions of desirability and feasibility in other well-executed studies of the innovative process (e.g., Jelinek & Schoonhoven, 1993). We can explore how existing inventories of barriers to innovation or corporate venturing reflect (or not) perceptions of desirability and feasibility (MacMillan, Block, & Narasimha, 1986; Kuratko, Montagno, & Hornsby, 1990).

We have a number of existing constructs (e.g., champions) that successfully explain facets of entrepreneurial behavior. We can test whether the intentions model explains their success. We can test whether successful champions influence entrepreneurial behavior indirectly through changing attitudes and intentions, as the model would predict. We can test the precipitating factors proposed by Shapero (1982, 1985) and Stopford and Baden-Fuller (1994). We can test whether the critical success factors of learning organizations (e.g., Senge, 1992) influence attitudes and intentions. That is, what aspects of the cognitive infrastructure support or inhibit organizational learning? Would it be valuable for organization members to perceive organization learning itself as an opportunity?

We often argue that innovative firms exhibit an innovation-friendly climate. If we examine existing inventories that measure barriers to innovation we find that many items directly reflect perceptions of personal desirability, social norms, personal efficacy and collective efficacy, as well as possible precipitating or inhibiting factors (MacMillan et all., 1986; Kuratko et al., 1990; Scott & Bruce, 1994). This suggests that the exploratory research that generated these inventories implicitly captures the intentional nature of entrepreneurial activity.

This model suggests that "barriers" and "climate" are also in the eye of the beholder. For example, we would predict that organizations that are both highly innovative and entrepreneurial would have a climate where organization members see "red tape" as "paying dues" rather than as a mechanism of intimidation.

Guiding Future Research

Intentions models such as the theory of planned behavior are already widely used in many settings. The intentions approach tells us that the effects of exogenous factors such as individual differences (e.g., personality, demographics) are indirect. This knowledge can help us identify stronger, more consistent effects from exogenous factors, enriching the explanatory and predictive power of our research.

Exploring Limitations

However, we should also explore the limits of this type of model. Does the scope of its applicability extend, for instance, to "really new" products? We may find even more valuable insights from applying other formal models of human cognition (e.g., Lord & Maher, 1990: Jelinek & Litterer, 1994).

For example, if the conventional wisdom is correct that teams are critical for innovation (e.g., Senge, 1992), then we need to explore ways to apply this framework to the team level of analysis.

Unanswered Questions

From Intent to Action Even more important is the critical issue of how intentions become reality. Figure 1 argues that exogenous factors can also precipitate, facilitate, or inhibit the realization of intentions. We have already noted Triandis's (1967) perceptions of resources availability and Shapero's (1982) propensity to act. Shapero (1982), Ajzen (1987), and Stopford-Fuller & Baden (1994) also offer other "likely suspects" for testing.

What catalyst serves to crystallize beliefs and attitudes into a salient intention? Shapero suggested the existence of some sort of personal propensity to act. However, does this propensity help attitudes coalesce into intentions or facilitate the realization of intentions? This would contribute to a broader understanding of intentions in general.

Intentions Toward Implementation? We also need to examine the specific path by which intentions are realized. To achieve the implementation of a new opportunity typically requires at least several steps along the way. The choice of intermediate actions is also an intentional process; thus we can examine why certain choices were made. That is, the intentions model should also help us understand specific aspects of a new venture. For example, consider a new perceived opportunity involving a new consumer product—there is still a choice of marketing channels and that choice should be influenced by intentions and the critical antecedents.

Changing Intentions? We can also track how changing perceptions change the opportunities (or lack thereof) perceived by organization members over time (e.g., Ropo & Hunt, 1995). We know surprisingly little about changing intentions; the study of intrapreneurial activity might thus contribute to our overall knowledge about intentions. We might gain a better understanding of how we recategorize strategic issues and how we cognitively convert threats into opportunities (as activity that we often prescribe to students and trainees).

A Deeper Look? We can look more deeply into how our beliefs influence our perceptions through how we process cues from the environment. For example, what individual differences (demographics, personality, etc.) appear to moderate relationships in this model? Parallel to this, we should look closely at how information is presented (e.g., framing effects, anchor-and-adjust processes, and other cognitive phenomena).

For another example, social cues may prove more important for perceived feasibility (through effects on collective and personal efficacy) than for perceived desirability. Each of these represents a useful contribution to the broader overall literature on intentions.

Qualitative Tests   This model also merits a formal qualitative test. One specific approach that we propose is action research to identify whether influencing attitudes does indeed influence opportunity perceptions (and thus behavior. Research should also explore the links between the attitudes and intentions of organization members and their organizations' entrepreneurial orientation (Lumpkin & Dess, 1996). What dimensions of cognitive infrastructure influence which dimensions of entrepreneurial orientation?

Practical Issues   The literature often prescribes perfusing the entire organization with a supportive corporate culture, but what if we can work with only one group—who should it be? Do we need to influence the intentions of the rank and file? Middle managers? Top managers? Perhaps the role of leadership (as with Jack Welch) here is to promote a desired cognitive infrastructure, not just with internal stakeholders, but also with external stakeholders. For example, this model suggests that the team level may be critical. Finally what else will be required to help managers to adopt and skillfully use this framework to promote and diagnose innovation in their organizations?

Collective Efficacy   Finally, this model suggests that an opportunity-friendly organization requires high levels of collective efficacy. The scarcity of research into collective efficacy further suggests that this will be a fruitful opportunity to advance both practical and theoretical knowledge.

Implications for Practice and Teaching

If, as Weick, Senge, and others argue, managers and leaders guide the sensemaking of their colleagues and subordinates, the most important implication is that this model offers guidelines for doing so. For example, a leader can frame even a large setback as simply "paying dues." Consider the example of Thomas Watson and the story of an executive who lost IBM $10 million. The manager offered his resignation, but Watson reputedly said, "Not a chance, not after I just invested $10 million in training you!" Even if apochryphal, such stories send a clear signal throughout the organization that top management supports a gallant failure. An organization that faces downsizing can use this model to help its members identify and pursue opportunities for growth.

Supportive Cognitive Infrastructure   If we accept the model, the most obvious implication is that enhancing its components should pay off in a higher level of entrepreneurial activity. Organizations must develop a cognitive infrastructure among its members, which increases and broadens what members see as desirable and perceive as feasible. The model can also be used to diagnose potential reasons why (and especially why not) organization members seek new opportunities and which specific opportunities are (and are not) identified. Was it a deficit in perceived desirability? In perceived feasibility?

A Possible Downside   However, the model also suggests the absence of panaceas; we must not assume that we fully understand how the perceptions of organization members change. We must avoid creating new dysfunctions such as replacing one blind spot with another (e.g., Zahra & Chaples, 1993). We might also risk being too successful. We might generate an obsession with innovation. We might generate over-optimistic perceptions of feasibility and desirability, setting the organization up for a rude awakening. The "can-do" spirit is a two-edged sword; the very spirit that facilitates change could lead an organization and its members to take needless risks.

Rethinking SWOT   However, this same intentions process gives us ample evidence to consider inverting the usual process of environmental analysis (e.g., SWOT). If perceptions of feasibility are critical, they can bias an organization's information search. Almost by definition, needs assessments are likely to anchor perceptions of feasibility. The very nature of intentionality argues that strategy formulation should be driven as much by external issues as it is by perceived capabilities, by learning and exploration as much as by existing capabilities. Thus, managers and entrepreneurs should benefit from looking first at potential opportunities before risking any biases introduced by assessing current strengths and weaknesses. That is, change the question from "Can we do it?" to "*How* can we do it?"

Hamel and Prahalad (1989) may argue for a focus on core competencies, but they also argue for an organization working hard to envision radical new opportunities (1994). Both Senge (1992) and Mintzberg (1994) would argue that strategic planning must fully incorporate learning. To do so also requires an appropriately supportive cognitive infrastructure to encourage an "opportunity-first" approach.

Conclusion

Perhaps the most critical antecedent of organizational action is the categorization of strategic issues into opportunities and threats. As with intentions, opportunities are constructed, not found (Mintzberg, 1994; Dutton & Jackson, 1987; Dutton, 1993). An organization that wishes to promote entrepreneurial activity must establish conditions where its members see the prospect of seeking new opportunities (and the uncertainty associated with it) itself as an opportunity, not as a threat.

Understanding what inhibits entrepreneurial activity in an organization requires understanding how intentions toward a prospective course of action are constructed. Mental models of what we intend reflect why we intend an action. Intentions-based models capture how individuals really formulate mental models. Based on well-developed theory and robust empirical evidence about intentions, we have proposed a social psychological model of how opportunities emerge.

Perceptions of desirability (personal and social) and perceptions of feasibility (personal and organizational) are critical to the construction of intentions toward important behaviors. An organization's cognitive infrastructure should enhance, not impede, these critical perceptions.

The pursuit of entrepreneurial opportunities appears quite amenable to the use of such models in teaching and practice as well as research. We look forward to further testing the model and its components.

References

Ajzen, I. (1987). Attitudes, traits, and actions: Dispositional prediction of behavior in social psychology. *Advances in Experimental Social Psychology, 20,* 1–63.

Ajzen, I. (1991). The theory of planned behavior. *Organizational Behavior & Human Decision Processes.* 50, 179–211.

Bandura, A. (1986). *The social foundations of thought and action.* Englewood Cliffs, NJ: Prentice Hall.

Bandura, A. (1995). Exercise of personal & collective efficacy in changing societies. In A. Bandura (Ed.). *Self-efficacy in changing societies.* New York: Cambridge University Press.

Baugh, G., & Roberts, R. (1994). Professional and organizational commitment among engineers: Conflicting or complementing? *IEEE Transactions on Engineering Management, 41*(2), 108–114.

Bird, B. (1988). Implementing entrepreneurial ideas: The case for intentions. *Academy of Management Review, 13*(3), 442–453.

Brazeal, D. (1993). Organizing for internally developed corporate ventures. *Journal of Business Venturing. 8,* 75–100.

Covin, J., & Slevin, D. (1991). A conceptual model of entrepreneurship as firm behavior. *Entrepreneurship Theory & Practice, 16*(1), 7–25.

Davidsson, P. (1991). Continued entrepreneurship. *Journal of Business Venturing, 6*(6), 405–429.

Day, D. (1994). Raising radicals: Different processes for championing innovative corporate ventures. *Organization Science, 5*(2), 148–172.

Dougherty, D. (1994). The illegitimacy of successful product innovation in established firms. *Organization Science, 5*(2), 200–218.

Dutton, J. (1993). The makings of organizational opportunities: Interpretive pathway to organizational change. In B. Staw & L. Cummings (Eds.), *Research in organizational behavior,* 15. Greenwich, CT: JAI Press.

Dutton, J., & Jackson, S. (1987). Categorizing strategic issues: Links to organizational action. *Academy of Management Review, 12*(1), 76–90.

Eden, D. (1992). Leadership & expectations: Pygmalion effects & other self-fulfilling prophecies in organizations. *Leadership Quarterly, 3*(4), 271–305.

Eisenhardt, K., & Schoonhoven, C. (1990). Organizational growth: Linking founding team, strategy, environment and growth among U.S. semiconductor ventures, 1978–1988. *Administrative Science Quarterly, 35,* 504–529.

Gertz, D., & Baptista, J. (1996). *Grow to be great.* New York: Free Press.

Guth, W., & Ginsberg, A. (1990). Guest editors' introduction: Corporate entrepreneurship. *Strategic Management Journal, 11*(Summer), 5–15.

Hamel, G., & Prahalad, C. (1989). Strategic intent. *Harvard Business Review,* May–June, 63–79.

Hamel, G., & Prahalad, C. (1994). Competing for the future. *Harvard Business Review,* July–August, 122–128.

Hoskisson, R., Hitt, M., & Hill, C. (1993). Managerial incentives & investment in R&D in large multi-product firms. *Organization Science, 4*(2), 325–341.

Jackson, S., & Dutton, J. (1988). Discerning threats & opportunities. *Administrative Science Quarterly, 33,* 370–387.

Jelinek, M., & Litterer, J. (1994). A cognitive theory of organizations. In C. Stubbart, J. Meindl, & J. Porac (Eds.), *Advances in managerial cognition and information processing,* 5:3–42. Greenwich, CT: JAI Press.

Jelinek, M., & Schoonhoven, C. (1993). *The innovation marathon: Lessons from high technology companies.* San Francisco: Jossey-Bass.

Kanter, R., & Richardson, L. (1991). Engines of progress: Designing & running entrepreneurial vehicles in established companies—The Enter-Prize Program at Ohio Bell, 1985–1990. *Journal of Business Venturing, 6,* 209–229.

Katz, J., & Gartner, W. (1988). Properties of emerging organizations. *Academy of Management Review, 13,* 429–441.

Kim, M., & Hunter, J. (1993). Relationships among attitudes, intentions and behavior. *Communication Research, 20,* 331–364.

Krueger, N. (1993). Impact of prior entrepreneurial exposure on perceptions of new venture feasibility and desirability. *Entrepreneurship Theory & Practice, 18*(1), 5–21.

Krueger, N., & Brazeal, D. (1994). Entrepreneurial potential & potential entrepreneurs. *Entrepreneurship Theory & Practice, 18*(3), 91–104.

Krueger, N., & Dickson, P. (1994). How believing in ourselves increases risk taking: Self-efficacy and perceptions of opportunity and threat. *Decision Sciences, 25*(3), 385–400.

Krueger, N., & Gertz, D. (1996). Growth or downsizing? A cognitive approach. Paper presented at the Strategic Management Society, Phoenix, Arizona.

Krueger, N., Reilly, M., & Carsrud, A. (in press). A competing models test of entrepreneurial intentions. *Journal of Business Venturing.*

Kuratko, D., Montagno, R., & Hornsby, J. (1990). Developing an intrapreneurial assessment instrument for effective corporate entrepreneurial environment. *Strategic Management Journal,* 11(Summer), 49–58.

Lord, R., & Maher, K. (1990). Alternative information-processing models and their implications for theory, research, and practice. *Academy of Management Review, 15*(1), 9–28.

Lumpkin, G. T., & Dess, G. (1996). Clarifying the entrepreneurial orientation construct & linking it to performance, *Academy of Management Review, 21*(1), 135–172.

MacMillan, I., Block, Z., & Narasimha, P. (1986). Corporate venturing: Alternatives, obstacles encountered & experience effects. *Journal of Business Venturing, 1*, 177–191.

MacMillian, I., & Katz, J. 1992. Idiosyncratic milieus of entrepreneurial research. *Journal of Business Venturing, 7*, 1–8.

McCall, M. (1992). Executive development as corporate strategy. *Journal of Business Strategy, 13*, 25–31.

McGrath, R. G. (1995). Advantage from adversity. *Journal of Business Venturing, 10*, 121–142.

McGrath, R., Tsai, M., Venkataraman, S., & MacMillan, I. (1996). Innovation, competitive advantage, & rent. *Management Science, 42*(3), 389–403.

Mintzberg, H. (1994). *The rise and fall of strategic planning.* New York: Free Press.

Mitchell, R., & Chesteen, S. (1995). Enhancing entrepreneurial expertise: Experiential pedagogy & the new venture expert script. *Simulation & Gaming, 26*(3), 288–306.

Reitan, B. (1997). Where do we learn that entrepreneurship is feasible, desirable, and/or profitable? Paper presented to the ICSB World Conference: San Francisco, CA.

Ropo, A., & Hunt, J. (1995). Entrepreneurial processes as virtuous & vicious spirals in a changing opportunity structure. *Entrepreneurship Theory & Practice, 19*(3), 91–111.

Scott, S., & Bruce, R. (1994). Determinants of innovative behavior: A path model of individual innovation in the workplace. *Academy of Management Journal, 37*(3), 580–607.

Senge, P. (1992). Mental models. *The Planning Review, 20*, 4–11.

Shane, S. (1994). Cultural values & the championing process. *Entrepreneurship Theory & Practice, 18*(4). 25 41.

Shapero, A. (1982). Some social dimensions of entrepreneurship. In C. Kent, D. Sexton, & K. Vesper (Eds.). *The encyclopedia of entrepreneurship.* Englewood Cliffs, NJ: Prentice Hall.

Shapero, A. (1985). *Managing professional people.* New York: Free Press.

Shepherd, D., & Douglas, E. (1997). Entrepreneurial attitude & intentions in career decision makers. Paper at ICSB.

Stevenson, H., & Jarillo, J. C. (1990). A paradigm for entrepreneurship: Entrepreneurial management. *Strategic Management Journal, 11*, 17–27.

Stopford, J., & Baden-Fuller, C. (1994). Creating corporate entrepreneurship. *Strategic Management Journal, 15*, 521–536.

Triandis, H. (1967). *Interpersonal behavior.* New York: Free Press.

Tubbs, M., & Ekeberg, S. (1991). The role of intentions in work motivation: Implications for goal-setting theory and research. *Academy of Management Review, 16*(1), 180–199.

Weick, K. (1979). *The social psychology of organizing* (2nd ed.). Reading, MA: Addison-Wesley.

Zahra, S., & Chaples, S. (1993). Blind spots in competitive analysis. *Academy of Management Executive, 7*(2), 7–28.

COMPREHENSIVE CASE STUDY

C A S E   SANDWICH GALAXY

Robert Letovsky and Tamara Mullarky

Part A
Sue Eldridge: A Prospective Franschisee

As soon as the phone rang, Sue Eldridge raced across the study in her home in Elmira, NY, to answer it. It was 1:45 AM, but Sue was still at work, poring over collateral forms from her bank and documents prepared by her attorney. She knew who the call was from, and she realized that she had to give the caller an answer. Perhaps she could stall until morning, but she was sure that if she didn't give Sandy Lithrow a firm commitment to go ahead by then, the whole deal would be off.

Flashback: A History of Sandwich Galaxy

Sandy Lithrow was the founder and owner of Sandwich Galaxy (SG), a chain of deli shops in and around Ithaca, NY. SG was searching for new store operators in the Ithaca area. Sue was an English teacher at one of the local high schools. However, she had decided several years ago to leave teaching if she could find a suitable business of her own. She had told several of her friends about her plans, and one of them put her in touch with Sandy Lithrow. Sue had no prior experience in the restaurant business, but she did enjoy dealing with people and was willing to put in the long hours often required in starting a restaurant.

Ithaca, NY, is a town of about 30,000 people located in western New York state's Finger Lakes district. It is the home to both Cornell University (student population 20,000) and Ithaca College (student population 4,500).

Sandwich Galaxy was an extremely popular lunch spot in Ithaca, not only among college students but also among local business people, office workers and construction crews. The chain was founded by Sandy Lithrow in 1986. She had been an administrator in one of the college's athletics department for several years, but left in 1984 because she felt that she would not be able to move up in the department. She then spent a year managing a health and fitness club in the Ithaca area.

Through her work at the club, Sandy met several people who ran foodcarts in downtown Ithaca. She spent some time with the cart operators, and found that she really enjoyed their outdoors lifestyle and their interactions with the customers. Sandy

This case was prepared by Robert Letovsky and Tamara Mullarky, Saint Michael's College, and is intended to be used as a basis for class discussion. The views represented here are those of the case authors and do not necessarily reflect the views of the Society for Case Research. Authors' views are based on their own professional judgments. The names of the organizations, individuals, locations and financial information have been disguised to preserve the organizations' and individuals' requests for anonymity.

decided to open a cart specializing in sandwiches. Her goal was to offer "a really nice sandwich at reasonable prices."

The cart opened in the summer of 1986. The actual pushcart was designed by Sandy herself, and reflected what would become her trademark commitment to quality and uniqueness: The cart had mahogany countertops, running water, a microwave, refrigerator, dry ice, and a phone jack so people could phone in orders. Sandy's cart was an instant hit: Customers lined up for Sandy's sandwiches, which always featured unique recipes and same-day fresh bread.

Although Sandy's product won instant acceptance, the business itself faced several problems. Being an outdoor stand, the business was entirely weather-dependent. Though sales easily topped $400 on a sunny day, rainy days were a complete loss. Meanwhile, while Sandy's cart was eye-catching, it also weighed over 1,000 pounds. Lacking pivoting casters, the cart frequently got stuck as it was being brought to its downtown site, especially on wet days. This situation drove Sandy to her next step: A mobile sandwich truck bearing the Sandwich Galaxy name. Sandy bought a used pickup, and had it remodeled by the same craftsman who had built her pushcart. The truck also had the mahogany countertops, as well as built-in stereo speakers. Sandy would drive the truck up to a site near one of the local colleges, turn on the music as loud as the speakers could handle, and sell pre-made sandwiches to students who wanted a break from cafeteria food. Sandy even arranged to have graduate students give lunchtime lectures to her clientele on topics ranging from political science to biology.

Though the truck was an improvement over the pushcart, Sandy still found herself too dependent on the weather. The truck format did not last past the fall. In the winter of 1987, Sandy opened her first store, a small deli counter in downtown Ithaca. Like the pushcart, the store was a hit. More importantly, the store offered Sandy some protection against the vagaries of weather. By the end of its first year of operation, between the original pushcart and the first retail outlet, Sandwich Galaxy managed to attain $260,000 in sales (Exhibit 1).

In the fall of 1989, Sandy took several giant steps toward expanding SG. In September, she opened a new outlet on downtown Ithaca's pedestrian mall known as The Commons. Then, in October, SG opened a store in Cortland, a college town twenty-five miles outside of Ithaca. In December 1989, Sandy moved from the first storefront to a 1,100 square foot (s.f.) site nearby. Two months later, she rented an additional 1,500 sf attached to the back of her new retail space and converted it to a large bakery/commissary. Her idea was that the bakery/commissary would prepare all the breads, soups, and salads for the various SG outlets. By having all the baking and preparation done at a central location, Sandy felt that she would be able to assure a consistent level of quality throughout all the stores.

At the same time that she rented the space for the bakery/commissary, Sandy rented an additional 1,200 sf on the second floor of the building to serve as her corporate headquarters. The total renovation costs for preparing the bakery and offices came to almost $55,000. The owner of the building agreed to amortize the renovation costs over five years by adding them to SG's monthly rental. Including the costs of the leasehold improvements, SG's monthly rent at the new location came to almost $7 per square foot, or almost $2,300 per month for the 3,800 square feet. This represented a huge commitment for SG, but Sandy Lithrow was confident that her rapidly expanding business could easily carry the load.

As all this expansion occurred, Sandy Lithrow was finding it increasingly difficult to juggle all of her responsibilities at SG. She was supervising retail staff at her downtown Ithaca location, overseeing operations at the central bakery/commissary,

EXHIBIT A-1   SANDWICH GALAXY

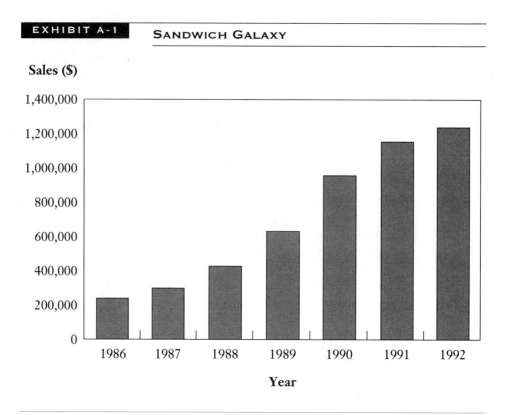

and constantly meeting with prospective new investors who wanted to open SG outlets. In January 1990, she asked a friend of hers, Dori McCloud, to join the business
as a partner. Dori brought several assets to SG. She was an experienced chef, having
worked in various cafes and restaurants for almost ten years. Dori would take over supervision of the central bakery/commissary. She was excited about having the chance
to introduce her ideas into SG's menu, and brought with her a number of unique
recipes from her previous jobs. More importantly, Dori's father, a wealthy food industry executive, agreed to lend SG $50,000, repayable over five years. In exchange, Mr.
McCloud became a silent partner and minority shareholder in SG. The loan came at
a critical time for SG, as the company was trying to digest the full impact of the expenses associated with opening the central bakery/commissary and the corporate offices upstairs. Despite their friendship, Sandy Lithrow knew that Dori could be
argumentative and even abrasive at times. However, Sandy felt that by having her run
the bakery/commissary, Dori would be insulated from dealing with customers.

Within the next three years, Sandwich Galaxy opened four other outlets in and
around Ithaca. Initially, each outlet was owned by the company, with in-store managers hired by Sandy. Employees were generally college students. Pay at Sandwich
Galaxy was good, to the point where word was out on the local student grapevine that
SG was a choice job for college students. Counter staff made a base of $3.50 per hour,
but with tips could make between $10 and $11 per hour. However, employees with
restaurant experience or cutting skills could start at as much as $5.50 per hour. Mean-
while, store managers earned between $7.00 and $10.00 per hour, and had health insurance paid for by the company.

In early 1991, Sandy approached Carol Fishman, the manager of the SG store in Cortland, with a proposal to buy the outlet and run it as a franchise. According to Sandy's original proposal, Carol Fishman would make an initial $28,000 up-front payment, which would cover purchase of the equipment in the store and the rights to the Sandwich Galaxy name. Fishman would also pay a royalty of 1% of gross sales each month. SG, in turn, would supply the store with all its daily needs for breads, salads, and soups at cost. Fishman's initial response was that she lacked the funds to even think about making the purchase. Sandy countered with a new proposal wherein Sandy would lend Carol $23,000 of the original up-front payment if Carol made an immediate down-payment of $5,000 and agreed to assume SG's unpaid back rent of almost $3,000 on the Cortland location. Carol Fishman managed to come up with $5,000 by liquidating savings and borrowing from her family, she negotiated a repayment schedule with the Cortland location's landlord, and then she signed a $23,000 promissory note to Sandy. The franchise deal was finalized in the spring of 1991.

In January of 1992, Roger Harris, a realtor from Geneva, NY, a small college town about 45 miles from Ithaca, contacted Sandy about opening a SG franchise in that town. Harris had been traveling through Ithaca one day and stopped for lunch at a SG outlet. He was impressed with the quality and uniqueness of the sandwiches, and thought that the "hip" SG image would be perfect for Geneva, a town of about 16,000 people. Geneva was home to two small colleges, though both were much smaller than Cornell and Ithaca. Geneva was also a popular tourist stop for visitors to the Finger Lakes district. Roger Harris owned a large retail space on Geneva's main shopping street. The original tenant, a clothing shop, had recently gone out of business and Harris was desperately trying to find a new tenant. He was carrying a mortgage on the property of almost $490,000, with a monthly mortgage payment of $3,800, and Harris realized that he couldn't afford to have the property sit empty for long. He had decided that if he couldn't find a suitable tenant, he would try to find a business to run on his own to occupy the space and generate the income needed to carry the mortgage.

Harris met with Sandy Lithrow in late January 1992. During their meeting, Harris was impressed with Sandy's enthusiasm and many ideas for expanding SG. At this point, SG was on a roll, with four outlets in and around Ithaca, and a solid reputation in town as the place to go for high quality, unique sandwiches at reasonable prices. Sandy herself was a local celebrity, and had recently been asked to participate in a special task force organized by Ithaca's mayor to travel to Russia to promote economic ties with the town's sister city. Even though Harris admitted to Sandy that he lacked any restaurant or retail experience, it seemed to him that Sandy was nonetheless extremely eager to sign him on as a SG franchisee. Under the deal they worked out, Harris would pay SG an up front fee of $30,000, paid in installments over the next three years. The first installment was only $4,000. This was done at the advice of SG's counsel, who told Sandy that any payment under $5,000 was not considered a franchise agreement in the eyes of the law, thus eliminating many of the disclosure provisions required under formal franchising agreements. Harris would also pay SG 2% of gross income for the first year of operation and 3% of gross in subsequent years.

In return for his up-front payment and ongoing royalties, Harris would be authorized to open a deli in his Geneva retail site under the SG name. Sandy would help him set up the business by assisting with the design of the store layout and selection of fixtures and equipment, training Harris' staff and sharing with Harris her recipes. Originally, Sandy wanted Harris to source his daily soup, salad, and bread needs from her central bakery/commissary in Ithaca. However, Harris felt that with the space that he had available, it would pay for him to install ovens right in his Geneva deli and fill all his store's baking and cooking needs right there. Sandy agreed, and so the Geneva store became the first SG outlet not dependent on the central commissary.

Roger Harris' SG outlet in Geneva opened in the summer of 1992. During the two months prior to opening day, Sandy Lithrow was there every day, supervising the renovation of the store and installation of the fixtures and equipment. She also sent two of her full-time staff from Ithaca, a baker from the central commissary and a manager from one of her stores, to spend a month in Geneva training Harris' newly hired employees. Lithrow even paid the salaries of two of Harris's staff who were sent up to the central commissary in Ithaca for a month to be trained.

Over the next two years, SG opened several new stores in and around Ithaca. However, several locations closed so the total number of SG outlets remained constant at five. Sandy Lithrow continued to be a fixture on the local business scene, frequently appearing as a speaker on the challenges of entrepreneurship for local community groups.

Sue Eldridge: A Decision Must Be Made

The package that SG was offering to Sue Eldridge was similar to the one Roger Harris had received. Eldridge would pay an up-front fee of $30,000, with an initial payment of $4,000 made upon signing and the balance payable over two years. Eldridge would also pay a royalty of 2% of gross revenue in her first year of operation, with the royalty increased to 3% for subsequent years. In return, she would have Sandy Lithrow's help in designing, setting up and opening an SG outlet in Elmira. SG would train Sue's staff, both at the new store and at the company's central commissary. Sue would source her daily bread, salad and soup needs from SG's central commissary. Sue would also benefit from volume discounts offered to SG outlets by the various purveyors of meats and condiments. Sandy had projected that Sue's new shop would average $700 per day in sales, resulting in an annual gross income of about $218,000. After expenses, Sandy forecast that Sue would earn between $35,000 and $40,000 per year from the venture, assuming that Sue worked in the store instead of hiring a manager.

Negotiations had been going back and forth for over three weeks. With each passing day, Sue sensed that Sandy seemed to be getting more and more anxious to close the deal. The phone calls from Sandy had been getting more and more frequent, to the point were it seemed that the only phone calls Sue was getting were from Sandy Lithrow. Sue's attorney had looked over the proposed agreement, and didn't seem to feel that it was too onerous. Meanwhile, Sue's banker was prepared to extend her a loan to cover the $30,000 up-front fee, though the loan was to be secured by a second mortgage on Sue's home.

SG seemed to be doing well, and this seemed to be the opportunity that Sue Eldridge had been waiting for to allow her to leave teaching and start her own business. Still, over the past two weeks she had been unable to get herself to simply say "yes" to the deal with SG. Maybe it was the amount of money involved, or the fact that she would be re-mortgaging her home. SG certainly seemed to be successful, and no one questioned its reputation as the leader in the local lunch trade. As she raced to answer the telephone, she frantically tried to come up with something to say to Sandy Lithrow.

EXHIBIT A-2	CHRONOLOGY

1986

Summer	Sandwich Galaxy (SG) begins as an outdoor "pushcart" in downtown Ithaca.
Fall	SG opens a second outdoor location at the local college: a pickup truck converted to serve as a mobile sandwich shop

1987

Winter	Sandwich Galaxy opens first store-front deli in downtown Ithaca. Pushcart and mobile shop are closed.

1989

Fall	SG opens second deli in Ithaca. SG opens additional outlet in Cortland.
Winter	Original SG deli moves to larger location in downtown Ithaca.

1990

Winter	Dori McCloud invests $50,000 and becomes a SG partner. SG rents additional space at its main downtown Ithaca deli; adds central bakery/commissary and office space.

1991

Winter	Sandy offers to franchise company-owned Cortland outlet to store manager, Carol Fishman.
Spring	Carol Fishman becomes first SG franchise owner.

1992

Spring	Roger Harris signs franchise agreement for a SG franchise in Geneva. Sue Eldridge becomes a SG franchise in Elmira.
Summer	Roger Harris opens a SG franchise in Geneva.

1990–1993

	Four new SG outlets open in and around Ithaca, others close; total stabilizes at five outlets.

CHAPTER

6

Assessment of Entrepreneurial Ventures

Key Topics

- **New-Venture Assessment: Critical Factors**

- **The Environment for New Ventures**

- **Key Steps for Industry Analysis**

- **The Evaluation Process**

New-Venture Assessment: Critical Factors

A number of critical factors are important in new-venture assessment. One way to identify and evaluate them is with the help of a checklist (Table 6.1). In most cases, however, such a questionnaire approach is too general; instead, the assessment must be tailor-made for the specific venture.

A new venture progresses through three specific phases: prestart-up, start-up, and poststart-up.

- The prestart-up phase begins with an idea for the venture and ends when the doors open for business.

- The start-up phase commences with initiation of sales activity and delivery of products and/or services and ends when the business is firmly established and beyond short-term threats to its survival.

TABLE 6.1	A NEW-VENTURE IDEA CHECKLIST

Basic Feasibility of the Venture

1. Can the product or service work?
2. Is it legal?

Competitive Advantages of the Venture

1. What specific competitive advantages will the product or service offer?
2. What are the competitive advantages of the companies already in business?
3. How are the competitors likely to respond?
4. How will the initial competitive advantage be maintained?

Buyer Decisions in the Venture

1. Who are the customers likely to be?
2. How much will each customer buy and how many customers are there?
3. Where are these customers located and how will they be serviced?

Marketing of the Goods and Services

1. How much will be spent on advertising and selling?
2. What share of market will the company capture? By when?
3. Who will perform the selling functions?
4. How will prices be set? How will they compare with the competition's prices?
5. How important is location, and how will it be determined?
6. What distribution channels will be used—wholesale, retail, agents, direct mail?
7. What are the sales targets? By when should they be met?
8. Can any orders be obtained before starting the business? How many? For what total amount?

(continued)

TABLE 6.1	**A NEW-VENTURE IDEA CHECKLIST** *(CONTINUED)*

Production of the Goods and Services

1. Will the company make or buy what it sells? Or will it be a combination of these two strategies?
2. Are there sources of supply available at reasonable prices?
3. How long will delivery take?
4. Have adequate lease arrangements for premises been made?
5. Can the needed equipment be available on time?
6. Are there any special problems with plant setup, clearances, or insurance? How will they be resolved?
7. How will quality be controlled?
8. How will returns and servicing be handled?
9. How will pilferage, waste, spoilage, and scrap be controlled?

Staffing Decisions in the Venture

1. How will competence in each area of the business be ensured?
2. Who will have to be hired? By when? How will they be found and recruited?
3. Will a banker, lawyer, accountant, or other advisers be needed?
4. How will replacements be obtained if key people leave?
5. Will special benefit plans have to be arranged?

Control of the Venture

1. What records will be needed? When?
2. Will any special controls be required? What are they? Who will be responsible for them?

Financing the Venture

1. How much will be needed for development of the product or service?
2. How much will be needed for setting up operations?
3. How much will be needed for working capital?
4. Where will the money come from? What if more is needed?
5. Which assumptions in the financial forecasts are most uncertain?
6. What will be the return on equity, or sales, and how does it compare with the industry?
7. When and how will investors get their money back?
8. What will be needed from the bank, and what is the bank's response?

SOURCE: Karl H. Vesper, *New Venture Strategies*, © 1990, p. 172. Adapted by permission of Prentice-Hall, Inc., Englewood Cliffs, New Jersey.

- The poststart-up phase lasts until the venture is terminated or the surviving organizational entity is no longer controlled by an entrepreneur.

This chapter focuses on the prestart-up and start-up phases, because they are critical segments for entrepreneurs. Five critical factors can determine the venture's success or failure during these two phases:

- The relative **uniqueness** of the venture
- The relative **investment** size at start-up
- The **expected growth** of sales and/or profits as the venture moves through its start-up phase
- The **availability of products**
- The **availability of customers.**

Uniqueness

A new venture's range of uniqueness can be considerable, extending from fairly routine to highly nonroutine. The amount of innovation required during the prestart-up phase separates the routine from the nonroutine, with this distinction being based on the need for new-process technology to produce services or products and/or on the need to service new-market segments. Venture uniqueness is further characterized by the length of time that a nonroutine venture remains nonroutine. For instance, will new products, new technology, and new markets be required on a continuing basis? Or will the venture be able to "settle down" after the start-up period and use existing products, technologies, and markets?

Investment

The capital investment required to start a new venture can vary considerably. In some industries, less than $50,000 may be required; in other industries, millions of dollars may be necessary. Moreover, in some industries only large-scale start-ups are feasible. For example, in the retail industry one can start a small venture with a small capital investment that can remain small or grow into a larger enterprise. By contrast, an entrepreneur attempting to break into the airline industry needs a considerable upfront investment.

Another critical finance-related issue is the extending and timing of funds needed to move through the venture process. To determine the amount of investment needed, questions such as the following must be answered:

Will industry growth be sufficient to maintain break-even sales to cover a high fixed-cost structure during the start-up period?

Do the principal entrepreneurs have access to substantial financial reserves to protect a large initial investment?

Do the entrepreneurs have the appropriate contacts to take advantage of various environmental opportunities?

Do the entrepreneurs have both industry and entrepreneurial track records that justify the financial risk of a large-scale start-up?

Sales Growth

Sales growth in the start-up phase is another critical factor. Key questions to ask include the following:

What is the anticipated growth pattern for new-venture sales and profits?

Are sales and profits expected to grow slowly or level off shortly after start-up?

Are large profits expected at some point with only small or moderate sales growth?

Are both high-sales growth and high-profit growth likely?

Will there be limited initial profits with eventual high-profit growth over a multi-year period?

In answering these questions, it is important to remember that most ventures fit into one of the three classifications:

- The primary driving forces of **lifestyle ventures** are independence, autonomy, and control. Neither large sales nor profits are important beyond providing an adequate, comfortable living for the entrepreneur.

- In **smaller profitable ventures,** financial considerations play a major role. Autonomy and control are also important in the sense that the entrepreneur does not want venture sales (and employment) to become so large that he or she must relinquish equity or ownership position, thus giving up control over cash flow and profits, which, it is hoped, will be substantial.

- In **high-growth ventures,** significant sales and profit growth are expected to the extent that it may be possible to attract venture capital money and/or funds raised through public or private placements.[1]

Product Availability

Product availability and the availability of a salable good or service are essential to the success of any venture at the time that the business opens its doors. Some ventures have problems in this regard because the product or service is still in development and needs further modification or testing. Others find that they bring their products to market too soon and subsequently these products must be recalled for additional work. A typical example is a software firm that rushes the development of its product and is then besieged by customers who find bugs in the program. Lack of product availability in finished form can affect both the company's image and its bottom line.

Customer Availability

If a product is available before the venture is launched, the odds are greater that the enterprise will be successful. Similarly, venture risk is affected by customer availability at start-up. At one end of the risk continuum is a venture that has customers who are willing to pay cash for its products or services before delivery. At the other end of the continuum is the enterprise that starts operations without knowing exactly who will buy its product. A critical consideration is how long it will take to determine who the customers are and what their buying habits are. As Ronstadt notes:

---

[1]Adapted from Robert C. Ronstadt, *Entrepreneurship*, (Dover, MA: Lord Publishing, 1984), 75.

The decision to ignore the market is an extremely risky one. There are, after all, two fundamental criteria for entrepreneurial success. The first is having a customer who is willing to pay you a profitable price for a product or a service. The second is that you must actually produce and deliver the product or service. The farther a venture removes itself from certainty about these two rules, the greater the risk and the greater the time required to offset the risk as the venture moves through the prestart-up and start-up periods.[2]

The Environment for New Ventures

There are many ways to construct an environmental assessment for a new venture, but generally these approaches are neither highly sophisticated nor heavily quantitative.[3] Being neither an economist nor a quantitative analyst, the average new-venture entrepreneur will stay within the confines of what he or she understands and can use to conduct an assessment. This approach often entails evaluating the general environment and compiling a detailed assessment of the industry characteristics, barriers to entry, and competitive analysis.

Evaluation of the industry environment is a critical step in the overall economic assessment of a new venture. Many major elements of industry structure exist, and hence an assessment of the entire industry structure can be detailed and comprehensive.[4] For our purposes here, we will examine only those segments of which entrepreneurs need to be aware.

Common Industry Characteristics

Although industries vary in size and development, certain characteristics are common to both new and emerging industries. The most important of these characteristics are discussed next.

Technological Uncertainty   A great deal of uncertainty usually exists regarding the technology of an emerging industry. What product configuration will ultimately prove to be the best? Which production technology will prove to be the most efficient? How difficult will it be to develop this technology? How difficult will it be to copy technological breakthroughs in the industry?

Strategic Uncertainty   Related to technological uncertainty is the wide variety of strategic approaches often tried by industry participants. Because no "right" strategy has been clearly identified, industry participants may formulate different approaches to product positioning, advertising, pricing, and the like, and they may adopt different product configurations or product technologies.

[2]Ibid., 79.

[3]Andrew H. Van de Ven, "The Development of an Infrastructure for Entrepreneurship," *Journal of Business Venturing* (May 1993): 211–230.

[4]See, for example, Michael E. Porter, *Competitive Strategy* (New York: Free Press, 1980); Michael E. Porter, *Competitive Advantage* (New York: Free Press, 1985); and Michael E. Porter, "From Competitive Advantage to Corporate Strategy," *Harvard Business Review* (May–June 1987): 43–59.

First-Time Buyers   The customers of an emerging industry's products or services are first-time buyers. The marketing task is thus one of substitution, or getting the buyer to make the initial purchase of the new product or service.

Short Time Horizons   The pressure to develop customers or produce products to meet demand is so great in many emerging industries that bottlenecks and problems are dealt with expediently rather than on the basis of an analysis of future conditions.[5] Short-run results are often given major attention, while long-run results receive too little consideration.

Barriers to Entry   In addition to the structural hurdles faced by an emerging industry barriers to entry must be overcome. These barriers may include proprietary technology (expensive to access), access to distribution channels (limited or closed to newcomers), access to raw materials and other inputs (for example, skilled labor), cost advantages due to lack of experience (magnified by technological and competitive uncertainties), or risk (which raises the effective opportunity cost of capital).

Some of these barriers decline or disappear as the industry develops. Nevertheless, it behooves entrepreneurs to be aware of them.

Competitive Analysis   Analyzing the competition in the industry involves consideration of the number of competitors as well as the strength of each rival. Both the quality and quantity of the competition must be scrutinized carefully.

When assessing the competition, it is important to keep in mind that various elements affect the profile. Figure 6.1 illustrates the components of a competitive analysis from two standpoints: what drives the competition and what the competition can do. The competition's current strategy and future goals help dictate its response. So, too, will the assumptions that each competitor makes about itself as well as its perceived strengths and weaknesses.

Figure 6.1 provides a framework that allows an entrepreneur to better assess the competition. A good competitive analysis is vital to the ultimate success of any new venture.

Key Steps for Industry Analysis

A number of useful steps can assist an entrepreneur in examining an industry. Following are five of the most helpful:

Clearly Define the Industry for the New Venture   The key here is to develop a relevant definition that describes the focus of the new venture. Definitions will vary, of course, depending on the venture and its specific target market. The more clearly the entrepreneur can define the industry for the new venture, the better the chance that the venture will get off to a sound start.

Analyze the Competition   An analysis of the number, relative size, traditions, and cost structures of direct competitors in the industry can help establish the nature of

---

[5]For a detailed discussion of this topic, see Porter, *Competitive Strategy*; and Michael E. Porter and Victor E. Millar, "How Information Gives You Competitive Advantage," *Harvard Business Review* (July–Aug. 1985): 149–160.

| FIGURE 6.1 | COMPONENTS OF A COMPETITIVE ANALYSIS |

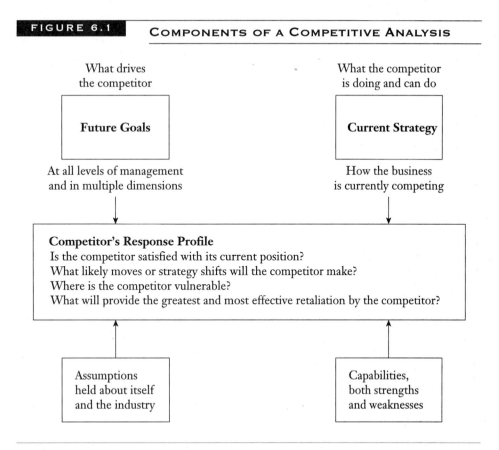

SOURCE: Adapted with permission of The Free Press, a division of Macmillan, Inc., from *Competitive Strategy: Techniques for Analyzing Industries and Competitors* by Michael E. Porter, p. 49. Copyright © 1980 by The Free Press.

the competition. Will competition become more or less intense as the number and characteristics of competitors change over time? This question can also be answered through detailed analysis. For instance, what will happen to the degree of competition if (1) market growth increases rapidly, (2) direct competitors equalize in size, (3) one or two direct competitors become substantially larger in size, or (4) product/service differentiation slows down?

Determine the Strength and Characteristics of Suppliers The important factor here is to establish the stance of the venture in relation to suppliers. How will the new firm be treated compared to other, more established firms? Do customers have a choice of many suppliers offering diverse services or must the new venture be prepared to accept limited services from a few?

Establish the "Value Added" Measure of the New Venture The concept of value added is a basic form of contribution analysis in which sales minus raw material costs equals the value added. This measure enables an individual to determine how much value is being added to the product or service by the entrepreneur. This analysis introduces the concept of integration, backward or forward. Backward integration is a buyer's movement to absorb the duties of a buyer. The likelihood of integration taking place is substantially influenced by the degree to which value added is essential to the final processing and consumption by the user.

Project the Market Size for the Particular Industry Markets are dynamic and prone to change over time. Therefore, it is important to examine the historical progression of the market, establish its present size, and extrapolate the data to project the likely potential of market growth. This assessment can be done by studying the industry life cycle, consumers (numbers and trends), product/service developments, and competitive analysis.

Although these five key points are not all-inclusive, they do represent an initial analysis of the industry environment faced by a new venture. This type of macro analysis is needed to establish the framework within which a venture will start, grow, and, it is hoped, prosper.

The Evaluation Process

A critical task in starting a new-business enterprise is to determine the feasibility of the product or service idea getting off the ground by undertaking solid analysis and evaluation. Entrepreneurs must put their ideas through this analysis to discover if they contain any fatal flaws.

Ask the Right Questions

Many important evaluation-related questions should be asked. Ten sets of preliminary questions that can be used to screen an idea are presented here:

1. Is it a new product or service idea? Is it proprietary? Can it be patented or copyrighted? Is it unique enough to get a significant head start on the competition? Or can it be easily copied?

2. Has a prototype been tested by independent testers who try to blow up the system or rip the product to shreds? What are its weak points? Will it stand up? What level of research and development should it receive over the next five years? If a service, has it been tested on customers? Will customers pay their hard-earned money for it?

3. Has it been taken to trade shows? If so, what reactions did it receive? Were any sales made? Has it been taken to distributors? Have they placed any orders?

4. Is the product or service easily understood by customers, bankers, venture capitalists, accountants, lawyers, and insurance agents?

5. What is the overall market? What are the market segments? Can the product penetrate these segments? Are there special niches that can be exploited?

6. Has market research been conducted? Who else is considered part of the market? How big is the market? How fast is it growing? What are the trends? What is the projected life cycle of the product or service? What degree of penetration can be achieved? Are there any testimonials from customers and purchasing agents? What type of advertising and promotion plans will be used?

7. What distribution and sales methods will be used—jobbers, independent sales representatives, company sales force, direct mail, door-to-door sales, supermarkets, service stations, company-owned stores? How will the product be transported: company-owned trucks, common carriers, postal service, or air freight?

8. How will the product be made? How much will it cost? For example, will it be produced in-house or by others? Will production be by job shop or continuous process? What is the present capacity of company facilities? What is the break-even point?

9. Will the business concept be developed and licensed to others, or developed and sold off?

10. Can the company get, or has it already lined up, the necessary skills to operate the business venture? Who are the workers? Are they dependable and competent? How much capital will be needed now? How much more in the future? Have major stages in financing been developed?[6]

Feasibility Criteria Approach

A single strategic variable seldom determines the ultimate success or failure of a new venture. Instead, in most situations, a combination of variables influences the outcome. Thus it is important to identify and investigate these variables before the new idea is put into practice. The results of a feasibility criteria approach enable the entrepreneur to judge the idea's business potential.

The feasibility criteria approach, developed as a criteria selection list from which entrepreneurs can gain insights into the viability of their venture, is based on the following questions:

1. *Is it proprietary?* The product does not have to be patented, but it should be sufficiently proprietary to permit a long head start against competitors and a period of extraordinary profits early in the venture to offset start-up costs.

2. *Are the initial production costs realistic?* Most estimates are too low. A careful, detailed analysis should be made so that no large unexpected expenses crop up.

3. *Are the initial marketing costs realistic?* Answering this question requires the entrepreneur to identify target markets, market channels, and promotion strategy.

4. *Does the product have potential for very high margins?* This potential is almost a necessity for a fledgling company. The financial community understands gross margins and, without the promise of high margins, obtaining funding can be difficult.

5. *Is the time required to get to market and to reach the break-even point realistic?* In most cases faster is better. In all cases the venture plan is tied to this answer, and an error here can spell trouble later on.

6. *Is the potential market large?* In determining the potential market, one must look three to five years into the future because some markets take that long

[6]John G. Burch, *Entrepreneurship* (New York: Wiley, 1986), 68–69.

to emerge. The cellular telephone, for example, had an annual demand of approximately 400,000 units in 1982. By 1991, however, this market had grown to 700,000 units annually.

7. *Is the product the first of a growing family?* If it is, the venture will be more attractive to investors. After all, if a large return is not made on the first product, it might be realized on the second, third, or fourth product.

8. *Is there an initial customer?* Financial backers are impressed when a venture can list its first ten customers by name. This pent-up demand also means that the first quarter's results are likely to be good and the focus of attention can be directed to later quarters.

9. *Are development costs and calendar times realistic?* Preferably, they should be zero. A ready-to-go product give the venture a major advantage over competitors. If there are costs, they should be complete and detailed and tied to a month-by-month schedule.

10. *Is this a growing industry?* Industry growth is not absolutely essential if profits and company growth are evident, but there is less room for mistakes. In a growing industry, good companies do even better.

11. *Are the product and the need for it understood by the financial community?* If financiers can grasp the concept and its value, chances for funding will increase. For example, a portable heart-monitoring system for postcoronary patient monitoring is a product that many will understand. Undoubtedly, some of those hearing the presentation for the product will have already had coronaries or heart problems of some sort.[7]

This criteria selection approach provides a means of analyzing the internal strengths and weaknesses that exist in a new venture by focusing on the marketing and industry potential that is critical to assessment. If the new venture meets fewer than six of these criteria, it typically lacks feasibility for funding. If the new venture meets seven or more of the criteria, it may stand a good chance of being funded.

Comprehensive Feasibility Approach

As a more wide-ranging and systematic feasibility analysis, the comprehensive feasibility approach incorporates external factors in addition to those outlined in the preceding questions. Figure 6.2 presents a breakdown of the factors involved in a critical feasibility study of a new venture: technical, market, financial, organizational, and competitive. A more detailed feasibility analysis guide is provided in Table 6.2, which identifies the specific activities involved in each feasibility area. Although all five of the areas presented in Figure 6.2 are important, two merit special attention: technical and market.

Technical Feasibility An entrepreneur should evaluate a new-venture idea by first identifying the technical requirements—the technical feasibility—for producing a

[7]Gordon B. Baty, *Entrepreneurship: Playing to Win* (Reston, VA: Reston Publishing, 1974), 33–34.

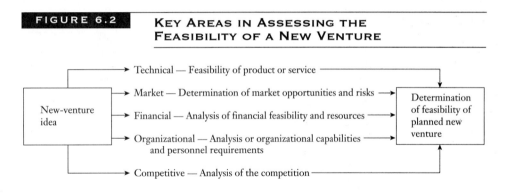

FIGURE 6.2   **KEY AREAS IN ASSESSING THE FEASIBILITY OF A NEW VENTURE**

product or service that will satisfy the expectations of potential customer. The most important of these follow:

- Functional design of the product and attractiveness in appearance

- Flexibility, permitting ready modification of the external features of the product to meet customer demands or technological and competitive changes

- Durability of the materials from which the product is made

- Reliability, ensuring performance as expected under normal operating conditions

- Product safety, posing no potential dangers under normal operating conditions

- Reasonable utility, an acceptable rate of obsolescence

- Ease and low cost of maintenance

- Standardization through elimination of unnecessary variety among potentially interchangeable parts

- Ease of processing or manufacture

- Ease in handling and use[8]

The results of this investigation provide a basis for deciding whether a new venture is feasible from a technical point of view.

Marketability   Assembling and analyzing relevant information about the marketability of a new venture are vital activities in judging its potential success. This type of analysis includes three major areas: (1) investigating the full market potential and identifying customers (or users) for the goods of service; (2) analyzing the extent to which the enterprise might exploit this potential market; and (3) using market analysis to determine the opportunities and risks associated with the venture. To address these

---

[8]Hans Schollhammer and Arthur H. Kuriloff, *Entrepreneurship and Small Business Management* (New York: Wiley, 1979), 58.

TABLE 6.2		SPECIFIC ACTIVITIES OF FEASIBILITY ANALYSES		

Technical Feasibility Analysis	Market Feasibility Analysis	Financial Feasibility Analysis	Analysis of Organizational Capabilities	Competitive Analysis
Crucial Technical Specifications	*Market Potential*	*Required Financial Resources*	*Personnel Requirements*	*Existing Competitors*
Design	Identification of potential customers and their dominant characteristics (e.g., age, income level, buying habits)	Fixed assets	Required skills levels and other personal characteristics of potential employees	Size, financial resources, market entrenchment
Durability		Current assets		Potential reaction of competitors to newcomer by means of price cutting, aggressive advertising, introduction of new products, etc.
Reliability		Necessary working capital	Managerial requirements	
Product safety	Potential market share (as affected by competitive situation)	*Available Financial Resources*	Determination of individual responsibilities	
Standardization				
Engineering Requirements	Potential sales volume	Required borrowing	Determination of required organizational relationships	Potential new competitors
Machines	Sales price projections	Potential sources for funds		
Tools	*Market Testing*	Cost of borrowing	Potential organizational development	
Instruments	Selection of test	Repayment conditions	Competitive analysis	
Work flow	Actual market test	Operation cost analysis		
Product Development	Analysis of market	Fixed costs		
Blueprints	*Market Planning Issues*	Variable costs		
Models	Preferred channels of distribution, impact of promotional efforts, required distribution points (warehouses), packaging considerations, price differentiation	Projected cash flow		
Prototypes		Projected profitability		
Product Testing				
Lab testing				
Field testing				
Plant Location				
Desirable characteristics of plant size (proximity to suppliers, customers), environmental regulations				

SOURCE: Hans Schollhammer and Arthur H. Kuriloff, *Entrepreneurship and Small Business Management* (New York: Wiley, 1979), 56.

areas, a variety of information sources must be found and used. General sources for a market feasibility analysis would include the following:

- *General economic trends*—economic indicators such as new orders, housing starts, inventories, and consumer spending.
- *Market data*—customers and customer demand patterns (for example, seasonal variations in demand, governmental regulations affecting demand).

- *Pricing data*—range of prices for the same, complementary, and substitute products, base prices, and discount structures.

- *Competitive data*—major competitors and their competitive strengths.

It is important to note the value of marketing research in the overall assessment and evaluation of a new venture.[9]

Thus, as demonstrated by Table 6.2, the comprehensive feasibility analysis approach is closely related to the preparation of a thorough business plan (covered in detail in Chapter 7). The approach clearly illustrates the need to evaluate each segment of the venture before initiating the business or presenting it to capital sources.

Exploring the Entrepeneurial Concepts

The following sections provide an "entrepreneurial library" that contains a journal reading on this chapter's subject and a comprehensive case study to illustrate the concept in practice. It is hoped that through the reading and discussion of the case, you will gain a greater understanding of the chapter.

THE ENTREPRENEURIAL LIBRARY

Reading for Chapter 6

PERCEIVED RISKS AND CHOICES IN ENTREPRENEURS' NEW VENTURE DECISIONS

David Forlani University of Colorado at Denver, Denver, Colorado
John W. Mullins University of Denver, Denver, Colorado

Address correspondence to David Forlani, Assistant Professor, College of Business Administration, University of Colorado at Denver, Box 165, Campus Box 173364, Denver, CO 80217; (303) 556-6616. Journal of Business Venturing **15**, 305–322 © Elsevier Science Inc. All rights reserved. 655 Avenue of the Americas, New York, NY 10010.

Executive Summary

Though risk plays a central role in most entrepreneurial decision making, little empirical research has explicitly examined how the elements of risk, risk perceptions, and entrepreneurs' propensities to take risks influence choices among potentially risky entrepreneurial ventures. This experimental study asked a sample of entrepreneurs leading America's fastest growing firms to make choices among a series of hypothetical new ventures. The results indicate that such choices are influenced by the risks inherent

---

[9]Gerald E. Hills, "Marketing Analysis in the Business Plan: Venture Capitalists' Perceptions," *Journal of Small Business Management* (Jan. 1985): 38–46. See also Gerald E. Hills and Raymond W. LaForge, "Research at the Marketing Interface to Advance Entrepreneurship Theory," *Entrepreneurship Theory and Practice* (Spring 1992): 33–60.

in the new ventures, as evidenced by the pattern of outcomes anticipated in each venture, the entrepreneurs' differing perceptions of those risks, and differences in their personal propensities to take risks.

The subjects in our sample of entrepreneurs tended not to choose ventures having a high degree of variability in their pattern of anticipated outcomes. This avoidance of outcome variability suggest that the sensitivity analyses commonly prescribed for examining new venture attractiveness may inhibit risk taking, and may deter potential investors from investing in their firms. New approaches to assessing and presenting new venture risk, other than the traditional best case/expected case/worst case approach, may be advisable, as well as sufficiently through market research to provide evidence of the degree to which market acceptance is likely for the venture's products or services.

We also found an effect of differences in risk propensities among entrepreneurs on their new venture choices. This effect suggests not only that entrepreneurs should be wary of any biases they bring to their new venture decisions, but that prospective investors should consider the degree to which entrepreneurs in whom they choose to invest are well matched to the investors' own risk-taking propensities.

Finally, while our sample of entrepreneurs tended to shun high levels of variability in their new venture choices, they appeared willing to accept a considerable degree of hazard, or possible downside, in their new venture choices, presumably in pursuit of potentially significant gains. Entrepreneurs are advised to seek a clear understanding of the downside entailed in their proposed ventures, and develop strategies to mitigate the likelihood of adverse outcomes. Thus they will not jeopardize chances for near-term success and attracting support of investors and others in later stages of the venture or in subsequent ventures.

Our research did not attempt to examine how our subjects' choices would have played out in terms of performance, but the apparent biases which entrepreneurs' risk propensities bring to their assessment of proposed new ventures is a potentially important issue that merits further scrutiny. On one hand, such biases may lead to patterns of suboptimal decisions. On the other hand, our results suggest that investors should entrust their new venture investments to entrepreneurs whose risk propensities (and perhaps other personal characteristics) best match the needs of both the opportunity at hand and the investor's objectives. As many venture capitalists attest, the management of a proposed new venture should lie at the heart of their investment decision. © 2000 Elsevier Science Inc.

Introduction

The image of entrepreneurs as bold, forward-thinking risk takers is a part of American business folklore. For entrepreneurs, risk is a central element in a variety of decision contexts, including those dealing with entry into new ventures or new markets (Dickson 1992; Timmons 1994), and new product introductions (Devinney 1992). Indeed, the uncertain nature of consumer and competitive responses to most entrepreneurial decisions makes consideration of risk an everyday task for most entrepreneurs, as well as for investors whose funds make possible entrepreneurs' pursuit of their dreams (Hall and Hofer 1993; Riquelme and Rickards 1992).

Given the significant failure rate among new ventures (Phillips and Kirchoff 1998; Reynolds 1986), and the rapidly changing markets in which today's new ventures are founded (Dickson 1992), a better understanding of risk and its role in new venture decision making has the potential to improve the quality of decision making in the risk-charged environments which most prospective founders of new firms face. Surprisingly, however, little empirical research has explicitly explored the role of risk in entrepreneurial decision making.

Prior research dealing with risk in entrepreneurial settings has focused largely on investors' decisions, and criteria and procedures used to manage investment risk (Sykes and Dunham 1995) and improve the performance of investment portfolios (e.g., Hall and Hofer 1993; Riquelme and Rickards 1992). Only recently have researchers begun to examine entrepreneurial risk-taking from the entrepreneur's point of view. Palich and Bagby (1995) found that entrepreneurs tend to view some business situations more positively than do nonentrepreneurs, perceiving strengths and opportunities where others seek weaknesses and threats. Their work suggests that entrepreneurs do not see themselves as risk takers, but that they pursue opportunities that others do not because they simply view such opportunities differently. Busenitz and Barney (1997) found that entrepreneurs tended to employ heuristics and biases to simplify and speed their decision making in the complex and risky decision environments which typify start-up situations. We extended this line of research into the perceptions and decision-making behavior of entrepreneurs to examine entrepreneurs perceptions of risk in new venture settings, as well as the choices entrepreneurs make among potentially risky new ventures.

Purpose

This paper's purpose is to improve our understanding of both the role and the antecedents of entrepreneurs' risk perceptions in their new venture decisions. Drawing on established traditions in both economics and behavioral decision theory, we first set forth a framework consisting of several factors likely to influence entrepreneurs' risk perceptions. This framework shows how these perceptions and other factors are linked to new venture decisions. We then experimentally test portions of the framework.

Our study attempts to shed some light on two specific research questions: 1) What factors lead entrepreneurs to perceive new ventures as risky? 2) Why do entrepreneurs sometimes pursue riskier ventures, and sometimes less risky ones? More specifically, we ask if variability in entrepreneurial risk-taking is due to differences in risk among different ventures, entrepreneurs' differing perceptions of such risks, or differences in the propensity of different entrepreneurs to take risks. Thus, we are concerned in this paper with both risk *perceptions* and risk *propensities* as they influence the risky choice *decisions* of entrepreneurs. In addition to addressing these research questions, our study seeks to build an interval scale of risky venture choices for use in this and subsequent empirical research.

A Brief Overview of the Role of Risk Perceptions in New Venture Decisions

Previous research involving the notion of risk in business decision-making contexts articulates two distinct views of risk (Fisher and Hall 1969; March and Shapira 1987), each of which holds implications for entrepreneurs' risk perceptions, and by implication, for risky decision making. Additionally, recent research suggests that factors other than the perceived risks associated with the decision alternatives may significantly influence risky choices (Krueger and Dickson 1994; Manimala 1992; Mullins 1996; Sitkin and Pablo 1992).

Drawing on the work of Sitkin and Pablo (1992), we argue that risk perceptions of entrepreneurs, venture characteristics, contextual effects, and traits of individual entrepreneurs play key roles in entrepreneurs' decisions to enter new ventures (see Figure 1). Stage 1 of our conceptual framework argues that managers' perceptions of new venture risks are driven principally by three sets of factors: a) the relative level of investment needed to fund the venture; b) variability in the anticipated outcomes of the venture; and c) any potential losses which may ensue. Perceived new venture risk is expected to be higher for ventures which entail greater investment (investing available capital in fewer

FIGURE 1   **A FRAMEWORK OF THE ROLE OF RISK PERCEPTIONS IN NEW VENTURE SELECTION**

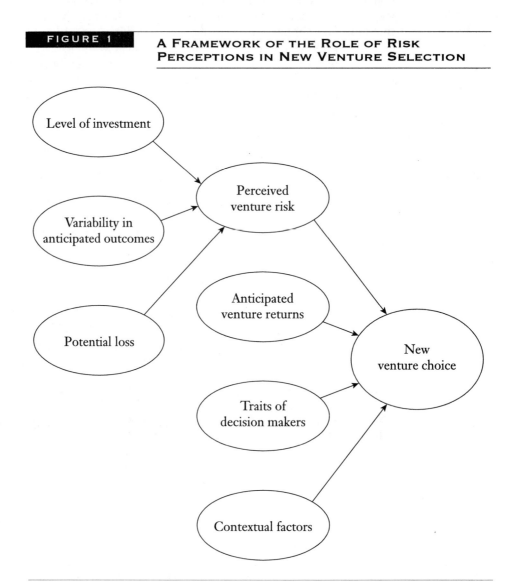

larger ventures limits opportunities for diversification, and there is more to lose on a given venture) and for ventures whose anticipated outcomes are either more uncertain (greater variability in anticipated returns) or entail the possibility of greater operating losses (March and Shapira 1987).

Stage 2 of our framework indicates that new venture choices are driven by the risk perceptions and anticipated returns of various alternative ventures, along with differences in personality traits of entrepreneurs considering such decisions, and a variety of other contextual factors. Such contextual factors include resource constraints, the fit of the venture with the entrepreneur's competencies and interest, and various organizational and environmental conditions operative at the time of the new venture decision (Baird and Thomas 1985). Space limitations require that we only develop and empirically test portions of our framework. Thus, in this paper, we focus on an examination of the effects of anticipated new venture outcomes as well as differences among individual entrepreneurs on risk perceptions and risk-taking behavior. We choose to direct our attention here because anticipated outcomes lie at the heart of the analysis which entrepreneurs are encouraged to undertake before launching new ventures (Sahlman 1997; Timmons 1994).

Implicit in our model is the notion that entrepreneurs' perceptions of risk and decisions involving risk are distinct and separate cognitive processes. This view is consistent with an abundant body of research into consumer decision-making that judgments about products and services and choices among them involve distinct cognitive operations that do not always work in parallel (cf. Bettman and Park 1980; Johnson and Russo 1984). Examining judgments and choices, or in our case, entrepreneurs' perceptions of risk and their decisions involving risk, as fundamentally different notions may offer new insights into how entrepreneurs view and respond to risk in new venture decision-making.

Theoretical Development

What Constitutes Risk?

Although considerable attention has been devoted to studying the conceptual and operational dimensions of risk (MacCrimmon and Wehrung 1986, 1990; Schneider and Lopes 1986; Shoemaker 1990), much less effort has been devoted to investigating the dimensions of the risk construct and their influences on risky choice behavior. Risk reflects the degree of uncertainty and potential loss associated with the outcomes which may follow from a given behavior or set of behaviors. Yates and Stone (1992) identify three elements of the risk construct: potential losses, the significance of those losses, and the uncertainty of those losses. In risky entrepreneurial contexts, where losses are almost always possible, it is the significance of any possible losses—or hazard, as we shall refer to it—and the uncertainty or variability of those losses that are likely to be most salient in driving risk perceptions and risky decision-making behavior. The hazard and variability dimensions of risk argue, respectively, that greater potential hazard for a proposed new venture and greater variability in anticipated returns for a proposed venture should lead entrepreneurs to view the venture as riskier than one having less hazard and less variability, all other factors equal. We employ the variability and hazard dimensions to develop our first two hypotheses.

The Variability Perspective and Entrepreneurs' Risk Perceptions

The economics literature typically defines risk as variability (Armour and Teece 1978; Fisher and Hall 1969), arguing that greater variability in economic returns constitutes greater risk. Variability, in turn, is defined as the probability of actual returns or outcomes deviating from the expected return or outcome. For example, investors might assess the risk of investing in a firm in terms of its chances for providing a given return based on the deviations in prior returns (Armour and Teece 1978; Bowman 1980; Fisher and Hall 1969). From this perspective, risk is seen as the possibility that an anticipated level of return will not be realized, and is typically operationalized as the standard deviation of an investment's historical returns.[1]

New ventures, by definition, typically do not have a flow of historical returns for entrepreneurs to examine, however, the risk-as-variability perspective may still be germane. Entrepreneurs use a variety of procedures for estimating the likely variability in future returns for proposed new ventures, including critical assumption planning (Sykes and Dunham 1995), risk analysis (Hertz 1964) and sensitivity analysis (Timmons 1994).

Sometimes such procedures are likely to produce rather subjective estimates of both the variability and magnitude of future returns for ventures involving new-to-the-world innovations. However, for less novel ventures, entrepreneurs can often draw on relevant experience gained from similar ventures in the past and produce risk and sensitivity estimates with greater confidence. Thus, the variability perspective suggests the following hypothesis:

> *H1:* The greater the variability in predicted outcomes of a proposed new venture, the greater will be its perceived risk.

The Hazard Perspective and Entrepreneurs' Risk Perceptions

March and Shapira (1987) studied executives' views of risk. They concluded that what the executive perceives as risk is not outcome variability, but hazard—if things go wrong, how much can we lose? "A risky choice is one that contains a threat of a very poor outcome" (March and Shapira 1987: 1407).[2] March and Shapira found that executives, in assessing risk, pay little attention to the probabilities associated with alternative outcomes, for several reasons. First, most managers do not treat uncertainty about positive outcomes as an important aspect of risk. Second, for most managers (and most entrepreneurs), risk is a concept having to do primarily with loss, not with probabilities. A study by Shapria (1995: 45) found that 95% of managers surveyed "described risk in terms of the magnitude of financial loss." Third, most managers show little desire to reduce risk to a single quantifiable construct.

Although this perspective incorporates the idea of variability in a range of possible outcomes, its emphasis is on the magnitude of potential losses. In a new venture context, march and Shapira's view leads to the following hypothesis:

---

[1]Although the standard deviation, as an operational measure of risk, encompasses both the magnitude and the probability distribution of historical returns, the emphasis in this theoretical stream is on the likelihood of achieving outcomes different from the historical mean.

[2]March and Shapira (1992: 172), in a different paper, also acknowledge the variability perspective: "Riskiness is associated with lack of certainty about the precise outcome of a choice and thus with variation in the probability distribution."

H2: The greater the magnitude of a proposed new venture's largest potential loss, the greater will be its perceived risk.

The Influence of Variability and Hazard in Risky Choice Decisions

Expected utility arguments indicate that decision alternatives having lower levels of perceived risk, whether due to high levels of variability or hazard, should be preferred to alternatives having higher levels of risk, other factors being equal (Yates 1990). Consistent with these arguments, March and Shapira's (1987) interviews found that managers are likely to avoid choosing decision alternatives for which the chances are high that the expected outcome will not occur. Indeed, Shapira (1995: 57) summarizes the section of his work on organizational risk-taking with the advice of an executive he interviewed: "Avoid risk taking would be my credo." Thus:

H3A: The greater the variability in predicted outcomes of a proposed new venture, the less likely it will be selected for funding.

H3B: The greater the magnitude of a new venture's largest potential loss, the less likely it will be selected for funding.

Individual Differences, Risk Perceptions, and Risky Choice Decisions

In a recent review of factors which influence risky business decisions, Sitkin and Pablo (1992: 9) posit that the "risk propensity (of the decision maker) dominates the actual and perceived characteristics of the situation as a determinant of risk behavior." In the new venture context, this statement suggests that the risk propensity of the entrepreneur making the decision as to which of several proposed ventures to enter is more important than the returns the alternative new ventures are expected to generate, their risks, and most other factors commonly considered in the analysis of such ventures. Sitkin and Pablo's assertion stands in sharp contrast to the expected utility perspective that dominates research and practice in the new venture decisions area.

Sitkin and Pablo define risk propensity as "the tendency of a decision maker either to take or to avoid risks" (p. 12). Sitkin and Pablo do not argue that all other factors, such as those whose effects we hypothesize above, are inoperative. They simply say that individual differences among actors in terms of their risk propensities are likely to explain a greater portion of variance in risky choice behavior. The impact of individual differences is supported by the work of Lopes (1987), who found that some individuals tend to base their actions on the upside of a range of possible decision outcomes, while others tend to act based on the downside. Thus, some individuals are motivated by upside potential, while others are motivated by security.

Recent research by Sitkin and Weingart (1995) has found that differences in risk propensities also influence risk perceptions. Individuals of higher risk propensity will perceive the risks associated with a particular decision alternative to be lower than those having lower risk propensities. Risk perceptions, in turn, are expected to influence choices among risky alternatives. Choices among alternatives in a decision set by a decision maker who perceives the set as less risky are expected to be riskier than for those who perceive the set as riskier (Yates 1990). The arguments of Sitkin and Pablo (1992); Sitkin and Weingart (1995); Lopes (1987); and Yates (1990) generate three additional hypotheses:

H4: The greater the risk propensity of the entrepreneur, the less will be the perceived risk associated with a particular new venture.

H5: The greater the risk propensity of the entrepreneur, the more likely he or she will be to select new ventures having higher levels of risk.

H6: The lower an entrepreneur's perceived risk across a set of decision alternatives, the more likely he or she will be to select new ventures having higher levels of risk.

Finally, the argument of Sitkin and Pablo (1992) that risk propensities dominate risky choice decisions, together with Lopes' (1987) theory that risk propensity consists largely of a tendency of individuals to attend to either the upside (i.e., the potential) or the downside (i.e., the hazard) of a situation, suggests that risk propensity should operate on March and Shapira's (1987) hazard conceptualization of risk, rather than on the variability dimension. If this is so, then for ventures of equal expected value, risk propensity is expected to influence choices among ventures which differ in amount of hazard and gain, but not necessarily among ventures which differ as to degree of variability. Based on Sitkin and Pablo's (1992) argument, this effect should be robust across different levels of variability in anticipated venture outcomes. Thus, for ventures of equal variability and expected value:

H7: The greater the risk propensity of the entrepreneur, the greater will be the likelihood of choosing a venture having higher levels of hazard.

Method

Design and Procedure

A 2 × 2 full factorial within subjects experimental design was employed to manipulate the variability and hazard associated with the outcomes of new ventures. We created, through several pretests, a series of descriptions of predicted outcomes for four new ventures (see Table 1). All four ventures have equal expected values, described as

TABLE 1	MEAN RISK STATISTICS AND CHOICES AMONG THE FOUR VENTURES				
Venture Name	Level of Variability	Level of Hazard	Mean Risk Score	Standard Deviation	Number of Subjects Choosing Venture
Green	High	High	5.57	1.22	10
Yellow	High	Low	4.53	1.43	3
Purple	Low	High	3.19	1.34	39
White	Low	Low	1.97	0.96	26
					Total 78

Differences between mean risk scores for all ventures are statistically significant (Tukey HSD test) at the 0.01 level.

---

[3]Given our criterion that expected values of all four ventures be equal, the ventures having greater hazard also have greater potential for gain. This operational condition permits us to gain insights into Lopes (1987) contention that differences in risk propensity consist largely of a tendency to pay attention to either the upside or the downside of an anticipated set of outcomes.

meeting the entrepreneur's requirements for return on investment (ROI) for new ventures. Two of the ventures have higher variability (a 40% chance of meeting target ROI with a 30% chance of being over target and a 30% chance of being under target versus an 80% chance of meeting target ROI with a 10% chance of being over target and a 10% chance of being under target), and two have greater hazard (possible outcomes $25 million over or under target versus $5 million over or under). In order to maintain equal expected values for all four ventures, potential for gain above target levels is equal to the potential for loss below target levels for each venture.[3]

Subjects were presented with a scenario which asked them to imagine that they were about to undertake a new venture. They were presented with the four potential new venture descriptions, and were told that all four were in the same industry, required similar and manageable levels of start-up capital, and that all met their target for return on investment. The ventures were rotated to eliminate possible order effects. The individual venture descriptions were repeated, one per page, on the next four pages, along with instructions for responding to the first dependent measure (see Table 1) provided on each page. This dependent measure, a three item scale, recorded the amount of risk the subject perceived in each venture (page ordering was matched to the venture rotation noted above). Next, a second dependent measure asked subjects to indicate which venture they would choose. Measures of the manipulation's effectiveness were collected next, followed by measures of individual differences and demographic items.

Sample

CEOs of the 540 firms listed in *INC*, *Fortune*, and *BusinessWeek* magazines on their combined 1994 and 1996 tabulations of the fastest growing public companies in the United States were contacted by fax to request their participation in the study. The 210 subjects who agreed to participate in the study (39% of those originally contacted, after three faxed requests) were then mailed the experimental instruments, and asked to return them via U.S. mail, to ensure confidentiality. After five weeks and two faxed reminders, 91 instruments (43% of those who had indicated they would participate in the study) had been returned. After discarding 13 incomplete or unusable instruments, we were left with a remaining subject pool of 78 entrepreneurs.

The entrepreneurs in the resulting sample had founded from 1 to 12 firms (mean 3.0 firms), and ranged from 28 to 66 years of age (mean 47.7). All were male. Their current firms ranged in size from 6 to 10,500 employees (mean 1,186), and $0.4 million to $1.2 billion in sales (mean $147.6 million). Of their current firms, 43.6% operate in manufacturing and 56.4% in service industries. In order to assess any possible nonresponse bias, we compared firm demographic data for our sample to mean data from the published lists from which our sample was drawn. Firms in our sample tended to be somewhat smaller than those on the published lists, in terms of revenue (mean of $147.6 million for the sample compared to $217.8 million for the listed firms) and number of employees (mean of 1,186 compared to 1,753). These data suggest that one should be cautious in generalizing our results to entrepreneurs who lead very large high-growth firms.

Independent Variables

The two manipulated variables were the variability and the degree of hazard (and gain) of the ventures' anticipated outcomes, as described previously (see Table 2). Risk propensity was operationalized using an adaptation of the established (Schneider and Lopes 1986) Risk Style Scale, as shown in Table 3. We chose this measure for our

TABLE 2	NEW VENTURE DESCRIPTIONS

Venture Green

There is a 30% chance of being under target by $25 million, a 40% chance of meeting target ROI and a 30% chance of going over target by $25 million. Graphically the distribution appears as:

Green's Outcomes

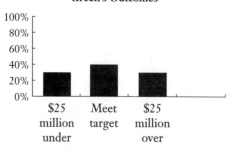

Venture White

There is a 10% chance of being under target by $5 million, a 80% chance of meeting target ROI and a 10% chance of going over target by $5 million. Graphically the distribution appears as:

White's Outcomes

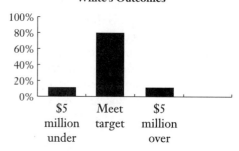

Venture Purple

There is a 10% chance of being under target by $25 million, a 80% chance of meeting target ROI and a 10% chance of going over target by $25 million. Graphically the distribution appears as:

Purple's Outcomes

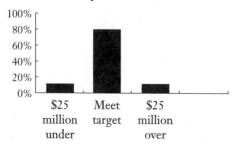

Venture Yellow

There is a 30% chance of being under target by $5 million, a 40% chance of meeting target ROI and a 30% chance of going over target by $5 million. Graphically the distribution appears as:

Yellow's Outcomes

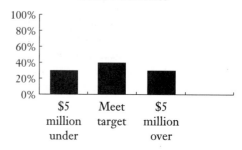

TABLE 3	SCALE OF RISK PROPENSITY

Please answer the following 5 items by circling the alternative ("a" or "b") you would feel most comfortable with.

1. a) an 80% chance of winning $400, or
   b) receiving $320 for sure

2. a) receiving $300 for sure, or
   b) a 20% chance of winning $1,500

3. a) a 90% chance of winning $200, or
   b) receiving $180 for sure

4. a) receiving $160 for sure, or
   b) a 10% chance of winning $1,600

5. a) a 50% chance of winning $500, or
   b) receiving $250 for sure

study because it deals with personal propensities toward financial risk taking (as opposed to other kinds of risks, such as those entailed in sky diving) and because of its efficacy in assessing the construct of interest (Schneider and Lopes 1986).

Dependent Measures

The dependent measure of *perceived new venture risk* for hypotheses H1, H2, and H4 was a scale of 3, 7-point items (see Table 4). The reliability of this scale is indicated by a coefficient alpha for a three item scale of 0.956.

The dependent measure of the riskiness of new venture choice for Hypotheses H3A, H3B, H5, H6, and H7 was the subject's selection of one of the four ventures to fund. The mean perceived risk scores for the four ventures indicate that this scale forms an approximately interval scale of the riskiness of the four ventures (see Table 5). As expected, the venture scoring the highest in perceived risk (Venture Green: mean perceived risk score 5.57) is the venture having high levels of both variability and hazard. The venture perceived as next most risky (Venture Yellow: 4.58) has high variability and low hazard. The venture perceived as third most risky (Venture Purple: 3.19) has low variability and high hazard. The venture judged least risky (Venture White: 1.97) is the venture having low levels of both variability and hazard (see Table 5). Pairwise comparisons between the perceived risk scores for all of the ventures were significant (Tukey's HSD test, $p < 0.01$).

TABLE 4	SCALE OF PERCEIVED NEW VENTURE RISK

For each scale below, kindly circle the number which you feel best assesses the amount of RISK associated with this scenario:

HIGH	1 2 3 4 5 6 7	LOW
MINIMAL	1 2 3 4 5 6 7	EXTREME
VERY RISKY	1 2 3 4 5 6 7	NOT RISKY

TABLE 5	MANIPULATION CHECK RESULTS

Independent Variable	Manipulation Check Mean Values	p Value
Variability		< 0.001
High	3.79	
Low	2.14	
Hazard[1]		< 0.001
High	4.32	
Low	1.97	

Mean values are points on a 5-point scale, with 3 as the midpoint.

[1] The manipulation of hazard also manipulated potential gain, in order to maintain equal expected values across ventures (see Table 2). A manipulation check for gain was also significant (means 4.40 and 1.90, $p < 0.001$).

Manipulation Checks

The effectiveness of the variability and hazard manipulations was assessed by comparing the mean scores on the manipulation check items (each a 5-point scale) for each venture across the two levels of each experimental condition. As shown in Table 2, all of the manipulations were effective.

Results

Antecedents of Risk Perceptions

A repeated measures analysis of variance procedure (Norusis 1990) was run to assess the effects of variability and hazard on perceptions of new venture risk. Main effects of both variability ($F(1.74) = 307.7$, $p < 0.001$) and hazard ($F(1.74) = 94.38$, $p < 0.001$) were found, thereby providing evidence in support of the impact of both the variability (H1) and hazard (H2) perspectives on risk perceptions. No significant interaction was found. To assess the effects of the subjects' risk propensities on the subjects' risk perceptions of each venture (H4), we ran a regression analysis of risk propensity on risk perception. The result was not significant ($\beta = -0.116$, $p = 0.13$).

Variability, Hazard, and New Venture Choices

Evidence to test H3A, which predicts greater likelihood of choice of ventures having less variability in anticipated returns, is found by comparing the number of higher versus low variability ventures chosen for funding (see Table 1). Thirteen subjects chose the high variability ventures (Ventures Green and Yellow), while 65 subjects chose the low variability ventures (Purple and White). A chi squared test rejects the null hypothesis that these differences are due to chance ($\chi^2(1 \text{ df}) = 34.67$, $p < 0.01$), thereby supporting H3A (see Table 1).

Evidence to test H3B, which predicts greater chance of choosing ventures having less magnitude of anticipated losses, is found by comparing the number of high vs. low hazard ventures chosen for funding (see Table 1). Forty-nine subjects chose the high hazard ventures (Green and Purple), while 29 subjects chose the low hazard ventures (Yellow and White). Thus, contrary to the prediction of H3B, entrepreneurs were more likely to choose high hazard than low hazard ventures, presumably to obtain the potential for the greater gains which went along with the high hazard condition. A chi squared test rejects the null hypothesis that these differences are due to chance ($\chi^2(1 \text{ df}) = 5.13$, $p < 0.05$).

Risk Perceptions, Propensity, and New Venture Choices

To examine H5 and H6, we ran a regression model in which the dependent variable was new venture choice, and the independent variables were subjects' risk propensity scores and their mean total *perceptions* of risk across the ventures.[4]

H5 predicts a positive relationship between risk propensity and new venture choices. This prediction was supported ($\beta = 0.26$, $p < 0.05$), thereby supporting the

---

[4]Tests of normality, homogeneity of variance, and multicolinearity were run to ensure that the regression model adequately fit the data (Neter, Wassermann, and Kutner 1990). No heteroskedasticity or lack of normality of multicolinearity problems was found.

prediction of Sitkin and Pablo (1992). The effect of risk perceptions on new venture choice (H6) was also significant ($\beta = -0.19$, $p < 0.05$). Thus, we find both risk propensity and risk perceptions influencing entrepreneurs' new venture choices. Given the inability, in this experimental research, to ascertain the relative "doses" of differences in risk perception brought about by our manipulations and differences in risk propensities of the entrepreneurs in our sample, we can draw no conclusive evidence of the relative importance of one factor compared to the other.

Finally, H7 predicts that, for ventures of equal expected value and equal variability, more risk-prone entrepreneurs will choose more risky ventures (i.e., those having higher levels of hazard and gain). For the two ventures having low variability, Ventures White (chosen by 26 subjects) and Purple (chosen by 39 subjects), the results of a logistic regression do not support this prediction ($\beta = 0.067$, $p = 0.74$). Similarly, comparing choices across the two high variability ventures, Yellow (chosen by three subjects) and Green (chosen by 10 subjects), the results of a second logistic regression also fail to support this prediction ($\beta = 2.14$, $p = 0.22$). Though the theories we relied on in developing our study did not predict that risk perceptions would drive these effects, we did include risk perception in the regression models to test H7. The effect of risk perception was significant for the Venture Purple vs. Venture White Comparison ($\beta = -0.648$, $p = 0.04$), but not for the Venture Green vs. Venture Yellow comparison ($\beta = 4.75$, $p = 0.18$).

Discussion

The results provide evidence which extends the work of March and Shapira (1987). Differences in entrepreneurs' new venture choices were influenced not only by differences in the risks inherent in the patterns of anticipated outcomes for different ventures, but by differences in our entrepreneurs' perceptions of those risks, as well as their propensities to take risk. Further, as March and Shapira predict, the degree of hazard in a decision alternative does influence the degree to which entrepreneurs perceive that alternative as risky, though greater perceived risk did not deter our subjects from making risky choices: the entrepreneurs in our study were more likely to choose high hazard than low hazard ventures (63% chose high hazard ventures, which also entailed high gain), contrary to our prediction. Apparently, high hazard ventures are acceptable as long as commensurate gains are sufficiently likely.

On the other hand, entrepreneurs appear to be more apprehensive about variability in possible outcomes, having overwhelmingly chosen ventures low in variability (83% chose either Venture White or Purple). Perhaps they are confident that they can intervene to increase their chances of achieving the desired outcome when probabilities of unexpected negative outcomes are relatively small. Indeed, a recent study suggests that the overconfidence of entrepreneurs enables them to start new ventures before many of the inherent uncertainties therein have been resolved (Busenitz and Barney 1997). When probabilities of unexpected negative outcomes are large, however, they may feel that they lack the control to bring in the venture on target.

As for risk propensities, as Sitkin and Pablo (1992) predicted, entrepreneurs who have greater risk propensities tend to choose riskier ventures. Interestingly, however, the subjects' risk propensities did not significantly influence their perceptions of venture risks, contrary to the prediction of Sitkin and Pablo. Thus, risk propensity appears to directly impact venture choice behavior, rather than indirectly affecting behavior through the perceptual process. The absence of an effect of risk propensity on risk perceptions is consistent with the findings of a recent study by Palich and Bagby (1995) that found a consistently optimistic pattern of categorization of business situations among entrepreneurs compared to nonentrepreneurs, in spite of no difference in risk propensity among the two groups. It may be that various cognitive patterns and processes of entrepreneurs are more important determinants of entrepreneurial behavior than their risk propensity. Indeed, such processes may constitute unobserved variables in our research that may be responsible for the effects we found. Our finding that risk propensity influences new venture choice behavior, but not risk perception, is parallel to research in consumer choice that judgment and choice tasks involve different cognitive operations (Bettman and Park 1980; Johnson and Russo 1984).

Our results, taken together with previous research findings by Palich and Bagby (1995) and Busenitz and Barney (1997), suggest that better understanding is needed about how entrepreneurs search for and process information about business situations (Copper, Folta, and Woo 1995; Manimala 1992), and how such information processing influences entrepreneurial behavior. Kahneman and Lovallo (1993) argue that the relative balance between what they call isolation errors (over-optimistic forecasting that ignores the statistics of the past on one hand, and overly timid evaluations of single risky opportunities that neglect possibilities to pool risks on the other) affect the risk-taking propensies of individuals. These and other errors or biases, including the well-known discrepancy (Kahneman and Tversky 1979) between the weights attached to losses and gains in evaluating risky decisions such as new venture opportunities, may explain why we found that hazard in anticipated new venture outcomes influenced perceptions of risk in our study, but did not deter the entrepreneurs in our sample from choosing riskier ventures. Additional research into the cognitions of entrepreneurs may offer additional insights to better explain entrepreneurial behavior.

Finally, our results indicate that the series of four hypothetical new ventures that we used as our dependent measure of new venture risk (See Exhibit 2) constitutes a scale having approximately interval properties (see Table 1). The availability of a valid scale of new venture risk should facilitate future experimental research into the role of risk in new venture decision making.

Limitations

Our study, like most experimental studies in business settings, suffers from several limitations. First, entrepreneurs in real situations may not behave as did our subjects in the hypothetical situations in which they were placed in our study. Given the likely difficulty, in a field study, of controlling for the broad array of factors which are posited to influence risky new venture decisions in natural settings, and to separate the effects of risk perceptions from "objective" risk, we elected to conduct an experimental study. This approach has advantages in internal validity for theory testing purposes, but may be criticized on grounds that the experimental task is not a real one with real payoffs. Given the early stage of research in this arena, and given our interest in testing theories, some of which have undergone little empirical scrutiny, we deemed the tradeoff acceptable.

Second, we chose to study decisions among a set of four new venture decision alternatives whose investments and expected values were all equal—such precise equality of investments and expected values across proposed ventures is unlikely in real situations. An additional limitation is the use of a measure of risk propensity borrowed from another literature, a measure which may not adequately capture the propensity of entrepreneurs to take risks in new venture situations. Bromiley and Curley (1992) argue that risk propensities are, to some degree, situation specific, and that measures from one situation may not work well in another situations.

Third, in manipulating hazard we also manipulated gain, in order to preserve the equality of the expected values in the anticipated outcomes of the four ventures from which our subjects were asked to choose. Had we not done so, there would have little motivation for our subjects to choose high hazard ventures (with little prospect for gain), and differences in choices would have been attributable to differences in expected value among the ventures, rather than to differences in risk propensity and risk perceptions, the variables of interest in our study.

Finally, we restricted our examination to only the effects of anticipated outcomes and differences in risk propensity on the decisions that were made. Potentially important contextual factors such as competencies and previous experience of the entrepreneur, incentives, and team decision process issues were not examined in our study. Future research is needed to explore these and other likely influences on new venture decisions.

Conclusions and Implications

Our study holds implications for investors who fund entrepreneurial ventures, as well as for entrepreneurs themselves, and for educators who train students hoping to join tomorrow's cadre of entrepreneurs.

To the extent that potential investors in new ventures behave similarly to the entrepreneurs in our study, the impact of variability in anticipated new venture outcomes on perceptions of risk entailed in, and choices among, new venture alternatives has implications for how entrepreneurs should employ sensitivity analyses and seek to reduce perceived outcome variability as they seek investment capital. High levels of hazard did not deter entrepreneurs from choosing ventures with potentially high levels of gain, therefore, ventures having high levels of variability, such as that often explicitly detailed in sensitivity analyses, were less likely to be chosen. Entrepreneurs may find it useful to find new ways, other than the traditional best case/expected case/worst case approach, to present to prospective investors the likelihood of deviation in future performance from desired outcomes. Our results may offer an explanation of why entrepreneurs are sometimes reluctant to engage in explicit risk and sensitivity analyses for proposed ventures. As Ulrich and Epplinger (1995: 256) suggest, "Often [decision makers] do not want to confront the true probabilities of bad outcomes." Rather than attempting to mask the outcome variability of presenting new ventures, entrepreneurs may be better advised to invest in sufficient market research to ascertain the level of market acceptance which the products or services of a proposed new venture are likely to enjoy, or to test the criticality of key assumptions underlying their plans (Sykes and Dunham 1995). Several new techniques of qualitative market research are able to provide tangible evidence of likely market acceptance, even for new-to-the-world products and services, thereby reducing perceptions of outcome variability and helping to build a solid foundation of customer needs on which to erect the new venture (Griffin and Hauser 1993; Griffin 1996; Zaltman 1997).

For entrepreneurs choosing among a set of proposed new venture alternatives, our results indicate that, where levels of investment and the expected values of returns are similar, ventures tend to be chosen based on differences in risk propensities among entrepreneurs, in addition to the risk entailed in the ventures' patterns of anticipated returns. This finding attests to the importance that venture capitalists and other investors place in the people who lead the ventures in which they invest (Heilemann 1997; Sahlman 1997).Entrepreneurs are advised to explicitly ask themselves whether their assessment of proposed ventures they consider are biased in any way by their propensities to take risks. Such biases could result in decisions which lengthen the already daunting odds for new venture success. Various approaches have been identified for overcoming decision biases, including the use of structured decision aids (Ghosh and Ray 1997) and treating a particular decision as an instance of a broader class of similar previous decisions about which outcome information is available (Kahneman and Lovallo 1993).

Additionally, entrepreneurs in search of new venture opportunities should think carefully about strategies for mitigating the hazard they appear willing to accept in search of potentially attractive gains. Failure to adequately understand and plan adverse outcomes not only may jeopardize chances for near term success, but they may make it more difficult to attract support from investors and others for subsequent financing (Sahlman 1997).

For teachers whose work it is to prepare a new generation of entrepreneurs to make wise choices among new venture opportunities and develop successful strategies to pursue them, our study suggests that providing would-be entrepreneurs with tools, techniques, and analytical frameworks for reducing the variability in their forecasts for new venture outcomes can play an important role in facilitating their pursuit of potentially attractive, but risky, opportunities. Potentially useful tools and techniques include various qualitative and quantitative market research approaches (cf., Griffin and Hauser 1993; Griffin 1996; Mahajan, Muller, and Bass 1990; Zaltman 1997); relevant analytical frameworks include critical assumption planning (Sykes and Dunham 1995) and risk analysis (Hertz 1964). Use of such tools and frameworks to provide a strong foundation of *evidence* on which to build a business plan provides two benefits to students as would-be entrepreneurs: first, stronger evidence supporting the attractiveness of a proposed venture is likely to enhance the likelihood of obtaining funding for the venture; second, as the results of our study suggest (recall that our subjects were more likely to choose ventures having less variability in anticipated outcomes), by eliminating uncertainty and reducing variability in anticipated outcomes, such evidence will make it more likely that the entrepreneur will, given favorable evidence, decide to pursue the venture. This psychological role of such evidence should not be underestimated.

Our results raise questions which call for additional research into the risky choice decisions of entrepreneurs. First, the person versus situation debate in organizational psychology (Mischel 1977, O'Reilly 1991) has wrestled in recent years with trying to better identify the kinds of situations in which individual differences tend to be relatively more or less important, compared to situational factors, in determining behavior. For risky new venture decisions such as those we have examined here, what situational or contextual factors are likely to moderate the importance of risk propensity and other individual differences in risky choice decisions? March and Shapira (1992) found, in a simulation study, that recent performance outcomes, accumulated resources, and the goals or reference points that decision makers attend to influence risky choice behavior. Baird and Thomas (1985) articulated a model of strategic risk taking which incorporated a broad array of environmental, organizational, industrial, decision maker, and problem variables. Few of these variables have been empirically studied as to their effects on risky choice decision making. These works suggest numerous directions for future empirical research.

How our subjects' venture choices would have played out in terms of new venture performance was not addressed in our study, but the apparent biases which individual differences in risk propensity generate in new venture decision making is a potentially important issue for future research. Viewed from one perspective, our findings suggest that patterns of suboptimal decisions are likely to be common, as managers' inertia (Sitkin and Pablo 1992) and proneness or aversity toward risk (Lopes 1987; Schneider and Lopes 1986) lead to consistently risk-prone or risk-avoiding decisions. Viewed from a more optimistic perspective, however, our results suggest that people matter in such decisions (Hitt and Tyler 1991). Entrusting new venture investments to individuals whose risk propensities and other individual characteristics best match the needs of the market opportunity and a prospective investor's objectives may help improve portfolio performance. The considerable effort which venture capitalists and other investors put forth in evaluating the individuals whose ideas and companies they fund attests to the importance of individual differences, including differences in risk taking propensity, for new firm success.

References

Armour, H. O. and Teece, D. J. 1978. Organization structure and economic performance: a test of multidivisional hypothesis. *Bell Journal of Economics* 9:106–122.

Baird, I. S. and Thomas, H. 1985. Toward a contingency model of strategic risk taking. *Academy of Management Review* 10(2):230–243.

Bettman, J. R. and Park, C. W. 1980. Effects of prior knowledge and experience and phase of the choice process on consumer decision processes: a protocol analysis. *Journal of Consumer Research* 7:234–248.

Bird, B. J. 1989. *Entrepreneurial Behavior.* Glenview, IL: Scott, Foresman and Company.

Bowman, E. H. 1980. A risk/return paradox for strategic management. *Sloan Management Review* 21 (Spring):17–31.

Bromiley, P. and Curley, S. P. 1992. Individual differences in risk taking. In J. F. Yates, ed., *Risk Taking Behavior.* West Sussex, England: John Wiley and Sons.

Busenitz, L. W. and Barney, J. B. 1997. Differences between entrepreneurs and managers in large organizations: biases and heuristics in strategic decision-making. *Journal of Business Venturing* 12:9–30.

Cooper, A. C., Folta, T. B. and Woo, C. 1995. Entrepreneurial information search. *Journal of Business Venturing* 10:107–120.

Devinney, T. M. 1992. New products and financial risk changes. *Journal of Product Innovation Management* 3:222–231.

Dickson, P. R. 1992. Toward a general theory of competitive rationality. *Journal of Marketing* 56:69–83.

Fisher, N. and Hall, G. R. 1969. Risk and corporate rates of return. *Quarterly Journal of Economics* 83:79–92.

Ghosh, D. and Ray, M. R. 1997. Risk, ambiguity, and decision choice: some additional evidence. *Decision Sciences* 28(1):81–104.

Griffin, A. 1996. Obtaining customer needs for product development. In M. D. Rosenau, ed., *The PDMA Handbook of New Product Development*, New York: John Wiley and Sons, pp. 153–166.

Griffin, A. and Hauser, J. R. 1993. The voice of the customer. *Marketing Science* 12(1):1–27.

Hall, J. and Hofer, C. W. 1993. Venture capitalists' decision criteria in new venture evaluation. *Journal of Business Venturing* 8:25–42.

Heilemann, J. 1997. The networker. *The New Yorker* August 11:28–36.

Hertz, D. B. 1964. Risk analysis in capital investment. *Harvard Business Review* (January–February): 96–106.

Hitt, M. A. and Tyler, B. B. 1991. Strategic decision models: integrating different perspectives. *Strategic Management Journal* 12:327–351.

Johnson, E. and Russo, J. E. 1984. Product familiarity and learning new information. *Journal of Consumer Research* 11:542–550.

Kahneman, D. and Lovallo, D. 1993. Timid choices and bold forecasts: a cognitive perspective on risk taking. *Management Science* 39(1):17–31.

Kahneman, D. and Tversky, A. 1979. Prospect theory: an analysis of decision under risk. *Econometrica* 47:263–290.

Krueger, N., Jr. and Dickson, P. R. 1994. How believing in ourselves increases risk taking: perceived self-efficacy and opportunity recognition. *Decision Sciences* 25(3):385–400.

Lopes, L. L. 1987. Between hope and fear: the psychology of risk. *Advances in Experimental Social Psychology* 20:255–295.

MacCrimmon, K. R. and Wehrung, D. A. 1986. *Taking Risks: The Management of Uncertainty.* New York: Free Press.

MacCrimmon, K. R. and Wehrung, D. A. 1990. Characteristics of risk taking executives. *Management Science* 36(4):422–435.

Mahajan, V., Muller, E. and Bass, F. M. 1990. New product diffusion models in marketing: a review and directions for research. *Journal of Marketing* 54 (January):1–26.

Manimala, M. J. 1992. Entrepreneurial heuristics: a comparison between high PI (pioneering-innovative) and low PI ventures. *Journal of Business Venturing* 7:477–504.

March, J. G. and Shapira, Z. 1987. Managerial perspectives on risk and risk taking. *Management Science* 33(11):1404–1418.

March, J. G. and Shapira, Z. 1992. Variable risk preferences and the focus of attention. *Psychological Review* 99(1):172–183.

Mischel, W. 1977. The interaction of person and situation. In D. Magnusson and N. S. Endler, eds., *Personality at the Crossroads: Current Issues in Interactional Psychology*, Hillsdale, NJ: Erlbaum.

Mullins, J. W. 1996. Early growth decision of entrepreneurs: the influence of competency and prior performance under changing market conditions. *Journal of Business Venturing* 11:89–105.

O'Reilly, C. A. III. 1991. Organizational behavior: where we've been, where we're going. *Annual Review of Psychology* 42:427–485.

Palich, L. E. and Bagby, D. R. 1995. Using cognitive theory to explain entrepreneurial risk-taking: challenging conventional wisdom. *Journal of Business Venturing* 10:425–438.

Phillips, B. D. and Kirchoff, B. A. 1988. An analysis of new firm survival and growth. *Babson Entrepreneurship Research Conference*, Calgary.

Reynolds, P. 1986. Predicting contributions and survival. In Ronstadt, et al. eds., *Frontiers of Entrepreneurship Research*. Wellesley, MA: Babson College.

Riquelme, H. and Rickards, T. 1992. Hybrid conjoint analysis: an estimation probe in new venture decisions. *Journal of Business Venturing* 7:505–518.

Sahlman, W. A. 1997. How to write a great business plan. *Harvard Business Review* (July–August):98–108.

Schneider, S. L. and Lopes, L. L. 1986. Reflection in preferences under risk: who and when may suggest why. *Journal of Experimental Psychology: Human Perception and Performance* 12(4):535–548.

Shapira, Z. 1995. *Risk Taking: A Managerial Perspective*. New York: Russell Sage.

Shoemaker, P. J. 1990. Are risk-attitudes related across domains and response modes? *Management Science* 36(12):1451–1463.

Sitkin, S. B. and Pablo, A. L. 1992. Reconceptualizating the determinants of risk behavior. *Academy of Management Review* 17(1):9–38.

Sitkin, S. B. and Weingart, L. R. 1995. Determinants of risky decision making behavior: a test of the mediating role of risk perceptions and risk propensity. *Academy of Management Journal* 38(6):1573–1592.

Sykes, H. B. and Dunham, D. 1995. Critical assumption planning: a practical tool for managing business development risk. *Journal of Business Venturing* 10:413–424.

Timmons, J. A. 1994. *New Venture Creation*. Homewood, IL: Irwin.

Ulrich, K. T. and Epplinger, S. D. 1995. *Product Design and Development*. New York: Mcgraw-Hill.

Yates, J. F. 1990. *Judgment and Decision Making*. Englewood Cliffs, NJ: Prentice-Hall.

Yates, J. F. and Stone, E. R. 1992. The risk construct. In J. F. Yates, ed., *Risk Taking Behavior*. West Sussex, England: John Wiley and Son.

Zaltman, G. 1997. Rethinking market research: Putting people back in. *Journal of Marketing* 34:424–437.

C A S E   "SHOULD I BUY THE 'JERRY'S
FAMOUS FROZEN DESSERTS' CHAIN?"

Todd A. Finkle, Ph.D., and Philip Greenwood, MBA, CPA

Dr. Finkle is an assistant professor of management at the University of North Carolina at Charlotte.
Mr. Greenwood owns Caminar Business Strategies Group, a consulting firm in Madison, Wisconsin.

As Phil Hogan lifted the final pages of his business plan out of his printer, he looked at the clock. It was almost midnight, which meant that he had about seven hours to get ready for another day at work.

But the idea of going to his job was not what was keeping him awake at this hour. No, it was the idea of owning his own business that invigorated him this night, as it had many nights, for many years.

It had started with a newspaper route—and the wish to be independent, make some money, call the shots. At age 12, he had sketched out a time line that included business ownership at age 30.

That didn't happen, of course. But now, at age 36, he was a CPA with a lot of valuable experience behind him, and he was ready. For that last five years, he had been a senior operations auditor, then a senior financial analyst, and now a marketing representative for Pfizer Laboratories. Before that he had been a senior internal auditor for McDonald's, and had worked for an accounting firm.

Lately, he had begun to think that if he was ever going to pull himself out of the corporate world, it would have to be now.

Now, stepping over the stacks of *Inc.* and *Entrepreneur* magazines on the floor by this desk, Phil took a moment to think about how the last year had gone:

January 1995: Contacted friends, business associates, and acquaintances to tell them he was interested in purchasing a small business that:

- had a net income of $50,000/year for the last five years,

- was located in the South,

- was a retail business,

- had an owner who was selling because of retirement, illness, or death.

March 1995: A former college roommate called to tell him about Jerry's Famous Frozen Desserts, three upscale frozen dessert stores that meet his criteria. Called the owner, Robert Hicks, to request more information. Received a letter from Mr. Hicks' accountant stating that before he shared this information, he wanted to see financial statements which verified Phil's financial capacity to purchase the company.

This article is reprinted from the *Small Business Forum*, the Journal of the Association of Small Business Development Centers, which is published by the University of Wisconsin–Extension Small Business Development Center. For information about subscriptions, reprints, or submissions, please write to us at 432 North Lake Street, Room 425, Madison, WI 53706, or call us at 608/263-7843.

April 1995: Contacted friends to ask if this was the proper procedure. They said it was. Began to look for a potential investor. Started to work on a business plan.

June 1995: A friend arranged a lunch with a potential investor, Terry Dunleavy, who owned 12 businesses, one of which invested in small businesses. After reading Phil's (unfinished) business plan, Mr. Dunleavy expressed an interest in investing, and agreed to provide a copy of his financial statements to send to Robert Hicks.

July 1995: Received the past four years of Jerry's financial statements.

Now Phil picked up those statements to look at them again. (See Exhibits 1 and 2).

Because they looked so good, Phil had visited the company and completed his research for his business plan.

With the plan in hand, he knew his next step would be to ask some experts to read the plan, and tell him what they thought of this investment opportunity.

EXHIBIT 1	JERRY'S FAMOUS FROZEN DESSERTS CONSOLIDATED INCOME STATEMENT FOR THE YEARS ENDED 1991–1994 (IN 000's)

	1991		1992		1993		1994	
	$	% Sales	$	% Sales	$	% Sales	$	% Sales
Sales:	$2,100	100%	$2,331	100%	$2,611	100%	$2,023	100%
Cost of Goods Sold:								
Food and Supplies	336	16%	396	17%	444	17%	445	22%
Direct Labor	179	9%	186	8%	183	7%	142	7%
Spoilage	11	1%	12	1%	13	1%	70	3%
Overhead	357	17%	373	16%	418	16%	324	16%
	882	42%	967	42%	1,057	41%	980	48%
Gross Profit	1,218	58%	1,364	59%	1,553	60%	1,043	52%
Operating Expenses:								
Depreciation	63	3%	70	3%	78	3%	61	3%
Administrative	147	7%	186	8%	209	8%	162	8%
Advertising	74	4%	140	6%	131	5%	101	5%
General	63	3%	70	3%	104	4%	61	3%
Total Operating Expenses	347	17%	466	20%	522	20%	384	19%
Income before Taxes	872	42%	897	39%	1,031	40%	659	33%
Taxes	261	12%	269	12%	309	12%	236	12%
Net Income	$610	29%	$628	27%	$722	28%	$423	21%

| EXHIBIT 2 | | JERRY'S FAMOUS FROZEN DESSERTS CONSOLIDATED BALANCE SHEET FOR THE YEAR ENDED DECEMBER 31, 1994 (IN 000's) | | | | | | | |

Assets	12/31/91	$ Total Assets	12/31/92	% Total Assets	12/31/93	% Total Assets	12/31/94	% Total Assets
Cash	$125	9%	$200	11%	$240	12%	125	5%
Inventory	40	3%	45	3%	50	2%	120	5%
Property & Equipment	1,200	86%	1,450	81%	1,600	79%	1,925	84%
Other	35	3%	100	6%	125	6%	125	5%
Total	$1,400	100%	$1,795	100%	$2,015	100%	$2,295	100%

Liabilities & Net Worth								
Accounts Payable	$35	3%	$45	3%	$50	2%	$90	4%
Long-Term Debt	225	16%	350	19%	225	11%	250	11%
Letter-of-Credit	125	9%	100	6%	85	4%	75	3%
Deferred Taxes	20	1%	50	3%	50	2%	20	1%
	405	29%	545	30%	410	20%	435	19%
Net Worth	995	71%	1,250	70%	1,605	80%	1,860	81%
Liabilities & Net Worth	$1,400	100%	$1,795	100%	$2,015	100%	$2,295	100%

The Business Plan

Robert Hicks and John Roberts, the founders of Jerry's Famous Frozen Desserts, did 18 months of research before starting their first frozen dessert store. Their initial location was an old deserted gas station in Austin, Texas. They financed their first store with $35,000 in savings, a Small Business Administration-backed loan of $55,000 from Texas Savings and Loan, and capital from their credit cards. In August 1986, the pair had transformed the gas station into Jerry's Famous Frozen Desserts. Successful from the beginning, they attributed their profitability to high quality products, giving back to the community, and such forms of advertising as word of mouth, radio stations, newspaper ads, and free press from business publications. As their stores increased in popularity, they expanded to three locations in the Austin area.

Jerry's sells high quality, super-premium regular and low-fat ice cream. Their upscale products include sundaes, malts, shakes, cones, and soft-serve. They also sell a limited number of products (e.g., pints of ice cream) for the take-home market. The best-selling products are soft-serve French silk and chocolate chip cookie dough. Jerry's products are more likely to have a chocolate than a fruit base. Their market research indicates the typical customer is between 24–45 years of age.

Several factors have contributed to Jerry's success. Establishing itself as the first upscale frozen dessert store in the Austin market in 1985 has given Jerry's the advantage of brand name recognition and being first to market. People recognize the name Jerry's Famous Frozen Desserts. Others have tried to overtake their lead in the market, but they have failed. Haagen-Dazs opened a store on University Boulevard two years ago, only to have it fail. Another regional chain out of Dallas, called Candee's Frozen Specialties, also failed after one year.

Competitive pressures from other upscale, retail frozen dessert companies are also limited. The only other national chains which compete with Jerry's are Haagen-Dazs and Ben & Jerry's Homemade. Currently, Ben & Jerry's and Haagen-Dazs are not located in the Austin area.

A major factor contributing to Jerry's success is *superior products.* Ingredients in their products are very high quality. The smooth (soft-serve) nature of Jerry's products is conducive to the needs of the fastest growing age segment in the U.S., 45–54 year olds. In addition, one of the owners, Robert Hicks, devotes 90 percent of his time to developing new types of products. Finally, Jerry's has developed an excellent reputation in Austin for its involvement with the community.

The following publicity and awards testify to the success of Jerry's Famous Frozen Desserts:

- Voted "Best in Business" for the month of June 1994 by *In Business* magazine.

- Voted best in places for dessert (ice cream/frozen yogurt) in Austin for 1992–1993, 1993–1994, 1994–1995 by the *Annual Guide to Austin.*

- Voted "Best Ice Cream in Texas" by *Texas Trails* magazine, The Magazine of Life in Texas, in 1993.

- Appeared in a 1990 feature article in the *Austin Chronicle*, Austin's daily newspaper.

Austin Demographics

Jerry's Famous Frozen Desserts is situated in beautiful Austin, Texas. The Austin area has consistently been ranked by *Money* magazine as one of the "Best Places to Live" in the United States. It is the capital of Texas and home to one of the largest and finest universities in the world, the University of Texas at Austin. Austin is located in Wilson County. The 1993 estimated population for Wilson County is 383,420 and for the city of Austin is 196,053. Projected increases in population are shown in Table 1. The

TABLE 1	PROJECTED POPULATION GROWTH FOR AUSTIN, TEXAS			
Projection	**Wilson County**	**% Increase**	**Austin**	**% Increase**
1980	323,545		170,616	
1990	367,085	13%	190,766	12%
2000	416,088	13%	209,523	10%
2010	454,699	9%	292,013	39%
2020	488,515	7%	NA	

SOURCE: Wilson County Regional Planning Commission and 1990 Census; figures include University of Texas at Austin students.

median estimate for household income in 1993 was $40,000 for Wilson County and $36,000 for the City of Austin.

The U.S. Frozen Dessert Industry

Total sales for the frozen dessert industry in 1993 were $10.7 billion, an increase of 5.2 percent over 1992 sales. *Frozen Food Digest* (July 1994), estimates that the sales of frozen desserts will exceed $12.8 billion by 1998, an increase of about 20 percent over 1993 sales. Growth will be in two areas: (1) full-fat products that appeal to indulgent consumers and (2) fat-free products that appeal to consumers' health and diet concerns.

Currently, 90 percent of U.S. households purchase ice cream, with consumption peaking in the summer. Ice cream is traditionally one of the most popular and profitable desserts in the United States. A survey by *Restaurants and Institutions* in 1993 showed that 40 percent of operators' menus have hard ice cream, 30 percent offer sundaes, and more than 25 percent offer ice cream specialties.

Industry Structure and Products The U.S. frozen dairy dessert industry is currently in the mature stage of the industry life-cycle. The market is segmented into the retail (dripping store) sector and the supermarket (take-home) sector. Recent attention has emphasized the supermarket sector where competitors such as Colombo, TCBY, and Swensen's have entered the market. Profits are becoming harder to sustain in the supermarket sector due to added competitive pressures from new firms entering the market.

Classification of various types of ice cream products is based on the percentage of butterfat and overrun (air content). Typically, higher quality ice creams contain fresh whole products, less air, and as much as 20 percent butterfat. The product segments are:

- *Superpremium ice cream* 16–20 percent butterfat and less than 40 percent overrun. A four-ounce scoop has 260 calories. Examples: Jerry's Famous Frozen Desserts, Haagen-Dazs, Ben & Jerry's Homemade, and Frusen Gladje.

- *Premium ice cream* 12–16 percent butterfat and 40–60 percent overrun. A four-ounce scoop has 180 calories. Examples: Breyer's, Edy's, and Sealtest.

- *Luxury ice cream* Specialty brands which are the most expensive, like Godiva.

- *Low calorie/low fat* Contains only 2–7 percent milk fat. Example: ice milk.

- *Frozen yogurt* Only about 1.7 percent milk fat at 120–125 calories per cup. Examples: TCBY and I Can't Believe It's Yogurt.

- *Novelty products* Bars, sticks, cones, sandwiches, parfaits. Account for 20–25 percent of total ice cream sales. Examples: Milky Way, Snickers, 3 Musketeers, Butterfinger, Nestle's Crunch, Bon Bons, and Dove Bar.

- *Soft-serve ice cream* Typically ice milk (3–10 percent butterfat). Children comprise 50 percent of sales in this segment.

- *Frozen custard* A form of ice cream which has a very high fat content, but not the highest. Example: Various frozen custard stores.

Industry Threats and Trends The Census Bureau estimates the total U.S. population annual growth rate will slow to a mere .9 percent per year for the remainder of the century (U.S. Department of Commerce, page 34). The fastest-growing age group will be the 45–54 year olds, increasing by 45 percent by the end of the decade. The changing demographics of the U.S. could have a negative effect on the frozen dessert industry. As people increase in age, their taste preferences change. This could drastically affect the sales of frozen dessert companies unless they adapt to the older generation's needs. Older people still buy dessert items, but they tend to shy away from products full of nuts and candy. To combat this trend, Ben & Jerry's Homemade has introduced a new line of "smoothie" ice cream. Therefore, Ben & Jerry's has appealed the taste buds of the older generation.

Currently, 30 percent of all family households are run by a single parent, of which 80 percent are women. The growing number of single-occupant and single-parent households combined with more working women and increased travel, is fueling a shift in demand towards the away-from-home market for consumer food and beverage spending (U.S. Department of Commerce, pages 16 and 17). This is a promising sign for the frozen dessert industry.

One of the biggest competitive pressures in the immediate future for the dripping store sector will be from supermarkets selling frozen dessert items. As more and more competitors sell through supermarkets, consumers will have a larger base of products to choose from. Furthermore, buying desserts at the store will be more economical. As Bob Vranek, a family man from Charlotte, North Carolina, states "Why would I want to take my four kids to a TCBY store and spend $14 when I can go to the supermarket and buy a half gallon of frozen yogurt for $3.50? What would you do?"

During the 1980s, the U.S. frozen dessert industry saw a redirection towards the health conscious consumer with the introduction of several new products (e.g., low-fat and fat-free products). NutraSweet® was introduced as a substitute to replace sugar. In addition, frozen yogurt, which contains little butterfat, sugar, or cholesterol, has become very popular in the 1980s and 1990s.

The trend in the 1990s is the "split personality" in consumer taste preferences. Consumers want to eat healthy, but they want products to taste rich and creamy. There is an increasing demand for very rich and light products. This has left a shrinking demand for mid-range products. The current trend is towards richer, mix-in, ingredient-packed premium products and lighter, health- and diet-oriented products.

In high demand are low-fat ice creams, with no more than three grams of fat per serving. ConAgra, a major corporation which competes in the grocery segment in the frozen dessert industry, reports there are 978 brands of regular and light ice cream, yogurt, and sherbet in the U.S. marketplace. Their Healthy Choice Premium Low-Fat Ice Cream ranks eighth in dollar sales. Their marketing strategy is the continual development of new healthy products such as low-fat flavors like Malt Caramel Cone, Cappuccino Chunk, and Black Forest. According to Ken Colnar, director of marketing and sales for ConAgra, "The key to success is you need to give consumers what they want—an ice cream so rich and creamy that they forget it's low in fat."

Further evidence of the trend away from ice cream is the frozen yogurt market, which is growing at a 12 percent annual rate (see Exhibit 3). New products are constantly being developed in the frozen yogurt market, including everything from fat-free fruit flavors to brands with chunks of nuts, brownies, and candy. Firms are developing two versions of frozen yogurt: a light line and another oriented towards indulgence.

Supermarket consumers will increasingly choose healthier products in the future Due to the passage of the Nutrition Labeling and Education Act of 1990, which took effect in May 1993, all products are now required to list calories and fat content on their labels. While the trend in supermarkets is changing, the effect of the Nutrition

EXHIBIT 3	FROZEN YOGURT SALES SOAR			
Brand	**Manufacturer**	**Sales ($ millions)**	**% Change from Year Earlier**	**Market Share**
Private Label	—	$94.0	–4.2%	16.8%
Dreyer's/Edy's	Dreyer's	74.5	34.9	12.5
Kemps	BolsWessanen	61.7	13.1	10.4
Ben & Jerry's	B & J Homemade	44.1	30.4	7.4
Breyers	Unilever	36.3	6.4	6.1
Colombo	General Mills	27.4	6.9	4.6
Haagen-Dazs	Grand Metropolitan	27.0	17.4	4.6

SOURCE: *The Wall Street Journal*, June 2, 1994

Labeling and Education Act on the dripping store segment is unknown at this time. The act should not have as significant an effect on the dripping store sector because customers will not have the luxury to examine the calorie and fat content on the dessert containers unless they buy packaged dessert items to go.

Competition in the U.S. Frozen Dessert Industry   Jerry's faces tough competition from two sectors—supermarkets and dripping stores.

Supermarkets

Grand Metropolitan:	Pet, Haagen-Dazs, and Baskin-Robbins.
Integrated Resources:	Steve's Homemade Ice Cream, Swensen's, and Heidi's.
Kraft General Foods:	Sealtest, Breyer's, Borden, Colombo, Frusen Gladje, and TCBY.
Other competitors:	Ben & Jerry's Homemade, Gelare, Breyer's, Friendly's, Dreyer's/Edy's, Mayfield's, Bassett's, Honey Hill Farms, Larry's, private local grocery brands, and other companies putting out novelty products (Bon Bons, Butterfinger, Dove, Eskimo, Milky Way, Nestle's Crunch, 3 Musketeers, Snickers).

Dripping Stores

National competitors:	Ben & Jerry's Homemade, Haagen-Dazs, TCBY, Baskin-Robbins, Colombo, Frusen Gladje, I Can't Believe It's Yogurt, and International Dairy Queen.
Regional competitors:	Honey Hill Farms, Swensen's, Friendly's, Steve's Homemade Ice Cream, Breyer's, and some other chains.

Competition of Dripping Stores in Austin   Jerry's competition from national chains is limited in the Austin area. There are six International Dairy Queens and only one TCBY. There is a large number of local competitors. Currently there are five Chocolate Ice Cream & Candy Stores, one Van Jordan's Ice Cream Co., two Mimi's Ice Cream Parlors, one Jamie's Chocolate Shoppe, and a variety of restaurants serving dessert items.

International Dairy Queen   Dairy Queen was founded in 1940 in Illinois and expanded by granting territory franchise rights for specific geographical areas. The company's current name, International Dairy Queen, was formed in 1962. The firm develops and services a system of quick-service restaurants which are franchised by the company to offer hard and soft-serve ice cream, limited menu items, and beverages under Dairy Queen, Brazier, and other trademarks.

The Brazier product line features hamburgers, hot dogs, barbecue, fish and chicken sandwiches, french fried potatoes, and onion rings. The Dairy Queen dairy dessert product lines include cones of various sizes as well as shakes, malts, sundaes, sodas, hardpacked products for home consumption, and specially frozen confections (frozen ice cream cakes and logs). The products are prepared in the store from the company's specialty formulated ingredients.

As of August 1993, the company had 6,068 franchised Dairy Queen units in the U.S., Canada, Japan, and several other countries. System-wide sales were over $2.1 billion. Dairy Queen has also diversified into the fast-food industry by acquiring the franchise rights to the following chains: Golden Skillet in 1981; Orange Julius in 1987; and Karmelkorn Shoppes, Inc., which sell popcorn, candy, and other treat items, in 1986.

International Dairy Queen has implemented the "Treat Center" concept. This franchising concept combines Dairy Queen treat items, together with either or both Orange Julius or Karmelkorn menu items, under one storefront within a shopping mall. The concept is based on the economies of leasing and improved sales volumes of the combined products. As of 1993, there were 105 Treat Centers units in the U.S. and in Canada. All were franchised by the company (Piper Jaffray, 1993).

TCBY   TCBY is the leading operator and franchisor of soft-serve frozen yogurt stores. Currently, 2,300 TCBY outlets exist in the U.S. and in nine foreign countries. Of these, 1,379 are franchised, 132 are company-owned, and 808 are nontraditional locations (e.g., airports, roadside travel plazas, hospitals, schools, and other noncommercial food service locations). TCBY's revenues come from the sale of frozen yogurt and yogurt products, company-owned yogurt shops, equipment sales, and franchise royalties and sales.

In addition to the sale of various frozen yogurt products, TCBY has been testing new menu items under the theme "Sensible Temptations." New products such as soups, salads, and sandwiches are available in certain stores which meet criteria (Stephens, Inc., 1994). These sales have helped keep some franchises in business.

TCBY has been accused in the past of opening up too many franchises in remote locations. This has seriously hurt the profitability of some franchises. Furthermore, TCBY's introduction of a product line in the supermarket sector has boosted its bottom line, but at the expense of some of its franchisees. Some franchisees are complaining about dwindling profits due to the easy and less expensive customer access to TCBY frozen yogurt in the supermarket sector.

Ben & Jerry's Homemade: A Potential Entrant   Ben & Jerry's currently is not in the Austin area. However, the threat of entry remains very possible over the near future as Ben & Jerry's expands its franchise areas. If this were to occur, they would be a main competitor of Jerry's Famous Frozen Desserts.

Ben & Jerry's Homemade was founded in 1978 after Bennett R. Cohen, a college dropout, and friend Jerry Greenfield, took a $5 correspondence class on how to make ice cream. Since opening their first ice cream shop in an old empty gas station, Ben & Jerry's Homemade Inc. has become a leading producer of superpremium ice cream, ice cream novelties, and both low-fat and nonfat frozen yogurt. Sales and net income increased between 1989 and 1993. Net sales have increased from $58 million to $140 million, while net income has increased from $2 million to $7.2 million. Ben & Jerry's current strategies are:

- *Differentiation*   Using the finest, high-quality, all-natural ingredients, they develop ice cream and yogurt products with large chunks of mix-ins. They differentiate themselves from the competition by having superior ingredients and a larger amount of mix-ins.

- *Product development*   They have developed several original flavors such as Rainforest Crunch, Chocolate Chip Cookie Dough, Praline Pecan, Chunky Monkey, Wavy Gravy, and Cherry Garcia. They are continually developing new innovative products.

- *Market development*   Since their inception, Ben & Jerry's has targeted two focus groups: (1) a frozen yogurt line oriented towards the health-conscious customer and (2) a "Smooth, No Chunks" line targeting the 35–54 age group. A Ben & Jerry's spokesperson states that their most popular frozen yogurt flavors are versions of their rich ice cream flavors. Their new smooth no-chunks line is oriented towards older customers who don't tend to like large pieces of mix-ins in their ice cream.

- *Social causes*   Another primary cause for their success is their belief in giving back to society. Ben & Jerry's founded an organization called Ben & Jerry's Foundation, Inc., which gives 7.5 percent of their pretax profit to charities. In 1993, they gave away $808,000 in 142 grants to assist with causes like AIDS, homelessness, immigrant rights, environment, and sexual harassment.

- *Geographical expansion*   They currently have over 100 franchises located all over the world. In addition, they sell their products in grocery stores throughout the U.S. To solve the problem of competing with their franchises, Ben & Jerry's sells a limited variety of their products at the same price as franchisees.

- *Advertising*   In 1994, Ben & Jerry's launched its first television advertising campaign to promote its new "Smooth, No Chunks!" line.

These strategies have allowed Ben & Jerry's competitive advantage in the frozen dessert industry. However, Ben & Jerry's fast growth has caused enormous managerial problems. Their CEO, Jerry Greenfield, recently resigned. They subsequently elected a new CEO. The new CEO will have to provide leadership and a vision to move the company forward. A related issue is executive compensation. In the past they have limited executive compensation to a mere seven times the lowest salary in the company. Recently, Ben & Jerry's has reluctantly decided to discontinue its policy of capping the highest-paid employee. This is likely to have a negative effect on their corporate culture.

Currently, Ben & Jerry's holds the number two market position, with 43 percent of the superpremium ice-cream market, compared with 54 percent for Haagen-Dazs. The fourth quarter 1994 was the first time the company had ever lost money following its initial public offering. This is mainly due to their current managerial problems and the recent passage of the Nutrition Labeling and Education Act of 1990. Most of Ben & Jerry's products tend to have a very high fat content.

Jerry's Weaknesses, Opportunities, and Threats

Weaknesses   One of the major weaknesses of Jerry's Famous Frozen Desserts is their current management, John Roberts, the business-oriented partner, died in 1994. The remaining partner, Robert Hicks, is the creative part of the company. As a result of Hicks' inexperience, within the last year, turnover at Jerry's has increased. This is thought to be the primary reason Hicks wants to sell the chain. The final weakness is the lack of products with different types of fruit in them. The menu is limited primarily to chocolate-based products.

Opportunities   Several opportunities exist for Jerry's. The most obvious is the huge potential for growth. Jerry's has a proven, successful concept and product base. They have the potential to grow by opening new corporate stores and/or franchising. Jerry's also has the potential to grow through nontraditional forms (e.g., selling at kiosk stands, carts, ball games, concerts, and other entertainment venues). Home delivery also offers growth opportunities. Currently, no firm delivers upscale frozen dessert products in the Austin area.

Product development offers another avenue for growth. Jerry's needs to continually develop new products to differentiate itself from the competition. The potential to take some of these products and sell them in other markets (e.g., supermarkets and restaurants) is enormous.

Another opportunity for Jerry's is the rising population base of the Austin area. Austin is expected to increase it population by one percent per year until the year 2000 and then by four percent per year from 2000 to 2010. The increase in the number of single-occupant and single-parent households will continue to fuel the trend toward away-from-home meals. In addition, the increasing number of two-income families will allow higher-income people the luxury of going out for desserts.

Since the fastest growing age group is 45–54 year olds, Jerry's has the opportunity to take advantage of the growth in this population segment by emphasizing the "smooth" aspect of their ice cream products.

Threats   The major threat to Jerry's is the mature stage of the industry life cycle with intense competition (from both supermarkets and dripping stores). Other threats are the increasing health consciousness of consumers, the aging population base which will bring a change in people's eating habits, the slowed population growth in the U.S., and the passage of the Nutrition Labeling and Education Act of 1990.

Management Team

Phil has gathered the following key people to be part of his management team following the acquisition. They have the experience and education to grow Jerry's into a national chain of frozen dessert stores.

Phil Hogan, CEO/President and Board Member   Mr. Hogan, age 36, holds both a B.S. (Accounting) and M.B.A. (Finance) from the University of Texas at Austin. He is also a CPA. Mr. Hogan brings a wealth of industry experience to Jerry's. He spent three years as a certified public accountant with Peat, Marwick, Mitchell, & Company in Dallas. This was followed by two years at McDonald's Corporation, where he was a senior internal auditor responsible for operational and financial audits of franchise restaurants. The audits focused on sales reporting, cash receipts, inventory controls, cash receipt and disbursement controls, and fraud reviews. After McDonald's, Mr. Hogan spent five years at Pfizer Laboratories in various positions such as senior operations auditor, senior financial analyst, and marketing representative for their alternate site production sales force. Mr. Hogan currently lives in the Houston area.

George Harris, Consultant and Board Member   Mr. Harris, age 38, has both a B.S. and M.B.A. in Business Administration specializing in entrepreneurship and small-business management from Babson College. Mr. Harris has been a successful entrepreneur for the past 15 years. He began his entrepreneurial background by working in his family's restaurant, and followed with 10 years of other work experience in the restaurant industry. Currently, Mr. Harris owns two very successful restaurants in the Kansas City, Missouri, area.

Dr. John Frank, Consultant and Board Member   Dr. Frank, age 55, holds both a B.S. and an M.B.A. in accounting from San Diego State University. He also has a Ph.D. in Business Administration from the University of Wisconsin–Madison and is a CPA. Dr. Frank is both an entrepreneur and an educator. He has started and grown two successful companies. Dr. Frank is world renowned in the area of entrepreneurship and small-business management. His current title is professor of management at the University of Texas at Austin Graduate School of Business.

Professional Advisers and Services

Accounting   The accounting firm which will be used in the acquisition process is the Austin Accounting Group. They will continue to be the accounting firm used following the acquisition.

Banking and Legal   Mr. Hogan has obtained the services of Doug Brady, an attorney in Austin, to assist with the acquisition process. Legal advice is also being obtained from friends of Hogan's, Kevin Sizemore and Gordon Goldstrom. Banking services have also been retained from Mike Jones, a branch manager at Southwest Bank in Austin.

Summary of the Company

The company had a successful track record for the past eight years. The owner wanted out due to the death of his partner. Furthermore, even though the U.S. frozen dessert industry was in its mature stage, Jerry's had created a very profitable niche. One of the major players, Haagen-Dazs failed against Jerry's. Jerry's had sustained a strong brand name within Austin. Additionally, Austin is a great part of the country to be in, with its warm weather, lakes, pretty country and apparently unlimited opportunity to grow the chain.

Field Notes

These are the notes made by the consultants who Phil Hogan turned to first. This case is based on an actual business and these notes reflect the first step in a real consulting relationship.

Knowing of our background in this area, Phil Hogan called us when he began to write his business plan. We provided some guidance to him during the writing of the plan, and we helped him sketch plans for the action (see Exhibits 4 and 5).

The next areas for discussion are financing and valuation. We explained to Phil that there are several ways to value companies and structure deals. Robert Hicks had previously stated that he needed at least $175,000/year after taxes. He stated that he would need at least $2 million in cash in order for this to occur.

We shared the following general guidelines on financing with Phil:

Financing Alternatives for Small-Business Acquisitions

Small business acquisitions can be structured through debt, equity, or a combination of both. The following briefly reviews some of these options.

Debt Financing   These are loans obtained for the purchase of a small business. The most popular forms of debt financing are:

- *Savings, friends, family, and credit cards*   Capital is obtained from savings, friends, family, or credit cards.

EXHIBIT 4   ACTION PLAN: ACQUISITION PROCESS

- Continue the negotiation process and obtain financial statements from the company. Line up potential investor(s).
- Have accountant analyze financial statements for irregularities and place an estimated value on the company
- Discuss negotiations and financials with attorney.
- Visit Jerry's: meet with owner; tour operations; interview customers, suppliers, and employees.
- Place a value on the company through financial and nonfinancial issues.
- Structure the deal.
- Write letter of intent.
- Negotiate the price of the business.
- Perform due diligence, write purchase agreement, and close the deal.
- Manage the acquisition.

EXHIBIT 5	ACTION PLAN: POST-ACQUISITION PROCESS

- Meet with employees and inform them of new management. Make them feel open enough to discuss problems, opportunities, threats, and weaknesses of the businesses. Let them know that open communication is encouraged. I will have a cellular phone and the managers can contact me if an important issue arises.

- Obtaining information from employees, customers (satisfaction surveys), and suppliers will be critical in the success of the venture. These activities will be done within the first month after the acquisition.

- The following managerial techniques will be implemented after the acquisition: empowerment, decentralization, pay-for-performance, and manage by walking around (MBWA)—style similar to Sam Walton of Wal-Mart.

- Management will emphasize the design of a person's job: by providing feedback, skill variety, job identity, significance and variety.

- A mission statement, objectives, and a new policy manual will be developed. Everyone in the company will have knowledge of the overall mission and objectives. Incentives will also be implemented for employees. The policy manual will be comprised of: expectations, compensation, employee rights, sexual harassment, health, safety issues, and other issues.

- To reduce the high cost of turnover, a strong effort will be made to retain employees. Selection, recruitment, and retention will have special areas of focus for management.

- Lower-level employees will have incentives. These have not been determined; however, some examples are: arriving for work every day on time will result in a 10 percent bonus at the end of the month; employees will be required to write one recommendation every week to assist the business (a prize for the best response will be given every month).

- A positive, supportive culture will be instituted. The culture will emphasize profitability, concern for employees, the environment, and ethical conduct.

- *Seller financing*   A portion of the selling price of the business is financed through the seller. Seller financing is sometimes partially structured through a consulting contract, whereby the seller will continue to work for the company and receive a yearly salary.

- *Government programs*   Federal, state and local government loan programs (e.g., Small Business Administration and local economic development programs) have money available for small-business acquisitions. These interest rates are usually cheaper than bank rates.

- *Commercial banks*   Loans that are available from commercial banks. The problem with this source of money is that banks usually require collateral before they will allow you to borrow funds.

- *Mezzanine financing*   This form of financing allows a bank to provide a term loan over an intermediate time period (usually 7–10 years) with an option to convert a balloon payment at the end, into some equity ownership.

- *Asset-based lenders (ABLs)*   These are companies that lend money based on a percentage of an existing company's equipment, accounts receivable, inventory, or other assets. They can be found in finance companies or departments of commercial banks.

Equity Financing   Equity capital is money in exchange for a percentage of owner-ship in a business. Some of the more popular forms of equity financing are:

- *Private investors*   Comprised of family, friends, suppliers, accountants, customers, business associates, business professionals, or attorneys.

- *Venture capital*   Money that can be obtained from private venture capital firms, small business investment companies (SBICs), minority enterprise small business investment companies (MESBICs), venture capital subsidiaries of large financial institutions, and industrial corporations. The cost of capital is very high (30–50 percent/year).

- *SBICs*   Small business investment companies (SBICs) are privately owned venture capital companies sponsored by the federal government. They provide straight debt or equity financing, or a combination of both.

At our next meeting, we plan to discuss financing alternatives in more detail, and we also plan to begin to explore the topic of valuation. We agreed to work with Phil on the topics of financing and valuation. In addition, we suggested that he contact his friends and business acquaintances for advice.

References

1. U.S. Department of Commerce, International Trade Administration (1994). *U.S. Industrial Outlook* 1994. 34-11-21.
2. Piper Jaffray (1993). Company Report: International Dairy Queen.
3. Stephens, Inc. (1994). Company Report: TCBY Enterprises, Inc.

Note: An update to this case study can be found on our Web site, http://www.harcourtcollege.com/management/kuratkoseg

7

Business Plans for Entrepreneurial Ventures

Key Topics

- **Defining a Business Plan**

- **Benefits of a Business Plan**

- **Developing a Well-Conceived Business Plan**

- **Guidelines to Remember**

Defining a Business Plan

A business plan is a written document that details a proposed venture. It must illustrate the current status, expected needs, and projected results of the new business.[1] Every aspect of the venture needs to be described: the project, marketing, research and development, manufacturing, management, critical risks, financing, and milestones or timetable. A description of all these facets of the proposed venture is necessary to give a clear picture of what the venture is, where it is projected to go, and how the entrepreneur plans to get it there. In other words, the business plan represents the entrepreneur's roadmap for a successful enterprise.[2]

The business plan is also sometimes referred to as a venture plan, a loan proposal, or investment prospectus. Whatever its name, this document is initially required by any financial source, and it allows the entrepreneur entrance into the investment-seeking process. Although it may be utilized as a working document once the venture is established, the major purpose of the business plan is to encapsulate strategic developments of the project in a comprehensive document that outside investors can scrutinize.

The business plan describes to potential investors and financial sources all of the events that may affect the proposed venture, including projected actions of the venture and their associated revenues and costs. It is vital to explicitly state the assumptions on which the plan is being based. For example, increases or decreases in the market or upswings or downswings in the economy during the start-up period of the new venture should be indicated.

The emphasis of the business plan should always be the final implementation of the venture. In other words, it is not just the writing of an effective plan that is important, but also the translation of that plan into a successful enterprise.[3] Thus a business plan should

- Describe every aspect of a particular business,
- Include a marketing plan,
- Clarify and outline financial needs,
- Identify potential obstacles and alternative solutions, and
- Serve as a communication tool for all financial and professional sources.

The business plan is the major tool used to guide the formation of the venture, as well as the primary document needed to manage it. But it is also more than a written document—it is a process that begins when the entrepreneur gathers information and then continues as projections are made, implemented, measured, and updated. Thus it is an ongoing process. (See Table 7.1 for a complete outline of a business plan.)

---

[1] Fred L. Fry and Charles R. Stoner, "Business Plans: Two Major Types," *Journal of Small Business Management* (Jan. 1985): 1–6.

[2] Donald F. Kuratko and Arnold Cirtin, "Developing a Business Plan for Your Clients," *National Public Accountant* (Jan. 1990): 24–28.

[3] James W. Henderson, *Obtaining Venture Financing* (Lexington, MA: Lexington Books, 1988), 13–14.

TABLE 7.1   COMPLETE OUTLINE OF A BUSINESS PLAN

Section I: Executive Summary

Section II: Business Description
  A. General description of the business
  B. Industry background
  C. Company history or background
  D. Goals and potential of the business and milestones (if any)
  E. Uniqueness of product or service

[handwritten: She doesn't use stats can. Rely's solely on London Free Press Article]

Section III: Marketing
  A. Research and analysis
    1. Target market (customers) identified
    2. Market size and trends
    3. Competition
    4. Estimated market share
  B. Marketing plan
    1. Market strategy—sales and distribution
    2. Pricing
    3. Advertising and promotions

Section IV: Location Segment
  A. Identify location
    1. Advantages
    2. Zoning *[handwritten: no]*
    3. Taxes *[handwritten: NO]*
  B. Proximity to supplies *[handwritten: not addressed]*
  C. Access to transportation

Section V: Management
  A. Management team—key personnel
  B. Legal structure—stock agreements, employment agreements, ownership, etc.
  C. Board of directors, advisers, consultants, etc.

Section VI: Financial
  A. Financial forecast
    1. Profit and loss
    2. Cash flow
    3. Break-even analysis
    4. Cost controls *[handwritten: reliant on chef. (not good.)]*
    5. Budgeting plans

[handwritten: not there]

Section VII: Critical Risks
  A. Potential problems
  B. Obstacles and risks
  C. Alternative courses of action

Section VIII: Harvest Strategy
  A. Transfer of assets
  B. Continuity of business strategy
  C. Identify successor

Section IX: Milestone Schedule
  A. Timing and objectives
  B. Deadlines and milestones
  C. Relationship of events

Section X: Appendix or Bibliography

SOURCE: Donald F. Kuratko, Jeffrey S. Hornsby, and Frank J. Sabatine, *The Breakthrough Experience: A Guide to Corporate Entrepreneurship* (Muncie, IN: The Midwest Entrepreneurial Education Center, College of Business, Ball State University, 1999).

Benefits of a Business Plan

The entire business-planning process forces an entrepreneur to analyze all aspects of the venture and prepare effective strategies to deal with the uncertainties that will undoubtedly arise. Thus a business plan may help an entrepreneur avoid a project that is doomed to failure. As one researcher states, "If your proposed venture is marginal at best, the business plan will show you why and may help you avoid paying the high tuition of business failure. It is far cheaper not to begin an ill-fated business than to learn by experience what your business plan could have taught you at a cost of several hours of concentrated work."[4]

The benefits derived from a business plan for both the entrepreneur and the financial sources that evaluate it are discussed next.

Financing   Venture capitalists and most banks require business plans. Generally, when the national economy declines, it becomes more difficult to obtain financing, and financiers increase their demands for documentation. Many entrepreneurs say that they write business plans only because their bankers or venture capitalists require them to do so.

Increased Knowledge   Many of these same entrepreneurs say that the process of actually putting the plan together is just as important as obtaining financing. Writing the plan forces them to review the business critically, objectively, and thoroughly.

Preventing Poor Investments   Business plans help entrepreneurs avoid projects that are poor investments. It is better not to begin a business that is destined to become a failed investment than to learn by experience what your business plan could have taught you.

Planning   Business plans force you to plan. Because all aspects of the venture must be addressed in the plan, the entrepreneur develops and examines operating strategies and their expected results. Goals and objectives are quantified so that forecasts can be compared with actual results. This type of planning can help keep you on track.[5]

Entrepreneurs who prepare all or most of the business plan themselves are the ones who tend to benefit the most. Conversely, those who delegate this job tend to gain the least. If an entrepreneurial team is involved in planning, then all of the key members should help write the plan, although it is important that the lead entrepreneur understand each member's contribution. If consultants are sought to help prepare a business plan, the entrepreneur must remain the driving force behind the plan. Seeking the advice and assistance of outside professionals is always wise, but owners need to understand every aspect of the business plan because it is they, and not the consultants, who will come under scrutiny of the financial sources. Thus the business plan stands as the entrepreneur's description and prediction for his or her venture, and it must be defended by the entrepreneur. Simply put, it is the entrepreneur's responsibility.

---

[4]Joseph R. Mancuso, *How to Write a Winning Business Plan* (Englewood Cliffs, NJ: Prentice-Hall, 1985), 44.

[5]See Donald F. Kuratko, "Demystifying the Business Plan Process: An Introductory Guide," *Small Business Forum* (Winter 1991): 33–40.

Developing a Well-Conceived Business Plan

Most investors agree that only a well-conceived, well-developed business plan can gather the necessary support that eventually leads to financing. The business plan must describe the new venture with excitement, yet complete accuracy.

The Components

A brief description of the ten components of a business plan is presented next.[6]

Executive Summary   The Executive Summary is the most important section because it must convince the reader that the business will succeed. In no more than three pages, you should summarize the highlights of the rest of the plan.

The Executive Summary must be able to stand on its own; it should not simply be an introduction to the rest of the business plan. Investors who review many business plans may read only the Executive Summary, so if it cannot gain the investor's confidence on its own, the plan will be rejected and never read in its entirety.

This section should discuss who will purchase the product or service, how much money is required for start-up, and what the payback is expected to be. You should also explain why you are uniquely qualified and skilled to manage the business.

Because this section summarizes the plan, it is often best to write it last.

Description of the Business   This section should provide background information about your industry, a history of your company, and a general description of your new product or service. Your product or service should be described in terms of its unique qualities and value to consumers.

Specific **short-** and **long-term objectives** must be defined. Clearly state what sales, market share, and profitability objectives your business should achieve.

Marketing   Two major parts make up the marketing section. The first part is the **research and analysis.** Here you should explain who will buy the product or service or, in other words, identify your target market. Measure your market size and trends and estimate the market share you expect to capture. Be sure to include support for your sales projections. For example, if your figures are based on published marketing research data, cite the source. Do your best to make realistic and credible projections. Describe your competition in considerable detail, identifying both their strengths and their weaknesses. Finally, explain how you will be better than your competitors.

The second part is your **marketing plan.** This critical section should include your market strategy, sales and distribution, pricing, advertising, promotion, and public awareness. You should also demonstrate how your pricing strategy will result in a profit, identify your advertising plans, and include cost estimates to validate the proposed strategy.

[6]See Donald F. Kuratko and Richard M. Hodgetts, *Entrepreneurship: A Contemporary Approach*, 5th ed. (Fort Worth, TX: Harcourt College Publishers, 2001), 295–310.

Research, Design, and Development (applicable only if R&D is involved)   This section includes **developmental research** leading to the design of the product. Industrial design is an art form that has successfully found its way into business, and it should not be neglected. Technical research results should be evaluated. Include the costs of research, testing, and development. Explain carefully what has already been accomplished (for example, prototype development, lab testing, and early development). Finally, mention any research or technical assistance that has been provided for you.

Location   This section should describe the advantages of your location in terms of zoning, tax laws, wage rates, labor availability, and proximity to suppliers and transportation systems. The requirements and costs of your facilities and equipment should also be outlined in this section. (Be careful—too many entrepreneurs underestimate this aspect of the plan.)

Management   Start by describing the **management team,** their unique qualifications, and your plans for their compensation (including salaries, employment agreements, stock purchase plans, levels of ownership, and other considerations). Discuss how your organization will be structured, and consider including a diagram illustrating who will report to whom. Also describe the potential contribution of the board of directors, advisors, and consultants. Finally, carefully delineate the legal structure of your venture (that is, sole proprietorship, partnership, or corporation).

Financial   This section of the business plan will be closely scrutinized by potential investors, so it is imperative that you give it the attention it deserves. Three key financial statements must be presented: a **balance sheet,** an **income statement,** and a **cash flow statement.** These statements typically cover a three-year period.

Determine the stages at which your business will require external financing and identify the expected financing sources (both debt and equity). Also, clearly show the return on investment that these sources will achieve if they invest in your business. The final item to include is a break-even chart, which should show the level of sales required to cover all costs.

If the work is done well, the financial statements should represent the actual financial achievements expected from the business plan. They also provide a standard by which to measure the actual results of operating the enterprise and become a valuable tool for managing and controlling the business in the first few years.

Harvest Strategy Segment   Every business plan should provide insights into the future harvest strategy. It is important for the entrepreneur to plan the orderly transition of the venture as it grows and develops. This section needs to deal with such issues as management succession and investor exit strategies. In addition, some thought should be given to change management—that is, the orderly transfer of the company assets if ownership of the business changes; continuity of the business strategy during the transition; and designation of key individuals to run the business if the current management team changes. With foresight, entrepreneurs can keep their dreams alive, ensure the security of their investors, and usually strengthen their businesses in the process. For this reason, a written plan for succession of your business is essential.

Critical Risks   Discuss **potential risks** before investors point them out. Outside consultants can often help identify risks and recommend alternative courses of action.

economy tanks, new gov't regulations, restaurant rat'g sys.

she hasn't outlined her objectives enough
→good service
→10% return

Here are some examples of potential risks: price cutting by competitors; potentially unfavorable industrywide trends; design or manufacturing costs that could exceed estimates; sales projections that are not achieved; production development schedules that are not met; difficulties or long lead times in procuring parts or raw materials; and greater-than-expected innovation and development costs needed to keep pace with new competition. The main objective of this section is to show that you can anticipate and control (to a reasonable degree) your risks.

Milestone Schedule   This section is another important segment of the business plan because its preparation requires you to determine what tasks must be accomplished to achieve your objectives. Milestones and deadlines should be established and monitored while the venture is in progress. Each milestone is related to all of the others, and together they form a network of the entire project.

Appendix   This section includes important background information that was not included in the other sections. It should include such items as résumés of the management team, names of references and advisors, drawings, documents, agreements, and any materials that support the plan. You may also wish to add a bibliography of the sources from which you drew information.

Acquiring information will probably be the most time-consuming part of the business-plan process. Following is a brief sampling of types of sources that may help you find the kind of information that you need.

Guidelines to Remember

The following points are a collection of recommendations by experts in venture capital and new-venture development.[7] These guidelines are presented as tips for successful business-plan development. You should adhere to them so that others will understand the importance of the various plan segments you are presenting. (Table 7.2 provides helpful hints for each segment of the plan.)

Keep the Plan Reasonably Short

Business plan readers are important people who refuse to waste time. Therefore, entrepreneurs should explain the venture not only carefully and clearly, but also concisely. (The plan should be no more than 40 pages long, excluding the Appendix.)

Appropriately Organize and Package the Plan

A table of contents, an Executive Summary, an Appendix, exhibits, graphs, proper grammar, a logical arrangement of segments, and overall neatness are critical elements in the effective presentation of a business plan.

---

[7]These guidelines are adapted from Jeffry A. Timmons, "A Business Plan Is More Than a Financing Device," *Harvard Business Review* (March–April 1980): 25–35; W. Keith Schilit, "How to Write a Winning Business Plan," *Business Horizons* (Sept.–Oct. 1987): 13–22; and William A. Sahlman, "How to Write a Great Business Plan," *Harvard Business Review,* (July–Aug. 1997): 98–108.

TABLE 7.2	HELPFUL HINTS FOR DEVELOPING THE BUSINESS PLAN

I. Executive Summary
- No more than three pages. This is the most crucial part of your plan because you must capture the reader's interest.
- What, how, why, where, and so on must be summarized.
- Complete this part after you have a finished business plan.

II. Business Description Segment
- The name of your business.
- A background of the industry with history of your company (if any) should be covered here.
- The potential of the new venture should be described clearly.
- Any uniqueness or distinctive features of this venture should be clearly described.

III. Marketing Segment
- Convince investors that sales projections and competition can be met.
- Use and disclose market studies.
- Identify target market, market position, and market share.
- Evaluate all competition and specifically cover why and how you will be better than your competitors.
- Identify all market sources and assistance used for this segment.
- Demonstrate pricing strategy since your price must penetrate and maintain a market share to *produce profits*. Thus the lowest price is not necessarily the best price.
- Identify your advertising plans with cost estimates to validate proposed strategy.

IV. Location Segment
- Describe the advantages of your location (zoning, tax laws, wage rates). List the production needs in terms of facilities (plant, storage, office space) and equipment (machinery, furnishings, supplies).
- Describe the access to transportation (for shipping and receiving).
- Indicate proximity to your suppliers.
- Mention the availability of labor in your location.
- Provide estimates of manufacturing costs—be careful; too many entrepreneurs underestimate their costs.

V. Management Segment
- Supply résumés of all key people in the management of your venture.
- Carefully describe the legal structure of your venture (sole proprietorship, partnership, or corporation).
- Cover the added assistance (if any) of advisors, consultants, and directors.
- Give information on how and how much everyone is to be compensated.

Orient the Plan Toward the Future

Entrepreneurs should attempt to create an exciting plan by outlining trends and forecasts that describe what the venture intends to do and what opportunities exist for the use of the product or service.

Avoid Exaggeration

Potential sales, revenue estimates, and the venture's potential growth should not be inflated. Many times, best-case, worst-case, and probable-case scenarios should be developed. Documentation and research are vital to the credibility of the plan.

Highlight Critical Risks

The Critical Risks segment of the business plan is important because it demonstrates the entrepreneur's ability to analyze potential problems and develop alternative courses of action.

TABLE 7.2   **(CONTINUED)**

VI. Financial Segment
- Give actual estimated statements.
- Describe the needed sources for your funds and the uses you intend for the money.
- Develop and present a budget.
- Create stages of financing for purposes of allowing evaluation by investors at various points.

VII. Critical-Risks Segment
- Discuss potential risks before investors point them out—for example,
  - Price cutting by competitors.
  - Any potentially unfavorable industry-wide trends.
  - Design or manufacturing costs in excess of estimates.
  - Sales projections not achieved.
  - Product development schedule not met.
  - Difficulties or long lead times encountered in the procurement of parts or raw materials.
  - Greater than expected innovation and development costs to stay competitive.
- Provide some alternative courses of action.

VIII. Harvest Strategy Segment
- Outline a plan for the orderly transfer of company assets (ownership).
- Describe the plan for transition of leadership.
- Mention the preparations (insurance, trusts, and so on) needed for continuity of the business.

IX. Milestone Schedule Segment
- Develop a timetable or chart to demonstrate when each phase of the venture is to be completed. This shows the relationship of events and provides a deadline for accomplishment.

Appendix or Bibliography

SOURCE: Donald F. Kuratko, Jeffrey S. Hornsby, and Frank J. Sabatine, *The Breakthrough Experience: A Guide to Corporate Entrepreneurship* (Muncie, IN: The Midwest Entrepreneurial Education Center, College of Business, Ball State University, 1999).

Present Evidence of an Effective Entrepreneurial Team

The Management segment of the business plan should clearly identify the skills of each key person as well as demonstrate how all such persons can effectively work together as a team to manage the venture.

Do Not Overdiversify

Focus the attention of the plan on one main opportunity for the venture. A new business should not attempt to create multiple markets or pursue multiple ventures until it has successfully developed one main strength.

Identify the Target Market

Substantiate the marketability of the venture's product or service by identifying the particular customer niche that is being sought. This segment of the business plan is pivotal to the success of the other parts. Market research must be included to demonstrate *how* this market segment has been identified.

Write the Plan in the Third Person

Rather than continually stating "I," "we," or "us," the entrepreneur should phrase everything as "he," "they," or "them." In other words, avoid personalizing the plan and keep the writing objective.

Capture the Reader's Interest

Because only a small percentage of the business plans that are submitted to investors are actually funded, entrepreneurs need to capture the reader's interest right away by emphasizing the venture's uniqueness. Use the title page and Executive Summary as key tools for capturing the reader's attention and creating a desire to read more.

Preparing a business plan will not guarantee success or remove risk or uncertainty, and it will not always result in financing. Nevertheless, business plans can help entrepreneurs make informed decisions. For this reason alone they almost always prove to be a good investment of time and effort.

Exploring the Entrepreneurial Concepts

The following sections provide an "entrepreneurial library" that contains a journal reading on this chapter's subject and a comprehensive cases study to illustrate the concept in practice. It is hoped that through the reading and discussion of the case, you will gain a greater understanding of the chapter.

THE ENTREPRENEURIAL LIBRARY

Reading for Chapter 7

HOW TO WRITE A GREAT BUSINESS PLAN

William A. Sahlman

Few areas of business attract as much attention as new ventures, and few aspects of new-venture creation attract as much attention as the business plan. Countless books and articles in the popular press dissect the topic. A growing number of annual business-plan contests are springing up across the United States and, increasingly, in other countries. Both graduate and undergraduate schools devote entire courses to the subject. Indeed, judging by all the hoopla surrounding business plans, you would think that the only things standing between a would-be entrepreneur and spectacular success are glossy five-color charts, a bundle of meticulous-looking spreadsheets, and a decade of month-by-month financial projections.

Nothing could be further from the truth. In my experience with hundreds of entrepreneurial start-ups, business plans rank no higher than 2—on a scale from 1 to 10—as a predictor of a new venture's success. And sometimes, in fact, the more elaborately crafted the document, the more likely the venture is to, well, flop, for lack of a more euphemistic word.

What's wrong with most business plans? The answer is relatively straightforward. Most waste too much ink on numbers and devote too little to the information that really matters to intelligent investors. As every seasoned investor knows, financial projections for a new company—especially detailed, month-by-month projections that stretch out for more than a year—are an act of imagination. An entrepreneurial venture faces far too many unknowns to predict revenues, let alone profits. Moreover, few if any entrepreneurs correctly anticipate how much capital and time will be required to accomplish their objectives. Typically, they are wildly optimistic, padding their projections. Investors know about the padding effect and therefore discount the figures in business plans. These maneuvers create a vicious circle of inaccuracy that benefits no one.

Don't misunderstand me: business plans should include some numbers. But those numbers should appear mainly in the form of a business model that shows the entrepreneurial team has thought through the key drivers of the venture's success or failure. In manufacturing, such a driver might be the yield on a production process; in magazine publishing, the anticipated renewal rate; or in software, the impact of using various distribution channels. The model should also address the break-even issue: At what level of sales does the business begin to make a profit? And even more important, When does cash flow turn positive? Without a doubt, these questions deserve a few pages in any business plan. Near the back.

What goes at the front? What information does a good business plan contain?

If you want to speak the language of investors—and also make sure you have asked yourself the right questions before setting out on the most daunting journey of a businessperson's career—I recommend basing your business plan on the framework that follows. It does not provide the kind of "winning" formula touted by some current how-to books and software programs for entrepreneurs. Nor is it a guide to brain surgery. Rather, the framework systematically assesses the four interdependent factors critical to every new venture:

The People. The men and women starting and running the venture, as well as the outside parties providing key services or important resources for it, such as its lawyers, accountants, and suppliers.

The Opportunity. A profile of the business itself—what it will sell and to whom, whether the business can grow and how fast, what its economics are, who and what stand in the way of success.

The Context. The big picture—the regulatory environment, interest rates, demographic trends, inflation, and the like—basically, factors that inevitably change but cannot be controlled by the entrepreneur.

Risk and Reward. An assessment of everything that can go wrong and right, and a discussion of how the entrepreneurial team can respond.

The assumption behind the framework is that great businesses have attributes that are easy to identify but hard to assemble. They have an experienced, energetic managerial team from the top to the bottom. The team's members have skills and experiences directly relevant to the opportunity they are pursuing. Ideally, they will have worked successfully together in the past. The opportunity has an attractive, sustainable business

Printed in the *Harvard Business Review*, July–August, 1997.

model; it is possible to create a competitive edge and defend it. Many options exist for expanding the scale and scope of the business, and these options are unique to the enterprise and its team. Value can be extracted from the business in a number of ways either through a positive harvest event—a sale—or by scaling down or liquidating. The context is favorable with respect to both the regulatory and the macroeconomic environments. Risk is understood, and the team has considered ways to mitigate the impact of difficult events. In short, great businesses have the four parts of the framework completely covered. If only reality were so neat.

The People

When I receive a business plan, I always read the résumé section first. Not because the people part of the new venture is the most important, but because without the right team, none of the other parts really matters.

I read the résumés of the venture's team with a list of questions in mind. . . . All these questions get at the same three issues about the venture's team members: What do they know? Whom do they know? and How well are they known?

What and whom they know are matters of insight and experience. How familiar are the team members with industry players and dynamics? Investors, not surprisingly, value managers who have been around the block a few times. A business plan should candidly describe each team member's knowledge of the new venture's type of product or service; its production processes; and the market itself, from competitors to customers. It also helps to indicate whether the team members have worked together before. Not played—as in roomed together in college—but *worked*.

Investors also look favorably on a team that is known because the real world often prefers not to deal with start-ups. They're too unpredictable. That changes, however, when the new company is run by people well known to suppliers, customers, and employees. Their enterprise may be brand new, but they aren't. The surprise element of working with a start-up is somewhat ameliorated.

Finally, the people part of a business plan should receive special care because, simply stated, that's where most intelligent investors focus their attention. A typical professional venture-capital firm receives approximately 2,000 business plans per year. These plans are filled with tantalizing ideas for new products and services that will change the world and reap billions in the process—or so they say. But the fact is, most venture capitalists believe that ideas are a dime a dozen: only execution skills count. As Arthur Rock, a venture capital legend associated with the formation of such companies as Apple, Intel, and Teledyne, states, "I invest in people, not ideas." Rock also has said, "If you can find good people, if they're wrong about the product, they'll make a switch, so what good is it to understand the product that they're talking about in the first place?"

Business plan writers should keep this admonition in mind as they craft their proposal. Talk about the people—exhaustively. And if there is nothing solid about their experience and abilities to herald, then the entrepreneurial team should think again about launching the venture.

The Opportunity

When it comes to the opportunity itself, a good business plan begins by focusing on two questions: Is the total market for the venture's product or service large, rapidly growing, or both? Is the industry now, or can it become, structurally attractive? Entrepreneurs and investors look for large or rapidly growing markets mainly because it is often easier to obtain a share of a growing market than to fight with entrenched competitors for a share of a mature or stagnant market. Smart investors, in fact, try hard to identify high-growth-potential markets early in their evolution: that's where the big payoffs are. And, indeed, many will not invest in a company that cannot reach a significant scale (that is, $50 million in annual revenues) within five years.

As for attractiveness, investors are obviously looking for markets that actually allow businesses to make some money. But that's not the no-brainer it seems. In the late 1970s, the computer disk-drive business looked very attractive. The technology was new and exciting. Dozens of companies jumped into the fray, aided by an army of professional investors. Twenty years later, however, the thrill is gone for managers and investors alike. Disk drive companies must design products to meet the perceived needs of original equipment manufacturers (OEMs) and end users. Selling a product to OEMs is complicated. The customers are large relative to most of their suppliers. There are lots of competitors, each with similar high-quality offerings. Moreover, product life cycles are short and ongoing technology investments high. The industry is subject to major shifts in technology and customer needs. Intense rivalry leads to lower prices and, hence, lower margins. In short, the disk drive industry is simply not set up to make people a lot of money; it's a structural disaster area.

The information services industry, by contrast, is paradise. Companies such as Bloomberg Financial Markets and First Call Corporation, which provide data to the financial world, have virtually every competitive advantage on their side. First, they can assemble or create *proprietary* content—content that, by the way, is like life's blood to thousands of money managers and stock analysts around the world. And although it is often expensive to develop the service and to acquire initial customers, once up and running, these companies can deliver content to customers very cheaply. Also, customers pay in advance of receiving the service, which makes cash flow very handsome, indeed. In short, the structure of the information services industry is beyond attractive: it's gorgeous. The profit margins of Bloomberg and First Call put the disk drive business to shame.

Thus, the first step for entrepreneurs is to make sure they are entering an industry that is large and/or growing, and one that's structurally attractive. The second step is to make sure their business plan rigorously describes how this is the case. And if it isn't the case, their business plan needs to specify how the venture will still manage to make enough of a profit that investors (or potential employees or suppliers, for that matter) will want to participate.

Once it examines the new venture's industry, a business plan must describe in detail how the company will build and launch its product or service into the marketplace. Again, a series of questions should guide the discussion. (See the insert "The Opportunity of a Lifetime—or Is It?")

Often the answers to these questions reveal a fatal flaw in the business. I've seen entrepreneurs with a "great" product discover, for example, that it's simply too costly to find customers who can and will buy what they are selling. Economically viable access to customers is the key to business, yet many entrepreneurs take the *Field of Dreams* approach to this notion: build it, and they will come. That strategy works in the movies but is not very sensible in the real world.

It is not always easy to answer questions about the likely consumer response to new products or services. The market is as fickle as it is unpredictable. (Who would have guessed that plug-in room deodorizers would sell?) One entrepreneur I know proposed to introduce an electronic news-clipping service. He made his pitch to a prospective venture-capital investor who rejected the plan, stating, "I just don't think the dogs will eat the dog food." Later, when the entrepreneur's company went public, he sent the venture capitalist an anonymous package containing an empty can of dog food and a copy of his prospectus. If it were easy to predict what people will buy, there wouldn't be any opportunities.

Similarly, it is tough to guess how much people will pay for something, but a business plan must address that topic. Sometimes, the dogs will eat the dog food, but only at a price less than cost. Investors always look for opportunities for value pricing—that is, markets in which the costs to produce the product are low, but consumers will still pay a lot for it. No one is dying to invest in a company when margins are skinny. Still, there is money to be made in inexpensive products and services—even in commodities. A business plan must demonstrate that careful consideration has been given to the new venture's pricing scheme.

The list of questions about the new venture's opportunity focuses on the direct revenues and the costs of producing and marketing a product. That's fine, as far as it goes. A sensible proposal, however, also involves assessing the business model from a perspective that takes into account the investment required—that is, the balance sheet side of the equation. The following questions should also be addressed so that investors can understand the cash flow implications of pursuing an opportunity:

- When does the business have to buy resources, such as supplies, raw materials, and people?
- When does the business have to pay for them?
- How long does it take to acquire a customer?
- How long before the customer sends the business a check?
- How much capital equipment is required to support a dollar of sales?

Investors, of course, are looking for businesses in which management can buy low, sell high, collect early, and pay late. The business plan needs to spell out how close to that ideal the new venture is expected to come. Even if the answer is "not very"—and it usually is—at least the truth is out there to discuss.

The opportunity section of a business plan must also bring a few other issues to the surface. First, it must demonstrate and analyze how an opportunity can grow—in other words, how the new venture can expand its range of products or services, customer base, or geographic scope. Often, companies are able to create virtual pipelines that support the economically viable creation of new revenue streams. In the publishing business, for example, *Inc.* magazine has expanded its product line to include seminars, books, and videos about entrepreneurship. Similarly, building on the success of its personal-finance software program Quicken, Intuit now sells software for electronic banking, small-business accounting, and tax preparation, as well as personal-printing supplies and on-line information services—to name just a few of its highly profitable ancillary spin-offs.

Now, lots of business plans runneth over on the subject of the new venture's potential for growth and expansion. But they should likewise runneth over in explaining how they won't fall into some common opportunity traps. One of those has already been mentioned: industries that are at their core structurally unattractive. But there are oth-

TABLE 1	THE OPPORTUNITY OF A LIFETIME—OR IS IT?

Nine Questions About the Business Every Business Plan Should Answer

☐ Who is the new venture's customer?

☐ How does the customer make decisions about buying this product or service?

☐ To what degree is the product or service a compelling purchase for the customer?

☐ How will the product or service be priced?

☐ How will the venture reach all the identified customer segments?

☐ How much does it cost (in time and resources) to acquire a customer?

☐ How much does it cost to produce and deliver the product or service?

☐ How much does it cost to support a customer?

☐ How easy is it to retain a customer?

---

ers. The world of invention, for example, is fraught with danger. Over the past 15 years, I have seen scores of individuals who have devised a better mousetrap-newfangled creations from inflatable pillows for use on airplanes to automated car-parking systems. Few of these idea-driven companies have really taken off, however. I'm not entirely sure why. Sometimes, the inventor refuses to spend the money required by or share the rewards sufficiently with the business side of the company. Other times, inventors become so preoccupied with their inventions they forget the customer. Whatever the reason, better-mousetrap businesses have an uncanny way of malfunctioning.

Another opportunity trap that business plans—and entrepreneurs in general—need to pay attention to is the tricky business of arbitrage. Basically, arbitrage ventures are created to take advantage of some pricing disparity in the marketplace. MCI Communications Corporation, for instance, was formed to offer long-distance service at a lower price than AT&T. Some of the industry consolidations going on today reflect a different kind of arbitrage—the ability to buy small businesses at a wholesale price, roll them up together into a larger package, and take them public at a retail price, all without necessarily adding value in the process.

Taking advantage of arbitrage opportunities is a viable and potentially profitable way to enter a business. In the final analysis, however, all arbitrage opportunities evaporate. It is not a question of whether, only when. The trick in these businesses is to use the arbitrage profits to build a more enduring business model, and business plans must explain how and when that will occur.

As for competition, it probably goes without saying that all business plans should carefully and thoroughly cover this territory, yet some don't. That is a glaring omission. For starters, every business plan should answer the following questions about the competition:

- Who are the new venture's current competitors?

- What resources do they control? What are their strengths and weaknesses?

- How will they respond to the new venture's decision to enter the business?

- How can the new venture respond to its competitors' response?

- Who else might be able to observe and exploit the same opportunity?

- Are there ways to co-opt potential or actual competitors by forming alliances?

Business is like chess: to be successful, you must anticipate several moves in advance. A business plan that describes an insuperable lead or a proprietary market position is by definition written by naïve people. That goes not just for the competition section of the business plan but for the entire discussion of the opportunity. All opportunities have promise; all have vulnerabilities. A good business plan doesn't whitewash the latter. Rather, it proves that the entrepreneurial team knows the good, the bad, and the ugly that the venture faces ahead.

The Context

Opportunities exist in a context. At one level is the macroeconomic environment, including the level of economic activity, inflation, exchange rates, and interest rates. At another level are the wide range of government rules and regulations that affect the opportunity and how resources are marshaled to exploit it. Examples extend from tax policy to the rules about raising capital for a private or public company. And at yet another level are factors like technology that define the limits of what a business or its competitors can accomplish.

Context often has a tremendous impact on every aspect of the entrepreneurial process, from identification of opportunity to harvest. In some cases, changes in some contextual factor create opportunity. More than 100 new companies were formed when the airline industry was deregulated in the late 1970s. The context for financing was also favorable, enabling new entrants like People Express to go to the public market for capital even before starting operations.

Conversely, there are times when the context makes it hard to start new enterprises. The recession of the early 1990s combined with a difficult financing environment for new companies: venture capital disbursements were low, as was the amount of capital raised in the public markets. (Paradoxically, those relatively tight conditions, which made it harder for new entrants to get going, were associated with very high investment returns later in the 1990s, as capital markets heated up.)

Sometimes, a shift in context turns an unattractive business into an attractive one, and vice versa. Consider the case of a packaging company some years ago that was performing so poorly it was about to be put on the block. Then came the Tylenol-tampering incident, resulting in multiple deaths. The packaging company happened to have an efficient mechanism for installing tamper-proof seals, and in a matter of weeks its financial performance could have been called spectacular. Conversely, U.S. tax reforms enacted in 1986 created havoc for companies in the real estate business, eliminating almost every positive incentive to invest. Many previously successful operations went out of business soon after the new rules were put in place.

Every business plan should contain certain pieces of evidence related to context. First, the entrepreneurs should show a heightened awareness of the new venture's context and how it helps or hinders their specific proposal. Second, and more important, they should demonstrate that they know the venture's context will inevitably change and describe how those changes might affect the business. Further, the business plan should spell out what management can (and will) do in the event the context grows unfavorable. Finally, the business plan should explain the ways (if any) in which management can affect context in a positive way. For example, management might be able to have an impact on regulations or on industry standards through lobbying efforts.

Risk and Reward

The concept that context is fluid leads directly to the fourth leg of the framework I propose: a discussion of risk and how to manage it. I've come to think of a good business plan as a snapshot of an event in the future. That's quite a feat to begin with—taking a picture of the unknown. But the best business plans go beyond that; they are like movies of the future. They show the people, the opportunity, and the context from multiple angles. They offer a plausible, coherent story of what lies ahead. They unfold possibilities of action and reaction.

Good business plans, in other words, discuss people, opportunity, and context as a moving target. All three factors (and the relationship among them) are likely to change over time as a company evolves from start-up to ongoing enterprise. Therefore, any business plan worth the time it takes to write or read needs to focus attention on the dynamic aspects of the entrepreneurial process.

Of course, the future is hard to predict. Still, it is possible to give potential investors a sense of the kind and class of risk and reward they are assuming with a new venture. . . . In reality, there are no immutable distributions of outcomes. It is ultimately the responsibility of management to change the distribution, to increase the likelihood and consequences of success, and to decrease the likelihood and implications of problems.

One of the great myths about entrepreneurs is that they are risk seekers. All sane people want to avoid risk. As Harvard Business School professor (and venture capitalist) Howard Stevenson says, true entrepreneurs want to capture all the reward and give all the risk to others. The best business is a post office box to which people send cashier's checks. Yet risk is unavoidable. So what does that mean for a business plan?

It means that the plan must unflinchingly confront the risk ahead—in terms of people, opportunity, and context. What happens if one of the new venture's leaders leaves? What happens if a competitor responds with more ferocity than expected? What happens if there is a revolution in Namibia, the source of a key raw material? What will management actually *do*?

Those are hard questions for an entrepreneur to pose, especially when seeking capital. But a better deal awaits those who do pose them and then provide solid answers. A new venture, for example, might be highly leveraged and therefore very sensitive to interest rates. Its business plan would benefit enormously by stating that management intends to hedge its exposure through the financial-futures market by purchasing a contract that does well when interest rates go up. That is the equivalent of offering investors insurance. (It also makes sense for the business itself.)

Finally, one important area in the realm of risk/reward management relates to harvesting. Venture capitalists often ask if a company is "IPOable," by which they mean, Can the company be taken public at some point in the future? Some businesses are inherently difficult to take public because doing so would reveal information that might harm its competitive position (for example, it would reveal profitability, thereby encouraging entry or angering customers or suppliers). Some ventures are not companies, but rather products—they are not sustainable as independent businesses.

Therefore, the business plan should talk candidly about the end of the process. How will the investor eventually get money out of the business, assuming it is successful, even if only marginally so? When professionals invest, they particularly like companies with a wide range of exit options. They like companies that work hard to preserve and enhance those options along the way, companies that don't, for example, unthinkingly form alliances with big corporations that could someday actually *buy* them. Investors feel a lot better about risk if the venture's endgame is discussed up front. There is an old saying, "If you don't know where you are going, any road will get you there." In crafting sensible entrepreneurial strategies, just the opposite is true: you had better know where you might end up and have a map for getting there. A business plan should be the place where that map is drawn, for, as every traveler knows, a journey is a lot less risky when you have directions.

The Deal and Beyond

Once a business plan is written, of course, the goal is to land a deal. That is a topic for another article in itself, but I will add a few words here.

When I talk to young (and old) entrepreneurs looking to finance their ventures, they obsess about the valuation and terms of the deal they will receive. Their explicit goal seems to be to minimize the dilution they will suffer in raising capital. Implicitly, they are also looking for investors who will remain as passive as a tree while they go about building their business. On the food chain of investors, it seems, doctors and dentists are best and venture capitalists are worst because of the degree to which the latter group demands control and a large share of the returns.

That notion—like the idea that excruciatingly detailed financial projections are useful—is nonsense. From whom you raise capital is often more important than the terms. New ventures are inherently risky, as I've noted; what can go wrong will. When that happens, unsophisticated investors panic, get angry, and often refuse to advance the company more money. Sophisticated investors, by contrast, roll up their sleeves and help the company solve its problems. Often, they've had lots of experience saving sinking ships. They are typically process literate. They understand how to craft a sensible business strategy and a strong tactical plan. They know how to recruit, compensate, and motivate team members. They are also familiar with the Byzantine ins and outs of going public—an event most entrepreneurs face but once in a lifetime. This kind of know-how is worth the money needed to buy it.

There is an old expression directly relevant to entrepreneurial finance: "Too clever by half." Often, deal makers get very creative, crafting all sorts of payoff and option schemes. That usually backfires. My experience has proven again and again that sensible deals have the following six characteristics:

- They are simple.

- They are fair.

- They emphasize trust rather than legal ties.

- They do not blow apart if actual differs slightly from plan.

- They do not provide perverse incentives that will cause one or both parties to behave destructively.

- They are written on a pile of papers no greater than one-quarter inch thick.

But even these six simple rules miss an important point. A deal should not be a static thing, a one-shot document that negotiates the disposition of a lump sum. Instead, it is incumbent upon entrepreneurs, before they go searching for funding, to think about capital acquisition as a dynamic process—to figure out how much money they will need and when they will need it.

How is that accomplished? The trick is for the entrepreneurial team to treat the new venture as a series of experiments. Before launching the whole show, launch a little piece of it. Convene a focus group to test the product, build a prototype and watch it perform, conduct a regional or local rollout of a service. Such an exercise reveals the true economics of the business and can help enormously in determining how much money the new venture actually requires and in what stages. Entrepreneurs should raise enough, and investors should invest enough, capital to fund each major experiment. Experiments, of course, can feel expensive and risky. But I've seen them prevent disasters and help create successes. I consider it a prerequisite of putting together a winning deal.

Beware the Albatross

Among the many sins committed by business plan writers is arrogance. In today's economy, few ideas are truly proprietary. Moreover, there has never been a time in recorded history when the supply of capital did not outrace the supply of opportunity. The true half-life of opportunity is decreasing with the passage of time.

A business plan must not be an albatross that hangs around the neck of the entrepreneurial team, dragging it into oblivion. Instead, a business plan must be a call for action, one that recognizes management's responsibility to fix what is broken proactively and in real time. Risk is inevitable, avoiding risk impossible. Risk management is the key, always tilting the venture in favor of reward and away from risk.

A plan must demonstrate mastery of the entire entrepreneurial process, from identification of opportunity to harvest. It is not a way to separate unsuspecting investors from their money by hiding the fatal flaw. For in the final analysis, the only one being fooled is the entrepreneur.

We live today in the golden age of entrepreneurship. Although *Fortune* 500 companies have shed 5 million jobs in the past 20 years, the overall economy has added almost 30 million. Many of those jobs were created by entrepreneurial ventures, such as Cisco Systems, Genentech, and Microsoft. Each of those companies started with a business plan. Is that why they succeeded? There is no knowing for sure. But there is little doubt that crafting a business plan so that it thoroughly and candidly addresses the ingredients of success—people, opportunity, context, and the risk/reward picture—is vitally important. In the absence of a crystal ball, in fact, a business plan built of the *right* information and analysis can only be called indispensable.

COMPREHENSIVE CASE STUDY

C A S E   GROUNDED: BUSINESS SOLUTIONS FOR TODAY'S TRAVELER

Jason O'Neil, Owner and CEO of Grounded

Table of Contents

IV.   Space and Area
V.   Layout
Critical Risks
Milestones

Executive Summary

Statement of Purpose

The purpose of this business plan is to obtain the attention, interest, and investment of four investors generating a total of $80,000. Mr. Jason A. O'Neil will contribute $31,000 and a bank loan of $50,000 will be obtained to complete the $161,000 needed to finance this business concept.

Description of Grounded LLC

Grounded proposes to be the Indianapolis International Airport's first and foremost full-service office center. The business will be dedicated to providing the business traveling community the ways and means to conduct their day-to-day business operations while on the road. Grounded offers travelers copy and printing services, fax services, a conference room and both private office facilities and pay per use computer terminals to access the Internet via ISDN and T-1 connections; these 13 computers will also be equipped with exhaustive software applications. Each of the seven private offices will be equipped with a Gateway PC, laptop data port, color printer, scanner, fax machine, and three-line conference telephone; all domestic long distance calls are included in the price of Grounded's services. Collectively, these amenities offer business travelers all facets of their respective offices while they are on the road.

Marketing Strategy

Grounded's market niche will be the business traveler whose day to day business functions hinge on their ability to stay in communication with their clients and companies. The specific market for Grounded's services is Indianapolis International Airport passengers who exhibit high income levels, spend a great deal of time at the airport, and have managerial or professional occupations. Persons with these characteristics made up 375,594 (10.3%) passengers who flew out of the Indianapolis International Airport in 1998.

    The business has determined that it can gain a 3.8% market penetration in the first year of operations, equating to 14,238 total clients. By the third year of operations, 20,007 clients are anticipated, accounting for a 5.3% market penetration.

Financial Projections

Sales were determined by the computation of survey results, and LapTop Lane's sales trends. LapTop Lane functions in a similar capacity to that of Grounded. Sales are anticipated to climb from 45 clients per day in the first month of operations to 70 clients per day in the middle of year three which is deemed to be maturity.

    By the beginning of the third year of operations, the business will reach its break-even point, yielding returns for Grounded, and its potential stakeholders.

Grounded has two long range options for growth or exit:

- Establish stores on a global front
- Sell out to LapTop Lane's parent company Softnet

LapTop Lane's twelve stores were recently acquired for $33 million by Softnet Systems; the purchase price equates to $2,750,000 per store. Investors will grow with the company as it undertakes global expansion, cash in their percentage of ownership into the capital generated from the sale, or convert their ownership into the parent company's stock.

Business Description

I. Company

State of the art office functions, complete computing capabilities, advanced telecommunications facilities, on-line collaboration, real-time sales reports, last minute revisions, a conference center, and knowledgeable client assistants—at the airport. Traveling can be both the most important and least productive activity in business."[1] Grounded is dedicated to providing its clients with all the amenities of their offices while they are traveling.

Grounded will operate in a space approximately 1,600 square feet in size across from the TWA and ATA ticket counters on the second floor of the Indianapolis International Airport (IIA). Clients will have access to high-speed Internet connections via ISDN and T-1 lines, all-inclusive private offices, black and white and color copiers as well as a conference room.

Six computers, with a full range of desktop publishing software, will be provided for clients to use as they please. These computers will be networked to both black-and-white and color laser printers. Keeping with the trend of providing sound means of communication, Grounded recognizes the necessity of privacy in today's business world. To combat the privacy issue, the store will be equipped with 7 private offices. These will be small in size, approximately 42 square feet; their purpose is to provide clients with a private, quiet, comfortable means to conduct their business. These offices will be fully equipped with a PC, printer, data port, wall plug, fax machine, scanner, and telephone. Clients will have the ability to plug in their laptops, access their company's information page, check their stocks on our PC, send a fax and make a phone call at the same time.

Overall, Grounded will supply the business traveler with everything he or she needs to keep pace with the ever-changing business environment while they are traveling.

II. Mission

To provide a platform for our clients to become more efficient, productive, and professional while traveling. Our client's objectives instantly become our primary objective and we will do anything in our power to meet these ongoing needs and wants; client satisfaction is paramount.

---

[1]Baker, Kim and Sunny. *Office on the Go*. Prentice Hall, 1993.

III. *Products and Services*

Grounded is a service business dedicated to providing its clients with office services, computing and Internet functions while offering a quiet and productive environment. The uniqueness of Grounded lies in its location. While similar businesses are currently operating successfully in today's market, Grounded will be located in the Indianapolis International Airport (IIA). The location of the business is crucial in providing clients with the convenience of fast, reliable Internet and computing services at a place where they otherwise could not use them. Grounded will serve as a forum for business travelers to complete or revise any work, check e-mail, make conference calls, or conduct a meeting.

Office Services Offered by Grounded:

- Private offices
- Black-and-white copying
- Color copying
- Stapling and grouping
- Phone (Domestic long distance included in charges of private offices)
- Fax (Domestic long distance included in charges of private offices)
- Access to computers
- Internet access
- Mailing

Computing Services Offered by Grounded:

- Gateway PCs
- Microsoft Office Professional 2000
- Laptop data ports
- Scanners
- Full range of software
- High-speed Internet access via ISDN and T-1

Products Offered by Grounded:

- Paper
- Cardstock
- Transparencies
- Mailing products and services

IV. Policies and Standards

Grounded will provide business travelers with the means they need to conduct businesses during downtime at the airport. A comfortable, productive, and professional atmosphere will be provided to meet the needs of its clients. Emphasis will be placed on time-honored traditions coupled with today's technology. Client assistants will be courteous, professional, knowledgeable, and helpful. Client satisfaction is paramount. Grounded is aware of the unique, enchanting, and sometimes odd needs of today's professional; to combat this, dedication will lie in the capability and willingness to go as far as possible to meet all client wants.

Internally, Grounded's client assistants are the most important part of the organization—without them all the technology, marketing, and clients will be worthless. Grounded believes that through extensive training, empowerment, and knowledge their client assistants will be equipped with the foundation to treat each client as their respective bosses. Clients will have the impression that each client assistant is in fact their personal assistant doing whatever it takes to solve their needs.

Standards Grounded and its client assistants will uphold:

- Unprecedented service

- Courtesy

- Professionalism

- Knowledge

V. Industry

An actual industry for this business concept fails to exist in documented form. For intensive purposes, this plan shall extrapolate information from industries such as Other Information Services and Business Services. LapTop Lane, which functions in a similar capacity as Grounded will be reviewed, as well as an analysis of current mobile communication options, comparable technologies, technological trends, business trends, and specific services currently available to business travelers. Finally, Internet usage will be examined. Focus will be placed on LapTop Lane, the Internet, and specific trends and options currently available to the business traveler.

During 1997, the U.S. Census Bureau reported that within the state of Indiana, other information services accounted for 59 established businesses with 314 employees, and an annual payroll of $7,503,000; these 59 businesses generated $39,585,000 in sales during that year.

The National Business Travel Association reported that a survey done by *Frequent Flyer* magazine uncovered some revealing facts about the habits specific to business travelers. The survey revealed that seven out of ten respondents continued to bring a laptop, and 47% use the Internet, or other on-line services while on the road, which has more than doubled since the 1996 poll. E-mail rose to the second most popular method of communication, rivaled only by voice mail, and overtaking faxes for the first time. "Technology has clearly changed the way we travel and continues to grow in importance among frequent business travelers. It enables travelers to stay in touch and be more productive while on the road, and this trend is certain to continue," according to Charlene Seoane, publisher of *Frequent Flyer* magazine.[2]

---

[2]http://travelvault.nbta.org

All areas of communication have become increasingly more important to Americans; a major indicator of this is how the general population, especially business people, have come to rely heavily on the use of mobile communication. Time is money; having easy access to a phone makes good business sense. It is estimated that nearly 75 percent of all cellular phone conversations are business related. In fact, cell phones have become such a necessary business tool, that there are an estimated 35 million cellular phones currently in use in the United States and that number could go as high as 80 million by the year 2000. Many of those will be employer-provided cell phones for employees who are on the road a majority of their working hours.[3]

According to the Personal Communications Industry Association (PCIA), Cahners (marketing firm) reports that nearly 50 million Americans are mobile, spending twenty percent or more of their time away from their desks. Additionally, 49 percent of business professionals say they would access the Internet several times daily (while on the road) if the price and service were right.[4] Individuals have mastered the art of using their cell phones as extensions of their offices, time that was previously wasted waiting, traveling, or in route can now easily be converted to fertile billable time by any professional.[5]

Having laid the groundwork for the necessity of mobile communication between business people, it must be recognized that the company LapTop Lane functions in a similar capacity to that of Grounded. LapTop Lane is currently operating in twelve airports throughout the United States, with plans to open four more in the future.

LapTop Lane's market is essentially the same as Grounded's—the business traveler. Their spin on the situation is to offer only private offices with all the amenities as that of Grounded. They do not offer independent workstations, a copy center, or a conference room. LapTop Lane has in turn experienced a great deal of success in their short two years of existence. In fact, the company has recently received so much attention that on March 14, 2000, a deal was struck involving a stock swap between Softnet Systems Inc., Compaq Computer Corporation, Nokia Corporation, and Cisco Systems Inc. in which SoftNet acquired LapTop Lane for one million shares of SoftNet trading at around $33. The deal is to be closed by late April; due to the size and nature of the deal, marketing, and financial information about the company are considered sensitive data. (*Note:* Nokia stock split 4:1 on April 11, 2000.)

This attention and high dollar figure indicates the amount of potential currently available in this market. It is apparent that SoftNet will become a major player in the market, and has serious plans for expansion.

Internet access stations are also popping up in airports, convention centers, and even local small business. These are stand-alone ATM type kiosks where users can pay about $2.50 for 10 minutes of Internet service.[6] These machines are a temporary solution for an ailing problem. While they serve the need for anyone who merely needs to check their e-mail—in scope they have many downfalls. First, only web access is available. As stated earlier, this suits someone who needs to merely send or receive e-mail, check a stock quote, or play a game. Second, they are stand-alone machines, meaning that the user is sitting in the middle of a terminal with no privacy which will cause them to be cautious when entering passwords and always be wondering about their baggage which is sitting next to them. Finally, the speed of these

---

[3]http://law.about.com/medianews/law/gi/dynamic/offsite.htm?site=http://www.saif.com/Safety%5Fartc/cell%5Fph.htm

[4]http://www.wirelesstoday.com/snaparchives/snap112299.html

[5]http://law.about.com/medianews/law/gi/dynamic/offsite.htm?site=http://www.saif.com/Safety%5Fartc/cell%5Fph.htm

[6]http://www.quickaid.com/qis

machines is not guaranteed; if someone puts in $7.50 to access the Internet for half an hour, it is questionable as to the connection they will receive.

These Internet access stations can easily be viewed as a threat because they can easily be located in terminals without taking up much space. At the same time it must be noted that none of these currently exist in the IIA, with that in mind, Grounded can easily set up these stations at a minimal cost and eliminate the threat.

As is widely recognized, the Internet is moving at lightning speed. Companies are tailoring their businesses to meet the needs and market gaps both created, and widened with the advent of this massive communication forum. During the past two years, the amount of time the average Internet user spends online each week has risen from 4.4 hours to 7.6 hours, an annual growth rate of 31.5%.[7]

Currently there are nearly 4,397 verified functioning cyber cafés in 135 countries.[8] These cafes are serving primarily travelers.[9] This is the reason for locating Grounded in major metropolitan airports. The growths of Internet usage, and computing services are climbing at an alarming rate. Nua Internet Consulting and Demographic Research suggests that there are currently 201 million Internet users worldwide.[10] During 1995 there were 18 million users in the United States. By July of 1999 that number had climbed to 106.3 million users accounting for 39.37% of the U.S. population.[11]

With more and more business offering on-line service, and the vast majority of companies communicating with employees via e-mail it is only natural that for anyone to achieve or maintain business success, accessible fast computing services are needed. Over 90% of survey respondents agree that cyber cafés in general are not a fad.[12]

While Grounded is not a cyber café in the functioning sense of the term, it is the intention to employ the philosophies and technologies used in starting and operating such businesses. The crux of Grounded lies in its specific niche to offer business people an upscale operation to perform their day-to-day business functions with the convenience and ease utilized in their respective offices.

VI. Customer Value

Grounded will be providing its clients with service and products paralleled only to their respective offices and support staff. Benefits include:

- Location in high traffic common area of the IIA

- Professional environment

- Knowledgeable and helpful client assistants

---

[7]Wright, Robert. *TIME.* "Will We Ever Log Off." http://www.pathfinder.com/time/magazine/articles/0,3266,39239.html

[8]http://Cybercaptiva.com. Cyber café search engine updated 12/1/1999.

[9]http://Cybercaptiva.com. Cyber café patron survey results as of January 1999. 71.9% of respondent's reason for visiting cyber cafés was travel or vacation.

[10]http://www.internetstats.com/whos_online/whos_online.html

[11]http://www.nua.ie/surveys/how_many_online/n_america.html

[12]http://Cybercaptiva.com. Cyber café patron survey results as of January 1999. 91% of respondents replied that cyber cafés are not a fad.

- Access to all modes of communication (Internet, e-mail, phones, fax)
- Conference room—seven person capacity
- Exhaustive software applications
- Private workstations

Every minute on the road is precious—but time and time again the minutes are wasted away in airports, hotels, and traffic. While the traditional business traveler still squanders time reading paperback books and dozing off while waiting in airports, the fully wired traveler spends his or her trips getting work done. This of course, is a major competitive advantage, because more productivity means new business and a better bottom line.[13]

Grounded brings with it the one thing that sets implausible productivity apart from standard productivity—efficiency; the advent of the technological revolution has brought with it a global yearning for such efficiency. In the 21st century, people from all socioeconomic backgrounds are engaged in communication facets once reserved only for a privileged few. Mobile phones, pagers, and computers are all exceptionally inexpensive and easy to use. More than 60 million people in the United States subscribe to wireless telephone services, and approximately 80 million people will own wireless telephones by the year 2000.[14]

VII. Growth Potential

Business travelers and airport patrons alike recognize that there is a specific need for the services that Grounded proposes to offer. Initial development of the proposed business, its strategies, and its promise will be fully explored in its first store located in the IIA; from there the possibilities are limitless. Aside from a few feeble technologies and one existing business this niche has yet to exploit on a global basis. Grounded will do exactly this.

In a short amount of time the proposed business will prove to be not only successful but equally needed as a means to utilize the technological revolution as it is meant to be—all encompassing. The business is unique only in that it gives travelers what they want where they want it, very similar to McDonald's or a Wal-Mart. For that specific reason the success of Grounded brings with it the threat of competition. This is an excellent indicator just how successful, profitable, and valuable a business concept of its nature is.

Travelers will come to recognize Grounded as a friendly, competent, professional establishment where work can be completed. Simply stated, the more accessible Groundeds are, the more they will be used, and the more profitable they will be.

With more stores, the less limited opportunity will be in scope. Clients will be able to have faxes sent wherever they land, they will be able to modify a proposal in the air, drop off the disk during their layover in Philadelphia, and pick up fifty copies of it when they arrive in London. The technology is here today—Grounded will provide the service.

---

[13] Baker, Kim and Sunny. *Office on the Go*. Prentice Hall, 1993.
[14] http://law.about.com/library/weekly/aa101999.htm

The long term potential of Grounded is to either sell out to the established Lap-Top Lane, or vast growth, becoming involved in direct competition with LapTop Lane.

Marketing

Market

Grounded will target the market of business travelers whose day to day business thrives on computing and the Internet in general. It will also serve as a forum for all travelers to communicate with anyone via email. It is estimated that more than 70% of time spent on business travel is wasted.[15] Grounded will offer these travelers a forum to productively utilize their time.

The IIA is an ideal location for Grounded due to its demographics. During 1997 and 1998, 51.6% of all enplanements (passengers getting on planes) held occupations in managerial fields, 35.1% reported a household income of over $80,000. Also, 70.6% of all respondents were between the ages of 25 and 54.[16] These are the characteristics of businesspersons that Grounded is targeting.

According to Kim Baker, computer expert, consultant and author of *Office on the Go*, numerous business people who should be traveling as a means to conduct their business are not due to the influx of travelers, inconvenience, and overall treatment in airports. In a phone interview he stated that many travelers are disenfranchised and are simply having no fun. Baker states that, Grounded will give this segment a break from the traditional airport atmosphere and a chance to "Get out of the crowd."[17]

II. Survey Data

Grounded administered 63 surveys to various persons in and around the city of Indianapolis. Due to IIA regulation and in compliance with their laws, Grounded was unable to distribute any surveys on the airport's property. The airport did, however, provide Grounded with in-depth passenger characteristics and marketing data, which will be referred to throughout this section. It is important to note that IIA passenger characteristics, and all numbers drawn from this data is for enplanements, passengers getting on planes. No data is used for passengers whose final destination was Indianapolis.

The surveying conducted by Grounded was done in various ways. These surveys were distributed at first, via E-mail and traditional mail to a number of persons who spend time traveling, or conduct business on a regular basis in other cities. Not satisfied with the number of surveys returned, a more random method of surveying was done in the downtown area of Indianapolis around the Convention Center, Hyatt Regency Hotel, RCA Dome, and other surrounding areas.

III. Market Share

Occupational Characteristics   Based on Grounded's survey results, 46% of respondents were in managerial occupations and 38% considered themselves professionals.

[15]Baker, Kim and Sunny. *Office on the Go*. Prentice Hall, 1993.

[16]Indianapolis International Airport passenger characteristics by enplanements.

[17]Phone interview with Kim Baker, February 17, 2000.

Based on the IIA's passenger profile for the period of June–July 1998, 51.6% of all passengers were in managerial fields.

The Indianapolis International Airport passenger profile does not distinguish between managerial and professional; with this in mind, Grounded has grouped these two occupations as managerial/professional to establish that 84% of all survey respondents hold occupations in these fields.

Based on Grounded's survey results, 75% of all managerial/professional occupation respondents stated they would use Grounded's services. With a total of 3,645,427 passengers during the said time period, 1,881,040 held occupations in managerial/professional fields. By extrapolating the 75%, Grounded has a maximum potential market share of 1,410,780 people, or 38.7% of the IIA's travelers hold managerial/professional positions and would use Grounded's services. The breakdown of these results can be viewed in Table 2.1.

Income Characteristics   Based on income characteristics, 71.4% of respondents who have household incomes of over $80,000 said they would use Grounded's services. According to IIA passenger characteristics, 35.1% (1,279,544) of all passengers have household incomes of over $80,000. Matched against Grounded's survey results, the maximum potential market share of passengers with incomes of over $80,000 who would use Grounded's services is 913,960 people.

Internet Usage by Income Level   By examining secondary data from an e-marketer, it is apparent to Grounded that households with incomes over $75,000 are twenty times more likely to have Internet access than those at lowest income levels; 58.9% of households in this income bracket are using the Internet.[18] The percentage of passengers at the IIA whose household income is above this $80,000 income level is 35.1%, which makes up 1,279,545 passengers. Assuming that 58.9% of these individuals use the Internet, it is apparent that there are 753,651 Internet users with incomes above $80,000 that fly out of the IIA on a yearly basis (Table 2.2).

These numbers confirm what Grounded's survey results unveiled: passengers with incomes over $80,000 are most likely to use the Internet. It is apparent that people in this income bracket readily rely on Internet service to do work, trade stocks, and communicate via E-mail.

Frequency of Visits   Through survey research by Grounded it is apparent that the more an individual visits the airport per month, the more likely he or she will be to use the services supplied by Grounded (Table 2.3).

Passenger Dwell Time   Passenger dwell time is the amount of time passengers actually spend at the airport, dwell time is a vital indicator of how much time passengers will have at the airport to use Grounded's services. According to Grounded's survey results, 30% of respondents reported spending between 30 and 60 minutes overall at the airport, 27% reported spending between 61 and 90 minutes there, and 14% said they spend 91 to 120 minutes. These results are consistent with the airport's finding, verifying the validity of Grounded's survey.

---

[18]http://www.emarketer.com/estats/071299_divide.html

| TABLE 2.1 | OCCUPATION VS. WOULD USE |

Occupation	Would Use	Would Not Use	Grand Total	Percent Would Use
Managerial	25	4	29	86%
Professional	15	9	24	62.5%
Technical	1	3	4	25%
Homemaker		1	1	0
Student	2		2	100%
Service	1	2	3	33.3%
Grand Total	44	19	63	69.8%

IIA Dwell Times:

- 18.2% of passengers spend between 30–60 minutes

- 33.4% of passengers spend between 61–90 minutes

- 21.3% of passengers spend between 91–120 minutes

- 16.8% of passengers spend between 121–180 minutes

- 9.1% of passengers spend over three hours at the airport

- Average passenger spends a total of 106 minutes at the airport, 18 minutes before security and 88 minutes after security

These numbers confirm what Grounded's survey results revealed, in fact, passengers spend a lot of time at the airport during each visit. It is clear through Grounded's results that passengers who spend more time at the airport are more apt to use its services (Table 2.4). Airline regulations request that passengers arrive at the airport one hour before scheduled departure for domestic flights, and two hours in advance of international flights. Due to the large number of respondents surveyed by the airport, the fact that all surveys took place within the airport, and the consistency with Grounded's results, the airport data is deemed to be accurate.

| TABLE 2.2 | INTERNET USAGE BY INCOME LEVEL |

Household Income	Percent of Passengers	Total Passengers	Number of Passengers	Percent of Internet Users	Passengers Who Use Internet
> $75,000	35.10%	3645427	1279544.877	58.90%	753,651

TABLE 2.3	NUMBER OF VISITS VS. WOULD USE			
# of Airport Visits per Month	Would Use	Would Not Use	Grand Total	Percent Would Use
< 1	9	10	19	47%
1 to 2	17	3	20	85%
3 to 4	13	5	18	72%
5 to 6	2		2	100%
> 6	3	1	4	75%
Grand Total	44	19	63	69%

From the airport's calculated passenger dwell time Grounded will use only the passengers who spend between one and two hours at the airport, accounting for 54.7% of the passengers.

Tables 2.4 and 2.5 illustrate the correlation between dwell time and propensity to use Grounded's services.

Deplanements As noted earlier, all passenger characteristics are for passengers getting on planes. It is assumed by Grounded that these passengers who leave Indianapolis also will arrive at Indianapolis, or have arrived earlier.

It is apparent to Grounded that passengers who are getting off of planes are less likely to use these services. However, as a means to account for these passengers, Grounded has taken a conservative estimate of 5% of enplaning passengers with trends exhibited by Grounded's potential passengers and counted them as potential clients on their return. These passengers will be motivated to use Grounded's services while they are waiting for baggage, a ride, or before checking into their respective hotels.

TABLE 2.4	TIME SPENT VS. WOULD USE			
Time Spent	Would Use	Would Not Use	Grand Total	Percent
Under 30 min.	2	1	3	3%
30 to 60 min.	19	7	26	30%
61 to 90 min.	17	3	20	27%
91 to 120 min.	6	6	12	9.5%
121 to 180 min.		2	2	0%
Grand Total	44	19	63	69%

TABLE 2.5	IIA PASSENGER DWELL TIME				
	Percent of Passengers	Total Passengers	Number of Passengers	% That Would Use	Total Clients
30 to 60 minutes	18.20%	3,645,427	663,467		
61 to 90 minutes	33.40%	3,645,427	1,217,572	27%	328,551
91 to 120 minutes	21.30%	3,645,427	776,475	9.5%	73,950
121 to 180 minutes	16.80%	3,645,427	612,431		
TOTAL					402,501

Total Potential Market Grounded has determined that an accurate potential market can be derived by taking the following characteristics of survey respondents:

- Respondents who hold managerial/professional occupations
- Respondents whose income levels exceed $80,000
- Respondents who spend between one and two hours at the airport

Table 2.6 illustrates the respondents who demonstrate all of these characteristics:
Based on Grounded's survey results, 23 out of 63 (36.51%) survey respondents fit all of these characteristics (Table 2.6). Of these 23 people, 10 of them "would use" Grounded's services, and rated primary services (PCs, Internet, Data ports, and E-mail) as either a "4" or "5" on their respective surveys. The breakdown is as follows:

Synopsis:

- Grounded's survey revealed that 43.74% of manager/professional occupations exhibited characteristics of having incomes over $80,000, and spending 1 to 2 hours at the airport.

TABLE 2.6	CHARACTERISTICS OF CLIENTS			
Time Spent	Income	Managerial	Professional	Grand Total
61 to 90 min	$100 to 150,000	2		2
	Over $150,000	9	3	12
61 to 90 min total		11	3	14
91 to 120 min	$80 to 100,000	1	2	3
	$100 to 150,000		1	1
	Over $150,000	5		5
91 to 120 min total		6	3	9
Grand Total		17	6	23

- 1,881,040 airport passengers are in managerial/professional occupations

- 1,881,040 × 43.74% = 822,766 airport passengers who exhibit all 3 characteristics

- 43.48% of respondents would use Grounded and ranked its 4 main services (PCs, data port, E-mail, and Internet) with a "4" or "5" on Grounded's survey

- 822,766 × 43.48% = 357,738 passengers

- 357,738 × 5% (deplanements) = 17,856 passengers

- 17,856 + 357,738 = 375,594

Daily Clients   A phone interview with LapTop Lane cyber concierge, Dwight Gregory, of the Raleigh Durham International Airport (RDI), revealed that on the average weekday, they attract about 45 patrons.[19] "We get anywhere from 20 to 100 people per day depending on flight schedules and a number of factors. A good average is 45 per day with weekends a bit slower . . . . about 20." Bruce Merrill, CEO of LapTop Lane, also confirmed these assumptions in a phone interview on April 3, 2000.[20]

RDI was used as a comparison airport due to its demographics, which are remarkably similar to the IIA, coupled with the fact that it too is a destination airport. At the time of the interview, the RDI LapTop Lane was 8 weeks old, also making ideal for a comparison store. Mr. Gregory, who has worked there since the store opened on February 10th, is anticipating much more traffic in months to come.

Potential clients who chose to use pay-per-use computers make up 22% of Grounded's survey respondents. Since LapTop Lane does not offer pay-per-use service, and many of their clients only check E-mail or use quick Internet functions, this percentage will be taken from the total projected clientele.

IV. Market Penetration

Grounded feels that it can attain the average sales volume of LapTop Lane RDI during the first months of operation; by doing this, Grounded is anticipating 45 clients per weekday; 35 of these are anticipated to use all inclusive offices, while 10 are expected to use pay-per-use computers. This equates to 945 clients on weekdays in the first month. Grounded is also anticipating 20 clients per weekend day, 15 who will use all-inclusive offices, and 5 who use pay-per-use computers. This equates to 180 clients on weekends for the first month. The grand total of clients in the first month is expected to be 1,125; total clients for the first year is expected to be 14,238 which is a 3.8% penetration of Grounded's total potential market.

TABLE 2.7	TOTAL POTENTIAL MARKET OF GROUNDED

Grounded's Potential Market	=	375,594 Airport Passengers

---

[19]Phone interview with LapTop Lane Cyber Concierge Dwight Gregory of Raleigh Durham International Airport on March 31, 2000.
[20]Phone interview with Bruce Merrill, CEO of LapTop Lane.

FIGURE 1

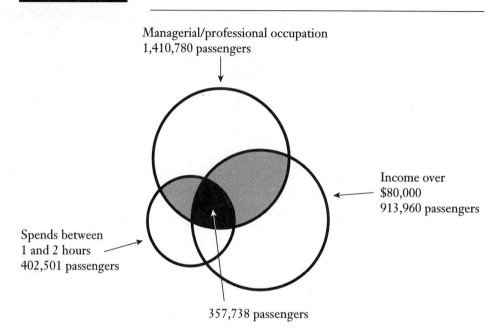

Managerial/professional occupation
1,410,780 passengers

Income over
$80,000
913,960 passengers

Spends between
1 and 2 hours
402,501 passengers

357,738 passengers

Mr. Merrill stated that these are appropriate market entry numbers based on airport size, size of location and a location outside of security. His pretense is that these numbers will increase steadily throughout the years consistent with the growth of LapTop Lane. "During maturity (about 2 years), we would expect 100 customers a day, having only one store you can expect 70, given it's only 1 location."

By Grounded's second year, 16,446 clients are expected; this equates to a 4.3% penetration of the total potential market. Also, by the third year of operation, 20,007 clients are expected, for a market penetration of 5.3%.

Average Time Spent at Grounded   The phone interview with LapTop Lane of RDI also revealed that the average patron spends approximately 40 minutes using their all inclusive office centers. "We have people that come in just to check their E-mail, and we have people who stay four or five hours. Overall the average person spends about 40 minutes though," stated Mr. Gregory.

Grounded will use this 40 minutes as an average base time for clients using all-inclusive private offices. This 40 minute time period is consistent with both Grounded's survey results as well as IIA passenger characteristics of the average passenger spending 118 minutes at the airport. Removing security time (18 minutes) and allowing time for clients to get to their gates and do other activities while at the airport, 40 minutes is deemed an appropriate average.

Passengers who opt to use pay-per-use services will most likely be using these computers to check E-mail, or browse on the Internet. Since time varies greatly in this situation it is deemed that 20 minutes is a very conservative estimate for these services.

V. Pricing

Grounded will have two primary pricing strategies for its computer rental. First, pricing for all-inclusive workstations will be $0.45 per minute. This rate will include all amenities in the offices including computing services, fax, printing, and long distance charges. This rate has been derived by survey results, which can be viewed in Table 2.8.

In accordance with current stand-alone Internet kiosks, Grounded will charge $0.30 per minute to use any of their other machines. Printing on such machines will be $0.40 per sheet for black and white, and $1.00 per sheet for color.

Copy machine prices will be on a sliding rate, black and white copying will be as follows: 1 to 10 copies at $0.20 each, 11 to 50 at $0.15 each, 51 to 100 at $0.10 each, over 100 at $0.07 cents each. Color copying will be as follows: $2.00 for 1 to 10, $1.75 for 11 to 50, $1.50 for 51 to 100, $1.25 for over 100 copies.

Conference room rental will be $100 for a two-hour block of time.

Usage As a means to determine which services clients prefer to use, Grounded reverts back to its core market of persons in managerial/professional occupations who make over $80,000, and spend between one and two hours at the airport. Of this market, 56.5% (13/23) indicated that they would prefer to pay for Grounded's services at an all-inclusive rate. In addition, 21.75% (5/23) stated they would prefer to pay for Grounded's services on a pay-per-use basis.

Based on survey results and interviews with LapTop Lane, it is estimated that every third customer will print two sheets on a pay-per-use computer; 75% of these are deemed to be black and white, and 25% are deemed to be color.

Based on survey results and interviews with LapTop Lane, it is estimated that 18% of all clients will use black and white copying and make 7 copies each. Color copies are estimated at 9% of total clients making 3 copies each.

Based on survey results, a conservative estimate has been made that 1% of total clients will desire conference room facilities.

VI. Growth

By the end of the first year, Grounded is anticipating 50 clients per day on weekdays, and 23 per day on weekend days for a total of 1,257 clients in the final month of the first year of operation. In the first year of operation, Grounded is anticipating 501,840 billable minutes, operating at 11% of its 4,352,400-minute capacity.

TABLE 2.8	BREAKDOWN OF SURVEY RESULTS: WOULD USE VS. PAYMENT METHOD AND AMOUNT			
Would Use	**Amount**	**Pay per Use**	**All Inclusive**	**Grand Total**
Would use	< 20 cents	2		2
	21 to 30	2		2
	31 to 40	5	7	12
	41 to 50	8	5	13
	> 50 cents		10	10

By the end of the second year, Grounded expects 60 clients per day on weekdays, and 27 on weekend days for a total of 1,503 clients during the final month of the second year of operation. In the second year, Grounded is anticipating 568,020 billable minutes, operating at 13% of its capacity.

By the end of the third year, Grounded expects 70 clients per day on weekdays, and 32 on weekend days, for a total of 1,758 clients in the final month of the third year of operation. By the end of the third year, Grounded is anticipating 674,909 billable minutes, operating at 15.5% of capacity.

VII. Competition

Direct Competition Within the confines of the IIA, the only service that functions in a similar capacity as proposed by Grounded is the US Airways Club. The club, located in Concourse D, offers travelers a sanctuary from the airport itself. The US Airways Club offers members a glorified lounge to relax, read, make phone calls, plug in laptop computers, or have a drink.

Amenities offered by the US Airways Club:

- Complimentary juice, coffee, cappuccino, espresso, soft drinks, breakfast pastries, and afternoon snacks

- Cocktail service, including premium spirits, wine, and beer

- Cable television, newspapers, and current periodicals

- Check-cashing privileges up to $100 at any US Airways ticket counter

Current membership fees range from $200 to $350 per year depending on individual frequent flyer miles. Potential members also have the option to buy a lifetime membership to the club for $2,950.

Initially, Grounded feels that itself and the US Airways Club will not engage in a great deal of competition. While each business offers some similar amenities, in the short run both will function independently and successfully. Grounded's clientele will be made up of business persons who truly desire to get work done in a private productive environment; in comparison, the US Airways Club clientele is composed of its members who wish to relax in an exclusive environment. The club effectively serves its purpose of giving its customers a comfortable, relaxing location to spend time before, after, or between flights.

To some degree, Grounded and the US Airways Club will be engaged in direct competition, however, Grounded's propitious niche, on the local front, will deter the club from altering the scope of their business as a means of competition. US Airways Club will be able to keep their clientele who use its service for its intensive purpose—to provide a relaxing atmosphere where travelers can get drinks, snacks, use the restroom, read the paper, etc. At the same time, Grounded has the opportunity to wean a percentage of their clientele from the private club to the public facility.

In the long run, as Grounded becomes the global frontrunner in airport communication, it is anticipated that this club and others similar to it will alter the scope of their business and services to provide the business traveler with amenities offered by Grounded.

Indirect Competition   Indirect competition will be faced by Grounded on multiple levels. First, today's traveler is much more wired with communication devices such as mobile phones and pagers. Second, Grounded will be in competition for every dollar spent at the airport, whether it be a pay phone call or a newspaper. Finally, the option to wait until the traveler gets home, to the office, or to the hotel will always be present. This final option does indeed prove that the business traveler is using, and has a need to use these functions in their own right. Grounded will simply and more conveniently solve the problem for the business traveler by offering the services while at the airport.

The primary indirect competition lays in current telecommunications technology, including mobile phones with Internet access, pay phones with data-ports, or pay fax machines. However, due to the nature of the technology involved in accessing the Internet via mobile phones, users are limited to only a few sights, and they can only receive real-time stock quotes, sports scores, weather reports, etc. The scope of E-mail functions on these phones is also very limited and unproven. Messages are often restricted to a few lines and replies are generally programmed responses. Also, all long distance and airtime charges apply when accessing the Internet through mobile digital technology.

The IIA has recently installed eight data ports into the pay phones in the newly renovated food court. This is an excellent indication by IIA that there is a need for such services; this is a feeble step towards a remedy. The primary problem with the data ports is the fact that they are located in the food court, while this is a very heavily traveled portion of the premises. It makes no suitable working environment.

VIII. *Advertising*

Since Grounded will initially be located only in the Indianapolis International Airport, advertising will not be a major issue. The location is approximately 1,600 square feet and is located in a very high traffic area of the airport. This location is in the central ticket lobby directly across from the Northwest Airline's, Trans World Airline's, and American Trans Airline's ticket counters. This location will provide a high amount of visibility from primary ticket counters. The rear of the store is a series of large windows, which look out on the curbside drop off area of the airport providing for even more visibility.

Though the location itself will be instrumental in attracting clients, it is recognized that numerous passengers who are layed over or catching connecting flights will not have knowledge of Grounded. To combat this issue an advertisement will be strategically placed within the confines of the airport.

Strategic Advertisement Location   The purpose of this advertising location is to gain the attention of travelers who would otherwise not know of Grounded's existence. The location will be responsible for gaining the attention of all travelers who fly into Concourse C or B, eat in the food court or nearby restaurants, or shop in the main shopping area of the airport.

This location was chosen because Concourses C and B had 2,281,912 passengers enplanements, collectively, in 1998, making up 62.6% of the airport's total passengers. It is also deemed that passengers who leave the gate area of Concourse A must walk by Grounded in order to get anywhere in the airport. Concourse A recorded 704,928 (19.3%) passengers in 1998. Concourse D was rejected as an advertising location due to the fact that it is so far out of the way, and only 638,587 (17.5%) passengers traveled through it in 1998. Also, only one primary airline services this concourse, and advertising is so expensive within the confines of the airport, it is deemed by Grounded that for the dollar, the cost of advertising there will not be worth the gain.

This advertisement will gain the attention of travelers, and creatively inform them of Grounded's existence and its ability to assist them in keeping their day-to-day business on track.

Through this interairport advertising strategy, Grounded will have the potential to reach all travelers who wander from their respective gates in search of food, shops, or a leisurely stroll through the airport.

Special Promotions   Grounded recognizes the need for its clients to be in constant communication. To effectively and efficiently satisfy the need, communication must be constant and two-way. Clients will have the option of receiving faxes or messages when they are not in the store. This simple but unique concept instantly makes any executive or sales person much more accessible to anyone; having a remote location to pick up faxes or an urgent message adds convenience, efficiency, and most of all peace of mind to all who desperately need a hard copy of a contract or sales report that they left at the office, or are waiting on while traveling.

This issue will be addressed by placing incoming phone and fax numbers on all receipts; clients will also be given business cards with these numbers on them.

Initially, these cards will only contain the numbers related to the Indianapolis location, however, as growth is sustained, the cards will contain the numbers of all Grounded locations worldwide.

Grounded will also attempt to achieve strategic alliances between local and national businesses in a means to provide any traveling members of their firm with state of the art communication facilities at a discounted corporate rate. Possible options and discounted rates will be fully explored through a determination of which corporations use this service as their primary means of communication at the airport. The reason for employing such a strategy is to curve a portion of the 60% credit purchases that Grounded is expecting.[21] The anticipation of high credit card sales is to the high usage of corporate credit cards clients will be using as a means to expense their visit to Grounded.

Technologies and Operations

I. Hardware and Software Specifications

Grounded's success hinges on its consistency to supply clients with fast, reliable, computing service along with current technologies. For these reasons Grounded has opted to employ top of the line machinery and software in its operations.

Computers   Grounded opts to use Gateway's business division to furnish itself with PCs. The specific PC decided upon is the Gateway GP7-550. Fourteen machines will be leased. Each system is quoted at $1,633. The specifications for the machines are as follows:

---

[21]Bruce Merrill, CEO, LapTop Lane

Processor:	Intel Pentium III processor 550 MHz with 512K cache
Memory:	128MB 100MHz SDRAM
Monitor:	EV700 17" Color Monitor
Video:	8MB AGP Graphics Accelerator
Hard Drive:	5.1 GB 5400RPM Ultra ATA hard drive
Floppy Drive:	3.5" 1.44 MB diskette drive
CD-ROM:	17X min./40X max. CD-ROM
Sound System:	Sound Blaster Audio PCI 128D
Case:	Mid Tower Case
Keyboard:	104+ keyboard
Mouse:	PS/2 Mouse and Gateway Mouse Pad
Operating System:	Microsoft Windows 98 Second Edition
Application Software:	Microsoft Office 2000 Professional
Antivirus Software:	Norton Antivirus Software
Expansion Slots:	4 PCI, 1 PCI/ISA and 1 AGP
Network Adapter	3 COM PCI 10/100 Twisted Pair Ethernet
Speakers	GC200 Speakers by Cambridge SoundWorks

Printers   Grounded's six pay per use computers will be networked to both a color and black and white printers. These are:

Hewlett-Packard Laser Jet 4050N network laser printer

- 1200 DPI
- 17 PPM
- 600 Sheet capacity

Tektronix Phaser 840

- 1000 DPI
- 10 PPM
- 200 Sheet capacity

Copy Machines   Grounded will operate with two copy machines; one black and white, and one color. Both will be acquired from IKON on a 48-month fair market value lease. All maintenance will also be done by IKON.

The black-and-white machine will be a Ricoh 450 which will include:

- Mainframe

- Document handler
- Offset stacker finisher
- 4 paper decks, 2000 sheet capacity

The color machine will be a Cannon clc 900 which will include:

- Mainframe
- Edit board

Private Office Printers   Grounded will supply a Hewlett-Packard OfficeJet T45 in every private office. Each machine has capabilities for:

- Color printing
- Color faxing
- Color scanning
- Color copying
- Color: 2 ppm
- B/W: 6 ppm

Leases   Grounded has opted to lease all hardware for a couple of reasons. First, the computers and printers are anticipated to receive heavy usage, and newer machines mean faster, more capable machines. Second, with the rapid growth trends in technologies, the two-year lease will be used to hedge the risk of computers becoming obsolete.

Software   All computers will be installed with Microsoft Office 2000 Professional Suite. This suite includes:

- Microsoft Word
- Microsoft Excel
- Microsoft Outlook
- Microsoft Publisher
- Microsoft Small Business Tools
- Microsoft Access
- Microsoft PowerPoint

Grounded will also employ Cyber-Time Software as the means for billing and time usage of all its computers. Cyber-Time is a comprehensive package for total management control of monitoring, billing, security, reporting, advertising, and marketing in a cyber business. It is currently installed in over 400 sites all over the world.[22]

---

[22]http://www.cybertimesoftware.com

Phone Service   As earlier specified, Grounded will assume the charges on all domestic local and long distance calls made by clients who opt to rent private offices. This is accomplished by utilizing a plan offered to Grounded by Spring—*All Calls All Day;* the plan specifies that all out-of-state calls, regardless of the time of day, be billed at $0.069 per minute. The details of the plan specify that after the first 16 seconds of each call, billing will be based on an 8 second continuum.[23] Under these stipulations, a two-page fax sent across the nation will cost Grounded under $0.03.

The reason for offering long distance calling to clients is to maximize client value and comfort while providing them with a needed service. Traditional calling cards are barely competing with the per minute rate proposed by this venture. A standard Sprint phone card runs the average person $0.40 per minute plus a surcharge from using a pay phone. Grounded offers their private offices with all of the aforementioned amenities for merely $0.05 more on a per minute basis.

Each private office, the conference room, and Grounded's desk will have a GE 3-line speakerphone telephone with LCD display.

II. Operations

Business Operations   The success of Grounded also hinges on its day-to-day operations and the way it conducts itself in the face of both prosperity and adversity. Grounded prides itself on its willingness and overall ability to consistently meet and exceed customer expectations. As specified in the mission, ". . . customer satisfaction is paramount." Through this simple statement Grounded will develop its reputation as global leader in service.

Grounded will refer to its employees as client assistants; this terminology accurately reflects the job each will perform. Each client will have the sensation that every client assistant is at his or her beck and call—they will be. Each client assistant will receive extensive training in customer service, technological aptitude, professionalism, and overall sense of the business being conducted.

To face the challenge of giving clients what they need or want, Grounded opts to empower its employees. In doing this, Grounded's client assistants will have a degree of latitude to solve customer problems and complaints. Each client assistant will also be provided with specific business knowledge generally reserved only for owners and managers. This will be done to continually demonstrate how each decision they make affects the bottom line and how individual performance on a broad scale is directly related to business development, performance, and growth.

Client Assistant Performance Incentive   The nature of the proposed lease agreement between Grounded and the IIA calls for specific rent credits or assessments based on periodic inspections. "Concessionaire acknowledges and agrees that Authority will conduct Quality of Service Monitor (QSM) surveys, . . . of airport passengers and visitors to insure the highest quality service standards are provided at all times by concessionaire."[24]

---

[23]Robert Repass, Sprint, 800 529 4259 ex 3715, February 16, 2000, **All calls all day**
[24]Concession Agreement, pages 39–43.

The said QSM is to encompass nine areas including:

- Overall rating

- Helpfulness and attitude of staff

- Speed of service

- Value for the money

- Choice/selection

- Quality

- Availability

- Specific cleanliness

- Overall cleanliness

If the QSM score is below satisfactory for an area, certain measures must be undertaken by Grounded to ensure corrective action. In the event that this does happen, Grounded will be assessed additional rent of $200 per area not in compliance. The said lease agreement also calls for a $200 rent credit to Grounded for each area QSM score above the arbitrary standard set by the airport.

The said lease agreement also stipulates that in the event of a QSM score falling below standard overall rating three consecutive times in an eighteen-month period, Grounded will be assessed additional rent of $2,000. Each ensuing unsatisfactory QSM score will warranty an additional $500 rent assessment. At the same time, if the QSM score for Grounded consistently is above the standard during an eighteen-month period, the unit will receive a rent credit in the amount of $2,000. The airport will also issue an additional $500 rent credit each consecutive time the QSM score rises after the first three occurrences.

As well as the QSM reports, it is acknowledged that the airport authority will conduct Secret Shop Evaluations. The said Secret Shop Evaluations will rate the unit in eight areas including:

- Customer approach

- Discovering customer needs

- Creating desire to buy

- Overcoming objectives

- Closing the sale

- Use of suggestive selling

- Speed of service

- Employee behavior and appearance

The monetary rent credit/assessment is virtually the same for the Secret Shopper Evaluations as for the QSM reports. A $200 per area rent credit/assessment will be applied for the first three evaluations. As with the QSM reports, three Secret Shopper Evaluations in an eighteen-month period with above standard scores will result in a $2,000 rent credit. Also, each consecutive occurrence above the said score will result in a $500 rent credit.

As a form of incentive, Grounded will issue each client assistant who is shopped, resulting in a shopper report warranting a rent credit, a bonus of $100 after taxes. Employees will be made aware of all criteria and evaluation forms used in the process in order for them to perform above par on a client-to-client basis.

This will prove to be a valuable incentive based program on multiple levels. First, the airport will use this system of checks and balances to ensure that standards are upheld. Grounded will use this system as an arbitrary means to judge both client assistant performance, and overall perception of the business. Finally, client assistants have the ability to be rated against other airport personnel as well as earn performance-based bonuses.

Employee Appearance   Employees of Grounded will be required to present themselves in a neat, clean, professional manner at all times. This includes proper grooming and personal hygiene. Specific uniform requirements will be as followed:

- Black pants, neatly pressed. Dockers' style (no pockets sewn on outside; this includes cargo style pants and jeans).
- Women may wear black skirts instead of pants granted these skirts are at a length within 2½ inches from the knee.
- Black belt.
- Black dress shoes and black socks.
- White or blue Polo style golf shirts with Grounded logo.
- Name-tag (supplied by Grounded).

Grounded will provide each client assistant with one shirt upon being hired. After that, additional shirts will be available at cost. Grounded's client assistants will be responsible for the rest of their uniform.

These uniforms will exude a professional, neat, and relaxed atmosphere. They are designed to be comfortable for client assistants to work in, as well as easy to maintain and keep clean. The purpose of the uniforms is to add to the ambiance generated by Grounded as a comfortable, efficient and productive atmosphere.

Hours of Operation   The hours of operation for Grounded are dictated in the lease agreement between the store and the Indianapolis International Airport. These hours will be on Monday through Friday from 5:30 AM until 9 PM, Saturday and Sunday 5:30–8:00. These hours are designed in an effort to optimize the time in which travelers are at the airport.

III. Core Values

Grounded recognizes that for it to become a large, financially sound, agile corporation with a global presence, it is imperative for the company to establish its core values while still in the inception stage. These values will serve as a road map during tough times and difficult decisions that are certain to come. The intention of these values is to lay down an understanding for every potential employee, client, or partner as to exactly why Grounded is in business.

Grounded is in the service business, this means that as an organization, itself and its client assistants will constantly and continually go above and beyond any job description to ensure client satisfaction. As a company, Grounded will always be committed to providing clients with the best quality product, as well as stay on the cutting edge of mobile communication services. Grounded's client assistants will come first in all organizational decisions; their freedom and organizational latitude will not be compromised so long as their decisions are made of sound mind with the client's best interests held in high regard.

As a budding business, Grounded is aware that every decision made does not stop with the client, it is imperative to recognize that the ultimate end user of Grounded's services will, in most cases, be the client's customer. This is in effect Grounded's reason for existence: To make others better at their jobs.

Management

I. Management

Grounded will operate under the sole management of Mr. O'Neil; his prior experience in numerous service businesses along with his degree from Ball State University in Management with an option in Entrepreneurship make him qualified to run the store. Under him will be nine client assistants who will be scheduled in accordance with Grounded's scheduling polices.

Mr. O'Neil will be responsible for the initial hiring of all client assistants, scheduling, compensation, performance reviews, as well as working in the store.

II. Employee Compensation and Scheduling

Grounded will operate between the hours of 5:30 and 9:00 on weekdays, and 5:30 and 8:00 on weekends. Two people will work from 5:30 until 2:00 each weekday, and one will work from 2:00 to 9:00 on weekdays. One person will be working during weekends.

All client assistants will be paid $10.00 an hour, which is what LapTop Lane pays their employees. Grounded will offer medical coverage to all full time employees. This coverage will be a 70/30 co-payment policy. Wages, and insurance benefits will be used as primary attraction and retention of client assistants.

Mr. O'Neil will draw an annual salary of $29,400.

III. Responsibilities

Each client assistant, as well as Mr. O'Neil, will be responsible for servicing all clients of Grounded. These duties will vary depending on the wants and needs of clients. They will vary from making copies, to assisting in computer tasks, to checking in clients.

IV. Professional Services

Grounded is anticipating special financial needs during the first three months of operations, during these months, Grounded will contract Mr. Howard May, CPA, at $75 per hour for four hours per month. During the ensuing months, Grounded is anticipating to use Mr. May's services for one hour per month. Grounded has also budgeted an additional $1,000 per year to be used on legal fees.

V. Legal Structure

Gounded will establish itself as a corporation in the form of a limited liability corporation (LLC). Legal arrangements to set up this form of corporation will cost Grounded $500.[25]

Financial

I. Financial Requirements

Mr. O'Neil requires $161,000 to for Gounded to initiate and sustain operations until profitability occurs. It is assumed that after $80,000 of preferred stock is sold, along with Mr. O'Neil's investment of $31,000, Grounded will be able to obtain a bank loan in the amount of $50,000. The loan will be amortized over ten years with a fixed interest rate of 11%. Also, Grounded will establish a money market account in which excess cash will be held; the account will yield an interest rate of 4.4%. This account will function similar to that of a sweep account. All monies needed to sustain the gap between sales and expenses during a given month will be with drawn from the money market account.

Preferred Stock	
Mr. O'Neil's investment	**$31,000**
Total investment from four other parties	**$80,000**
Bank Loan	**$50,000**
Total Financial Needs	**$161,000**

II. Financial Statement Assumptions

1. **Sales** Projected sales are split into four primary categories: all-inclusive computer rental, pay per use computer rental, copy sales, and conference room rental. The figures are based on 45 clients per weekday in the first month and consistently increasing to 70 clients per weekday by the end of the third year. Computer rental sales were figured by the percentage of the clients who would use all-inclusive service (approx. 70%) and the percentage of clients who would use pay per use service (approx. 30%). It is assumed that clients who use all-inclusive services will stay for 40 minutes at a rate of $0.45 per minute. It is also assumed that clients who opt for pay per use services will stay for 20 minutes at a rate of $0.25 per minute. Black and white copy sales were figured by taking 18% of total clients to gather the number of clients who will use copy service. It is estimated that each client will make 7 black and white copies at $0.20 per copy. Color copy sales were figured by taking 9% of all clients to gather the number of clients who will use color copy service. It is assumed that each color copy client will make 3 copies at $2.00 each. Conference room rental was figured by taking 1% of all clients to gather how many clients will use conference room facilities. Conference room facilities will cost $100 for a two-hour block of time.

---

[25]Quote from David Wallace of Warner, Wallace, McLaren, & Dague.

2. **Phone Service**   It is assumed that 70% of all clients will spend 80% of their time on the phone. This service is included in the cost of all-inclusive offices and will cost Grounded $0.069 per minute for all long distance calls.

3. **Credit Card Discount**   It is estimated that 60% of all clients will pay for Grounded's services with a credit card. All credit cards will carry a 1.65% handling fee and a $0.20 batch-processing fee.[26]

4. **Total Cost of Sales**   Sum of phone service fees and the credit card discount.

5. **Sales Profit**   The total amount of revenue taken in via sales.

6. **Interest Accrued**   This is the amount of interest earned monthly from the money market account which yields 4.4%.

7. **Gross Profit**   Sales less cost of goods sold plus interest from money market account.

8. **Salaries and Wages**   Grounded will have 2 client assistants for 8.5 hours per day, and 1 for 6 hours a day on weekdays. During weekends, Grounded will have 1 employee for 14.5 hours per day. All client assistants will be paid $10 per hour. Mr. O'Neil will draw an annual salary of $29,400, which equates to $2,450 per month.

9. **Employee Benefit Insurance**   The policy is established to offer health insurance to all full-time employees. Premiums are based on ten employees at $770 per month.

10. **Payroll Taxes**   Payroll tax includes Social Security (7.65%), State and Federal Unemployment (3.5% of the first $7,000 per employee).

11. **Rent**   The amount of rent specified by the IIA will be 15% of total sales.

12. **Parking**   Parking fees at the airport will be $7.50 per employee per month.

13. **Utilities**   As indicated by Indianapolis Power and Light (IPL) fees for a service such as Grounded's will be approximately $750 per month.

14. **Insurance**   Expense will cover comprehensive general liability, product liability, operations coverage, property damage, bodily injury liability, automobile liability, and workers compensation insurance as required by Indiana law. The premium on the policy will be $3,145.[27]

15. **Telephone**   This covers all monthly costs of $2,000, for phone lines and service, especially those to be used for Internet connection. This also includes the ISDN and T-1 Internet connections which will be employed.[28]

16. **Copy Machines**   Grounded's black-and-white and color machines will be leased on a 48-month fair market value lease. Black and white Ricoh 450 will cost $335 per month while a Canon clc 900 will cost $428 per month.

---

[26]Quote from Electronic Merchant Systems.

[27]Quote from Mr. John Parker, First Merchants Insurance.

[28]Quote from Susan Center, Time Warner.

17. **B/W Machine Maintenance**   This $47 per month will cover all supplies except paper and staples, up to 3000 copies, for the black and white copy machine. Overage on the 3,000 copies will be billed at $0.0154 per copy.

18. **Color Machine Maintenance**   This will cost Grounded $0.22 per copy and include all supplies except paper and staples.

19. **Paper**   This expense will be incurred as needed every month. Paper expense will cover 10 reams (5,000 sheets) of multipurpose paper every other month for $50.00, and 3 reams (1,500 sheets) of laser paper every third month for $15.00.

20. **Computer/Printer Lease**   This expense will cover all 14 computers, 1 server, 8 HP OfficeJets, 1 black and white laser printer, and 1 color laser printer. These will all be on a 24-month fair market value lease at $1,568 per month.[29]

21. **Advertising**   One advertising site within the airport will cost $1,800. A 25% discount is applied in lieu of Grounded's presence inside of the facility. This location will cost a total of $1,350 per month.[30]

22. **Professional Fees**   Grounded is anticipating special accounting needs during the first 3 months of business. For this purpose, Grounded has budgeted 4 hours per month during these months to use the services of Mr. Howard May, CPA, at $75 per hour. Thereafter, Grounded is anticipating using such accounting services for one hour per month. Grounded has also budgeted $1,000 per year for legal services.

23. **Depreciation**   The phone system is worth $810 and has an estimated economic life of 5 years. All office furniture is valued at $6,860 and has an estimate economic life of 7 years. In the year these assets were acquired, $1/2$ year of depreciation was applied. Phone system is depreciated at $81.00 for the first year, and $162 for all subsequent years. Furniture is depreciated at $432.00 for the first year, and $864.00 for subsequent years. Leasehold improvement are valued at $50,000; the life of the lease is to be five years. For these purposes, $10,000 will be depreciated for leasehold improvements each year. Total depreciation for the first year will be $10,513 and the total for subsequent years will be $11,026.

24. **Office Expenses**   It is estimated that $150 will purchase the initial office supplies need such as staplers, staples, pens, pencils, paper clips, etc. After the initial month, $25 will suffice to upkeep these supplies. Office expense will also include new printer cartridges, 1 for $49.99 every 14 months for pay per use printing, and 7 for $26.49 every 18 months.

25. **Operating Profit (Loss)**   Gross profits less total operating expenses.

26. **Interest Expense**   This includes the interest expense on the bank loan and line of credit. The bank loan is assumed to have an interest rate of 11% while the line of credit is assumed to have a rate of 10.75%.

---

[29]Quote from Geoff Schomacker, Gateway Business Division.

[30]Quote from Sue Rearick, Sky Sites.

27. **Net Profit Before Taxes**   Operating profit less interest expense.

28. **Income Tax**   No income tax will be paid in the first year because of an operating loss. The same first year loss will be used to offset income incurred during the second year. State income tax is figured by multiplying 5% by the state taxable income, which is equal to net profit before taxes. Federal income tax if further figured by multiplying the result of net profit before tax, less state income tax times 25%.

29. **Cash Sales**   Cash sales are figured at 40% of all sales.

30. **Credit Sales**   Credit card sales are figured at 60% of all sales.[31]

31. **Money Market W/D**   This is the amount of money that will be taken out of the money market fund to keep the business in positive numbers with an $800 balance at the start of each month.

32. **Preferred Stock Sale**   Grounded assumes to sell four lots of preferred stock for $20,000 each.

33. **Loans Received**   Grounded will obtain a business loan in the amount of $50,000 at an interest rate of 11% for a ten-year period.

34. **Leasehold Improvements**   This expense will only occur during the start-up period and cover all initial renovations to the premises.

35. **Furniture and Fixtures**   This expense will only be incurred during the start-up period and cover the expense of all fixtures and furnishings on the premises.

36. **Loan Repayments (Principal)**   This expense will be the amount of loan repayments that are directed towards the principal amount of the $50,000 loan.

37. **Interest Expense (LT)**   This expense will be the amount of loan repayments that are directed towards the interest incurred on the $50,000 loan.

38. **Total Cash Disbursements**   This is the total amount of all cash expenses incurred in a given period.

39. **Cash Flow Surplus/Deficit (–)**   This is the amount of cash that Grounded has after paying all incurred expenses in a given period.

40. **Preferred (Capital) Stock**   This is derived from the initial $31,000 Mr. O'Neil put into the business, along with the $80,000 invested by four investors.

41. **Retained Earnings**   This shows the accumulated net profit (loss) over the span of three years.

42. **Closing Cash Balance**   This is the amount of cash left over after a given period. This expense is carried forward to the beginning cash balance of the ensuing month. Grounded will begin each month with a cash balance of around $800.

---

[31]As stated by Bruce Merrill, CEO of LapTop Lane.

43. **Total Liabilities and Shareholders Equity** Total Current Liabilities + Long Term Debt + Capital Stock + Retained Earnings.

Location

I. Indianapolis

During the past decade the city of Indianapolis has come to be renowned for its diversity, culture, and commitment to growth. In a nutshell, the business climate in Indy can be described as friendly to business, hostile to red tape and taxes, and alive with opportunity.[32] Low unemployment, high tourism, and a continuing commitment to technology have been the basis for numerous accolades collected by the city in recent years:

- According to *Entrepreneur* Indianapolis is the eleventh ranked large city in nation for entrepreneurial growth.

- *Entrepreneur* also ranked Indianapolis first in the central nation area for entrepreneurial growth.

- In November 1997, *Fortune* magazine named Indianapolis one of the top 10 "Most Improved Cities" for business in the United States. Indianapolis was ranked No. 7 based on cost of living, educational opportunities, quality of life and business issues.

- Indianapolis has the 11th strongest economy in the nation, according to a 1998 economic analysis by Florida-based Police Corp. The analysis studied factors such as employment, per capita personal income and construction, and retail employment.

- The analysis also ranked the central Indiana region as having the strongest economy in the Midwest. According to Policom: "The Indianapolis area economy continues to outperform its competition."

- *Employment Review*'s June 1998 issue placed Indianapolis 15th among America's 20 Best Places to Live and Work. The magazine noted: "Indianapolis has a track record of making the most out of what it has and it continually addresses the need to have a diverse economy."

- Indianapolis was cited as one of the top 10 metropolitan areas in the nation as a hot spot for starting and growing young companies, according to a 1998 study by Cognetics, a research firm in Cambridge, Mass. The survey measured the number of significant start-up firms created during the last 10 years and the number of 10-year-old firms that grew substantially during the last four years.[33]

These accolades are not without merit, the startling growth in tourism as well as business growth have given the city the foundation needed to undertake the possibilities that lie in the near future. Countless businesses are starting and expanding, more

---

[32]www.indianapolis.org.

[33]Compiled at www.indianapolis.org.

TABLE 7.1   GROUNDED INCOME STATEMENT 2000–2001

	Start-Up	Nov	Dec	Jan	Feb	Mar	Apr	May	Jun	Jul	Aug	Sep	Oct	Year End
Sales														
All-inclusive computer rental		$15,660	$15,660	$16,038	$16,038	$16,038	$16,038	$16,416	$16,416	$16,578	$16,578	$16,956	$16,956	$195,372
Pay-per-use computer rental		1,530	1,530	1,530	1,530	1,710	1,710	1,710	1,710	1,836	1,836	1,836	1,836	20,304
Copy sales		891	891	908	908	931	931	948	948	972	972	988	988	11,276
Conference room rental		1,125	1,125	1,146	1,146	1,176	1,176	1,197	1,197	1,227	1,227	1,248	1,248	14,238
Printing pay-per-use		94	94	94	94	105	105	105	105	112	112	112	112	1,241
Other														—
Total Sales		19,300	19,300	19,715	19,715	19,960	19,960	20,376	20,376	20,725	20,725	21,141	21,141	242,431
Cost of Sales														
COS—phone service		1,345	1,345	1,377	1,377	1,377	1,377	1,410	1,410	1,423	1,423	1,456	1,456	16,776
Credit card discount		135	326	329	333	336	339	341	345	349	352	355	359	3,899
Total Cost of Sales		1,480	1,671	1,706	1,710	1,713	1,716	1,751	1,755	1,772	1,776	1,811	1,815	20,675
Sales Profit		17,820	17,629	18,009	18,005	18,246	18,244	18,625	18,621	18,953	18,949	19,330	19,326	
Interest accrued (MM)		317	295	276	259	243	227	211	196	182	168	154	142	2,669
Gross Profit		18,137	17,923	18,286	18,264	18,489	18,471	18,836	18,817	19,134	19,117	19,484	19,467	224,425
Operating Expenses														
Salaries and wages	9,890	9,890	9,890	9,890	9,890	9,890	9,890	9,890	9,890	9,890	9,890	9,890	9,890	128,570
Employee benefits (Insurance)	763	763	763	763	763	763	763	763	763	763	763	763	763	9,919
Payroll taxes	1,103	1,103	1,100	958	958	958	958	958	958	958	944	757	757	12,370
Rent		2,895	2,895	2,957	2,957	2,994	2,994	3,056	3,056	3,109	3,109	3,171	3,171	36,365
Parking	75	75	75	75	75	75	75	75	75	75	75	75	75	975
Utilities	750	750	750	750	750	750	750	750	750	750	750	750	750	9,750
Insurance	262	262	262	262	262	262	262	262	262	262	262	262	262	3,407
Telephone	2,000	2,000	2,000	2,000	2,000	2,000	2,000	2,000	2,000	2,000	2,000	2,000	2,000	26,000
Copy machines	763	763	763	763	763	763	763	763	763	763	763	763	763	9,919
B/W machine maintenance	47	47	47	47	47	47	47	47	47	47	47	47	47	611
Color machine maintenance	67	67	67	68	68	70	70	71	71	73	73	74	74	913
Paper	65			50	15	50		65		50	15	50		360
Computer and printer lease	1,568	1,568	1,568	1,568	1,568	1,568	1,568	1,568	1,568	1,568	1,568	1,568	1,568	20,384
Advertising	1,350	1,350	1,350	1,350	1,350	1,350	1,350	1,350	1,350	1,350	1,350	1,350	1,350	16,200
Professional fees	384	384	384	384	159	159	159	159	159	159	159	159	159	3,083
Office Supplies	500	25	25	25	25	25	25	25	25	25	25	25	25	450
Depreciation	150	876	876	876	876	876	876	876	876	876	876	876	876	10,513
Other														—
Total Operating Expenses	18,003	22,818	22,715	22,787	22,527	22,600	22,550	22,679	22,614	22,718	22,669	22,580	22,530	289,788
Operating Profit (Loss)	(18,003)	(4,680)	(4,792)	(4,501)	(4,262)	(4,111)	(4,079)	(3,843)	(3,797)	(3,584)	(3,552)	(3,096)	(3,063)	(65,363)
Interest Expense		458	453	447	441	435	429	423	417	411	405	398	392	5,107
Net Profit Before Tax	(18,003)	(5,138)	(5,244)	(4,948)	(4,703)	(4,546)	(4,508)	(4,266)	(4,214)	(3,995)	(3,957)	(3,495)	(3,455)	(70,471)
Taxes														
State														
Federal														
Net Profit After Tax	$(18,003)	$(5,138)	$(5,244)	$(4,948)	$(4,703)	$(4,546)	$(4,508)	$(4,266)	$(4,214)	$(3,995)	$(3,957)	$(3,495)	$(3,455)	$(70,471)

TABLE 7.2 GROUNDED INCOME STATEMENT 2001–2002

	Nov	Dec	Jan	Feb	Mar	Apr	May	Jun	Jul	Aug	Sep	Oct	Year End
Sales													
All-inclusive computer rental	$16,956	$16,956	$16,956	$17,496	$17,496	$17,874	$17,874	$18,414	$18,414	$18,792	$18,792	$19,170	$215,190
Pay-per-use computer rental	1,836	1,890	2,016	2,016	2,142	2,196	2,322	2,322	2,448	2,502	2,628	2,628	26,946
Copy sales	988	996	1,012	1,036	1,053	1,076	1,093	1,117	1,133	1,157	1,174	1,190	13,025
Conference room rental	1,248	1,257	1,278	1,308	1,329	1,359	1,380	1,410	1,431	1,461	1,482	1,503	16,446
Printing pay-per-use	112	116	123	123	131	134	142	142	150	153	161	161	1,647
Other													—
Total Sales	21,141	21,214	21,385	21,979	22,150	22,640	22,811	23,405	23,576	24,065	24,236	24,652	273,254
Cost of Sales													
COS—phone service	1,456	1,456	1,456	1,502	1,502	1,535	1,535	1,581	1,581	1,614	1,614	1,646	18,478
Credit card discount	359	361	365	375	379	387	391	401	405	414	418	424	4,679
Total Cost of Sales	1,815	1,817	1,821	1,877	1,881	1,922	1,926	1,982	1,986	2,027	2,031	2,070	23,156
Sales Profit	19,326	19,397	19,564	20,102	20,269	20,718	20,885	21,423	21,590	22,038	22,205	22,581	250,098
Interest accrued (MM)	130	116	103	91	80	70	60	52	45	39	34	29	848
Gross Profit	19,455	19,514	19,667	20,193	20,349	20,787	20,945	21,474	21,635	22,077	22,239	22,611	250,946
Operating Expenses													
Salaries and wages	9,890	9,890	9,890	9,890	9,890	9,890	9,850	9,890	9,890	9,890	9,890	9,890	118,680
Employee benefits (Insurance)	763	763	763	763	763	763	763	763	763	763	763	763	9,156
Payroll taxes	1,103	1,103	1,000	958	958	958	958	958	958	958	944	757	11,614
Rent	3,171	3,182	3,208	3,297	3,323	3,396	3,422	3,511	3,536	3,610	3,635	3,698	40,988
Parking	75	75	75	75	75	75	75	75	75	75	75	75	900
Utilities	750	750	750	750	750	750	750	750	750	750	750	750	9,000
Insurance	262	262	262	262	262	262	262	262	262	262	262	262	3,145
Telephone	2,000	2,000	2,000	2,000	2,000	2,000	2,000	2,000	2,000	2,000	2,000	2,000	24,000
Copy machines	763	763	763	763	763	763	763	763	763	763	763	763	9,156
B/W machine maintenance	47	47	47	47	47	47	47	47	47	47	47	47	564
Color machine maintenance	74	75	76	78	79	81	82	84	85	87	88	89	977
Paper			50	15	50	65	65	50	50	15	50		295
Computer and printer lease	1,568	1,568	1,568	1,568	1,568	1,568	1,558	1,568	1,568	1,568	1,568	1,568	18,816
Advertising	1,350	1,350	1,350	1,350	1,350	1,350	1,350	1,350	1,350	1,350	1,350	1,350	16,200
Professional fees	159	159	159	159	159	159	159	159	159	159	159	159	1,908
Office Supplies	25	75	25	25	25	210	25	25	25	25	25	25	535
Depreciation	919	919	919	919	919	919	919	919	919	919	919	919	11,026
Other													—
Total Operating Expenses	22,919	22,980	22,905	22,919	22,981	23,191	23,098	23,124	23,200	23,241	23,288	23,115	276,960
Operating Profit (Loss)	(3,464)	(3,467)	(3,237)	(2,726)	(2,631)	(2,404)	(2,153)	(1,649)	(1,566)	(1,164)	(1,050)	(504)	(26,014)
Interest Expense	386	379	373	366	359	353	346	339	332	326	319	312	4,189
Net Profit Before Tax	(3,849)	(3,846)	(3,610)	(3,092)	(2,991)	(2,757)	(2,499)	(1,989)	(1,898)	(1,490)	(1,368)	(815)	(30,203)
Taxes													
State													
Federal													
Net Profit After Tax	$(3,849)	$(3,846)	$(3,610)	$(3,092)	$(2,991)	$(2,757)	$(2,499)	$(1,989)	$(1,898)	$(1,490)	$(1,368)	$(815)	$(30,203)

TABLE 7.3 GROUNDED INCOME STATEMENT 2002–2003

	Nov	Dec	Jan	Feb	Mar	Apr	May	Jun	Jul	Aug	Sep	Oct	Year End
Sales													
All-inclusive computer rental	$19,332	$19,710	$19,710	$20,250	$20,250	$20,628	$20,628	$21,168	$21,168	$21,546	$21,546	$21,546	$247,482
Pay-per-use computer rental	2,754	2,808	2,934	2,934	3,060	3,114	3,240	3,240	3,366	3,366	3,366	3,366	37,548
Copy sales	1,214	1,238	1,255	1,278	1,295	1,319	1,335	1,359	1,376	1,392	1,392	1,392	15,846
Conference room rental	1,533	1,563	1,584	1,614	1,635	1,665	1,686	1,716	1,737	1,758	1,758	1,758	20,007
Printing pay-per-use	168	172	179	179	187	190	198	198	206	206	206	206	2,295
Other													
Total Sales	25,001	25,490	25,662	26,256	26,427	26,916	27,087	27,681	27,852	28,268	28,268	28,268	323,177
Cost of Sales													
COS—phone service	1,660	1,692	1,692	1,739	1,739	1,771	1,771	1,818	1,818	1,850	1,850	1,850	21,250
Credit card discount	431	440	444	454	458	466	470	480	484	491	491	491	5,600
Total Cost of Sales	2,091	2,132	2,137	2,192	2,197	2,238	2,242	2,298	2,302	2,341	2,341	2,341	26,851
Sales Profit	22,910	23,358	23,525	24,063	24,230	24,678	24,846	25,383	25,551	25,927	25,927	25,927	296,326
Interest accrued (MM)	27	24	23	22	22	22	22	22	22	22	22	22	273
Gross Profit	22,937	23,382	23,548	24,085	24,252	24,701	24,868	25,406	25,573	25,949	25,949	25,949	296,600
Operating Expenses													
Salaries and wages	9,890	9,890	9,890	9,890	9,890	9,890	9,890	9,890	9,890	9,890	9,890	9,890	118,680
Employee benefits (Insurance)	763	763	763	763	763	763	763	763	763	763	763	763	9,156
Payroll taxes	1,103	1,103	1,000	958	958	958	958	958	958	958	944	757	11,614
Rent	3,750	3,824	3,849	3,938	3,964	4,037	4,063	4,152	4,178	4,240	4,240	4,240	48,477
Parking	75	75	75	75	75	75	75	75	75	75	75	75	900
Utilities	750	750	750	750	750	750	750	750	750	750	750	750	9,000
Insurance	262	262	262	262	262	262	262	262	262	262	262	262	3,145
Telephone	2,000	2,000	2,000	2,000	2,000	2,000	2,000	2,000	2,000	2,000	2,000	2,000	24,000
Copy machines	763	763	763	763	763	763	763	763	763	763	763	763	9,156
B/W machine maintenance	47	47	47	47	47	47	47	47	47	47	47	47	564
Color machine maintenance	91	93	94	96	97	99	100	102	103	104	104	104	1,188
Paper	—	—	50	15	50	—	65	—	50	15	50	—	295
Computer and printer lease	1,568	1,568	1,568	1,568	1,568	1,568	1,568	1,568	1,568	1,568	1,568	1,568	18,816
Advertising	1,350	1,350	1,350	1,350	1,350	1,350	1,350	1,350	1,350	1,350	1,350	1,350	16,200
Professional fees	159	159	159	159	159	159	159	159	159	159	159	159	1,908
Office Supplies	25	25	75	25	25	25	25	25	25	25	25	210	535
Depreciation	919	919	919	919	919	919	919	919	919	919	919	919	11,026
Other													
Total Operating Expenses	23,515	23,590	23,614	23,578	23,640	23,665	23,757	23,783	23,860	23,889	23,910	23,858	284,660
Operating Profit (Loss)	(578)	(208)	(66)	507	612	1,035	1,110	1,622	1,713	2,061	2,040	2,092	11,939
Interest Expense	304	297	290	283	275	268	260	253	245	237	230	222	3,164
Net Profit Before Tax	(883)	(505)	(356)	224	337	767	850	1,370	1,467	1,823	1,810	1,870	8,775
Taxes													
State													
Federal													
Net Profit After Tax	$(883)	$(505)	$(356)	$224	$337	$767	$850	$1,370	$1,467	$1,823	$1,810	$1,870	$8,775

TABLE 7.4 — GROUNDED CASH FLOW STATEMENT 2000–2001

	Start-up	Nov	Dec	Jan	Feb	Mar	Apr	May	Jun	Jul	Aug	Sep	Oct
Beginning Cash	$ —	$ 500	$ 800	$ 800	$ 800	$ 800	$ 800	$ 800	$ 800	$ 800	$ 800	$ 800	$ 800
Cash Inflows													
Cash sales	0	7,128	7,052	7,204	7,202	7,299	7,298	7,450	7,448	7,581	7,580	7,732	7,730
Collections from credit sales	0	10,692	10,577	10,806	10,803	10,948	10,946	11,175	11,172	11,372	11,369	11,598	11,595
Interest accrued (MM)		317	295	276	259	243	227	211	196	182	168	154	142
Money market W/D		5,191	5,003	4,712	4,473	4,322	4,290	4,054	4,008	3,795	3,763	3,307	3,274
Preferred stock sale	80,000												
Loans received	50,000												
Owners Contribution (Stock)	31,000												
Total Cash Available	161,000	23,828	23,726	23,798	23,538	23,611	23,561	23,690	23,625	23,729	23,680	23,591	23,541
Less Cash Disbursements													
Computer lease	1,568	1,568	1,568	1,568	1,568	1,568	1,568	1,568	1,568	1,568	1,568	1,568	1,568
Copy machine leases	763	763	763	763	763	763	763	763	763	763	763	763	763
B/W machine maintenance	47	47	47	47	47	47	47	47	47	47	47	47	47
Color machine maintenance	67	67	67	68	68	70	70	71	71	73	73	74	74
Paper	65	65	0	50	15	50	0	65	0	50	15	50	0
Salaries and wages	9,890	9,890	9,890	9,890	9,890	9,890	9,890	9,890	9,890	9,890	9,890	9,890	9,890
Employee benefits	763	763	763	763	763	763	763	763	763	763	763	763	763
Payroll taxes	1,103	1,103	1,000	958	958	958	958	958	958	958	944	757	757
Rent	2,895	2,895	2,895	2,957	2,957	2,994	2,994	3,056	3,056	3,109	3,109	3,171	3,171
Utilities	750	750	750	750	750	750	750	750	750	750	750	750	750
Insurance	262	262	262	262	262	262	262	262	262	262	262	262	262
Telephone	2,000	2,000	2,000	2,000	2,000	2,000	2,000	2,000	2,000	2,000	2,000	2,000	2,000
Office supplies	150	25	25	25	25	25	25	25	25	25	25	25	25
Advertising	1,350	1,350	1,350	1,350	1,350	1,350	1,350	1,350	1,350	1,350	1,350	1,350	1,350
Professional fees	500	384	384	384	159	159	159	159	159	159	159	159	159
Parking	75	75	75	75	75	75	75	75	75	75	75	75	75
Bank charges													
Leasehold Improvements	50,000												
Furniture and Fixtures	6,932												
Loan repayments (Principal)		629	635	640	646	652	658	664	670	676	683	689	695
Interest expense (LT)		458	453	447	441	435	429	423	417	411	405	398	392
Tax payments													
Other													
Total Cash Disbursements	74,935	23,028	22,926	22,998	22,738	22,811	22,761	22,890	22,825	22,929	22,880	22,791	22,741
Cash Flow Surplus/Deficit (−)	86,065	800	800	800	800	800	800	800	800	800	800	800	800
Money Market Acct dep	85,565												
Closing Cash Balance	500	800	800	800	800	800	800	800	800	800	800	800	800
Money market	86,565	80,374	75,372	70,660	66,186	61,864	57,574	53,520	49,512	45,717	41,954	38,646	35,373
Money Market W/D		5,191	5,003	4,712	4,473	4,322	4,290	4,054	4,008	3,795	3,763	3,307	3,274
Money Market W/D (acum)		10,193	10,193	9,715	14,188	18,510	22,800	26,854	30,862	34,657	38,421	41,728	45,002

TABLE 7.5   GROUNDED CASH FLOW STATEMENT 2001–2002

	Nov	Dec	Jan	Feb	Mar	Apr	May	Jun	Jul	Aug	Sep	Oct
Beginning Cash	$ 800	$ 800	$ 800	$ 800	$ 800	$ 800	$ 800	$ 800	$ 800	$ 800	$ 800	$ 800
Cash Inflows												
Cash sales	7,730	7,759	7,826	8,041	8,108	8,287	8,354	8,569	8,636	8,815	8,882	9,033
Collections from credit sales	11,595	11,638	11,739	12,061	12,162	12,431	12,531	12,854	13,954	13,223	13,323	13,549
Interest Accrued (MM)	130	116	103	91	80	70	60	52	45	39	34	29
Money Market W/D	3,632	3,635	3,406	2,894	2,800	2,572	2,321	1,818	1,734	1,332	1,218	671
Loans received												
Other												
Total Cash Available	23,887	23,949	23,873	23,887	23,949	24,159	24,066	24,092	24,169	24,209	24,257	24,082
Less Cash Disbursements												
Computer Lease	1,568	1,568	1,568	1,568	1,568	1,568	1,568	1,568	1,568	1,568	1,568	1,568
Copy Machine leases	763	763	763	763	763	763	763	763	763	763	763	763
B/W machine maintenance	47	47	47	47	47	47	47	47	47	47	47	47
Color machine maintenance	74	75	76	78	79	81	82	84	85	87	88	89
Paper	—	—	50	15	50	—	65	—	50	15	50	—
Salaries and wages	9,890	9,890	9,890	9,890	9,890	9,890	9,890	9,890	9,890	9,890	9,890	9,890
Employee benefits	763	763	763	763	763	763	763	763	763	763	763	763
Payroll taxes	1,103	1,103	1,000	958	958	958	958	958	958	958	944	757
Rent	3,171	3,182	3,208	3,297	3,323	3,396	3,422	3,511	3,536	3,610	3,635	3,698
Utilities	750	750	750	750	750	750	750	750	750	750	750	750
Insurance	262	262	262	262	262	262	262	262	262	262	262	262
Telephone	2,000	2,000	2,000	2,000	2,000	2,000	2,000	2,000	2,000	2,000	2,000	2,000
Office supplies	25	75	25	25	25	210	25	25	25	25	25	25
Advertising	1,350	1,350	1,350	1,350	1,350	1,350	1,350	1,350	1,350	1,350	1,350	1,350
Professional fees	159	159	159	159	159	159	159	159	159	159	159	159
Parking	75	75	75	75	75	75	75	75	75	75	75	75
Bank charges												
Leasehold Improvements												
Furniture and Fixtures												
Loan repayments (Principal)	702	708	714	721	728	734	741	748	755	762	769	776
Interest Expense (LT)	386	379	373	366	359	353	346	339	332	326	319	312
Tax payments												
Other												
Total Cash Disbursements	23,087	23,149	23,073	23,087	23,149	23,359	23,266	23,292	23,369	23,409	23,457	23,283
Cash Flow Surplus/Deficit (−)	800	800	800	800	800	800	800	800	800	800	800	799
Closing Cash Balance	800	800	800	800	800	800	800	800	800	800	800	799
Money Market	31,740	28,105	24,700	21,806	19,006	16,434	14,113	12,295	10,561	9,229	8,011	7,340
Money Market W/D	3,632	3,635	3,406	2,894	2,800	2,572	2,321	1,818	1,734	1,332	1,218	671
Money Market W/D (acum)	48,634	52,269	55,675	58,569	61,368	63,941	66,262	68,079	69,813	71,145	72,363	73,034

TABLE 7.6 GROUNDED CASH FLOW STATEMENT 2002–2003

	Nov	Dec	Jan	Feb	Mar	Apr	May	Jun	Jul	Aug	Sep	Oct
Beginning Cash	$ 799	$ 797	$ 771	$ 746	$ 1,085	$ 1,528	$ 2,395	$ 3,337	$ 4,792	$ 6,336	$ 8,228	$ 10,100
Cash Inflows												
Cash sales	9,164	9,343	9,410	9,625	9,692	9,871	9,938	10,153	10,220	10,371	10,371	10,371
Collections from credit sales	13,746	14,015	14,115	14,438	14,538	14,807	14,907	15,230	15,330	15,556	15,556	15,556
Interest Accrued	27	24	23	22	22	22	22	22	22	22	22	22
Money Mkt Dep	745	350	209	—	—	—	—	—	—	—	—	—
Loans received												
Other												
Total Cash Available	24,481	24,530	24,529	24,831	25,337	26,229	27,263	28,743	30,364	32,285	34,177	36,049
Less Cash Disbursements												
Computer Lease	1,568	1,568	1,568	1,568	1,568	1,568	1,568	1,568	1,568	1,568	1,568	1,568
Copy Machine leases	763	763	763	763	763	763	763	763	763	763	763	763
B/W Machine maintenance	47	47	47	47	47	47	47	47	47	47	47	47
Color machine maintenance	91	93	94	96	97	99	100	102	103	104	104	104
Paper	—	—	50	15	50	—	65	—	50	15	50	—
Salaries and wages	9,890	9,890	9,890	9,890	9,890	9,890	9,890	9,890	9,890	9,890	9,890	9,890
Employee benefits	763	763	763	763	763	763	763	763	763	763	763	763
Payroll taxes	1,103	1,103	1,000	958	958	958	958	958	958	958	944	757
Rent	3,750	3,824	3,849	3,938	3,964	4,037	4,063	4,152	4,178	4,240	4,240	4,240
Utilities	750	750	750	750	750	750	750	750	750	750	750	750
Insurance	262	262	262	262	262	262	262	262	262	262	262	262
Telephone	2,000	2,000	2,000	2,000	2,000	2,000	2,000	2,000	2,000	2,000	2,000	2,000
Office supplies	25	25	75	25	25	25	25	25	25	25	25	210
Advertising	1,350	1,350	1,350	1,350	1,350	1,350	1,350	1,350	1,350	1,350	1,350	1,350
Professional fees	159	159	159	159	159	159	159	159	159	159	159	159
Parking	75	75	75	75	75	75	75	75	75	75	75	75
Bank charges												
Leasehold Improvements												
Furniture and Fixtures												
Loan repayments (Principal)	783	790	797	804	812	819	827	834	842	850	858	865
Interest Expense (LT)	304	297	290	283	275	268	260	253	245	237	230	222
Tax payments												
Other												
Total Cash Disbursements	23,683	23,758	23,783	23,747	23,809	23,834	23,926	23,951	24,028	24,057	24,078	24,026
Cashflow Surplus/Deficit (−)	$ 797	$ 771	$ 746	$ 1,085	$ 1,528	$ 2,395	$ 3,337	$ 4,792	$ 6,336	$ 8,228	$ 10,100	$ 12,023
Closing Cash Balance	797	771	746	1,085	1,528	2,395	3,337	4,792	6,336	8,228	10,100	12,023
Money Market	6,595	6,245	6,036	6,036	6,036	6,036	6,036	6,036	6,036	6,036	6,036	6,036
Money Market W/D	745	350	209	—	—	—	—	—	—	—	—	—
MoneyMarket W/D (acum)	73,779	74,129	74,338	74,338	74,338	74,338	74,338	74,338	74,338	74,338	74,338	74,338

TABLE 7.7   Grounded Balance Sheet 2000–2001

	Start-up	Nov	Dec	Jan	Feb	Mar	Apr	May	Jun	Jul	Aug	Sep	Oct
ASSETS													
Current Assets													
Cash	500	800	800	800	800	800	800	800	800	800	800	800	800
Marketable securities	85,565	80,374	75,372	70,660	66,186	61,864	57,574	53,520	49,512	45,717	41,954	38,646	35,373
Accounts receivable, net													
Inventory													
Prepaid expenses													
Other													
Total Current Assets	86,065	81,174	76,172	71,460	66,986	62,664	58,374	54,320	50,312	46,517	42,754	39,446	36,173
Long-Term Assets													
Property & Equipment	56,932	56,932	56,056	55,180	54,304	53,428	52,552	51,676	50,799	49,923	49,047	48,171	47,295
Less accumulated depreciation		876	876	876	876	876	876	876	876	876	876	876	876
Net property & Equipment	56,932	56,056	55,180	54,304	53,428	52,552	51,676	50,799	49,923	49,047	48,171	47,295	46,419
Other long-term assets													
Total Long-Term Assets	56,932	56,056	55,180	54,304	53,428	52,552	51,676	50,799	49,923	49,047	48,171	47,295	46,419
Total Assets	142,997	137,230	131,351	125,763	120,414	115,216	110,049	105,119	100,235	95,564	90,925	86,741	82,592
LIABILITIES AND SHAREHOLDERS' EQUITY													
Current Liabilities													
Current maturities of long-term debt													
Accounts payable													
Income taxes payable													
Accrued liabilities													
Other													
Total Current Liabilities	0	0	0	0	0	0	0	0	0	0	0	0	0
Long-Term Liabilities													
Long-term debt less current maturities	50,000	49,371	48,737	48,096	47,450	46,798	46,140	45,476	44,805	44,129	43,446	42,757	42,062
Deferred income taxes													
Other long-term liabilities													
Total Long-Term Liabilities	50,000	49,371	48,737	48,096	47,450	46,798	46,140	45,476	44,805	44,129	43,446	42,757	42,062
Shareholders' Equity													
Common stock	111,000	111,000	111,000	111,000	111,000	111,000	111,000	111,000	111,000	111,000	111,000	111,000	111,000
Additional paid-in capital													
Retained earnings	(18,003)	(23,141)	(28,385)	(33,333)	(38,036)	(42,582)	(47,090)	(51,356)	(55,570)	(59,565)	(63,521)	(67,016)	(70,471)
Money Market Acct													
Total Shareholders' Equity	92,997	87,859	82,615	77,667	72,964	68,418	63,910	59,644	55,430	51,435	47,479	43,984	40,529
Total Liabilities and Shareholders' Equity	142,997	137,230	131,351	125,763	120,414	115,216	110,049	105,119	100,235	95,564	90,925	86,741	82,592

TABLE 7.8 GROUNDED BALANCE SHEET 2001–2002

	Nov	Dec	Jan	Feb	Mar	Apr	May	Jun	Jul	Aug	Sep	Oct
ASSETS												
Current Assets												
Cash	800	800	800	800	800	800	800	800	800	800	800	799
Money Market	31,740	28,105	24,700	21,806	19,006	16,434	14,113	12,295	10,561	9,229	8,011	7,340
Money Market W/D (acum)												
Accounts receivable, net												
Inventory												
Prepaid expenses												
Other												
Total Current Assests	32,540	28,905	25,500	22,606	19,806	17,234	14,913	13,095	11,361	10,029	8,811	8,139
Long-Term Assets												
Property & Equipment	46,419	45,500	44,581	43,663	42,744	41,825	40,906	39,987	39,068	38,150	37,231	36,312
Less accumulated depreciation	919	919	919	919	919	919	919	919	919	919	919	919
Net property & Equipment	45,500	44,581	43,663	42,744	41,825	40,906	39,987	39,068	38,150	37,231	36,312	35,393
Other long-term assets												
Total Long-Term Assests	45,500	44,581	43,663	42,744	41,825	40,906	39,987	39,068	38,150	37,231	36,312	35,393
Total Assets	78,041	73,487	69,162	65,349	61,631	58,140	54,900	52,164	49,511	47,259	45,123	43,532
Liabilities and Shareholders' Equity												
Current Liabilities												
Line of Credit												
Current maturities of long-term debt												
Accounts payable												
Income taxes payable												
Accrued liabilities												
Other												
Total Current Liabilities	—	—	—	—	—	—	—	—	—	—	—	—
Long-Term Liabilities												
Long-term debt less current maturities	41,361	40,653	39,938	39,217	38,490	37,755	37,014	36,266	35,512	34,750	33,982	33,206
Deferred income taxes												
Other long-term liabilities												
Total Long-Term Liabilities	41,361	40,653	39,938	39,217	38,490	37,755	37,014	36,266	35,512	34,750	33,982	33,206
Shareholders' Equity												
Common stock	111,000	111,000	111,000	111,000	111,000	111,000	111,000	111,000	111,000	111,000	111,000	111,000
Additional paid-in capital												
Retained earnings	(74,320)	(78,166)	(81,776)	(84,868)	(87,859)	(90,615)	(93,114)	(95,103)	(97,001)	(98,490)	(99,859)	(100,674)
Other												
Total Shareholders' Equity	36,680	32,834	29,224	26,132	23,141	20,385	17,886	15,897	13,999	12,510	11,141	10,326
Total Liabilities and Shareholders' Equity	78,041	73,487	69,162	65,350	61,631	58,140	54,900	52,164	49,511	47,260	45,123	43,532

TABLE 7.9   GROUNDED BALANCE SHEET 2002–2003

	Nov	Dec	Jan	Feb	Mar	Apr	May	Jun	Jul	Aug	Sep	Oct
ASSETS												
Current Assets												
Cash	$ 797	$ 771	$ 746	$ 1,085	$ 1,528	$ 2,395	$ 3,337	$ 4,792	$ 6,336	$ 8,228	$ 10,100	$ 12,023
Money Market	6,595	6,245	6,036	6,036	6,036	6,036	6,036	6,036	6,036	6,036	6,036	6,036
Accounts receivable, net												
Inventory												
Prepaid expenses												
Other												
Total Current Assets	$ 7,392	$ 7,016	$ 6,782	$ 7,120	$ 7,564	$ 8,431	$ 9,373	$ 10,827	$ 12,372	$ 14,264	$ 16,135	$ 18,059
Long-Term Assets												
Property & Equipment	35,393	34,474	33,555	32,637	31,718	30,799	29,880	28,961	28,042	27,124	26,205	25,286
Less accumulated depreciation	919	919	919	919	919	919	919	919	919	919	919	919
Net property & Equipment	34,474	33,555	32,637	31,718	30,799	29,880	28,961	28,042	27,124	26,205	25,286	24,367
Other long-term assets												
Total Long-Term Assests	34,474	33,555	32,637	31,718	30,799	29,880	28,961	28,042	27,124	26,205	25,286	24,367
Total Assets	41,867	40,572	39,418	38,838	38,363	38,311	38,334	38,870	39,495	40,469	41,421	42,426
LIABILITIES AND SHAREHOLDERS' EQUITY												
Current Liabilities												
Line of Credit												
Current maturities of long-term debt												
Accounts payable												
Income taxes payable												
Accrued liabilities												
Other												
Total Current Liabilities	—	—	—	—	—	—	—	—	—	—	—	—
Long-Term Liabilities												
Long-term debt less current maturities	32,423	31,633	30,836	30,032	29,220	28,401	27,574	26,740	25,898	25,048	24,190	23,325
Deferred income taxes												
Other long-term liabilities												
Total Long-Term Liabilities	32,423	31,633	30,836	30,032	29,220	28,401	27,574	26,740	25,898	25,048	24,190	23,325
Shareholders' Equity												
Common stock	111000	111000	111000	111000	111000	111000	111000	111000	111000	111000	111000	111,000
Additional paid-in capital												
Retained earnings	(101,557)	(102,061)	(102,418)	(102,193)	(101,856)	(101,089)	(100,239)	(98,869)	(97,402)	(95,579)	(93,769)	(91,899)
Other												
Total Shareholders' Equity	9443.5	8938.557	8582.3	8806.634	9143.517	9910.86	10760.88	12130.55	13598.04	15421.19	17231.28	19101.25
Total Liabilities and Shareholders' Equity	41,867	40,572	39,419	38,838	38,363	38,312	38,335	38,870	39,496	40,469	41,422	42,426

hotels are being planned and built, and the airport is on the doorstep of a multibillion-dollar renovation; all of this is being done to prepare the city to follow the growth trend justly established in the past decade.

II. Tourism

The tourism industry in Indianapolis is booming. During 1996 5.4 million person visits were logged. The average group for travelers to Indianapolis has 4.7 people in their party and stays almost 2 days—90% of the travelers stay in hotels. Another factor is the city's increased hotel inventory. Between 1984 and 1998, 64 new hotels with 8,779 rooms opened in Indianapolis/Marion County. Countless other hotels have undergone major renovations and/or expansions. Citywide, Indianapolis has 20,158 rooms in 154 hotels.[34]

III. Indianapolis International Airport (IIA)

Along with the rest of the city, the IIA is dedicated to growth and recognizes the potential in the future. The airport is currently finishing up a $6 million renovation of its food and beverage service, which will bring in 15 new options for quests.

IIA Facts:

- Largest airport in the United States to be managed by a private firm–BAA, the same British firm that also operates London's Heathrow and Gatwick airports.

- A 12-minute drive from downtown.

- 7.9 million passengers in 1998.

- More than 175 daily departures and 76 direct and nonstop destinations.

- Currently undergoing an $8 million general renovation.

- Site of United Airlines Indianapolis Maintenance Center.

- Cargo hubs: FedEx package sorting hub and US Postal Service Eagle Network hub.

- Headquarters of American Trans Air.

- Served by 18 airlines.

IV. Space and Area

The uniqueness of Grounded lies in its location, by locating Grounded in Airports, it will have the ability to reach the relatively untapped market of travelers in need of means of modern communication. The Indianapolis International Airport provides the large facility, which will in turn offer business travelers a forum to conduct their office work while they are not at their offices.

---

[34]www.indianapolis.org

| FIGURE 2 | ACTIVITIES OF VISITORS WHILE IN INDIANAPOLIS |

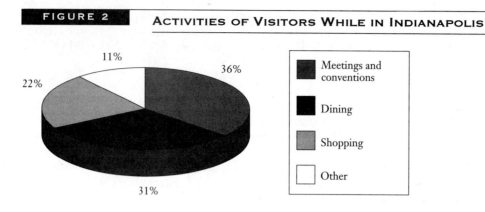

The specific location within the airport is on the second floor across from the TWA and ATA ticket counters in the Central Ticket Lobby; the space is approximately 1600 square feet in size. Due to the high amount of traffic generated in this area, and its high visibility, this is an ideal location for Grounded.

The airport logged 3,645,427 enplanements during 1998, and 1,737,938 as of June 1999.[35] Of these enplanements in 1998, 704,928 people, or 19% of this group, had to walk directly by Grounded's proposed location in order to reach their terminal (Concourse A). With over 90% of all ticketing counters being located in the Central Ticket Lobby, these characteristics will allow Grounded to gain a high degree of visibility.

Location Outside of Security   Grounded's location outside of security poses a potential problem for the business. However, this is not deemed to be a problem in the IIA due to its layout. The IIA is one of the few airports whose main shopping area, including food court, are outside of the security points. These business are currently prospering, proving that passengers are willing to leave their respective concourses in search of food or shops.

V. Layout

Grounded will operate in a space approximately 1600 square feet in size. Within the space, Grounded will supply seven private offices, six additional computers, one black and white copy machine, one color copy machine, one black and white network printer, one color network printer, as well as other amenities used in any office.

Private offices include:

- Laptop data port

- Wall plug for laptop

- Gateway PC

- Telephone

---

[35]Indianapolis International Airport passenger characteristics by enplanements.

- All domestic long distance calling and faxing

- Hewlett-Packard Office Jet includes Black and White and Color:

  - Printing

  - Faxing

  - Scanning

All computers in the facility will be wired with ISDN and high-speed T-1 cables to ensure a high-speed internet connection at all times.

Clients have the option to either rent a private office for $0.45/minute, or use one of the other PCs at a rate of $0.30/minute and pay per use rates when printing, copying, faxing, etc.

Job Market   Locating in the Indianapolis area will prove to be very beneficial to Grounded in lieu of the strong Job market. Unemployment levels are high, but not so high that Grounded will not be able to attract responsible workers; as a means of attraction, Grounded will use its high wages coupled with its medical insurance package both as means of attraction and retention.

It must also be noted that the IIA is within a twenty-minute drive of two colleges, Butler and IUPUI. These campuses will be used as marketing tools to attract potential part-time employees who will already be able to exhibit a degree of computer proficiency.

Critical Risks

Grounded has taken account of possible risks that could be critical to the day-to-day operations of the business, Grounded's operations, and Grounded's market share as a whole. Foresight has been used to first, identify these risks and finally determine feasible alternative solutions to combat these potential risks.

Grounded has determined its critical risks to be:

- Advent of new affordable multimedia solutions which will make Grounded's traditional internet access obsolete

- Hiring and retention of reliable client assistants

- Management experience

- Death

Multimedia Solutions

With rapid growth of all forms of multimedia, it is possible that future developments will bring technologies such as capable Internet browsers on mobile phones. This technology is currently available, however the minute usage rate is about the same as Grounded's all-inclusive minute rate. These quasi browsers are very limited in scope, and users are limited to specific sites. The future could bring with it such technologies that eliminate these barriers.

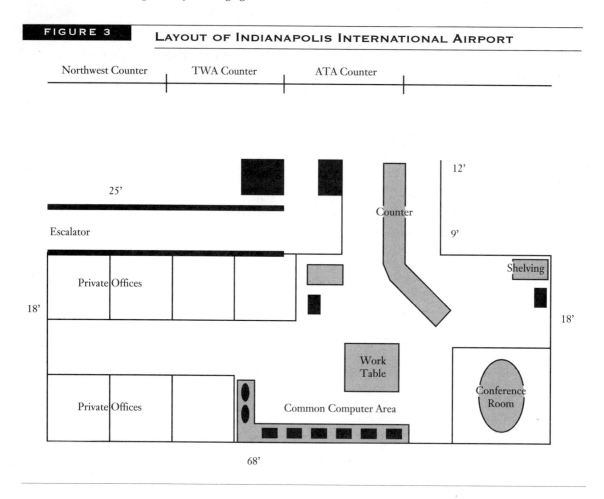

FIGURE 3   LAYOUT OF INDIANAPOLIS INTERNATIONAL AIRPORT

Grounded has pledged to stay abreast to latest technological changes in doing this, Grounded will be able to recognize these trends. It is also assumed that current multimedia solutions will affect the sector as a whole. Following the current trends, the Internet, and desktop applications should always stay ahead of mobile communication possibilities. For these reasons, Grounded may need to change services and methods offered to stay abreast of market needs. This is also the reason for setting up two year leases on all hardware; after the two-year period, new machinery will be brought in.

Hiring and Retention of Reliable Client Assistants

Grounded's business hinges on the reliability, personality, and overall attitude of its employees. Grounded has taken a proactive stance on this issue by offering top wages and solid benefits to its employees. If, however, Grounded is unable to retain quality individuals, new compensation methods will be reviewed.

Management Experience

Mr. O'Neil has little management experience in regards to managing such a technical service business. To combat this issue, Mr. O'Neil will retain financial and legal services as a means to make certain that operations are running as they should.

Death

In the event of death of Mr. O'Neil, the day-to-day business operations of Grounded will be severely interrupted. This unlikely event will have adverse effects on the business as a whole.

Milestones

September 2000

- Construction begins.
- Interview process begins.

October 2000

- Interviews and hiring will be completed.
- Computers, printers, copiers, etc., delivered.
- Phone system installed.
- Construction on Grounded will be completed.
- Training for all employees will take place.

November 2000

- Grounded will open for business.

January 2002

- Grounded's target break-even point.

8

Family Business Succession Strategies

Key Topics

- Family-Owned Businesses

- Advantages and Disadvantages
  of a Family Business

- Problems in Family Businesses

- The Succession Issue

- Prescriptions

In many cultures, male–female distinctions have been dichotomized into wage-earner, warrior, and external interfacer (male) and housekeeper, child-bearer, internally focused (female) roles. These traditional stereotypic conceptions are reinforced through accepted norm and behaviors that define individuals and their tasks. The family is the social unit that helps blend these tasks together and smooths over the rough edges when conflict arise concerning individuals' roles.

A unique combination arises in **family businesses** that blends economic considerations with the traditional roles of the family social unit. Fathers, mothers, and children take on additional or modified responsibilities in family businesses as they seek to integrate the roles of employer, employee, owner, and supervisor with their family member roles.

Family businesses are usually defined according to ownership (for instance, whether the company is closely held and controlled by the family), the existence and extent of family investors, and the number of family members employed in the business.

Family-Owned Businesses

Sixty to seventy percent of all U.S. small businesses define themselves as family-owned, according to a recent survey conducted by Arthur Andersen Enterprise Group and National Small Business United.[1] The survey found that "family-owned" also means "family-operated."

Nearly 40 percent of small-business owners hire a spouse, and 37 percent have children on the payroll (see Figure 8.1). A smaller percentage—17 percent—employ parents. It also appears that these owners are less anxious to have a sibling around: Only 12 percent hire brothers or sisters.

The real cold shoulder, however, is reserved for in-laws. Those hoping to get ahead by marrying the boss's son or daughter should know that only 3 percent of all U.S. family-owned businesses employ in-laws. Family business experts say that many in-laws stay out of the family business because they fear that the strain of working with their in-laws might hurt their marriages. Another reason for this hesitancy in employing in-laws is that the possibility of divorce discourages some business owners from bringing in-laws into the corporate fold. Marriages may end, but the business must go on.

The next generation to take over a family business can assume any of a variety of roles. Which role is played depends on the individual's needs, interests, and personal qualities. The decision to join a family venture is both subtle and dynamic, and it can take many years and several periods in and out of the business to solidify.

Three categories of roles can be identified for younger-generation workers:

- **Helper or faithful apprentice**—Learning from the "bottom up," the helper sometimes stays on as the dutiful apprentice, sometimes not having a formal title or position but expected to perform all kinds of tasks.

- **Stepping stone**—An individual may gain job experience by using the family firm as a stepping stone on a career path. This role provides an opportunity for personal growth and the development of business skills necessary to move into

---

[1] Arthur Andersen Enterprise Group and National Small Business United, *Survey Results of Small and Middle Market Businesses* (July 1992): 19.

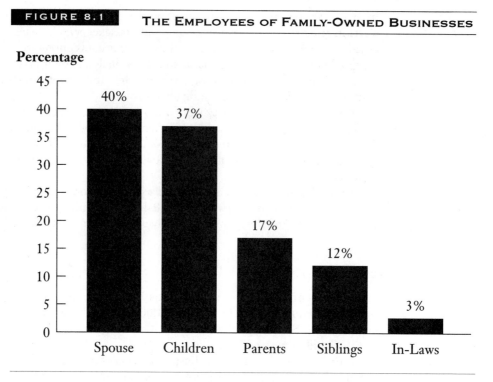

FIGURE 8.1 THE EMPLOYEES OF FAMILY-OWNED BUSINESSES

SOURCE: Arthur Andersen Enterprise Group and National Small Business United, *Survey Results of Small and Middle Market Businesses* (July 1992): 19.

the next stage of a career. It also fulfills the sense of personal obligation that members of the younger generation are likely to feel toward the family business.

- **Socialized successor**—When younger-generation individuals join the family business, they become socialized with the strong likelihood of becoming the next-generation president. Thus they have an opportunity to be creative, innovative, and goal-oriented.[2]

Several complications can arise as a younger-generation person enters the family business. Sometimes it is difficult to establish boundaries between the business and family life, resulting in tensions that spill over into both domains. This individual also runs the risk of becoming a permanent person-in-waiting as owners-founders unconsciously may prefer not to let go or may want to prove that no one can fill their shoes. A related issue is establishing credibility, which represents a slow and gradual process between parent and child. Founding parents have difficulty believing that the children will ever grow up. Although they may expect their offspring to enter the business, they often fail to give them authority or encouragement. Many family business owners have higher expectations of family members, thereby implying that because they are family, praise is not necessary.[3]

---

[2]Wendy C. Handler, "The Family Venture," in William A. Sahlman and Howard H. Stevenson, *The Entrepreneurial Venture* (Cambridge, MA: Harvard Business School Publication, 1992), 311–321.
[3]Ibid.

Advantages and Disadvantages of a Family Business

Some economic development economists believe that the family is a major barrier to entrepreneurial activity. They contend that instead of encouraging and supporting entrepreneurial endeavors, the family dampens incentives to achieve, discourages risk taking, and impedes the mobilization of capital. The obligation to share the wealth with family members or elders to provide support and security may deter the potential entrepreneur from building a nest egg large enough to invest in a business. In addition, the fruits of an investment may be subject to family sharing, so the child of a family business owner may not view the benefits of entrepreneurship as positively as does a nonfamily member.

The counter argument is based on a **resource dependency model,** which contends that the family may be instrumental in helping the entrepreneur establish a business. Perhaps the entrepreneur is dependent on his or her family for initial capital, room and board, building space, tools, encouragement, and moral support to help start the business. "The family may also help the fledgling entrepreneur obtain access to suppliers, merchants, creditors, market authorities, local officials, and persons with economic power and influence." (for example, extension of credit when the family guarantees payment).[4] Table 8.1 provides an overview of some key advantages and disadvantages of family-controlled firms.

Conflicts sometimes arise when relatives look at the business from differing perspectives. Those who are engaged in daily operations may choose to conserve their salary so as to retain capital for future investment and growth in the company. Conversely, relatives not involved in operations—such as silent partners, directors, or stockholders—may prefer to receive higher levels of payout in the form of dividends.

Other conflicts are generated when "favorite" children are promoted to executive positions ahead of others. This problem is aggravated when those family members who are promoted are viewed as less competent than others. Weak offspring of company founders or those relatives who must be "taken care of" eventually lead to more serious problems later. In come cases, a nonrelative may enter the firm, become a superstar in terms of management talent, become indispensable, and then demand a portion of the business.

Figure 8.2 illustrates the normal overlap of family and business systems, as well as a situation in which the overlap leads to excessive, destructive conflict.

Common Cultural Patterns in Family Firms

Similar patterns in family firms recur frequently across a wide variety of circumstances and demographic changes. These patterns are related to different methods of dealing with authority, goal attainment, decision making, and coping with conflict. Three patterns have been discovered in the research:

1. **The patriarchal or matriarchal family** is characterized by a dominant authority figure, and family life revolves around the needs and wishes of that person. All major decisions about the family are made by this person and family members are expected to follow obediently. The family leader sets the goals for the entire family, with the spouse and children playing subservient

---

[4]Wayne E. Nafziger, "The Effect of the Nigerian Extended Family on Entrepreneurial Activity," *Economic Development and Cultural Change* (1968): 19–24.

TABLE 8.1	ADVANTAGES AND DISADVANTAGES OF FAMILY-CONTROLLED FIRMS

Advantages	Disadvantages
• Long-term orientation	• Less access to capital markers may curtail growth
• Greater independence of action —Less (or no) pressure from stock market —Less (or no) takeover risk	• Confusing organization —Messy structure —No clear division of tasks
• Family culture as a source of pride —Stability —Strong identification/commitment/motivation —Continuity in leadership	• Nepotism —Tolerance of inept family members as managers —Inequitable reward systems —Greater difficulties in attracting professional management
• Greater resilience in hard times —Willing to plow back profits	• Spoiled kid syndrome
• Less bureaucratic and impersonal —Greater flexibility —Quicker decision making	• Internecine strife —Family disputes overflow into business
• Financial benefits —Possibility of great success	• Paternalistic/autocratic rule —Resistance to change —Secrecy —Attraction of dependent personalities
• Knowing the business —Early training for family members	• Financial strain —Family members milking the business —Disequilibrium between contribution and compensation
	• Succession dramas

(handwritten notes: "- flexible hours - $ stay in family - Trust?" and "→ may lead to an informal/comfortable orgn (atmosphere)")

SOURCE: Manfred F. R. Kets de Vries, "The Dynamics of Family-Controlled Firms: The Good and the Bad News," *Organizational Dynamics* (Winter 1993): 61.

roles. In setting goals for the family, the leader is often secretive about these activities, rarely taking children or even the spouse into his or her confidence.

2. **The collaborative family** share the power. The head of the family often takes the spouse and children into his or her confidence and relies on them for information and ideas when making decisions. The family creates and shares goals and values, and it places a high priority on maintaining family solidarity. Family members see the interdependencies in their relationship and make every effort to work cooperatively. Difficult situations such as death, retirement, choosing a successor, and estate planning are discussed and debated. Collaborating on these kinds of problems can lead to increased understanding within the family and increased family solidarity.

3. **The conflicted family** does not share goals, with individual/personal motives and desires guiding each member's action. Family members are distrustful of one another and seem to be constantly defending themselves against the designs of others. Relationships are counter-dependent in nature and are always

FIGURE 8.2	NORMAL AND EXCESSIVE FAMILY-BUSINESS OVERLAPS

In a "normal" situation, the overlap is within reasonable limits and thus manageable.

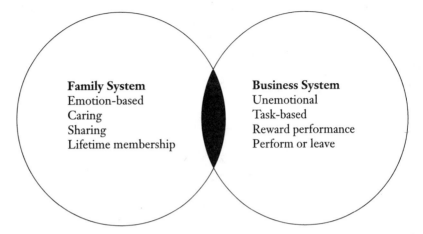

When the overlap is excessive, conflict can be destructive.

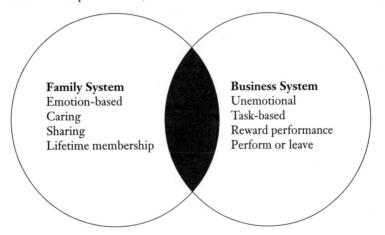

SOURCE: Adapted from Paul Rosenblatt, Leni de Mik, Roxanne Marie Anderson, and Patricia A. Johnson, *The Family in Business* (San Francisco, CA: Jossey-Bass, Inc. 1985), 131–135.

in conflict. Family members rarely communicate with one another, avoid, or rely on lawsuits to establish their position. This type of family is characterized by mistrust, alienation, and conflict. Member are unable to develop problem-solving mechanisms to resolve their differences.[5]

A similar set of cultural patterns can be outlined based on the family's philosophy about business decisions, as described in Table 8.2. Three philosophical orientations can be identified:

---

[5]W. Gibb Dyer, Jr., *Cultural Change in Family Firms* (San Francisco: Jossey-Bass, 1986).

1. Some families choose **business first,** supporting what is best for the company, including its customers, employees, and shareholders. They select sound business principles and policies to administer such matters as compensation, hiring, and titles. They believe that these principles constitute excellent criteria by which they will be able to make tough decisions, even if they lead to unequal treatment of family members.

2. Those families that choose the **family first** philosophy believe that the family's happiness and cohesiveness should come before anything else. Their decisions favor family equality and unity, even if they come at some expense to the company's future. Such families will allow every family member to enter the business, pay everyone equally, and guarantee their jobs for life. Differences in quality of decision making and contributions generally are not recognized.

3. The third philosophy seeks a **balance** between the two previous orientations and posits that any decision must provide for both the satisfaction of the family and the economic growth of the business. This family enterprise approach implies a long-term commitment to the future of the business and the family, and it requires the family to creatively resolve conflicts between the two interests.

TABLE 8.2	FAMILY PHILOSOPHY'S IMPACT ON BUSINESS DECISIONS		
Business Decision	**Business First**	**Family First**	**Family Enterprise First**
Entry rules	For specific job, if qualified	All welcome	Opportunities will be developed for all individuals in or out of the business, depending on family business needs
Compensation	As job description warrants	Equal pay for all members of same generation	Acceptable family standard of living assured for everyone
Stock ownership	According to business philosophy (that is, all to chief executive or distributed according to contribution or possibly among nonfamily employees)	Equal to branch of family	Equal values of all—some in business stock, others in passive investments or entrepreneurial opportunities
Dividends	None	Stable, fair return to capital	Variable, modest return of capital
Titles and authority	Based on merit in a business hierarchy honoring the principle of each person having only one boss	Equal titles for all members of same generation and role in decision making for all shareholders	Equal roles for all those with high degree of competence
Governance	Board of outside directors	Broad family consensus	Representative family council
Role in community	Leadership	Voluntary	Active according to family needs and individual interests

SOURCE: John Ward, *Keeping the Family Business Healthy* (San Francisco: Jossey-Bass, 1987).

Competitive Advantages of Family Firms

Individuals are attracted to work in family firms as opposed to careers in corporations for many reasons. For example, they may prefer to work with and report to a family member in whom they can confide. By growing with the firm, they viscerally understand what makes their colleagues and business tick. The best family businesses convert this understanding into an efficiency that breeds more effective management. Also, compared with large corporations, family firms afford more flexibility, control, compatibility, trust, and opportunity.

Externally, in a world dominated by images and perceptions, the experience of dealing with a family member can reassure a customer as much as speaking to a firm's president. Internally, few people in business with family members have cause to second-guess their partners' motives. A sense of trust has the potential to make family partners more secure, more open, and more informed than any team of unrelated persons could be. Presenting themselves as a family operation, owners can convey an image of stability, suggesting that the company is in business for the long haul and will provide continuity for customers and employees alike.[6]

Family values and influences can have positive effects on the operation of a business. According to researcher Peter Davis, three advantages may be forthcoming:[7]

- **Preserving the humanity of the workplace.** A family business can easily demonstrate higher levels of concern and caring for individuals than are found in the typical corporation.

- **Focusing on the long run.** A family business can take the long-run view more easily than corporate managers who are being judged on year-to-year results.

- **Emphasizing quality.** Family businesses have long maintained a tradition of providing quality and value to the customer.

Problems in Family Businesses

Problems in family businesses often differ from the problems that confront non-family-owned businesses. When close relatives work together, social and emotional variables often interfere with business decisions. Over time, many problems may be acknowledged, but others may lurk silently in the background, sometimes ultimately having serious, or even fatal, consequences for the family business.

Narrow or Outdated Viewpoints

Originators of family businesses tend to view their creation as their "baby." Those relatives who are silent partners, stockholders, or directors often see only dollar signs when judging capital expenditures, growth, and other major matters. Relatives who are engaged in daily operations may judge major patterns from the viewpoint of production, sales, and personnel necessary to make the company successful. Often these three perspectives clash. Because the family business owner is usually the boss, his or

---

[6]Leslie Brokaw, "Why Family Businesses Are Best," *Inc.* (March 1992): 20–22.
[7]Peter Davis, "Realizing the Potential of the Family Business," *Organizational Dynamics* (Summer 1983): 53–54.

her decisions may go largely unquestioned by other family members. But what will happen after the death of the owner, when the ownership becomes diffused among members of the family? Sons, daughters, grandchildren, and the spouse may be in conflict and perhaps compete for financial advantage. Disagreements that remained latent during the life of the original owner can materialize after his or her death.

Not Matching Rewards with Contributions

A typical unrecognized problem in a family business is the proliferation of family members within the company, particularly after the firm's profitability has been established. Members of the owner's family frequently hold positions and draw salaries that are not commensurate with their contributions to the company. Sometimes key personnel are added long before they are needed. In other cases, an owner might be inclined to hold down expenses and not hire needed personnel. The family business owner often is subject to the "I'd rather do it myself" syndrome, failing to delegate adequately.

The Sky Is the Limit

Setting realistic goals and objectives is a process generally ignored within the small business, particularly in terms of long-run opportunities. The family business owner usually is involved in day-to-day operations and finds it difficult to plan for the long term. Often action is not taken today to adjust for almost-certain changes in business conditions that could have substantial implications for the business tomorrow. In many cases, the family business owner neglects to set realistic goals and objectives in the intermediate or short term.

Brother-in-Law Needs a Job

One of the most common problems in a family business is the hiring of relatives who do not have talent. When a close relative says, "Bob needs a job badly," the emotional aspect tied to the family relationship is difficult to resist. It will be problematic to fire Bob if he turns out to cost more money than his presence is worth.

   The major concern is not necessarily the actual relative, but how he or she affects other employees. In some cases, a relative can demoralize the organization by his or her dealings with other employees. For example, he or she may loaf on the job, avoid unpleasant tasks, take special privileges, or make snide remarks about family members.

My Family Is the Greatest

Every parent has a natural tendency to favor his or her children over others. The family business owner often believes that his or her child will naturally succeed to the ownership and management of the business and that the child has the competence and ability to operate a successful enterprise. It is difficult to recognize that a son, daughter, son-in-law, or daughter-in-law might have other needs and interests that preclude his or her entry into the family business. In addition, some family members may not have the ability to successfully operate the small business. What, then, does the family business owner do about the management succession problem? Should professional management be hired?

High Nonfamily Turnover

Some family-owned companies are plagued with high turnover among their nonfamily employees. Sometimes relatives are responsible. They may resent outside talent and, at best, make things unpleasant for nonfamily executives. In other cases, top-notch managers and workers leave because promotions are closed to them. They see relatives being promoted to executive positions and their own career advancement at a dead end.

The Aging Entrepreneur

When relatives in a family-owned business grow older, they may develop a tendency to prefer the status quo over change. That is, they may be afraid of risk. With this attitude they can—and often do—block growth in their family's business.

After years of effort devoted to building a successful enterprise, an aging owner may become tired and know that he or she cannot continue indefinitely as the head of the family business. Should the owner retain the business for his or her family or should the business be sold or merged? The owner probably feels a lifelong sentimental attachment to the enterprise and would be gratified to have the family continue the business as an external monument in memory of its founder. Indeed, the family business owner is apt to be quite emotional on this subject, and he or she may not fully appreciate the fact that monuments do not pay for food, clothing, and shelter for the surviving family.

The same personal traits that made a family business owner so successful can, in turn, impede the growth and profitability of the business. The drive for accomplishments, ego involvement, willingness to make decisions, and dedication to hard work sometimes limit the owner's perspective as to when he or she needs assistance in decision making.

The Inflated Ego Problem

The egotistical and confident family business owner believes that he or she is indispensable to the success of the business and must have a say in every phase of the business, often denying well-educated, well-trained children or key employees the opportunity to demonstrate their competence. It is difficult for this owner to recognize the need for successor management. Yet, the owner is aging, and his or her decision-making competence is diminishing.

The Key Personnel Problem

The family business owner who is getting on in years may decide not to sell or merge the business, but recognize the value and contributions of key employees—the people who often provide continuity of management during the owner's lifetime and after his or her demise. The owner must then determine how best to keep these key employees within the business. What type of compensation package might be suitable and attractive to them?

The Key Personnel–Absentee Ownership Problem

A unique problem occurs when ownership of the business passes to family members who do not play an active role in it. Key personnel might be quite competent to provide continuity of good management, but also might be resentful of absentee owners receiving what seems to be a disproportionate share of earnings through dividends. This problem can be accentuated if a family member succeeds to the presidency of the business without first having been active in the business and having gained the respect of key personnel. Without a respected member of the family active in the business and at the helm, will the key personnel exert their best efforts on behalf of the business? What can be done to motivate them?

Role Reversal and Sibling Rivalry

A family business owner can find himself or herself in an awkward position when employing a parent. This role reversal may prove to require a difficult adjustment given the history of relating as a son or daughter. The parent may experience resentment, especially if the work is tedious, unrewarding, or difficult. Sibling rivalry problems of jealousy, power, and competitiveness, perhaps existing since childhood, may now become exacerbated in the more stressful functional setting.

Many times when members of a family are active in the business, it is difficult for them to make objective decisions about the skills and abilities of each other. For example, one might say about another relative, "He was lazy when we were kids, and he's still lazy." Or a distinguished wife might say about an aunt, "What does she know about the business? She's only here because of her father's money."[8]

The Succession Issue

One problem that most family businesses experience is planning how to pass control of the business on to the next generation. It is important to review some of the family

TABLE 8.3	BARRIERS TO SUCCESSION PLANNING IN FAMILY FIRMS	
Founder/Owner	**Family**
• Death anxiety	• Death as taboo
• Company as symbol	—Discussion is a hostile act
—Loss of identity	—Fear of loss/abandonment
—Concern about legacy	• Fear of sibling rivalry
• Dilemma of choice	• Change of spouse's position
—Fiction of equality	
• Generational envy	
—Loss of power	

SOURCE: Manfred F. R. Kets de Vries, "The Dynamic of Family Controlled Firms: The Good News and the Bad News," *Organizational Dynamics* (Winter 1993), 68.

---

[8]Adapted from R. Levinson, *Problems in Managing a Family-Owned Business*, U.S. Small Business Administration, Management Aid #.004, 1987; and Benjamin M. Becker and Fred Tillman, *Family Owned Business*, 2nd ed. (Chicago: Commerce Clearinghouse, Inc., 1978).

business's major concerns (see Table 8.3). The cruel, hard fact is that one generation succeeds the other with biological inevitability. Despite this certainty, most family-owned businesses never formulate a succession plan.

A number of reasons explain this failure to plan for an orderly transfer of family businesses. In some cases the owner-founder presents the roadblock due to his or her anxiety over death. Psychologist Manfred Kets de Vries states: "Some presidents of family firms act as if death were something that happens to everyone except themselves. Talking about death is taboo. Raising the topic is viewed as a hostile act, and may be interpreted as a wish to have the person in question dead."[9] Owners may also fear losing their identity by turning over the company or simply hate losing their power base.

In other cases, the family may represent the roadblock. Not only can family members be hampered by the death anxiety already mentioned, but they may also suffer from the fear of sibling rivalry or a change in their position or status.

Whatever the reason, Leon Danco, founder of the Center for Family Business, states:

> It is a daily miracle that there are any owner-managed businesses left in the world with so few making plans for their own continuity. The toughest thing for the business owner to realize is that time is running out on him.[10]

Death and retirement are facts of life, and a well-conceived succession plan must take both into consideration. Transferring a family business is always difficult and often emotional; it affects family members, bankers, employees, managers, competitors, lawyers, spouses, and friends. The only sure thing is that *failing* to plan will make the transfer more difficult and painful.

The Next Generation

A first generation's failure to successfully pass ownership of a business to the next generation is well documented. Many small businesses go out of existence after ten years, and only three out of ten survive into the second generation.[11] More significantly, only 16 percent of all family enterprises make it to the third generation.[12] The average life expectancy for a family business is 24 years—interestingly, the average tenure for the founder of a business.[13]

At first, succession planning seems to pose no major problem: The older generation must simply designate which heirs will inherit the business. Ideally, the older generation will train one or more heirs and then let the younger generation take over while the founder is still alive. Unfortunately, this task is often easier said than done.

---

[9]Manfred F. R. Kets de Vries, "The Dynamics of Family Controlled Firms: The Good News and the Bad News," *Organizational Dynamics* (Winter 1993): 68.

[10]Leon A. Danco, *Inside the Family Business* (Cleveland, Ohio: Center for Family Business, University Press, 1985).

[11]Donald F. Kuratko and Richard M. Hodgetts, "Succession Strategies for Family Business," *Management Advisor* (Spring 1989): 22–30.

[12]John L. Ward, *Keeping the Family Business Healthy* (San Francisco, CA: Jossey-Bass Publishers, 1987).

[13]Richard Beckhard and W. Gibb Dyer, "Managing Continuity in the Family-Owned Business," *Organizational Dynamics* (Summer 1983): 7–8.

One researcher, Wendy C. Handler, has examined the importance of the next generation in family business and contends that the quality of the succession experience is based on both individual and relational influences. Figure 8.3 illustrates a descriptive framework of these factors.[14] **Individual influences** are associated with the individual and affect his or her personal experience of the succession process. They include personal needs fulfillment (career, psychosocial, and life stage) as well as the ability to personally influence the fulfillment of those needs in the context of a family business. **Relational influences** involve the next generation's relation to a group or other individuals. Two of these influences—mutual respect between generations and sibling accommodation—are interpersonal. The remaining two issues—commitment to family business perpetuation and separation strains due to family involvement—are intergroup. That is, they are a function of the overlap between family and business systems. As re-

---

FIGURE 8.3   **A DESCRIPTIVE FRAMEWORK OF THE SUCCESSION EXPERIENCE**

Individual Influences

> • Personal needs fulfillment
>   Career (interest)
>   Psychosocial (personal identity)
>   Life stage (exploration, advancement, balance)
>
> • Personal influence

Quality of Succession Experience

Relational Influences

> • Mutual respect and understanding between generations
> • Sibling accommodation
> • Commitment to family business perpetuation
> • Separation strains due to family involvement

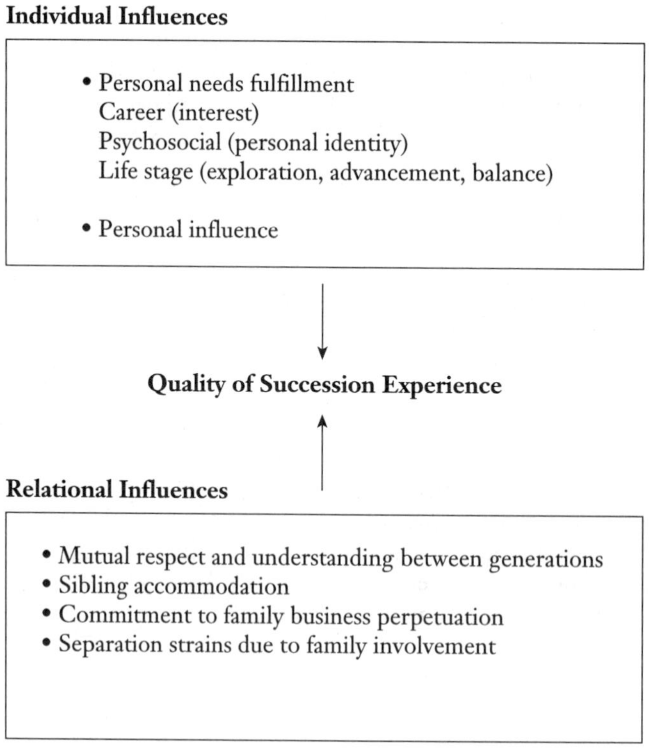

SOURCE: Wendy C. Handler, "The Succession Experience of the Next Generation," *Family Business Review*, (Fall 1992): 288.

---

[14]Wendy C. Handler, "The Succession Experience of the Next Generation," *Family Business Review* (Fall 1992): 283–308.

search continues to focus on these influences for the next generation, we will learn more about the quality of succession and should better understand the succession process.

Effective management succession can reduce the legal problems associated not only with ownership, but also with taxes and inheritance. As with many of the challenges confronting family business, professional advice is useful in effectuating proper succession plans.[15] Nevertheless, despite all of the recommendations to properly plan, finance, and manage a family firm, many business owners eventually watch their firms self-destruct because they have not confronted the challenge of succession. In attempting to avoid problems and prepare for succession, there are four critical steps to remember.[16]

Identify a Successor   Difficult as the task might be, every owner-manager should identify a successor or at least the characteristics and experience needed in such an individual. The basic question that must be answered is, Who can do the best job in keeping the firm going? Survival and growth should be the primary areas of concern. The major hurdle is getting the key manager(s) to select someone. If one relative is designated as the heir apparent, how will the other relatives react? Some founders, not wishing to hurt anyone, never make a decision. If no successor is identified, the next two steps are also ignored.

Groom an Heir   In some firms, the entrepreneur will pick a successor and let that fact be known. Many owners, however, waiver when it comes to actually announcing a choice. Perhaps one person appears to have the inside track or the successor will be chosen from a small group of candidates, but no one knows for sure who will get the job and thus no formal grooming takes place. Regardless of who eventually heads the firm, precious time is lost in learning the job. Even if the heir is designated, the founder may find it difficult to relinquish the authority necessary for effective grooming. The ego factor can prove to be a major stumbling block.

Agree on a Plan   Effective succession requires a plan. Usually, a detailed person-to-person discussion is needed to decide how responsibilities will be transferred to the successor. No owner wants to step aside for a person who will change things dramatically; no entrepreneur wants to see a lifetime of effort unraveled. If the person leaving the position has any power to influence future decision making, now is the time to use it—if only by spelling out a philosophy or general course of action.

During this step, attention should be given to day-to-day operations. Such consideration helps eliminate (or at least reduce) feuding. At this point, it can be helpful to bring into the plan those who will be most affected by it. This participatory approach will often co-opt some critics and alleviate the fears of others. In any event, it is a useful management tactic for helping to create unity behind the new person.

Consider Outside Help   Promotion from within the family can be a mistake. When the top person does a poor job, does promoting the next individual in line solve the problem? The latter may be the owner's clone. Or consider family-owned businesses that

[15]Glenn R. Ayers, "Rough Family Justice: Equity in Family Business Succession Planning," *Family Business Review* (Spring 1990): 3–22; and Ronald E. Berenbeim, "How Business Families Manage the Transition from Owner to Professional Management," *Family Business Review* (Spring 1990): 69–110.

[16]Donald F. Kuratko and Richard M. Hodgetts, *Entrepreneurship: A Contemporary Approach*, 5th ed. (Fort Worth, TX: Harcourt College Publishers, 2001), 592–616. See also Ivan Lansberg, "Twelve Tasks in Succession," *Family Business* (Summer 1993): 18–24.

have begun to outgrow the managerial ability of the top person. Does anyone in the family really have the requisite skills for managing the operation? The question that must be answered is, How can the business be run effectively and who has the ability to do it? Sometimes this task calls for an outside person. In addition, the ego factor is ever-present in family businesses. Does the owner have the wisdom to step aside and the courage to let someone else make strategic decisions? Or is the desire for control so great that the owner prefers to run the risks associated with personally managing the operation?[17]

Prescriptions

The term "family business" connotes and projects positive images based on values held in high esteem by many different people. One reason for this image is the entrepreneurial culture and management practices that allow for continuity from one generation to the next. It is important to create a cross-generational culture and continuously reinforce these values and practices over various stages in the life cycle of the firm. Table 8.4 suggests ways to integrate the requirements of strategy and culture in easing the firm through its intergenerational stages.

By means of strategic exploration, organizational development, financial restructuring, and behavioral modification, the stage can be set for renewal and growth of the family firm. Innovations in reward or information systems, diversification, specialization where in-house expertise already exists, or other creative changes can stimulate necessary regeneration throughout the enterprise's life cycle.

In an early-stage operation, several questions may be asked:

- What, exactly, is the area of responsibility of each family member, and to whom is he or she responsible?

- What is the compensation—salary, bonus, equity shares, or some mixture?

- What will be done in the event of a disagreement or if one family member is not pulling his or her weight?

- What is the ante—can it be redeemed if a joining family member changes his or her mind?

The regeneration process requires new blood and fresh initiatives to maintain and grow the business. Individuals planning to enter an early-stage family business should ask themselves several questions:

- What are my strengths and what do I need to work on?

- What other aspects of the business do I need to learn?

- Do I have the qualities to be a leader?

---

[17]Johannes H. M. Welsch, "The Impact of Family Ownership and Involvement on the Process of Management Succession," *Family Business Review* (Spring 1993): 31–54.

[18]Handler, "The Family Venture," 320.

TABLE 8.4	INTEGRATING STRATEGIES FOR CROSS-GENERATIONAL SUCCESS	
	Requirements	**Strategy**
Strategy	Knowledge of product and manufacturing process technology Knowledge of market Overcoming absence of growth vision	Specialization Diversification Entrepreneurial approximations
Organization	Role differentiation and separation between family and business and between owners and managers Focused structures Communication and problem solving Overcoming distance from customers and employees	Task and business terms Reward systems Rationalize duties and responsibilities
Finance	Creating an information-rich decision-making environment Funding of new ventures Overcoming obsession with data and the "nervous money" syndrome	Information systems Family venture capital company
Family	Equity structures that support "focused" organization structure and a distinction between active and inactive owners Commitment and sense of ownership by nonfamily employees Overcoming inappropriate roles and boundaries between founder, family, and business Overcoming perception of high social risk	Ownership equity structures Programmed training for family members Human resource policies and practices Competence based job opportunities

SOURCE: Adapted from Ernesto J. Poza, "Managerial Practices That Support Entrepreneurship and Continued Growth," *Family Business Review*, 1, no. 4 (Winter 1988).

- Am I happy working in the business?
- Is there anything else I should do to meet my goals?[18]

In addition, Wendy Handler suggests that family member applicants are more likely to achieve success for themselves and the business when they are clear about their needs and communicate them directly to the owner in charge. Learning as much as they can about the business, followed by a specialization stage to acquire specific skills, is part of this strategy. Then the applicant must become a generalist to learn how to manage. By developing a relationship with a mentor or several people who can act as coach, protector, moderator, role model, counselor, or even friend, the new employee has support on several fronts. This person should also look to respected individuals outside the family for counseling and long-term development, because parents may have difficulty accepting the reality that their children are grown up. Acquiring practical business experience and confidence is also likely to enhance the applicant's credibility with employees who may be skeptical about qualifications of family members.

Other strategies have also been suggested, such as establishing communication mechanisms (both informal sessions for sharing and formal sessions for planning and exchange). For example, the creation of a family council—composed of all family members critical to the future of the business such as the founder, spouse, and children, as well as other relatives who have a significant interest in the business—could be a workable solution. A council can help establish open communication, understanding, and trust and serve as a planning forum for both the family and the business. It can also allow the airing of problems or differences that might otherwise be ignored.

Family members should take responsibility for the development of both the business and their own personal goals by asking themselves the following questions:

- Am I cultivating an "entrepreneurial mind" (that is, entrepreneurial attitudes and behaviors)?

- What are the critical skills and know-how required in the business now and in the immediate future?

- In what ways will my personal needs be satisfied through the family venture?

- If we plan to double the size of the business in the next three, five, or ten years, what are the likely requirements?

- What do I bring to the team now, and later?

- What are my strengths and what do I need to work on?

- What additional relevant "chunks" of experience do I need and how can I get them?

- What other aspects of the business do I need to learn?

- Do I have the qualities necessary to be a leader?

- Am I happy working in the business and does it "give me energy"?

- Is there anything else I need to do to meet my goals?[19]

Conclusion

Family businesses have been in existence for many centuries and they will undoubtedly continue to survive, split, merge, and continue in a new vein in the future. The U.S. government has discovered the economic development, job creation, and taxation advantages of family businesses and is currently designing legislation intended to help keep businesses within the family. John L. Ward, for example, suggests that family business is an old idea whose time has come.[20]

Family businesses are unique combinations of rationality and emotion. Family business members claim that such firms are special because they are a labor of love. Building a company with people you care about can be more fulfilling than building a firm with people who do not share so fundamental a connection. Common sacrifices

---

[19]Jeffry Timmons, *New Venture Creation*, 3rd ed. (Homewood, IL: Irwin, 1990)

[20]John L. Ward, "What Is a Family Business and How Can We Help?" *Small Business Forum* (Winter 1990/1991): 63–71.

and success enable individuals to achieve a real sense of pride in accomplishing the dual goals of business growth and family happiness.

Exploring the Entrepreneurial Concepts

The following sections provide an "entrepreneurial library" that contains a journal reading on this chapter's subject and a comprehensive case study to illustrate the concept in practice. It is hoped that through the reading and discussion of the case, you will gain a greater understanding of the chapter.

THE ENTREPRENEURIAL LIBRARY

Reading for Chapter 8

IMPORTANT ATTRIBUTES OF SUCCESSORS IN
FAMILY BUSINESSES: AN EXPLORATORY STUDY

James J. Chrisman, Jess H. Chua, Pramodita Sharma

James J. Chrisman is associate dean of research and Ph.D. programs and on the faculty of management at University of Calgary, Alberta, Canada. Jess H. Chua is associate dean of academics and on the faculty of management at the University of Calgary, Alberta, Canada. Pramodita Sharma is an assistant professor in the school of business administration at Dalhousie University, Halifax, Nova Scotia, Canada.

Respondents from 485 family firms in Canada rated integrity and commitment to the business as the most important attributes of a successor. Results indicated that the older the family business and the longer the respondent's tenure in that business, the more important these attributes became. Birth order and gender were rated the least important, despite the attention the literature has given to those attributes.

Introduction

The topic of succession has dominated research in the field of family business (Wortman, 1994; Dyer & Handler, 1994). Surprisingly, who is considered the most desirable successor has not received much attention. The literature has suggested a number of successor attributes that may lead to an effective succession. This paper reports some preliminary results from a survey of what family firms consider the most important successor attributes.

Included here is a review of successor attributes found in the literature as well as details of the methodology we used for this study. In addition, we discuss the ratings for different attributes and exploratory results on the factors affecting these ratings.

Family Business Review, vol. XI, no. 1, March 1998 © Family Firm Institute, Inc.

We conclude with a summary of our findings and a discussion of the implications for family business managers and consultants.

Literature Review of Desirable Attributes of Successors

This literature survey focuses on identifying and discussing those attributes that researchers considered important, rather than providing an exhaustive treatment of each attribute. To facilitate the discussion, we grouped the desirable successor attributes, according to the literature, into six categories: (i) relationship to the incumbent, (ii) relationships to other members of the family, (iii) family standing, (iv) competence, (v) personality traits, and (vi) current involvement in the family business.

Potential Successor's Personal Relationship with the Incumbent

Literature on both family business and executive succession emphasize the importance of the relationship between the successor and the incumbent in determining the process, timing, and effectiveness of the succession. A smooth succession requires the cooperation of the incumbent and the successor (Handler, 1992; Hollander & Elman, 1988). If the incumbent is unwilling to let go (Christensen, 1953; Firnstahl, 1986; Levinson, 1971) or if family members from the next generation are unwilling to take over (Barry, 1975; Blotnick, 1984), succession will be ineffective. A good personal relationship between these individuals (Grusky, 1959; Friedman, 1986; Kesner & Sebora, 1994, Lansberg, 1988) will contribute to the training and development of the successors (Fiegener, et al., 1994; Seymour, 1993) and is key to a successful transition (Barnes & Hershon, 1976; Davis & Tagiuri, 1989; Handler, 1992; Stempler, 1988). Based on these finding, we included "personal relationship with CEO" in our list of desirable attributes.

Davis's and Tagiuri's (1989) research indicated that the life-cycle stage of the potential successor relative to that of the incumbent affects the quality of the father–son work relationship. For example, such relationships are typically at their most problematic when the successor is in his or her late thirties, with relationships improving thereafter. This suggests that "age of the successor" would be another important attribute.

Aside from personal rapport, Levinson (1971) and Helmich and Brown (1972) suggested that compatibility of goals also influences the choice of successor. Therefore, we also included "compatibility of goals with those of the CEO" in the criteria.

Potential Successor's Personal Relationships with Other Members of the Family

Family harmony is very important for family firms (Churchill & Hatten, 1987; Malone, 1989). In fact, Davis (1968, p. 416) stated that "personal relations among relatives often take precedence over maximum profit" in family firms. Therefore, a potential successor must have the trust of family members actively involved in the business (Goldberg & Woolridge, 1993; Horton, 1982; Lansberg & Astrachan, 1994). Also the trust and respect of family members not actively involved in the business may arguably be just as important because the most influential family members may not necessarily be active in the business (Gillis-Danovan & Moynihan-Bradt, 1990; Barnes & Hershon, 1976). We used four variables to describe the successor's relationship with the family: "respect of actively involved family members," "respect of non-involved family members," "trust of family members," and "ability to get along with family members."

Family Standing

The choice of primogeniture has remained widely used to transfer power in the family business (Levinson, 1971; Cates & Sussman, 1982, Dumas, 1989), although it is now more frequently acknowledged that the eldest may not always be the best and sons may not necessarily be better than daughters (Ayres, 1990; Goldberg & Woolridge, 1993; Kaye, 1992; Lyman, Salganicoff, & Hollander, 1985). Barnes (1988) suggested that one reason for this persistence in choosing the eldest is that incongruity develops between the successor's standing in the business and the family when a younger son or a daughter takes over the business, which thus leads to ambiguity and rivalry within the family. As a result, incumbents, in order to preserve family harmony, may be discouraged from choosing a younger son or a daughter as successor. We therefore added "birth order" and "gender" to our list of attributes.

Different views prevail about choosing an "in-law" as the family business leader. Researchers such as Syms (1994) believed that in-laws are not normally considered for succession. Whereas others (Fiegener, et al., 1994) believed that in-laws are usually included in the short list of succession candidates. As a result, we included "blood relation" as a potential attribute of the successor.

Competence

Although competence is undeniably desirable in a leader, measuring or even establishing competency is difficult. The literature uses "education," "experience in the family business," "experience outside the family business," and "past performance" as proxies for competence, and we do likewise.

Educational attainment is believed to indicate an individual's knowledge, skills, receptivity to innovation, and cognitive and problem-solving abilities (Fiegener, et al., 1994; Hambrick & Mason, 1984; Cooper, Gimeno-Gason, & Woo, 1991). Experience in the family business enables the successor to develop relationships within the company and understand the culture and intricacies of the business (Danco, 1982; Lansberg & Astrachan, 1994; Nelton, 1986). Experience outside the company helps the successor develop an identity and prepare for a wider range of problems that may confront the organization (Barnes, 1988; Correll, 1989; Donnelley, 1964; Danco, 1982; Hambrick & Mason, 1984; Lansberg & Astrachan, 1994). To determine which skill set is considered important, we included in the list of desirable attributes the following: "financial skills," "marketing/sales skills," "strategic-planning skills," "technical skills," "decision-making abilities," and "interpersonal skills."

Personality Traits

The literature provided a long list of personality characteristics (e.g., aggressiveness, creativity, and integrity) that are considered desirable in successors. This list included the following: "aggressiveness" (Malone & Jenster, 1992), "creativity" (Schumpeter, 1934), "independence" (Correll, 1989; Goldberg & Woolridge, 1993; Levinson, 1971), "integrity" (Levinson, 1971), "intelligence" (McMullan & Long, 1990), "self-confidence" (Goldberg & Woolridge, 1993; Sapienza, Herron, & Menendez, 1991), and "willingness to take risk" (Sexton & Bowman, 1983). The list also included complex psychological characteristics, such as locus of control and need for achievement, which we did not include because we believed that respondents would be unable to rate their importance without involved explanation.

Current Involvement with the Family Business

A potential successor may be involved with the family business through share ownership or active participation. A family member owning a large share of the business has a greater stake in the continuing health of the company than a smaller shareholder. Because agency theory suggests that owners may make decisions that are more consistent with business effectiveness than the decisions that nonowners make (Jensen & Meckling, 1976; Shane, 1997), potential successors who have a greater ownership stake may be preferred by the incumbents. We therefore included "current ownership share" in our list of desirable attributes.

A potential successor's participation in the company may vary in intensity and quality. Quality is obviously more important than quantity. Because opposition by nonfamily managers can be a barrier to succession planning (Lansberg, 1988), we included "respect of employees." Finally, because recent studies have shown that the incumbent's confidence in the successor's willingness to take over the business has a direct correlation to the ease with which power and authority are transferred (Goldberg & Woolridge, 1993), we included "commitment to business" as another variable.

The Survey

Sample

There are no national statistics on family business, perhaps because no uniformly accepted definition of a family business exists. Therefore, empirical research has relied on convenience samples, such as the membership lists of professional associations (e.g., Goldberg & Woolridge, 1993; Lansberg & Astrachan, 1994) or the mailing lists of family business consultants (e.g., Geeraerts, 1984). This study uses both.

Following the first approach, we used the mailing list of the Canadian Association of Family Enterprises (CAFE). CAFE is the largest national association of Canadian family firms, with a membership of 585 businesses (approximately 10% family business consultants and bankers) at the time of data collection (fall, 1994). Included in that mailing list were approximately 1,000 nonmember family firms.

Based on the second approach, we also selected a random sample of 500 family firms from the more than 4,000 names on the mailing list of Deloitte & Touche (Canada). After eliminating names that were obviously not family firms (e.g., account managers in banks and lawyers in large law firms) and duplications, questionnaires were sent to 1,725 Anglophone Canadian family firms. These included 483 members and 1,242 nonmembers of CAFE. To decrease the possibility of including those that were not family firms, respondents that did not consider themselves family businesses were asked to return their questionnaires unanswered.

Data Collection

Two mailings of the questionnaire—initial and follow-up—were made to the sample firms in order to increase the response rate and check for possible response bias. Questionnaires returned from CAFE members and nonmembers totaled 211 and 274, respectively. This yielded a response rate of 44% for CAFE members and 22% for nonmembers and an overall rate of 28%. We attributed the higher response rate of CAFE members to the strong endorsement given by the officers of CAFE.

Variables and Measures Used

The questionnaire included three parts pertinent to this study: the importance of each successor attribute, information about the business, and information about the respondent. In the successor attributes section, respondents were asked to rate the importance of 30 attributes on a seven-point Likert scale. A low score of 0 meant the attribute was considered "not important" and a high score of 6 meant that it was "critically important." The other two parts were included to determine how the characteristics of the family business and the respondent influenced the ratings for the attributes.

The business information section included questions about the age of the business, its industry sector (retail, service, wholesale, manufacturing, natural resources, and construction), legal form, size (geographical distribution and number of locations and full-time employees), gross revenues and profitability, number of family and nonfamily managers in the business, the family's share of ownership, the likelihood of the current president retiring in the next 10 years, the generation running the business, and the number of family and nonfamily members on the board of directors.

The respondent information section requested information about the respondent's gender, age, number of male and female children, current position in business, share ownership, years of active involvement in the family business, outside management experience (in number of years), and type of work experience outside the business. It also asked whether the respondent was a founder.

Data Validation Tests

First, we tested for nonresponse bias. For this, the responses were divided into five batches according to when they were received. ANOVA and MANOVA tests indicated no statistically significant differences between the early and late responses. Second, we tested for homogeneity in the responses from different provinces. Again, tests indicated no statistically significant differences.

We did, however, observe significant differences between member and nonmember responses to the importance of past performance, interpersonal skills, birth order, ability to get along with family members, and respect of actively involved family members. It is difficult to imagine that family firms within a nation would face different types of succession/issues and thus look for different types of successors simply because of membership in an association. Besides, nonmembers can easily become members by simply paying the membership dues. Therefore, we believe that differences in the operating conditions of family businesses lead to different succession issues that, in turn, influence whether or not a family business joins CAFE. For example, member firms are, on average, older and larger than nonmember firms, probably because age and size, among other things, influence a family firm's sensitivity to succession issues and the perceived value of membership in CAFE. Accordingly, data from members and nonmembers were combined to form one sample.

The Respondents

Business Profiles

The average age of the responding firms was 38 years (see Table 1). Median number of employees was 45 and the mean was 108. Median gross revenues were $5.3 million.

Around 41% were run by first generation family members, and 97% of the families owned 50% or more of the companies' equities. Manufacturing (23%), service (20%), wholesale (19%), and retail (17%) businesses dominated the sample.

Personal Profiles

About 85% of the respondents were male (see Table 1); 39% were founders of their businesses; 65% were presidents; and 23% were board chairs. The average member had been involved in the business for 19 years.

TABLE 1	PROFILES OF SAMPLE FIRMS AND RESPONDENTS

Firm Profile

Years in Business		Gross Revenue	
Average	38	Median ($ million)	$5–$10
Minimum	1	< $100K	2%
Maximum	169	> $50 Million	9%

Type of Business		Generation Managing the Business	
Retail	17%	1st	41%
Wholesale	19%	2nd	37%
Manufacturing	23%	3rd	15%
Service	20%	4th	5%
Construction	8%	5th	1%
Other	13%	6th	1%

Number of Employees		Share Ownership	
Median	45	< 50%	3%
Mean	108	50% to 99.99%	15%
0	1%	100%	82%
> 500	4%		

Respondent Profile

Gender		Current Position in Firm*	
Male	85%	Chairperson	23%
Female	15%	President	65%
		Vice president	14%
Years in the Family Business		Directors	31%
Mean	19		
Median	17		
Longest	50	% who are founders	39%

Note: Percentages add to more than 100% because some respondents held more than one position.

Ranking the Attributes

Before dividing the sample by demographic characteristics, we first sought to determine the relative importance of the successor attributes for the entire sample. The mean ratings of 30 successor attributes were arranged in descending order in Table 2 along with the standard deviations. To ascertain that overall the mean ratings were indeed different, we conducted Hotelling's *T*-squared test on the means. The results indicated that the attributes differ significantly in importance. Next, two tailed *t*-tests were used to determine whether an attribute's importance differed significantly from that of the attributes ranked above and below it. The results are also presented in Table 2. In general, the standard deviation increased as the mean rating decreased. This indicated that there is more agreement among respondents about the importance of a highly rated attribute than of a low-rated one.

On a 0 to 6 scale, a score of 3 would represent an average rating. Therefore, overall, the results indicated that all but 4 of the 30 attributes were of higher-than-average importance in selecting a successor. This was a preliminary confirmation that the attributes suggested by the literature are, in general, appropriate. Of the six attribute groups, personality traits and current involvement with the business were the most important, followed by competence, relationships with other family members, relationship with the incumbent, and finally, family standing.

Among our thirty attribute variables, the family firms in our sample considered "integrity" and "commitment to the business" the two most important. Two tailed *t*-tests indicated that these two attributes were rated significantly higher than any others. We believe that these two attributes were considered the most important because they contribute to both trustworthiness and the performance of the business. For others to trust the successor, they must be sure about the successor's honesty, intentions, ability to implement, and timeliness of communication (Astrachan, 1997). We believe that integrity would be related to honesty, intentions, and timeliness of communication, whereas commitment to the business would be related to intentions. Our findings indicated that integrity and "commitment to the business" contribute more than trustworthiness because "trusted by family members" received a rating of 12. We believe this may indicate that respondents considered "integrity" to encompass dealings with employees, suppliers, and customers in addition to family members. This is an important finding because the succession literature is unclear as to whether competence (Trow, 1961) or relationship (Miller & Rice, 1988) is the more critical factor. These results suggested that, at least in the family business, relationships are likely to be more important than competence.

Next in importance was the respect of employees, another attribute related to the quality of the successor's current involvement in the family business. In terms of competence, decision-making abilities and interpersonal skills—the fourth- and fifth-highest-rated attributes—are rated significantly higher than any other skills. Superficially, one might expect interpersonal skills to rank higher because of all the family relationship issues usually associated with running a family business (Lansberg & Astsrachan, 1994; Levinson, 1971). We interpreted this ranking to mean that family firms view interpersonal skills without integrity as "slick" and ineffective in the long run. Among the other personality traits, intelligence, self-confidence, and creativity were also highly rated. Aggressiveness, willingness to take risk, and independence were rated further down on the scale. The low ratings of these traits normally associated with the entrepreneur (McMullan & Long, 1990), and that outside managerial experience ranks significantly

TABLE 2			
MEANS, STANDARD DEVIATIONS, AND SIGNIFICANCE TESTS FOR DIFFERENCES IN MEAN RATINGS			

Attribute and Number		Mean	S.D.	Significantly Different from Attribute Number*
1	Integrity	5.54	0.86	3–30
2	Commitment to business	5.50	0.80	3–30
3	Respect from employees	5.18	0.98	6–30
4	Decision-making abilities and experience	5.12	0.86	8–30
5	Interpersonal skills	5.10	0.98	8–30
6	Intelligence	5.08	0.91	8–30
7	Self-confidence	5.05	0.93	8–30
8	Creativity	4.87	0.93	13–30
9	Experience in business	4.82	1.14	13–30
10	Past performance	4.81	1.06	13–30
11	Respect from actively involved family members	4.81	1.43	13–30
12	Trust by family members	4.79	1.55	14–30
13	Marketing skills/sales skills	4.66	1.08	15–30
14	Ability to get along with family members	4.56	1.50	19–30
15	Financial skills/experience	4.53	1.04	20–30
16	Strategic-planning skills	4.53	1.08	21–30
17	Aggressiveness	4.47	1.11	21–30
18	Willingness to take risk	4.43	1.04	21–30
19	Respected by non-involved family members	4.37	1.71	22–30
20	Independence	4.36	1.16	21–30
21	Education level	4.18	1.26	23–30
22	Compatibility of goals with current CEO	4.06	1.50	24–30
23	Technical skills	3.98	1.27	25–30
24	Outside management experience	3.87	1.43	26–30
25	Personal relationship with CEO	3.78	1.72	26–30
26	Age of successor	3.14	1.40	27–30
27	Blood relation	2.58	1.93	28–30
28	Current ownership share	1.91	1.90	29–30
29	Gender	1.60	1.67	30
30	Birth order	1.10	1.34	

*Note: This column lists the attributes with ratings significantly lower at the 5% level than that of the variable in the row, using a two tailed *t*-test.

lower than the education level of successors, may suggest that family firms do not want successors who are eager to make radical changes. Obviously, whether these personality traits are necessary for maintaining the competitiveness of the business will depend on the competitive structure of the business environment.

Birth order and gender were the two lowest-ranked attributes. Birth order and gender rate at one-fifty and one-third, respectively, compared with the top two attributes. These results were very surprising because of the academic literature's preoccupation with their importance.

Determinants of the Attributes' Importance Ratings

Exploratory tests were conducted to determine whether the observed differences in attribute ratings could be explained by the business and respondent profile variables. MANOVA and ANOVA were used on the attributes. We dropped four profile variables because they were highly correlated with each other. MANOVA tests were conducted on the remaining profile variables. The tests showed that importance ratings were affected by 10 profile variables. Univariate tests were conducted to determine the relationship between each attribute and each profile variable. The results are in Table 3. Appendix [A] provides the definitions of the attribute and profile variables listed in the table.

Apparently the longer the respondent was involved in the business (YRSBUS), the more important the attributes became. Length of time at the company affected positively the ratings of 18 attributes. As explained in the literature survey section, we included this variable because researchers suggested that duration in the business improved the successor's understanding about the culture and intricacies of the business (Danco, 1982; Lansberg & Astrachan, 1994; Nelton, 1986). Therefore, we interpreted this variable's influence to mean that longer involvement increased the respondent's appreciation of a well-rounded leader in terms of competence and trustworthiness by both family and nonfamily members.

The size of the firm (GRSREV) affected the ratings of nine attributes. These included personal traits, involvement in the business, competence, and relationships with family members. Most interesting, was that as the firm grew, technical skill apparently became less important. This suggests that larger firms looked for successors with strategic rather than operational skills. The tendency for larger firms to value a wider variety of attributes more than small firms do was somewhat surprising because the literature suggested that the former do not appear any more likely to engage in business continuity planning (Malone, 1989).

The number of nonfamily managers (NONFAM) also influenced the ratings of nine attributes. As the number of nonfamily managers increased, the need for the successor to have technical skills also decreased, but the need for interpersonal skills increases. In fact, this is the only profile variable that affects the rating of interpersonal skills. It is also the only profile variable that affects the rating of goal compatibility between the successor and the incumbent (GOAL). We think this is because nonfamily managers tend to be people committed to the incumbent's goals (e.g., Lansberg, 1988). Therefore, when the successor's goals differ from the incumbent's and there is a large number of these managers, the probability is higher that there will be conflicts and turmoil in the succession process that will have a negative impact on a company's performance (Levinson, 1971).

Because a large number of descendants complicates succession planning (Ward, 1987), it is not surprising that the number of potential successors (NOMPOT) affects the ratings of eight attributes. Numerous descendants influence negatively the ratings of integrity and whether the successor is a blood relation or an in-law. We expected both relationships to be positive. The more potential successors there were, the more important integrity should have been because the successor should be expected to have the highest integrity to be trusted and to continue to work with the other potential successors. As far as blood relatives, we expected that family firms would pick in-laws only when sons and daughters were unavailable.

Five attributes were affected when a firm is facing its president's retirement in the next 10 years (RETIRE). The relationship between the successor and the incumbent

TABLE 3										

RESULTS OF UNIVARIATE TESTS OF RELATIONSHIPS

Attribute	BRD FAM	FAM NUM	FOUN DER	GEN RUN	GRS REV	NON FAM	OWN PCT	NUMPOT	RET IRE	YRS BUS
INTEGR							*(+)	*(−)		**(+)
COMMIT					*(+)	**(+)		*(+)		*(+)
RESPEMP					**(+)	**(+)	**(+)	**(+)		*(+)
DMSK						*(+)		*(+)		**(+)
IPSK						*(+)				
INTEL					**(+)					**(+)
SELF										**(+)
CREATE			*(+)		*(+)					**(+)
EXPBUS		**(+)						*(+)		*(+)
PASTP					**(+)	**(+)		*(+)		
RESPAFM	**(+)	**(+)		**(+)						**(+)
TRUSTFM		**(+)								
MARKSK		*(+)	*(+)							
ALNGFM	**(+)	**(+)		**(+)	**(+)					**(+)
FINSK										
PLANSK										
AGGRES					*(+)				**(+)	**(+)
RISK	*(−)		*(+)				*(+)			**(+)
RESPNAFM					*(+)	*(+)		*(+)		*(+)
INDEP			*(+)							*(+)
EDUC										*(+)
GOAL						*(+)				
TECHSK					**(−)	**(−)			*(+)	
OUTEXP										
RELCEO	*(−)								**(+)	**(+)
AGE	*(−)								**(+)	**(+)
BLOOD	**(+)							**(−)	**(+)	
CUROWN	*(+)	**(+)		*(+)			**(−)			*(+)
GENDER										
BIRTH	*(+)	**(+)				*(−)	*(−)		**(+)	

Note: *Indicates significance at 0.05 level; ** indicates significance at 0.01 level; (+) and (−) indicate the direction of the relationship. Definitions of the variables are in Appendix [A].

became more important (Fiegener, et al., 1994) as did the successor's standing in the family in terms of birth order and gender. When the respondent was the founder, personality traits associated with an entrepreneur (creativity, independence, willingness to take risk, and marketing and sales skills) are more highly rated.

Interestingly, among the statistically significant determinant variables, founder status and the generation that was running the business (GENRUN) affected only four and three attributes, respectively, the least number of attributes to be affected. In contrast, the number of family members on the board of directors (BRDFAM) affected eight attributes, the number of family members actively involved in the business (FAMNUM) affected seven, and the family's percentage of ownership in the business (OWNPCT) affected five, all three of these variables influenced the ratings of relatively more attributes.

Conclusion

One of the major issues that family firms face is choosing a successor. The literature has suggested a number of desirable attributes, and a clear knowledge of successor attributes that are considered important can help potential successors determine their suitability for the top position in the family firm. Moreover, knowing what to look for and what to develop in potential successors can also help incumbents in the succession process. This study attempted to answer the call for confirmatory research made by some scholars (e.g., Handler, 1992; Wortman, 1994). This study presents the way family business managers rank the importance of various attributes, as suggested in the literature.

We found that respondents considered "integrity" and "commitment to business" the most important attributes of successors. Conversely, gender and birth order were rated least important. These findings suggest that incumbents based the succession decision on personal qualities rather than gender, age, or bloodline.

Concerning the business and personal characteristics governing the perceptions of desirable attributes, it appears that a manager's years of experience in the family business is the most important. That experience engenders a greater appreciation of the human and economic difficulties of business leadership and a desire to select a successor with the best mix of personal qualities, business and interpersonal skills, and experience. It is also noteworthy that business size had a large impact on the ratings. Such factors as commitment to the business, respect of employees, intelligence, and creativity seemed to become more important as a firm grew, whereas technical skills faded in significance. Finally, it is somewhat surprising that variables such as founder status and the generation running the business—both proxies for the age of a firm—did not have a great effect on the ratings. Although too early to make definitive statements, an organization's age or stage of development apparently has less of an impact on the qualities sought in a potential successor than the literature might imply (cf. Barnes & Hershon, 1976).

Based on the findings of this exploratory study, future researchers should consider proceeding in at least three general directions: First, this study should be replicated using different samples, particularly samples drawn from other countries. Second, it would be useful to determine how incumbents actually select successors, whether they in fact use the criteria they indicated were important, and what other factors may come into play in the process. In this respect, the difference between what we have found concerning important attributes and what the literature and prior practice suggested (e.g., regarding gender and blood relationships) deserves further investigation. The process used to choose a successor may not be as linear as one might imagine. Certain attributes may be considered important at different stages in the process. In other words, the criteria used to select a pool of candidates may be somewhat different from the criteria used to select a successor from the candidate pool. Although merely a conjecture at this point, research into the other kinds of selection processes—for example, the process venture capitalists use to make investments (Hall & Hofer, 1993)—may be worthwhile.

Finally, it would also be very valuable to determine the relationship between different attributes of successors and the subsequent performance of a family business. Our research has provided some insight into what family business managers look for in a successor, but that does not necessarily ensure that they make the right choices or that the attributes they believed were most important actually were the most important in terms of the effectiveness and efficiency of the family business. Furthermore, although the current study suggests a greater homogeneity of opinion concerning desirable attributes than might have been expected, it also indicates clearly that a number of important characteristics of the business and the decision maker influence the type of successor sought. Therefore, future research should not assume that what made the best successor in one case will make the best successor in another.

Implications for Family Business Managers and Consultants

Assuming that the combined wisdom of nearly 500 family business managers was used as a guide, this study implies primarily that integrity and commitment to the business should not be sacrificed for competence. Of course, competence is an important factor in selecting a successor, as evidenced by the fact that decision-making and interpersonal skills were rated fourth and fifth in importance. However, it is even more important to find a person who can be depended on to make decisions that are in the best interest of the business as well as the family. Competence without integrity or commitment does not provide that assurance. There is no better way of discouraging a founder from making a clean break than to select a successor who cannot be trusted to be honest, make decisions in the interest of the business, and communicate with other stakeholders, no matter how well qualified that person may be in other respects. Thus, incumbents should be encouraged to go with their gut instincts in this regard; likewise successors must demonstrate their business commitment and character. Consultants should also keep these findings in mind when advising family businesses on succession selection.

A second implication of this study is that different family businesses have different needs and different family managers have different perceptions of those needs. What is best for one family business is not necessarily best for another. Family-business professionals must understand that successor selection must be carefully tailored to these needs and perceptions. In particular, the incumbent's years in the business, the size of the firm, the number of nonfamily managers, the number of successors, and the number of family members on the board of directors appear to have the greatest potential influence on these decisions.

The final implication of this study is that in contemporary family businesses, gender and birth order do not appear valid as criteria for selecting a successor. The family-business managers in our survey recognized that for the good of the business and the good of the family an evaluation of a potential successor's integrity, commitment to the business, respect of employees, and decision-making and interpersonal skills must guide the selection process. If the best candidate is not the first-born male, so be it. On the other hand, family-business managers and their advisors must acknowledge the potential difficulties that can occur when status in the business and status in the family do not coincide (Barnes, 1988) and then devise approaches to overcome such difficulties. Potential successors should also keep this in mind, make sure they understand what is required to be successful in the family business, and take the necessary preparatory steps to assume leadership when the time comes.

References

Astrachan, J. H. (1997). Personal communications.

Ayres, G. A. (1990). Rough family justice: Equity in family business succession planning. *Family Business Review, 3*(1), 3–22.

Barnes, L. B. (1988). Incongruent hierarchies: Daughters and younger sons as company CEOs. *Family Business Review, 1*(1), 9–21.

Barnes, L. B., & Hershon, S. A. (1976). Transferring power in the family business. *Harvard Business Review, 54*, 105–114.

Barry, B. (1975). The development of organization structure in the family firm. *Journal of General Management, 1*, 42–60.

Blotnick, S. (1984). The case of the reluctant heirs. *Forbes, 134*, 180.

Cates, J. N., & Sussman, M. B. (1982). Family systems and inheritance. *Marriage and Family Review, 5*, 1–24.

Christensen, C. (1953). *Management succession in small and growing enterprises.* Boston: Harvard Business School, Division of Research.

Churchill, N. C., & Hatten, K. J. (1987). Non-market based transfers of wealth and power: A research framework for family businesses. *American Journal of Small Business, 11*, 51–64.

Cooper, A. C., Gimeno-Gason, F. J., & Woo, C. Y. (1991). A resource-based prediction of new venture survival and growth. Academy of Management Best Papers Proceedings.

Correll, R. W. (1989). Facing up to moving forward: A third-generation successor's reflections. *Family Business Review, 2*(1), 17 29.

Danco, L. (1982). *Beyond survival: A guide for the business owner and his family.* Cleveland, OH: University Press.

Davis, S. M. (1968). Entrepreneurial succession. *Administrative Science Quarterly, 13*, 402–416.

Davis, J. A., & Tagiuri, R. (1989). The influence of life-stage on father–son work relationships in family companies. *Family Business Review, 2*(1), 47–74.

Donnelley, R. (1964). The family business. *Harvard Business Review, 42*, 93–105.

Dumas, C. (1989). Understanding the father–daughter and father–son dyads in family-owned businesses. *Family Business Review, 2*(1), 31–46.

Dyer, W. G., Jr., & Handler, W. (1994). Entrepreneurship and family business: Exploring the connections. *Entrepreneurship Theory and Practice, 19*, 71–83.

Fiegener, M. K., Brown, B. M., Prince, R. A., & File, K. M. (1994). A comparison of successor development in family and nonfamily businesses. *Family Business Review, 7*(4), 313–329.

Firnstahl, T. W. (1986). Letting go. *Harvard Business Review, 64*, 14–18.

Friedman, S. D. (1986). Succession systems in large corporations: Characteristics and correlates of performance. *Human Resource Management, 2*, 191–303.

Geeraerts, G. (1984). The effect of ownership on the organization structure in small firms. *Administrative Science Quarterly, 29*, 232–237.

Gillis-Danovan, J., & Moynihan-Bradt, C. (1990). The power of invisible women in the family business. *Family Business Review, 3*(2), 153–167.

Goldberg, S. D., & Woolridge, B. (1993). Self-confidence and managerial autonomy: Successor characteristics critical to succession in family firms. *Family Business Review, 6*(1), 55–73.

Grusky, O. (1959). Role conflict in organizations: A study of prison officials. *Administrative Science Quarterly, 3*, 463–467.

Hall, J., & Hofer, C. W. (1993). Venture capitalists' decision criteria in new venture evaluation. *Journal of Business Venturing, 8*, 25–42.

Hambrick, D. C., & Mason, P. A. (1984). Upper echelons: The organization as a reflection of its top management. *Academy of Management Review, 9*(2), 193–206.

Handler, W. C. (1992). The succession experience of the next generation. *Family Business Review, 5*(3), 283–307.

Helmich, D. L., & Brown, W. B. (1972). Successor type and organizational change in the corporate enterprise. *Administrative Science Quarterly, 17*, 371–181.

Hollander, B. S., & Elman, N. S. (1988). Family-owned businesses: An emerging field of inquiry. *Family Business Review, 1*(2), 145–164.

Horton, T. P. (1982). The baton of succession. *Management Review, 71*, 2–3.

Jensen, M., & Meckling, W. (1976). Theory of the firm: Managerial behavior, agency costs, and ownership structure. *Journal of Financial Economics, 3*, 305–360.

Kaye, K. (1992). The kid brother. *Family Business Review, 5*(3), 237–256.

Kesner, I. S., & Sebora, T. C. (1994). Executive succession: Past, present, and future. *Journal of Management, 20*(2), 337–372.

Lansberg, I. (1988). The succession conspiracy. *Family Business Review, 1*(2), 119–143.

Lansberg, I., & Astrachan, J. H. (1994). Influence of family relationships on succession planning and training: The importance of mediating factors. *Family Business Review, 7*(1), 39–59.

Levinson, H. (1971). Conflicts that plague family businesses. *Harvard Business Review, 49*, 90–98.

Lyman, A., Salganicoff, M., & Hollander, B. (1985). Women in family business: An untapped resource. *SAM Advanced Management Journal, 50*, 46–49.

Malone, S. C. (1989). Selected correlates of business continuity planning in the family business. *Family Business Review, 2*(4), 341–353.

Malone, S. C., & Jenster, P. V. (1992). The problem of plateaued owner manager. *Family Business Review, 5*(1), 25–41.

McMullan, W. E., & Long, W. A. (1990). *Developing new ventures: The entrepreneurial option.* Orlando, FL: Harcourt Brace Jovanovich.

Miller, E. J., & Rice, A. K. (1988). The family business in contemporary society. *Family Business Review, 1*(2), 193–210.

Nelton, S. (1986). *In love and in business: How entrepreneurial couples are changing the rules of business and marriage.* New York: Wiley.

Sapienza, H. R., Herron, L., & Menendez, J. (1991). The founder and the firm: A qualitative analysis of the entrepreneurial process. In *Frontiers of entrepreneurial research.* Wellesley, MA: Babson College.

Schumpeter, J. A. (1934). *The theory of economic development.* New Brunswick, NJ: Transaction.

Sexton, D. L., & Bowman, N. B. (1983). Comparative entrepreneurship characteristics of students. In *Frontiers of entrepreneurship research.* Wellesley, MA: Babson College.

Seymour, K. C. (1993). Intergenerational relationships in the family firm: The effect on leadership succession. *Family Business Review, 6*(3), 263–281.

Shane, S. A. (1997). Hybrid organizational arrangements and their implications for firm growth and survival: A study of new franchisers. *Academy of Management Journal, 39*, 216–234.

Stempler, G. L. (1988). *A study of succession in family owned businesses.* Unpublished doctoral dissertation, George Washington University.

Syms, M. (1994). *Mind your own business—And keep it in the family.* New York: Mastermedia.

Trow, D. B. (1961). Executive succession in small companies. *Administrative Science Quarterly, 6*, 228–239.

Ward, J. L. (1987). *Keeping the family business healthy.* San Francisco: Jossey-Bass.

Wortman, M. S., Jr. (1994). Theoretical foundations for family-owned businesses: A conceptual and research based paradigm. *Family Business Review, 7*(1), 3–27.

APPENDIX A — DEFINITIONS OF ATTRIBUTE AND PROFILE VARIABLES

Attribute Variables

INTEGR	Integrity
COMMIT	Commitment to the business
RESPEMP	Respected by employees
DMSK	Decision making abilities and experience
IPSK	Interpersonal skills
INTEL	Intelligence
SELF	Self confidence
CREATE	Creativity
EXPBUS	Experience in the business
PASTP	Past performance
RESPAFM	Respected by actively involved family members
TRUSTFM	Trusted by family members
MARKSK	Marketing and sales skills
ALNGFM	Ability to get along with family members
FINSK	Financial skills and experience
PLANSK	Strategic planning skills
AGGRES	Aggressiveness
RISK	Willingness to take risk
RESPNAFM	Respected by non-involved family members
INDEP	Independence
EDUC	Education
GOAL	Compatibility of goals with incumbent
TECHSK	Technical skills
OUTEXP	Outside experience
RELCEO	Personal relationship with incumbent
AGE	Age of successor
BLOOD	Blood and not marital relationship
CUROWN	Current share ownership of the successor
GENDER	Gender of the successor
BIRTH	Birth order of the successor

Profile Variables

BRDFAM	Number of family members on the board of directors
FAMNUM	Number of family members actively involved in the business
FOUNDER	Whether the respondent is the founder
GENRUN	The generation currently managing the business
GRSREV	Gross revenues of the business
NONFAM	Number of nonfamily managers in the business
OWNPCT	The family's percentage ownership of the business
NUMPOT	Number of potential successors
RETIRE	Whether the incumbent is expected to retire in the next ten years
YRSBUS	Years respondent has been involved in the business

C A S E   Stew Leonard's Dairy

Charles B. Shrader, Steven A. Rallis, and Joan L. Twenter

Stewart (Stew) J. Leonard's father, Leo Leonard, owned and operated a small dairy route with four milk trucks. As a young boy, Stew often helped his father with deliveries. By the time Stew was in high school he was operating his own milk route (Leonard, 1993). Stew pursued a college education in hopes that it would prepare him to one day run the dairy. After Stew's graduation from college, his father passed away and Stew took over the dairy.

In the late 1960s, the state of Connecticut decided to build a highway through the land used for the dairy. Furthermore, the proliferation of supermarkets and refrigerators had made the cost of running a milk delivery route prohibitive. So Stew decided to move and start a new store. In 1968 the Small Business Administration loaned Stew $500,000, the largest loan granted to that date, to start a dairy store in Norwalk, Connecticut. Leonard and his wife, Marianne, knew they were risking their net worth of $100,000, but on the basis of his experience selling dairy products since he was a child, he was convinced his ideas would work. He expected to be competitive with other area stores by stocking mostly his own products in a specialized dairy store (Fishman, 1985).

Stew Leonard and his wife formed a partnership. He refused to form a corporation because he wanted to be liable for any losses (Fishman, 1985). Before opening, he visited many food stores across the country gathering information on what worked and what did not (Slater, 1991). During one visit he met a farmer who was bottling and selling milk on the premises (Fishman, 1985). Leonard decided his store would do the same. Calculating the cost of the SBA loan and other credit, Leonard estimated he needed to sell $20,000 a week to survive. Through long hours and attention to detail, Leonard realized $21,850 in his first week in business. By mid-week he was so optimistic about reaching the $20,000 mark that he took his wife on a trip to Grenada in the Caribbean.

The following week, an incident occurred that was to become the foundation of the Stew Leonard management philosophy. The incident began when a customer complained that the eggnog she recently purchased was sour. Stew tasted the eggnog and concluded that the customer was wrong. He told her so and added, "We sold over 300 half-gallons of eggnog this week, and you're the only one who's complained." The customer angrily left the store and stated she would never come back (Leonard, 1987). Later that evening Leonard could not get the scene out of his mind. Upon reflection, he acknowledged that not only had he failed to empathize with the customer, but he had ignored the potential repercussions of the complaint. His wife, Marianne, said that her husband had just lost a valuable customer over a $.99 carton of eggnog. This was a customer who may have later spend thousands of dollars on groceries, money that Stew Leonard's dairy store would now never see. This mistake led Stew Leonard to a mission statement for his business:

Rule 1: The customer is always right!
Rule 2: If the customer is ever wrong, reread Rule 1!

These rules, which were engraved on a 6,000-pound boulder and placed at the entrance of the store, became the credo upon which Stew Leonard built his business (Leonard, 1987). By the end of the 1980s, the store had grown from two cash registers, 6,000 square feet, and $20,000 a week in sales to a retail grocery with more than 2 dozen registers, 37,000 square feet, and annual sales in excess of $100 million (Penzer, 1991). By 1991, a second store had been opened on a 40-acre complex in Danbury, Connecticut. Although the mission statement formed the backbone of the strategy which enabled the organization to expand 27 times in roughly 20 years, Stew Leonard implemented additional strategies to achieve his business's remarkable growth—a growth so remarkable that Stew Leonard's did more business per square foot than any business of any kind in the world (Raphel, 1989).

Marketing and Customer Relations

Initially, Stew Leonard stocked his dairy store with just under a dozen items. Eventually, the store topped out at 800 items (the typical supermarket stocked 15,000). Stew differentiated his store by eliminating the middleman and passing the savings on to his customers (Suters, 1991).

Stew also sold the idea of freshness. Customers knew they could count on the freshest produce, milk, cheese, meats, and baked goods. A glass-enclosed milk processing plant was located in the center of the store, where customers could see their milk being produced (Fishman, 1985). Beth Leonard, Stew's daughter, ran the bakery which filled the store with the aroma of croissants, cookies, and muffins (Adams, 1991). Free samples and recipes were always made available to customers.

To further distinguish itself from other food stores, Stew Leonard's added entertainment to the marketing mix (Englander, 1989). A petting zoo with barnyard animals was placed in the parking lot, encouraging parents to bring children. Animated singing animals filled the store and employees roamed the aisles in cow, chicken, and duck costumes (Leonard, 1993). All of this was part of Leonard's emphasis on making grocery shopping an enjoyable experience (Slater, 1991).

Building on the mission statement, *The Customer is Always Right*, Stew Leonard's adopted other customer service systems. A liberal return policy provided internal checks and balances which required employees to constantly monitor quality. Even if a Stew Leonard "team member" knew that a customer was returning an item the store did not sell, the customer got his or her money back (Adams, 1991). Stew once said:

Our attitude is that everybody's honest. If we occasionally run into someone who isn't, we just take it on the chin. But the important point is that 999 out of 1,000 customers are honest. We simply refuse to let one dishonest customer determine how we are going to treat the other 999.
(Stew Leonard, *Management Review*, October 1987)

Stew Leonard's exhibited a special commitment to following up on customers' comments. A suggestion box was filled to capacity each day (Englander, 1989). By 11:00 a.m. each morning, all the complaints and suggestions were typed and submitted to the appropriate department. Mangers held weekly meetings to report what had been done with the customers' suggestions.

Customer feedback was also gathered through in-store focus groups. Each month 10 specially selected customers were given $20 worth of store gift certificates in return for which they met with store managers and offered suggestions on what items should be stocked and how items should be displayed (Bennett, 1992).

There were other small acts of kindness, as well. For example, free ice cream cones were given randomly to customers, customers' pictures with Stew Leonard's shopping bags were posted near the entrance, and elderly customers were given free rides to the dairy in a bus provided by the store (Englander, 1989; Feldman, 1989). By conducting business in this manner, Stew Leonard's earned tremendous customer trust and loyalty over the years (Hill, 1993).

Employee Relations

Employees, referred to as team members, were well-trained in customer relations. Many employees were also Leonard family members.

The large number of family members working for the company contributed to the company's culture. Of the company's 1200+ employees, 25 percent had worked at Stew Leonard's for at least five years and over half had family as co-workers (Leonard, 1993). Stew believed in nepotism (*Review of Business*, 1991). He was an ardent supporter of employing relatives as team members; he believed they worked much harder because the presence of a relative was like another boss watching over them (Fishman, 1985).

Team members understood that a job at Stew Leonard's required that they provide superior customer service (Weinstein, 1993). The company's two stores were open 364 days a year, and team members were required to work during various times of the day and on holidays. Also, team members were expected to be well groomed and display positive attitudes. As a result of Stew's hiring practices, the store had a 60 percent turnover rate—much better than the supermarket industry average of 82 percent (Weinstein, 1993).

Curiosity about Stew Leonard's training and customer relations methods ran strong among business firms. Inquiries from companies like Kraft, Citibank, and IBM led to the creation of Stew Leonard University by Stew's daughter, Jill (Adams, 1991). "Stew U" was a four-hour seminar intended to give insight into Stew Leonard's operation. Throughout the seminar, attendees were taught methods of how to handle dissatisfied customers, appropriate behaviors of team members, and management tips for motivating team members (Adams, 1991).

Stew Leonard's offered its employees a variety of incentive programs to heighten the level of customer service, such as:

1. A monthly "One Idea Club," where 10 team members and a department manager went to other supermarkets and on the basis of that experience made suggestions for improving store departments (Englander, 1989).

2. A "Superstar of the Month," nominated by co-workers and department managers for achievement of safety, cleanliness, and attendance. Winners had their photographs posted in the store and were awarded $100 (Bolger, 1988; Englander, 1989).

3. "Ladders of Success" charts placed near checkout lanes demonstrating team members' career progression. Stew Leonard's company fully supported a promotion-from-within policy (Bolger, 1988; Englander, 1989).

4. Retail gift certificates valued up to $500 if team members' ideas were implemented (Bolger, 1988).

5. Fifty dollar awards to team members who referred new hires (Bolger, 1988).

6. An ABCD (Above and Beyond the Call of Duty) award—a polo shirt embroidered with "ABCD Award"—to employees who performed beyond the duties of their jobs (Bolger, 1988).

7. A "Hall of Fame," which consisted of workers who performed admirably during their careers (Bolger, 1988).

8. An Outstanding Performance Award given to three high achievers at the annual Christmas party (Englander, 1989).

9. A recreation program, supplemented by employee vending machine funds, providing outings and trips to workers at discount rates (Englander, 1989).

10. A "Stew's News" company newsletter—called the ultimate company newsletter by *Inc.* magazine—filled with information about bonus plans, contests, and customer comments. Births, parties, anniversaries, illnesses, and organization successes were included (Adams, 1991).

11. A "Name Game" reward for cashiers who thanked customers by name. Customers dropped cashiers' names in a box, and at the end of each week, the three cashiers who thanked the most customers by name received $30 (Penzer, 1991).

These activities were used by Stew Leonard Dairy to focus team members on the mission statement. Leonard knew everybody was motivated by different things. Occasionally, Stew would place extra dollars in pay envelopes along with thank-you notes (which he wrote hundreds of every year) for employees who performed exceptionally well (Penzer, 1991). Impromptu inducements were often granted to team members. It was not uncommon for Stew Leonard or the other managers to hand out lunch or dinner certificates for special performance such as coming in on a day off (Penzer, 1991).

The Organization

Stew Leonard's overall company goal—customer satisfaction—determined the design of the organization. It was a simple, relatively informal structure. Because the business was a partnership, there was no board of directors or shareholders. There were also no required annual reports or meetings. The partners gained and lost in proportion to the success of the business, and were personally liable for financial obligations. The partnership paid no taxes as an entity; rather, Stew and Marianne were taxed directly for their portion of the business' income.

All four of Stew Leonard's children were actively involved in the business and held corporate titles. Stew Jr., the oldest, was President. He originally planned on working for an accounting firm after earning his M.B.A. at UCLA, but became involved in every detail of the company. Tom managed the Danbury store which opened in the fall of 1991. Beth, after obtaining her masters degree in French and working for a croissant distributor, originated and managed the high volume in-store bakery (Fishman, 1985). Jill Leonard was the Vice President of Human Resources (Weinstein, 1993). And, of course, Marianne, Stew's Sr.'s wife, continued to provide support as she had from the beginning.

Marianne's brothers Frank H. Guthman and Stephen F. Guthman served as Executive Vice President and Vice President of Finance, respectively (Pastore, 1993). Most company decisions were made by the family. However, lower-level employees were allowed a great deal of discretion, especially in the area of customer service.

The company preferred "in-house" control practices. Customers were asked to pay cash for gift certificates and were encouraged to use cash for other purchases (Levy, 1993). Stew did not make much use of outside consultants in his business. He preferred using the in-house customer focus groups for business advice. Being privately held, the company did not publicly reveal its profits (Bolger, 1988). Profits, however, were significant enough to fund the store's numerous expansions as well as a large second home for Stew and his children. The second home, located in St. Maarten in the Caribbean, was named "Carpe Diem" (Latin for "seize the day") (Steinberg, 1993).

As the business grew from a small dairy to super retailer to world's largest dairy store, the Stew Leonard's story was one of customer satisfaction, employee development, and tremendous growth. Over the years the store received numerous awards and accolades. For example:

- An award for entrepreneurial excellence from President Ronald Reagan

- The Connecticut Small Business Advocate of the Year Award

- A citation from the *Guinness Book of World Records* for doing more business per square foot than any store of any kind in the world

In addition, a certified in-house Dale Carnegie training school, attended by *Fortune* 500 firms, was operated in conjunction with Stew Leonard University. In 1991, Stew Leonard's Dairy was nominated for the Malcolm Baldridge National Quality Award in the service category in 1991, and might have become the first retail organization ever to win the award had not the company decided to withdraw from the competition.

In addition to all the other awards, a 1993 issue of *Chief Information Officer (CIO)*, a publication for data processing and computer programming professionals, named Stew Leonard's as one of the 21 recipients of their customer service award (Pastore, 1993). Criteria for winning this award included a company's successful integration of management information systems and customer service. The store was commended for its ability in tracking sales and using point-of-sale data. The sophisticated system also helped managers anticipate heavy traffic periods so that cash registers could be staffed adequately and product shortages avoided.

Trouble Looms

On August 25, 1991, Stew Leonard Sr. was questioned by a Norwalk, Connecticut, reporter about a visit from the Criminal Investigation Division of the Internal Revenue Service. On August 9, 1991, the IRS raided the homes of several company officers, seizing boxes of records and cash (Kanner, 1993). Stew Leonard said that the raid "came out of the blue" and that he was "as surprised as anyone else" (Heller,

1991). But U.S. customs agents had stopped him back in June of 1991 when, with $80,000 in cash, he boarded a flight to St. Maarten in the Caribbean (Kanner, 1993). Leonard had not filled out the forms required for taking large sums of money out of the country, and this eventually led to the IRS confiscation of store records (Levy, 1993). Nevertheless, Leonard maintained that he did not know what prompted the IRS agents to enter the store with a search warrant on August 9th (IRS probing records, 1991).

Leonard and his son, Tom, manager of the Danbury store, told the news reporters and the public that the IRS was simply conducting a routine audit. However, the Criminal Investigation Division of the IRS did not conduct "audits," which involved possible civil violations; it investigated possible criminal violations of internal revenue laws (Heller, 1991).

Most people in the community reacted with disbelief to news of the investigation. Many of Stew Leonard's customers found it impossible to believe that any wrongdoing had taken place, regarding the Leonard family as a pillar of honesty in the community. Ironically, it was Stew Leonard's sophisticated computer system that gave the IRS the primary evidence it needed to charge Leonard and other executives with tax evasion.

The Guilty Plea

On July 22, 1993, the U.S. Department of Justice announced that Stewart J. Leonard Sr., Frank H. Guthman, Stephen F. Guthman, and company general manager Tiberio (Barry) Belardinelli had pleaded guilty in federal court to federal tax conspiracy charges. The four defendants admitted that between 1981 and August 9, 1991, they had defrauded the IRS by skimming more than $17 million from Stew Leonard's Dairy in Norwalk, Connecticut. It had taken the IRS almost two years to determine the full extent of the tax evasion scheme. Along with paper records and large sums of cash, the IRS found other items indicating the executives' aversion to paying taxes (Steinberg, 1993).

According to the IRS, Stew Leonard had avoided $6.7 million in taxes between 1981 and 1991 by not reporting $17 million in sales during that period (Wamae, 1993). They also reported that it was the largest computer-driven criminal tax evasion case in United States history, calling the fraud a crime of the twenty-first century (Levy, 1993).

Stew Leonard Jr., president of the Norwalk store, was cited as having knowledge of the tax conspiracy (Kanner, 1993). A *New York Times* article reported that part of the plea bargain arrangement was that no charges would be brought against Stew Jr. (Steinberg, 1993). Observers speculated that the IRS may have given Stew Jr. immunity in order to persuade his father to plead guilty. According to the IRS, Stew Sr. was initially turned in by an employee who had recently been fired (Berman, 1996).

The "Equity Program"—Skimming

In Frank Guthman's basement, in a hollowed-out edition of the 1982 *New England Business Directory*, the Criminal Investigation Division of the IRS discovered a computer program that the executives had named "Equity" (Ingram, 1993). Apparently, the program had been developed in the latter part of 1981 by Jeffrey Pirhalla, Stew

Leonard's computer programmer. Frank Guthman had instructed the programmer to create the program in order to reduce sales data stored on Stew Leonard's computer. Frank Guthman had also directed Pirhalla to write the program so that it would reduce Stew Leonard's financial and bank deposit data.

Witnesses in the court proceedings testified that Stew Leonard Sr. and the other executives were informed of the use of this tax evasion tool. In general, the program enabled the defendants to enter a dollar figure that matched a cash receipt withdrawal for the day. Typical cash diversions were $10,000 to $15,000 per day. Furthermore, the program allowed the company to keep dual books that generated accounting spreadsheets disclosing "actual" and "reported" sales. To appease previous IRS auditors, Stew Leonard's had provided "reported" sales data while the actual sales were utilized only for store operations.

As part of the scheme, Belardinelli and the Guthmans set up a system that transferred Universal Product Code (UPC) scanner information from the cash registers to two different computer record systems. One set of records systematically understated sales by a predetermined amount. Belardinelli destroyed the tapes with the "real" sales data generated daily from the cash registers. Then he secretly removed cash from bank deposit bags in his office, and the skimmed cash was hidden in "vaults" and "fireplaces" constructed specifically for the execution of this crime. Correspondingly, investigators identified personal and partnership tax forms that were falsely submitted to the IRS.

Shortweighting

To make matters worse, on July 23, 1993, a day after the tax evasion announcement, the Connecticut State Consumer Products Department charged Stew Leonard's with violating state labeling laws (Baron, 1993). A series of inspections involving a check of 2,658 products in the Norwalk store revealed that 730 of the products checked weighed less than what the label stated—they were "shortweighted"—and 500 items carried no labels or were improperly labeled (Tosh, 1993). The Consumer Products Commissioner reported that this rejection rate, 46.3 percent, was much greater than the statewide average of 5 percent (Ingram, 1993).

Some industry experts believed that shortweighting charges were not fair and were merely the bureaucratic attempt of a vengeful state to embarrass the family (O'Neill, 1996). They maintained that store scales were accurate and that the variance noted by investigators was not atypical of other stores. Stew Jr. argued that because the company sold so many handpacked and precooked items, product weight could not always be perfectly accurate (Kanner, 1993; Zemke, 1993).

Each of the 1,230 violations was subject to a $500 maximum fine (Barron, 1993). Stew Leonard's had already been assessed fines of $10,500 for similar violations at the Danbury store. The company planned to appeal the Danbury store fines as well as the potentially costly fines on the alleged 1,230 violations (Barron, 1993; Zwiebach, 1993).

The Aftermath

News of the crime drew harsh criticism from industry professionals and the media, but caused only a minor decline in sales (Zwiebach, 1993). Some customers condemned the elder Leonard and the store for being hypocritical (Ingram, 1993). The majority of Stew Leonard's clientele was angrier about the shortweighting than the tax evasion. Indeed, many people believed that the tax fraud was a private rather than a business issue (Ingram, 1993). Several shoppers even expressed sympathy for Leonard and his family and pledged they would continue to support the company (Crispens, 1993). As had happened early in the investigation, in 1991, some community members thought the IRS was overreacting, even harassing the company. One customer stated that it was okay for the store to cheat the government because everybody else does it (Crispens, 1993). *The Danbury News Times* polled 5,323 of its readers and 4,556 said they would continue to shop at Stew Leonard's (Kanner, 1993). Employees of Stew Leonard', including Leonard Jr., stated that business was good and that they were 100 percent behind the fallen founder (Ingram, 1993).

Stew Leonard was sentenced to 52 months in prison and ordered to pay $15 million in back taxes, penalties, and interest (IRS interview, 1995). He was also fined $850,000 for court and probation costs, but this fine was later reduced to $650,000 by a federal appeals court judge (Silvers, 1994). The resulting $650,000 was still much larger than the usual $100,000 fine for tax fraud, because Leonard had profited so greatly from the scheme (Silvers, 1994). Leonard's brothers-in-law, Frank H. Guthman and Stephen F. Guthman, were sentenced to 41-month and 18-month prison terms, respectively (Wamae, 1993). Frank Guthman's plea agreement provided that he pay $335,000 in tax, penalties, and interest. Stephen Guthman was not fined. Belardinelli received no prison sentence but was fined $15,000 and put on probation for two years (Wamae, 1993).

Leonard gave no reason for the crime he committed, although he did apologize to customers and employees. At one point, the Leonards insinuated that the tax scheme had been suggested by their lawyer (now deceased) as a way to raise capital for expansion (Kanner, 1993). Later, in 1994, after reflecting on the crisis while in prison, Leonard commented that "Somehow, I just lost sight of my core values" (Silvers, 1994). After the incident, the company continued to grow, and was even planning to open a third store. Stew Leonard was scheduled to be released from a Schuylkill, Pennsylvania prison in December 1997 (Suters, 1995; Berman, 1996).

Damage Control

Once Stew Sr. was in prison, Stew Jr. had to step up and fill the leadership void. Stew Jr. began running the Norwalk store, which was still in his mother's name. Stew Jr., Tom, and their sisters, Jill and Beth, owned and operated the new Danbury store (Berman, 1996). They were now faced with monumental decisions regarding damage control. How would they be able to maintain the business? How could they regain goodwill and customer confidence? How could they overcome the stigma associated with skimming and shortweighting? Would they be able to get along without Stew Sr.? What steps could they take to ensure that wrongdoing like this wouldn't happen again? How could they restore the company's reputation?

There were other worries as well. Stew Sr.'s health was in question. Prior to entering prison, he had to have a heart valve and hip replaced (Farrelly, 1993).

To make matters worse, in early 1996, it was reported that Tom was under a grand jury investigation for skimming cash from store vending machines (Berman, 1996). According to investigators, Tom had been skimming cash from pop machines, hot dog vendors, and other vending locations in the store. Stew Jr. would almost certainly be called to testify before the grand jury.

Stew Jr. had been responsible for withdrawing from the Baldridge Award competition in 1991, a move he had made only because of the criminal investigations (O'Neill, 1996). Now he wondered if he could put the store back into contention for the prestigious award.

Young Stew Jr. knew he must direct his attention immediately to the challenges facing him. He knew his father would want to return to store management and that it was his mission to pave the way. He pondered how he would be able to regain customers' faith and redeem the Leonard family name.

References

Adams, M. "The udder delights of Stew U." *Successful Meetings*, 403, March 1991: 59–61.

Barron, J. "Stew Leonard's Is Cited for Shorting Customers." *The New York Times*, July 24, 1993: L24.

Bennett, S. "What Shoppers Want." *Progressive Grocer*, 71(10), October 1992: 73–78.

Berman, P. "Like Father, Like Son." *Forbes*, May 20, 1996: 44–45.

Bolger, B. "Stew Leonard: Unconventional Wisdom." *Incentive*, 162(11), November 1988: 36–40.

Crispens, J. "The Reaction from Shoppers: Luke-Warm to Mildly Stewed." *Supermarket News*, Aug. 2, 1993: 42.

Englander, T. "Stew Leonard's: In-store Disneyland." *Incentive*, 163(1), January 1989: 26–30.

Farrelly, P. T. Jr. "Leonard to Begin Sentence Today at Medical Facility." *The Hour*, Norwalk, CT, Nov. 29, 1993: 1–2.

Feldman, D. "Companies Aim to Please." *Management Review*, 78(5), May 1989: 8–9.

Fishman, Davis K. *Stew Leonard's—The Disney World of Supermarkets*, Curtis Brown Publishers, New York, Mar. 11, 1985.

Heller, J. "At Stew Leonard's Business as Usual Despite IRS Audit." *The Fairpress* (Norwalk, weekly edition), sec. CG, Aug. 15, 1991: 54.

Hill, J. M. "Supermarkets Can Beat Warehouse Clubs, But Not on Price Alone." *Brandweek*, 34(1), January 1993: 25.

"IRS Crime Unit Probing Records." *The Advocate* (Stamford, CT), Aug. 22, 1991.

IRS. Telephone interview with Larry Marini, state investigator, Criminal Investigation Division, Connecticut, March 1995.

Ingram, B. "Stew, We Hardly Knew Ye." *Supermarket Business*, September 1993: 157–158.

Kanner, B. "Spilled Milk." *New York*, 26(42), Oct. 25, 1993: 68–74.

Leonard, S. "Love That Customer!" *Management Review*, 76(10), October 1987: 36–39.

Leonard, S. Jr. "The Customer Is Always Right." *Executive Excellence*, 10(8), 1993: 16–17.

Levy, C. J. "Store Founder Pleads Guilty in Fraud." *The New York Times*, July 23, 1993: B1, B4.

O'Neill, H. Telephone interview with consultant who worked with Stew Leonard's in making the Baldridge Award application, August 1996.

Pastore, R. "A Virtual Shopping Spree." *CIO*, 6, August, 1993: 70–74.

Penzer, E. "Secrets from the Supermarket." *Incentive*, 165(8), August 1991: 67–69.

Raphel, M. "Confidence Is Number One." *Direct Marketing*, 52(5), September 1989: 30, 32.

Silvers, S. 1994, October 27. "Judge Reduces Stew's Fine." *Connecticut Post*, A1, A13.

Slater, Les. Interview in *Review of Business*, 13, Summer/Fall 1991: 10–12.

Steinberg, J. "Papers Show Greed Calculation and Betrayal in Stew Leonard Case." *The New York Times*, Oct. 22, 1993.

Stew Leonard's Fact Sheet, 100 Westport Avenue, Norwalk, CT.

Suters, E. T. "Stew Leonard: Soul of a Leader." *Executive Excellence*, 8(6), June 1991: 13–14.

Suters, E. Telephone interview, April 1995. Author, *The Unnatural Act of Management*.

Tosh, M. "Mislabeling Charge May Be More Taxing." *Supermarket News*, Aug. 2, 1993: 43.

Wamae, C. H. "Leonard Checks in at Federal Hospital." *Connecticut Post*, Nov. 30, 1993: A7.

Weinstein, S. "How to Hire the Best." *Progressive Grocer*, 72(7), July 1993: 119–122.

Zemke, R. "Piling On." *Training*, 30(10), October 1993: 10.

Zwiebach, E. "Stew Leonard's Reports Sales Dip." *Supermarket News*, Aug. 2, 1993: 42–43.

III

Growth Options for Strategic Impact

9

Corporate Entrepreneurship: Developing Internal Innovation

Key Topics

- **Entrepreneurial Thinking**

- **Defining the Concept**

- **Elements of a Corporate Intrapreneuring Strategy**

- **A Continuum of Intrapreneurial Activity**

- **Models of Corporate Entrepreneurship (Intrapreneurship)**

Entrepreneurial Thinking

Progress in understanding the process of corporate entrepreneurship may help the development of new managerial approaches and innovative administrative arrangements to facilitate the collaboration between entrepreneurial individuals and the organizations in which they are willing to exert their entrepreneurship.[1]

The past two decades have seen corporate strategies focused more heavily on innovation. This new emphasis on entrepreneurial thinking developed during the entrepreneurial economy of the 1980s. Peter Drucker (1984), the renowned management expert, has described four major developments that explain the emergence of this economy. First, the rapid evolution of knowledge and technology has promoted the use of high-tech entrepreneurial start-ups. Second, demographic trends such as double-income families, continuing education for adults, and the aging population have fueled the proliferation of newly developing ventures. Third, the venture capital market has become an effective funding mechanism for entrepreneurial ventures. Fourth, American industry has begun to learn how to manage entrepreneurship.

The contemporary thrust in entrepreneurship as the major force in American business has led to a desire to foster this type of activity *inside* enterprises. Although some researchers have concluded that entrepreneurship and bureaucracies are mutually exclusive and cannot coexist, others have described entrepreneurial ventures within the enterprise framework. Successful corporate ventures have been used in many different companies, including 3M, IBM, Hewlett-Packard, AT&T, General Electric, and Polaroid. Today, a wealth of popular business literature describes a new "corporate revolution," which is attributable to the infusion referred to as **corporate entrepreneurship** or **intrapreneurship**.[2]

In 1985, Gifford Pinchott coined the term *intrapreneurship* to describe entrepreneurial activity inside the corporation where individuals (intrapreneurs) "champion" new ideas from development to complete profitable reality.[3] Other authors have expanded this definition to include sanctions and resource commitments for the purpose of innovative results. On the surface, this concept may appear straightforward. Nevertheless, a number of authors have concluded that intrapreneurship may take several forms. One researcher, Hans Schollhammer, proposed five broad types of internal entrepreneurship: administrative, opportunistic, imitative, acquisitive, and incubative.[4] Incubative entrepreneurship most closely resembles the intrapreneurial model, because it refers to the creation of semi-autonomous units within the existing organization for the purposes of sensing external and internal innovative developments; screening and assessing new-venture opportunities; and initiating and nurturing new-venture developments.

Researcher Karl Vesper identified three major types of corporate venturing: new strategic direction, initiative from below, and autonomous business creation.[5] Vesper

[1] Robert A. Burgelman, "Designs for Corporate Entrepreneurship," *California Management Review* (1984): 154-166.

[2] Peter F. Drucker, "Our Entrepreneurial Economy," *Harvard Business Review* (Jan.–Feb. 1984): 59–64. See also Donald F. Kuratko and Richard M. Hodgetts, *Entrepreneurship: A Contemporary Approach*, 5th ed. (Fort Worth, TX: Harcourt College Publishers, 2001).

[3] Gifford Pinchott, *Intrapreneuring* (New York: Harper & Row, 1985).

[4] Hans Schollhammer, "Internal Corporate Entrepreneurship." In C. Kent, D. Sexton, and K. Vesper, eds., *Encyclopedia of Entrepreneurship*, (Englewood Cliffs, NJ: Prentice-Hall, 1982).

[5] Karl H. Vesper, "Three Faces of Corporate Entrepreneurship: A Pilot Study." In *Frontiers of Entrepreneurship Research* (Wellesley, MA: Babson College, 1984): 294–320.

believed that corporate venturing could be any one of these individual types, as well as any or all possible combinations of them. Similar to Schollhammer's incubative form, the "initiative from below" approach, where an employee undertakes something new (that is, an innovation), best represents the type of corporate entrepreneuring activity that has become recognized as intrapreneurship. While all of these forms of intrapreneuring are considered important, the factors that are essential in developing an entrepreneurial environment are the focus of this chapter. If an organization's atmosphere does not support innovative efforts, then intrapreneuring (in any form) will probably not occur.

Over the past few years, there has been a growing interest in intrapreneurship (corporate entrepreneurship) as a way for corporations to enhance their employees' innovative abilities and, at the same time, increase corporate success through the potential creation of new corporate ventures. The creation of corporate entrepreneurial activity can prove difficult, however, because it involves radically changing traditional forms of internal organizational behavior and structure.

The desire to pursue corporate entrepreneurship has arisen from a variety of pressing problems, including the following:

- Required changes, innovations, and improvements in the marketplace to avoid stagnation and decline

- Perceived weaknesses in the traditional methods of corporate management

- The turnover of innovative-minded employees who are disenchanted with bureaucratic organizations.

The loss of talented employees is intensified by entrepreneurship's new appeal as a legitimate career and the increased ability (and willingness) of the venture capital industry (as well as informal capitalists) to finance more new ventures.

Continuous innovation (in terms of products, processes, and administrative routines and structures) and an ability to compete effectively in international markets are among the skills that are expected to increasingly influence corporate performance in the twenty-first century's global economy. Corporate entrepreneurship is seen as a process that can facilitate firms' efforts to innovate constantly and cope effectively with the global economy's competitive realities, which companies inevitably encounter when competing in international markets. Thus entrepreneurial attitudes and behaviors are necessary for firms of all sizes to prosper and flourish in competitive environments.[6]

The pursuit of corporate entrepreneuring as a strategy to counter these problems, however, creates a newer and potentially more complex set of challenges on both a practical and a theoretical level. On a practical level, organizations need guidelines to direct or redirect their resources toward establishing effective intrapreneuring strategies. On a theoretical level, researchers must continually reassess the components or dimensions that predict, explain, and shape the environment in which corporate entrepreneuring flourishes. Recently, several studies have focused on the factors contributing to or enhancing the establishment of corporate venturing. This chapter presents an overview

---

[6]Bruce R. Barringer and Alan C. Bluedorn, "Corporate Entrepreneurship and Strategic Management," *Strategic Management Journal*, 20 (1999): 421–444. See also Jeffrey G. Covin and Morgan P. Miles, "Corporate Entrepreneurship and the Pursuit of Competitive Advantage," *Entrepreneurship Theory and Practice* (March 1999): 47–64.

of the concept of intrapreneurship from an organizational perspective by outlining recommended steps to implement a strategy of corporate entrepreneurship based on organizational factors that would encourage the development of innovative-minded employees.

Defining the Concept

Operational definitions of corporate entrepreneurship have evolved over the last 30 years through many scholars' work. For example, one researcher noted that corporate innovation is a very broad concept that includes the generation, development, and implementation of new ideas or behaviors. An innovation can be a new product or service, an administrative system, or a new plan or program pertaining to organizational members.[7] In this context, corporate entrepreneurship centers on reenergizing and enhancing the firm's ability to acquire innovative skills and capabilities.

Researcher Shaker A. Zahra observed that "corporate entrepreneurship may be formal or informal activities aimed at creating new businesses in established companies through product and process innovations and market developments. These activities may take place at the corporate, division (business), functional, or project levels, with the unifying objective of improving a company's competitive position and financial performance."[8] William D. Guth and Ari Ginsberg have stressed that corporate entrepreneurship encompasses two major types of phenomena: new-venture creation without existing organizations and the transformation of organizations through strategic renewal.[9]

Following a thorough analysis of the entrepreneurship construct and its dimensions, recent research has defined corporate entrepreneurship as a process whereby an individual or a group of individuals, in association with an existing organization, creates a new organization or instigates renewal or innovation within the organization. Thus strategic renewal (organizational renewal involving major strategic and/or structural changes), innovation (the introduction of something new to the marketplace), and corporate venturing (corporate entrepreneurial efforts that lead to the creation of new business organizations within the corporate organization) are all important and legitimate parts of the corporate entrepreneurship process.[10]

Elements of a Corporate Intrapreneuring Strategy

What conditions or steps must be followed for a corporate intrapreneuring program to succeed? The flowchart in Figure 9.1 outlines the prescribed steps. These steps, in turn, are described in the following sections.

---

[7]Fariborz Damanpour, "Organizational Innovation: A Meta-analysis of Determinant and Moderators," *Academy of Management Journal*, 34 (1991): 355–390.

[8]Shaker A. Zahra, "Predictors and Financial Outcomes of Corporate Entrepreneurship: An Exploratory Study," *Journal of Business Venturing* 6 (1991): 259–286.

[9]William D. Guth and Ari Ginsberg, "Corporate Entrepreneurship," *Strategic Management Journal*, 11 (1990): 5–15.

[10]Pramodita Sharma and James J. Chrisman, "Toward a Reconciliation of the Definitional Issues in the Field of Corporate Entrepreneurship," *Entrepreneurship Theory and Practice* (Spring 1999): 11–28.

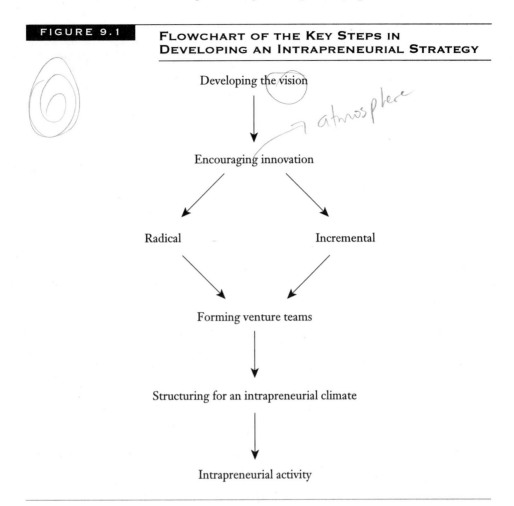

FIGURE 9.1

FLOWCHART OF THE KEY STEPS IN DEVELOPING AN INTRAPRENEURIAL STRATEGY

Developing the Vision

The first step in planning an intrapreneurship strategy for the enterprise is sharing the vision of innovation that the corporate leaders wish to achieve. As corporate entrepreneuring results from the creative talents of people within the organization, employees need to know about and understand this vision. The importance of a shared vision is therefore a critical element for a strategy that seeks high achievement. Developing this shared vision requires identification of specific objectives for corporate entrepreneuring strategies and the programs needed to achieve those objectives. Author and researcher Rosabeth Moss Kanter has described three major objectives and their respective programs designed for venture development within companies (Table 9.1).[11]

---

[11]Rosabeth M. Kanter, "Supporting Innovation and Venture Development in Established Companies," *Journal of Business Venturing* (Winter 1985): 47–60.

TABLE 9.1	OBJECTIVES AND PROGRAMS FOR INTERNAL VENTURE DEVELOPMENT

Objectives	Programs
Make sure that the current system, structures, and practices do not present insurmountable roadblocks to the flexibility and fast action needed for innovation.	Reduce unnecessary bureaucracy and encourage communication across departments and functions.
Provide the incentives and tools for entrepreneurial projects.	Use internal "venture capital" and special project budgets. (This resource has been termed *intracapital* to signify a special fund for intrapreneurial projects.) Allow discretionary time for projects (sometimes referred to as "bootlegging" time).
Seek synergies across business areas so that new opportunities are discovered in new combinations.	Encourage joint projects and ventures among divisions, departments, and companies. Allow and encourage employees to discuss and brainstorm new ideas.

SOURCE: Adapted by permission of the publisher from Rosabeth Moss Kanter, "Supporting Innovation and Venture Development in Established Companies," *Journal of Business Venturing* (Winter 1985): 56–59. Copyright © 1985 by Elsevier Science Publishing Co., Inc.

Encouraging Innovation

The next step for a corporation seeking to establish an intrapreneurial strategy is to encourage innovation among employees as the key element in its strategy. This element is a critical component of contemporary competitive strategies. Innovation has been described as chaotic and unplanned by some authors; other researchers insist it is a systematic discipline. Both positions can be true depending on the nature of the innovation. One way to understand this concept is to recognize two types of innovation—radical and incremental.[12]

Radical innovation represents unprecedented breakthroughs (for example, personal computers, Post-it Notes, disposable diapers, and overnight mail delivery). These innovations take experimentation and determined vision that are not necessarily managed, but *must* be recognized and nurtured. **Incremental innovation**, on the other hand, refers to the systematic evolution of a product or service into newer or larger markets. Examples include microwave popcorn, popcorn used for packaging (to replace styrofoam), and frozen yogurt. Many times incremental innovation will take over after radical innovation introduces a breakthrough. A corporation's traditional functional areas, such as marketing, financing, and so forth, as well as its formal systems can help implement incremental innovation. (See Table 9.2).

Both types of innovation require vision and support.[13] This support, in turn, requires different steps for effective development. For example, it has been widely

---

[12]Harry S. Dent, Jr., "Reinventing Corporate Innovation," *Small Business Reports* (June 1990): 31–42.

[13]Dean M. Schroeder, "A Dynamic Perspective on the Impact of Process Innovation Upon Competitive Strategies," *Strategic Management Journal* 2 (1990): 25–41.

TABLE 9.2	CHARACTERISTICS OF RADICAL VERSUS INCREMENTAL INNOVATION

Radical	**Incremental**
Stimulate through challenges and puzzles	Have flexible funds for opportunities that arise
Remove budgetary and deadline constraints when possible	Reward with freedom and capital for new projects and interests
Encourage technical education and exposure to customers	Set systematic goals and deadlines
Allow technical sharing and brainstorming sessions	Stimulate through competitive pressures
Give personal attention—develop relationships of trust	Encourage technical education and exposure to customers
Encourage praise from outside parties	Hold weekly meetings that include key management and marketing staff
	Delegate more responsibility
	Set clear financial rewards for meeting goals and deadlines

SOURCE: Adapted from Harry S. Dent, Jr., "Growth through New Product Development," *Small Business Reports* (Nov. 1990): 36.

recognized that entrepreneurial activity needs a champion—a person with a vision and the ability to share it. In addition, both types of innovation require top management to educate employees about innovation and entrepreneurship—a concept known as **top management support.**

Encouraging innovation requires a willingness to not only tolerate failure, but also to learn from it. For example, one of the founders of 3M, Francis G. Oakie, had an idea to replace razor blades with sandpaper. He believed that men could rub sandpaper on their face rather than use a sharp razor. He was wrong and the idea failed, but his concept evolved until he developed a waterproof sandpaper for the auto industry, a blockbuster success!

In this way, 3M's philosophy of innovation was born. According to the company, innovation is a numbers game; the more ideas you have, the better your chance for a successful innovation. In other words, to master innovation you must learn to tolerate failure. This philosophy has paid off for 3M. Antistatic videotape, translucent dental braces, synthetic ligaments for knee surgery, heavy-duty reflective sheeting for construction signs, and, of course, Post-it Notes are just some of the great innovations developed at 3M. Overall, the company has a catalog of 60,000 products that has contributed to more than $10.6 billion in sales.[14]

Today, 3M follows a set of innovative rules that encourage employees to foster ideas. The key rules include the following:

---

[14]See Russell Mitchell, "Masters of Innovation," *Business Week* (April 10, 1989): 58–63.

- *Don't kill a project.* If an idea can't find a home in one of 3M's divisions, a staffer can devote 15 percent of his or her time to prove it is workable. For those who need seed money, as many as 90 Genesis grants of $50,000 are awarded each year.

- *Tolerate failure.* By encouraging plenty of experimentation and risk taking, the company has more chances for a new-product hit. 3M's goal: divisions must derive 25 percent of sales from products introduced in the past five years. The target may be boosted to 30 percent.

- *Keep divisions small.* Division managers must know each staffer's first name. When a division gets too big, perhaps reaching $250 million to $300 million in sales, it is split up.

- *Motivate the champions.* When a 3M employee comes up with a product idea, he or she recruits an action team to develop it. Salaries and promotions are tied to the product's progress. The champion has a chance to someday run his or her own product group or division.

- *Stay close to the customer.* Researchers, marketers, and managers visit with customers and routinely invite them to help brainstorm product ideas.

- *Share the wealth.* Technology, wherever it is developed, belongs to everyone.

Forming Venture Teams

A third step in developing an intrapreneurial strategy is to focus on **venture teams.** Venture teams and the potential they hold for producing innovative results are being increasingly recognized as the productivity breakthrough of the nineties. There is little doubt that their popularity is on the rise. Companies that have committed to a venture team approach often label the change a "transformation" or "revolution." Indeed, this type of work team has been adopted by many firms. The teams are often referred to as self-directed, self-managing, or high-performance, though most venture teams include all of these descriptions.

By examining many of the successful entrepreneurial developments within established corporations, it can be shown that entrepreneurship is not the sole province of the company's founder or its top managers. Rather, it is diffused throughout the company. Experimentation and development go on continually, as the company searches for new ways to build on the knowledge already accumulated by its workers. Former U.S. Labor Secretary Robert B. Reich has referred to this effort by using the term **collective entrepreneurship**, where individual skills are integrated into a group and their collective capacity to innovate becomes something greater than the sum of its parts.[15] Over time, as group members work through various problems and approaches, they learn about one another's abilities. Specifically, they learn how they can help one

---

[15]Robert B. Reich, "The Team as Hero," *Harvard Business Review* (May–June 1987): 81.

another perform better, what each can contribute to a particular project, and how they can best take advantage of one another's experience. Each participant is constantly on the lookout for small adjustments that will speed and smooth the evolution of the project as a whole.

The net result of many such small-scale adaptations, effected throughout the organization, is to propel the enterprise forward. In keeping with this focus on collected entrepreneurship, venture teams offer corporations the opportunity to utilize the talents of individuals but with a sense of teamwork. An excellent example of project team development is Signode Industries, Inc., a $750 million-per-year manufacturer of plastic and steel strapping for packaging and materials handling, located in Glenview, Illinois. The corporate leaders wanted to chart new directions to become a $1 billion-plus firm. In pursuit of this goal, Signode set out to devise an aggressive strategy for growth by developing "new legs" for the company to stand on. According to Robert F. Hettinger, a venture manager with Signode, the firm formed a corporate development group to pursue markets outside the company's core business but within the framework of its corporate strengths.

Before launching the first of its venture teams, Signode's top management identified the firm's global business strengths and broad areas with potential for new product lines: warehousing/shipping; packaging; plastics for nonpackaging, fastening, and joining systems; and product identification and control systems. The goal of each new business opportunity suggested by a venture team was to generate $50 million in business within five years. In addition, each opportunity had to build on one of Signode's strengths: its industrial customer base and marketing expertise, systems sales and service capabilities, containment and reinforcement technology, steel and plastic process technology, machine and design capabilities, and productivity and distribution know-how.

The criteria were based on business-to-business selling, because Signode did not want market directly to retailers or consumers. The basic technology to be employed in the new business had to already exist and there had to be a strong likelihood of attaining a major market share within a niche. Finally, the initial investment in the new opportunity had to be $30 million or less. Based on these criteria, Signode began to build its "V-Team" (venture team) approach to intrapreneurship. It took three months to select the first team members. The six initial teams had three traits in common: high risk-taking ability, creativity, and the ability to deal with ambiguity. All were staffed by multidisciplinary volunteers who would work full-time developing new consumer product packaging ideas. The team members came from such backgrounds as design engineering, marketing, sales, and product development. They set up shop in rented office space located five miles from the firm's headquarters. Although, all six teams were not able to develop remarkable new ventures, the efforts did pay off for Signode. One venture team developed a business plan to manufacture plastic trays for frozen food entrees that could be used in either regular or microwave ovens. The business potential for this product was estimated to be in excess of $50 million per year within five years. In addition, the V-Team experience rekindled enthusiasm and affected moral throughout the organization. Most importantly, the V-Team approach became Signode's strategy to invent its future rather than waiting for things to happen.[16]

---

[16]Interview with Robert F. Hettinger of Signode Industries and Brian S. Moskal, "Inventing the Future," *Industry Week* (Sept. 30, 1985): 45–46.

Structuring for an Intrapreneurial Climate

In reestablishing the drive to innovate in today's corporations, the final—and possibly most critical—step is to invest heavily in an **entrepreneurial structure** that allows new ideas to flourish in an innovative environment. This concept, when coupled with the other elements of a strategy for innovation, can enhance the potential for employees to become venture developers. In fact, in developing employees as a source of innovation for corporations, research has shown that companies need to provide more nurturing and information-sharing activities. In addition to establishing entrepreneurial ways and nurturing intrapreneurs, companies need to develop a climate that will help innovative-minded people reach their full potential. The perception of an innovative climate is critical for stressing the importance of management's commitment to not only the organization's people, but also the innovative projects.

As a way for organizations to develop key structural factors for intrapreneurial activity, one group of researchers developed an Intrapreneurship Training Program (ITP) to induce the change needed in the work atmosphere. We will not completely detail the content of the training program here, but rather present a brief summary of the actual program to provide a general understanding of how it is designed to introduce an intrapreneurial environment in a company. The award-winning ITP program was intended to create an awareness of intrapreneurial opportunities within an organization. It consisted of six four-hour modules, each designed to train participants to be able to support intrapreneurship in their own work area.[17] The modules and a brief summary of their contents follow:

1. *Introduction*—This module consists of a review of management and organizational behavior concepts, definitions of intrapreneurship and related concepts, and a review of several intrapreneurship cases.

2. *Personal creativity*—This module attempts to define and stimulate personal creativity. It involves a number of creativity exercises and has participants develop a personal creative enrichment program.

3. *Intrapreneuring*—A review of the current literature on the topic is presented here, as well as in-depth analysis of several intrapreneuring organizations.

4. *Assessment of current culture*—A climate survey is administered to the training group for the purpose of generating discussion about the current facilitators and barriers to change in the organization.

5. *Business planning*—The intrapreneurial business planning process is outlined and explained. The specific elements of a business plan are identified and illustrated, and an example of an entire business plan is identified and illustrated.

6. *Action planning*—In this module, participants work in teams and create action plans designed to bring about change to foster intrapreneurship in their own workplaces.

---

[17]Donald F. Kuratko and Ray V. Montagno, "The Intrapreneurial Spirit," *Training and Development Journal* (Oct. 1989): 83–87.

To validate the training program's effectiveness, a questionnaire entitled the "Intrapreneurship Assessment Instrument (IAI)" was developed to measure key entrepreneurial climate factors. The responses to the IAI were statistically analyzed and identified five such factors: management support for intrapreneurship, risk-taking activity, rewards, resource availability, and organizational boundaries.[18]

The results indicated that organizations seeking to introduce an intrapreneurial strategy need to focus on an underlying set of internal environmental factors. The research revealed that these factors matched those that were consistently mentioned in the literature: top management support, risk-taking activity, organizational structure, rewards, and resource availability. These factors support the critical steps involved in introducing an intrapreneurial strategy.

After reviewing these elements, it becomes apparent that change in the corporate structure is inevitable if entrepreneurial activity is to prosper. In the change process, people, corporate goals, and existing needs all undergo change. In short, the organization can encourage innovation by relinquishing controls and altering the traditional bureaucratic structure.[19]

A Continuum of Intrapreneurial Activity

Overall, the major elements of an intrapreneurial strategy point to a proactive change in the existing corporate status quo that leads to a newer, more flexible organization. It should be recognized, however, that an intrapreneurial strategy cannot be effected all at once. It must proceed through a progression of activity using the steps identified earlier in this chapter. Figure 9.2 provides an illustrative look at the dimensions of intrapreneurial activity.

The continuum depicted in Figure 9.2 first presents ventures that may be considered corporate-assigned projects, which are characterized by a great deal of corporate control and commitment, and then progresses through Management by Objectives (MBO) projects, Strategic Team projects, and Corporate R&D projects, all of which feature increased individual autonomy and decreased corporate control. The degree of project control and corporate commitment pushes certain projects toward greater corporate control and, therefore, assignment and supervision. The need for autonomy and freedom to run a project will push other projects toward the ideal of intrapreneurship—completely self-appointed champions of new venture development.

Various forms of intrapreneurial activity can exist between the two extremes. Projects that seem semi-intrapreneurial (due to corporate control) or involve semi-corporate research (due to freedom given to an individual project leader) all fall within the scope of entrepreneurial behavior. Intrapreneurship is a risk, but it has to start somewhere—even if it starts small and is kept under corporate control. Once initiated, there is a good chance that this effort will progress through the steps of the continuum. Over time, people tend to become more comfortable with the idea, confidence builds, results occur, and soon the first corporate-assigned projects evolve into more autonomous ventures that involve the innovative abilities of all team members. The key steps of

---

[18]Donald F. Kuratko, Ray V. Montagno, and Jeffrey S. Hornsby, "Developing an Intrapreneurial Assessment Instrument for an Effective Corporate Entrepreneurial Environment," *Strategic Management Journal* 11 (1990): 49–58.

[19]See Donald F. Kuratko, Jeffrey S. Hornsby, Douglas W. Naffziger, and Ray V. Montagno, "Implementing Entrepreneurial Thinking in Established Organizations," *Advanced Management Journal* (Winter 1993): 28–33.

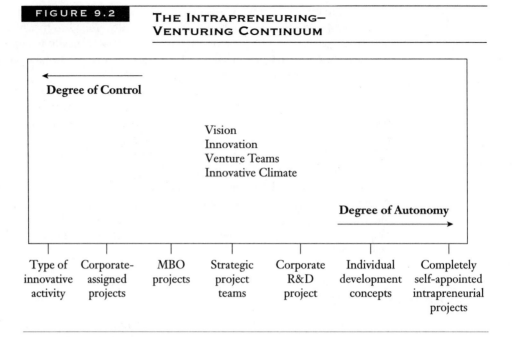

FIGURE 9.2 THE INTRAPRENEURING–VENTURING CONTINUUM

vision development, innovation encouragement, venture teams formation, and emergence of an innovative climate need to occur within an organization, each in its own turn. This phased development is a realistic approach of which managers should be aware.

The major thrust behind intrapreneurship is a revitalization of innovation creativity and managerial development in corporations. The strategies and insights presented here can serve as a foundation for understanding the current increase in entrepreneurial interests inside corporations. Intrapreneurship may possess the critical components needed to boost the future productivity of our organizations. If so, then managers need to recognize the objectives, prerequisites, and range of potential activities required to establish an intrapreneurship program strategy.

Models of Corporate Entrepreneurship (Intrapreneurship)

Research concerning corporate entrepreneurship has been rapidly increasing over the past few years. A number of leading research journals have published articles that describe exploratory work in this emerging field. In addition, a variety of models have been developed that attempt to provide a better framework for future understanding and study of intrapreneurial activity.

A Domain Model for Corporate Entrepreneurship

One model developed by William D. Guth and Ari Ginsberg attempted to provide a framework for tracking the research in corporate entrepreneurship.[20] According to

---

[20]William D. Guth and Ari Ginsberg, "Corporate Entrepreneurship," *Strategic Management Journal* 11 (Summer 1990): 5–15.

these researchers, the domain of corporate entrepreneurship encompasses two types of processes: **internal innovation,** or venturing through the creation of new businesses within existing organizations, and the **strategic renewal** of key corporate ideas that transform organizations. Figure 9.3 illustrates this model. Key components in this model include the environment, strategic leaders, organization form, and organization performance. Each component is an important element within the domain of corporate entrepreneurship.

A Conceptual Model of Firm Behavior

In examining the behaviors of entrepreneurs and their impact on the firm's actions, researchers Jeffrey G. Covin and Dennis P. Slevin developed an organization-level model.[21] They contend that entrepreneurial behavior at the firm level is affected by the firm's particular strategies, structures, systems, and cultures. Figure 9.4 depicts the key elements of this model. The major purpose of this behavioral model is to allow for considerable managerial intervention and thus reduce the view of corporate entrepreneurship as serendipitous or mysterious.

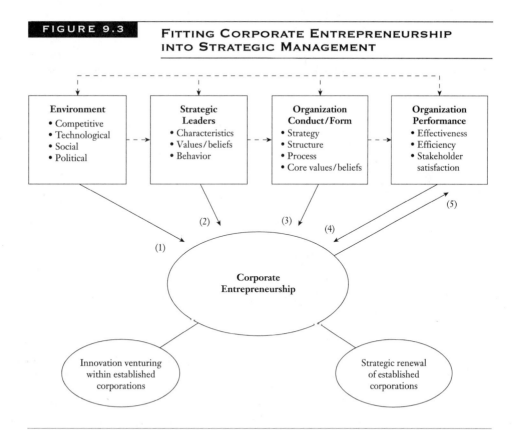

| FIGURE 9.3 | FITTING CORPORATE ENTREPRENEURSHIP INTO STRATEGIC MANAGEMENT |

---

[21]Jeffrey G. Covin and Dennis P. Slevin, "A Conceptual Model of Entrepreneurship as Firm Behavior," *Entrepreneurship Theory and Practice* (Fall 1991): 7–25.

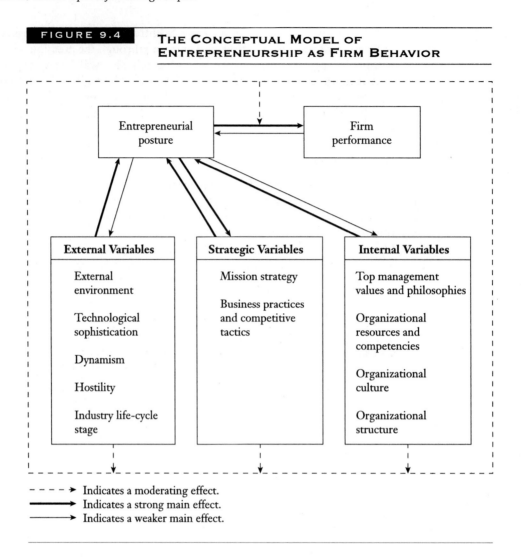

FIGURE 9.4   THE CONCEPTUAL MODEL OF ENTREPRENEURSHIP AS FIRM BEHAVIOR

- - - - ▶ Indicates a moderating effect.
━━━━━▶ Indicates a strong main effect.
──────▶ Indicates a weaker main effect.

An Organizational Model for Internally Developed Ventures

In defining corporate venturing as "an internal process that embraces the ultimate goal of growth through the development of innovative products, processes, and technologies" that should be institutionalized as a process geared toward long-term prosperity, researcher Deborah V. Brazeal created a framework model to explain this concept.[22] Figure 9.5 illustrates this model. The focus of this approach is a *joint function* between innovative-minded individuals and organizational factors. Thus, for an organization to promote innovation among its employees, careful attention must be given to the melding of an individual's attitudes, values, and behavioral orientations with the organizational factors of structure and reward. Ultimately, the key objective is to enhance a firm's innovative abilities through an organizational environment that is supportive of these individuals.

---

[22]Deborah V. Brazeal, "Organizing for Internally Developed Corporate Ventures," *Journal of Business Venturing* 8 (1993): 75–90.

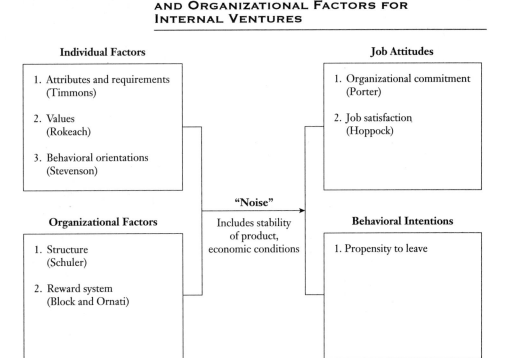

FIGURE 9.5 THE JOINT FUNCTION OF INDIVIDUAL AND ORGANIZATIONAL FACTORS FOR INTERNAL VENTURES

An Interactive Model of the Intrapreneurial Process

The final model presented in this section is based on the same concepts as the model developed by Brazeal; however, researchers Jeffrey S. Hornsby, Douglas W. Naffziger, Donald F. Kuratko, and Ray V. Montagno have attempted to describe the interaction of organizational factors and individual characteristics that is ignited by a precipitating event that leads to successful intrapreneurship. Figure 9.6 illustrates this interactive model.[23] The precipitating event could be a change in company management, a merger or acquisition, development of a new technology, or an event that acts as the impetus for the interaction between individual characteristics and organizational factors.

Exploring the Entrepreneurial Concepts

The following sections provide an "entrepreneurial library" that contains a journal reading on this chapter's subject and a "comprehensive case study" to illustrate the concept in practice. It is hoped that through the reading and discussion of the case, you will gain a greater understanding of the chapter.

[23]Jeffrey S. Hornsby, Douglas W. Naffziger, Donald F. Kuratko, and Ray V. Montagno, "An Interactive Model of the Corporate Entrepreneurship Process," *Entrepreneurship Theory and Practice* (Spring 1993): 29–37.

| FIGURE 9.6 | AN INTERACTIVE MODEL OF CORPORATE ENTREPRENEURING |

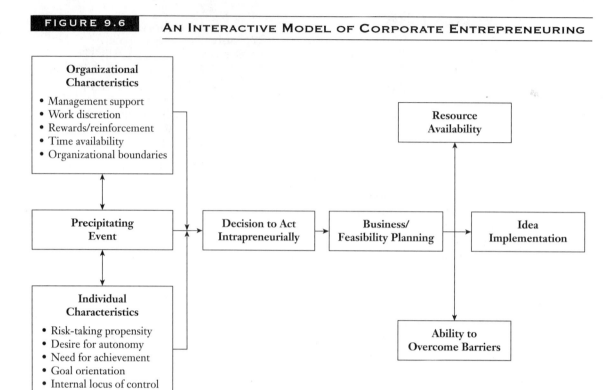

THE ENTREPRENEURIAL LIBRARY

Reading for Chapter 9

THE ANTECEDENTS AND CONSEQUENCES OF FIRM-LEVEL ENTREPRENEURSHIP: THE STATE OF THE FIELD

Shaker A. Zahra, Georgia State University
Daniel F. Jennings, Texas A&M University
Donald F. Kuratko, Ball State University

We acknowledge with gratitude the comments of Julie Carleton and Patricia H. Zahra. The support of the Beebe Institute for the first author is also acknowledged with appreciation.

Empirical research into firm-level entrepreneurship spans over a quarter of a century. This article reviews the current state of this research by identifying key trends in 45 published empirical studies; examining the key issues addressed and methods used to examine them; and outlining six key areas that need greater attention in future research.

Research in the nature, antecedents, and effects of firm-level entrepreneurial activities has grown rapidly over the past 25 years. Starting with Peterson and Berger's (1972) seminal study, this research has sought to identify organizational and environmental factors that affect a company's entrepreneurial activities. Earlier researchers gave special attention to the process by which established firms venture into new business fields and discussed the factors that influence the success of corporate ventures (Burgelman, 1983a, 1983b; Scholl-hammer, 1982). Likewise, Burgelman's (1983c) research into corporate venturing processes added considerable richness to the literature by documenting the interplay between autonomous and formal strategic behaviors that exist in a firm's entrepreneurial activities. Miller's (1983) paper, however, was a key turning point in the research on firm-level entrepreneurship. Authors from the U.S. and other countries have used Miller's theory and research instruments to examine the key linkages between environmental, strategic, and organizational variables, and a company's entrepreneurial activities. Research into these complex linkages continues to grow rapidly in scope and depth.

This article reviews the published research on the antecedents and consequences of firm-level entrepreneurship. It identifies issues covered, methods used, types of analyses conducted, and conclusions to be drawn from this research. The review also seeks to identify the shortcomings and contributions of past research efforts, hoping to set the stage for future research studies. Toward this end, the article outlines research questions worthy of greater attention in future study.

Two comments about the scope of this review are in order. First, given that several researchers (Jennings & Lumpkin, 1989; Covin & Slevin, 1991; Kuratko, Hornsby, Naffziger, & Montagno, 1993; Hornsby, Naffziger, Kuratko, & Montagno, 1993; Zahra, 1991, 1993a) have offered models of firm-level entrepreneurial activities, we have opted not to offer a new model. We believe that existing models are appropriate, but greater creativity is needed in testing the relationships depicted in, or proposed by, these models. Second, while we have reviewed diverse conceptual and empirical contributions as well as case studies, this paper emphasizes past empirical studies that have shaped the evolution of research in this area. Consequently, we have attempted to be as thorough and comprehensive as possible in assembling and reviewing these articles from refereed journals. This has led us to exclude some proceedings papers and book chapters. Still, we have made extensive use of many of these papers in developing our arguments and explaining key trends in the literature. Below, we present a listing of the articles we reviewed together with the variables we studied. In discussing each of these key variables, we have also stated the contributions and limitations of prior studies. Finally, the implications of our analysis of the state of the field for future research and scholarship are outlined.

Articles Reviewed

Table 1 presents the articles that we reviewed. These articles were selected from the journals identified by MacMillan (1993) as an appropriate publication forum for entrepreneurial research, with two exceptions. The first was Schollhammer's (1982) classification of internal corporate ventures and the second was Vesper's (1994) empirical classification of corporate ventures. Both classifications have been widely cited in the literature and, consequently, were included in the analysis.

As stated earlier, we examined only empirical studies so that we could follow the evolution of research in the area of firm-level entrepreneurship. The classification of

TABLE 1

ARTICLES REVIEWED

Conceptual Contribution	1	2	3	4	5	6	7	8	9	10	11	12	13	14	15	16	17	18	19
Schultz (1975)	X	X																	X
Webster (1977)		X	X																
Roberts (1980)											X								
Schollhammer (1982)								X	X	X	X	X							
Burgelman (1983)			X				X			X		X	X						
Gartner (1985)							X					X	X						
MacMillan & George (1985)			X				X				X		X						
Nielsen, Peters, & Hisrich (1985)				X															
Roberts & Berry (1985)						X	X		X										
Kanter (1985)	X	X	X				X					X			X				
Quinn (1985)	X	X	X								X	X				X			
Reich (1987)					X											X			
Wortman (1987)				X															
Gartner (1988)													X						
Rule & Irwin (1988)				X											X				
Sathe (1989)		X													X	X			
Guth & Ginsbert (1990)			X				X				X		X	X				X	
Howell & Higgins (1990)																	X		
Kanter, North, Bernstein, & Williamson (1990)	X																	X	X
Starr & MacMillan (1990)				X			X									X			
Stevenson & Jarrillo (1990)	X		X	X					X										
Chittipeddi & Wallet (1991)	X	X	X	X														X	
Covin & Slevin (1991)	X	X	X																
Cunningham & Lischeron (1991)				X															
Fulop (1991)		X																	
Herron (1992)			X	X		X	X	X		X									
Lengnick-Hall (1992)			X	X		X	X		X	X	X				X				
Jones & Butler (1992)								X	X		X							X	

362

TABLE 1   **ARTICLES REVIEWED**

Conceptual Contribution	1	2	3	4	5	6	7	8	9	10	11	12	13	14	15	16	17	18	19
Kelly (1993)	X															X		X	
Zahra (1993a)		X	X													X	X	X	
Kuratko (1993)			X												X	X			
Kuratko, Hornsby, Naffziger, & Montagno (1993)		X																	
Ginsberg & Hay (1994)				X				X		X						X			
Stopford & Baden-Fuller (1994)	X	X		X													X	X	
Dougherty (1995)														X					
Ghosal, Bauman, & Bartlett (1995)			X									X	X			X			
Guth (1995)			X								X								
Hill & Levenhapen (1995)		X	X								X							X	
Krachhardt (1995)											X		X						
Muzyka, Koning, & Churchill (1995)										X		X						X	
Yeoh & Jeong (1995)								X		X									X
Rope & Hunt (1995)										X							X		X
Brazeal & Herbert (1996)	X	X														X			
Dess, Lumpkin, & McGee (1996)												X						X	X
Johnson (1996)													X					X	
Lumpkin & Dess (1996)	X	X	X				X	X	X	X	X			X				X	X
Teese (1996)			X				X	X	X					X				X	X
Chung & Gibbons (1997)																			X	X
Johannison & Monsted (1997)										X									
Tercine, Harvey, & Buckley (1997)														X		X		X	
Tiessen (1997)				X	X								X						
Peterson & Berger (1971)														X			X		
Von Hipple (1977)							X												
Biggradike (1979)						X	X						X						
Fast (1981)						X	X						X						
Miller & Friesen (1982)	X	X	X													X		X	X

(continued)

TABLE 1   ARTICLES REVIEWED (CONTINUED)

Conceptual Contribution	1	2	3	4	5	6	7	8	9	10	11	12	13	14	15	16	17	18	19
Miller (1983)	X	X	X																
Vesper (1984)						X	X	X											
Miller & Camp (1985)						X	X												
Covin & Slevin (1986)													X						
MacMillan, Block, & Subbanarsimha (1986)			X			X	X												
Hisrich & Peters (1986)							X									X	X	X	
Sykes (1986)		X										X				X	X	X	
Covin & Slevin (1988)																		X	
Jennings & Lumpkin (1989)		X											X					X	
Jennings & Young (1990)			X																
Kuratko, Montagno, & Hornsby (1990)											X								
Zahra (1991)					X													X	
Larson (1992)			X			X													X
Russell & Russell (1992)												X						X	X
Deshpande, Farley, & Webster (1993)			X																
Katz (1993)		X																	
Kolvereid, Shave, & Westhead (1993)								X											X
Morris, Avila, & Aallen (1993)			X															X	
Zahra (1993b)			X															X	X
Zahra (1993c)			X											X					
Dougherty & Heller (1994)																			
Morris, Davis, & Allen (1994)	X															X		X	X
Sebora, Hartman, & Tower (1994)			X											X					
Dougherty & Bowman (1995)			X								X							X	
Fiol (1995)			X															X	
Fisenhauer (1995)												X							
Morris & Lewis (1995)	X																		X

TABLE 1 — ARTICLES REVIEWED

Conceptual Contribution	1	2	3	4	5	6	7	8	9	10	11	12	13	14	15	16	17	18	19
Sayles & Steward (1995)	X	X	X							X							X		
Scott (1995)			X																X
Zahra (1995)			X					X	X	X									
Brazeal (1996)			X												X			X	
Morris & Sexton (1996)																	X	X	
Zahra (1996)											X								
Dennis (1997)	X																	X	
Kuratko, Hornsby, & Naffziger (1997)															X				
Park & Kim (1997)												X		X					
Pearce, Kramer & Robbins (1997)	X										X							X	
Vesper & Gartner (1997)	X		X																
Wright, Robbie, & Ennew (1997)										X		X							
Westhead & Wright (1998)												X						X	X

1 = Proactiveness, 2 = Risk Taking, 3 = Innovation, 4 = Intrapreneurship, 5 = Internal Alliances, 6 = External Alliances, 7 = Incubative Ventures, 8 = Initiative Venturing, 9 = Acquisitive Venturing, 10 = Opportunistic Venturing, 11 = Administrative, 12 = Venture Capital, 13 = Business Definition, 14 = Competitive Approach, 15 = Appropriate Use of Rewards, 16 = Management Support, 17 = Resource Availability, 18 = Organizational Structure, 19 = Environment.

variables used to construct Table 1 was developed simply by listing the variables mentioned in previous research. Thus, no a priori conceptual typology guided the development of the categories of the classification. Using this post hoc categorization of past writings has allowed us to capture the richness of the literature without imposing our biases or personal preferences on prior contributions.

Publication Timeline

A comprehensive search of the literature yielded 45 empirical papers on firm-level entrepreneurship. Table 1 shows that three papers appeared on the topic in the 1970s, 10 were published in the 1980s, and the remaining 32 papers were published in the 1990s. Three factors account for this dramatic increase in the number of papers published in the past decade. First, the growth of the field of entrepreneurship itself has added legitimacy to research into firm-level entrepreneurship. This growth also resulted in the creation of entrepreneurship-related journals that were especially interested in research into firm-level phenomena. Indeed, most of the papers on the topic have appeared in specialized entrepreneurship journals such as *Journal of Business Venturing (JBV)* and *Entrepreneurship Theory and Practice (ET&P)*. Second, the growth of publications in this area mirrored a societal interest in the U.S. and elsewhere in revitalizing established companies and improving their ability to innovate and take calculated risks. Third, the availability of reliable instruments that capture entrepreneurial activities has made it easier for researchers to examine this complex phenomenon. The instruments developed and validated by Miller (1983) have become the standard in this area. Covin and Slevin's (1988) extensions and refinements of this instrument were also influential in promoting empirical research on firm-level entrepreneurship.

Trends in Samples, Location, and Data Collection

Countries

Most past research into firm-level entrepreneurship has been conducted in the U.S. or by researchers working in U.S.-based universities. Only a few studies have been published using data from non-U.S. companies including: Canadian (Miller, 1983); Norwegian (Knight, 1997); Japanese (Deshpande, Farley, & Webster, 1993); Swedish (Wiklund, 1998); and South African and Portuguese (Morris, Davis, & Allen, 1994) companies. However, more and more papers are being contributed by researchers from non-U.S. universities or by researchers using data from different countries. Researchers have also begun to explore factors that differentiate entrepreneurial research conducted in other countries from the U.S. model of scholarship. A noteworthy example is Huse and Landstrom's (1997) special issue devoted to European-based research on entrepreneurship. Without doubt, this research will increase our understanding of the profound effect of national cultures and unique resource endowments in promoting firm-level trend entrepreneurship.

Economic Sectors Studied

Another trend in published research into firm-level entrepreneurship is the predominance of data collected from manufacturing companies (85%). Service companies, which represent one of the fastest growing sectors in the global economy, have received only modest attention. One possible reason for the disproportionate attention given to manufacturing companies is the public concern over the global competitive status of manufacturing companies. Another reason is that some researchers do not understand service companies' operations.

Samples

Researchers have also relied for the most part on data collected from established companies (average age across samples = 42 years, sd = 3.5). This focus on established companies is understandable because of the interest in renewing and revitalizing companies' ongoing operations (Drucker, 1985; Peters & Waterman, 1982; Pinchot, 1985). However, with the exception of the Covin and Slevin (1990) study, we do not know the effect of the stages of the industry life cycle (ILC) on companies' entrepreneurial activities or whether the payoff from these activities varies across these stages. Economists (e.g., Porter, 1980) have long recognized the importance of inter-industry variations in explaining entrepreneurship and determining its effect on company performance.

Eighty-five percent of prior studies that have used manufacturing samples have also collected data from multiple industries. However, there is no uniformity in controlling for inter-industry variations, a factor that increases concern about the validity of past results. Only 37% of the studies controlled for industry effects. Even when statistical controls are used, we fear that researchers miss the opportunity to capitalize on inter-industry differences in structures and competitive dynamics in theorizing about the nature of entrepreneurship and its implications for company performance.

Researchers have also made extensive use of mail surveys in collecting data on entrepreneurial activities. Our analysis shows that 19% of the studies reviewed have used only mail surveys to collect data; 7% used interviews; 6% employed both interviews and mail surveys; and 68% used a combination of mail surveys and secondary data. The predominance of survey data is understandable because gaining access to information about companies' entrepreneurial activities is exceedingly difficult.

Reliance on surveys has well-known side effects such as an overemphasis on the content of entrepreneurial activities (rather than their process) and difficulties in making strong causal attributions. Use of survey data might have contributed to an overemphasis on the formal aspects of entrepreneurial activities, overlooking informal entrepreneurial activities and their contributions to a company's performance. As noted by several observers (Drucker, 1985; Kanter, 1985, 1989; Kuratko, 1993; Kuratko & Hornsby, 1996; Peters & Waterman, 1982; Pinchot, 1985; Wortman, 1987; Zahra, 1991), informal aspects of entrepreneurship can and do play an important role in enriching a company's performance. Field studies, experiments, and interviews can be more revealing about the role of autonomous entrepreneurial activities (Burgelman, 1983c, 1991).

We certainly do not suggest that mail surveys are not a viable approach to data collection; we have in fact made extensive use of them in our own research. Rather, we would like to see more energy devoted to using multiple sources of data in research on firm-level entrepreneurship in validating measures, testing hypotheses, and developing theories.

The problems associated with the use of survey data are further magnified by researchers' reliance on a single respondent. When mail surveys are used (87% of the articles reviewed), nearly all studies relied on a single respondent. Almost all past studies targeted CEOs or the firm's most senior managers who are assumed to know a great deal about companies' entrepreneurial activities (Zahra, 1991). A few studies (19%) have attempted to establish inter-rater reliability by contacting a second respondent (typically a senior executive). Of course, evidence of significant inter-rater reliability increases confidence in the quality of data used in prior studies. However, senior executives may not be fully aware of the many autonomous initiatives undertaken by their firms' divisions; middle managers are usually more positioned at the center of these activities (Burgelman, 1991; Floyd & Wooldrige, 1992; Peters & Waterman, 1982; Pinchot, 1985). Middle managers are also better informed about how formal and informal entrepreneurial activities unfold (Kanter, 1985) and therefore can better evaluate the success or failure of these efforts. Given that most prior studies have attempted to link entrepreneurial activities to the firm's overall financial performance, important insights can be gained from surveying or interviewing middle managers (Kuratko, Montagno, & Hornsby, 1990).

The Many Faces of Firm-Level Entrepreneurship

A close examination of published papers reveals that authors have not been consistent in the label they attach to the phenomenon they purport to study (Wiklund, 1998). Authors have used labels that include: entrepreneurship (Miller, 1983), corporate entrepreneurship (Peterson & Berger, 1971; Morris & Paul, 1987; Zahra, 1991, 1993a, 1993b, 1996; Zahra & Covin, 1995), intrapreneurship (Kuratko, 1993; Kuratko, Montagno, & Hornsby, 1990), entrepreneurial posture (Covin & Slevin, 1991), strategic posture (Covin & Slevin, 1988; Covin, Slevin, & Covin, 1990; Merz, Parker, & Kallis, 1990), and entrepreneurial orientation (Dess, Lumpkin, & Covin, 1997; Miles, Arnold, & Thompson, 1993). Yet, despite the ubiquity of labels used, most researchers have used Miller and Friesen's (1982) measure of firm-level entrepreneurship (Merz et al., 1990) or a modified version of this instrument (Covin & Slevin, 1988, 1991; Covin et al., 1990; Miles et al., 1993; Zahra, 1991).

Miller's (1983) conceptualization focuses on three related dimensions of firm-level entrepreneurship: proactiveness, innovation, and risk taking. Some earlier studies attempted to extend and modify Miller's (1983) conceptualization. Covin and Slevin (1988) extended Miller's measure to gauge a firm's entrepreneurial activities. Zahra (1991) argued that Miller's instrument captured disposition toward rather than actual entrepreneurship (Wiklund, 1998). Miller's measure did not capture, however, external entrepreneurial activities by the firm, focusing instead on internal entrepreneurial activities. Zahra (1991) further asserted that Miller's measure did not capture those informal entrepreneurial activities that take place in a firm (e.g., Pinchot, 1985; Wortman, 1987).

When Guth and Ginsberg (1990) reviewed the status of the field a decade ago, they concluded that firm-level entrepreneurship embodied two key components: innovation (of all types) and new business creation through venturing. However, we were able to locate only one study that captured both dimensions (Zahra, 1993b). Apparently, Miller's conceptualization has evolved into the instrument of choice in examining firm-level entrepreneurship. One unanticipated consequence of this practice is that research into corporate venturing, therefore, has not been fully integrated into discussions of firm-level entrepreneurship or entrepreneurial orientation.

Perhaps the time has come to conceptually integrate Miller's (1983) and Guth and Ginsberg's (1990) classifications of firm-level entrepreneurship. A unified typology (Zahra, 1991) would highlight three dimensions. The first is the content of the entrepreneurial act, which corresponds to Miller's (1983) conceptualization and Guth and

Ginsberg's (1990) innovation and venturing. The second dimension focuses on the locus of this act; it separates internal from external entrepreneurial activities. Internal activities are conducted within a firm's boundaries, as happens when two divisions of the same company join forces to develop a new product. External entrepreneurial activities transcend the firm's boundaries, as occurs when a firm joins another to pursue new product development. The third and final dimension indicates the source of the entrepreneurial act: whether formal or informal. This last dimension corresponds directly to Burgelman's (1983c, 1991) distinction between autonomous and formal strategic actions. Combining these three dimensions produces an eight-cell matrix that represents different entrepreneurial activities that can occur within established companies. Each of these eight cells offers interesting research possibilities into the antecedents, process, and consequences of entrepreneurial activities.

While no single typology is all encompassing, the above classification (Figure 1) suggests that some dimensions of firm-level entrepreneurial activities have not been closely examined. Informal, whether internally or externally focused, entrepreneurial activities have not been studied, and more research is needed to understand the conditions that foster these activities. The cells overlooked in this typology are among the areas that are receiving attention beyond the traditional boundaries of the field of entrepreneurship. Formal alliances that support corporate venturing are one example. Another example is research on external networks, the ties that bond their members, and their effects on a company's innovation and risk taking. These issues are receiving attention from strategic management and international business scholars. Future entrepreneurship research would benefit greatly from examining these issues, thus filling voids in our knowledge of the nature, dimensions, and effects of these variables on firm-level entrepreneurship.

Method and Analysis

Understanding the contributions of past research requires that we consider several issues: the statistical treatment of the entrepreneurship construct; the statistical controls employed in past designs; and the types of analytical tools used.

Statistical Treatment of the Entrepreneurship Construct   Most past studies (45%) used a measure of entrepreneurship as their dependent variable (76%). Most prior research examined the determinants of firm-level entrepreneurship by exploring the effects of a company's external environment, strategy, structure, and organizational culture. Researchers were keenly interested in uncovering those variables that enhanced companies' willingness to be entrepreneurial. This research, we believe, responded to a societal need to identify the sources of variations in entrepreneurial activities. Through the 1980s and 1990s, belief persisted that once these variables were identified and understood, strategic change and organizational renewal were achievable.

A smaller number of studies, however, treated entrepreneurship as an independent variable (Brazeal, 1993). Most of these studies have explored the effect of a company's entrepreneurial activities on financial or nonfinancial outcomes. In many ways, these studies enhanced the legitimacy of research into firm-level entrepreneurship by documenting the effects of entrepreneurship on company performance. Collectively, these studies suggested that entrepreneurship was a significant correlate of a company's performance.

FIGURE 1	A TYPOLOGY OF FIRM-LEVEL ENTREPRENEURSHIP LOCUS ON ENTREPRENEURIAL ACTIVITY

Internal	External	Internal	External
Informal	Informal	Informal	Informal
Formal	Formal	Formal	Formal
Venturing	Innovation	Venturing	Innovation

Still a third group of researchers treated entrepreneurship as both a dependent and independent variable (Zahra, 1991). They sought to clarify the antecedents and effects of certain variables on firm-level entrepreneurship and examine the effect of entrepreneurship on an outcome variable such as the company's financial performance. Most of these studies were guided by the configuration approach that dominated the literature in the late 1980s and early 1990s. This approach focused on finding constellations of organizational variables that influenced entrepreneurship while determining their potential association with measures of performance.

Upon examining published studies, one cannot help but notice the general lack of attention to the lagged effect that might exist among the sets of antecedents, entrepreneurship, and performance variables examined. The overwhelming majority of prior studies give the reader the impression that antecedent variables affect entrepreneurship almost instantly, and that entrepreneurship improves company performance as quickly. We were able to find two studies that recognized the possibility that the effect of entrepreneurship is long-term in nature (Zahra, 1991; Zahra & Covin, 1995), and both of these studies have several limitations. One of these studies (Zahra, 1991) examined the effect of entrepreneurship on performance measures for only one or two years after the data for the entrepreneurship variable were collected. Obviously, the long-term effects of entrepreneurship on a company's performance are unclear. The other study (Zahra & Covin, 1995) used a three-year time lag, but the attrition among companies in the sample was so high that survivor bias might have been magnified in the results. Companies that survived might have pursued different entrepreneurial ventures from firms that failed, or pursued the same ventures but did so differently from failing companies. Whether this is true or not cannot be gleaned from the results. Further, many organizational changes have occurred in the firms studied by Zahra and Covin (1995), raising a question about the sources of performance differences observed in the sample.

In summary, most prior studies have treated "entrepreneurship" as either an independent or dependent variable. However, because these studies have not examined the lag effect that might exist between antecedent variables and entrepreneurship, and between entrepreneurship and outcomes (e.g., performance), the causal sequence among these variables is unclear.

Measures There has been an unusually high degree of consistency in the way researchers measured firm-level entrepreneurship. Most researchers used the measures developed by Miller and Friesen (1982) and published by Miller (1983). This consistency is remarkable, especially because researchers have not used the same labels (or even the same constructs) in their research, as we noted earlier. Consequently, we fear that the quest for consistency has caused a serious *misfit* between construct and measures, raising a question about the meaning of what has been found and its theoretical and practical importance. One exception was the study by Jennings and Lumpkin (1989) in which they utilized the work of Schumpeter (1947), Ansoff (1965), and Hambrick (1983) to define firm-level entrepreneurship as the extent to which new products are developed. Jennings and Lumpkin (1989) also used archival data to measure new product additions.

Another source of concern is that few researchers have attempted to validate the popular measures developed by Miller and Friesen (1982), who were careful to show evidence of the reliability and validity of their measure. Zahra (1991, 1993b) correlated secondary and survey data to demonstrate the validity of Miller's (1983) index, supporting the reliability and validity of the measure. In another effort, Covin and Slevin (1988) used factor analysis to establish the dimensionality of a revised (expanded) measure of Miller's index. However, Jennings and Young (1990) found no significant difference between Jennings and Lumpkin's (1989) measurement of firm-level entrepreneurship and that of Miller and Friesen (1982). Thus, the dimensionality of Miller's measure has escaped close examination until recently, when Knight (1997) used LISREL to compare the stability (hence, comparability) of the structure of this measure using data from Norway and the U.S.

We appreciate the need for the use of consistent measures of entrepreneurship. Indeed, the Miller (1983) measure and the Covin and Slevin (1988) extensions have both served the field well, and no one can question their merit. We remain concerned that researchers might have prematurely agreed on a common measure without establishing its dimensionality or other psychometric properties. Triangulation also is clearly absent in this area of research, which opens the door for many interesting possibilities to be explored in future studies to validate, revise, and refine measures of firm-level entrepreneurship. In particular, these improvements should also emphasize a closer connection between constructs and empirical measures.

Statistical Controls Over the past decade researchers have become more attentive to the issues of reliability, evidenced by the fact that nearly all studies (84%) report a measure of internal scale consistency (usually Cronbach's alpha). They have also increased their attention to demonstrating internal reliability (73% of the studies). Further, researchers have controlled for variables that might affect the relationship

372 • **Part Three** *Growth Options for Strategic Impact*

between entrepreneurial activities and firm performance, including: company age (6%), size (14%), industry types (5%), and past performance (9%). While researchers have used different ways to perform these controls, it is clear that researchers are aware that these variables can confound their results.

One variable that has not been recognized in prior research is a company's past entrepreneurial activities. The laws of inertia may work both ways: conservative companies are likely to behave in this way over time, while innovative and entrepreneurial companies are likely to engage in more and more entrepreneurial activities. Given that most past research has focused on companies' entrepreneurial "disposition" or "orientation," future researchers need to control for a company's past entrepreneurial orientation.

Analytical Tools Used   Most past studies have used regression analysis as the primary technique in analyzing their data (59%); one study used both cluster analysis and multivariate analysis of variance (Covin et al., 1990); one study used structural equation modeling (LISREL) techniques (Knight, 1997); one study used canonical analysis (Zahra, 1991); and one study used time series analysis (Zahra & Covin, 1995). It is noteworthy, however, that the use of techniques other than regression analysis increased in the 1990s, reflecting the growing maturity of research in this area, the entry of researchers with a strong grasp of these techniques, and the availability of databases that permit the use of advanced analyses. We anticipate and suggest even greater diversity in the use of the analytical techniques employed in future studies.

Future Directions

Throughout this analysis of the literature, we have attempted to outline areas of potential importance for future research. In this section, we will only highlight the most important conceptual, methodological, and analytical issues that deserve greatest attention in future studies.

(1) There is a need to explore different conceptualizations of firm-level entrepreneurship. Future researchers are encouraged to distinguish between entrepreneurial disposition (Miller, 1983; Covin & Slevin, 1988), orientation (Lumpkin & Dess, 1996), and actions (Zahra, 1991, 1993b). Orientation does not always gauge actions. Lumpkin and Dess (1996) have made an important contribution to the field by identifying the various dimensions of firm-level entrepreneurship, and their classification system can guide future research. Entrepreneurial actions can be captured by companies' actual strategic choices and moves; they embody the firm's innovations (process, product, and organization) and venturing activities, as noted by Guth and Ginsberg (1990). Researchers can also help validate the results reported in prior research and summarized in this review by using alternative classifications of firm-level entrepreneurship.

(2) The literature would benefit also from revisiting the various units of analysis used in research into firm-level entrepreneurship. To date, and perhaps predictably, the literature has focused on overall firm-level activities. Greater attention should be given to entrepreneurship at the divisional (strategic business unit) level of the analysis. A great many entrepreneurial activities occur at the level of organizational divisions (Kuratko, Montagno, & Hornsby, 1990; Peters & Waterman, 1982; Pinchot, 1985; Zahra, 1993a, 1993b).

Researchers need also to give attention to the antecedents and effects of particular entrepreneurial events. These events provide important glimpses into a company's unfolding entrepreneurial activities and, therefore, can help improve our understanding of the contributions of entrepreneurship to company performance (Pinchot, 1985). Prior researchers, who have shown a consistent interest in entrepreneurial disposition or orientation, have not given sufficient attention to the factors that encourage firms to undertake particular actions. For example, rather than using the creation of a new venture as an indicator of firm-level entrepreneurship (which it is), future researchers should consider isolating the factors that may have led a company to undertake such an effort (Kuratko, Hornsby, & Naffziger, 1997).

(3) Greater diversity in the geographic and industry scope is also needed in future research into firm-level entrepreneurship. One area that requires greater attention is the nature of entrepreneurial activities across national cultures. Most past research has used data collected from U.S. companies; future researchers need to explore the stability of these results by collecting data from other countries. A related area of potential interest is the effect of national cultures on entrepreneurship. Shane's (1993) research clearly shows that national cultures play a profound role in explaining the differences in rates of entrepreneurship among societies. Research by Morris et al. (1994) also shows that national cultural variables can also influence firm-level entrepreneurship activities. However, more studies are needed to show how national cultures affect the rates and types of firm-level entrepreneurship and the resultant outcomes of entrepreneurial activities.

One area that needs more research is the interaction of national and organizational cultures on firm-level entrepreneurship. These two variables have been analyzed separately, though theory clearly indicates that national cultures influence organizational cultures (Morris et al., 1993), which, in turn, determine firm-level entrepreneurship. Does this mean that organizational culture mediates the national culture–entrepreneurship relationship? An answer to this question must await future research.

(4) Different conceptualizations of the link between entrepreneurial activities and company performance are needed. Both the popular press and the practitioner-oriented literature claim that entrepreneurial activities are inherently linked to higher company performance. However, this relationship is an important empirical question. There is the implicit assumption that first-mover firms that incur the greatest business and financial risk and spend the most on innovative activities would always be rewarded in the marketplace. However, many firms, such as Lincoln Electric and Emerson Electric, which are stellar performers, aggressively pursue cost leadership strategies and de-emphasize innovation and risk taking (Dess, Lumpkin, & McGee, 1996). Also, as noted by Nelson and Winter (1982), research has indicated that firms may enjoy a greater long-term benefit from imitation strategies than from high levels of innovativeness. Further, the notion of equifinality suggests that organizations can utilize different orientations to reach the same objective and achieve the same outcome(s). Consequently, there may be no performance differences between entrepreneurial and conservative firms (Jennings & Seaman, 1994). The relationship between performance and entrepreneurial activity remains a fruitful area for future research. Austrian economics would suggest a further need to examine different entrepreneurial actions (tactical vs. strategic) and relate them to a company's performance (see Grimm & Smith, 1997).

(5) An area that needs more attention is the firm's international operations. Entrepreneurial activities abound in the firm's internationalization efforts (Zahra & Garvis, 2000). As companies expand globally, researchers have a golden opportunity to examine

entrepreneurial orientations, activities, and processes. Researchers may study companies' international expansion activities or the joint activities of companies from different countries. Studying the entrepreneurial activities of the subsidiaries of multinationals is another fertile area for empirical research (Birkinshaw, 1997).

(6) Qualitative and quantitative studies should be combined in ways that enrich our understanding of firm-level entrepreneurship. These studies can help clarify the relative importance of antecedent variables on entrepreneurial activities or orientations. These studies can also help to define the effect of organizational context on entrepreneurial variables of interest. One notable area that would benefit from integrating qualitative and quantitative studies is the role of organizational cultures in explaining entrepreneurial activities or the effect of these activities on company performance. Another area that deserves attention is national cultures, as noted previously. A third area is the effect of top managers (or owners) on firm-level entrepreneurship. Ownership variables vary considerably across countries and, therefore, can influence a company's entrepreneurial activities quite differently. Future studies can improve our appreciation of how and why the characteristics of senior executives can affect a company's entrepreneurship. Obviously, research opportunities on the nature and process of entrepreneurship and its implications for organizational performance are abundant.

Conclusion

Research on firm-level entrepreneurship has grown in scope and depth over the past 25 years. This research has enriched and extended the literature in significantly and important ways. The results of the theoretical research during this time period suggest that companies that engage in entrepreneurial activities achieve superior performance. Our review of the state of the art in this area, however, indicates that many research questions still need attention. We hope our review encourages future researchers to continue to explore some of the important issues we have highlighted in this paper.

References

Ansoff, I. (1995). *Corporate strategy*. New York: McGraw-Hill.

Biggadike, R. (1970). The risky business of diversification. *Harvard Business Review, 57*(3), 103–111.

Birkinshaw, J. (1997). Entrepreneurship in multinational corporations: The role of subsidiary initiative. *Strategic Management Journal, 18*(3), 207–229.

Brazeal, V. D. (1993). Organizing for internally developed corporate ventures. *Journal of Business Venturing, 8*(1), 75–90.

Brazeal, V. D. (1996). Managing an entrepreneurial organizational environment. A discriminant analysis of organizational and individual differences between autonomous unit managers and department managers. *Journal of Business Research, 35*(1), 55–67.

Brazeal, V. D., & Herbert, T. T. (1996). Towards conceptual consistency in the foundations of entrepreneurship: Change, innovations and creativity. Working Paper, California State Polytechnic University.

Burgelman, R. A. (1983a). A model of the interaction of strategic behavior, corporate context, and the concept of strategy. *Academy of Management Review, 8*(1), 61–70.

Burgelman, R. A. (1983b). Corporate entrepreneurship and strategic management: Insights from a process study. *Management Science, 29*(12), 1349–1363.

Burgelman, R. A. (1983c). A process model of internal corporate venturing in the diversified major firm. *Administrative Science Quarterly, 28*(2), 223–244.

Burgelman, R. A. (1991). Intraorganizational ecology of strategy making and organizational adaptation: Theory and field research. *Organizational Science, 2*(3), 239–262.

Chittipeddi, K., & Wallet, T. (1991). Entrepreneurship and competitive strategy for the 1990s. *Journal of Small Business Management, 29*(1), 94–98.

Chung, H. L., & Gibbons, T. P. (1997). Corporate entrepreneurship: The roles of ideology and social capital. *Group & Organization Management, 22*(1), 10–30.

Covin, J. G., & Slevin, D. P. (1986). The development and testing of an organizational level entrepreneurship scale. In R. Ronstadt, J. A. Hornaday, R. Peterson, & K. H. Vesper (Eds.), *Frontiers of entrepreneurship research—1986*, pp. 628–639, Wellesley, MA: Babson College.

Covin, J. G., & Slevin, D. (1988). The influence of organization structure on the utility of an entrepreneurial top management style. *Journal of Management Studies, 25*(3), 217–234.

Covin J. G., & Slevin, D. P. (1990). New venture strategic posture, structure and performance: An industry life cycle analysis. *Journal of Business Venturing, 5*(2), 123–135.

Covin, J. G., & Slevin, D. (1991). A conceptual model of entrepreneurship as firm behavior. *Entrepreneurship Theory & Practice, 15*(4), 35–50.

Covin, J. G., Slevin, D., & Covin, T. J. (1990). Content and performance of growth-seeking strategies: A comparison of small firms in high- and low-technology industries. *Journal of Business Venturing, 5*(6), 391–412.

Cunningham, J., & Lischeron, J. (1991). Defining entrepreneurship. *Journal of Small Business Management, 29*(1), 45–61.

Dennis, W. J., Jr. (1997). More than you think: An inclusive estimate of business entries. *Journal of Business Venturing, 12*(3), 175–196.

Deshpande, R., Farley, J. U., & Webster, F. E. (1993). Corporate culture, customer orientation, and innovativeness in Japanese firms: A quadrad analysis. *Journal of Marketing, 57*(1), 23–37.

Dess, G. G., Lumpkin, G. T., & Covin, J. G. (1997). Entrepreneurial strategy making and firm performance: Tests of contingency and configurational models. *Strategic Management Journal, 18*(9), 677–695.

Dess, G. G., Lumpkin, G. T., & McGee, J. E. (1996). Linking corporate entrepreneurship to strategy, structure, and process: Suggested research directions. Working Paper, University of Kentucky.

Dougherty, D. (1995). Managing your core incompetencies for corporate venturing. *Entrepreneurship Theory and Practice, 19*(3), 113–136.

Dougherty, D., & Bowman, E. H. (1995). The effects of organizational downsizing on product innovation. *California Management Review, 37*(4), 28–45.

Dougherty, D., & Heller, T. (1994). The illegitimacy of successful product innovation in established firms. *Organization Science, 5*(2), 200–218.

Drucker, P. (1985). *Innovations and entrepreneurship.* New York: Harper & Row.

Fast, N. D. (1981). Pitfalls of corporate venturing. *Research Management,* March 21–24.

Fiol, C. M. (1995). Thought worlds colliding: The role of contradiction in corporate innovation processes. *Entrepreneurship Theory and Practice, 19*(3), 71–91.

Fisenhauer, J. G. (1995). The entrepreneurial decision: Economic theory and empirical evidence. *Entrepreneurship Theory and Practice, 19*(4), 67–80.

Floyd, S. W., & Woodridge, B. (1992). Middle management involvement in strategy and its association with strategic type: A research note. *Strategic Management Journal, 13*(special issue), 153–167.

Fulop, L. (1991). Middle managers: Victims or vanguards of the entrepreneurial movement? *Journal of Management Studies, 28*(1), 25–44.

Gartner, W. B. (1985). A conceptual framework for describing the phenomenon of new venture creation. *Academy of Management Review, 10*(4), 696–706.

Gartner, W. B. (1988). "Who is an entrepreneur?" is the wrong question. *American Journal of Small Business, 12*(4), 11–32.

Ghoshal, S., Bauman, P. R., & Bartlett, C. (1995). Building the entrepreneurial corporation: New organizational processes, new managerial tasks. *European Management Journal, 13*(2), 139–158.

Ginsberg, A., & Hay, M. (1994). Confronting the challenges of corporate entrepreneurship: Guidelines for venture managers. *European Management Journal, 12*(4), 382–389.

Grimm, C. M., & Smith, K. G. (1997). *Strategy as action: Industry rivalry and coordination.* Cincinnati, OH: South-Western College Publishing.

Guth, W. D. (1995). Theory from field research on firm level entrepreneurship: A normal science overview. *Entrepreneurship Theory and Practice, 19*(3), 169–173.

Guth, W. D., & Ginsberg, A. (1990). Guest editor's introduction: Corporate entrepreneurship. *Strategic Management Journal,* 11, 5–16.

Hambrick, D. C. (1983). Some tests of the effectiveness and functional attributes of Miles and Snow's strategic types. *Academy of Management Journal, 26*(1), 5–26.

Herron, L. (1992). Cultivating corporate entrepreneurs. *Human Resource Planning, 15*(4), 3–15.

Hill, R. C., & Levenhapen, M. (1995). Metaphors and mental models: Sensemaking and sensegiving in innovative and entrepreneurial activities. *Journal of Management, 21*(6), 1057–1075.

Hisrich, R. D., & Peters, M. P. (1986). Establishing a new business venture unit within a firm. *Journal of Business Venturing, 1*(3), 307–322.

Hornsby, J. S., Naffziger, D. W., Kuratko, D. F., & Montagno, R. V. (1993). An interactive model of the corporate entrepreneurship process. *Entrepreneurship Theory & Practice, 17*(2), 29–37.

Howell, J. M., & Higgins, C. A. (1990). Champions of technological innovation. *Administrative Science Quarterly, 35*(2), 317–341.

Huse, M., & Landstrom, H. (1997). European entrepreneurship and small business research: methodological openness and contextual differences. *International Studies of Management & Organization, 27*(3), 3–27.

Jennings, D. F., & Lumpkin, R. J. (1989). Functioning modeling corporate entrepreneurship: An empirical integrative analysis, *Journal of Management, 15*(3), 485–502.

Jennings, D. F., & Seaman, S. L. (1994). High and low levels of organizational adaptation: An empirical analysis of strategy, structure, and performance. *Strategic Management Journal, 15*(6), 459–475.

Jennings, D. F., & Young, D. M. (1990). An empirical comparison between objective and subjective measures of the product innovation domain of corporate entrepreneurship. *Entrepreneurship Theory and Practice, 15*(1), 53–66.

Johannison, B., & Monsted, M. (1997). Contextualizing entrepreneurial networking: The case of Scandinavia. *International Studies of Management and Organization, 27*(3), 109–128.

Johnson, R. A. (1996). Antecedents and outcomes of corporate refocusing. *Journal of Management, 22*(3), 439–484.

Jones, G. R., & Butler, J. E. (1992). Managing internal corporate entrepreneurship: An agency theory perspective. *Journal of Management, 18*(4), 733–749.

Kanter, R. M. (1985). Supporting innovation and venture development in established companies. *Journal of Business Venturing, 1*(1), 47–60.

Kanter, R. M. (1989). *When giants learn to dance.* New York: Simon and Schuster.

Kanter, R. M., North, J., Bernstein, A., & Williamson, A. (1990). Designing and running entrepreneurial vehicles in established companies. *Journal of Business Venturing, 5*(6), 415–427.

Katz, J. A. (1993). How satisfied are the self-employed: A secondary analysis approach. *Entrepreneurship Theory and Practice, 17*(3), 35–52.

Kelly, J. (1993). Executive behavior: Classical and existential. *Business Horizons, 36*(1), 16–27.

Knight, G. A. (1997). Cross-cultural reliability and validity of a scale to measure firm entrepreneurial orientation. *Journal of Business Venturing, 12*(3), 213–225.

Kolvereid, L., Shave, S., & Westhead, P. (1993). Is it equally difficult for female entrepreneurs to start businesses in all countries? *Journal of Small Business Management, 31*(4), 42–52.

Krackhardt, D. (1995). Entrepreneurial opportunities in an entrepreneurial firm: A structural approach. *Entrepreneurship Theory and Practice, 19*(3), 53–70.

Kuratko, D. F. (1993). Intrapreneurship: Developing innovation in the corporation. *Advances in Global High Technology Management–High Technology Venturing,* 3, 3–14.

Kuratko, D. F., & Hornsby, J. S. (1996). Developing entrepreneurial leadership in contemporary organizations. *Journal of Management Systems, 8*(1), 17–27.

Kuratko, D. F., Hornsby, J. S., & Naffziger, D. W. (1997). An examination of owner's goals in sustaining entrepreneurship. *Journal of Small Business Management, 35*(1), 24–34.

Kuratko, D. F., Hornsby, J. S., Naffziger, D. W., & Montagno, R. V. (1993). Implementing entrepreneurial thinking in established organizations. *SAM Advanced Management Journal, 58*(1), 28–35.

Kuratko, D. F., Montagno, R. V., & Hornsby, J. S. (1990). Developing an entrepreneurial assessment instrument for an effective corporate entrepreneurial environment. *Strategic Management Journal,* 11, 49–58.

Larson, A. (1992). Network dyads in entrepreneurial settings: A study of the governance of exchange relationships. *Administrative Science Quarterly, 37*(1), 76–104.

Lengnick-Hall, C. A. (1992). Innovation and competitive advantage: What we know and what we need to learn. *Journal of Management, 18*(2), 399–429.

Lumpkin, G. T., & Dess, G. G. (1996). Clarifying the entrepreneurial orientation construction and linking it to performance. *Academy of Management Review, 21*(1), 135–173.

MacMillan, I. C. (1993). The emerging forum for entrepreneurship scholars. *Journal of Business Venturing, 8* (5), 377–381.

MacMillan, I. C., Block, Z., & Subbanarasimha, P. (1986). Corporate venturing: Alternatives, obstacles encountered, and experience effects. *Journal of Business Venturing, 1*(2), 177–191.

MacMillian, I. C., & George, R. (1985). Corporate venturing: challenges for senior managers. *Journal of Business Strategy, 5*(3), 34–44.

Merz, G. R., Parker, B. J., & Kallis, M. J. (1990). Resources-related dependencies: Marketing strategies of technological-based firms. *European Journal of Marketing, 23*(4), 44–65.

Miles, M. P., Arnold, D. R., & Thompson, D. L. (1993). The interrelationship between environmental hostility and entrepreneurial orientation. *Journal of Applied Business Research, 9*(4), 12–23.

Miller, A., & Camp, B. (1985). Exploring determinants of success in corporate ventures. *Journal of Business Venturing, 1*(1), 247–259.

Miller, D. (1983). The correlates of entrepreneurship in three types of firms. *Management Science, 29*(7), 770–791.

Miller, D., & Friesen, P. H. (1982). Innovation in conservative and entrepreneurial firms: Two models of strategic momentum. *Strategic Management Journal, 3*(1), 1 25.

Morris, M. H., Avila, R. A., & Allen, J. (1993). Individualism and the modern corporation: Implications for innovation and entrepreneurship. *Journal of Management, 19*(3), 595–613.

Morris, M. H., Davis, D. L., & Allen, J. W. (1994). Fostering corporate entrepreneurship: Cross-cultural comparisons of the importance of individualism versus collectivism. *Journal of International Business Studies, 25*(1), 65–90.

Morris, M. H., & Lewis, P. S. (1995). The determinants of entrepreneurial activity: Implications for marketing. *European Journal of Marketing, 29*(7), 31–49.

Morris, M. H., & Paul, G. W. (1987). The relationships between entrepreneurship and marketing in established firms. *Journal of Business Venturing, 2*(3), 247–259.

Morris, M. H., & Sexton, D. L. (1996). The concept of entrepreneurial intensity: Implications for company performance. *Journal of Business Research, 36*(1), 5–13.

Muzyka, D., Koning, A. D., & Churchill, N. (1995). On transformation and adaptation: Building the entrepreneurial corporation. *European Management Journal, 13*(4), 346–362.

Nelson, R. R., & Winter, S. G. (1982). *An evolutionary theory of economic change.* Cambridge, MA: Belknap Press.

Nielsen, R. P., Peters, M. R., & Hisrich, R. D. (1985). Intrapreneurship strategy for internal markets—Corporate, nonprofit, and government institution cases. *Strategic Management Journal, 6*(2), 181–189.

Park, S. H., & Kim, D. (1997). Market valuation of joint ventures: Joint venture characteristics and wealth gains. *Journal of Business Venturing, 12*(2), 83–108.

Pearce, J. A. II, Kramer, T. R., & Robbins, D. K. (1997). Effect of managers' entrepreneurial behavior on subordinates. *Journal of Business Venturing, 12*(2), 147–160.

Peters, T. J., & Waterman, P. H. (1982). *In search of excellence: Lessons from America's best run companies.* New York: Harper & Row.

Peterson, R., & Berger, D. (1972). Entrepreneurship in organizations. *Administrative Science Quarterly, 16*, 97–106.

Pinchott, G. III. (1985). *Intrapreneuring.* New York: Harper & Row.

Porter, M. E. (1980). *Competitive strategy.* New York: Free Press.

Quinn, J. B. (1985). Managing innovation: Controlled chaos. *Harvard Business Review, 63*(3), 43–59.

Reich, R. B. (1987). Entrepreneurship reconsidered: The team as hero. *Harvard Business Review, 65*(3), 7–83.

Roberts, E. (1980). New ventures for corporate growth. *Harvard Business Review, 58*(4), 130–144.

Roberts, E. G., & Berry, C. A. (1985). Entering new businesses: Selecting strategies for success. *Sloan Management Review*, Spring, 3–17.

Ropo, A., & Hunt, J. G. (1995). Entrepreneurial process as virtual and vicious spirals in a changing opportunity structure: A paradoxical perspective. *Entrepreneurship Theory and Practice, 19*(3), 91–111.

Rule, E. G., & Irwin, D. W. (1988). Fostering intrapreneurship: The new competitive edge. *Journal of Business Strategy, 9*(3), 44–47.

Russell, R. D., & Russell, C. J. (1992). An examination of the effects of organizational norms, organization structure and environmental uncertainty on entrepreneurial strategy. *Journal of Management, 18*(4), 639–657.

Sathe, V. (1989). Fostering entrepreneurship in large diversified firms. *Organizational Dynamics, 18*(10), 20–32.

Sayles, L. R., & Steward, A. (1995). Belated recognition for work flow entrepreneurs: A case of selective perception and amnesia in management thought. *Entrepreneurship Theory and Practice, 19*(3), 7–23.

Scott, S. (1995). Uncertainty avoidance and the preference for innovation championing roles. *Journal of International Business Studies, 26*(1), 47–69.

Schollhammer, H. (1982). Internal corporate entrepreneurship. In C. A. Kent, D. L. Sexton, & K. H. Vesper (Eds.), *Encyclopedia of entrepreneurs*, pp. 209–223. Englewood Cliffs, NJ: Prentice Hall.

Schultz, T. W. (1975). The value of the ability to deal with disequilibria. *Journal of Economic Literature, 13*(3), 827–846.

Schumpeter, J. (1947). *Capitalism, socialism and democracy* (2nd ed.). New York: Harper & Row.

Sebora, C. T., Hartman, A. E., & Tower, B. C. (1994). Innovative activity in small businesses: Competitive context and organization level. *Journal of Engineering and Technology Management, 11*(3,4). 253–272.

Shane, S. (1993). Cultural influences on national rates of innovation. *Journal of Business Venturing, 8*(1), 59–73.

Starr, J. A., & MacMillian, I. C. (1990). Resources co-optation via social contracting: Resource acquisition strategies for new ventures. *Strategic Management Journal, 11* 79–92.

Stevenson, H. H., & Jarillo, J. C. (1990). A paradigm of entrepreneurship: Entrepreneurial management. *Strategic Management Journal, 11* 17–27.

Stopford, J. M., & Baden-Fuller, C. W. F. (1994). Creating corporate entrepreneurship. *Strategic Management Journal, 15*(7), 521–536.

Sykes, H. B. (1986). The anatomy of a corporate venturing program: Factors influencing success. *Journal of Business Venturing, 1*(3), 215–230.

Teece, D. J. (1996). Firm organization, industrial structure, and technological innovation. *Journal of Economic Behavior and Organization, 31*(2), 193–224.

Tercine, R., Harvey, M., & Buckley, M. (1997). Shifting organizational paradigms: Transitional management. *European Management Journal, 15*(1), 45–57.

Tiessen, J. H. (1997). Individualism, collectivism, and entrepreneurship: A framework for international comparative research. *Journal of Business Venturing, 12*(5), 367–384.

Vesper, K. H. (1984). Three faces of corporate entrepreneurship: A pilot study. In J. A. Hornaday, F. A. Tarpley, J. Timmons, & K. H. Vesper (Eds.). *Frontiers of entrepreneurship research*, pp. 294–320. Wellesley, MA: Babson College.

Vesper, K. H., & Gartner, W. B. (1997). Executive forum measuring progress in entrepreneurial education. *Journal of Business Venturing, 12*(5), 403–421.

Von Hipple, E. (1997). Successful and failing internal corporate ventures: An empirical analysis. *Industrial Marketing Management, 6*(3), 163–174.

Webster, F. A. (1977). Entrepreneurs and ventures: An attempt of classification and clarification. *Academy of Management Review, 2*(1), 54–61.

Westhead, P., & Wright, M. (1998). Novice, portfolio, and serial founders: Are they different? *Journal of Business Venturing, 13*(3), 173–204.

Wiklund, J. (1998). *Small firm growth and performance.* Unpublished doctoral dissertation, Jonkoping University.

Wortman, M. S., Jr. (1987). Entrepreneurship: An integrating typology and evaluation of the empirical research in the field. *Journal of Management, 13*(2), 207–222.

Wright, M., Robbie, K., & Ennew, C. (1997). Venture capitalists and serial entrepreneurs. *Journal of Business Venturing, 12*(3), 227–249.

Yeoh, P. L., & Jeong, I. (1995). Contingency relationsh channel structure and environment: A proposed co *European Journal of Marketing, 29*(8), 95–116.

Zahra, S. A. (1991). Predictors and financial outcome exploratory study. *Journal of Business Venturing, 6*(4

Zahra, S. A. (1993a). A conceptual model of entrepre extension. *Entrepreneurship Theory and Practice, 17*

Zahra, S. A. (1993b). Environment, corporate entrep taxonomic approach. *Journal of Business Venturing*

Zahra, S. A. (1993c). New product innovation in est industry and strategy variables. *Entrepreneurship '*

Zahra, S. A. (1995). Corporate entrepreneurship an agement leveraged buyouts. *Journal of Business V*

Zahra, S. A. (1996). Governance, ownership and cc impact of industry technology opportunities. *Academy of Management j....* 1713–1735.

Zahra, S. A., & Covin, J. G. (1995). Contextual influences on the corporate entrepreneurship–performance relationship: A longitudinal analysis. *Journal of Business Venturing, 10*(1), 43–58.

Zahra, S. A., & Garvis, D. (2000). International corporate entrepreneurship and firm performance: The moderating effect of international environmental hostility. *Journal of Business Venturing*, in press.

COMPREHENSIVE CASE STUDY

C A S E **INDEPENDENCE DAY: EDS SPLIT-OFF FROM GENERAL MOTORS**

Patricia A. Ryan, Drake University

> There is no other image overshadowing this company. We are on the threshold of a new era.
>
> Lester M. Alberthal, Jr., Chairman and CEO, EDS
> June 10, 1996

It was June 10, 1996, just minutes before the beginning of another trading day on Wall Street. This, however, was no ordinary day for Les Alberthal, Chairman and CEO of Electronic Data Systems (EDS), the world's largest provider of information technology services, offering its clients a continuum of services, including the management and operation of computers, networks, information systems, information processing facilities, business operations, and management consulting services. Alberthal was bequeathed with the honor of ringing the opening bell, signifying the opening of the largest stock market in the world and the birth of EDS as a corporation separate from its parent of twelve years, General Motors.

This case was prepared by Patricia A. Ryan, Drake University, and is intended to be used as a basis for class discussion. The views represented here are those of the case author and do not necessarily reflect the views of the Society for Case Research. The author's views are based on her own professional judgment.

A lot had happened in Alberthal's twenty-two year tenure with the company, but nothing as exciting and challenging as what he was facing now. EDS paid General Motors $500 million for the separation; was the price of divorce too high? Would the company be able to maintain or exceed the growth they had enjoyed in the past decade? On June 10, 1996, EDS stock traded at around $57. Was this an accurate value of the company's stock? How should one best approach valuation for a recently split-off company in this growing industry? How do the issues related to the split-off affect cash flow estimation? Where would the dawn of the new millennium take EDS and how would the company respond to rapid industry and market changes? EDS had an opportunity to capitalize on the fate of companies facing what had become known as the "Year 2000" problem. This problem pertained to operating systems and software using only a two digit date for the year. Unless resolved, data generated immediately after midnight on January 1, 2000 would be inaccurate. Rather than the date being reflected as January 1, 2001, the date would be interpreted as January 1, 1901, since only the last two digits of the year were used in the original computer coding. This presented an opportunity for EDS to gain new clients and expand current business, but it was not without inherent risks. Alberthal knew timing was everything, and now it was time for EDS to strike out on its own.

History of Electronic Data Systems

After 10 years with IBM, H. Ross Perot left the company in frustration because the computer company was not receptive to his proposals to offer clients electronic data processing management services. Perot founded Electronic Data Systems (EDS) on June 27, 1962, with an initial investment of $1,000 and a staff of two former IBM colleagues. Two months and 78 calls later, EDS secured its first contract from Collins Radio in Cedar Rapids, Iowa. Over the next year, EDS gained several additional clients, including Mercantile Security Life and Frito Lay. Three years after earning his first entrepreneurial dollar, Perot gained the lucrative Medicare and Medicaid claims processing account, which by 1968 made up 25% of EDS revenues. The continuance of a strong growth pattern enabled EDS stock to go public in 1968 for $16.50

Perot heartily took to gaining business from his former employer, IBM. He recruited many of IBM's best employees and provided a reward system that rewarded those who gained business from Big Blue.[1] Perot was multifaceted in nature; he wanted the best and would accept no less. Through EDS, he became so powerful that the U.S. government and Wall Street officials pleaded with him to help save the faltering brokerage firm of du Pont, Glore Forgan, and Company. He put it this way:

> I was encouraged by virtually everybody at a senior level in government in Washington, and certainly by everybody running a major New York bank, to step in to avoid what they perceived to be an impending disaster, because there was no specific legislation to bail out a failing firm.
>
> Ross Perot, as quoted in *Barrons*
> February 23, 1987

At first glance this sounds heroic. The commentary would not be complete without the recognition that EDS provided du Pont's data processing services, a client that was reportedly worth 10 and 12% of EDS' business. Like him or not, Ross Perot was a true entrepreneur at heart.

Perot was known for expecting extraordinary dedication from his employees, often for relatively low pay. In response to the question, "What is an EDSer?", he responded, "An EDSer is a person that goes anywhere, anytime, 24 hours a day, seven days a week, to make sure that EDS is the finest computer company in the world and that nobody beats us in competition."[2] How did Perot find the right people for such jobs?

> Finding the best man for the job was Perot's specialty. Although he was one of the most successful self-made men in the history of American capitalism, he was not the world's greatest computer expert, or the world's greatest salesman, or even the world's greatest business administrator. He did just one thing superbly well: pick the right man, give him the resources, motivate him, then leave him alone to do the job.
>
> Excerpt from *On Wings of Eagles*, p. 59.

With the proliferation of computers in the business sector, more and more companies sought to outsource their data processing as a means of reducing costs and eliminating the need to invest in large, soon to be obsolete mainframe processors. EDS thrived on this increased demand and continued to grow by leaps and bounds. In the early eighties, EDS and Ross Perot attracted the attention of General Motors Chairman, Roger Smith.

Enter General Motors

In his unauthorized biography of GM Chairman Roger Smith, former GM writer Albert Lee described Smith as "enamored with the entrepreneurial spirit Perot has infused into EDS and equally infatuated with the folk hero founder."[3] Lee described Perot as demonstrative and philanthropic and Smith as private and parsimonious. Smith appeared willing to pay a significant premium to purchase EDS. It appeared as though he hoped EDS's 13,800 employees would pervade the stiff GM's 800,000 employee corporate environment. Part of this process entailed the transfer of 10,000 GM data processing employees to EDS.

On June 27, 1984, exactly 22 years after it founding, EDS was sold to General Motors for $2.55 billion. Key in the contract was the right for EDS to maintain its own key personnel and management style. (Refer to Exhibit 1.) After the merger was finalized on October 18, EDS became a wholly owned subsidiary of GM. In a move unusual for GM, Perot was to remain at the helm of EDS and in addition was guaranteed a seat on GM's board, a move that some say Smith later regretted. Furthermore, in an effort to separate the conglomerate from its independent entities, GM issued a special class of stock, GM Class E, for which value was derived from the performance of EDS.

In the purchase, it made sense for EDS to take over GM's data processing and, in the process, Smith hoped the Perot spirit would be infused into GM. EDS joined GM and took control of the parent company's $6 billion annual data processing account.

Meanwhile, EDS continued international expansion to Canada, Australia, Mexico, and several European and South American countries in the mid-eighties and succeeded in tripling revenues in the first year following the GM acquisition.

Les Alberthal, a twelve-year veteran of EDS, became President and CEO in June of 1986. EDS maintained a strong market position under the helm of Alberthal. In

1988, *Fortune* magazine named EDS the leading company in diversified services and the well-respected Gallagher report named Alberthal as one of the ten top executives of companies with annual revenues in excess of $1 billion. Under Alberthal's guidance, EDS gained the reputation as a hard-driving, results-oriented organization with a strict, almost militarian management. It was these features that were largely to credit for the company's record revenues and growth. EDS discerned the shifting needs of clients and in a continued effort to expand, the company focused on new, innovative markets. One example of such would be co-sourcing, when EDS would enter into a partnership-type arrangement with the client to provide data services.

Although initially the relationship between Smith and Perot appeared to be based on admiration, the honeymoon between the merged companies soon ended. The relationship between Perot and GM was rocky at best. Perot summed up his perception of the relationship in the following comment:

> I come from an environment where, if you see a snake, you kill it. At GM, if you see a snake, the first thing you do is organize a committee on snakes. Then you go hire a consultant who knows a lot about snakes. Then you talk about it for a year.[4]

While Smith's style of management was seen as reserved, Perot suggested that senior management should mingle with union workers at company dinners. The two leaders compromised at times, but in an awaited separation, Perot sold his stock to GM for approximately $700 million in 1986. GM succeeded in removing Perot from GM's board and removed his direct influence on EDS. Typical of his entrepreneurial spirit and spunk, Perot started another competitor for EDS, Perot Systems, and over the years battled with GM and EDS over territorial rights and legal infringements. (Refer to Exhibit 2.)

The computer services giant worked hard to decrease its dependence on GM for revenue development and continued international expansion in Asia. In 1988, EDS purchased China Management Services, Taiwan's leading information services company. In 1993, partially due to rapid growth and expansion of other lines, GM's business represented only 39% of total EDS revenue, down from 73% seven years earlier. By 1996, EDS' presence was felt in 42 countries.

In 1995, EDS acquired A. T. Kearney, a global management consulting firm for $300 million in cash, notes, and contingency payments. The Kearney acquisition allowed EDS to diversify interests and gain a substantial presence in the high growth field of consulting.

Talks [were] fueled of a split-off. In the mid nineties, it was rumored on Wall Street that EDS had outgrown GM, or perhaps the other way around depending on whom one listened to. Regardless of how it would occur and how the fine details would be ironed out, General Motors appeared to lack strategic fit with EDS.

Exit General Motors

> At EDS, we like to focus on four strategic directions for customer growth: Better, Bigger, Broader, and Bolder. We call these—the "Killer Bees."
> Lester M. Alberthal, Jr., Chairman and CEO, EDS
> April 26, 1995

Clearly, Alberthal felt it was time for EDS and GM to part ways. In August 1995, both companies announced plans for a split-off of EDS from GM. Plans were finalized on December 31, 1995 when a tax-free transfer was approved by the IRS and it appeared as though the split-off would proceed within six months.

Alberthal stated the intention of the split-off was to accomplish three critical objectives for EDS.[5] First, the company wanted to improve its ability to participate in major strategic alliances. Second, and arguably a major factor in the decision to separate, [it wanted] to remove limitations on EDS' ability to obtain business from companies that compete with GM or its subsidiaries. Finally, EDS wanted to enhance its access to capital necessary for future growth.

> We know that there will be no boundaries in the frontier of the future. That much is plain to see. And today's data deluge offers a couple of simple choices. We can either be washed away with the tide—or we can learn to harness its power and surf the waves of the future.
>
> Lester M. Alberthal, Jr., Chairman and CEO, EDS
> October 25, 1995

The Price of Freedom

In April of 1996, the board of General Motors approved the EDS proposed split-off with the stipulation that EDS pay a parting dividend to GM of $500 million. In turn, however, EDS would receive a ten year, $40 billion contract to continue providing computer services to GM.[6] After June 7, GME stock would become EDS stock on a one for one transfer basis. That is, each share of GME common stock would be exchanged for one share of EDS stock.

EDS had grown to 95,000 employees in 42 countries and as an independent entity, ranked as one of the 100 largest U.S. based public companies. (Refer to Exhibits 3–7 for EDS' new board, summary income statements, balance sheets, cash flow statements, stock and market statistics.) The market murmured as to the true value of EDS. While the company was gaining its independence from General Motors and would be able to compete for additional contracts, there was an increased probability that EDS may lose some of their GM business as contracts began to expire over the next decade.

One *ValueLine* analyst shared his mixed views in the following commentary:

> The re-negotiation of the GM contract seems less favorable than originally expected . . . specifically the agreement allows GM to solicit competitive bids on its Information Technology outsourcing . . . Assuming the split-off occurs, the likely inclusion of EDS shares in the S&P 500 index could mean additional demand of as many as 25–30 million shares from market index funds . . . we think independence will enable EDS to grow earnings more quickly.
>
> R. Daniel Oshinskie
> June 7, 1996

Although he could not predict everything the future held for EDS, Alberthal was sure of one thing. He anticipated EDS would increase in value as an independent entity. The company had seen significant growth over the past decade and most indications were positive that the growth would continue after the split-off. On June 10, EDS was trading in the $57 range. Alberthal summed up his thoughts:

This is a significant day in EDS' history. Last year, we determined that we'd have better opportunities to grow if we became an independent company. We have attained that goal and look forward to the increased flexibility we'll have to respond quickly to customer and industry opportunities.

Lester M. Alberthal, Jr., Chairman and CEO, EDS
June 10, 1996

new objr's

Given the significance of the event, analysts were challenged to determine the value of the newly split-off EDS. What should Alberthal and his senior management team emphasize over the next few years to insure EDS maintains its position in the marketplace? What special factors come into play when valuing a recent split-off entity? What factors are most difficult to estimate in this valuation and why? What rate of growth did EDS enjoy over the past decade? Is this rate of growth likely to be maintained in the future? Why or why not? What is the intrinsic value of EDS stock on June 10, 1996? What is the per share value of the stock? Is the market overvaluing, undervaluing, or pricing the stock correctly? These were all valid questions to be answered before investment decisions could be made.

EXHIBIT 1	MISSION STATEMENTS

General Motors' Mission Statement

The fundamental purpose of General Motors is to provide products and services of such quality that our customers will receive superior value, our employees and business partners will share in our success, and our stockholders will receive a sustained, superior return on their investment.

—Roger B. Smith, in *Building on 75 Years of Excellence*

Electronic Data Systems Statement of Intent

EDS will be the leader in shaping how information is created, distributed, shared, enjoyed and applied for the benefit of enterprises and individuals worldwide. (1996).

| EXHIBIT 2 | POTENTIAL COMPETITORS FOR EDS |

Key Competitors[*]

Arthur Anderson Consulting

Computer Sciences Corporation

IBM Services Division

Other Potential Competitors[†]

ADP

Advantis

American Software

Arthur Anderson

AT&T

Cap Gemini Sogeti

Compucom Systems

Computer Sciences

Continuum

Coopers and Lybrand

Deloitte and Touche

IBM

Intelligent Electronics

MCI

Perot Systems

Policy Management Systems

SHL Systemhouse

System Software Associates

[*]Interview with Roxanne Curry, Investor Relations, EDS, August 22, 1997.
[†]*Hoover's Handbook of American Business*, 1995 edition.

EXHIBIT 3	EDS' POST SPLIT-OFF BOARD OF DIRECTORS (APPROVED APRIL 1, 1996)	
Name	**Title**	**Age**
Lester M. Alberthal, Jr.	Chief Executive Officer and Chairman of the Board, EDS.	52
James A. Baker, III	Senior partner of Baker and Botts, LLP law firm. Former White House Chief of Staff, 1981–85, 1992–93.	66
Richard B. Cheney	Chairman, President and CEO, Halliburton. Former Secretary of Defense, 1989–1993.	55
Gary J. Fernandes	Vice Chairman, EDS. Joined EDS in 1969.	52
Ray J. Groves	Former Chairman and CEO of Ernst and Young, LLP.	60
Jeffrey M. Heller	President and Chief Operating Officer, EDS. Senior Vice President prior to split-off.	56
Ray L. Hunt	Chairman and CEO, Hunt Oil Company.	52
C. Robert Kidder	Chairman and CEO, Borden, Inc. Previously Chairman and CEO of Duracell.	51
Judith Rodin	President, University of Pennsylvania.	51
Enrique J. Sosa	Executive Vice President, Amoco. Former President of Dow North America.	56

SOURCE: *EDS 1995 Annual Report* and EDS news release, April 2, 1996.

EXHIBIT 4

CONSOLIDATED STATEMENTS OF INCOME, EDS (IN MILLIONS, EXCEPT PER-SHARE DATA)

Years Ended Dec. 31	1995	1994	1993	1992	1991	1990	1989	1988	1987	1986
Systems & other contracts revenue										
Outside customers	8,531.0	6,412.9	5,183.6	4,806.7	3,666.3	2,787.5	2,384.6	1,907.6	1,444.8	1,127.7
GM and affiliates	3,891.1	3,547.2	3,323.7	3,348.5	3,362.2	3,234.2	2,988.9	2,837.0	2,883.3	3,195.1
Total revenues	12,422.1	9,960.1	8,507.3	8,155.2	7,028.5	6,021.7	5,373.5	4,744.6	4,328.1	4,322.8
Costs & expenses										
Cost of revenues	$9,601.6	$7,529.4	$6,390.6	$6,205.8	$5,415.1	$4,639.0	$4,168.6	$3,749.5	$3,452.5	$3,463.1
Selling, general, & administrative	1,291.5	1,187.1	1,005.4	969.3	761.9	663.0	605.2	500.0	447.0	434.8
Total costs & expenses	10,893.1	8,716.5	7,396.0	7,175.1	6,177.0	5,302.0	4,773.8	4,249.5	3,899.5	3,897.9
Operating income	1,529.0	1,243.6	1,111.3	980.1	851.5	719.7	599.7	495.1	428.6	424.9
Interest & other income, net	(62.0)	40.6	20.0	20.7	42.2	69.0	80.6	94.3	95.7	39.1
Income before income taxes	1,467.0	1,284.2	1,131.3	1,000.8	893.7	788.7	680.3	589.4	524.3	464.0
Provision for income taxes	528.1	462.3	407.3	365.3	330.7	291.8	245.0	205.3	201.2	203.1
Net income before cumulative effect of accounting change	938.9	821.9	724.0	635.5	563.0	496.9	435.3	384.1	323.1	260.9
Cumulative effect of accounting change**	—	—	—	—	(15.5)	—	—	—	—	—
Separate consolidated net income	$938.9	$821.9	$724.0	$635.5	$547.5	$496.9	$435.3	$384.1	$323.1	$260.9
EPS available to GM Class E common stock	$1.96	$1.71	$1.51	$1.33	$1.14	$1.04	$0.90	$0.79	$0.66	$0.53

| EXHIBIT 5 | CONSOLIDATED BALANCE SHEETS, EDS (IN MILLIONS) | | | | |

Years Ended Dec. 31	1995	1994	1993	1992	1991
Assets					
Current Assets					
Cash & cash equivalents	$ 548.9	$ 608.2	$ 383.4	$ 421.9	$ 260.6
Marketable securities	89.7	149.6	224.1	166.0	155.2
Accounts receivable	2,872.0	2,082.1	1,412.5	1,214.0	1,237.2
Receivables: GM & affiliates	297.0	65.4	112.6	41.1	45.8
Inventories	181.2	137.8	130.7	88.5	66.9
Prepaids & other	392.7	311.0	243.5	225.5	179.9
Total current assets	4,381.5	3,354.1	2,506.8	2,157.0	1,945.6
Property & equipment, at cost	6,561.8	5,437.5	4,520.4	3,888.9	3,401.8
Less accumulated depreciation	(3,319.4)	(2,680.9)	(2,405.7)	(2,168.2)	(1,850.2)
Net property & equipment	3,242.4	2,756.6	2,114.7	1,720.7	1,551.6
Operating & other assets					
Land held for development	105.1	97.4	94.4	148.1	148.9
Investment in leases & other	1,573.5	1,308.8	1,159.9	1,231.4	1,167.7
Software, goodwill, & other intangibles	1,529.9	1,269.6	1,066.3	866.3	889.4
Total operating & other assets	3,208.5	2,675.8	2,320.6	2,245.8	2,206.0
Total assets	10,832.4	8,786.5	6,942.1	6,123.5	5,703.2
Liabilities & Equity					
Current liabilities					
Accounts payable	$ 603.9	$ 571.1	$ 359.8	$ 348.0	$ 387.9
Accrued liabilities	1,704.5	1,451.0	996.0	918.4	960.9
Deferred revenue	629.3	536.7	429.7	295.8	299.2
Income taxes	75.9	111.0	202.2	66.0	167.8
GM & affiliate advances				5.5	16.0
Notes payable	247.8	203.4	172.7	269.4	564.9
Total current liabilities	3,261.4	2,873.2	2,160.4	1,903.1	2,396.7
Deferred income taxes	739.7	659.8	641.5	595.9	414.3
Deferred revenue					
Notes payable	1,852.8	1,021.0	522.8	560.6	275.9
Advances from GM & affiliates				0.5	6.0
Total liabilities	5,853.9	4,554.0	3,324.7	3,060.1	3,092.9
Stockholder's equity					
Common stock	517.7	455.1	421.2	365.9	323.4
Retained earnings	4,460.8	3,777.4	3,196.2	2,697.5	2,286.9
Total stockholder's equity	4,978.5	4,232.5	3,617.4	3,063.4	2,610.3
Total liabilities & equity	10,832.4	8,786.5	6,942.1	6,123.5	5,703.2

| EXHIBIT 5 | (CONTINUED) | | | | |

Years Ended Dec. 31	1990	1989	1988	1987	1986
Assets					
Current Assets					
Cash & cash equivalents	$ 407.1	$ 400.5	$ 379.2	$ 507.6	$ 235.3
Marketable securities	308.3	280.7	348.4	459.6	298.3
Accounts receivable	719.0	551.2	419.0	428.0	306.3
Receivables: GM & affiliates	63.2	95.5	6.3	16.4	151.6
Inventories	75.5	46.3	57.9	64.0	23.7
Prepaids & other	143.3	83.7	128.6	102.2	63.8
Total current assets	1,716.4	1,457.9	1,339.4	1,577.8	1,079.0
Property & equipment, at cost	2,774.2	2,349.5	2,081.2	1,836.2	1,354.1
Less accumulated depreciation	(1,577.1)	(1,266.4)	(1,004.6)	(729.4)	(361.5)
Net property & equipment	1,197.1	1,083.1	1,076.6	1,106.8	992.6
Operating & other assets					
Land held for development	134.5	119.9	106.3	103.4	122.3
Investment in leases & other	992.9	778.1	479.2	235.4	168.0
Software, goodwill, & other intangibles	524.4	479.2	414.5	83.5	47.7
Total operating & other assets	1,651.8	1,377.2	1,000.0	422.3	338.0
Total assets	4,565.3	3,918.2	3,416.0	3,106.9	2,409.6
Liabilities & Equity					
Current liabilities					
Accounts payable	$ 210.4	$ 165.1	$ 152.2	$ 108.4	$143.0
Accrued liabilities	706.6	557.2	518.2	520.9	393.2
Deferred revenue	373.5	356.4	329.8	189.5	95.5
Income taxes	74.7	74.1	66.8	99.0	37.3
GM & affiliate advances	104.1	218.5	225.7	311.9	189.7
Notes payable	184.6	123.2	84.5	108.0	12.5
Total current liabilities	1,653.9	1,494.5	1,377.2	1,337.7	871.2
Deferred income taxes	444.5	333.7	230.6	181.8	113.7
Deferred revenue			2.4	2.6	4.7
Notes payable	263.1	210.9	88.6	25.4	19.8
Advances from GM & affiliates	22.0	115.5	313.3	505.9	601.9
Total liabilities	2,383.5	2,154.6	2,012.1	2,053.4	1,611.3
Stockholder's equity					
Common stock	272.5	237.5	213.6	173.7	143.1
Retained earnings	1,909.3	1,526.1	1,190.3	879.8	655.2
Total stockholder's equity	2,181.8	1,763.6	1,403.9	1,053.5	798.3
Total liabilities & equity	4,565.3	3,918.2	3,416.0	3,106.9	2,409.6

EXHIBIT 6	CONSOLIDATED STATEMENT OF CASH FLOWS, EDS (IN MILLIONS)		

Years Ended December 31	1995	1994	1993
Cash flows from operating activities			
Net income	$ 938.9	$ 821.9	$ 724.0
Adjustments to reconcile net income to net cash provided by operating activities:			
Depreciation & amortization	1,107.8	771.1	626.8
Deferred compensation	58.8	62.0	33.8
Other	33.0	30.9	(17.7)
Changes in assets & liabilities, net of effects of acquired companies:			
(Increase) in accounts receivable	(611.5)	(605.4)	(200.8)
(Increase) decrease in accounts receivable from GM & affiliates	(227.8)	51.1	(56.0)
(Increase) in inventory	(41.9)	(1.9)	(15.5)
(Increase) in prepaids & other	(59.7)	(57.0)	(26.8)
Increase (decrease) in accounts payable & accrued liabilities	(76.0)	453.2	27.4
Increase in deferred revenue	81.0	79.1	137.1
Increase (decrease) in taxes payable	56.4	(72.5)	188.7
Total adjustment	320.1	710.6	697.0
Net cash provided by operating activities	1,259.0	1,532.5	1,421.0
Cash flows from investing activities			
Proceeds from sales of marketable securities	163.6	370.0	234.2
Proceeds from lease investments & other assets	87.8	134.6	217.3
Payments for purchases of property & equipment	(1,261.5)	(1,186.0)	(816.4)
Payments for lease investments & other assets	(356.3)	(395.7)	(170.6)
Payments related to acquisitions, net of cash acquired	(234.9)	(186.6)	(122.1)
Payments for purchases of software & other intangibles	(92.0)	(77.0)	(119.0)
Payments for marketable securities	(100.9)	(248.9)	(292.5)
Other	12.7	49.9	1.4
Net cash used in investing activities	(1,781.5)	(1,539.7)	(1,067.7)
Cash flows from financing activities			
Proceeds from notes payable	7,466.7	10,821.0	2,527.7
Payments on notes payable	(6,776.3)	(10,300.7)	(2,648.7)
Net decrease in current notes payable with maturities less than 90 days		(102.9)	(99.0)
Employee stock transactions & related tax benefit	26.0	20.2	33.9
Dividends paid	(251.3)	(231.1)	(192.1)
Net cash provided by (used in) financing activities	465.1	206.5	(378.2)
Effect of exchange rate changes on cash & cash equivalents	(1.9)	25.5	(13.6)
Net increase (decrease) in cash & cash equivalents	(59.3)	224.8	(38.5)
Cash & cash equivalents at beginning of year	608.2	383.4	421.9
Cash & cash equivalents at end of year	$ 548.9	$ 608.2	$ 383.4

EXHIBIT 7

*STOCK STATISTICS, EDS

Years Ended Dec. 31	1995	1994	1993	1992	1991	1990	1989	1988	1987	1986
Stock Price										
High	$52.63	$39.50	$35.88	$34.00	$33.06	$20.06	$14.40	$11.22	$12.75	$12.40
Low	$36.88	$27.50	$26.00	$25.25	$17.50	$12.19	$10.62	$8.37	$6.00	$6.18
Close	$52.00	$38.37	$29.25	$32.87	$31.50	$19.31	$13.65	$11.21	$9.62	$6.21
Dividend per Share	$0.52	$0.48	$0.40	$0.36	$0.32	$0.28	$0.24	$0.17	$0.13	$0.10
Shares in Dividend Base (millions)	483.7	481.7	480.97	479.3	478.0	478.6	477.4	487.6	487.6	487.6
P/E ratio	26.5	22.4	19.4	24.7	26.9†	18.6	15.2	14.2	14.6	11.7
Dividend Payout Ratio‡	26.5%	28.1%	26.5%	27.1%	27.4%†	26.9%	26.7%	21.5%	19.7%	18.9%
Dividend Yield	1.0%	1.3%	1.4%	1.1%	1.0%	1.5%	1.8%	1.5%	1.4%	1.6%
Book Value	$10.29	$8.79	$7.52	$6.39	$5.46	$4.56	$3.69	$2.88	$2.16	$1.64
Stockholder's Equity (mil.)	$4,978.5	$4,232.5	$3,617.4	$3,063.4	$2,610.3	$2,181.8	$1,763.6	$1,403.9	$1,053.5	$798.3
Total Market Value ($ mil.)	25,152.4	18,485.2	14,066.3	15,757.0	15,057.0	9,243.2	6,519.4	5,470.4	4,693.2	3,032.4

SOURCE: EDS Fact Book, 1996.

EDS's stock beta on June 7, 1996 (per *ValueLine*): 1.2
Number of shares outstanding on June 10, 1996: 485.71 million

Market Statistics§	Estimated Annual Rate
90-day Treasury bill	5.7%
10-year Treasury bond	6.9%
Average market risk premium (1926–1995)	8.6%

SOURCE: EDS Fact Book, 1996.

*Statistics are adjusted for two-for-one splits in 1990 and 1992.
†Before cumulative effect of accounting change.
‡The dividend policy in effect in 1989 was to pay dividends of 25% of the prior year's earnings. In 1989, the payout policy was increased to 30%.
§The rates for the 90-day Treasury bill and the 10-year Treasury bond are from the *Wall Street Journal*, June 10, 1996, and the market risk premium is from Ibbotson Associates.

References

Barrons, February 23, 1987.

EDS Annual Reports.

EDS 10K & 10Q Statements filed with the SEC.

EDS Fact Book, 1996.

EDS Home Page: http://www.eds/com

EDS News Releases

General Motors Annual Reports

General Motors 10K & 10Q Statements filed with the SEC.

General Motors News Releases.

Hoovers Handbook of American Business, 1995 edition, edited by Gary Hoover, Alta Campbell, & Patrick Spain Reference Press, p. 470–471.

Interview with Roxanne Curry, Investor Relations, EDS, August 22, 1997.

Smith, Roger B. *Building on 75 Years of Excellence: The General Motors Story*, Speech presented to & published by the Newcomen Society of the United States, 1984.

Levin, Doron P. *Irreconcilable Differences: Ross Perot Versus General Motors*, Signet Publishing, 1992.

Follett, Ken. *On Wings of Eagles*, William Morrow & Company, 1983.

Lee, Albert. *Call Me Roger*, Contemporary Books, 1988.

Keller, Maryann. *Rude Awakening*, William Morrow & Company, 1989.

ValueLine Investment Survey Report by R. Daniel Oshinskie, June 7, 1996.

Endnotes

1. Drake, Jacob, Carri Karuhn, and Joyce Werges. *Ross Perot: What Does He Stand for?* (1992), p. 31.
2. *Texas Monthly*, December 1998.
3. Lee, Albert, *Call Me Roger* (1988), p. 12.
4. Keller, Mary Ann. *Rude Awakening* (1989), p. 189.
5. EDS News Release, June 10, 1996.
6. *Wall Street Journal*, April 2, 1996.

10

Embracing Rapid Expansion:
The Franchise Option

Key Topics

- **The Franchising Choice**

- **How Franchising Works**

- **The Growth of Franchising**

- **Advantages of Franchising**

- **Trends in Franchising** → Gov't Role.

- **Franchising Your Business**

- **The Uniform Franchising Offering Circular**

Strategic growth and rapid expansion are accomplished in a variety of ways—acquisitions, mergers, internal growth, and so forth. One of the most popular forms of expansion is the franchise option. This option has many different aspects that need to be understood before it is undertaken. In this chapter we review some of the most important elements of this unique—and popular—form of business expansion.

The Franchising Choice

A franchise is a system of distribution that enables a supplier (the *franchisor*) to arrange for a dealer (the *franchisee*) to handle a specific product or service under certain mutually agreed-on conditions. In most cases, the franchisee is given the right to distribute and sell goods or services within a specific area. The business itself is owned by the franchisee, and the franchisor is paid a fee and/or a commission on sales. In essence, two types of franchising arrangements exist: the franchising of a product or service, and the franchising of an entire business enterprise.

Product or Service Franchise

When a *product* is franchised, the franchisee receives the goods from the franchisor and then sells them through a wholesale or retail outlet. An auto dealership provides an illustration of this arrangement. The dealership owner receives cars from an auto manufacturer and has an exclusive right to sell them. Retail purchasers cannot buy directly from the factory. Instead, they must go through a dealer who has a franchise.

Another illustration of product franchising is the local General Electric dealer. This business owner receives the product from the company and, in turn, sells it to the consumer. Retail firms that sell a wide variety of goods have franchise agreements with many different manufacturers for all kinds of products: General Electric for air-conditioners, RCA for radios, Magnavox for televisions, Whirlpool for washers and dryers, and so forth. In all of these cases, the supplier exerts only a small measure of control over the retailer, and this control is limited to the particular franchised product. The franchisor does not attempt to control the operations of the business itself.

When a *service* is franchised, the franchisee receives a license for a trade name and the particular services to be sold. Again, the franchisor does not attempt to control the operation of the business itself. The franchisee directs daily activities—hiring and firing of employees, operational business decisions, and budgeting concerns—whereas the franchisor maintains control over standard features expected of all franchisees.

Business Franchise

When the word *franchise* is used today, it often refers to the franchising of an *entire business enterprise*.[1] Common examples include McDonald's, Pizza Hut, and Burger King. In these cases, the franchisee operates the unit under a common trade name. The business operation, the establishment's appearance, the merchandise, and even the operating procedures are standardized to a high degree. In an effort to maintain this standardized image and marketing approach for the general buying public, the franchisor usually retains a strong, formalized system of control over the business op-

---

[1]J. Donald Weinrauch, "Franchising an Established Business," *Journal of Small Business Management* (July 1986): 1–7.

eration. In this type of a franchise arrangement, the responsibilities of both parties (the franchisor and the franchisee) are spelled out in the franchise contract and usually are considered to be of mutual advantage to both parties. The remainder of this chapter focuses on the franchising of the entire enterprise as opposed to the franchising of a particular product, product line, or service.

Conversion Franchising

Conversion franchising refers to the conversion of independent, ongoing concerns into franchise-system members. These independents usually come from the same product or service category as the franchisor whose name they adopt. Struggling independent firms that face strong competition and adverse results may seek greater success by turning to a franchise's nationally known brand name, access to additional customers, marketing assistance, promise of cost savings through mass purchasing power, and improved business procedures and operations. Franchisors use a conversion strategy to achieve rapid growth and selective market entry.

Conversion franchising has been particularly successful in the highly competitive and domestically mature industries of restaurants (Subway Sandwiches & Salads), hotels (Best Western), and real estate (Century 21).[2]

How Franchising Works

Business franchise systems for goods and services generally work in the same way. The franchisee (an independent businessperson) contracts for a complete business package. This contract usually requires the individual to do one or more of the following:

- Make a financial investment in the operation.

- Obtain and maintain a standardized inventory and/or equipment package usually purchased from the franchisor.

- Maintain a specified quality of performance.

- Follow the specific operating procedures and promotional efforts of the franchisor.

- Pay a franchise fee as well as a percentage of the gross revenues to the franchisor.

- Engage in a continuing business relationship with the franchisor.

In turn, the franchisor provides the following types of benefits and assistance:

- The company name. For example, if someone bought a Burger King franchise, this name would provide the business with drawing power. A well-known name, such as Burger King, ensures higher sales than an unknown name, such as Ralph's Big Burgers.

---

[2]John F. Preble, "Franchising: A Growth Strategy for the 1990s," *Mid-American Journal of Business* (Spring 1992): 35–41; and Patrick J. Kaufman, "Franchising and the Choice of Self-Employment," *Journal of Business Venturing* (July 1999): 345–362.

- Identifying symbols, logos, designs, and facilities. For example, all McDonald's units have the same identifying golden arches on the premises. Likewise, the facilities are similar inside.

- Professional management training for each independent unit's staff.

- Sale of specific merchandise necessary for the unit's operation at wholesale prices. Usually provided are all of the equipment to run the operation and any food or materials needed for the final project.

- Financial assistance, if needed, to help the unit in any way possible.

- Continuing aid and guidance to ensure that everything is done in accordance with the contract.[3]

The Growth of Franchising

Franchising has proved to be one of the most popular vehicles for individuals to pursue a career as an entrepreneur. Franchised businesses currently account for more than one-third of all U.S. retail sales, with projections increasing to 50 percent by the year 2005. In recent years, franchising has reacted favorably to many of the trends that have adversely affected other business segments. This option's ability to meet subtle, yet rapid shifts in consumer demands, demographic changes, and technological breakthroughs indicates that it is likely to remain a strong business segment regardless of the general state of the economy.

The franchising statistics are certainly stunning. More than half a million franchise businesses exist in the United States alone, employing 8 million people; 600,000 franchise/small business owners are involved in the industry. Sales revenues from franchising operations, which currently total $800 billion per year, are expected to account for 50 percent of the nation's retail sales by the year 2005.[4] (See Table 10.1 for franchise facts.)

More important than the growth statistics are the attitude and satisfaction of franchise owners, as well as the success rate of franchise operations. According to a study carried out by the accounting firm Arthur Andersen, of 366 franchise companies in 60 different industries, nearly 86 percent of all franchise operations that had opened in the previous five years remained under the same ownership; only 3 percent of those businesses had gone out of business.

Franchising also has opened up opportunities for minorities and women. For example, of the 2,177 franchisors recently surveyed by the federal government, 572 reported a total of 10,142 units owned by minority businesspersons. Included in this group were 3,615 African Americans, 2,808 persons with Spanish surnames, 3,616 Asian Americans, and 103 Native Americans. The most minority-owned franchises involved auto products and service businesses, restaurants, food stores, and convenience stores.[5]

---

[3]For a complete resource book on franchising, see Robert Justis and Richard Judd, *Franchising* (Cincinnati: South-Western, 1989); and Kurk Shivell and Kent Banning, "What Every Prospect Franchisee Should Know," *Small Business Forum* (Winter 1996/1997): 33–42.

[4]U.S. Department of Commerce, *Franchising in the Economy: 1991–1993* (Washington, DC: U.S. Government Printing Office, 1994), Chart 1, 2; and the International Franchise Association, 1997.

[5]U.S. Department of Commerce, *Franchising in the Economy*, 11; and Rajiv P. Dant, Candida G. Brush, and Francisco P. Iniesta, "Participation Patterns of Women in Franchising," *Journal of Small Business Management* (April 1996): 14–28.

TABLE 10.1   FRANCHISE FACTS

Franchised businesses accounted for $803 billion in annual sales.

Franchises represent 42 percent of all U.S. retail sales.

Franchise sales equal 20 percent of the gross national product.

Total franchise sales are projected to reach $1 trillion by 2003.

One out of every 12 business establishments is a franchised business.

A new franchise business opens every eight minutes of every day.

There are more than 600,000 franchised establishments in the United States.

There are more than 8.5 million people employed by franchise establishments, with an average of 8 to 15 employees per establishment.

Seventy-five industries use franchising to distribute goods and services to consumers.

The average initial investment level for nearly eight out of ten franchises, excluding real estate, is less than $250,000.

Average royalty fees range from 3 percent to 6 percent of monthly gross sales.

Most franchise companies have fewer than 100 units.

The average length of a franchise contract is ten years.

SOURCE: International Franchise Association, 2000.

Expansion into foreign markets by U.S. franchisors has continued to increase. In 1971, 156 companies operated 3,365 units in overseas locations. In 1990, 374 franchisors had 35,046 overseas units.[6] By the mid-1990s, approximately one-third of U.S. franchisors had foreign outlets. Within this group of internationally active franchisors, approximately 22 percent earned at least 10 percent of their income from these foreign sources.[7] In most cases, the franchisor sells the outlets to the franchisee either directly or through a master licensee who holds the right to develop the franchisor's system in a specific country or region of the world. In a small percentage of cases, the franchisor runs the unit directly or engages in a joint venture with local operating partners.

In a study conducted for the International Franchise Association, the Gallup Organization surveyed 1,001 current U.S. franchisees and found that an overwhelming majority—nearly nine of ten (88 percent)—said they would recommend purchasing a franchise to someone rather than opening a nonfranchise business of their own. Nearly all—93 percent—believed that being associated with a franchise system gave them an advantage. The most important advantages, in order, were name recognition, support from the franchisor, knowledge, advertising, buying power, networking, and training.[8] (See Table 10.2 for some of the common myths of franchising.)

---

[6]U.S. Department of Commerce, *Franchising in the Economy: 1986–1988* (Washington, DC: U.S. Government Printing Office, 1988), 9.

[7]Christopher Melly, *Franchising* (Washington, DC: Office of Industries, U.S. International Trade Commission, 1995), 21.

[8]International Franchise Association Educational Foundation, Washington, DC, 2000.

■ TABLE 10.2	FRANCHISING MYTHS

Myth: "Franchising is fast food."
Fact: Franchising spans 75 industries, with food being only one industry. Examples include, but are not limited to, carpet dyeing, personnel testing, accounting, wood restoration, and interior plantscaping.

Myth: "Franchises are expensive."
Fact: The fastest-growing segment of the franchise industry is home-based business. The initial investments for quality opportunities range from $15,000 to $35,000.

Myth: "I must invest a lot of money to own a business that will allow me to earn a lot of money."
Fact: There is no correlation between the amount of initial investment and potential earnings from a single unit. For example, annual earnings from a home-based business are often five to ten times the initial investment because operating expenses are relatively low.

Myth: "I need business experience to own a franchise."
Fact: Quality franchise systems have proven records of teaching and supporting their franchisees to successfully run all aspects of the business.

Myth: "Most franchisors are big companies."
Fact: Only 6.5 percent have more than 100 franchise outlets.

Myth: "Franchising is the same as other forms of business opportunity."
Fact: "Franchising" is a legal term. It is federally regulated, whereas multilevel marketing, distributorships, and other forms of licensing are not. Franchisors must give you their offering prospectus before you invest, which is annually registered with the Federal Trade Commission. It explains 23 categories of information you need to know, including a list of all franchisees.

SOURCE: www.frannet.com.

Despite the growing popularity of franchises, the potential franchisee needs to be aware that many franchise operations fail. Table 10.3 lists the most common reasons for such failures and suggests how these major pitfalls might be avoided.[9]

Advantages of Franchising

As stated previously, a number of advantages are associated with franchising.[10] Some of the most important advantages follow:

- Training and guidance are provided by the franchisor.

- The franchise offers brand-name appeal.

- The track record of other franchisees shows proof of success.

- Financial assistance can be secured from the franchisor.

The following sections examine each of these advantages.

---

[9]See Gary J. Castrogiovanni, Robert T. Justis, and Scott D. Julian, "Franchise Failure Rates: An Assessment of Magnitude and Influencing Factors," *Journal of Small Business Management* (April 1992): 105–114.

[10]See Alden Peterson and Rajiv P. Dant, "Perceived Advantages of the Franchise Option from the Franchisee Perspective: Empirical Insights from a Service Franchise," *Journal of Small Business Management* (July 1990): 46–61; see also Darrell L. Williams, "Why Do Entrepreneurs Become Franchisees? An Empirical Analysis of Organizational Choice," *Journal of Business Venturing* (Jan. 1999): 103–124.

TABLE 10.3	REASONS FOR FAILURE AND SUCCESS IN FRANCHISING
Reason for Failure	**Prescription for Success**
Bad location	Excellent physical location
Stiff competition	Prosperous ongoing small business
Inadequate capital	Financial strength
Management "spread too thin"	Solid management team
Inappropriate business concept	A unique and protected process or marketable idea
Weak organizational structure	Simple, well-defined concept that franchisees can easily implement
Poor legal/contractual framework	Appropriate legal structure
Poor quality control	Quality control for products and services
Selling franchise outlets too quickly	Strong financial backing
Unexpected operating expenditures	Healthy gross margins
Changing consumer tastes	Long-term market prospects

SOURCE: J. Donald Weinrauch, "Franchising an Established Business," *Journal of Small Business Management* (July 1986): 3. Reprinted by permission.

Training and Guidance

Perhaps the greatest advantage of buying a franchise, as compared to starting a new business or buying an existing one, is that the franchisor usually will provide both training and guidance to the franchisees. As a result, the likelihood of success is much greater for national franchisees who have received this assistance than for small business owners in general. For example, it has been reported that the ratio of failure for small enterprises to franchised businesses may be as high as five to one.

Some of the best-known training programs are those offered by McDonald's and Holiday Inn. At McDonald's, the owner is sent to "Hamburger U" before starting the business. There the individual learns how to make hamburgers, manage the unit, control inventory, keep records, and deal with personnel problems. Other national franchisors provide the same kind of training. For example, the Mister Donut franchise requires each owner to attend an eight-week training course in which it covers topics such as doughnut making, merchandising, production scheduling, labor scheduling, advertising, and accounting. One of the greatest advantages of these training programs is that they provide an individual who has only a limited amount of business training with the opportunity to pick up a great deal of practical information that can spell the difference between success and failure.

Another benefit relates to continuing assistance. A well-operated franchise system stays in continual contact with the franchisees, providing them with practical business tips, follow-up training, and pamphlets and manuals designed to make the overall operation more efficient.

Brand-Name Appeal

An individual who buys a well-known national franchise, especially a big-name one, has a good chance to succeed. The franchisor's name acts as a drawing card for the establishment.

Consumers often are more aware of the product or service offered by a national franchise and prefer it to those offered by lesser-known outlets. One way that the large franchisors create such brand-name appeal is through advertising. Consider the television commercials you see and hear every day from Burger King, McDonald's, Papa Johns, Denny's, and a host of other national franchises. They all have catchy jingles that help create the all-important brand-name appeal.

A Proven Track Record

The third major benefit of buying a franchise is that the franchisor has already proved that the operation can be successful. Of course, if someone is the first individual to buy a franchise, this benefit is not assured. If the organization has been around for five to ten years and has 50 or more units, however, it should not be difficult to check on its success. If all of the units are still in operation and the owners report that they are doing well financially then, one thing is certain: The franchisor has proved that the layout of the store, the pricing policy, the quality of the goods or service, and the overall management system are successful. If a person buys a successful business from another individual, it may be difficult to determine how much of its success is a function of the seller's personality or drive. In contrast, when one buys into a franchise organization that has had many successes, it is likely that the franchising concept accounts for the success rather than the managerial skills or drive of a single individual. (Table 10.1 provides some interesting statistics on the successful tenure of franchise operations.)

Financial Assistance

Another reason that a franchise can be a good investment is that the franchisor may be able to help the new owner secure the financial assistance needed to run the operation. For example, many bankers will think twice about lending a business owner money to open an automobile transmission-repair operation. However, if it is an AAMCO franchise, the story might be different. The banker knows that if the prospective businessperson is associated with a national chain, the chances of bankruptcy will be reduced greatly, because the franchisor will stand behind the individual and try to help in every way possible. In fact, in some cases, franchisors have helped franchisees get started by lending them money and not requiring any repayment until the operation is up and running smoothly. In short, buying a franchise is often an ideal way to ensure assistance from the financial community.

The Decision: It's Up to the Investor

After the prospective investor has gathered all of the necessary information, it is up to him or her to make the final decision on the matter. As with buying an ongoing business, however, asking the "right questions" can help.

Trends in Franchising

Trends in franchising include systemwide changes in the way of doing business. Some of the most prominent changes follow:

- *Internet franchising.* The franchisor Internet explosion has begun. A significant increase has occurred in both Internet pages as a means of communicating within franchise organizations and Internet advertising by franchises.

- *Globalization of franchising.* Many franchisors overseas are either expanding vertically (growing rapidly in certain narrow industries, such as fast food or retail) or horizontally (many small U.S. franchisors entering the market).

- *Home-based franchises.* The growth in this sector is "explosive, more than doubling in the past two years."[11] Many of these franchise opportunities exist in business-to-business services, which are usually direct-sales franchises.

- *Rural franchises.* These small markets are fertile ground if a franchisor can develop a concept that works rurally. The key to success in rural markets is the ability to provide quality services combined with low start-up construction so that the franchise can prosper even with low levels of unit volume.[12]

In addition to these trends, the legal considerations associated with franchising continue to change. Changes are taking place in the legal environment for both franchisers and franchisees. For example, in 1993, the franchisor-controlled International Franchise Association (IFA) agreed to accept franchisees as members for the first time. This move illustrates that the balance of power is now shifting from franchisors to franchisees. In addition, numerous franchise hearings have taken place in the U.S. House of Representatives' Small Business Committee. These hearings have spurred the Federal Trade Commission (FTC) to more strictly enforce its Franchise Disclosure Rule as well as prompting the passage of improved franchise laws within individual states. Over the next ten years, more legislation will be passed to regulate franchising. Franchisors themselves admit that greater regulation is one of the major problems they will have to face. Pending legislation and court rulings all promise to make franchising more confusing.

The retail environment throughout the United States is becoming increasingly complex. This trend merely means that the franchisee must be a better businessperson than his or her predecessors. Many of the laws will not injure, but rather protect the franchisee from unfair practices by unscrupulous franchisors.[13] In addition, retailing undoubtedly will change in terms of product mix, store design, and layout. For example, some supermarkets are fighting fast-food outlets by installing fast-food departments in their own stores. In short, survival in the retail environment will require creative marketing. Franchising will play an important role in this environment. The need for entrepreneurs with the ability and daring to assume the challenges and risks that will be inherent in franchise operations will be the challenge of the next decade.

---

[11]Janean Chun, "Franchise Frenzy," *Entrepreneur* (Jan. 1997): 161.

[12]Chun, "Franchise Frenzy," 60–163.

[13]For a legal discussion of franchising laws, see Roger Miller and Gaylord A. Jentz, *Business Law Today*, 4th ed. (St. Paul, MN: West, 1997), 630–635.

Franchising Your Business

The other side of the franchising equation involves the entrepreneur acting as the developer of the franchise idea and business. According to Francorp, Inc., a franchise management consulting firm, the future for franchising is bright. Fundamental changes in business and society are opening up many opportunities for new franchisors. Among the factors promoting franchising are a cleaner environment, the "graying" of America, the popularity of niche restaurants and speciality retailing, the emergence of personal and business services, and the growth of direct sales to business.[14]

How does one get the next franchise business off the ground? Assume you are a successful entrepreneur considering franchising your business. First, it's important to recognize that you would be creating a business, but not the same one you already created. Second, you need to try to determine whether the idea is franchisable. Simply having a successful business does not always mean that it is a good franchise candidate. What are the growth opportunities? Is it a business with growth potential that will exceed its ability to fund its own expansion? Is it a business where any one unit will serve only a limited number of locations? How quickly could you grow on your own versus growing by selling franchises? Will a lack of rapid growth have a negative impact on your business's survival?

Before putting together a franchise plan, you must make many decisions. For every issue a prospective franchisee would consider, you now must make a decision as the franchisor.[15] The shoe is on the other foot; these are very important choices. What should my franchise fee be? What royalties will I charge? Sections V and VI of the Uniform Franchise Offering Circular (UFOC) address the issue of initial and ongoing franchise fees. What service do I give the franchisee? What rights do the franchisees have? How much control do I want to retain? Who will write the franchise agreement? Once franchisees sign on, what training will I give them and where? Will I offer any financing? What sales territory rights will I give? Section XII of the UFOC covers details about how much territory the franchisee can operate within. But how will I select the franchises themselves? The list goes on and on. Experienced legal counsel is highly recommended.

The development of a new franchise business will be a complex process. For the same reason that you would develop a business plan for any other type of business, it is essential that you develop a comprehensive business plan for your new franchising firm. It is also recommended that you develop a model business plan for prospective franchisees. This model business plan needs to be modified to accommodate the unique or unusual situations of individual franchises. You must also remember that you're now in several businesses. Here are more guidelines:

Developing a Franchise Business   You must develop operating systems for your own business—that is, the headquarters business. You will need to develop functional areas such as human resources, information systems, accounting, purchasing and logistics, training for home-office employees and franchisees, and methods for franchisee evaluation.

---

[14]Kevin D. Thompson, "Driving for Diversity," *Black Enterprise* (Sept. 1992): 49–60; and Erika Kotite, "Franchising Comes Alive!" *Entrepreneur* (April 1991): 9–101.

[15]Tham Jambulingam and John R. Nevin, "Influence of Franchisee Selection Criteria on Outcomes Desired by the Franchisor," *Journal of Business Venturing* (July 1999): 363–396.

Selling Franchises   Your success depends not only on your ability to manage the business you have created, but also on the expansion of your sales base by adding franchises to the firm. This effort is marketing of a different sort. Your firm must prospect to develop leads, market itself through appropriate channels, and screen these prospective franchisees. Careful franchisee selection is key to building a strong outlet network.

Servicing Franchises   Provision of necessary business support services by the franchisor is one of the main reasons people purchase franchises. If you cannot or do not offer them enough in return, such as marketing assistance and support, for their franchise fee or royalties, you'll have a revolution among the ranks. Other areas of franchisee support you need to develop include dependable suppliers, ideas, strategies for dealing with the competition, and training for the franchise owners and their employees.

The Uniform Franchise Offering Circular

In 1979, the Federal Trade Commission established a Franchise Disclosure Rule requiring franchisors to make full presale disclosure nationwide. To comply with this ruling, the UFOC was developed for franchisors.

The UFOC is divided into 23 items that provide different segments of information for prospective franchisees. Summaries of the sections follow.

Sections I–IV: cover the franchisor, the franchisor's background, and the franchise being offered

Sections V–VI: delineate the franchise fees, both initial and ongoing

Section VII: sets forth all of the initial expenses involved to established the entire franchise

Sections VIII–IX: detail the franchisee's obligation to purchase specific goods, supplies, services, and so forth from the franchisor

Section X: provides information on any financing arrangements available to franchisees

Section XI: describes in detail the contractual obligations of the franchisors to the franchisees

Section XII: clearly outlines the geographic market within which the franchisee must operate

Sections XIII–XIV: disclose all pertinent information regarding trademarks, trade names, patents, and so forth

Section XV: outlines the franchisor's expectations of the franchisee (day-to-day operations)

Section XVI: explains any restrictions or limitations

Section XVII: sets forth the conditions for renewal, termination, or sale of the franchise

Section XVIII: discloses the actual relationship between the franchise and any celebrity figure used in advertising for the franchise

Section XIX: provides a factual description of any potential "earnings claims," including their assumptions and actual figures

Section XX: lists the names and addresses of all existing franchises in the state where the proposed franchise is to be located

Sections XXI–XXIII: provide certified financial statements for the previous three fiscal years and a copy of the actual franchise contract

In 1993, the FTC revamped the UFOC guidelines to require more detailed information in the sections, to remove the legal language to promote easier understanding, and to provide franchisees with a clear picture of their obligations.[16]

Exploring the Entrepreneurial Concepts

The following sections provide an "entrepreneurial library" that contains a journal reading on this chapter's subject and a "comprehensive cases study" to illustrate the concept in practice. It is hoped that through the reading and discussion of the case, you will gain a greater understanding of the chapter.

THE ENTREPRENEURIAL LIBRARY

Reading for Chapter 10

FRANCHISING AND THE CHOICE OF SELF-EMPLOYMENT

Patrick J. Kaufmann Boston University

Executive Summary

This paper reports the findings of a study of the decision to purchase a franchise within the broader context of the decision to become self-employed. The sample is taken from individuals who had indicated an interest in self-employment and franchising three years prior to the current study. In the interim, some had purchased franchises, some had opened or bought independent businesses, and some had remained employed by others. The differences among these groups are examined. Some support was found for the posited relationship between the personal benefits of self-employment and the decision to purchase a franchise or independent business. The importance attached to the financial and business benefits of franchising is positively related to the decision to pur-

---

[16]David J. Kaufmann and David E. Robbins, "Now Read This," *Entrepreneur* (Jan 1991): 100–105.

Address correspondence to Dr. P. J. Kaufmann, Professor of Marketing, School of Management, Boston University, Boston, MA 02215; (617) 353-4278; Fax: (617) 353-4078; E-mail: patk@bu.edu

This research was conducted while the author was on the faculty of Georgia State University and was made possible through the generous support of the Carl R. Zwerner Chair of Family Owned Enterprises, Georgia State University. Thanks also to Jaime Durand for his assistance.
Journal of Business Venturing **14**, 345–362. © 1999 Elsevier Science Inc. All rights reserved.

chase a franchise. Finally, there was some evidence that franchising offered greater choice of sectors. Franchisees were less likely than independent business owners to operate within sectors where they had previous experience.

Introduction

Franchising is often touted as a way to be in business for yourself but not by yourself (International Franchise Association 1988). Although its current growth rate may be slowing (Trutko et al. 1993; Stanworth et al. 1997), franchising's phenomenal growth over the past four decades can be traced, in part, to the belief that it permits much of the independence sought by would-be small business owners while providing training, support, and (arguably) some reduction in the risk associated with starting an independent business (International Franchise Association Educational Foundation and Horwath International 1990; but see also Bates 1995).

Individuals decide to become self-employed for a variety of reasons. Whatever the reasons, however, the benefits of self-employment are always gained at the cost of increased risk. One obvious way to reduce the risk of opening an independent small business is to leverage one's business experience by operating within a familiar sector (Perry 1994). An experienced cook might open his or her own restaurant, or an experienced mechanic might open his or her own service station. The personal human capital gained as someone else's employee is invested in the new business and augmented by the new business owner's own personal insight or unique understanding (Cooper 1981). This allows the new owner to create a novel product or service offering while operating generally within a familiar area.

Franchising, on the other hand, offers would-be small business owners the benefit of choice. Franchisees typically need little direct experience in the type of business their franchise represents. Instead, they can rely on the franchisor to train them and provide the institutionalized knowledge necessary to successfully operate the franchised concept (Perry 1994). This opens a wide area of choice that might not be considered by independent entrepreneurs.

Franchising, however, also presents costs that are not associated with starting an independent business. In addition to the fees and royalties, there are the expected restrictions on the free operation of the franchise. These restrictions may include relocation, operational controls, restrictions on transfer of the franchise, and even restrictions of family member succession (Sullivan and Robins 1996). In making his or her decision, the prospective franchisee must address all of the issues that a prospective independent entrepreneur must face, as well as the issues that are occasioned by the franchise relationship itself. Thus, the would-be owner of a small business considering franchising has a more complex choice that not only includes whether to go into business for oneself, but also whether to start a business from scratch or purchase an existing business, the type of business, the organizational form (independent or franchised), and if relevant, the franchise system itself. Consequently, by examining the decision process of a prospective franchisee, we gain a unique perspective on the more general issues surrounding the creation of small businesses.

In this paper, the decision to purchase a franchise is explored within that broader context of the decision to become self-employed. The results are reported of a longitudinal study of individuals who were chosen initially because they had demonstrated an interest in becoming franchisees. Variables are used from two sets of data obtained three years apart, spanning the period from consideration, to decision, to result. The paper begins with a review of the literature as it relates to the decision to open a franchise, and the antecedents, expectations, and perceptions of the franchise opportunity compared with employment and self-employment. A model is presented that places the franchise decision within a decision process that leads from the decision to become self-employed to the choice of a particular franchise system. Several hypotheses are proposed that link contextual constructs to the various decision nodes in that process. Proposed antecedents to the decision to become self-employed, to the decision as to organizational form, and to the decision as to sector are examined. In doing so, questions are raised relating to the employment of family members, to the conflict between work and family life, the relative benefits of franchise operation, and the impact of prior work experience. Further hypotheses are proposed and tested and the findings reported along with some follow-up analysis. Finally, these results are discussed and suggested interpretations of the findings are offered.

Antecedents of the Decision to Become a Franchisee

The Franchisee's Decision

The academic literature on franchising has demonstrated a preoccupation with the decision of the franchisor and has given noticeably less attention to the franchisee's decision to purchase a franchise. The business press, while devoting a great deal of attention to the franchisee's decision, has simply provided a laundry list of caveats and noted the issues to explore before taking the plunge. Whether franchising is a response to the need for financial capital (Oxenfeldt and Kelly 1968; Caves and Murphy 1976), a solution to the incentive problem of geographically dispersed outlets (Rubin 1978; Brickley and Dark 1987; Lafontaine 1992), or both (Kaufmann and Dant 1996), or the result of a more idiosyncratic motivation, is not entirely clear (Dant 1995). It is clear, however, that the decision of the franchisee to accept the offered contract is just as important as the decision of the franchisor to offer it.

In the traditional economic analysis of contracts, the identity of the parties is not important. In franchising, however, there is reason to question that assumption. Most franchisors are corporate entities even if the founder still controls the company. Franchisees, on the other hand, are more likely to be physical (not just legal) persons (Oxenfeldt and Kelly 1968).[1] In other words, franchisees have finite life expectancies and often have families. Issues such as retirement and succession, irrelevant to a corporate franchisor, are of critical concern to human franchisees. Franchisees face income constraints (Mathewson and Winter 1985) which, taken together with the liquidity requirements of franchise systems (Kaufmann and Lafontaine 1994), can influence the decision to purchase a franchise. Franchisees have idiosyncratic life experience and skill sets that cannot be augmented in the same way an organization can acquire those inputs. Finally, franchisees have personal goals that, while they often include financial returns, may well extend beyond those unidimensional objectives to include such things as family employment.

---

[1]Although many franchisees organize their businesses as partnerships or closely held corporations (often for tax and liability reasons), franchise agreements typically require the primary individual named as franchisee to hold the majority of the outstanding stock. In addition to these restrictions on the assignment of franchise rights, franchise agreements may also contain the obligation of the individual franchisee to personally manage or control the franchise (Keating 1987). Thus, the human nature of the franchisee generally is relevant whatever the legal configuration of the business.

The implication of these differences between franchisor and franchisee is that small business research in general, and franchise research in particular, should include a closer examination of the franchisee's decision process and not assume symmetry of motives between franchisor and franchisee. Bhattacharyya and Lafontaine (1995) have incorporated the franchisee's decision more directly into standard economic analysis through the concept of double-sided moral hazard. This approach, however, still focuses on only one aspect of the franchisee's decision calculus, that of creating incentives for the franchisor to maintain support for the franchisee during the life of the relationship. Many of the other issues, enumerated above, are ignored.

When researchers have examined the franchisee's decision to purchase a franchise, they have focused only on existing franchisees. The respondents typically are asked to reconstruct their purchase decision and indicate the issues that were important to them (Knight 1986; Bannock and Stanworth 1990; Peterson and Dant 1990). Noticeably absent from these studies are those individuals who have considered purchasing a franchise and have decided against it. This is similar to doing market research only on a firm's customers. You know why they bought, but you don't know why the others didn't.

Other studies of the decision to purchase a franchise have focused on individuals before the decision is made (Bradach and Kaufmann 1988; Stanworth and Purdy 1994; Kaufmann and Stanworth 1995; Stanworth and Kaufmann 1996). In those studies, prospective franchisees were asked what criteria they would use to make their decision. This solved some of the retrospective problems, but again in each case, the prospective franchisees were never linked with the ultimate outcome of the decision process. To fully understand the decision and the factors affecting it, both purchasers (i.e., franchisees) and nonpurchasers (i.e., those who have considered franchising and have rejected it) must be included in the study. This permits the researcher to examine the franchise decision process, not just the real or expected outcome. To do this, however, requires the recognition that the decision to become a franchisee itself is embedded in a series of related decisions, and is contingent on the more general decision to become self-employed (see Figure 1).

FIGURE 1   THE DECISION TO PURCHASE A FRANCHISE: PROCESS MODEL

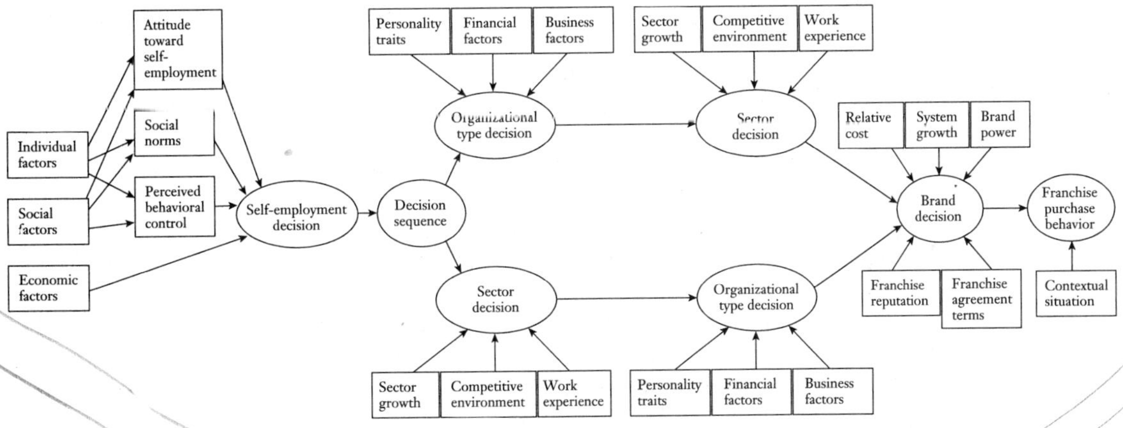

There is very little reported research of this type. In one of the few examples of longitudinal research involving self-employment decisions and entrepreneurial success, Schiller and Crewson (1997) found that unsuccessful entrepreneurs resembled nonentrepreneurs. Carroll and Mosakowski (1987) used a retrospective-based methodology to examine respondents' cycles of employment and self-employment, and found that self-employment was dependent on prior self-employment and family member self-employment. In the only franchising research of this kind, Hatcliffe et al. (1995) conducted a follow-up study of respondents two years after they had attended a franchising exposition in the U.K. The authors achieved a 33% response rate with a final sample of 169. They do not report the results of any tests for non-response bias nor do they test any specific hypotheses, however, they do provide a number of descriptive statistics relevant to the present study. Thirty-three percent of their respondents had become self-employed, with 20% purchasing franchises, and 13% purchasing or opening independent businesses. Seventy-four percent of the franchisees joined sectors in which they had no previous work experience. Forty-five percent of the franchise purchasers had never been self-employed, 17% had been but were not currently self-employed, and 38% were self-employed when they purchased the franchise. Ninety-four percent of those purchasing franchises decided to do so within one year of attending the exposition.

General Process Model of Self-Employment

Self-employment is not the equivalent of entrepreneurship. An individual wishing to become self-employed may form a new and unique enterprise or merely purchase an existing business (Kolvereid 1996a). In this study, the focus is on status choice, i.e., the choice of self-employment (Katz 1992), and not only on the creation of a new enterprise. The status of self-employment, therefore, can be achieved through entrepreneurial activity, purchase, or inheritance of an independent business, or purchase of a franchise.

As depicted in Figure 1, the decision process leading ultimately to the purchase of a franchise is posited to begin with the antecedents to the general decision to become self-employed. Once that intention is formed, a sequencing decision is made that determines the order in which the organizational form and business sector are decided. Subsequent to those decisions, the brand decision is made, and subject to the impact of exogenous situational variables, the intention is transferred to actual purchase behavior in accordance with Ajzen's (1991) theory of planned behavior.

Personal, family, and social considerations have been linked with the initial status choice. The personal factors that have been associated with the choice of self-employment have both demographic and psychographic components (Dyer 1994) and have included gender and work experience (Matthews and Moser 1995), personality traits (Begley and Boyd 1987), and psychosocial values such as autonomy (Katz 1992). The family factors have included such variables as the existence of parental role models (Carroll and Mosakowski 1987) and family support (Cooper 1981). The social factors have included social networks (Aldrich and Zimmer 1986) and culture-based components (Dyer 1994). Dyer (1994) also suggests the impact of a third set of economic variables such as alternative employment opportunities.

Drawing on both Shapiro's (1975) entrepreneurial event model and Ajzen's (1991) theory of planned behavior, Kolvereid (1996b) suggest three direct antecedents to status choice; the individual's attitude toward self-employment, the perceived social norms surrounding that choice, and the perception of behavioral control. Included in the attitude toward self-employment construct are preferences for such values as autonomy, challenge, and self-realization. The social norms construct includes the individual's beliefs regarding the value put on self-employment by his or her family. Finally, behavioral control reflects the level of control the individual feels he or she has over the decision and its success. Demographic and tracking variables such as gender and personal and family self-employment history are seen to act through these intervening constructs to predict status choice.

Findings within franchising research are consistent with some of these ideas and models, and so are better understood with reference to the overall self-employment decision process than merely the franchise decision. For example, both Knight (1986) and Peterson and Dant (1990) report that franchisee respondents identified personal independence (or autonomy) as a key benefit of owning a franchise. Clearly, the comparison is to employment by others, not to owning an independent outlet. Given that any form of self-employment (either franchise or independent business ownership) would provide the benefit of independence, the construct is more properly linked to the initial decision to become self-employed than to the more specific decision to buy a franchise. The more detailed decision process model offered in Figure 1 is an attempt to disentangle some of these constructs and relationships. In the case of autonomy, i.e., the importance attached to independence or direct involvement in running the business, the link would be to the decision to become self-employed. Thus the first hypothesis:

> *H1:* The greater the importance attached to the personal benefits of independence and control, the more likely the individual is to become self-employed.

Social issues are also critical to that initial decision to become self-employed. Some antecedents relate directly to the social value placed on entrepreneurial activity. Others relate to family interaction and the association between family and work. For example, the conflict that an individual feels between the requirements of his or her work and the individual's role as family member will impact the decision as to whether to become self-employed. Boles (1996) has argued that the role of work/family conflict is an especially important issue in the management of small businesses. Work/family conflict is defined as the pressure that arises from incongruity between an individual's role at work and in the family (Greenhaus and Beutell 1985). In one of the few studies to focus on the work/family conflict of the small business owner/operator, Boles (1996) found a significant relationship between work/family conflict and job satisfaction. Although this study provided significant insight into the role of work/family conflict in small business, it did not directly compare small business owners (either independent or franchisees) with employees, nor did it attempt to predict what role work/family conflict might have in the decision to become self-employed.

One of the sources of work/family conflict is the unanticipated competition for an employee's time (Greenhaus and Beutell 1985). Family problems are often not addressed because of the inflexibility of work requirements. For example, a parent is unable to get time off to take a child to an unplanned doctor's appointment. One way to alleviate this inflexibility is to take control over one's own work life. It should be noted that the increased stress placed on the self-employed individual (e.g., changes in the concept of job security) may ultimately create more work/family conflict than is alleviated through the greater ability to react to unforeseen family demands. Nevertheless, to an employee, the independence that self-employment promises can offer a solution to some of the sources of work/family conflict that they are currently experiencing. As posited in H1, this independence is a valued benefit of self-employment generally, and has been shown to be an important benefit of being a franchisee (Knight 1986; Peterson and Dant 1990). Employees experiencing relatively high levels of work/family conflict in their current jobs may be expected to seek relief through self-employment.

> *H2:* The greater the level of work/family conflict in one's current employment, the more likely the individual is to become self-employed.

The personal control associated with self-employment extends beyond the ability to react to family emergencies or other unforeseen time demands. Business ownership also permits the solution to family employment problems or the desire to socialize family members into business practice. Because many non-family businesses have explicit policies against nepotism, the more an employee values the ability to provide employment for family members, the more likely he or she is to seek the control over that decision provided by self-employment. Thus, the importance attached to employing family members and being able to leave the business to one's heirs, are other examples of social antecedents to the self-employment decision.

> *H3a:* The greater the importance an individual attaches to providing employment for family members, the more likely the individual will become self-employed.
> *H3b:* The greater the importance an individual attaches to leaving the business to one's heirs, the more likely the individual will become self-employed.

Finally, an interest in entrepreneurship has been linked with past self-employment (Scott and Twomey 1988; Matthews and Moyers 1995), and with the socialization that comes from role models and parental employment history (Cooper 1981; Dyer 1994). It is likely therefore, that these historical factors also will influence the choice of self-employment status.

> *H4a:* Employees with a history of self-employment will be more likely to choose the status of self-employment than those without that history.
> *H4b:* Employees with a history of parental self-employment will be more likely to choose the status of self-employment than those without that history.

Once the decision to become self-employed has been made, two more decisions precede the actual franchise purchase: the choice of organizational form and the choice of industry sector. The first refers to the choice between operating as a franchise or operating as an independent business, and the second refers to the determination of the type of business to operate (e.g., hardware store, grocery store, restaurant). The sequencing of these two decisions has been the focus of some prior research. Bradach and Kaufmann (1988) found that 63% of the respondents thought that they would first choose the type of business and then decide whether to become a franchisee or open an independent business. Kaufmann and Stanworth (1995) found that same percentage to be 75%. Note that in each study, the actual decisions were yet to be made, and that in many cases the respondents never did make the initial decision to become self-employed.

The sequencing of the decisions has significant consequences for the model presented here. Although the antecedent constructs are posited to be the same for each decision no matter in which order they are made, the impact of these constructs may be expected to vary. For example, prior work experience will be a much more important determinant of the sector chosen if the sector decision is made first than it will be if the organizational form decision is made first. In the former case, the choice of a sector will reflect directly the individual's willingness to accept the risk associated with operating a business in an unfamiliar sector. In the latter case, the choice of the franchise form, and the training and support implicit in that decision, will obviate much of the need for experience in a particular sector. Similarly, if the choice of sector is made first, the impact of such constructs as the importance of business support on the organizational form decision will be lessened because the chosen sector may not provide good franchising options.

Empirical studies of franchisees' decision criteria consistently reveal the importance of both business and personal benefits derived from franchising. The business benefits typically include such things as the proven brand name (Stanworth 1977; Knight 1986; Peterson and Dant 1990), and franchisor support of the franchisee (Hough 1986; Stanworth, Curran, and Hough 1984; Withane 1991). As discussed above, the more general personal benefits, such as independence, normally found important in franchisee studies are not specific to franchising and relate rather to self-employment (Peterson and Dant 1990). Interestingly, the issue most often suggested in the economic literature, i.e., the financial benefits to the franchisee, typically is not directly included. This may be due to the fact that in these studies the respondents are all franchisees who have come to view process-oriented issues [as] more relevant to their ongoing operations than basic questions of financial return. The lack of importance that respondents in previous studies afforded the financial aspects of the decision, therefore, may reflect the methodological shortcomings of the research rather than their actual level of importance in the decision process.

It was argued above that the frame of reference for the personal benefits attached to franchising in previous studies was the comparison of franchising with employment. Thus, franchising delivered the benefits of independence. Similarly, the financial and business benefits associated with franchising in prior studies must also be examined in terms of their frame of reference. Clearly, that comparison is to operating an independent business. For example, training and an established brand are seen as important issues in the franchise decision because they are compared with operating independently, not with corporate employment. Issues such as attractive levels of risk and available financing are again compared with an independent business, not corporate employment. Unlike the personal benefits associated with self-employment, these benefits relate to the decision between franchising and independent business, once the initial self-employment decision has been made. The more value placed on such features, the greater the relative attractiveness of the franchise option. Thus,

H5: The greater the importance attached to the financial and business benefits of franchising, the more likely the purchase of a franchise.

The first five hypotheses relate to the decision to become self-employed, and the decision to become either a franchisee or an independent business owner. As discussed above, two of the key business benefits of franchising are training and ongoing support from the franchisor. Training and support are valued benefits because they not only allow franchisees to share in the institutional knowledge of the franchise system, thereby avoiding costly mistakes, but also enable franchisees to consider a wider range of sectors in which to work. Prospective entrepreneurs often draw on prior work experience for the skills and industry knowledge they need to operate a new venture (Cooper 1981). Franchising provides a means by which a prospective small business owner can break free of the restrictions of his or her work experience and pursue other sector options. Although some small business owners may be willing to open businesses in sectors where they have no specific experience, to do so they are accepting additional risk. Thus,

> *H6:* Franchisees are more likely than independent small business owners to open businesses in sectors where they have had no previous work experience.

It is clear that many other antecedents will impact the various decision nodes represented in the model in Figure 1. For example, personality traits are important in the decision to purchase a franchise. Perry (1994) warns real entrepreneurs who chafe at control to avoid franchising. Similarly, the choice of a sector will not just reflect the individual's work history, but also the relative attractiveness of the sector (captured in such constructs as growth rate and competitive activity). The hypotheses here are simply a sampling of the relationships suggested in the overall model.

The Study

Sample

The sampling frame for this study was a subset of the respondents from a previous study of prospective franchisees that took place in April 1994. In that study, individuals were intercepted as they were leaving a Franchise Exposition and asked to complete a questionnaire. Respondents were also asked to include their name and address, although this was voluntary. Three hundred and thirteen respondents provided ostensibly usable names and U.S. addresses and those were used as the mailing list for the second study in April 1997. Eighty-six questionnaires were returned as undeliverable, not surprising given the length of time between studies. This provided an effective mailing of 227, from which 63 returned usable questionnaires, yielding a response rate of 28%.

Because of the relatively small number in the final sample, it was particularly important to examine both the power of the test and the representativeness of the sample. As shown below, the power of the test was acceptable, in the 0.8 range. To determine whether the respondents represented an unbiased sample of the population from which it was drawn, a direct comparison was made between the respondents in the current study and those of the first study on a number of key variables. Two follow-up comparisons were also made to determine whether the respondents in the current study adequately represent the sampling frame and whether the sampling frame adequately represents the respondents to the first study (see Table 1).

The comparison variables were chosen so as to identify any bias relevant to the likelihood of purchase of a franchise and included whether the respondent had ever owned his or her own business, or had a parent who had owned his or her own business, and the sequencing of the decision (organizational form or sector first). Also included was the self-reported likelihood of purchasing a franchise, along with importance attached to employing family members or leaving the business to one's heirs. The only significant differences found were those that related to the importance attached to employing family members and leaving the business to one's heirs. Respondents to the original study attached significantly greater importance to both than did respondents to the current study, even though the sampling frame adequately represented the original study respondents.

TABLE 1 — REPRESENTATIVENESS OF STUDY RESPONDENTS: COMPARISONS ON VARIABLES OF INTEREST

Comparison 1: Respondents vs. Sampling frame

Dichotomous Variables (Equal Proportion Test)

Owned Business	n	p	q	z	sig.
Respondents	63	0.444	0.556	0.844	0.398
Sampling frame	520	0.500	0.500		
Parents Owned					
Respondents	61	0.377	0.623	0.637	0.523
Sampling frame	494	0.419	0.581		
Decision Sequence					
Respondents	59	0.814	0.186	0.922	0.356
Sampling frame	478	0.764	0.236		

Continuous Variables (Equal Means Test)

Employ Family	n	μ	σ	t	sig.
Respondents	63	2.49	1.33	1.74	0.085
Sampling frame	507	2.80	1.43		
Leave to Heirs					
Respondents	63	2.78	1.48	2.53	0.014
Sampling frame	505	3.28	1.51		

Categorical Variables (Nonparametric Test)

Likelihood of Purchase	n	Mean Rank	z	sig.
Respondents	62	274.3	0.614	0.539
Sampling frame	509	287.4		

Comparison 2: Sampling frame vs. Study 1 population

Dichotomous Variables (Equal Proportion Test)

Owned Business	n	p	q	z	sig.
Sampling frame	311	0.434	0.566	1.85	0.064
Study 1 population	520	0.500	0.500		
Parents Owned					
Sampling frame	301	0.412	0.588	0.194	0.844
Study 1 population	494	0.419	0.581		
Decision Sequence					
Sampling frame	295	0.763	0.237	0.032	0.976
Study 1 population	478	0.764	0.236		

Continuous Variables (Equal Means Test)

Employ Family	n	μ	σ	t	sig.
Sampling frame	309	2.91	1.42	0.987	0.324
Study 1 population	507	2.80	1.43		
Leave to Heirs					
Sampling frame	311	3.35	1.50	0.676	0.499
Study 1 population	505	3.28	1.51		

Categorical Variables (Nonparametric Test)

Likelihood of Purchase	n	Mean Rank	z	sig.
Sampling frame	309	399.6	0.977	0.328
Study 1 population	509	415.5		

Measures

Of the respondents, 16% had purchased a franchise at the time of the second study, and an additional 30% had opened their own independent business. This is somewhat greater than the 33% switch to self-employment in the U.K. data (Hatcliffe et al. 1995), but the difference is most pronounced relative to opening independent businesses (30% vs. 13%). Respondents also indicated when they had purchased the franchise or independent business. The first four hypotheses related the decision to become self-employed (either as a franchisee or independent business person) to the importance attached to personal attitudinal factors (H1), to the level of work/family conflict felt in the previous employment (H2), to the desire to provide current employment for family members (H3a), to be able to leave the business to one's heirs (H3b), and to the history of one's own self-employment (H4a), and that of one's parents (H4b). The fifth hypothesis suggested that the decision to purchase a franchise would be related to the importance attached to the perceived attributes associated with franchising (H5). The sixth hypothesis suggested the relationship between being a franchisee and whether the individual had prior work experience in the chosen sector (H6).

The decision to become self-employed was a categorical variable computed from variables reporting the individual's current employment status and the individual's status at the time of the first study. To be categorized as making a positive self-employment decision, the respondent must have been employed by someone else at the time of the first study, and own a franchise or an independent business at the time of the second study. The importance attached to the personal benefits of self-employment (independence and the level of personal involvement in running the business) was measured on a two-item scale comprised of 5-point Likert type scale items asked in the context of the franchise purchase decision. The two items were highly correlated (0.385, $p < 0.01$). The measure for work/family conflict was adapted from Boles (1996). The respondent was asked to rate the level of work/family conflict occasioned by the job he or she had at the time of the previous study. The WFC scale was tested for reliability and was highly reliable ($\alpha = 0.93$) (Nunnally 1978). The desire to employ family members was operationalized using the self-reported importance measured on a 5-point Likert scale variable from the first study (Litz 1995). Similarly, the desire to leave a business to one's heirs was also measured on a 5-point Likert type scale. The individual's personal history of self-employment and that of his or her parents were measured as categorical yes/no variables reporting whether either had ever owned their own business.

In the second study, two multi-item composite scales were created using 5-point Likert scale items. The scales asked the respondents to rate the importance of possible considerations in the decision whether to purchase a franchise. The items were randomly mixed in the questionnaire. The two scales were constructed to reflect maximum face validity and reliability and were factor analyzed. Varimax rotation confirmed the two distinct factors (see Table 2). Average factor loading was 0.73 (minimum 0.64) with average cross loading 0.2 (maximum 0.34) and 60% of variance explained. The first scale was designed to reflect the financial interest of the franchisee. The items making up the Financial scale were: 1) Level of financial risk, 2) Amount of capital required to start and develop the business, 3) Available financing, 4) Presence of earnings disclosure. The reliability of the scale was tested and produced an acceptable $\alpha = 0.74$ (Nunnally 1978). The second scale was designed to reflect the benefits derived from the provisions of the franchise agreement. The items

TABLE 2	FACTOR ANALYSIS OF BENEFIT IMPORTANCE SCALES		

Two Factors Extracted (Eigenvalue > 1)

Factor	Eigenvalue	Pct of Var	Cum Pct
1	3.53121	44.1	44.1
2	1.22240	15.3	59.4

VARIMAX Rotator Factor Matrix:	Factor 1	Factor 2
Established and recognized trade name of brand	0.08905	0.71644
Proven business concept	0.12074	0.80726
Amount and quality of training	0.28023	0.71172
Territorial protection	0.32697	0.66825
Level of financial risk	0.80412	0.20159
Amount of capital required to start and develop business	0.84888	0.05639
Available financing	0.66383	0.21492
Presence of earnings disclosure	0.64038	0.34591

making up the Business scale were: 1) Established and recognized trade name or brand, 2) Proven business concept, 3) Amount and quality of training, 4) Territorial protection. The reliability of the scale was tested and produced an acceptable $\alpha = 0.75$ (Nunnally 1978).

Previous work experience in the sector chosen was measured by comparing the self-reported work experience by sector in the first study with the sector in which the franchisee or independent business owner was operating in the second study. It was a categorical variable.

Analysis

As indicated above the measure of status choice was operationalized as the actual change in status from employed to self-employed across the period of the two studies. This meant that the construct of decision or intent to become self-employed envisioned in the model was not directly observed or measured (Kolvereid 1996b), and that any situational variables that may have intervened between the intent and the behavior were not controlled for. It should also be noted that the decision to purchase a franchise or independent business is an event in the individual's history that could occur at any time. Because the second data collection took place three years after the initial indication of interest in becoming self-employed, it was believed that the decision whether to change one's status was likely to have been made by that time. However, it is clear that changes made subsequent to the second data collection would not be captured in the data. In other words, the data are right censored.[2]

To analyze the first four hypotheses, therefore, a Cox regression was run using the date that the franchise or independent business was purchased as the time censoring variable and the purchase itself as the event. The date of the second study censored the data. The hypothesized correlates were: the personal benefits of self-employment (H1), the level of prior work/family conflict (H2), the importance of employing family members (H3a), the importance of leaving a business to one's family (H3b), the individual's history of self-employment (H4a), and the individual's parent's history of self-employment (H4b). The results of the Cox regression are reported in Table 3. The overall model was significant ($p < 0.05$). The measure of the personal benefits of self-employment was marginally significant ($p = 0.05$), positive, and therefore supportive of H1. The individual's prior self-employment was negatively related to the self-employment decision ($p < 0.01$) and was counter to H4a. The level of prior work/family conflict was negatively related to the self-employment decision, and moderately significant ($p < 0.1$). This was also the opposite of the hypothesized relationship (H2). None of the other independent variables were significant.

TABLE 3	COX REGRESSION OF CHOICE OF SELF-EMPLOYMENT STATUS

Dependent Variable: Date of purchase
Event: Self-employment—Purchase of franchise or independent business

Events	Censored
20	22 (52.4%)

	Chi-Square	df	Sig
Overall (score)	14.068	6	0.0289

Variable	B	S.E.	Wald	df	Sig	R	Exp(B)
Personal benefits (H1)	0.9603	0.4970	3.7327	1	0.0534	0.1117	2.6124
Work/family conflict (H2)	−0.1155	0.0619	3.4756	1	0.0623	−0.1030	0.8909
Employ family (H3)	−0.1035	0.1882	0.3026	1	0.5823	0.0000	0.9016
Leave to heirs (H3a)	0.2663	0.1733	2.3604	1	0.1245	0.0509	1.3051
Owned business (H4a)	−1.4710	0.5528	7.0803	1	0.0078	−0.1912	0.2297
Parents owned (H4b)	0.0286	0.5101	0.0031	1	0.9553	0.0000	1.0290

---

[2]Right censoring refers to the fact that the focal event, here the decision to become self-employed, could still occur after the time of the study. The data are right censored because only those respondents who have made the decision before the measures were taken for the study are counted as positive events. Right censoring means that the time dimension is truncated at the time of the study. In the analysis, therefore, the dates of observed positive events become relevant to determine the likelihood that all eventual positive events are included.

As described above, in the Cox regression there was no support for H2 (i.e., that employees experiencing high levels of work/family/[conflict] are more likely to go into business for themselves). Another way to explore this issue, however, is to ask whether self-employed individuals currently experience lower levels of work/family conflict than employees. This question was examined using a test for differences in the means of the *current* work/family conflict between groups comprised of 1) franchisees and independent business persons, and 2) those employed by someone else. There was no significant difference between the groups. Interestingly, however, as a group, all of the respondents to the second study reported greater work/family conflict at their previous jobs than they reported for their current employment. This difference was significant ($p < 0.05$).

H3a posited that the desire to provide employment for family members should be related to the decision to become self-employed. As reported, the Cox regression offered no support for the hypothesis. Related to this hypothesis was the question of whether those individuals who ultimately became franchisees or independent business persons had ever intended to employ other family members, and whether they followed through on those intentions. In the first study, 69% of the respondents who subsequently became self-employed indicated their intention to employ family members if they purchased a franchise or independent business. By the time of the second study, however, only 26% of those same individuals were operating as a family business. Once they had begun operation as a franchisee or small business, nearly three quarters changed their minds. Conversely, 33% of the respondents who had indicated originally that they did not intend to employ family members subsequently reported doing so. Overall, only 40% of the respondents behaved as intended with respect to the employment of family members.

In one final exploratory test, an attempt was made to determine whether the employment of family members in the business either ameliorated or exacerbated work/family conflict. The respondents were again separated into two groups, this time based on whether they employed any other family members, either part-time or full-time, in the business. The mean scores for the composite work/family conflict scale for the respondent's current job were compared. There was no significant difference between the groups.

H5 and H6 were tested using MANOVA. Only those who had decided to become self-employed were included in the analysis. The two group factor was the categorical decision outcome: purchase of a franchise or purchase of an independent business. The effect of the factor was evaluated in terms of the two benefits' importance scales (BUSINESS, FINANCIAL), and whether the individual had previous experience in the particular sector chosen. In accordance with the overall model (Figure 1), the sequencing of the decision (i.e., whether the organizational form or sector was decided first) was posited to alter the relationship between the factor and the evaluated variables and was used as the covariate. The results are reported in Table 4. The MANOVA was significant ($F = 6.813$, $p < 0.01$) with associated statistical power of 0.94, and the effect size (η^2) was 0.546. All three variables were significant ($p < 0.05$); FINANCIAL ($\eta^2 = 0.315$, power = 0.79), BUSINESS ($\eta^2 = 0.33$, power = 0.83), and PREVIOUS ($\eta^2 = 0.30$, power = 0.77). This offers support for both H5 and H6.

Hypothesis 6 was also tested without the decision sequencing covariate using a simple test of the differences in proportions. In the first study, respondents were asked to indicate the various sectors in which they had full-time work experience. In the second study, those who had purchased a franchise or opened an independent business were asked the sector in which they were operating. In the case of franchisees,

TABLE 4	MANOVA ANALYSIS OF FRANCHISE OR INDEPENDENT BUSINESS PURCHASE

Factor: Purchase of Franchise or Independent Business
Covariate: Decision sequence (organizational form or sector)

Overall Model:	Value	Exact F Hypoth.	DF	Error DF	Sig. of F	Effect Size	Power
Wilks	0.42415	8.59835	3	19	0.001	0.576	0.98

(Multivariate effect size and observed power at 0.0500 level)							
Variable	Hyp. SS	Error SS	Hyp. MS	Error MS	F	Sig.	η^2	Power
BUSINESS	2.04523	6.07530	2.04523	0.29830	7.06960	0.015	0.252	0.711
FINANCIAL	2.15146	6.17711	2.15146	0.29415	7.31422	0.013	0.258	0.726
Previous Exper.	3.97835	12.83494	3.97935	0.61119	6.51084	0.019	0.237	0.675

70% had purchased franchises in business sectors in which they had no specific work experience. In the case of those who had opened independent businesses, 50% had opened their businesses in a sector in which they had no specific work experience. The likelihood that the population proportions are the same is less than 0.15, and the difference in not significant. It would appear, therefore, that ignoring the sequencing of the decision masks the relationship between the choice of franchise or independent business and previous experience.

Discussion

The purchase of a franchise is part of a larger more complex process; one that begins with the antecedents to the intent to become self-employed and ends with the purchase of the franchise itself. Some of the factors associated in the literature with the purchase of a franchise are more properly thought of in relation to earlier steps in this process. For example, some personal benefits frequently associated with being a franchisee, such as independence and the personal involvement in running a business, are equally associated with owning an independent business. The value an individual puts on such personal benefits, therefore, should predict the more general decision to become self-employed. There was some support for this proposition in the analysis of the first hypothesis.

The results with respect to H2 and H4 are surprising. It was hypothesized that higher levels of work/family conflict and prior business ownership should be predictive of the choice of self-employment. Work/family conflict was seen as creating a social norm in favor of a more independent self-controlling life style. Instead, lower levels of work/family conflict were linked to the choice of self-employment. It is possible that self-employment is not seen as a solution to work/family conflict, and in fact may be seen as inducing higher levels of stress in a family. Those for whom it has not been a problem may be more likely to take the risk of heightening it. It may also mean that low levels of work/family conflict allow the individual the flexibility to explore self-employment.

Another explanation is that the level of work/family conflict experienced in the previous employment (i.e., at the time of the first study) was measured retrospectively at the time of the second study, subsequent to any change in employment status. Those who had become self-employed may have been biased in their recreation of the level of work/family conflict they had experienced in their prior work (Fischhoff 1975). If newly self-employed individuals are currently experiencing higher levels of work/family conflict than expected, they may be adjusting their perceptions of the earlier levels downward, remembering the earlier experience as better than it actually was. In any event, it would seem useful in future studies to examine the various sources of work/family conflict separately (Greenhaus and Beutell 1985) to tease out some of these more complex relationships.

The finding that prior business ownership was negatively related to the decision to become self-employed was also troubling. Most of the literature suggests that one's personal employment history is predictive of future intent. It should be noted that in this study for a respondent to be classified as a positive event case for purposes of the Cox regression analysis, the respondent had to change his or her status from employed at the time of the first data collection to self-employed at the time of the second data collection. This excludes all those who were currently self-employed at the time of the first study. To be further categorized as having had a history of self-employment, the respondent had to have owned a business sometime before the first study and have given it up (e.g., sold it or closed it) by the time of that study. Because this method of measurement has produced a sample of individuals with a discontinued history of self-employment, it is possible that it may have created a bias toward those whose history of self-employment has not been a positive experience.

The central focus of this study was the decision between franchise and independent business. In the test of H5, the data supported the association between the importance attached to financial and business benefits and the decision to purchase a franchise. In fact, financial considerations play a more important role than previously indicated in studies confined to existing franchises. It is possible that the different sampling frame in this study, where individuals who had decided to purchase an independent business instead of a franchise were included along with franchisees, accounts for this difference. The more people cared about, and attended to, the financial issues relating to franchising, the more likely it was that they purchased a franchise. This may suggest that franchisors are successfully presenting an attractive financial picture to prospective franchisees. The importance attached to business considerations was also significantly related to the ultimate purchase decision. It is important to note, however, that the sequencing of the decision (organizational form vs. sector) was an important covariate. No antecedents were offered to the sequencing decision, and the literature is silent as to what predicts this important, but relatively unexplored, construct.

Franchisees were more likely to purchase a franchise outside their area of expertise than within, i.e., 70% did so. In fact, they were significantly more likely to do so than independent business owners as demonstrated in the MANOVA. This supports H6 and suggests that franchising does, in fact, offer choice to prospective entrepreneurs. Again, it is important to remember that the sequencing of the organizational form/sector decisions had an important impact on this relationship. None of the respondents who chose the organizational form first ended up working in a sector where they had previous work experience. On the other hand, when the sector was chosen first, half of the respondents ended up working in a sector where they had previous work experience.

As suggested throughout, it is important to examine the franchise purchase decision within the general context of the decision to become self-employed, and to do so in a way that incorporates the dynamics of the decision process. Longitudinal studies of the type reported here, therefore, are important, but the deterioration of the original sample base over time is one of the problems inherent in such an effort. In this study, 25% of the original sampling frame was unavailable after only 3 years. Consequently, the sample here was quite small, and although there was some insight gained, the ability to discern complex relationships or use more sophisticated methods of analysis was clearly constrained. An alternative approach is to forego statistical tests of specific hypotheses and use a combination of descriptive statistics and in-depth interviews of the individuals who had purchased franchises (Hatcliffe et al. 1995). Whatever the methodology, it is important to examine the decision to purchase a franchise from the perspective of both those who did purchase and those who decided not to do so.

References

Aldrich, H. and Zimmer, C. 1986. Entrepreneurship through social networks. In H. Aldrich, ed., *Population Perspectives on Organizations*. Uppsala, Sweden: Universitatis Upsaliensis, pp. 13–28.

Ajzen, I. 1991. The theory of planned behavior. *Organizational Behavior and Human Decision Processes* 50:179–211.

Bannock, G. and Stanworth, J. 1990. *The Making of Entrepreneurs*. London: Small Business Research Trust Monograph.

Bates, T. 1995. A comparison of franchise and independent small business survival rates. *Small Business Economics* 7:377–388.

Begley, T. M. and Boyd, D. P. 1987. Psychological characteristics associated with performance in entrepreneurial firms and smaller businesses. *Journal of Business Venturing* 2(1):79–93.

Bhattacharyya, S. and Lafontaine, F. 1995. Double-sided moral hazard and the nature of share contracts. *Rand Journal of Economics* 26:761–781.

Boles, J. S. 1996. Influences of work-family conflict on job satisfaction, life satisfaction, and quitting intentions among business owners: The case of family-operated businesses. *Family Business Review* 9(1):61–74.

Bradach, J. and Kaufmann, P. J. 1988. Franchisee or independent businessperson: some observations on the decision process. In G. E. Hills & W. LaForge, eds., *Research at the Marketing/Entrepreneurship Interface*. Chicago: University of Illinois at Chicago, pp. 38–48.

Brickley, J. A. and Dark, F. H. 1987. The choice of organizational form. *Journal of Financial Economics* 18:401–420.

Carroll, G. R. and Mosakowski, E. 1987. The career dynamics of self-employment. *Administrative Science Quarterly* 32(4):570–589.

Caves, R. E. and Murphy, W. F. 1976. Franchising: firms, markets and intangible assets. *Southern Economic Journal* 42(4):572–586.

Cooper, A. C. 1981. Strategic management: new ventures and small business. *Long Range Planning* 14(5):39–45.

Dant, Rajiv P. 1995. Motivation for franchising: rhetoric versus reality. *International Small Business Journal* 14(1):10–32.

Dyer, W. G. 1994. Toward a theory of entrepreneurial careers. *Entrepreneurship Theory and Practice* 19(2):7–21.

Fischhoff, B. 1975. Hindsight ≠ foresight: The effect of outcome knowledge on judgement in uncertainty. *Journal of Experimental Psychology: Human Perception and Performance* 1(3): 288–299.

Greenhaus, J. J. and Beutell, N. J. 1985. Sources of conflict between work and family roles. *Academy of Management Review* 10(1):76–88.

Hatcliffe, M., Mills, V., Purdy, D., and Stanworth, J. 1995. *Lloyds Bank Plc/IFRC franchising in Britain report Vol 1, No.1 "Prospective Franchisees."* London: Lloyds Bank and International Franchise Research Centre, Westminster University.

Hough, J. 1986. *Power & authority and their consequences in franchise organizations—A study of the relationship between franchisors and franchisees.* Unpublished Ph.D. thesis, London: University of Westminster.

International Franchise Association. 1988. *Franchising: how to be in business for yourself nor by yourself.* Videocassette #349. Washington, D.C.: International Franchise Association.

International Franchise Association Educational Foundation and Horwath International. 1990. *Franchising in the economy 1988–1990.* Washington, D.C.: International Franchise Association.

Katz, J. 1992. A psychosocial cognitive model of employment status. *Entrepreneurship Theory and Practice* 17:29–36.

Kaufmann, P. J. and Dant, R. P. 1996. Multi-unit franchising: growth and management issues. *Journal of Business Venturing* 11(5):343–358.

Kaufmann, P. J. and Lafontaine, F. 1994. Costs of control: the source of economic rents for McDonald's franchisees. *Journal of Law and Economics* 37(2):417–453.

Kaufmann, P. J. and Stanworth, J. 1995. The decision to purchase a franchise. *Journal of Small Business Management* 33(4):22–33.

Keating, W. J. 1987. *Franchising Advisor.* Colorado Springs, CO: Shepard's/McGraw Hill.

Knight, R. M. 1986. Franchising from the franchisor and franchisee points of view. *Journal of Small Business Management* July:8–15.

Kolvereid, L. 1996a. Organizational employment versus self-employment: Reasons for career choice intentions. *Journal of Business Venturing* Spring:23–31.

Kolvereid, L. 1996b. Prediction of employment status choice intentions. *Journal of Business Venturing* Fall:47–57.

Lafontaine, F. 1992. Contract theory and franchising: some empirical results. *Rand Journal of Economics* 23:263–283.

Litz, R. A. 1995. The family business: toward definitional clarity. *Academy of Management Journal, Best Papers Proceedings 1995*, pp. 100–104.

Mathewson, G. F. and Winter, R. A. 1985. The economics of franchise contracts. *Journal of Law and Economics* 28(October):503–526.

Matthews, C. H. and Moser, S. B. 1995. Family background and gender: Implications for interest in small firm ownership. *Entrepreneurship and Regional Development* 7(4):365–377.

Nunnally, J. C. 1978. *Psychometric Theory, 2nd ed.* New York: McGraw Hill.

Oxenfeldt, A. R. and Kelly, A. O. 1968. Will successful franchise systems ultimately become wholly-owned chains? *Journal of Retailing* 44(4):69–87.

Perry, R. L. 1994. *The 50 Best Low-Investment, High-Profit Franchises, 2nd ed.* Englewood Cliffs, N.J.: Prentice-Hall.

Peterson, A. and Dant, R. P. 1990. Perceived advantages of the franchise option from the franchisee perspective: empirical insights from a service franchise. *Journal of Small Business Management* 28(3):46–61.

Rubin, P. H. 1978. The theory of the firm and the structure of the franchise contract. *Journal of Law and Economics* 21 (April):223–233.

Schiller, B. R. and Crewson,. P. E. 1997. Entrepreneurial origins: a longitudinal study. *Economic Inquiry* 35(July):523–531.

Shapiro, A. 1975. The displaced, uncomfortable entrepreneur. *Psychology Today* 9(Nov.):83–88.

Stanworth, J. 1977. *A Study of Franchising in Britain.* London: University of Westminster.

Stanworth, J., Curran, J. and Hough, J. 1984. The franchised small business: Formal and operational dimensions of independence. In J. Lewis, J. Stanworth, and A. Gibb, eds., *Success and Failure in Small Business.* Aldershot, England: Gower Publishing:157–177.

Stanworth, J. and Kaufmann, P. J. 1996. Similarities and differences in UK and US franchise research data: towards a dynamic model of franchisee motivation. *International Small Business Journal* 14(3):57–70.

Stanworth, J. and Purdy, D. 1994. *The Blenheim/University of Westminster franchise survey no. 1.* London: International Franchise Research Centre, University of Westminster.

Stanworth, J., Purdy, D., and Price, S. 1997. Franchise growth and failure in the U.S. and the U.K., a troubled dreamworld revisited. *Proceedings of the 1997 Society of Franchising Conference.* Spriggs, M., Ed. Minneapolis, MN: Society of Franchising.

Sullivan, K. M. and Robins, L. A. 1996. Keeping the family business in the family. *Franchising World* (May/June):31.

Trutko, J., Trutko, J., and Kostecka, A. 1993. *Franchising's growing role in the U.S. economy.* Washington, D.C.: U.S. Small Business Administration.

Williams, D. L. 1994. Why do entrepreneurs become franchisees?: An empirical analysis of organizational choice. *Working Paper, Department of Economics,* University of California at Los Angeles.

Withane, S. 1991. Franchising and franchisee behavior: An examination of opinions, personal characteristics, and motives of Canadian franchisee entrepreneurs. *Journal of Small Business Management* 29(1):22–29.

COMPREHENSIVE CASE STUDY

C A S E   ROCKY MOUNTAIN CHOCOLATE FACTORY, INC. (RMCF)

Walter Greene, University of Texas–Pan American
Jeff Totten, Bemidji State University

Introduction

The first Rocky Mountain Chocolate Factory (RMCF) was opened in 1981 in Durango, Colorado, on the western slope of the Rocky Mountains. Franklin E. Crail, one of the co-founders of RMCF, was the company's chairman of the board, president, treasurer, and director. The company began operations with the objective of becoming the premier chocolatier in the U.S. and in the world through product excellence and expansion of its franchise system. Frank Crail was now rethinking the Company's future business expansion strategy.

Rocky Mountain Chocolate Factory had two store segments. The first focused on the traditional retail chocolate candy market through the 200 RMCF stores across the U.S., Canada and Guam. The second segment focused on the hard candy retail market and was called Fuzziwig's Candy Factory. However, in late 1997, RMCF executives decided that the Fuzziwig's store segment did not meet its strategic long-term goals, and adopted a plan to divest itself of these operations by July 31, 1998.[1]

History

Frank Crail first operated a computer software company in the San Diego, California, area in the 1970s. He and his wife decided to move to Durango, Colorado, for a change in lifestyle. After literally walking up and down the streets of Durango, asking people what was needed in the city, Crail went back to San Diego and researched the candy business. Then he opened the first RMCF store in 1981 in Durango.[2]

This case was prepared by Walter Greene, University of Texas–Pan American, and Jeff Totten, Bemidji State University, and is intended to be used as a basis for class discussion. The views represented here are those of the case authors and do not necessarily reflect the views of the Society for Case Research. The authors' views are based on their own professional judgments. This case is based on field research work.

In 1982, the first franchise operation was opened in Colorado Springs, Colorado. The next major event for RMCF was the construction of a 12,000 square ft. factory in Durango, Colorado. In 1986, the company had grown enough to go public. RMCF is listed on the NASDAQ National Market Exchange. In 1993, RMCF opened its one-hundredth store and only a year later, in 1994, the 150th store was opened in Orlando, Florida. In that time, the Durango factory had been expanded twice, the first time to 28,000 square ft. and the second time to 53,000 square ft. As of April 30, 1998, the company had a total of 222 stores, 185 of them being franchises of RMCF and 37 being company-owned stores operating in 43 states, Canada, and Guam. In addition, the company recently completed a master franchise agreement to establish a number of RMCF stores in Taiwan.[3]

Mission Statement

"Rocky Mountain Chocolate Factory manufactures high quality chocolate products, which are presented in unique, fun and inviting packaging and offered for sale to the general public in accessible, diverse environments.

Our goal: To become America's Chocolatier.™

Our image: American-made, old fashioned quality presented with charm and excitement.

Our vision: For our Company and employees to build upon our reputation for honesty, integrity, creativity, and customer service guided by common sense, fairness, and caring."[4]

Company Objectives

RMCF had four main goals which it followed in order to fulfill its strategic goal of continuing to be a leading franchiser and operator of retail chocolate stores in the United States:

1. To manufacture a wide variety and assortment of world-class chocolates of the highest quality while at the lowest possible cost.

2. To have company-owned stores that serve as profit generators and as training and support leaders for the franchised operations.

3. To be the support system for the franchisees to insure their long-run success and profitability.

4. To provide merchandising and marketing support to company-owned operations as well as franchised stores.

Company Structure

The RMCF was composed of company-owned stores and franchises located in regional malls, tourist-oriented retail areas, ski resorts, specialty retail centers, airports, neighborhood centers, and factory outlet malls. Locations were selected on the basis of high tourism traffic. The company also had a factory, located in Durango, Colorado. RMCF had two different types of stores, the RMCF and Fuzziwig's Candy Factory. The factory manufactured fine chocolates for both the company-owned stores and franchises; however, high quality chocolate candies were also hand-made at every RMCF store. The Durango factory made approximately 1.9 million pounds of chocolate confections annually. One hundred twenty-five (125) people were employed at the plant; overall company employment was 350.[5]

The focus of RMCF was on franchise retailing, not on mail order. In 1995–96, *Success* magazine placed Rocky Mountain in the seventh position of a list of the top 100 franchisers in the nation.

> "We literally had to learn everything from scratch," Crail says. "How to be a retailer, how to be a manufacturer, how to be a franchiser, how to be a marketer. We develop all our own packaging." . . . "We have a tremendous amount of vision as to where retail is going. We're more than just a chocolate company; our real expertise is in the franchise industry." . . . "We're a full-service franchiser, . . . We find the location, negotiate the lease, design the store, coordinate the build-out, bring the franchisee here for training, send a district manager to the store opening, and have ongoing field support and regional and national conventions. . . . We do everything we can to give our franchisees the tools to be successful."[6]

Store Segments

Rocky Mountain Chocolate Factory stores were decorated in a distinctive early country Victorian design, which made an attractive setting for up to a variety of approximately 250 fine chocolates. Each store also had a selection of other items such as brittle, carmel apples, and fudge. Not all products were manufactured at the Rocky Mountain factory. Many chocolates were also prepared in the stores from company recipes. The franchise fee was $19,500; the total investment required for a RMCF franchise license and to open a retail store was between $113,475 and $213,460, depending upon store size and location.[7] Candy making shows and demonstrations were a grand attraction for store customers. These stores tended to attract a "typically adult female market."[8] A line of sugar-free/no-sugar-added candies was introduced in fiscal year 1998, among 25 new products introduced.[9]

The first Fuzziwig's Candy Factory was opened in 1995, and it was a completely different atmosphere than that of Rocky Mountain Chocolate Factory stores. Fuzziwig's sold more than 250 varieties of non-chocolate candies. Selections consisted of hard-candies, fruit-flavored chewy candies, sugar-free candies, and some chocolate covered confections. Fuzziwig's store environment was geared toward families and children, because of its animated characters, props, lighting and sound. Fuzziwig's Candy Factories were decorated in the style of an Industrial Revolution Era factory, complete with the character of Professor Fuzziwig.[10] As the fastest-growing segment of the candy industry, hard candy was a lucrative business, with a customer base that spanned all age groups. Fuzziwig's was designed not only to appeal to the largest audience possible but also to stand out in the market.[11]

By the end of fiscal year 1997, the company had established fourteen Fuzziwig's stores, two of which were franchised. As Frank Crail admitted, store growth "has been slower than expected as a result of several factors, the most important one of which is the high cost of build-out and a larger 'footprint' of the store than can be economically justified in the most fruitful store environments. The Company is currently in the process of redesigning the Fuzziwig's store plan, including fixtures and animation, with the goal of reducing cost, allowing 'scalability' to lower space requirements with the goal of improving store economics."[12]

The company even licensed physical space in two Toys R Us stores.[13] Yet, by late 1997, the company decided to discontinue the Fuzziwig's hard candy concept, due to lack of sufficient repeat business, according to Frank Crail. The concept and assets were to be sold in June 1998 to an unnamed buyer for $1.6 million.[14]

Competitive Factors

The retailing of confectionery products was extremely competitive. Many of RMCF's competitors had more name recognition, capital, marketing and other resources, e.g., Godiva (Belgian), Perugina (Italian), See's (American), and Teuscher (Swiss). In addition, there was strong competition among retailers for future outlets, store personnel and qualified franchisees. According to Susan Smith, Vice President, Chocolate Manufacturers Association of the U.S.A., the 170-member companies who wholesale chocolate produce approximately three billion pounds of chocolate each year for an estimated market of $12–13 billion retail. Smith noted that it's hard to estimate the industry's size given that it's so fragmented. Chocolate factories go up against independent companies who retail their own products.[15] A recent check of chocolate candy companies with web pages on the Internet yielded a list of at least 125 companies, many of whom could be considered competitors for Rocky Mountain's stores. A search of "RMCF" on the Internet leads to about a dozen or so franchise store web sites; however, the company itself did not appear to have a web site.

While fine chocolates are primarily sold in specialty stores, RMCF also faces secondary competition from less expensive chocolates (e.g., Russell Stover and Whitman's), which are sold in drug, grocery and discount stores. According to the National Confectioners Association and the Chocolate Manufacturers Association, 1997 confectionery sales increased 2.9 percent in food, drug and mass merchant outlets. Sales of boxed chocolates increased 10.5 percent over 1996 sales. "Mass merchants led the way in 1997 with a 4.7 percent increase in dollar sales over 1996. Food stores produced a 3.5 percent increase while drug store sales were off 0.4 percent. Convenience store confectionery sales were even against 1996."[16]

In addition, fine chocolates compete with other product forms of snack foods, e.g., candy bars and nuts, for the consumer's snacking pleasure. Additional confectionery consumption statistics are shown in Table 1.

According to Crail, Rocky Mountain's strengths include:

1. A well known name;

2. Known for excellence, value, assortment and incomparable quality of its products;

3. Store ambiance;

4. Intelligence and background in implementing stringent standards for new store sites;

5. Specialization in retailing and distribution of chocolate and other candy products; and

TABLE 1	CONFECTIONERY CONSUMPTION STATISTICS

- U.S. per capita consumption of confectionery grew from 17.9 pounds per person in 1983 to 25.5 pounds per person in 1997.

- Each American consumed an average of 11.7 pounds of chocolate in 1996.

- U.S. per capita chocolate consumption was 10.8 pounds in 1994, 11.5 pounds in 1995, and 12.1 pounds in 1997.

- In 1997, chocolate consumption totaled 3.23 billion pounds.

- Production of U.S. chocolate products grew from 1,126,400 metric tons in 1988 to 1,370,100 metric tons in 1995.

- Estimated seasonal sales (in millions) of confectionery for 1997 and 1998 were:
  - Halloween $1,708 $1,767
  - Easter   1,495   1,670
  - Christmas   1,460   1,525
  - Valentine's   955   1,033

SOURCE: Several reports under the category, "Stats" from the CandyUSA web page, *http://www.candyusa.org/*, Chocolate Manufacturers Association & National Confectioners Association, downloaded on 10/27/1998.

6. Enforcement of important procedures and techniques at its franchised and company-owned outlets. By managing the production of its own chocolate output, RMCF sought to improve its production quality standards for those products, extend proprietary products, control costs, manage production and delivery schedules and identify potentially new distribution channels.

A survey conducted by *Money* magazine (February 1995) demonstrated that not all chocolate candies were created equal. The magazine's staff decided to test out the best premium-quality chocolates and ordered the "Forrest Gump" sampler ("You never know what you're gonna get."), a half pound assortment box, from six of the most popular chocolatiers. A panel of 30 blindfolded judges (staff tasters) all agreed that the best chocolate was from Rocky Mountain Chocolate Factory. Here are some of the remarks made by the judges about RMCF chocolates and its competitors:
(Note: second place was a tie, therefore two companies are listed in second place.)

5th   Fanny May—Affordable, yes—but "too salty"

4th   Godiva—overly "chemical taste" from the world-famous Belgian house, which has 116 U.S. stores.

3rd   Teuscher—Swiss candymaker's package featured a mix of filled chocolates and truffles—the box's best stuff—but they lost points by sending the wrong order first time around.

2nd   Perugina—Deemed "uneven", the Italian maker's sampler contained several marvelous dark pieces as well as some banana-flavor ditties described as, well, "yuckie."

2nd   See's Candies—America's old-fashioned sweetheart, founded in 1921, turns out well-priced, "very good" chocolate.

1st   Rocky Mountain Chocolate Factory—Overall, Rocky Mountain won the coveted three-heart rating in our blind taste test because of "superior flavor" and "no chemical aftertaste," "richest chocolate," with intense, "natural" flavor.[17]

Economic Factors

The late 1980s and early 1990s were a period of high risks and uncertainty for all businesses in the U.S. Candy retailers and manufacturers were not immune to these risks. According to Rocky Mountain's management team, inflationary factors such as increases in the costs of ingredients and labor immediately affected company operations. Various facility leases had provisions for cost-of-living adjustments and required the company to pay taxes, insurance and maintenance costs, all of which were exposed to inflation. Furthermore, projected lease costs for new store buildings included potential escalating cost of land and construction. The company would likely not be able to pass on its expansion costs to its customers.[18]

In addition, RMCF's sales and earnings were seasonal, with significantly higher sales and earnings occurring during the Christmas holidays and summer vacation seasons. This seasonality created irregularities in its quarterly production outputs. Furthermore, quarterly results had been, and would likely continue to be, affected by the timing of new outlet openings and the sale of franchises.[19]

Financial Results and Operations

Rocky Mountain Chocolate Factory's sales increased approximately $5 million between fiscal years 1995 and 1996 and between 1996 and 1997. At the same time, the company experienced increases in cost of sales, retail operating expenses, and store closure expenses. As a result, RMCF had a net loss of approximately $1.36 million in fiscal year 1997 after posting net incomes in preceding years, as shown in Exhibit B. Nine company-owned stores were not making sufficient profits and had to be closed in 1997.[20] While store closure expenses remained a dragging factor in fiscal year 1998 along with the discontinuation of the Fuzziwig's retail concept, RMCF managed to post a positive net income, as shown in Exhibit D.

Balance sheets for fiscal years 1996 and 1997 are shown in Exhibit A.[21] Statements of operations are provided in Exhibit B for three years (1995–1997).[22] The 1998 fiscal year balance sheet and statement of operations are provided in Exhibit C and D.[23] Note that sales and marketing expenses are shown separately from franchise costs for fiscal year 1998 (Exhibit D). In the previous years, these expenses were listed as part of franchise costs (Exhibit B). This change in reporting was made to reflect the increased focus on sales and marketing by the company, in terms of new products, customer service, additional promotional programs and alternative distribution sales personnel.[24]

Expansion Strategy

Sales of candy were primarily impulse driven. RMCF was building its name recognition so it could become a destination chocolatier. In other words, consumers would automatically recall the brand name when they wanted to give or get chocolate. If consumers began to seek out RMCF chocolates, the company would see an increase in the size of its gift business. Candy makers such as Fanny Farmer and Russell Stover had stronger gift business because of name recognition and longevity. Domestically, there was room for geographical expansion. RMCF stores were primarily located in the Rocky Mountain, Pacific and Midwest regions of the Unites States. The Sunbelt and Eastern Seaboard regions offered possibilities, assuming premium high-traffic retail locations could be determined and acquired. The company was also considering foreign operations, including further expansion into the Canadian Market.[25] Several of its retail outlets had home pages on the Internet, and offered consumers the opportunity to purchase products online.[26]

With the decision to divest the Fuzziwig's Candy Factory store segment, which did not meet the strategic long-term goal of becoming a premier chocolatier, RMCF started pursing distribution of products outside the franchised and company-owned stores. With limited viable real estate available and a desire to increase its market share, brand awareness and customer base, RMCF began implementing an expansion strategy in fiscal 1998 and beyond. A major pilot program was launched with Sam's Club to offer selected company products in approximately eighty Sam's Club locations throughout the United States. The number of Sam's Club locations was to be expanded to 105 by October 1998, with more locations added in fiscal year 2000. A franchised store was opened on Guam and a master franchise agreement for Taiwan was also planned. Additionally, RMCF had received a commitment from AAFES (Army Air Force Exchange Services) to test candy-owned RMCF stores in two of AAFES largest domestic bases. The first military base store opened on August 1, 1998. Also, AAFES agreed to sell RMCF products in approximately 50 base exchanges by February 1999.[27]

Frank Crail provided this challenge in his letter to shareholders:

> "Managing our brand will be the strategic focus for the future. Our continued growth and success in the market place can only be achieved through creating a loyal and diverse customer base for our products. The progress we made in fiscal year 1998 was exciting, but merely sets the standard for future performance."[28]

Endnotes

1. Rocky Mountain Chocolate Factory, Inc. *FORM 10-K*, February 28, 1998, p. 3.
2. Bruce Goldberg, "Candy a Dandy Colorado Business," *Colorado Business Magazine* (September 1996): pp. 56+; downloaded from the Internet on 10/27/1998.
3. Rocky Mountain Chocolate Factory, Inc. *FORM 10-K*, February 28, 1998, p. 1.
4. Mission Statement, Rocky Mountain Chocolate Factory, *1998 Annual Report*, p. 1.
5. Goldberg, pp. 56+.
6. Goldberg, pp. 56+.
7. Rocky Mountain Chocolate Factory, Inc., *Facts About Franchising with Rocky Mountain Chocolate Factory, Inc.*, Revised 6/98.
8. Fuzziwig's web site was at *http://www.fuzziwigs.com/index.htm* (as of 1/14/98).
9. Franklin E. Crail, Letter to Our Shareholders, Rocky Mountain Chocolate Factory, *1998 Annual Report*, p. 2.
10. Rocky Mountain Chocolate Factory, Inc., *Annual Report, 1996*, p. 11.
11. "Fuzziwig's creates Candyland," *Chain Store Age Executive with Shopping Center Age*, v. 72, n. 10, (October 1996): p. 74.
12. An Interview with CEO Frank Crail, "Rocky Mountain Chocolate Factory, *1997 Annual Report*, pp. 6–7.

13. Bruce Horovitz, "Discovering candyland. Toymakers spy sweet success in confections," *USA Today*, (March 4, 1997): p. 1B.
14. Franklin E. Crail, Letter to Our Stockholders, Rocky Mountain Chocolate Factory, *1998 Annual Report*, p. 2.
15. Robert Schwab, "Sweet Deal," *The Denver Post*, (February 10, 1997): p. C-01.
16. "A Review of Issues and Trends in the Confectionery Industry by the NCA," *Candy Industry*, (June 1998): A2.
17. Elif Sinanoglu, "Smart Spending," *Money*, (February 1995): p. 171.
18. *1998 Annual Report*, p. 8.
19. Ibid., p. 8
20. Dina Bunn, "Nine Candy Stores Get Sour News," *Rocky Mountain News*, (April 15, 1997): p. 3b.
21. *RMCF Annual Report*, 1997, p. 20–21.
22. Ibid., p. 22.
23. *1998 Annual Report*, pp. 9–10.
24. *1998 Annual Report*, pp. 6.
25. Susan Tiffany, "Rocky Mountain Candy Factory Celebrates 15 'Beary' Good Years," *Candy Industry*, v. 161, n. 8, (August 1996): p. 24–29.
26. For example, see the outlets at Ocean City, MD *(http://www.rmcfactory.com)*, Naperville, IL *(http://www.napercafe.com/rmcf)*, Breckenridge, CO *(http://www.mefbreck.com/factory.htm)*, and Burlington, WA *(http://www.emcf-wa.com/main.htm)*. These web sites were all active as of 4/4/98.
27. RMCF *FORM 10-K*, February 28, 1998, p. 5; "Rocky Mountain Chocolate Factory, Inc. Reports Record Revenue Income," *PR Newswire* (10/1/98): pages 1–3 downloaded from *http://investing.lycos.com* on 10/28/1998.
28. Frank Crail, *1998 Annual Report*, p. 2.

EXHIBIT A	**BALANCE SHEET**
	RMCF

	Feb. 28, 1997	**Feb. 29, 1996**	**Feb. 28, 1995**
ASSETS			
CURRENT ASSETS			
Cash and cash equivalents	$ 792,606	$ 528,787	$ 382,905
Accounts and notes receivable— trade, less allowance for doubtful accounts of $202,029 in 1997 and $28,196 in 1996	1,729,971	1,463,901	1,179,019
Inventories	2,311,321	2,504,908	1,687,016
Deferred income taxes	22,595	59,219	68,586
Other	81,133	224,001	110,105
Total current assets	5,737,626	4,780,816	3,427,631
PROPERTY AND EQUIPMENT —AT COST			
Land	122,558	122,558	122,558
Building	3,644,357	3,596,905	2,453,069
Leasehold improvements	2,213,116	1,753,165	803,160
Machinery and equipment	6,446,612	4,898,174	2,917,148
Furniture and fixtures	2,667,420	2,330,057	1,086,282
Transportation equipment	246,499	228,816	197,346
	15,340,562	12,929,675	7,579,563
Less accumulated depreciation and amortization	3,565,194	2,468,084	1,690,118
	11,775,368	10,461,591	5,889,445
OTHER ASSETS			
Accounts and notes receivable— trade, due after one year	82,774	111,588	136,132
Goodwill, net of accumulated amortization of $277,344 in 1997 and $253,740 in 1996	312,656	336,260	359,864
Deferred income taxes	43,044		
Other	638,637	624,185	368,098
	1,077,111	1,072,033	1,072,033
TOTAL ASSETS	$18,590,105	$16,314,440	$10,181,170

EXHIBIT A	(CONTINUED)		

	Feb. 28, 1997	Feb. 29, 1996	Feb. 28, 1995
LIABILITIES AND STOCKHOLDERS' EQUITY			
CURRENT LIABILITIES			
Short-term debt	$ —	$ 1,000,000	$ —
Current maturities of long-term debt	847,881	134,538	182,852
Accounts payable—trade	799,671	998,520	839,117
Accrued compensation	465,338	335,926	222,713
Accrued liabilities	867,961	214,460	272,593
Income taxes payable	—	54,229	283,330
Deferred income	93,000	—	—
Total current liabilities	3,073,851	2,737,673	1,800,605
LONG-TERM DEBT, less current maturities	5,737,312	2,183,877	2,313,895
DEFERRED INCOME TAXES	—	275,508	159,863
COMMITMENTS AND CONTINGENCIES	—	—	—
STOCKHOLDERS' EQUITY			
$1.00 cumulative convertible preferred stock—authorized 250,000 shares, $0.10 par value, issued and outstanding, 14,160 shares in 1995	—	—	1,462
Common stock—authorized 7,250,000 shares, $.03 par value, issued 3,041,302 shares in 1997 and 3,034,302 in 1996	91,239	91,029	79,029
Additional paid-in capital	9,730,872	9,703,985	4,700,527
Retained earnings	972,565	2,338,267	1,130,522
	10,794,676	12,133,281	5,911,540
Less common stock held in treasury, at cost—129,003 shares in 1997, 129,153 shares in 1996, & 4,303 shares in 1995	1,015,734	1,015,899	4,733
	9,778,942	11,117,382	5,906,807
TOTAL LIABILITIES	$18,590,105	$16,314,440	$10,181,170

| EXHIBIT B | STATEMENTS OF OPERATIONS
RMCF
FOR THE YEARS ENDED |

	Feb. 28, 1997	Feb. 29, 1996	Feb. 28, 1995
REVENUES			
Sales	$21,674,485	$16,094,995	$11,427,700
Franchise and royalty fees	2,597,985	2,648,303	2,188,434
	24,272,470	18,743,298	13,616,134
COSTS AND EXPENSES			
Cost of sales	11,508,384	8,598,798	5,985,970
Franchise costs	1,999,964	1,803,506	1,376,820
General and administrative	1,989,958	1,436,551	1,234,002
Retail operating expenses	8,087,052	4,746,026	2,749,511
Provision for store closure	1,358,398	—	—
Impairment loss—retail operations	597,062	—	—
Loss on write-down of assets	330,587	—	—
	25,871,405	16,584,881	11,346,303
Operating (loss) profit	(1,598,935)	2,158,417	2,269,831
OTHER INCOME (EXPENSES)			
Interest expense	(473,618)	(299,792)	(152,592)
Interest income	28,637	57,620	22,580
	(444,981)	(242,172)	(130,012)
Litigation settlements	(154,300)	—	—
Income (loss) before income tax expense	(2,198,216)	1,916,245	2,139,819
INCOME TAX EXPENSE (BENEFIT)			
Current	149,414	583,488	749,516
Deferred	(981,928)	125,012	39,871
	(832,514)	708,500	789,387
NET INCOME (LOSS)	(1,365,702)	1,207,745	1,350,432

EXHIBIT C	RMCF FISCAL YEAR 1998 BALANCE SHEET

Assets
Current Assets

Cash and cash equivalents	$1,795,381
Accounts and notes receivable, less allowance for doubtful accounts ($214,152 & $202,029)	2,174,618
Refundable income taxes	483,448
Inventories	2,567,966
Deferred income taxes	257,176
Other	103,195
Net current assets of discontinued operations	44,351
Total current assets	7,426,135
Property and Equipment, Net	9,672,443
Other Assets	
Net noncurrent assets of discontinued operations	1,555,681
Accounts and notes receivable	279,122
Goodwill, less accumulated amortization	596,152
Other	338,359
Total other assets	2,769,314
Total assets	$19,867,892

Liabilities and Stockholders' Equity
Current Liabilities

Current maturities of long-term debt	$1,132,900
Accounts payable	1,296,769
Accrued salaries and wages	707,737
Other accrued expenses	339,481
Deferred income	—
Total current liabilities	3,476,887
Long-Term Debt, Less Current Maturities	5,993,273
Deferred Income Taxes	378,272

Stockholders' Equity

Common stock, $0.03 par value; 7,250,000 shares authorized; 2,912,449 and 2,912,299 shares issued and outstanding	87,373
Additional paid-in capital	8,719,604
Retained earnings	1,212,483
Total stockholders' equity	10,019,460
Total liabilities and stockholders' equity	$19,867,892

EXHIBIT D	STATEMENTS OF OPERATIONS

RMCF

FOR THE YEAR ENDED FEBRUARY 28, 1998

REVENUES	
Sales	$20,659,076
Franchise and royalty fees	3,104,906
	23,763,982
COSTS AND EXPENSES	
Cost of sales	10,960,966
Franchise costs	1,106,172
Sales and marketing	1,290,516
General and administrative	1,763,757
Retail operating expenses	6,043,810
Provision for store closure	—
Impairment loss—retail operations	—
Loss on write-down of assets	—
	21,165,221
OPERATING INCOME (LOSS)	2,598,761
OTHER INCOME (EXPENSES)	
Interest expense	(664,852)
Litigation settlements	—
Interest income	114,732
Other, net	(550,120)
INCOME (LOSS) BEFORE INCOME TAX EXPENSE	2,048,641
INCOME TAX EXPENSE (BENEFIT)	788,640
INCOME (LOSS) FROM CONTINUING OPERATIONS	1,260,001
DISCONTINUED OPERATIONS	
Income (Loss) net of taxes	(90,849)
Provision for estimated loss on disposition	(929,234)
Total	(1,020,083)
NET INCOME (LOSS)	$239,918

11

The Challenges of Global Expansion

Key Topics

- **Venturing Abroad**

- **Why Internationalize?**

- **Researching the Foreign Market**

- **International Product Adaptation**

- **The Global Manager/Entrepreneur**

- **International Threats and Risks**

- **Key Questions and Resources**

Venturing Abroad

For many years, U.S. entrepreneurs shuddered at the thought of "going international" because it was just too big a step, too risky, and too uncertain. On the other side of the ocean, Lenin wrote that foreign investment represented the final stage of capitalism. It is therefore ironic that the world's greatest boom in foreign investment took place in the years when Lenin's communism was dying. From 1983 to 1990, foreign investment grew four times faster than world output and three times faster than world trade. Entrepreneurs rushed enthusiastically to those countries that were blighted by communism, state socialism, or authoritarian, isolationist governments. Prime targets included China, India, other parts of Asia, Latin America, and Eastern Europe.

Historically, the United States had been a major exporter—especially after World War II, when goods were in short supply and the worldwide market was insatiable. After production of more goods began in other countries, U.S. exporters found themselves being squeezed out of markets by European and Japanese producers, who took the initiative away from them. Japanese businesses have learned that they have to "export or die." In contrast, American businesspeople have grown up saying, "I'd rather die than export." For many entrepreneurs, exporting remains the biggest hurdle to their expansion.

Marx and Lenin taught their pupils to fear business initiatives from abroad. They believed that foreign entrepreneurs were ruthless and greedy and that they would inevitably exploit the poor, manipulate governments, and flout popular opinion.

Why Internationalize?

Countries vary with respect to the quantity and proportion of resources they possess, which forms the basis for a competitive advantage of nations. **Resource-rich countries** (those having extractive assets) include the OPEC bloc nations and many African nations. Labor-rich, rapidly developing countries include Brazil, Sri Lanka, India, the Philippines, and the countries of South and Central America. **Market-rich countries,** such as Europe, Brazil, Mexico, and the United States, have purchasing power, in contrast to India or China, which possess large populations but suffer from lack of purchasing power. Each country has something that others need, leading to an interdependent international trade system.

Internationalization can be viewed as the outcome of a sequential process of incremental adjustments to changing conditions of the firm and its environment. This process progresses step by step, as risk and commitment increase and as entrepreneurs acquire more knowledge through experience. The entrepreneur's impression of the risks and rewards of internationalizing can be determined by feasibility studies of the potential gains to be won from this course of action.

An entrepreneur's willingness to move into international markets is also affected by whether he or she has studied a foreign language, has lived abroad long enough to have experienced culture shock, and is internationally oriented. Another factor is the entrepreneur's confidence in the company's competitive advantage in the form of price, technology, marketing, or financial superiority. This advantage might include an efficient distribution network, an innovative or patented product, or possession of exclusive information about the foreign market.

Decentralization is the key to Nebraska-based American Tool Company's international marketing strategy. Gunnar Birnum, director of marketing for the firm's international division, says, "We delegate responsibility for running the local operations in foreign countries to our resident managers. They are, almost exclusively, natives of the country. They know the subtleties and peculiarities of their homeland the way no outsider can. The point is to bring as much responsibility to our local managers as possible. This is really the same approach most Japanese manufacturers use to market here in the United States. They hire Americans to move their products through our distribution chain—as we know, that's worked rather well for them.[1]

Deteriorating market conditions at home may propel entrepreneurs to seek foreign markets to help offset declining business. Alternatively, a countercyclical market might be sought to balance the fluctuations of a single market subject to one set of local economic conditions.[2]

Some small businesses internationalize immediately and do not wait to expand their horizons. Multinational from inception, these companies break with the traditional expectation that a business must enter the international arena incrementally, becoming global only as it grows older and wiser. (Table 11.1 describes proactive and reactive reasons to internationalize.)

According to Oviatt and McDougal, successful global start-ups share seven characteristics:

1. Global vision from inception

2. Internationally experienced management

3. A strong international business network

TABLE 11.1 **MAJOR REASONS TO INTERNATIONALIZE SMALL BUSINESS OPERATIONS**

Proactive Reasons	Reactive Reasons
Increased profit	Competitive pressures
Unique goods or services	Declining domestic demand
Technological advantage	Overcapacity
Exclusive market information	Proximity to customers
Owner-manager desire	Counterattack foreign competition
Tax benefits	
Economies of scale	

SOURCE: Richard M. Hodgetts and Donald F. Kuratko, *Effective Small Business Management*, 7th ed. (Fort Worth, TX: Harcourt College Publishing, 2001).

---

[1]William A. Delphos, ed., *The World Is Your Market: An Export Guide for Small Business* (Washington, DC: Braddock Communications, 1990).

[2]A. Kuriloff, J. Hemphill, and D. Cloud, "Managing International Trade." In *Starting and Managing the Small Business*, 3d ed. (New York: McGraw-Hill, 1993), 273–308.

4. Preemptive technology or marketing

5. A unique intangible asset

6. A linked product or service

7. Tight organizational coordination worldwide.[3]

As global opportunities expand, entrepreneurs are becoming more open-minded about internationalizing. The primary advantage of trading internationally is that a company's market is expanded significantly and growth prospects are greatly enhanced. Other advantages include utilizing idle capacity; minimizing cyclical or seasonal slumps; getting acquainted with manufacturing technology used in other countries; learning about products not sold in the United States; learning about other cultures; acquiring growth capital more easily in other countries; and having the opportunity to travel for business and pleasure.[4]

Researching the Foreign Market

Before entering a foreign market, it is important to study the unique culture of the potential customers. Concepts of how the product is used, demographics, psychographics, and legal and political norms usually differ from those in the United States. Therefore, it is necessary to conduct market research to identify these important parameters.

- *Government regulations:* Must you conform to import regulations or patent, copyright, or trademark laws that would affect your product?

- *Political climate:* Will the relationship between government and business or political events and public attitudes in a given country affect foreign business transactions, particularly with the United States?

- *Infrastructure:* How will the packaging, shipping, and distribution system of your export product be affected by the local transportation system—for example, air, land, or waste?

- *Distribution channels:* What are the generally accepted trade terms at both wholesale and retail levels? What are the normal commissions and service charges? What laws pertain to agency and distribution agreements?

- *Competition:* How many competitors do you have and in what countries are they located? On a country-by-country basis, how much market share does each of your competitors have, and what prices do they charge? How do they promote their products? What distribution systems do they use?[5]

- *Market size:* How big is the market for your product? Is it stable? What is its size, country by country? In what countries are markets opening, expanding, maturing, or declining?

- *Local customs and culture:* Is your product in violation of cultural taboos?

---

[3]B. Oviatt and P. McDougal, "Global Start-ups," *Inc.* (June 1993): 23.

[4]R. Anderson and J. Dunkelberg, *Managing Small Business* (Minneapolis: West, 1993), 510.

[5]Kuriloff et al., "Managing International Trade."

How can small businesses learn about international cultures and thus know what is acceptable and what is not? A number of approaches can be employed. One of the most helpful is international business travel, which provides the individual with first-hand information regarding cultural dos and don'ts. Other useful activities include participating in training programs, undertaking formal educational programs, and reading the current literature.

As example of how culture affects business, researchers have recently reported that it is useful to follow these nine lessons when doing business in Mexico:

1. Exploit and become a functioning partner in Mexican social and business networks.

2. Allow Mexican employees to reveal failure or error without losing face.

3. Do not underestimate Mexican expertise and adaptability in cutting-edge technologies.

4. Work within Mexican cultural parameters for male/female workplace relationships.

5. Clarify expectations at the start and throughout the working relationship.

6. Embrace Mexican cultural values that enhance and facilitate teamwork.

7. Tailor employee reward systems to cultural and economic circumstances.

8. Cultivate and support employee initiative and decision making.

9. Understand and adapt to the transitional aspects of Mexican business and culture.[6]

International Product Adaptation

Every small business would like to sell the same product on a worldwide basis. Such standardization is not always desirable, however. In many cases, the good must be adapted for different local markets if it is to be accepted. Two reasons for this requirement are the nature of the product and the culture.

In some cases, a product will need little adaptation. An industrial good, such as a factory robot, will need only minor adaptation because the most important factor is the way the machine works. Although the company may need to rewire the unit to meet local electrical standards, very few other changes are usually necessary. In contrast, consumer goods often require much more adaptation. For example, in some countries in the Middle East, toothpaste is given a spicy taste; in Latin countries, some soft drinks are sweeter than they are in the United States.

Culture affects product adaptation because the basic product needs to be changed to meet the values and beliefs of the local culture. For example, in Japan, Levi's jeans are snugger than they are in the United States because Japanese like tighter-fitting pants. Similarly, in Japan, the McDonald's trademark character's first name is Donald (not Ronald) because it is easier for the Japanese to pronounce this word. Inside the

[6]Gregory K. Stephens and Charles R. Greer, "Doing Business in Mexico: Understanding Cultural Differences," *Organizational Dynamics* (Summer 1995): 50–54.

fast-food franchise in Germany, beer is sold; in France, wine is sold in McDonald's restaurants.

Another factor in product adaptation is governmental regulation. For example, in many countries, imported liquid products must identify their contents in metric measurements, such as liters. Many nations also regulate the content of products and do not allow aerosol-spray containers or food processed with particular chemicals. Some of these regulations are related to consumer or environmental safety. In other cases, they are formulated to protect to local industries. Auto exporters, for example, often find that they must modify their cars to sell them in most other countries. Japan carefully regulates the import of all pharmaceutical products, which must be tested in Japanese laboratories. In Europe, many countries require that all postal and telecommunication equipment be developed according to uniform standards, thus forcing all exporters to modify their machines.[7]

Consider the case of pizza. Although Domino's Pizza executives in Ann Arbor, Michigan, believed they could sell a pizza anywhere, it took a few modifications to succeed in selling their products in certain foreign markets. After all, everyone might like pizza—but not necessarily the same kind.

In Germany, where pizzas are smaller and eaten individually, Domino's delivered personal-size pizzas. In Japan, pizzas were also reduced in size because people would not buy bigger portions, according to David M. Board, Domino's vice president for international operations. Other modifications were made to suit regional tastes. For example, popular toppings in Japan are tuna and sweet corn; in Australia, prawns and pineapple are favorites. The basic recipe and menu choices, however, have remained primarily standard Domino's fare—two sizes, 12 topping choices, and a cola beverage.

In some instances, Domino's promotional themes also needed slight alterations. In England, the "One call does it all," slogan could hardly be used, because the king's English considers a "call" the same thing as a personal visit. In Germany, where pizza is seen as a snack food, the company advertisements were designed to emphasize pizza's nutritional value and its appeal as a full meal so as to expand the market potential. For a company that prides itself on consistency, the diversity of international markets has posed some interesting challenges—challenges that have been met only with flexibility and minor modifications.[8]

By making use of market research done for its Russian restaurants, McDonald's has managed to create a gleaming island of quality, service, and satisfaction in a country where indifferent waiters, filthy surroundings, and ghastly food were commonplace. Opening just three years ago, serving 40,000 customers per day, and selling more food in three weeks than the average McDonald's restaurant sells in a year, the Moscow location is the busiest McDonald's in the world.

In 1990, journalists predicted that the Moscow McDonald's would fail: Within a few months the restrooms would be trashed, employees would grow nasty, and the food would turn rancid. Not only has this scenario not materialized, but three years later two smaller restaurants in downtown Moscow have been opened. McDonald's accomplished its foreign objectives with liberal doses of clout and savvy and huge amounts of patience.

[7]Richard M. Hodgetts and Donald F. Kuratko, *Effective Small Business Management*, 7th ed. (Fort Worth, TX: Harcourt College Publishers, 2001), 379.

[8]Delphos, *The World Is Your Market*.

As the examples of Domino's Pizza and McDonald's illustrate, understanding where to find information on the selected foreign market may be the most important step in internationalizing a business. Common sources of secondary research include the U.S. government and foreign governments, international organizations, service organizations, trade organizations, directories and newsletters, and databases.

The U.S. Government Printing Office publishes *Country Studies* for more than 100 countries. Each of these publications offers a wealth of information to small firms interested in doing business abroad. The government also provides information through the Department of State, Department of the Treasury, U.S. Trade Department, and American embassies abroad. Other countries also offer information, such as trade data and information related to domestic industries. This information often can be obtained from the respective country's embassy or consulate in the United States.

Some international organizations provide statistical data on trade and on specific products exported and imported on a country-by-country basis, as well as population and other demographic information. Examples include the following:

- The *Statistical Yearbook*, published by the United Nations

- The *World Atlas*, published by the World Bank and providing information on population, growth trends, and gross national products

- The Organization for Economic Cooperation and Development, which publishes quarterly and annual trade data on its member countries

- The International Monetary Fund and the World Bank, which publish periodic staff papers that evaluate region- or country-specific issues in depth

In addition, a large number of service organizations, such as accounting firms, airlines, universities, and banks, provide data on international business practices, legislative and regulatory requirements, political stability, and trade. For example, PriceWaterhouse Coopers, the internationally known accounting firm, offers a series of publications titled *Information Guide for Doing Business in* [Name of Country]. The Language and Intercultural Research Center of Brigham Young University publishes *Briefing Programs* for more than 60 countries, and a more extensive series called *Building Bridges for Understanding with the People of* [Name of Country]. The Hong Kong and Shanghai Banking Cooperation offers a *Business Profile Series* that is particularly useful, especially for firms seeking to do business in the Middle East.[9]

The Global Manager/Entrepreneur

Individuals who internationalize and carry out a coordinated strategy are characterized as being **integrators;** that is, they work across country boundaries to ensure the dissemination and development of core competence. "They create personal relationships to increase the speed and effectiveness of programs being implemented. They understand and mediate conflicts between divisions and worldwide product and country operations, with a decidedly overall local focus. Their travels and contacts make

---

[9]Hodgetts and Kuratko, *Effective Small Business Management*, pp. 373–375.

them useful for the collection and dissemination of information that is vital to the establishment of feedback and control systems."[10]

Global entrepreneurs are opportunity-minded and open-minded, able to see different points of view and weld them into a unified focus. They rise above nationalistic differences to see the "big picture" of global competition without abdicating their own nationalities. They have a core language plus working knowledge of others. They confront the learning difficulties of language barriers head-on, recognizing that ignorance can generate such obstacles. The global entrepreneur is required to wear many hats, taking on various assignments, gaining experience in various countries, and seizing the opportunity to interact with people of different nationalities and cultural heritages.[11]

International Threats and Risks

Capturing foreign markets is not as simple as picking fruit from a vine. Instead, a series of potential dangers must be monitored carefully. *Ignorance* and *uncertainty*, combined with *lack of experience* in problem solving in a foreign country, top the list of threats. *Lack of information* about resources to help solve problems contributes to the unfamiliarity. *Restrictions* imposed by the host country often contribute to the risk. For instance, many host countries demand development of their export markets and insist on training and development of their nationals. They can also demand that certain positions in management and technological areas be held by nationals. Many seek technologically based industry rather than extractive industry, hoping to turn the technology to their later advantage. In other cases, the host country may require that it own controlling interest and/or limit the amount of profits or fees that entrepreneurs can remove from the country.

Political risks include unstable governments, disruptions caused by territorial conflicts, wars, regionalism, illegal occupation, and political ideological differences. *Economic risks* that should be monitored include changes in tax laws, rapid rises in costs, strikes, sudden increases in the cost of raw materials, and cyclical or dramatic shifts in GNP. *Social risks* include antagonism among classes, religion conflict, unequal income distribution, union militancy, civil war, and riots. *Financial risks* encompass fluctuating exchange rates, repatriation of profits and capital, and seasonal cash flows.[12]

> The costs and penalties for not complying with export regulations can be substantial. For example, an Irvine, California, company was recently fined $100,000 for violating the Export Administration Act by failing to obtain a "Swiss Blue" import certificate, which would have protected the company's product from unauthorized re-export.
>
> In another instance, a New York electronics company executive was given a three-year suspended prison sentence for failing to notify the Department of Commerce of changes in his license application to export a high-tech integrated circuit test system. Penalties for other violations can reach into the millions of dollars.[13]

---

[10]L. Hrebiniak, "Implementing Global Strategies," *European Management Journal* (Dec. 1992): 399.

[11]Ibid.

[12]John Burch, *Entrepreneurship* (New York: Wiley, 1986).

[13]Delphos, *The World Is Your Market.*

Import regulations applied by foreign government can also affect a company's ability to export its products successfully. These regulations represent an attempt by foreign governments to control their markets—to protect a domestic industry from excessive foreign competition; to limit health and environmental damage; or to restrict what they consider excessive or inappropriate cultural influences.

Most countries have import regulations that represent potential barriers to export products. Exporters, therefore, need to be aware of import tariffs and consider them when pricing their products. Although most countries have reduced their tariffs on imported goods, other major restrictions to global trade persist, such as nontariff barriers (NTB). They include prohibitions, restrictions, conditions, or specific requirements that can make exporting products difficult and sometimes costly. An example of an NTB is when a country requires all labels and markings to appear in a specified language.

> In France, all labels, instructions, and other printed material for imported goods must be in French. In addition, certain products must now be labeled with their country of origin when foreign merchandise has a trademark or name that suggests that the product may have originated in France.
>
> In Sweden, sanitary certificates of origin testifying to the good condition of a product and its packaging at the time of export are required for meat, meat products, and other items of animal origin, margarine, vegetables, fresh fruits, and plants.[14]

Most entrepreneurs avoid international trade because they believe it is too complicated and fraught with bureaucratic red tape. They also believe that international trade is profitable only for large companies that have more resources than smaller businesses. Other perceived drawbacks of international trade include the following:

- The chance of becoming too dependent on foreign markets
- Foreign government instability that could cause problems for domestic companies
- Tariffs and import duties that make it too expensive to trade in other countries
- Products manufactured in the United States that may need significant modification before they are accepted by people in other countries
- Foreign cultures, customs, and languages that make it difficult for Americans to do business in some countries[15]

Table 11.2 identifies some additional complications of international operations. International sales were not a problem for Thermal Bags by Ingrid of Des Plaines, Illinois. A single trade show in England led to the sale of $160,000 worth of insulated bags. Yet when the company ran into difficulty financing the sale, President Ingrid Skamser thought that it might have to pass on the large English orders because the firm lacked the capital to produce enough bags. "Up to this point, we thought we had no

[14]Ibid.

[15]Anderson and Dunkelberg, *Managing Small Business.*

TABLE 11.2 COMPARING U.S. AND INTERNATIONAL OPERATIONS

Factor	U.S. Operations	International Operations
Language	English used almost universally	Domestic language must be used in many situations
Culture	Relatively homogeneous	Varies between countries and within a country
Politics	Stable and of varying importance	Often volatile and of decisive importance
Economy	Relatively stable	Wide variations among countries and between regions within countries
Government interference	Minimal and reasonably predictable	Extensive and subject to arbitrary interventions
Labor	Skilled labor available	Skilled labor often scarce, requiring training or redesign of production methods
Financing	Well-developed financial markets	Poorly developed financial markets; capital flows subject to government interference
Market research	Data easy to collect	Data difficult and expensive to collect
Advertising	Many media available; few restrictions	Media limited; many restrictions; low literacy rates rule out print media in some countries
Currency	U.S. dollar used without restriction	Must change from one currency to another; changing exchange rates and government restrictions are problems
Transportation/communication	Among the best in the world	Often difficult and sporadic
Control	Ability to define when centralized control will be effective	A worse problem; must walk a tightrope between over-centralizing and losing control through too much decentralizing
Contracts	Once signed, are binding on both parties, even if one party makes a bad deal	Can be voided and renegotiated if one party becomes dissatisfied
Labor relations	Collective bargaining; can lay off workers easily	Often cannot lay off workers; may have mandatory worker participation in management; workers may seek change through political process rather than collective bargaining
Trade barriers	Nonexistent	Extensive and complicated

SOURCE: Adapted from R. G. Murdick, R. C. Moor, R. H. Eckhouse, and T. W. Simmerer, *Business Policy: A Framework for Analysis*, 4th ed. (Columbus, OH: Grid, 1984).

choice but to get full payment in advance—a policy that lost us a lot of orders," she said. When Skamser contacted the Illinois District Export Council, however, she was pleasantly surprised to learn that financial assistance was available to her from the

Foreign Credit Insurance Association and the Illinois Export Authority. As a result, Thermal Bags by Ingrid was able to fulfill the international orders it received at the trade show.[16]

McDonald's Corporation has also encountered some difficulties with its overseas operations. In Russia, employee theft is a problem even though company-issued uniforms have only a single small pocket. Worker discontent is also rising over salaries that are not keeping pace with Russia's runaway inflation. Employees who press their case for labor unions are threatened with dismissal. Workers also claim that they can earn faster promotions if they are willing to act as informers against their fellow employees. The entrepreneur running the franchise claims that his 51 percent partner, the City of Moscow, is not pulling its share of the weight, yet it is getting half of the profits. Some of the raw materials needed by McDonald's, such as iceberg lettuce, grow outside Russia in a country where an ethnic group is fighting for its own independence. The firm must also deal with other negative factors, such as a shabby man who hawks pornography just outside the front door, and young toughs packing handguns that protrude from beneath their leather jackets who barge to the front of the entrance line.

However, by withdrawing from Russia, McDonald's would be abandoning its $77 million investment and the tantalizing prospect of huge future earnings. Russia would lose fresh tax revenues and thousands of new jobs. Neither side can afford to fail.[17]

Key Questions and Resources

International marketing research is critical to the success of small business efforts to sell goods and services in overseas markets. Although small enterprise owners can tap a host of sources to obtain the needed information, these efforts should be directed toward answering three questions:

1. *Why is the company interested in going international?* The answer to this question will help the firm set its international objectives and direct the marketing research effort. For example, if the entrepreneur wants to establish and cultivate an overseas market, then the firm will be interested in pinpointing geographic areas where the market potential is likely to be high. If the business owner wants to use the market to sell off current overproduction, then the company will be interested in identifying markets that are most likely to want to make immediate purchases. Regardless of which path is chosen, the firm will have established a focus for its marketing research efforts.

2. *What does the foreign market assessment reveal about the nature and functioning of the market under investigation?* The answer to this question, which often is comprehensive in scope, helps identify market opportunities and provide insights into the specific activities of individual markets. For example, if the firm identifies potential markets in Spain, Italy, and Mexico, the next step is to evaluate these opportunities. This goal can be accomplished by gathering information related to the size of each market, the competition that exists in each, the respective government's attitude toward foreign businesses, and steps that must be taken to

---

[16]Delphos, *The World Is Your Market.*

[17]H. Witt, "The Big Mac Revolution," *Chicago Tribune Magazine* (July 25, 1993): 11–15.

do business in each location. Based on this information, a cost-benefit analysis can be performed and a decision made regarding which markets to pursue.

3. *What specific market strategy is needed to tap the potential of this market?* Answering this question requires a careful consideration of the marketing mix: product, price, place, and promotion. What product should the firm offer? What specific features should it contain? Does it need to be adapted for the overseas market, or can the firm sell the same product as it sells domestically? At what stage in the product life cycle will this product be? How much should the firm charge? Can the market be segmented so that several prices can be charged? How will the product be moved through the marketing channel? What type of promotional efforts will be needed—advertising, sales promotion, personal selling, or a combination of these?

Once these questions have been answered, the small business owner will be in a position to begin implementing the international phase of the firm's strategy.

International Web Resources

Many excellent resources are available on the Web for entrepreneurs concerning global business opportunities. Entrepreneurs can research markets, countries, trade barriers, currencies, legal issues, financing, cultural issues, tax issues, and investment and partnerships opportunities, among others.

http://ciber.bus.msu.edu/busres.htm
Michigan State University's Center for International Business Education and Research (CIBER) Web site has excellent links and resource offerings for entrepreneurs. This site is a must-see for entrepreneurs interested in international business opportunities.

http://www.bg.org/guides.html
This site provides in-depth "Doing business guides" for more than 50 countries.

http://www.state.gov/www/about_state/business/com_guides/
The U.S. Bureau of Business and Economic Affairs offers business reports for nearly every industrial country in the world. The reports are updated annually by the U.S. embassies located in the given countries.

http://www.inc.com/challenges/details/0,6279,CHL10,00.html
Inc. Online Global provides a wealth of valuable information for entrepreneurs.

http://www.sbaonline.sbs.gov/OIT/info/Guide-To-Exporting/
The SBA's guide to small business exporting is found here.

http://www.InternationalWorkz.com
This site provides a variety of resources for global small business.

http://www.ita.doc.gov/tic/
This U.S. Department of Commerce Web site offers country-specific information as well as tariff, legal, financing, and exporting information and information on a wide variety of other topics.

Exploring the Entrepreneurial Concepts

The following sections provide an "entrepreneurial library" that contains a journal reading on this chapter's subject and a "comprehensive cases study" to illustrate the concept in practice. It is hoped that through the reading and discussion of the case, you will gain a greater understanding of the chapter.

THE ENTREPRENEURIAL LIBRARY

Reading for Chapter 11

INTERNATIONALIZATION OF SMALL FIRMS: AN EXAMINATION OF EXPORT COMPETITIVE PATTERNS, FIRM SIZE, AND EXPORT PERFORMANCE

James A. Wolff and Timothy L. Pett

Dr. Wolff is an assistant professor in the W. F. Barton School of Business at Wichita State University in Wichita, Kansas. His research interests include small business internationalization, international entrepreneurship, and cooperative strategies.

Dr. Pett is an assistant professor in the W. F. Barton School of Business at Wichita State University. His research interests include small firm strategy and market regionalization.

Analysis of data taken from 157 small firms actively exporting to markets outside the U.S. revealed that small firms differ among themselves with respect to the competitive pattern used in their export activities. Larger (small) firms exhibited competitive patterns consistent with their size-related resource base. However, smaller (small) firms did not exhibit competitive patterns that could be viewed as consistent with their size-related resource base. In addition, no significant difference in export intensity across three size categories was found. The implications of these findings with respect to the explanatory power of the stage theory of international development and the resource-based theory of the firm are discussed.

The why and how of internationalization in small businesses are subjects of significant and ongoing research. An export strategy is the primary foreign-market entry mode used by small businesses in their internationalization efforts (Leonidou and Katsikeas 1996). Exporting fits the capabilities of small business by offering a greater degree of flexibility and minimal resource commitment yet limits the firm's risk exposure (Young et al. 1989). Exporting can be an engine for individual firm growth and profitability, and for the nation's economic growth as well. In the U.S., small manufacturing firms

We wish to thank Dr. Dharma deSilva (Director, Center for International Business Advancement, W. F. Barton School of Business and Chair, World Trade Council of Wichita, Kansas), Dr. Ann Sweeney, and Dr. Art Sweeney for providing data from the Kansas International Trade Data Bank. The Data Bank was made possible by funding from the USDE-IB Research Project and the World Trade Council of Wichita. We also thank Professors Cynthia Lengnick-Hall, Lawrence Inks and the anonymous reviewers for the *Journal of Small Business Management* for their valuable assistance on this article.

(those with fewer than 500 employees) make up 98.7 percent of manufacturers (U.S. Bureau of the Census 1993) and play a major role in the economy. With increased internationalization, the economic growth potential afforded by small-business exporting may be quite significant (Dichtl et al. 1984; Hardy 1986). However, only a minority of all small U.S. manufacturing firms are currently engaged in any type of export activity.

Since Johanson and Vahlne's (1977) pioneering study on the internationalization process of small firms, much research has addressed how small firms pursue internationalization. This research stream proposes that small firms internationalize their activities through a series of progressive stages (Anderson 1993; Barkema, Bell, and Pennings 1996; Bilkey and Tesar 1977). Recently, however, Oviatt and McDougall (1994) proposed that at least some small firms are international (that is, involved in significant cross-border business activities) at their inception. Obviously, such firms do not follow the successive stages that some research suggests.

Based on this new insight, the literature now suggests two discreet ways that small firms internationalize—"international-at-founding" (Oviatt and McDougall 1994) and "international-by-stage" (Johanson and Vahlne 1977). However, it is still an open question whether there are only two means by which small firms internationalize. The two methods may actually represent the end points of a continuum for internationalization. The question, "Might there be firms that are not 'international-at-founding' but that are able to circumvent or skip stages in their efforts to internationalize?" has received increased attention (for example, Oviatt and McDougall 1994; Reuber and Fisher 1997). Stated more generally, does the stage theory of small-business internationalization apply to all "domestic-at-founding" firms, or is it a special-case explanation for how (some) small businesses internationalize?

With increasing global competition, falling barriers to international trade, and improved international communication and information networks, many small firms are pressed to compete in international markets. Exporting may offer an effective means for firms to achieve an international position (Ohmae 1990; Porter 1990) without overextending their capabilities or resources (Young et al. 1989). The potential ability to skip stages in the export-development process could create a relative advantage vis-à-vis those firms that follow a stepwise path.

There is an extensive and well-developed body of literature that examines many issues in small-firm internationalization. Examples include the stage theory of export development (see Leonidou and Katsikeas 1996 for a thorough review) and research into differences between exporters and non-exporters (Baird, Lyles, and Orris 1994; Calof 1993). Other areas that have received significant attention are the decision to export (Dichtl et al. 1984), export performance predictors (Naidu and Prasad 1994), and small-firm export attitudes and consequent behaviors (Axinn et al. 1994). However, research that seeks to understand how small firms are able to develop their export capabilities at an early life-stage or circumvent steps in an export development process is less developed. Investigation into these issues may add to our understanding of small-firm export development and may also provide insight into the capacity of (some) small firms to leapfrog steps in the export-development process.

The purpose of this study is to examine the export activities that small-firms use in pursuing an internationalization strategy. First, we explore the question of whether there are discernable patterns in the competitive actions used by small firms in carrying out export activity. Second, we examine the influence that firm size may have within the "small-firm category" of businesses. Specifically we address the question: Is there a relationship between size and competitive pattern in exporting? Lastly, we seek to determine the relationship among size, competitive pattern, and export performance for small exporting firms. We begin with a brief overview of theory and empirical research that underpin our research questions. Next, the methodology used in this research is described, followed by a discussion of the results from the analysis. In the last section we present conclusions and implications from our findings and offer some suggestions for future research.

Background

One of the most developed streams of research examining small-firm exporting is the stage theory of internationalization. In this view, internationalization is accomplished by establishing an export capability through a developmental and sequential process (for examples, see Crick 1995; Johanson and Vahlne 1977; Johanson and Wiedershheim-Paul 1975). Empirical tests include as many as six distinct stages in a firm's progression to becoming an established and consistent exporter. In their review of stages-theory literature, Leonidou and Katsikeas concluded that the sequence of activities in the export-development process "can be divided into three broad phases: pre-engagement, initial, and advanced" (1996, p. 524). The "pre-engagement" step includes firms that are active in their domestic market but are not exporting. Firms included in the "initial" phase are sporadic or experimental exporters evaluating future export actions. Those firms in the "advanced" phase are actively and consistently engaged exporters. Stage theory broadly suggests that firms undertake export activity incrementally to gain information, experience, and know-how with which they can expand into additional markets. One can infer that incremental success builds confidence, leading to more extensive export activity, and hence to greater internationalization, while failure likely leads to reevaluation and possibly retrenchment to an earlier stage.

The developmental aspect of the stage model is intuitively appealing and consistent with some elements in the resource-based view of the firm proposed by Barney (1991). "Learning the ropes" of internationalization requires development of the requisite skills and know-how. Dierickx and Cool (1989) described a path-dependent process of investment flows (effort, dollars, and learning) to create a stock of know-how (resource base) that can lead to firm success and ultimately to a competitive advantage. Firms that develop superior resources and capabilities will generate superior profits (Barney 1991). Thus, to internationalize, firms are more likely to establish a base of operations, either figuratively or literally, from which they can begin to test the waters of export activity and develop the tacit knowledge necessary for export success. Once the requisite skills and know-how are sufficiently developed, exporting may become a natural extension of their current business activities. This natural progression, it is argued, affords the successful firm growth opportunities and increased profitability through a stepwise progression toward internationalization.

However, the stage model has been criticized (Leonidou and Katsikeas 1996). The underlying premise of the stage approach is that firms progress from a less-involved export position to a more-involved position in a given market. Empirical confirmation that firms follow a stepwise progression is inferred from cross-sectional data (Bilkey and Tesar 1977; Johanson and Vahlne 1977). These cross-sectional empirical investigations of stage theory verify that the firms sampled fit within one or another of the stages proposed. However, dynamic progression, which can be confirmed by longitudinal research designs, has not been reported. Hence, with the absence of any longitudinal corroboration, assumptions about export-stage progression may, at best, be premature.

Additionally, and possibly more important, recent research has used resource-based theory (Barney 1991) to propose that small firms need not always progress through stages. Oviatt and McDougall (1994) and McDougall, Shane, and Oviatt (1994) present convincing arguments and evidence that some firms are international at inception. Oviatt and McDougall (1994) attributed the international-at-founding phenomenon in part to advances in communications, information flow, transportation, and the growing trend by entrepreneurs to view markets internationally rather than domestically. An additional attribution may be trade-facilitating agreements exemplified by the North American Free Trade Agreement (NAFTA), the European Community (EC), and the Association of Southeast Asian Nations (ASEAN). Over time, as managerial views toward internationalization change and barriers to international trade are further reduced, managerial actions to internationalize may also change to meet the opportunities. Additionally, new business start-ups could be founded solely to take advantage of new environmental conditions. Indeed, Reuber and Fischer (1997) argue that the knowledge and experience of a firm's top management team—a critical firm resource—is a contributing factor to early exporting and internationalization. Hence, certain resource types under the control of a small firm may substitute for another resource type gained through path-dependent developmental stages.

Thus small businesses may have the opportunity or, due to competitive pressure, may be forced to internationalize by exporting. Through strategic action, firms may circumvent, skip, or compress stages in the export development process to the point that these stages are no longer meaningful distinctions (Sullivan and Bauerschmidt 1990; Welch and Loustarinen 1988). Those firms able to shorten the route to effective export activity may be more likely to derive greater benefit from coupling conservation of effort and resources with more rapid growth and profitability. In short, we are proposing a challenge to the general notion that all or most small businesses progress (or should progress) through specific stages of export development.

Competitive Patterns in Export Activity

To unravel the complex issues involved in extending small business activities internationally via exporting, our first step is to attempt to sort out some of the ways that small firms undertake export activity. Following the resource-based view, firms implement strategic actions that are consistent with the resources and capabilities available to them. Because firms are heterogeneous with respect to their resources and capabilities (Barney 1991), they are likely also to differ in the actions taken to formulate and implement strategy. Baird, Lyles, and Orris (1994) concluded that small firms become global competitors when this strategic action fits their unique resources. Further, as Galbraith and Kazanjian (1986) effectively argued, there are multiple paths firms may take to reach a similar outcome. One may conclude that with unique resource combinations there will be infinite variance in strategic actions. However, we believe that meaningful competitive patterns do emerge from company-specific variance.

It is well accepted that large firms compete in their respective product markets using one of three generic business-level strategies (Dess and Davis 1984; Porter 1980). Chaganti, Chaganti, and Mahajan (1989) supported the contention that Porter's framework also applies to small businesses. Hence, just as large and small firms pursue different strategies because of different resource endowments, so too are their strategic actions likely to differ. Specifically related to exporting, Namiki's (1988) exploratory work revealed four competitive patterns that small firms use in pursuit of export markets: (1) "competitive pricing; brand identification; control over distribution; advertising; and innovation in marketing techniques and methods"; (2) "capability to manufacture specialty products for customers, broad range of products; and new product development"; (3) "technological superiority of products and new product development"; (4) "customer service and high quality products" (Namiki, 1988, p. 35). Consistent with Namiki's work, we propose that there are discernable patterns of action undertaken by small firms to carry out export activity. We expect to find meaningful and different activity patterns within our sample of small exporters.

As indicated earlier in the discussion, the stage theory of export development is conditionally compatible with the resource-based view of the firm. Following Dierickx and Cool's (1989) path-dependence arguments, the development of resources and capabilities through time implies that firms seeking to export would do so from a well-developed base of activity in the firm's domestic market. Hence, larger firms are more likely to have the resource base necessary to pursue an export strategy effectively. Moini's (1995) results indicate that firm size is positively correlated with export activity and export success. Calof (1993) found that small firms (measured by dollar-volume of sales) exhibited greater export intensity as measured by the ratio of export sales to total sales. However, Leonidou and Katsikeas' review reported that "the empirical testing of several models found no significant relationship between firm size and the degree of export development" (1996, p. 535).

Conflicting or confusing results across studies may suggest that an important dynamic related to firm size might be at work. We believe that this dynamic is the way in which small firms carry out export activities. Very small firms, because they lack the broad resource base generally associated with larger firms, may be able to compensate by focused use of a narrow but critical set of skills. For example, Reuber and Fisher (1997) [found] that internationally experienced top managers move a small firm toward internationalization more quickly than their counterpart firms without such resources. Such limited skill sets may also allow small firms to pursue a relatively narrow, albeit international, market segment. In other words, very small firms may be able to pursue a focused strategy (Porter 1985) internationally by employing a specific skill base. At the same time, larger (small) firms, with more broad-based skill sets and capabilities, may likely approach internationalization in a way that is commensurate with their breadth of skills.

To illustrate the preceding arguments more clearly, we call attention back to Namiki's (1988) four competitive patterns. For a firm to compete successfully using pattern one (pricing, branding, distribution, advertising, and marketing innovation) requires significant sophistication in the marketing function. Brand recognition takes time to develop and requires significant organizational effort on a sustained basis. Similar requirements exist for well-developed distribution systems and innovation in marketing effort. Likewise, the second pattern requires significant organizational resources to tailor products, to make broad product offerings available, and to innovate. These patterns of activity are more likely to be present in firms that have sufficiently developed their resource base. As an organization grows, it is more likley to acquire or develop the resources necessary to be successful when using either Namiki's first or second competitive pattern.

In contrast, competitive patterns three (technological superiority and product innovation) and four (customer service and high quality) can be argued to require a much narrower resource base. Break-through products and innovations can be accomplished by very small or start-up firms and marketed internationally without pricing, distribution, or innovative marketing capabilities as part of the internal resource base. The same logic holds for a firm that focuses on the quality of its (possibly narrow) product line and the service it offers. Taken together, patterns one and two are likely to require a greater resource base or a broad-based skill set than are patterns three and four. The broad-based skill set is more likely to be found in larger firms, while smaller firms are more likely to use a focused skill set. Thus, this discussion suggests the following relationship:

H_{1A}: Very small exporting firms use a competitive pattern of focused export activity.
H_{1B}: Larger small exporting firms use a competitive pattern of broad-based export activity.

The last element in our study examines whether an exporting firm's size is related to its export performance. According to the stage theory, export activity develops as an outgrowth of a firm's success in its domestic market. In other words, domestic success allows a firm the ability to extend its competitive reach into foreign markets that seem relatively similar to its domestic environment (Johanson and Vahlne 1977). Once familiarity is gained or learning occurs, the know-how gained facilitates extension and growth into additional foreign markets (Barkema, Bell, and Pennings 1996). Therefore, one would expect to see an increase over time in the ratio of export sales to total sales and export intensity. In other words, the larger (small) firms will exhibit greater export intensity.

However, recent propositions and empirical findings presented by Bonaccorsi (1992), Calof (1993), Oviatt and McDougall (1994), and Reuber and Fisher (1997) raise significant questions about the preceding logic. Increased emphasis on international activities, more internationally savvy managers and entrepreneurs, government trade policies and pacts, and technological changes may be changing the business environment sufficiently that very small manufacturers are pursuing export activities out of necessity, early and often. Additionally, very small firms may be able to focus resources and efforts narrowly enough to be as export-effective as their larger counterparts.

In summary, empirical results that demonstrate a positive relationship between firm size and export intensity [are] supportive of the stage theory. Conversely, the finding of no relationship would support the recent stream of research derived from the resource-based view of the firm. Thus, we state our second hypothesis consistent with the premises of stage theory, with the recognition that the finding of no relationship, or a negative relationship, supports recent resource-based results.

H_2: There is a positive relationship between firm size and export intensity. Larger (small) firms exhibit greater export intensity than do very small firms.

Methodology

Sample

Our sample is composed of small firms that are headquartered in a Midwestern U.S. state. This study used the criterion for a small-business designation that is accepted in the export literature—500 employees or fewer (Moini 1995; Seringhaus 1993). As for the decision to restrict the sample to a particular region, it was reasoned that firms within the same region execute their export activities under similar influence from environmental conditions and complexity (Robinson and Pearce 1988). For example, legal, political, and taxation issues are likely to be relatively homogeneous within geographic locations and heterogeneous across geographic regions (such as across states in the U.S.).

Data obtained from a questionnaire administered to the membership of a regional trade association were used to provide answers to the research questions for this study. The questionnaire was mailed to the owners or top executives of 1,600 trade-association member firms as part of an international business research project that covered a broad range of topics related to internationalization. A follow-up phone reminder was made to each nonresponding firm approximately three weeks after the original mailing. A total of 511 firms responded (a 32 percent response rate), with 242 respondents (15 percent) providing complete information. The research questions explored issues faced by active exporters. Of the complete responses, 157 firms (10 percent of the original sample) were active exporters. These 157 firms comprise the sample used in this study. Questionnaire items were adapted from instruments published in the export literature (see Czinkota 1982).

Measures

Competitive Patterns   Using a five-point Likert scale, respondents were asked to indicate their perceptions of the relative importance of items on nine dimensions relative to their firm's export decision-making policies and practices. The scale for each of these items ranged from 1 = "strongly disagree" to 5 = "strongly agree." Although we had a priori expectations, based on previous research, that meaningful patterns would emerge from the data analysis, the instrument was not designed specifically to corroborate or confirm prior research. Hence, we deemed exploratory analysis to be the appropriate manner in which to proceed with the study.

The responses were analyzed using principal components factor analysis with varimax rotation. The analysis resulted in a three-factor solution.[1] Following Nunnally's (1978) criteria, the results presented in Table 1 appear to be quite robust, as indicated by the eigenvalues (>1.0) and unique variable loadings (>.60) for each factor.

The three-factor solution represents distinct competitive patterns used by firms when undertaking export activity. While the interpretation of the underlying constructs represented by the factors is subjective, we find important similarities between our three-factor results and those found by Namiki (1988). Although we were not able to duplicate precisely the competitive patterns reported by Namiki, three robust patterns did emerge in this study. Since our hypotheses are framed within the context of Namiki's competitive patterns, we must explain the issues raised by the lack of direct correspondence in the results.

First, the questionnaire scale used by this study differed from Namiki's (1988), thereby precluding a confirmatory analysis approach that may have otherwise verified Namiki's competitive patterns. However, using a different scale to measure competitive patterns does provide a means for triangulation to validate the competitive pattern construct. Second, little research to date has explored the competitive patterns of

---

[1]In the analysis, we forced a four-factor solution which resulted in an eigenvalue of 0.83 for the fourth factor, well below the 1.0 rule-of-thumb threshold. The additional variance explained by the fourth factor was sharply lower than the added variance explained by the third factor. As well, the interpretability of the four-factor solution was confusing and did not result in meaningful constructs.

TABLE 1	COMPETITIVE PATTERNS IN EXPORT ACTIVITIES		
	Factor Loading		
Items	**Factor 1: Service Pattern**	**Factor 2: Marketing Pattern**	**Factor 3: Operations Pattern**
Availability of capital to finance exports	0.702		
Post sale servicing specific to the products	0.714		
Unique technology/product/services	0.738		
In-house research on foreign markets		0.692	
Entry strategy for new foreign markets		0.861	
Promotions designed for foreign markets		0.674	
Production capacity to meet foreign demand		0.684	
Personnel with expertise in export activities		0.641	
Price competitiveness		0.760	
Eigenvalues	3.22	1.20	1.17
Variance explained (percent)	35.7	13.3	13.1
Cronbach's alpha	.674	.725	.682

small firms that internationalize their business activities. Thus, without either a theoretically developed typology or an empirically confirmed taxonomy, we chose to proceed with three competitive patterns to test the hypotheses stated above.

Based upon our interpretation of the analysis, we designated the three factors as follows: (1) the customer service pattern; (2) the marketing pattern; and (3) the operations pattern. The customer service pattern is associated with the firm's ability to arrange export financing, provide post-sale product service, and/or provide unique technology, products, or services specifically to better satisfy customer needs. This factor exhibits characteristics that are consistent with a combination of Namiki's (1988) competitive patterns three and four. Factor two was labeled a marketing pattern due to the association between the firm's foreign market intelligence, market entry mode, and promotional activity in the foreign market. These activities are consistent with Namiki's (1988) competitive pattern one. We designated the final factor the operations pattern because of its emphasis on production capacity, need for exporting expertise by personnel, and product-price competitiveness. Our results differ from Namiki in that he considered price competitiveness a part of the marketing pattern rather than part of the production pattern. However, it is not unreasonable to think that respondents may associate pricing with a product or production orientation rather than with a marketing orientation.

Following the logic from which H_{1A} and H_{1B} were derived and the discussion above, we consider the service pattern one in which a comparatively focused resource base would be effective. In contrast, the marketing and operations competitive patterns imply a relatively broad resource base for a firm to be successful. Thus, to complete our analysis, a mean value by firm was computed for each competitive pattern and these values were used for further analysis.

Firm Size   Beyond the inclusion criterion of 500 or fewer employees, we were interested in the differences among firms within this "small business" category. Firms included in our sample responded to questions about the total number of individuals employed and about the total number of employees directly involved with export activities. We used total number of employees as our measure of firm size. We divided the sample into three groups that would, first, yield a similar sample size for each group, and, second, closely reflect the three size categories used by the U.S. Department of Commerce. Accordingly, for statistical analysis our groups were: (1) under 25 employees (very small); (2) 26 to 100 employees (mid-range); and (3) 101 to 500 (larger) small firms.

Export Performance   Firms are often reluctant to provide information concerning how well or poorly they are performing, especially small privately held businesses. This fact partially explains the severe reduction in usable surveys for this study. Study participants were asked to provide their firm's total export dollar sales and the percentage of total sales derived from exporting. Total dollar sales were computed from these responses. The primary performance indicator in which we were interested was effectiveness of export activities. Export intensity (the ratio of export sales to total sales) is a frequently used measure in the export literature (see, for example, Calof 1993; Czinkota and Johnson 1993). The reasoning is that higher export intensity indicates a greater degree of internationalization and is therefore a measure of the effectiveness with which a firm has internationalized its activities.

Data Analysis

The purpose of our study was to examine: (1) the differences in competitive patterns of exporting among small firms; (2) whether size plays a role in those differences; and (3) the relationship between these two factors and export performance. To address these issues, analysis of variance (ANOVA) was used to determine whether any differences among the three firm-size groups were statistically significant. The results provide some interesting findings concerning the relationships among different competitive patterns in exporting, firm size, and export performance.

Results

Table 2 presents the means for competitive pattern, export intensity, log of export sales, and log of total sales for each of the three firm-size categories. The overall mean for number of employees was 95.06 employees (s.d. 119.14). The very small category (1–25 people) consisted of 49 firms with a mean of 12.32 employees (s.d. 8.07; the mid-range category (26–100 people) contained 60 firms with a mean of 51.19 (s.d. 21.11); and the larger category (101–500 employees) included 48 firms with a mean of 245.09 (s.d. 125.88).

The first set of results addresses the question of whether firm size is related to the competitive pattern used by the firm in its export activities. The findings indicate some significant differences among the three size categories and the competitive pattern used by the various size groups. Very small groups (Group 1) recorded the lowest mean score for the service competitive pattern and are significantly different from both medium-size (Group 2) and larger (Group 3) firms. The medium-sized category reported the highest mean response ($F = 5.50$, $p < .01$) for the service pattern. With respect to the marketing pattern, no statistically significant differences were found among the groups.

TABLE 2	ANOVA RESULTS OF GROUP DIFFERENCES FOR SMALL EXPORTING FIRMS		
	Very Small (1–25 employees) $n = 49$	**Medium-Sized (26–100 employees)** $n = 60$	**Larger (101–500 employees)** $n = 48$
Competitive Patterns			
Service Pattern	$3.16^{**a,b}$	3.94^{**a}	3.77^{*b}
Marketing Pattern	3.52	3.41	3.44
Operations Pattern	3.68^{**b}	3.97	4.22^{**b}
Performance			
Export Intensity	$.20$	$.17$	$.15$
Sales			
Log of Export Sales	6.79^{***c}	8.32^{***c}	9.62^{***c}
Log of Total Sales	4.29^{***c}	5.63^{***c}	6.89^{***c}

[a]Group 1 different from Group 2.
[b]Group 1 different from Group 3.
[c]All groups different.
$^*p < .10$
$^{**}p < .05$
$^{***}p < .01$

Results for the operations pattern indicate a significant difference ($F = 3.11$, $p < .05$) between the very small category and the large category (which reported the highest overall value). These results suggest that different-sized small firms do indeed approach exporting in different ways. However, support for the hypothesized pattern proposed by H_{1A} and H_{1B} is mixed—H_{1A} is not supported while H_{1B} is supported.

The lack of support for H_{1A} may be due more to the measurement of competitive pattern than to the inadequacy of the theoretical relationship. As previously, our analysis yielded three competitive patterns rather than the four on which the hypotheses were based. Because our exploratory factor analysis may have produced at least one factor that is not clearly either broad-based or focused in its resource requirements, the measures may not be wholly adequate to test the hypothesized relationship. This situation indicates a limitation of the present study that future research should investigate.

The performance section of Table 2 shows the performance differences across the three size categories in our study. We include the descriptive information for export sales and total sales in the table for comparison purposes. These descriptive values show that there is a monotonic relationship exhibited between export sales compared to size and total sales compared to size. Medium-sized firms exhibit significantly greater export sales and total sales than very small firms but are significantly lower in both areas than the larger firms in the sample. The relationship between sales and size is not surprising and was expected. However, when we examine the performance measure "export intensity," some very surprising results come to light.

As one can see from Table 2, very small firms exhibited the highest absolute level of export intensity followed by medium-sized firms and then large firms. While the absolute values reported indicate a monotonic pattern opposite to that expected, the differences among the groups are not statistically significant ($F = .41$, n.s.). As we discussed above in our development of H_2, stage theory predicts that larger firms are likely to be more effective exporters. However, this contention and, consequently, H_2 are not supported. The results suggest that very small and medium-sized firms, at minimum, export as effectively as their larger counterparts.

Discussion

Before we discuss the conclusions that can be drawn from this study, we must note some important limitations. First, the data used to examine the research questions framing this study and the results reported above are self-report responses to a survey questionnaire. This suggests two important possible limitations: self-report bias and self-selection bias. While we believe the problems associated with self-report bias are minimal, the usual problems must be considered. The issues surrounding self-selection bias are more serious. The randomness of the respondent firms cannot be assured, and, therefore, the representativeness of the sample can be questioned.

Second, the survey sample was constrained to small firms in a Midwestern state. Inasmuch as the sample may represent a unique group of firms in an isolated business environment, the generalizability of the findings to all small exporters is questionable. The following discussion must be viewed with these limitations in mind.

In spite of these limitations, we believe the results of this study offer some interesting insights into small firm exporting. We sought to determine whether small firms exhibit different competitive patterns when undertaking export activities. The analysis suggests that small firms do use different competitive patterns of export activity and that these patterns are consistent with the competitive patterns observed by Namiki (1988). The findings here are also consistent with the principle of equifinality (the principle that there are different ways in which firms can achieve similar goals). When taking strategic action (exporting, in this case), small firms seem to play to their particular strengths and capabilities. This conclusion is consistent with propositions forwarded in the resource-based literature (for example, Barney 1991).

However, when we consider the relationship between firm size and the competitive patterns exhibited, the results are less straightforward than the general relationships hypothesized. Our fundamental premise was that small firms, because they are less likely to have the breadth of resources larger firms do, seek to focus effort where they will gain maximum benefit from limited resources. We reasoned that limited resources might lead very small firms to follow a competitive pattern consistent with the focused use of a narrow skill set. Conversely, the likelihood that larger organizations possess a more broadly developed resource base leads one to expect that they will exhibit a competitive pattern consistent with a broad resource base. This argument was supported by the data. However, with respect to smaller firms in the sample, the hypothesized relationship did not hold. Surprisingly, the very small and medium-sized firms did not conform to the notion that limited resources preclude them from a given competitive pattern. Therefore, we interpret our findings to mean that it is not the breadth or quantity of resources but the types of resources available to the firm that determine a firm's competitive patterns and competitive action.

When we introduced the performance variable (export intensity) into our analysis, the above conclusions were strengthened. Export intensity is a well established measure of export-firm performance (for example, Calof 1993). Following stage-theory expectations, there should be a direct relationship between firm size and export performance (Samiee and Walters 1990). Larger (small) firms should out-perform mid-range or very small firms in exporting. However, the expected pattern is not supported. There was no statistically significant difference among the performance levels for any of the size categories. In other words, the export intensity of the very small firm group was no different from that of either the medium-size or the large category (see Table 2).

These findings are consistent with previous research in this area. Our work shows that given the appropriate *type* of resource, a small firm can execute competitive patterns also used by larger firms and perform as effectively. Reuber and Fisher (1997) concluded that internationally experienced management is a key ingredient in early internationalization by small firms. Hence, a key resource type—internationally experienced managers—may allow small firms to effectively compete in a domain heretofore deemed better suited to larger firms. While we agree that management experience is a critical resource in the internationalization of small firms, we question whether it is necessary or sufficient for small-firm internationalization. One contribution this research makes is support for the contention that resource type is important. Therefore, a fruitful direction for future research would be to identify resource types that may complement management experience in small firm internationalization efforts.

A second contribution made by this study is to dispel the notion that very small firms, though resource-constrained because of size, are restricted in the choice of competitive pattern they follow to internationalize. Further, although medium-sized small firms may have resource endowments greater than their small counterparts, they do not necessarily undertake competitive patterns that reflect their comparative resource base. These findings suggest that the relationship between size, resource base, and competitive pattern is not monotonic. Hence, future research should recognize the nonlinear nature of the relationship among these variables and seek to explain why this may hold.

A third contribution is to provide an additional piece to the growing body of literature comprising a resource-based view of small firm internationalization. Managers' views toward international markets and globalization are changing (Leonidou and Katsikeas 1996; Oviatt and McDougall 1994). Some of this change may be due in part to greater international emphasis in business education and the reality of the increased internationalization of the competitive environment (Ohmae 1990). Also, technological advances have greatly facilitated communication and information processing at a global level, and trade agreements in all areas of the world have removed many barriers to international business activity. As a result, very small firms may now be more inclined to see that their efforts for growth and survival must be toward international or global markets (Oviatt and McDougall 1994). We believe that the findings in this study support the contention that some very small firms have developed the resource base to circumvent, compress, or leapfrog stages in the internationalization process.

The empirical evidence that lends support and credence to the stage model cannot be ignored. The literature clearly suggests that stage theory does depict the export-development process for at least some small firms. However, while some firms may follow the stepwise progression of export development and internationalization, at least some other firms—contingent upon their resources—are able to circumvent the stepwise approach and follow a different path to internationalization (Bonaccorsi 1992; Oviatt and McDougall 1994; Reuber and Fisher 1997).

The primary implication here is that the stage model of the internationalization process is no longer the only representation of how small firms pursue an international strategy. These findings are wholly consistent with the contentions of Bonaccorsi (1992), Oviatt and McDougall (1994), and Reuber and Fisher (1997). Extending this implication to practice, managers of small firms who are convinced that their business activities must be established on a sound domestic base before any efforts are taken to internationalize may miss significant growth opportunities. Given the results of this study, firms that follow the stepwise progression of activities to internationalize may be bypassed by more nimble competitors that conceptualize the market for their product or services in global terms as well as domestic.

References

Anderson, Otto (1993). "On the Internationalization Process of Firms: A Critical Analysis," *Journal of International Business Studies* 24(2), 209–231.

Axinn, Catherine N., Ron Savitt, James M. Sinkula, and Sharon V. Thach (1994). "Export Intention, Beliefs, and Behaviors in Smaller Industrial Firms," *Journal of Business Research* 32, 49–55.

Baird, Inga S., Marjorie A. Lyles, and J. B. Orris (1994). "The Choice of International Strategies by Small Businesses," *Journal of Small Business Management* 32 (January), 48–59.

Barkema, Harry, John Bell, and Johannes Pennings (1996). "Foreign Entry, Cultural Barriers, and Learning," *Strategic Management Journal* 17 (February), 151–166.

Barney, Jay B. (1991). "Firm Resources and Sustained Competitive Advantage," *Journal of Management* 17, 99–120.

Bilkey, Warren J., and George Tesar (1977). "The Export Behavior of Small-Sized Wisconsin Manufacturing Firms," *Journal of International Business Studies* (Spring/Summer), 93–98.

Bonaccorsi, Andrea (1992). "On the Relationship between Firm Size and Export Intensity," *Journal of International Business Studies* 23 (Fourth Quarter), 605–635.

Calof, Jonathan L. (1993). "The Impact of Size on Internationalization," *Journal of Small Business Management* 31 (October), 60–69.

Crick, Dave (1995). "An Investigation into the Targeting of UK Export Assistance," *European Journal of Marketing* 29(8), 76–94.

Czinkota, Michael R. (1982). *Export Development Strategies*. New York: Praeger.

Czinkota, Michael R., and Wesley J. Johnston (1983). "Exporting: Does Sales Volume Make a Difference?" *Journal of International Business Studies* (Spring/Summer), 47–153.

Dess, Gregory G., and Peter S. Davis (1984). "Porter's Generic Strategies as Determinants of Strategic Group Membership and Organizational Performance," *Academy of Management Review* 27, 467–488.

Dichtl, E., M. Leibold, H.-G. Köglmayr, and S. Müller (1984). "The Export-Decision of Small and Medium-Sized Firms: A Review," *Management International Review* 24 (February), 49–60.

Dierickx, Ingmar, and Karel Cool (1989). "Asset Stock Accumulation and Sustainability of Competitive Advantage," *Management Science* 35, 1504–1513.

Galbraith, Jay R., and Robert Kazanjian (1986). *Strategy Implementation: Structure, Systems and Process*, 2nd edition. New York: West.

Hardy, Kenneth G. (1986). "Key Success Factors for Small/Medium-Sized Canadian Manufacturers Doing Business in the United States," *Business Quarterly* 51 (March), 67–73.

Johanson, Jan, and Finn Wiedershheim-Paul (1975). "The Internationalization of the Firm: Four Swedish Cases," *Journal of Management Studies* 12 (October), 305–322.

Johanson, Jan, and Jan-Erik Vahlne (1977). "The Internationalization Process of the Firm: A Model of Knowledge Development and Increasing Foreign Commitments," *Journal of International Business Studies* 8(1), 23–32.

Leonidou, Leonidas C., and Constantine S. Katsikeas (1996). "The Export Development Process: An Integrative Review of Empirical Models," *Journal of International Business Studies* 27 (Third Quarter), 517–551.

McDougall, Patricia Phillips, Scott Shane, and Benjamin M. Oviatt (1994). "Explaining the Formation of International New Ventures: The Limits of Theories from International Business Research," *Journal of New Business Venturing* 9 (November), 469–487.

Moini, A. H. (1995). "An Inquiry into Successful Exporting: An Empirical Investigation Using a Three-Stage Model," *Journal of Small Business Management* 33 (July), 9–25.

Naidu, G. M., and V. Kanti Prasad (1994). "Predictors of Export Strategy and Performance of Small and Medium-Sized Firms," *Journal of Business Research* 31, 107–115.

Namiki, Nobuaki (1988). "Export Strategy for Small Business," *Journal of Small Business Management* 26 (April), 32–37.

Nunnally, Jum C. (1978). *Psychometric Theory.* New York: McGraw-Hill.

Ohmae, Kenichi (1990). *The Borderless World.* New York: Harper Business.

Oviatt, Benjamin M., and Patricia Phillips McDougall (1994). "Toward a Theory of International New Ventures," *Journal of International Business Studies* 25 (First Quarter), 45–64.

Porter, Michael (1980). *Competitive Strategy.* New York: Free Press.

——— (1985). *Competitive Advantage: Creating and Sustaining Superior Performance.* New York: Free Press.

——— (1990). *The Competitive Advantage of Nations.* New York: Free Press.

Reuber, A. Rebecca, and Eileen Fisher (1997). "The Influence of the Management Team's International Experience on the Internationalization Behaviors of SMEs," *Journal of International Business Studies* 28 (Fourth Quarter), 807–825.

Robinson, Richard, and John Pearce (1988). "Planned Patterns of Strategic Behavior and their Relationships to Business-Unit Performance," *Strategic Management Journal* 9 (January–February), 43–60.

Samiee, Saeed, and Peter G. P. Walters (1990). "Influence of Firm Size and Export Planning and Performance," *Journal of Business Research* 20 (May), 235–248.

Seringhaus, F. H. Rolf (1993). "Comparative Marketing Behavior of Canadian and Austrian High-Tech Exporters," *Management International Review* 33(3), 247–269.

Sullivan, Daniel, and Alan Bauerschmidt (1990). "Incremental Internationalization: A Test of Johanson and Vahlne's Thesis," *Management International Review* 30 (January), 19–30.

U.S. Bureau of the Census (1993). *Statistical Abstract of the United States,* Washington, D.C.: Government Printing Office.

Welch, L., and R. Loustarinan (1988). "Internationalization: Evolution of a Concept," *Journal of General Management* 14(2), 34–55.

Young, Stephen, James Hamill, Colin Wheeler, and J. Richard Davies (1989). *International Market Entry and Development.* Englewood Cliffs, NJ: Prentice-Hall.

COMPREHENSIVE CASE STUDY

C A S E KRASTYAZHMASH

Richard C. Insinga, State University of New York at Oneonta

Vladimir A Kureshov, Higher Business School, Krasnoyarsk, Russia

"This is going to be tough," Dr. George Stevens said aloud as he gazed out of his office window on an August afternoon in 1994. He had only one more week left on his three-month stay in Russia, and it was time to present his analysis and recommendations at a mid-week meeting.

This case was prepared by Richard C. Insinga, State University of New York at Oneonta, and Vladimir A. Kureshov, Higher Business School in Krasnoyarsk, Russia, and is intended to be used as a basis for class discussion. The views represented here are those of the case authors and do not necessarily reflect the views of the Society for Case Research. The authors' views are based on their own professional judgments.

Dr. Stevens, an American, was sent to Russia by the U.S. government to help newly privatized Russian companies with, the assignment stated, their "transition to a market economy." As a professor of business, a consultant, and with years of industry experience, Stevens was considered a business strategy expert.

Egor Ol ("owe-ul"), General Director of Krastyazhmash ("kraz-tee-ya-zh-mah-sh"), was eagerly awaiting Stevens' recommendations. Ol had asked Dr. Stevens, "What should I do with this company?" Ol specifically asked for Stevens' strategic analysis, which would assist him in preparing a new strategic plan. For three months, Stevens was given full access to the company. He had met with senior managers, toured the company's facilities, read reports prepared by Russian consultants, reviewed financial statements, and gathered market information.

The situation in Krastyazhmash, a manufacturer of heavy equipment for coal mining, was typical of the other companies Stevens had worked with during his stay, but Krastyazhmash was especially important to him. Krastyazhmash was his primary assignment, and its General Director had been most helpful. He said to himself, "I don't envy Russian managers," as he gathered his materials to start on the analysis.

Introduction

In 1991, Russian President Boris Yeltsin ushered in a new era in Russian history. He reformed the Russian economy and political environments, moving toward a market economy and a democratic government. One of the changes involved the privatization of state enterprises. While these changes were initially welcomed, Russian managers soon found that they were not adequately prepared. They lacked the training and experience for managing a business in a market economy.

The privatization process included the selling off of government enterprises. Shares were distributed to managers and workers of the enterprises, and a certain percentage of ownership as made available to the general public. Managers received the larger portion of the shares.

Krastyazhmash, a manufacturer of excavators and draglines[1] for coal mining, was located about 20 kilometers from the city of Krasnoyarsk ("kras-noy-yersk"). This modern-looking city of one million people was in central Siberia, about 3,600 kilometers east of Moscow and to the north of China. It was the capital of the Krasnoyarsk territory,[2] a vast region encompassing one-tenth the area of Russia (and about the size of Western Europe).

Krastyazhmash was placed in this location because about 40 percent of Russia's coal deposits were in the Krasnoyarsk territory. Its remote location made transportation especially important. Krasnoyarsk was a stop on the famous Trans-Siberian Railroad, the Siberian Highway passed through it, and it also was a major seaport on the Yenisey ("yen-ees-say") River, one of the world's longest rivers, which flowed northward to the Arctic Ocean. Rail transportation also was available to China.

The Company

There was a significant difference between the Krastyazhmash that existed under the Soviet Union and the Krastyazhmash that was created by the privatization program. Under the Soviet Union, it had been organized as one integrated plant (*zavod* in Russian), although Americans might call it a "complex." Each part of this complex worked together to produce coal-mining excavators and related equipment.

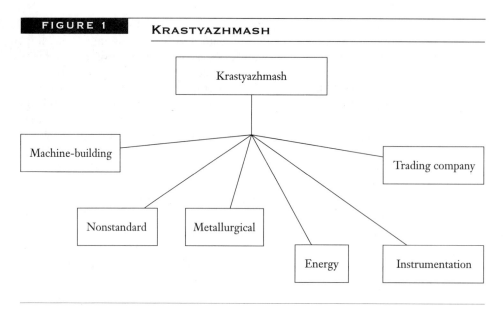

SOURCE: Krastyazhmash management.

The privatized Krastyazhmash was a holding company with subsidiary companies, because in the privatization program, it was decided that separate companies should be created for each of the plants in the complex. The major subsidiaries[3] are shown in Figure 1.

Krastyazhmash was one of four major producers of large coal-mining equipment in the Soviet Union. Table 1 shows the production of these four producers in 1991, the year preceding the breakup of the Soviet Union. Krastyazhmash had been under construction as a coal-mining equipment plant for more than ten years, and it was just beginning to produce excavators in 1991. The plan was to place a producer of coal-mining equipment in the Siberian region of Russia, close to its vast coal fields. The breakup of the Soviet Union curtailed the flow of investment funds to the plant from the central ministry, and the subsequent privatization of Krastyazhmash left it in a partially completed state, pending the raising of investment capital.

Krastyazhmash offered a line of excavators and draglines over a wide range of sizes. It had fewer models than its Russian competitors (Table 2), and its strengths tended to be in the mid-to-large products, which were sold in lesser numbers than small excavators. Krastyazhmash had the benefit of location, being the only excavator manufacturer in the Asian part of Russia near large deposits of coal, but the advantage was constrained by the market for coal, which was larger in the more populous European part of Russia where its major competitors were located.

Stevens had written the following impressions of the complex and each of its plants from his many visits to the facility over the three-month period.

The Krastyazhmash Complex Krastyazhmash was situated near a highway and had a rail line running to it. The complex covered a large area (more than 150 hectares) of mostly flat terrain. A high fence surrounded it. A visitor entered through the main gate, went past the guardhouse and along an interior road to reach the main administrative office building. Some of the major buildings of the complex were visible, but it was

TABLE 1	EXCAVATOR PRODUCTION IN 1991[*] (WITH BUCKET CAPACITY OF 4M³ AND OVER)			

	Amount of Production			
Manufacturer	**In Number of Units Produced**	**Percent of Total**	**In Bucket Capacity (m³) of Units Produced**	**Percent of Total**
Krastyazhmash	16	3.1	230	6.3
UralMash	366	70.4	1,977	53.9
Izhora	110	21.2	1,150	31.4
(Ukraine)	28	5.3	308	8.4
Total	520	100.0	3,665	100.0

[*]Note: Planned production for 1992 would have placed Krastyazhmash at 7 percent of units and 12.9 percent of bucket capacity.

SOURCE: Krastyazhmash internal reports.

not possible to see all of the buildings from any one location, due to the vastness of the area covered. One got the correct impression from the weed-covered and scrap-strewn appearance that, although the buildings were completed, the equipment inside the buildings was not fully operational.

Machine-Building   This plant was the centerpiece of the "old" Krastyazhmash, because it was where the coal-mining excavators were assembled. The plant was very large, with high ceilings throughout. Parts were moved by truck, an internal rail system, and heavy overhead cranes. There were many large milling machines for cutting large-diameter (3 to 6 meters) circular gears. There were workstations for assembly and welding of large sections. Overhead cranes moved the excavator in sections to each workstation. At one end of the plant, there was a high bay area where excavators were assembled and tested before being disassembled for loading onto rail cars for shipment. An excavator headed for China was observed being packed and loaded. While excavators were observed being manufactured, it was clear from the size of the plant that production was at a very low level of capacity utilization.

The Machine-Building plant also made transmissions in a range of sizes to serve the several electric motors that control the excavators. There was a flexible manufacturing system in a state of partial completion. This system was purchased from an Italian company to produce large transmissions. Although the system was about half installed, there were no signs that installation was continuing.

Metallurgical   The Metallurgical plant produced steel. This plant was also very large, with high ceilings. It used a modern steel-making process involving electric arc crucibles. There were locations for 12 to 14 crucibles, but equipment for only six crucibles was in place. Just two of these showed signs of recent use.

The plant was idle. The only visible occupants were two stray dogs and a cat. Besides the electric arc furnaces, the largest part of the plant was dedicated to hot and cold rolling mills. These mills were in a partial state of completion (perhaps 40 percent).

| TABLE 2 | PRODUCT LINES OF MAJOR PRODUCERS |

		Theoretical Productivity (m³/hr)			
Model	Bucket Capacity (m³)	Krastyazhmash	Izhora	UralMash	(Ukraine)
ЭКГ-5	5		600		
ЭКГ-5	5.2			810	
ЭКГ-8	8		1,030		
ЭКГ-8	8	820			
ЭКГ-10	10		1,380		
ЭШ 11.70	11				730
ЭКГ-12	12		1,350		
ЭКГ-12	12	1,350			
ЭКГ-12	12			1,540	
ЭШ 14.50	14				930
ЭКГ-15	15	1,920	1,920		
ЭШ-15.80	15				930
ЭКГ-20	20		2,570		
ЭКГ-20	20			2,570	
ЭШ 20.90	20			1,200	
ЭШ 20.65	20				1,380
ЭШ 40.85	40	2,400			
ЭШ 40.85	40			2,400	
ЭШ 65.100	65			3,600	

SOURCE: Krastyazhmash internal reports.

There was an extensive system of hoppers for feeding additives (in powder form) to the steel, and the plant had an environmental control system for air and water. As was required for electric arc furnaces, one area of the plant had a rail car unloading station filled with steel scrap, which was abundant in the region. Finished steel was transported to the other plants via a railway system within the Krastyazhmash plant complex.

Instrumentation The translation, "instrumentation," did not fittingly describe this plant. A better term would be "tool making." This sizable plant was dedicated to producing tools for the other parts of Krastyazhmash. It mainly made cutting tools, but its machinery was capable of making a variety of other products. The plant was essentially a large machine shop with many lathes and a few heat-treating furnaces. This plant also produced electric mixers until they were no longer able to obtain the small electric motors from Germany that they needed. A fair amount of activity was observed during the tour. Perhaps 30 percent of the plant was being utilized.

A mold for making plastic baby bibs was seen being produced. This was an example of production orders that they were able to obtain to keep busy. At one end of the plant was a pile of steel reinforced concrete slabs, which were used for construction of garages. Apparently some workers were paid in-kind (i.e., getting a slab in place of cash) and received income from a sideline construction business.

Nonstandard   The Nonstandard plant produced hoppers, conveyors, and other coal-mining equipment. It was a joint stock company that was established in an earlier round of privatization, so it had been a separate company for a couple of years. Its relationship with Krastyazhmash was that it leased plant space and purchased utilities. The plant also continued to get marketing assistance from the Trading Company (discussed later in this section). The Nonstandard plant was more versatile, being capable of producing products other than coal-mining equipment. Its progressive management had been discussing ventures with foreign companies that wanted to gain access to the regional market.

The Nonstandard plant seemed very busy. There were a number of products being produced, and the employees had a certain *esprit*, which was missing at the other plants of Krastyazhmash. It appeared to be the best-run plant of the group. The building was similar to the others, with high ceilings and an internal railway system (for large carts). The machinery was similar to the tool making plant in one area, where they made their own tools rather than purchase them from the Instrumentation plant. Much of the fabrication involved cutting and bending metal sheets, then assembling the sheets and painting the final product.

Energy   The Energy plant was not really a single plant, but rather a series of facilities that provided all sorts of utilities to the plants of Krastyazhmash and its surrounding areas. For example, it provided water, sewer, electricity, steam, hot water, and natural gas. The Energy plant did not generate its own electricity; it merely operated a switching station and the power lines to deliver electric power that was received from the gigantic Krasnoyarsk Dam. Water for the plant was taken from the Yenisey River at a location in the city of Krasnoyarsk, 20 kilometers away, and transported to the plant via conduits that were owned and maintained by this plant.

There was a sewage treatment plant with primary and secondary treatment plus oil removal, but it was in need of an upgrade. It was interesting to look at the water flow through this plant, because one could see that it was only about 20 percent of the way up to a watermark, which indicated the high flow point. This gave an indication of the level of production at the plants of Krastyazhmash. (In terms of volume, the water was mainly from the cooling of parts during machining.) An inspection of the water storage and pumping station, the gas control facility, and the steam and hot water production facility showed that, overall, the facilities were in decent condition.

The Energy plant was trying to expand its business to customers outside of the Krastyazhmash complex. For example, the Energy plant supplied electricity and other utilities to Solnetchny ("soul-nitch-ny"), a nearby apartment complex for Krastyazhmash employees, where about 5,000 people lived. It also supplied utilities to other companies that had located nearby in a form of industrial park. One was a timber processing company, which needed natural gas to run drying ovens. The Energy plant also produced carbon dioxide, a byproduct of their hot water boilers, for use in soda (i.e., carbonated beverage) production.

Trading Company   The Trading Company had several functions. It had been the marketing department of Krastyazhmash, and them split off into a separate company. This left the Machine-Building plant totally dependent on it for customer contact, a situation that did not please the Machine-Building plant's management. The Trading Company began to pursue its own interests rather than those of the Machine-Building plant. Since the arrangement clearly was not beneficial to Krastyazhmash, the General Director of Krastyazhmash worked out a new arrangement to better coordinate the activities of the Trading Company with the interests of Krastyazhmash as a whole.

The Trading Company did marketing, installation, and service for Krastyazhmash's heavy excavators. It had its own production facilities to make or refurbish parts for maintenance and repair purposes. It was a profitable business, since it was a combination of a service business and a spare parts business.

Due to the declining economy, coal mines were seeking to extend the useful life of their excavators rather than purchase new ones, which was good for the Trading Company's service business, but not good for the Machine-Building plant. This service business was not assured, however, because some coal mines were starting to perform their own maintenance and refurbishment in order to cut costs. Trading Company management was considering whether to expand its service business by taking on the maintenance and repair of excavators produced by other manufacturers. Previously, the Trading Company only serviced excavators from Krastyazhmash, and the management of the Machine-Building plant was concerned that servicing other manufacturers could undermine its sales of new excavators.

The Trading Company had good relationships with China, where many of the most recently built Krastyazhmash excavators were shipped. Krastyazhmash was currently working on an order from China for 10 excavators. (Excavators sold for about 2 billion rubles each.) Another part of the Trading Company's function, which it did not like, was the responsibility for changing bartered goods, particularly coming from China, into cash. They mentioned getting a large quantity of canned pork as payment and had problems selling it, because the pork was of poor quality.

Dr. Stevens thought about all of these plants and the way that they were separated. This posed difficulties for the General Director in managing the complex. Currently, each of these separate companies was going its own way, trying to develop its own product lines and business opportunities. This approach might help the individual companies to survive, but it tended to undercut the integration required for production of excavators, which depended on the plants working together. Perhaps something should be said about this in his report, but he set this aside for now. Stevens decided that the primary question was whether Krastyazhmash could be viable in the excavator business and, if so, what business strategy might Krastyazhmash pursue? For this, he turned his attention to the Machine-Building plant, where the excavators were assembled.

The Machine-Building Plant

During 1994, financial statements were being prepared for the first time for these plants. (Previously, under the Soviet system, Western-style financial statements were not done.) Stevens was given the Balance Sheet, which just had been completed in June during his stay. The Balance Sheet for the Machine-Building plant is shown in Table 3. One of the problems with the figures was that the valuation of fixed assets was based on costs from previous times, which have been adjusted for the rapid inflation of

TABLE 3	BALANCE SHEET FOR KRASTYAZHMASH MACHINE-BUILDING PLANT (IN THOUSANDS OF "OLD" RUBLES)	

Item	On January 1, 1994	On April 1, 1994
Assets		
Cash	27,632	4,066
Accounts receivable	667,798	1,794,153
Inventories	3,182,626	4,361,747
Prepaid expenses	14,482	25,425
Total Current Assets	3,892,538	6,185,391
Machinery and equipment	130,757,944	130,396,991
Less: Accumulated depreciation	(36,462,268)	(37,221,358)
Net machinery and equipment	94,295,676	93,175,633
Other assets	1,621,324	1,437,857
Total Assets	**99,809,538**	**100,798,881**
Liabilities and Equities		
Accounts payable	2,177,853	3,135,645
Taxes payable	939,728	1,449,159
Salaries payable	254,140	689,175
Current portion of long-term debts	630,957	624,576
Total Current Liabilities	4,002,678	5,898,555
Other liabilities	1,306,764	463,349
Shareholders capital	241,316	241,316
Additional paid-in capital	94,258,780	94,195,661
Total capital	94,500,096	94,436,977
Total Liabilities and Equities	**99,809,538**	**100,798,881**

Note: In April 1994, the ruble was valued at about 1,600 to the U.S. dollar. The "old" ruble was converted to the "new" or current ruble in 1998 by exchanging 1 new ruble for 1,000 old rubles.

SOURCE: Poisk report provided by Krastyazhmash.

the early 1990s according to an index provided by the Russian government. As a result, the values assigned to fixed assets are not reliable estimates of liquidation value.

Kitsov's Comments

In addition, Stevens met with the General Manager of the Machine-Building plant, Anatoly Kitsov, to get his perspective on the situation facing Krastyazhmash, and Kitsov subsequently wrote some comments for Stevens to consider. Stevens began to review Kitsov's comments, which follow.

Economic and Financial Conditions

Production output in first four months of 1994 was at the level of 55.7 percent of the planned volume. Only 2.7 billion rubles worth of products were actually produced versus the planned 4.9 billion rubles worth of output. (*Note:* These are not capacity utilization figures, since the plant was operating well below its full capacity. If it had been operating according to the Soviet era plan, product output should have been

25.5 billion rubles.) Planned sales levels were not achieved, which made it impossible for the plant to repay its debts for taxes, credits, services, and inventory.

The total number of employees was 1,390. Their average wages were considerably lower than those at most other Krasnoyarsk enterprises, and salary payments were often delayed. Since most of the output was mining machinery with a long manufacturing cycle, payments for supplied products as well as advance payments from mining enterprises (i.e., customers) were often delayed. As a result, the plant was forced to manufacture various other products that often were not strategically optimal, just to keep the plant operating. The plant was situated outside the city and did not have a large staff of security guards, so if it stopped production, it would be impossible to resume the production later due to the risk of pilfering. For this reason, it was necessary to employ the workforce with whatever orders were obtainable, no matter what the nature of the products.

At present, it was not possible to sell the manufactured products inventories on the plant's premises. Practically all money entering the plant was used to pay taxes. Because of the difficult financial situation, not one unit of the plant had received full wages since the previous December.

Technical Conditions

The plant had 685 metalworking machines and 96 cranes. The utilization factor was about 21 percent. The plant was built to produce mining machinery, such as walking and rotary excavators, so it was equipped with large and unique machines. It was often difficult or impossible to use those machines to manufacture different products. The plant had unused machinery which had a book value of 22 billion rubles, including 33 unique large metalworking machines and 14 cranes with large load ratings. Amortization costs for the installed equipment summed up to 4.3 billion rubles a year.

Efforts Being Made and Necessary Assistance

1. Considerable effort was being expended to employ the main workforce with spare parts and the manufacturing of other products in order to prevent a stoppage of production.

2. The plant's managers had concluded an agreement with a bank, allowing for a decrease in credit interest rates from 280 percent to 215 percent per annum, as well as changing the conditions of the credit contracts. According to the new conditions, repayments were postponed, but the plant cannot get new credit.

3. A list of equipment with its actual condition had been created. Now it was necessary to decide what to do with the unused equipment, since the cost of its maintenance, guarding, and amortization were too high.

   a. One possible way to employ that equipment was to begin manufacturing excavator types that were formerly produced by a different plant in the Ukraine.

   b. It was also possible to join one of the conversion programs, with the help of the Holding Company or the Union of Producers and Entrepreneurs, to modernize cement factories. There were eight cement factories in Russia, including one in Krasnoyarsk, that were in need of modernization. The Machine-Building plant could supply metalworking machines and spare parts, as well as services, to those factories. A contract with the Krasnoyarsk Cement Factory had already been signed.

    c. Another possibility was to ask for relief from the property taxes on these machines.

    d. It might be possible to find orders for some new products that could be manufactured with the equipment.

    e. A better approach might be to sell the unused equipment and purchase something useful.

4. In order to cut expenses, the plant stopped heating certain underutilized production and administrative sections on the 1st of April.

5. A large walking excavator was being manufactured for Vostsibugol (the Eastern Siberia Coal Company). The plant cannot collect progress payments for it because of Vostsibugol's financial difficulties. As a result, the plant had to seek the assistance of Rosugol (the Russian Coal Ministry) to finance the contract.

6. The plant produced large excavators for China and sold them through the Trading Company. The plant had contracts with the Trading Company, and the Trading Company had corresponding contracts with a Chinese company. For some reason, the plant was unable to get progress payments for excavators from the Trading Company or the Chinese. A mutual understanding with the Trading Company on this matter had been difficult to reach, so it was necessary either to work with China directly or to ask the General Director of Krastyazhmash to help in negotiations with the Trading Company or between the Trading Company and the Chinese customer

7. The plant had partly installed the flexible manufacturing system "Rino Berardi" for gear body manufacturing. Its cost, when purchased in 1989, was $24.9 million. The system may be used for manufacturing of gear bodies for oil-extracting, metallurgical, cement machinery, large molds, dies, etc. To complete the installation of all equipment and start production will take about 2 years and 1.5 billion rubles, but the plant needs financial aid to do it.

8. Finally, there were negotiations in progress with U.S. companies on joint production, and other efforts were being made to improve the plant's financial condition.

Auditor's Report

Dr. Stevens joined the group of auditors who were preparing financial statements for the company during several of their meetings. At the completion of their work, the auditors presented a report, giving their views and advice on the situation. Stevens next reviewed their report, which follows.

The audit company, *Poisk* ("poy-sk"), based upon work done in May–June 1994, prepared this report. The object of investigation was the Krastyazhmash Machine-Building plant. The investigation covered the operating period October 1993 to March 1994. Methods of work were investigation and analysis of accounting documents and summary financial reports, evaluation of accounting operations in comparison to proper methods, consideration of existing systems of production management, review of management documents, and conversations with managers and workers at the plant.

The auditors found the following:

1. Production capacities were not completely used; unused equipment was 70 percent.

2. The account structure was complex, with internal departments having separate independent balances that make bookkeeping and control laborious.

3. There existed a considerable amount of unemployed, defective equipment.

4. Marketing was absent. To some extent, marketing functions were carried out by the holding company subsidiary, "Trading Company."

5. Because of the economic situation in Russia, the high cost for transportation underscored the importance of plant location for producing equipment and providing services to the coal-mining industry. As a result, the Machine-Building plant did not practically have any competitors in the East market at the present time.

6. Materials and purchased products made up 30 to 50 percent, wages 20 to 35 percent, depreciation 27 percent, management expenses 25 to 30 percent of the production cost.

7. Of the total excavator weight, irretrievable scrap made up 250 metric tons, including 50 metric tons of nonferrous materials.

8. Prices were usually set lower than costs.

9. The plant produced goods that were not in demand. There was higher demand for excavators of lower capacity (bucket capacity of 5–8 m^3), not the larger ones that the plant was capable of producing.

10. There were neither the means nor well-prepared personnel for the efficient reconstruction of the plant at the present time.

11. The number of workers was constantly being reduced.

12. According to the financial statement dated April 1, 1994, the results of economic activity were negative. Losses were 470,697 thousand rubles.

In conclusion, the plant was in a difficult financial state with a falling liquidity ratio. According to the Russian Federation Resolution N498 dated May 20, 1994, the plant was considered to be bankrupt and was in need of serious reforms of its economic-financial activity.

Stevens paused to reflect on what he had learned from Kitsov and Poisk. Typical of Russia at this time, the numbers were not always in agreement, but the message seemed quite clear. The situation was not good.

The Market for Excavators

Dr. Stevens then reviewed the information he had about the market for excavators. He looked at an excerpt from an old plan that he had received from Egor Ol, a U.S. Department of Commerce report, and articles on the Chinese market.

Krastyazhmash's Market Projections

The (old) plan for Krastyazhmash was prepared in the late 1980s, before the transition to a market economy. He extracted information from this plan and created the following table. The plan estimated that, from 1993 to 2000, 248 draglines were needed by the mining industry, as show below.

Dragline Size	Quantity	Percent
11–15 m^3	160	67
20–25 m^3	78	28
40–100 m^3	10	5
Total	248	100

In addition, mining enterprises were estimated to need 422 excavators in the same period, not counting the demand of the gold industry or ore mining. However, if all Russian excavator-manufacturing plants worked at their full 1990 capacity, then excavator production, beginning in 1993 and ending in 2000, would be 3,990 excavators.[4]

He concluded that there was clearly too much capacity built during the Soviet era.

The Russian Mining Equipment Industry[5]

Before leaving the United States, Dr. Stevens had obtained a report on the Russian mining-equipment industry from the U.S. Department of Commerce. While the purpose of that report was to inform U.S. companies about business opportunities in Russia, its discussion of the Russian market for coal-mining equipment was helpful for his work with Krastyazhmash. Steven's summary of a few pertinent portions follows.

Overview

The Russian mining and mining-equipment sector was vast. Coal mining represented 57 percent of the overall mining activity in Russia. (Iron ore was 42 percent, and the remainder included a variety of other ores.)

In 1992, Russian coal mines produced 327 million tons of coal, with 45 percent from underground mines and 54 percent from surface mines. (Krastyazhmash excavators were used in surface mining.) This production level was only 95 percent of the production in 1991, and the level had continued to decline. The production of coal took place in nearly 300 facilities in Russia, of which 208 were underground mines and 65 were surface mines.

Managers of Russian mining operations generally regarded Russian produced equipment as adequate. Additionally, the shortage of funds and other severe problems in the industry presented serious obstacles to foreign companies seeking to export to Russia. Nonetheless, several niche opportunities existed. Among heavy excavators, the "best prospects" included:

- Draglines for overcasting in surface mining operations
- Excavators with bucket capacities exceeding 11.9 cubic meters
- Excavators with boom lengths exceeding 70 meters
- Field maintenance and repair
- Spare parts

Competitive Situation Russian manufacturers had a competitive advantage over foreign companies because of their experience in, and proximity to, the market for mining equipment. The following Russian companies were suppliers of much of this equipment.

Company (Location)	Major Products
UralMash (Yekaterinburg)	excavators, crushing machines
Izhorsky (Kolpino)	excavators
Krastyazhmash (Krasnoyarsk)	excavators
Nokokramatorsk (Novokramatorsk)	excavators

In 1992, there were 433 excavators and buckets in use (of which 51 are bucket-wheel systems). These had an average bucket capacity of 11.9 cubic meters. Buckets with 4 to 8 cubic meter capacity made up 75 percent of the total.

Field researchers contacted users and manufacturers of mining equipment and learned the following:

- Russian equipment producers were strongly entrenched in the market.

- Equipment purchasers at the mines were technically quite particular about their needs and extremely sensitive to prices.

- Mining operators preferred excavators from UralMash and Izhorsky to the other two manufacturers, i.e., Krastyazhmash and Nokokramatorsk.

- Military plants in Tula and Ulyanovsk, for example, were now trying to produce equipment previously supplied by plants in Ukraine and Byelorussia, but production was just beginning.

- Equipment producers had little experience with pricing or marketing their products to end users.

- Efficiency and cost had become major concerns for mine operators.

- Manufacturers were seeking relationships with foreign firms and were exporting some equipment to C.I.S.[6] and other countries.

Overall, there appeared to be 47 plants in Russia that produced mining equipment. Only a very small number of these plants—perhaps only four—produced integrated systems. The remainder provided discrete units or subassemblies either to the mines or the integrated systems producers. Perhaps as many as 27 of these plants were military plants that had just begun to produce equipment for the mining sector.

Difficulties for Foreign Competitors While foreign firms had made some penetration into this market, they were at a disadvantage regarding price. For example, respondents mentioned the "very expensive prices" of American equipment. A quote from a Russian mining official helped to set the tone: "The Russian equipment is very good. We are satisfied with it. We don't see any reason for spending money on imports." Additionally, American-made excavators, although operating satisfactorily in Russia for ten years, were criticized for having weak teeth and weak motors for lateral movements.

One approach to market entry by a foreign competitor could be to develop a partnership with a local Russian equipment provider to either jointly assemble or manufacture equipment for use both in Russia and for export. This approach was perhaps the only one that would enable a foreign firm to compete in terms of price in the Russian market.

The Chinese Market for Excavators

Finally, because of Krastyazhmash's sales to China, Dr. Stevens did an Internet search to find information on the Chinese market for excavators and other mining equipment. Unfortunately, he did not locate a report with the depth of the one on the Russian mining-equipment market, but he was able to obtain two relevant full-text articles.

Electric Power Needs

The first article, "China's Booming Power Demand Continues Unabated,"[7] reported that China was sticking to its ambitious target of nearly doubling electric generating capacity, mostly using coal, from the 1992 year-end level of 165 GW to 310 GW by 2000. The need for electricity was driven by China's economic boom. China's power sector was caught in a spiral of perpetual catch-up, with a seemingly never-ending demand-supply gap.

The article further reported that, according to the *People's Daily*, at least one-third of China's industry was now idle for lack of electricity. Lost output last year was worth more than Yuan 700bn ($1.7bn). If anything, the situation was worsening, with national power supply falling 15 to 20 percent short of demand each year. For example, factories in Guangdong were closing for three, even four days a week, the article said.

Steel Needs

The second article, "China's Industrial Push Is Requiring a Lot More Steel,"[8] reports that the Chinese government was working hard to develop its agricultural, energy, transportation, communication, and raw material sectors in the 1990s. As one of the important raw materials, steel was vital for building a developing economy like China's.

The article reported that, in the 1980s, China's steel output increased rapidly, from 37.12 million metric tons in 1980 to 66.04 million tons in 1990, representing an annual average increase of 3 million tons. China had been the world's fourth largest steel producer since 1982. Targets had been set for 72 million tons of steel output for 1995 and more than 80 million tons for 2000.

With regard to energy, China's steel industry consumes 10 percent of the country's total annual output. China had abundant energy resources. Its economically recoverable fossil energy reserves were the third highest in the world. China also ranked third in total energy consumption. The remarkable feature of energy consumption in China was that coal held a dominant share, which in 1985 was 75.95 percent. Coal amounted to over 70 percent of the energy consumption in the steel industry.

Energy, according to the article, was in short supply in China and the unit energy consumption of the steel industry was much higher than the international average. The comprehensive energy consumption per ton of crude steel produced (energy consumed by mining, ore dressing, coking, etc.) was 2.04 tons of coal in 1980 and 1.62 tons in 1990. In comparison, the international average for energy consumption per ton crude steel was roughly 1 ton of coal. To reduce the gap, China was adopting advanced technology to improve its energy consumption levels. Energy consumption per ton of crude steel produced will be decreased to 1.55 and 1.45 in 1995 and 2000, respectively, while the internationally comparable energy consumption for the major iron and steel enterprises will be decreased to 0.985 and 0.977 ton of coal.

While neither article gave specific information on the demand for coal-mining excavators, Stevens recognized that the demand for coal in China was growing, which was favorable to selling Krastyazhmash's excavators.

Mulling Over the Situation

Over the three months, Dr. Stevens worked in the evenings on his laptop computer, writing notes to himself, sometimes in the form of questions and answers. This process helped him to organize his thinking and to test some hypotheses. He reviewed these notes, which follow.

Observations on the Situation

Ol and the other managers inherited plants that were built for a different economic system. Now that the central planning authorities are no longer placing the orders, old "customers" no longer were required to purchase the company's output and could shop around for other sources of equipment. Krastyazhmash needed to get its financial house in order so that it could support production and sales and finish construction of the plant. The whole situation was made more difficult as a result of a general decline in the economy.

Ownership did not bring much cash (Table 3), and the economic situation did not provide many orders for production. When the privatization era began, expectations and hopes were high. It soon became apparent to managers that their companies faced a crisis for which they were not well prepared. They lacked education and training in how to operate a business in a market economy, while the sharp downturn in Russia's economy would be a challenge to managers everywhere.

The most serious problem was a lack of cash flow. Even though Krastyazhmash had production orders, customers wanted to pay with barter, which Krastyazhmash had to accept of necessity since there was no alternative in order to make the sale. Realizing cash from the sale of bartered goods was not a skill that the technical employees of the Machine-Building plant had. Furthermore, to produce excavators, they needed materials and supplies, but their suppliers wanted payments and, unlike the excavator company, were unwilling to accept barter.

An important issue for the management was to keep the company. Now that they owned it, there was a promise that it would be a very profitable business for them. In addition to ownership, they had ties to the city and region and were concerned about the well-being of their employees. These attachments gave them further incentive to want the company to succeed.

Questions Considered

Several questions were raised by people who Stevens spoke with and by Stevens himself. He had written notes to address some of the more significant questions.

1. *Should the Machine-Building plant remain in business at all?*

   Looking at the balance sheet (Table 3) and the auditor's report, it appeared that the most prudent financial decision would be to liquidate the plant and distribute the proceeds to shareholders. For instance, on a Boston Consulting Group (BCG) matrix, the plant might be characterized as a "dog." This course of action was discussed, but rejected by Krastyazhmash management. Management could benefit more from operating the plant, even if it was losing money, since they enjoyed the trappings of ownership and could realize the fruits of liquidation at a slow pace. There was always the possibility that the economy would improve, and in the meanwhile, they were able to use the plant in a sort of moonlighting way to produce some income. Besides, alternative jobs were not plentiful for them.

The government and the workers, many of whom were shareholders, had an interest in keeping the plant operating. A decision to liquidate would not have been well received and could have precipitated action to block it.

2. *Does Krastyazhmash need to develop a smaller excavator?*

The *Poisk* (auditor's) report recommended developing a smaller excavator, which had a higher demand in terms of units. One might use a Growth Directions matrix to illustrate that this was a "product development/penetration" strategy. It had the advantage of being a new product for a known, existing market, but there were disadvantages as well.

For one, the possibility of doing this was quite low. Funds for new product development were not available, the manufacturing process was geared to the larger excavators, and there was the question of how long it would take to get a product onto the market. The mine operators were quite satisfied with smaller excavators that were made by other producers. It was not clear that a Krastyazhmash small excavator could successfully enter this market.

3. *What should Krastyazhmash do to survive until the time that the economy improves?*

Krastyazhmash had a good location for serving the needs of coal mines in the coal-rich Krasnoyarsk region, but demand for coal was tied to the state of the general economy, which was not good at the moment. As the Commerce Department Market Report indicated, Russian excavators are preferred by Russian mine operators, so perhaps the strategy should be to remain in business until the economy improves.

With the economic decline, mine operators were not buying new excavators. There were two possible approaches to ride out the market decline. First, Krastyazhmash could emphasize other types of production in order to provide some revenues. The types of products were difficult to select, because much of the production machinery was not very adaptable to general purposes, but there were possibilities. Management had begun to assemble a list of possible products (e.g., oil drilling equipment and large steel containers). The second approach was to emphasize the service business for excavators and focus on making spare parts for repairs. In this way, Krastyazhmash could continue to produce parts for its and perhaps others' excavators and could maintain relationships with the coal mines that would eventually want to purchase new excavators. (This approach fits the classification of "market penetration" in the Growth Directions matrix.) Since the Trading Company was already in the service business, some form of profit sharing might be needed to sustain the Machine-Building plant.

4. *Should it consider mergers or foreign affiliations, and what might the thrust of these be?*

A quicker way to enter the market for a small excavator, for example, would be to merge with (or license a product from) one of the other producers in Russian, or even with a foreign company. This approach would make Krastyazhmash a regional producer for the local coal mines and the accessible Asian countries. This approach was attempted, and for a while, there was an arrangement with an American company, but the difficulties of doing business in Russia (laws, taxes, etc.) and the lack of demand, brought an end to the collaboration. Understandably, it seemed that foreign companies were more interested in selling their products to Krastyazhmash's customers than they were interested in keeping the Machine-Building plant in operation. This same observation applied to other Russian excavator producers.

The possibility of setting up production outside of the region or outside of Russia was also discussed. The technology of Krastyazhmash's excavators was not superior to foreign models, and in most cases, their excavators would be at a price (too high) and features (not enough) disadvantage.

5. *What should be its relationship with the Trading Company?*

The Trading Company seemed to hold the key to the survival of Krastyazhmash. Its former marketing and service department had spun off and was now in the best position for surviving (see Question 3 above). Because the Machine-Building plant lacked a marketing and sales staff, it was almost totally dependent on the Trading Company for its survival. In fact, the Trading Company might wish to diversify into other "brands" of excavators for sales.

Recognizing this possibility, the management of Krastyazhmash exercised its operational control of the company and pressured the Trading Company to work in a more integrated fashion with the other plants of Krastyazhmash, particularly the Machine-Building plant. In addition to management direction, incentives were put into place to encourage efforts that supported the interests of the whole.

6. *How can it manage its cash needs during the lengthy and expensive process of producing an excavator?*

This was the gravest of their problems (Table 3). Some of it was handled by negotiations that insisted on some cash payments. Another effort was made to improve collections from customers. But the usual practices were instituted: delays in paying employees, suppliers, and anyone who could be put off. Some pieces of equipment were sold off to generate cash. Production of a variety of products was undertaken in order to generate some funds. And cost-cutting measures, including turning off the heat (which was a major step in the Siberian winter), were instituted. There was also a slow, but steady, reduction in the number of employees.

Back to Stevens

After reviewing this information, George Stevens decided that he needed to focus on the "big" questions.

1. Considering the business environment, what business/market strategy should Krastyazhmash pursue for its excavator and dragline line?

2. The organization of the plants into separate companies bothered Stevens. Also, he wondered if it was good for each company to pursue its own business opportunities. Was there something that should be done in terms of company structure or operating policies? How is this related to business strategy?

3. Finally, he thought about acceptance of his report, which got him thinking about Krastyazhmash's shareholders. Who are the stakeholders, what are the stakeholders' interests, and how might he orient the report to address them?

He thought that the answers to these questions would give Ol the requested input to a strategic plan. He wished that he had more information, but this was all that was available to him at this time. He would have to make the best of it. Stevens turned on his laptop and began working.

Endnotes

1. A dragline is similar to an excavator in that they are both types of earth-moving equipment. The excavator is more familiar and operates as a shovel. The dragline has a large bucket that is dragged along by cables, picking up earth as it goes. Draglines typically can pick up more earth than excavators.
2. A Russian territory (or *krai*) is comparable to a U.S. state. The top official of a *krai* is its governor.
3. The word "plant" might be creating confusion. In the United States, the term is used somewhat loosely. Often people speak about "going to the plant," when they are referring to a large complex with many buildings where production is performed. At other times, they might refer to one of the buildings in such a complex as "the plant." That building might contain the production for one component of the product that is being made at the complex. In this terminology, Krastyazhmash is a plant complex made up of plants. The situation becomes more complicated because Krastyazhmash (the plant complex) was privatized into companies (formerly its plants) and turned into a holding company for the individual plants/companies, now called subsidiaries.
4. Krastyazhmash estimates.
5. This section is based on "The Market for U.S. Mining Equipment in Russia," published by the BISNIS office of the U.S. Department of Commerce, June 1994. FYI Information Resources, Washington, DC, wrote the report.
6. The C.I.S. is the Commonwealth of Independent States. It is made up mostly of the republics of the former Soviet Union, which are now independent countries.
7. *Power in Asia*, October 25, 1993, published by Financial Times Business Information Ltd.
8. *American Metal Market*, Oct. 7, 1991, v99 n192 p. 16A (1).